D0071064

Assembly Language
for the IBM PC Family

Second Edition

William B. Jones
California State University
Dominguez Hills

Scott/Jones Inc. Publishers • P. O. Box 696 • El Granada, CA 94018
voice: (415) 726-2436 • FAX (415)726-4693
e-mail: scotjones2@aol.com
WEB: http://www.scotjonespub.com

Assembly Language for the IBM PC, second edition
William B. Jones

Copyright © 1997 by Scott/Jones, Inc.

ISBN 1-57676-001-4

Text Design, Composition, and Illustrations: William B. Jones
Editor: Heather Bennett
Book Manufacturing: Malloy Lithographing, Inc.

987   YZ

ADDITIONAL TITLES OF INTEREST FROM SCOTT/JONES

The Windows 95 Textbook: Standard Ed.
The Windows 95 Textbook: Extended Ed.
A Short Course in Windows 95
  by Stewart Venit

The DOS-6 Coursebook
Visual Basic Programming
QuickStart in Visual Basic
The Visual Basic 4 CourseBook
  by Forest Lin

Visual Basic with Business Applications
  by Mark Simkin

Computer Architecture and Assembly Language: The MC 68000
  by G. M. Prabhu and Charles Wright

Fortran for Scientists & Engineers, 2nd ed.
  by Gary Bronson

QuickStart in C++
  by William B. Jones

C by Discovery, 2nd ed. (emphasis on ANSI C)
  by L. S. Foster

C Through Objects
  by John Connely

Problem Solving with C
  by Jacqueline Jones and Keith Harrow

The DOS Primer and More, 2nd ed.
  by Dorothy Calvin

FORTHCOMING TEXTS FROM SCOTT/JONES

The Windows NT Textbook
  by Stewart Venit

Principles of Programming using Visual Basic
  by Gary Bronson

Contents

Preface

This is a book on Assembly Language Programming for IBM PCs and PC Clones using the two predominant commercial assemblers, Microsoft MASM and Borland Turbo Assembler (TASM). I also cover some of their related utility programs, particularly their interactive debuggers. Such a book raises several questions. First among them,

▶ **Why learn assembly language?**

- In order to write high-level languages such as C/C++ and Pascal well, it is necessary to have some knowledge of the assembly language they translate into.
- Even with modern optimizing compilers, programs written in high-level languages will generally be larger and slower than if they were written in assembly language In situations where size or speed is critical, it may be necessary to write all or part of the program in assembly language. This is particularly true of code for operating systems and programs that can make use of special-purpose instructions, such as those for decimal arithmetic.
- To debug high-level language programs, it may be necessary to look at them at the level of the assembly language they generate. I have found bugs in high-level languages this way.
- Even though compilers are generally written in a high-level language (often in their own language), the compiler writer must know how to write assembly language in order to have the compiler do code generation.
- Writing assembly language is fun!

The IBM PC was chosen because it is by far the most available (and inexpensive) platform for such a study. We will emphasize good old clunky DOS and except towards the end, all of our programs will run on the original 8088 model. The next question therefore is

▶ **Why an obsolete chip in an obsolete environment?**

- The 8088 CPU is the basis of all CPUs that came after it, up to and including the Pentium. To understand the Pentium, you have to understand the 8088 first.
- The alternative to programming in DOS would be to program in Microsoft Windows, and to get to the point where you could do that in a meaningful way would require a whole

other course first, in which the assembly language part would be lost.

- If you need to use assembly in a Windows environment, you can call assembly language programs from high-level languages, or even drop into assembly language where needed in all of the popular high-level languages. (For instance, Microsoft's Visual C++ and Borland's C++ and Turbo Pascal; see chapter 13.)

This, the second edition, has much of the same texture and flavor of the first, so you may ask

▶ **What's new in the second edition?**

- Many changes are due to several professors who used the first edition and made numerous detailed suggestions based on their classroom experience.
- More roadsigns are given to allow the instructor or the reader to chart an independent path through the material.
- Motivation and examples are more clearly separated from expository material. For example, subprocedures and separate compilation are treated first, in a separate chapter, before substantial examples involving the construction of procedures for numeric I/O. The latter can be easily skipped or delayed.
- Keyboard input has been moved later in the book, to the point where it is first used.
- Many details on address arithmetic, byte swapping, and various other advanced topics were moved from the old Chapter 4 to a position much later in the book, where they become essential.
- The debuggers, which now seem to have stabilized, are treated mostly in separate chapters called Debug Workshops, which have their own numbering.
- A substantial chapter has been added on the use of the Floating Point Unit. Routines for reading floating point numbers from the keyboard and writing them to the display have been added to the library on the disk that comes with this book.
- Many corrections have been made. Interfacing with high-level languages is easier than the first edition indicated, and VGA graphics is a little more complicated.
- Internal formats of instructions is now covered, as well as its relationship to speed of execution. This material is optional and easily skipped.
- There is a move away from examples using Pascal, with many examples being given in C or C++.

There is probably more material here than could be covered in a two semester course. Therefore one asks

▶ **What material should be covered?**

- **Absolute bare minimum**: Cover Chapters 1–6 (includes arithmetic, decisions, looping, simple I/O, and subprograms), some Chapter 9 (shifting for multiplication, and the `test` instruction), Chapter 10 (Arrays), part of Chapter 12 (Segments), and part of Chapter 15 (Interrupts) and the corresponding Debug Workshops.
- **What I cover**: in addition to the above, Chapter 7 (Numeric I/O routines), Chapter 8 (Macros), Chapter 9 (Logical Operations) and the beginning of Chapter 13 (More on the Procedure interface) if time.

- **Alternatives**: Many chapters and parts of chapters can be treated more or less indepen-dently. In particular, I suggest choosing from Chapters 11 and 14 (the latter does multiple precision numbers and a good random number generator), Chapter 18 (String Processing instructions), Chapter 19 (Video) and Chapter 20 (Floating Point).

▶ **What visual cues should the reader look for?**

- Advisable things to do are listed in bold text preceded and followed by bars:

Buy this book!

- Selected exercises, marked ✓, have answers given in a section near the end of the book.

- All chapters that introduce new registers or new uses of registers begin with a diagram showing the complete register set in the upper right corner of the first page, with the treated registers shown in black. See the beginning of Chapter 2 for an example.

- **Model Programs** are shown in shaded boxes, with a top line indicating what the program does:

Have a Healthy Life
Exercise Everything in Moderation   (including moderation)

- Things you should not do are crossed out, as in

Eat ✖ Raw Lard

- Debug Workshops are indicated are indicated by gray rectangles on the outside edges of their pages.

As in the first edition, the disk that accompanies this book contains useful libraries of macros and utility programs, as well as the source of all the utilities and all of the complete programs that appear in this book.

I designed and typeset this book using Adobe PageMaker 6.0 and 6.01, a frustrating experience which I will not repeat. The illustrations were done with Adobe Illustrator 5.5 and 6.0, which con-tinues to be a fine program. I do wish it previewed type correctly.

The following adoptees reviewed the book, many of them giving an exceptional amount of time and insight to the task.

Bill Cole
Sierra College

Charles Crittenden
Weber State University

Joe Dumas
University of Tennessee,
  Chatanooga

Jacqueline Jones
Brooklyn College, CUNY

Richard Glass
Nassau Community College

Maria Kolatis
Morris County College

Laszlo Szuecs
Fort Lewis College

Richard Roiger
Mankato State University

William Pervin
University of Texas, Dallas

Jim Thomas
Ohlone College

Elizabeth Alpert
Hartnell College

Isabeth Comisky
Mohawk Valley Community
  College

Masood Towhidenejad
Embry-Riddle Aeronautical
  University

Noe Lopez-Benitez
Texas Tech University

David Sarchet
Embry-Riddle Aeronautical
  University

Glenn Jackson
Oakland University

Finally, I would like to thank my developmental editor Joan Venegas, my editor, Heather Bennett, and my publisher, Richard Jones, for their constant help and encouragement.

Bill Jones
Hermosa Beach, CA
e-mail: wbj@research.csudh.edu
WEB: http://csc.csudh.edu

Chapter 1

Preliminaries

This chapter covers more or less unrelated introductory topics. Most readers will be somewhat familiar with each of them. The sections can be read in any order (but 1.3 after 1.2), or skipped and returned to later when necessary.

1.1 • Hardware Overview

In this section, the following important terms will be defined:

address	fetch-execute cycle	memory
assembler	general register	operation code
assembly language	firmware	register
bit	I/O device	RAM
byte	instruction	RISC
CISC	instruction pointer (IP)	ROM and ROM BIOS
computer chip	machine cycle	stack pointer (SP)
CPU	machine language	stored program

There are three levels on which we can describe the IBM PC hardware:

I.   General properties of personal computers,
II. IBM PC hardware, and
III. Software, called *firmware*, which gives the IBM PC its particular character.

Levels I and II represent the actual hardware. Level III is a part of the hardware, in the sense that it is permanently "burned" into integrated circuit memory chips. In fact, though, it is programs superimposed onto the hardware to make a new *virtual* machine, that is, to add new capabilities and characteristics to the machine which make it more convenient to use. We will discuss levels I and II, as well as III briefly, in this section. Much of the rest of the book will involve further discussion of levels II and III.

1.1.1 • Level I: General Properties of Personal Computers

A simple digital computer can be thought of as consisting of three basic parts:

- The **Central Processing Unit**, or CPU
- The **Memory Unit**, containing both the program to be executed and its data
- Input/Output (**I/O**) devices

In a typical personal computer, the pieces are related as follows:

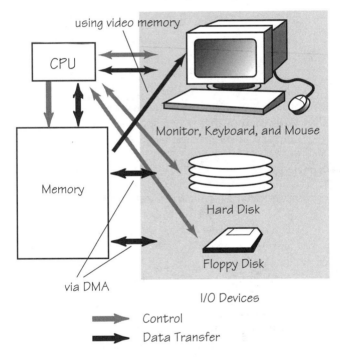

The CPU is contained in a single Integrated Circuit (IC) **computer chip**. The Pentium chip, for instance, is a piece of silicon perhaps 3/4 inch square, mounted in a two-inch square plastic slab, and contains the equivalent of over three million transistors. Speed of CPUs is usually expressed in MHz (Megahertz, or millions of **machine cycles** per second; each machine instruction takes one or more machine cycles to execute).

The control from I/O devices to the CPU is minimal—it is mostly messages like "I have finished something." Low-speed devices such as the keyboard and mouse do their I/O directly through the CPU, while the monitor takes its data directly from memory, in a process that will be explained further below. High-speed devices, such as disks, would slow down the CPU substantially if all data to and from them flowed through the CPU, so for them, the CPU *initiates* data transfer, which then takes place directly to or from memory using **Direct Memory Access** (DMA).

Computer memory is a collection of **bits**. A bit (short for **bi**nary dig**it**) is a component with two stable states, off and on, usually represented as 0 and 1, respectively. Bits are arranged in groups of eight as **bytes**. Memory bytes are numbered from 0 to $N-1$ where N is the number of bytes in the memory. A byte's number is called its **address**. (In a few computers, the address may refer to a unit of memory containing anything from 16 to 64 bits, depending on the computer). A particular byte is called a **memory location**. Each bit of memory is always contained in the same byte at the same address. Each bit always has a *value* too, but the value of the bit can change.

A useful analogy might be as follows: Think of memory as a large apartment building, with each apartment having a number (its address) and exactly eight light switches. Each of those switches represents one bit of binary information, off = 0 and on = 1. One can get information (the current light switch settings) from a particular memory location (apartment) or set information in the light switch settings of an apartment, but whatever happens, each apartment will always have the same location, its switches will always have *some* settings, and there will always be exactly eight of them in the apartment.

At the time of this writing, a typical memory package consists of three small computer chips supplying four million bytes of memory.

A computer can execute programs only when they reside in the computer's memory. The actions of the program are broken down into small steps or **instructions** such as add, move data item, etc., and encoded in binary in a method which is unique to each type of computer. Each instruction usually begins with a byte specifying the operation, called the **operation code**, which may be followed by one or more operands—perhaps addresses of data in memory.

The idea of storing programs as well as data in the same memory, called the **stored program concept**, is probably the most important concept in modern computers. Some of the advantages of the stored program are

- Programs can be set up and executed very rapidly, under computer control.

- The same memory can be used for a large program with little data and a small program with a great deal of data

- When a large memory is available, many programs can be in memory at the same time, optimizing usage of computer resources by allowing one program to execute while other programs in memory wait on relatively slow I/O devices or terminal input.

At one time the list of "advantages" would also have included that stored programs can modify themselves. It is now recognized that self-modifying programs are very undesirable. They are hard to debug, and can execute more slowly on timesharing systems.

Originally all programs were written in **machine language**—the actual numbers that went into the computer's memory. Say you wanted to add the contents of memory location 4278 to the contents of memory location 3133, and the operation code for addition was 31. Then you would write the instruction 3142783133. (Actually, the binary version would be used.) **Assembly language** allows us to use symbolic names for operations, and also to attach symbolic names to memory locations. Our add instruction might appear as ADD NET_PAY, BONUS. An assembly program is then processed by a fairly simple table lookup program called an **assembler** to get the machine language version. (Since actual machine language is virtually never used now, and assembly language is just a symbolic form of it, the term "machine language" is often used to refer to assembly language.)

High-level languages such as Ada, C/C++, Fortran, or Pascal bear no relationship to machine language on *any* computer. A statement in such a language may translate into many or few machine instructions, and it may be hard to predict which from looking at the source statement. Also, the same high level language statement can be translated into the machine languages of many very different machines. An assembly language, on the other hand, is associated with one particular type of computer.

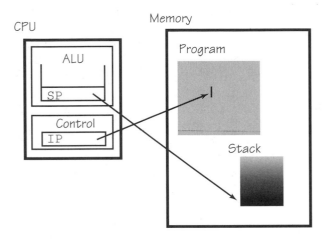

The CPU is organized in two parts, the **Arithmetic and Logic Unit** or **ALU** which performs computations and the **Control Unit** which fetches information from and stores information into the Memory Unit, and tells the ALU and the Input/Output devices which operations to perform. In addition the CPU contains **registers,** which are temporary storage for information, intermediate computation results, etc. The registers can be thought of as a special small, fast memory. Registers which can be used for all types of arithmetic, as well as for addresses (pointers, subscripts, etc.) are called **general registers**.

Two (non-general) registers which are commonly available are a **stack pointer**, or SP, in the ALU and an **instruction pointer**, or IP, in the control unit. (The latter is sometimes also called the program counter.)

The instruction pointer contains the address in memory of the next instruction to be executed by the CPU. One of the main functions of the Control Unit is to perform an infinite loop of fetching the instruction at the IP, updating the IP to point to the next instruction, and then executing the fetched instruction. This loop is called the **fetch-execute cycle**:

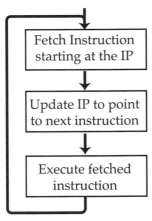

Fetch Instruction starting at the IP

Update IP to point to next instruction

Execute fetched instruction

There is no way of telling from looking at memory whether a piece of memory is program or data. If the IP is pointing to it, it is *assumed* (sometimes erroneously) to be program and if the program tries to manipulate it, it is assumed to be data.

The `stack` data structure has become so important in computing that most modern computers implement a stack, and the instructions to manipulate it, in hardware. In particular, a hardware stack is a powerful means of implementing procedure call and return (see chapter 7) and handling interrupts (see chapter 15), as well as storage for procedure parameters and local variables (see chapter 13). The actual stack is a block of memory locations, and the stack pointer register in the ALU contains the address of one of them, called the 'top' of the stack. For more information on the stack and how it is used, see the chapters referenced above.

An important way of classifying computer memory is to distinguish between **RAM** (*Random Access Memory*) and **ROM** (*Read Only Memory*). The terms RAM and ROM are somewhat misleading, as ROM is also random access. 'Random access' means that you can get or store information in any part of memory in a time that is independent of where you last looked in the memory. Nonrandom access memory includes disks, which have an arm that must be moved different distances to get to data depending on where the arm was last. The *real* distinction between RAM and ROM is that RAM can be changed as the computer operates (and its contents disappear when the computer is turned off) while the contents of ROM are permanent.

ROM is usually used for standard data and standard basic parts of the computer's operating system. The CPU always starts up with a fixed address in the IP. A computer is designed so that the start-up location is an address in ROM of a **bootstrap** routine. The bootstrap code usually looks in a fixed place on a disk, or on a series of disks, for the code to load the rest of the operating system. The term 'bootstrap' comes from the expression "pulling oneself up by one's bootstraps," and the whole process is called **booting** the machine.

The programs in ROM are considered to lie somewhere between hardware and software and as a result they are called **firmware**. (Programs which have been promised but not yet delivered are often called *vaporware*.)

There are two basic philosophies used for designing the instruction set of a CPU. The more recent method is called **RISC,** for Reduced Instruction Set Computing. In response, the older one has been called **CISC**, for Complex Instruction Set Computing. (They are pronounced "risk" and "sisk", respectively.) CISC strove to improve efficiency by using complex instructions which did many things, perhaps taking many machine cycles. The principle of RISC is that each instruction should be very simple and execute in a single machine cycle. The RISC CPU usually has many internal registers and most operations are performed by loading data into registers and then performing operations among registers. All of the CPU chips used in IBM PCs use the CISC philosophy. The PowerPC chips used on recent models of Macintosh computers use the RISC philosophy. There has been something of a melding of the two philosophies in recent years. The technology of computer chips has advanced so rapidly that CISC computers are able to execute many of their simple instructions in a single cycle. Also, certain sets of instructions, such as those for manipulating floating point (real) numbers, are so complex that they would be far too slow if implemented by a sequence of RISC instructions, so even RISC machines generally have CISC-type instructions. Schmit's book, pp. 273-282 (see the bibliography) has an excellent section comparing RISC to CISC, and in particular the Pentium to the PowerPC. He says "Every major CPU architecture developed in the last decade (or more) is a RISC design … [but] the 80X86 [IBM PC] and 680X0 families have consistently outsold RISC systems because of the installed base of software … and the highly competitive consumer market."

1.1.2 • Level II: IBM PC Hardware

Personal computer CPUs generally come from one of three families:

- The Intel 8088, 8086, 80286, 80386, 80486, and Pentium (80586) chips, called collectively the **80X86**. These chips are used mainly in IBM PCs, and their clones (copies).

- The Motorola 68000, 68010, 68020, 68030, and 68040 chips, called collectively the **680X0**. These chips are used in Apple Macintosh, Amiga, and Atari computers and in many workstations, which are in effect more elaborate personal computers.

- The PowerPC 601, 604, and others, which use RISC architecture and are used mostly in recent Macintosh computers.

We will be concerned with the 80X86 family with the attached special-purpose hardware and firm-

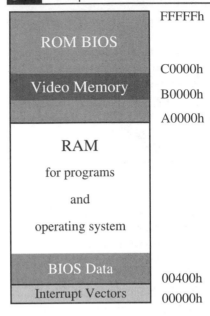

FFFFFh

C0000h

B0000h

A0000h

00400h

00000h

ware that makes it an IBM PC, or PC *clone* (copy). Except for Chapters 20 and 21, all of our programs will be written for the most primitive member of the family, the 8088, and will work on all CPUs in the 80X86 family. Much professional software is also written for all CPUs, although increasingly, advanced software like word processors work only for the later models.

Addresses in computer memory are generally a fixed number n of binary digits, so the maximum number of bytes in memory is 2^n. On the 8086/88, n is 20, so memory can in principle contain up to $2^{20} = 1,048,576$ bytes, or 1 *Mega*byte (MByte, one *million* bytes), of information. Higher numbered 80X86 CPU chips can address memory in the *Giga*Byte (GByte, one *billion* byte) range, but not under control of the usual DOS operating system. Microsoft Windows based systems typically deal (even require) these larger memories, but that is beyond the scope of this book.

The general arrangement of IBM PC memory is shown in the illustration at the left. The numbers followed by 'h' are hexadecimal addresses (base 16; see Section 1.2).

If you haven't already learned them, now is as good a time as any to present you with the following table of common multipliers.

$$n = nano = 1 \text{ billionth } (10^{-9})$$
$$\mu = micro = 1 \text{ millionth } (10^{-6})$$
$$m = milli = 1 \text{ thousandth } (10^{-3})$$

$$G = giga = 1 \text{ billion } (10^9 \approx 2^{30})$$
$$M = mega = 1 \text{ million } (10^6 \approx 2^{20})$$
$$K = kilo = 1 \text{ thousand } (10^3 \approx 2^{10})$$

$\approx$ means "is approximately equal to." As is common practice, with the positive powers, we will be vague as to whether we mean powers of ten or powers of two. Thus a Mega something might be either a million or $2^{20} = 1,048,576$ somethings. 1 MByte is usually 2^{20} bytes while 1 MHz is usually 1 million cycles per second.

The IBM PC makes special use of parts of its 1 MByte address space. The Intel 80X86 chip uses the first 1024 bytes for **interrupt vectors**, which we will explain in Chapter 15. The PC itself makes special use of memory in locations above 640K = A0000h.

It is the ROM on the IBM PC (called the **ROM BIOS**, or Basic Input Output System) which most distinguishes it from just any old 80X86 system. Whether or not a PC clone is a "true compatible" depends largely on how good a job its ROM BIOS does of mimicking that of the IBM PC. (The BIOS is level III of our hardware hierarchy.) As the name indicates, most of what the BIOS does is related to Input/Output, where its function is to present the programmer with simpler, more machine and device independent I/O operations.

The BIOS Data area consists of variable storage for the BIOS. It is set up by the bootstrap program in ROM.

Most personal computers have a simple and ingenious method of displaying information on the CRT screen. A fixed set of memory locations called **video memory** is an exact image of what is displayed on the screen. We can think of the CRT as a window that views video memory, which is usually in the address range B0000h-BFFFFh. To display the character 'M' at a particular place on the CRT screen, all we have to do is move 'M' (using a standard data movement instruction) to the corresponding place in video memory.

Most IBM PCs have a **video board** which contains the necessary video memory and also the electronic circuitry to draw and redraw the contents of that memory on the CRT screen. There are many different types of video boards for the PC—MDA, CGA, EGA, and VGA to name a few. We will discuss two of the simplest and most widely available, MDA and CGA, and one of the more capable, VGA, in Chapter 19 of this book.

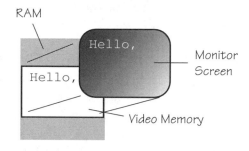

The upshot of all the special purpose memory discussed above is that the only RAM that's available for general purposes is the addresses 1024–655,359 or in hex, 400h–9FFFFh (640K = 655,360; 9FFFFh = A0000h – 1). User programs can use only the part of this memory above the BIOS Data and memory-resident part of the operating system. (In some PCs, some pieces of memory above A0000h are unused as ROM or video and can be used by later versions of DOS for small programs. The available parts of this area are called the **High Memory Area**.)

1.1.3 • More on Memory (Optional)

This section can be omitted with no loss of continuity. I have glossed over an important fact about the 80X86: the actual mechanism for addressing memory is quite a bit more complicated than I've indicated here. I will put off exposing you to its complexities until Chapter 12 when it can no longer be avoided. There are other questions about memory though that are even more complex than that, and are far beyond the scope of this book (or in fact any other *textbook* I have seen). These questions concern the subject of extending memory beyond the 1 Megabyte boundary.

It must have seemed to the designers of the 8086/88 that they were supplying all the memory anyone could ever want. After all, the 8080, its predecessor, could only handle 64 KB of memory, and here they were allowing sixteen times as much! The original IBM PC was not only designed so that other uses were prescribed for memory beyond 640 K, it was assumed that no one would want to expand their memory beyond 256 K. (Then again, the original Macintosh was designed years later with a maximum (and minimum) of 128 K of user memory and one 400 K floppy disk.)

Before long, of course, it was clear that even 640 K of RAM was insufficient, and Lotus, Intel, and Microsoft combined to define a kludge called the **expanded memory specification** (**EMS**) which allowed memory to exist beyond the 1 MByte boundary. Sixteen KByte chunks are shuttled in and out of memory below the 1 MByte limit and then accessed with normal methods. (A *kludge* (pronounced klooj) is a word of computerese meaning "an ill-sorted collection of poorly matching parts, forming a distressing whole.")

With the advent of the 80286 and beyond, access to memory above the 1 MByte limit was built into the CPU. To differentiate from expanded memory, this technique is called the **extended memory specification** (**XMS**). It stabilized with the 80386, and that is what we will discuss here.

With XMS, memory addresses continue above 1 MByte, up to a maximum of 4 GigaBytes (4 *billion* bytes), depending on how much memory is physically installed. Addressing this memory is even more complicated, and is far beyond the scope of this book. (See Chappell, *Undocumented DOS*, pp. 349-584, or Williams, *DOS 6, A Developer's Guide*, pp. 631-654 and 701-720. This topic is *not* for the faint of heart.)

Since anyone with the money to buy expanded memory has for years had the much more attractive prospect of buying a computer with extended memory, which is also much faster, EMS is effectively dead.

1.2 • The Decimal, Binary, and Hexadecimal Numbering Systems

All modern digital computers use combinations of **bits** to represent information. A bit is a component with two stable states, called 0 and 1. A moment's thought should convince you that just about any information should be representable as a collection of bits—consider for instance the modern scoreboard which consists of a large array of light bulbs that are either on or off (1 or 0). Unfortunately, such a representation isn't very useful for doing arithmetic.

Normally computers represent numbers in the **binary** (base 2) number system. Just as the ordinary decimal (base 10) system has digits 0, 1, ..., 9, the base 2 number system has digits 0 and 1. A group of n binary digits can represent 2^n different quantities: each bit can have two different values, independently of all the other bits, so the total number of different values is

$$2 \times 2 \times \ldots \times 2 \ (n \text{ times}) = 2^n$$

The smallest standard group of bits is the **byte**, which is 8 bits long. Thus a byte can hold 2^8 = 256 different pieces of information. Other units of information on the IBM PC are groups of bytes, and include the **word** (2 bytes = 16 bits), the **double word** (2 words = 4 bytes = 32 bits) and the **quad word** (4 words = 8 bytes = 64 bits). (A byte is almost always eight bits, but word size varies from computer to computer. A rule of thumb is that the larger the word size, the more powerful the computer.)

In addition to the binary number system, assembly language programmers need to know the **hexadecimal** number system (base 16, **hex** for short). Hex is in effect a shorthand representation of binary numbers which is often easier for humans to manipulate. To use base 16, we use the letters A through F (upper or lower case insignificant) to represent the 'digits' 10 through 15, respectively

In the assemblers we will be discussing, the Microsoft Assembler MASM or the Turbo Assembler TASM, binary numbers are indicated by following them with the letter B (or b), hexadecimal numbers by following them with the letter H (or h), with no intervening space. A typical binary number might be 1101101010010B and a typical hex number might be 3A9BH.

A small problem arises with something like EACH, which could be a programmer-defined name of some kind or a three hexadecimal digit number. The rule is

---
A number in assembly language must start with a digit 0 through 9. A hex number which would otherwise start with a letter must be preceded by a 0.

Thus in order for EACH to be interpreted as a number, it would have to be written 0EACH.

The remainder of Section 1.2 discusses the binary and hexadecimal number systems and conversions between these systems and decimal. If you are already familiar with the material, skip to the exercises at the end of the section to check your knowledge.

1.2.1 • The Binary Number System

The binary number system as used by computers is a *positional* number system, just like the decimal number system. In the decimal number 95243, the last position, containing the 3, has a weight of 10^0, the next to last position, containing 4, has a weight of 10^1, and so on up through the first position, containing a 9, which has a weight of 10^4. Thus the value of 95243 is

$$9 \times 10^4 + 5 \times 10^3 + 2 \times 10^2 + 4 \times 10^1 + 3 \times 10^0$$

There is a similar formula for binary numbers. The value of 1011010B is

$$1 \times 2^6 + 0 \times 2^5 + 1 \times 2^4 + 1 \times 2^3 + 0 \times 2^2 + 1 \times 2^1 + 0 \times 2^0$$
$$= 64 + 16 + 8 + 2 = 90$$

1.2.2 • Conversions between Binary and Decimal

In general, there are two ways of converting a number representation to another base—multiplication or division by the base. Each works from any base to any other base. The difference is the base in which the operations are performed.

▶ **Binary to Decimal**

One way to convert binary to decimal is to start at the right end of the number, writing 1 over the last digit. Then working your way to the left, double the number you write over each successive digit. Circle and add up the numbers over 1s and the result is the value of the binary number:

$$\boxed{64} \quad 32 \quad + \boxed{16} + \boxed{8} \quad 4 \quad + \boxed{2} \quad 1 = 90$$

$$1 \qquad 0 \qquad 1 \qquad 1 \qquad 0 \qquad 1 \qquad 0$$

We are simply multiplying digits by their positional value and adding them up (in the new base, decimal.) An equivalent method, based on Horner's method * for efficient evaluation of polynomials, uses

$$1 \times 2^6 + 0 \times 2^5 + 1 \times 2^4 + 1 \times 2^3 + 0 \times 2^2 + 1 \times 2^1 + 0 \times 2^0 =$$
$$(((((1 \times 2 + 0) \times 2 + 1) \times 2 + 1) \times 2 + 0) \times 2 + 1) \times 2 + 0$$

The sequence of numbers computed is 1, 2, 2, 4, 5, 10, 11, 22, 22, 44, 45, 90, 90. This method is fairly fast and can be done in your head for short numbers, but it quickly becomes unwieldy and error-prone even for numbers the size of the example.

The multiply and add technique used here works from any base to any base. The arithmetic is performed in the new base, so generally humans use this method to convert from another base to *decimal* and computers use this method to convert from another base to *binary*.

▶ **Decimal to Binary**

Conversion from decimal to binary is the reverse of Horner's method: it consists of repeatedly

---

* **Horner's Method** is a method for evaluating polynomials that uses the least number of multiplications and additions (n each for a polynomial of degree n). It makes use of the following identity: $a_n x^n + a_{n-1} x^{n-1} + \ldots + a_1 x + a_0 = (\ldots((a_n x + a_{n-1})x + a_{n-2})x + \ldots + a_1)x + a_0$

dividing by 2. The sequence of remainders *in reverse order* is the binary representation for the number. For instance, let's apply the technique to 90 (whose binary representation we already know). We will write the quotient of dividing each number by 2 under the number and the remainder to the right of the quotient:

	quotients	remainders	
90:	45	0	
	22	1	
	11	0	↑ Read result upwards
	5	1	to get 1011010B
	2	1	
	1	0	
	0	1	

The method of division can also be used to convert between any two bases, but as the division is done in the original base, humans generally use this method to convert from *decimal* to another base, while computers use it to convert from *binary* to another base.

1.2.3 • The Hexadecimal Number System

The main problem with the binary number system for humans is that decimal numbers of reasonable size are long and cumbersome in binary. For instance

$$1000 \text{ (decimal)} = 1111101000B$$

and one million is 20 binary digits long. Hexadecimal (base 16) is used as a convenient shorthand for binary numbers.

1.2.4 • Conversions Involving Hexadecimal

You should commit to memory the table of equivalents of hex digits and their binary and decimal values shown on the top of the next page.

▶   **Hex to Binary**

Each hex digit corresponds exactly to four binary digits. To convert a hex number to binary, just convert each individual hex digit to binary:

$$0EACH = 0000\ 1110\ 1010\ 1100\ B$$

Although welldisguised, the method above is, in fact, the multiplicative conversion method—we are expressing each digit in its representation in the new base, multiplying by its position value (which is particularly easy here since the base is 16 = 10000B and multiplying by 16 involves adding four zeroes to the right in binary), and adding.

Hex	Decimal	Binary
0	0	0000B
1	1	0001B
2	2	0010B
3	3	0011B
4	4	0100B
5	5	0101B
6	6	0110B
7	7	0111B
8	8	1000B
9	9	1001B
A	10	1010B
B	11	1011B
C	12	1100B
D	13	1101B
E	14	1110B
F	15	1111B

▶ **Binary to Hex**

The method here is similar to hex-to-binary. The only trick is that you must start from the *right*, marking off your binary number in groups of four bits, (which makes a difference when the number of digits isn't divisible by 4). Thus 1100111001011B is divided up as

$$1\ \ 1001\ \ 1100\ \ 1011B = 19CBH$$

Once again we are using the division method. Marking off groups of four from the right is, in fact, the same as repeated division by 16 = 10000B.

It is so easy to translate between hex and binary that programmers often speak of numbers as being in binary when in fact they are displayed or entered in hex. With a little practice it is possible to look at a hex number and directly visualize the binary.

▶ **Decimal to Hex**

Of course we could convert between decimal and hex by going through binary, but it is useful to have a direct method. For decimal to hex, use a method similar to the decimal to binary procedure, dividing by 16 instead of 2. Thus to convert 6841 to hex:

$$
\begin{array}{r}
427 \\
16\,)\,\overline{6841} \\
64 \\
\hline
44 \\
32 \\
\hline
121 \\
112 \\
\hline
9
\end{array}
\quad = \text{last digit}
$$

$$
\begin{array}{r}
26 \\
16\,)\,\overline{427} \\
32 \\
\hline
107 \\
96 \\
\hline
11
\end{array}
\quad = \text{next to last digit} = B
$$

$$
\begin{array}{r}
1 \\
16\,)\,\overline{26} \\
16 \\
\hline
10
\end{array}
\quad = \text{next to first digit} = A
$$

$$
\begin{array}{r}
0 \\
16\,)\,\overline{1} \\
0 \\
\hline
1
\end{array}
\quad = \text{first digit}
$$

so 6841 = 1AB9H.

▶ **Hex to Decimal**

Either of the methods suggested for binary to decimal will also work for hex to decimal with 2 replaced by 16 in appropriate places. For instance,

$$
\begin{aligned}
1AB9h &= (\ (1 \times 16 + \boxed{0Ah}\ ) \times 16 + \boxed{0Bh}\ ) \times 16 + 9 \\
&= (\ (1 \times 16 + \boxed{10}\ ) \times 16 + \boxed{11}\ ) \times 16 + 9 \\
&= (\ \boxed{26} \times 16 + 11\ ) \times 16 + 9 \\
&= (\ \boxed{416} + 11\ ) \times 16 + 9 \\
&= \boxed{427} \times 16 + 9 \\
&= \boxed{6832} + 9 = 6841
\end{aligned}
$$

1.2.5 • Addition in Binary and Hex

Addition in binary or hex is a straightforward modification of the usual decimal methods. In binary, one must simply remember that 1B + 1B = 2 = 10B = 0 carry 1 and that 1B + 1B + 1B = 11B = 1 carry 1. For instance we add 111101011B and 10100110B, working right to left as follows:

```
    1111 111         (Carries)
     111101011B
   +  10100110B
   1010010001B
```

Adding numbers in hex is similar, if trickier. One could either convert the numbers to binary and add *or* convert pairs of hex digits to decimal, add, and convert the result back to hex. The problem above, in hex, would be

```
     11               (Carries)
     1EBh
   + 0A6h
     291h
```

(0Bh + 6 = 11 + 6 = 17 = 11h = 1 carry 1. 1 + 0Eh + 0Ah = 1 + 14 + 10 = 25 = 19h = 9 carry 1. 1 + 1 + 0 = 2 = 2h. Two other important cases are 1 + 9 = A (hex) and 1 + F = 10h.)

Subtraction will be discussed in Section 1.3, when we discuss computer representation of signed numbers.

Exercises 1.2

1. Convert to binary: 2483   3E8Ah

2. Convert to decimal: 1011000111B   3E8Ah

3. Convert to hex: 1011000111B   2483

4. Perform the following additions in binary:

$$\begin{array}{r} 11010101B \\ +\ \ \ 1110011B \\ \hline \end{array} \qquad \begin{array}{r} 10011111B \\ +\ \ \ \ 100001B \\ \hline \end{array}$$

5. Perform the following additions in hex:

$$\begin{array}{r} 8A3Fh \\ +\ 38CDh\ \checkmark \\ \hline \end{array} \qquad \begin{array}{r} 9B34h \\ +\ 5AE6h \\ \hline \end{array}$$

Note: The answers to exercises, or parts thereof, marked by ✓ are given in the **answers section** in the back of the book.

1.3 • Negative Numbers; 2's Complement Arithmetic

Representing negative numbers in binary gets a little tricky. In a computer, where numbers occupy a fixed-length piece of storage (a 16-bit word or 8-bit byte on the IBM PC) it seems reasonable to pick one bit to act as the sign. Traditionally it is the left-most bit and also traditionally, 0 represents a '+' sign and 1 represents a '−' sign. (Probably the reason for both conventions is that when we are representing positive numbers, these conventions don't get in the way. In fact we don't have to care if we are dealing with signed or unsigned numbers.)

Once the sign has been agreed upon, consensus vanishes. There are at least three different methods which have been used at various times by various computers. (And the PC uses one method for integers and another for reals!)

1.3.1 • Sign-Magnitude Representation

The most obvious method is to do as humans do: represent a negative number as the corresponding positive number (its *magnitude*) together with a minus sign. Thus if we are considering 8-bit numbers,

$$51 = \boxed{0}\ 0110011B$$
$$-51 = \boxed{1}\ 0110011B$$

Sign-magnitude seems such an obvious choice that you may be surprised that it is seldom used any more except in special cases. There are two problems with it:

- Arithmetic is very complicated. For instance, consider the rule for adding two signed numbers: If the two numbers have the same sign, add and use that sign as the sign of the result; if they have different signs, subtract the smaller magnitude from the larger and give the result the sign of the larger.

- 0 has two different representations: in 8-bit numbers, as 00000000B and 10000000B.

Of course humans have both of these problems to deal with and have managed to do so successfully for hundreds of years, but we shouldn't let our humanity prejudice us in trying to come up with a better solution for computers.

1.3.2 • 1's Complement Representation

In this representation, the negative of a number is represented as the **1's complement** of the corresponding positive number. The 1's complement of a binary number is obtained by changing all zeroes to ones and ones to zeroes. Thus

$$51 = 00110011B$$
$$-51 = 11001100B$$

The term *1's complement* is used because

$$-51 = 11001100B = 11111111B - 00110011B$$
$$= 11111111B - 51$$

A positive number has a sign bit which is 0 (= +), so its 1's complement will have a sign of 1 (= '–').

1's complement numbers solve the arithmetic problem in a rather miraculous way: To add two 1's complement numbers, just add them, treating them as unsigned! The only special thing to do is that if there is a carry out the left end, it must be added back into the right end—called an **end-around carry**. Subtraction is almost as easy: Take the 1's complement of the number to be subtracted and then add.

The trouble with 1's complement is that it doesn't solve the second problem, that of two zeroes. In 1's complement, +0 = 00000000B, –0 = 11111111B. (On one machine of the author's acquaintance, +0 = –0 *and* +0 > –0!)

1.3.3 • 2's Complement Representation.

The method actually used by the IBM PC and most other modern computers for representing signed integers is 2's complement. The operation of taking the **2's complement** of a number is obtained by taking the 1's complement and adding 1. Thus the 2's complement of an 8-bit number X would be

$$11111111B - X + 1 = (11111111B + 1) - X = 100000000B - X = 2^8 - X$$

which gives us an idea of where the name came from. In general, the n-bit 2's complement of X is 2^n – X. You can also see that the 2's complement of the 2's complement of X is X back again, as $2^n - (2^n$

$- X) = 2^n - 2^n + X = X.$

▶ **Quick 2's Complement**.

There is a simple algorithm for computing 2's complements in one step which you are welcome to use if you wish. Starting from the right end of the number, keep all zeros unchanged until you get to the first '1' from the right. Leave it alone too, but change all further digits. Thus

$$11010\ 100 \qquad \text{(The number)}$$
$$\text{Change} \rightarrow \mid \leftarrow \text{Keep the same}$$
$$00101\ 100 \qquad \text{(The 2's complement))}$$

The 2's complement *representation* of –X is the result of applying the 2's complement *operation* to the representation of X

Be sure to distinguish:
• 2's complement *representation*
• 2's complement *operation*

00110011B is the 8-bit 2's complement *representation* of 51
11001101B is the 8-bit 2's complement *representation* of –51

The 2's complement *operation* applied to 00110011B (= 51) is 11001101B (= –51)
The 2's complement *operation* applied to 11001101B (= –51) is 00110011B (= 51)

▶ **Addition of 2's Complement Numbers**

To add two 2's complement numbers, we simply add the numbers as though they were unsigned, and if there is any carry out the left end, *throw it away*! Suppose for instance we wish to add 74 and –51 in **8-bit** 2's complement form. 74 = 01001010B, 51 = 00110011B, and so –51 = 11001100B + 1 = 11001101B. The sum is

$$\mid \leftarrow 8 \text{ bits} \rightarrow \mid$$
$$\begin{array}{r} 1\ \ 1\ \ \ 1 \qquad \text{(Carries)} \\ 74\ =\ \ \ 01001010 \\ \underline{-51\ =\ +11001101} \\ \cancel{1}\,00010111\ =\ 17h\ =\ 23 \end{array}$$

as expected. (The carry out the left end was discarded.) On the other hand, if we compute –74 + 51, –74 = 10110101+1 = 10110110B, and

$$
\begin{array}{rl}
& 11\ \ 11 \qquad\qquad \text{(Carries)} \\
-74\ =\ & 10110110 \\
\underline{\ 51\ =\ } & \underline{+00110011} \\
& 11101001 \\
=\ & -\,(2\text{'s comp of }11101001) \\
=\ & -\,00010111B\ =\ -17h\ =\ -23
\end{array}
$$

(The result is a negative number since its first bit is 1.) Finally, consider –74 + –51:

$$
\begin{array}{rl}
& 1\ \ 11111 \qquad\qquad \text{(Carries)} \\
-74\ =\ & 10110110 \\
\underline{-51\ =\ } & \underline{+11001101} \\
& 10000011 \\
=\ & -\,(2\text{'s comp of }10000011) \\
=\ & -01111101B\ =\ -7Dh\ =\ -125
\end{array}
$$

as expected.

2's complement arithmetic is even easier than 1's complement (though computing 2's complements is slightly harder) and the negative zero problem is finally solved: –00000000B = 11111111B + 1 = 00000000B (when the carry out the left end is discarded).

Unfortunately we have added a new problem: We now have a negative number for which there is no corresponding positive number. In 8-bit 2's complement, that number is 10000000B = –128. If you take its 2's complement, you get 01111111B + 1 = 10000000B!

There is no way to avoid this anomaly. For any representation of positive and negative numbers and zero by a fixed number of bits, either one number will be represented more than once or a different number of positive numbers than negative will be represented. In fact, a fixed number of bits has an even number of different values. Therefore if 0 has only 1 representation, there are an odd number of nonzero (positive and negative) representations. If no values have two representatives, there can't be the same number of positive and negative values represented.

Having a number with no negative doesn't commonly present problems in 2's complement because the anomaly is out at the fringes, but often that number must be tested for and treated specially.

▶ **2's Complement in Hex**

One can find the 2's complement of numbers in hex by converting to binary, taking the complement, and converting back to hex, but it is also easily done directly in hex. Taking the 1's complement is equivalent to subtracting the number from all ones in binary, from all Fs in hex. It's probably easiest to subtract from hex F by mentally converting each digit to decimal, performing the subtraction, then converting back to hex. Once the 1's complement is obtained, add one to get the 2's complement, being sure to remember that 1 + 9 = A, **not** 10, and 1 + F = 10 (hex).

For example, obtain the 2's complement of 3DA6h:

$$
\begin{array}{r}
\mathrm{FFFF} \\
-\underline{\mathrm{3DA6}} \\
\mathrm{C259} \\
+\underline{1} \\
\mathrm{C25A}
\end{array}
$$

$\mathrm{C259} = $ 1's complement

$\mathrm{C25A} = $ 2's complement

so the 2's complement is 0C25Ah.

▶ Which 2's Complement Hex Numbers are Negative

It's not hard to recognize negative 2's complement numbers in hex. Suppose the number of bits is divisible by 4, the usual case. If the first hex digit is in the range 8-F, the first bit is 1 so the number is negative, and if the first hex digit is in the range 0-7, the first bit is 0 and the number is positive .

▶ Range of Signed and Unsigned Numbers

A word or byte can be considered to hold either a signed or unsigned number. For instance, a word can hold signed numbers in the range –32768…32767 or unsigned numbers in the range 0…65535. It is up to the programmer to make the decision and act accordingly. For positive numbers in the range 0…32767, unsigned and signed words are identical— the words with first bit 0. For the ranges of signed and unsigned bytes, see Exercise 1.3—4.

▶ Changing Lengths of 2's Complement Representations

Of course, it takes more bits to represent large numbers than it does small numbers. However,

---

In 2's complement arithmetic, all operands must be the same length.
The first bit is always interpreted as the sign.

(In our examples above, that length is eight bits.) Since operands must be the same length, there may be occasions when we have to increase or decrease the number of bits in our representation, and we need to know how to do it.

It is in fact very easy. To shorten a 2's complement representation, you can remove as many bits as you like from the beginning, as long as they are all the same as the sign bit and you leave a sign bit in the first bit position.

Shortening 2's complement numbers

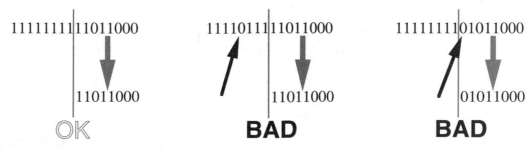

Lengthening 2's complement numbers always works, as one might expect. One simply copies the sign bit into as many positions to the left as are necessary to give the required length, a process called **sign extension**.

Lengthening 2's complement numbers

When the number of bits is divisible by 4, these operations are also easy in hex. Zeroes can be removed from the front end as long as the first remaining digit is in the range 0–7. F's can be removed as long as the first remaining digit is in the range 8–F. On the other hand, if the first digit is in the range 8–F, the number can be lengthened by adding F's on the left, and if the first digit is in the range 0–7, the number can be lengthened by adding zeroes.

▶ **Overflow**

The shortening operation above naturally gives rise to the question of what happens when the result of an arithmetic operation is too big to be represented with the number of bits we are using. In that case, we say **overflow** has occurred. For instance in an 8-bit representation:

$$
\begin{array}{rl}
87 = & 01010111 \\
+42 = & +00101010 \\
\hline
& 10000001 = -127
\end{array}
$$

and

$$
\begin{array}{rl}
-87 = & 10101001 \\
(+) \quad -42 = & +11010110 \\
\hline
& 1\,01111111 = 127
\end{array}
$$

both of which are the WRONG answer.

The reason these results are incorrect is that it isn't possible to represent the true answers, 129 and –129, as 8-bit 2's complement numbers.

Overflow is one of the recurring problems with computer arithmetic. How do we tell if it has occurred? It is quite easy for a human computer to determine when overflow has occurred. There are two cases:

- If we are adding two numbers with *different* signs, then there are enough bits to hold the result since the result is closer to zero than at least one of the addends. There is never any overflow in this case.
- If we are adding two numbers with the *same* sign, then overflow has occurred if the sign of the result is different.

Thus we have

01010111	10101001	11001011	11001011
+00101010	+11010110	+11010110	+01010110
10000001	1 01111111	10100001	00100001

    Overflow   **Overflow**   No **overflow**   No **overflow**

Exercises 1.3

1. Convert the following 8-bit binary numbers to decimal

    00101101B ✓   11101011B   11111111B ✓   10000000B   01000101B

    a) Assuming that they are signed 2's complement numbers.
    b) Assuming that the numbers are unsigned.
(For example, as a signed number, 11110101B = –(2's complement of 11110101 = –(00001011) = –11; as an unsigned number, 11110101B = 255 – 10 = 245.)

2. Convert the following 8-bit hex numbers to decimal:

    0FFh   88h ✓   3Fh ✓   0F0h

    a) Assuming that they are signed 2's complement numbers.
    b) Assuming that the numbers are unsigned.
(For example, as a signed 8-bit number, 0AAh = –(2's complement of AAh) = –(55h + 1) = –56h = – 86 as an unsigned number, 0AAh = 10 × 16 + 10 = 176. Remember that the leading 0 in 0AAh doesn't indicate a digit position; it merely indicates that the number is hex.)

3. Do the following addition exercises by translating the numbers into 8-bit 2's complement binary numbers, performing the arithmetic, and translating the result back into a decimal number. Indicate where overflow occurs and why, based on the *binary* arithmetic.

47	–47	47	–47
38	38 ✓	–38	–38

47	–47	47	–47
88	88	–88	–88 ✓

4. ✓ What is the range of *signed* numbers that can be represented by a byte? What is the range of *unsigned* numbers that can be represented by a byte? What range of numbers have the same representation in a byte whether it is interpreted as signed or unsigned?

5. a) Give the 16-bit 2's complement form of the following 8-bit 2's complement numbers:

    94h   33h ✓   AEh ✓   FFh

    b) Which of the following 16-bit 2's complement numbers can be shortened to 8 bits and maintain their value? For example, FE88h = –178h, while its shortened version, 88h = –78h ≠ FE88h. On the other hand, FF94h = –6Ch = 94h.

00A9h ✓   003Bh ✓   FF94h   FCF3h ✓   FF3Ch

6.   A positive binary number is even precisely when its last digit is 0. When is a negative 2's complement number even?

7.   (optional) There is nothing particularly magical about 2's complement in binary, other than that the computations are particularly easy in base 2. We could also do 10's complement arithmetic in normal decimal numbers. Suppose for instance that we use only three digit decimal numbers. Then the 10's complement of such a number x is 1000 – x. Thus the 10's complement of 423 is 577. We can represent negative numbers as the 10's complement of the corresponding positive number. Do the arithmetic in problem 3 in 3 digit 10's complement decimal arithmetic

1.4 • The ASCII Character Set

Another way to represent data with bits is to encode letters, digits, and punctuation as sequences of binary digits and then use those characters to represent data. The encoding scheme used by all personal computers is **ASCII**, the American Standard Code for Information Interchange.

A character set which contains the 52 upper- and lower-case letters, the 10 digits, and the 30 or so commonly used punctuation and math symbols clearly requires at least seven bits to represent each character.* The ASCII code uses exactly seven bits, giving a total of 128 possible characters. If we take the number represented by those seven bits, we can consider that an ASCII character is represented by a number between 0 and 127. Our assemblers denote the ASCII value of a character by surrounding that character with single quotes or double quotes. We will stick to single quotes for consistency. Thus 'A' represents the number which represents the first upper case letter of the alphabet, which happens to be 65.

It is normally unnecessary to know the actual values of ASCII characters (you should use the 'x' form wherever possible), but certain relationships are helpful and should be learned.

- The characters represented by the numbers 0 to 31 are **non-printing characters** and are used for more or less standard control purposes. The most commonly occurring of these are

> 13 = carriage return
> 10 = line feed
> 9 = tab

Character 127 is also non-printing, and is generally the character assigned to the delete key. The characters corresponding to 0–31 and 127 can be represented in assembly language *only* by their numeric values The characters 1 through 26, in addition to having various standard interpretations, are also called **control characters** and are identified with letters of the alphabet. Control-A is 1, control-B is 2, etc. Thus a carriage return is also control-M.

- The blank character ' ' (which is considered a printing character) is 32

---

* There are character sets which, like Morse Code, use different length representations for different characters—commonly, shorter representations for more frequently occurring characters. Such representations aren't in common use in computers.

- The digit characters run continuously: the digit '0' = 48, the digit '1' is 49, etc. Thus

$$\text{digit-character} = \text{'0'} + \text{digit value}$$

that is, for example, '7' = '0' + 7.

Do not confuse the ASCII value of a digit character with its actual numerical value.
'3' = '0' + 3 = 48 + 3 = 51 ≠ 3!

- The letters of the alphabet are in two continuous ranges, one for uppercase and one for lowercase. We have formulae for letters which are similar to those for digits:

$$n\text{th uppercase letter} = \text{'A'} + n - 1$$

$$n\text{th lowercase letter} = \text{'a'} + n - 1$$

and thus the important formula

$$\text{lower-case-letter} = \text{corresponding upper-case-letter} + (\text{'a'} - \text{'A'})$$

Another way to view the formula above is that obviously $'x' = 'X' + ('x' - 'X')$ for any letter x, and $('x' - 'X')$ is the same for all letters x, in particular, it is equal to $('a' - 'A')$. As a matter of possible interest, $'a' - 'A' = 32$ but I prefer using $('a' - 'A')$ as it more clearly describes what is going on.
- Once a character gets into the computer's memory, the computer has no way of telling it from a number. Thus for instance, 'A' and 65 are indistinguishable.

Since the seven bits used for the ASCII code is an inconvenient number in a binary computer, eight bits are usually used. The eighth bit may either be ignored, used for error-checking, used to carry other information (it is used for formatting information in one well-known word processor), or used to create another set of 128 characters. IBM has taken the last route, with an **extended ASCII** character set. The characters above 128 are used for foreign language and graphic (box-drawing) characters. Also in certain circumstances on the PC, the non-printing control characters from 0 to 31 print a graphic symbol instead of performing their control function.

For a complete table of the extended ASCII character set, see Appendix A.

Exercises 1.4

1. Write each of the following expressions in the form 'x' (i.e., as a single quoted character):

   '0' + 3   'A' + 1   '3' + 2 ✓   '8' – 3   '9' – 9   'f' – 5   'x' – 32

2. Write the numeric value of each of the following expressions (without using an ASCII table):

   'B' – 'A'   'd' – 'a'   'b' – 'A' ✓   '8' – '3'

1.5 • Pseudocode

At various times throughout this book, it will prove advantageous to express code in some high-level language—before writing the corresponding assembly language, as comments to explain assembly language, or in exercises to be translated into assembly language. We will be quite loose in our use of such pseudocode but with the help of this section, anyone familiar with a high-level language should be able to follow it.

The most basic construct is the *expression*. In what follows, all of our arguments will be assumed to be integers, and we will use five basic operations: +, –, * (times), / (integer division with integer result), and **mod** (remainder from integer division; the % operator in C). Simple examples are

$$2 - 3 = -1 \qquad 2 * 3 = 6 \qquad 2 + 3 = 5 \qquad 240 / 43 = 5 \qquad 240 \textbf{ mod } 43 = 25$$

For expressions with more than one operator, the usual rules of evaluation order hold:

- Operations within parentheses are evaluated before operations outside:

$$5 * (3 + 6) = 45 \qquad (20 + 4) / (5 - 2) = 8$$

- *, /, and **mod** operations are performed before + and –:

$$5 * 3 + 6 = 15 + 6 = 21 \qquad 20 + 4 / 5 - 2 = 20 + 0 - 2 = 18$$

- Several *, /, or **mod** operations or several + or – operations are performed left to right:

$$36 / 2 * 3 = 18 * 3 = 54, \text{ not } 6 \qquad 5 - 4 + 3 = 1 + 3 = 4, \text{ not } 5 - 7$$

Statements may be separated with semicolons, for readability.

The *assignment* statement *variable := expression* is used to give a value to a variable. Note the double symbol ':=', which can be read 'becomes' or 'is set to'. Notice also the distinction between ':=' and '=': The former is a command to compute its right-hand side and store the result in its left-hand side, whereas the latter is a statement of fact. (When used in logical expressions, '=' represents a test whose value can be true or false.)

The **if** statement is of the form

<table>
<tr><td>

if *condition* **then**
  statement
  ...
  statement
end if

</td><td>

or

</td><td>

if *condition* **then**
  statement
  ...
  statement
else
  statement
  ...
  statement
end if

</td></tr>
</table>

and looping is described by the **while** statement:

while *condition* **do**		W1:	**if** *condition* is false **go to** W2
statement	*which is*		*statement*
...	*equivalent to*		*...*
statement			*statement*
end while			**go to** W1
		W2:	

I will generally be quite free with these, omitting the **end if**/**while** statements, for instance, and depending on indentation or an understanding of the algorithm to group statements correctly. I will also often omit **then** and **do** to save space. The following pseudocode example computes $p = x^n$ (by in effect converting n to binary using the division technique we learned in Section 1.2).

p := 1; p2 := x		p := 1; p2 := x
while n > 0 **do**		**while** n > 0
if n is odd **then**		**if** n is odd
p := p * p2	*or*	p := p * p2
end if		n := n / 2
n := n / 2		p2 := p2 * p2
p2 := p2 * p2		
end while		

We will use <>, <=, and >= for the relations $\neq$, $\leq$, and $\geq$, respectively, when we don't go ahead and use the latter, and will use **and**, **or**, and **not** for the usual logical operations.

SUMMARY

Binary numbers are denoted in assembly language by a suffix of 'b' or 'B', hexadecimal numbers by a suffix of 'h' or 'H'. You should be able to convert between representations of positive integers in binary, decimal, and hexadecimal (hex).

1 byte	= 8 bits		
1 word	= 2 bytes	= 16 bits	
1 double word	= 2 words	= 4 bytes	= 32 bits
1 quad word	= 4 words	= 8 bytes	= 64 bits

Binary numbers can be considered either signed or unsigned. Signed representations have a fixed length and the left bit is interpreted as the sign, 0 for +, 1 for –. The IBM PC uses 2's complement notation, in which the negative of a number is found by taking the 2's complement: Change all 0s in the numbers to 1s and vice versa, and then add 1 to the result. For 2's complement to be meaningful, there must be a fixed length for the representation (which is generally longer than the length required to represent the magnitude of the number).

An n bit number can represent numbers from 0 to $2^n - 1$ as unsigned numbers and numbers from -2^{n-1} to $2^{n-1} - 1$ as signed 2's complement numbers.

Addition of binary 2's complement numbers is the same as addition of unsigned numbers. Any carry out the left end is discarded.

Subtraction is done by taking the 2's complement and adding.

Overflow occurs on addition if the signs of the addends are the same, and differ from the sign of the result.

A 2's complement representation is shortened by removing bits from the left end as long as only bits equal to the original sign are removed and at least one sign bit is left. Representations are lengthened by sign extension.

The following are some useful facts about the ASCII character set:

- The characters with values 0-31 and 127 are normally non-printing.
- $' \ ' = 32$
- Digit Character = Digit + $'0'$
- Lowercase letter character
$$= \text{corresponding uppercase letter character} + ('a' - 'A')$$

Chapter 2

A First Program

registers discussed

ah	AX	al
bh	BX	bl
ch	CX	cl
dh	DX	dl

SI
DI
BP
SP
DS
ES
SS
CS
IP

o d i t s z c

Here we learn how to create a simple assembly program and start to explain its structure.

2.1 • Creating an Assembly Language Program

The purpose of this section is to describe how to solve the following

Programming Problem 2.1

Write, assemble, link, and execute a program which displays your name on the screen.

The rest of this section will describe how to create and translate the program, and the remainder of the chapter will be devoted to discussing the general structure of PC assembly language programs, as related to this one, and to describing how this one works. The text of the program is at the top of page 27.

The overall process of creating an assembly language program involves the creation of three types of **files**. In computerese, a file is merely an arbitrary collection of information, stored on the computer's hard disk or on a removable floppy disk. DOS, the PC operating system, names files with a name of up to eight characters, followed by a period and an **extension** of up to three characters. Our three file types will be indicated by the following extensions:

.ASM Assembly language source programs; these are what the programmer writes.

.OBJ Object files; the output produced by the assember from an input .ASM file.

.EXE Executable files produced by the linker utility combining one or more .OBJ files.

For instance, in the creation of our first program, we will have three related files, FIRST.ASM, FIRST.OBJ, and FIRST.EXE. The overall process can be visualized as follows:

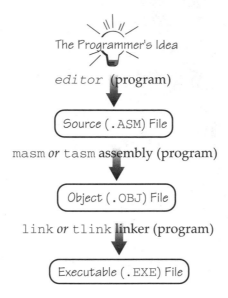

The .ASM file contains the human-readable program and is written directly by the programmer using a program called an **editor**. A wide variety of editors are available. Recent versions of DOS come with an editor called edit, and you can also use the NotePad program that comes with Microsoft Windows. A word processing program can also be used as long as you faithfully remember to save your files in text-only mode.

Two editors that are particularly useful for programming in assembly language are ed, which is supplied on the disk that comes with this book and a shareware program called WinEdit, for which the disk contains customization files. Ed is used in a DOS environment or a DOS window within Windows, and WinEdit is used strictly in a Windows environment. Their installation and particular use in assembly is discussed in Appendix C.

The .ASM file created with an editor is called the **source program**. The source program is translated into an **object program** (extension .OBJ) using an **assembler**. Finally, one or more object programs are combined using a **linker**, resulting in an **executable program** (extension .EXE). The assembler and linker are purchased as a package from a software vendor. The two packages discussed here are the Microsoft Assembler (assembler MASM and linker LINK) and the Borland Turbo Assembler (assembler TASM and linker TLINK).

▶ **Creating the Source (.ASM) Program**

Use the editor of your choice to create the source program file FIRST.ASM which is given at the top of the facing page. It is just about the simplest program which accomplishes anything visible. It displays the line 'Hello, my name is Bill Jones' on the CRT screen. The actual text to be entered begins with the line ;; FIRST.ASM... and ends with the line containing END HELLO. You should, of course, substitute your name for mine.

```
 First column
          First tab stop
             Second tab stop
                ...      A convenient tab stop

;; FIRST.ASM—Our first Assembly Language Program.  This program
;;   displays the line 'Hello, my name is Bill Jones' on the CRT

          .MODEL SMALL

          .STACK 100h

          .DATA
Message   DB     'Hello, my name is Bill Jones', 13, 10, '$'

          .CODE
Hello     PROC
          mov    ax, @data
          mov    ds, ax
          mov    dx, OFFSET Message
          mov    ah, 9h ;     Function code for 'display string'
          int    21h ;        The standard way to call MSDOS
          mov    al, 0 ;      Return code of 0
          mov    ah, 4ch ;    Exit back to MSDOS
          int    21h
Hello     ENDP

          END    Hello ;      Tells where to start execution
```

UPPER and lower case can be used interchangeably

except where I specifically state to the contrary. I use case to help indicate types of operators and operands and I would suggest you follow my example. (The systematic use of case is particularly important when using the customized WinEdit.) *All punctuation is important!* Assembly language is not nearly as free-form as high-level languages, and you should maintain my arrangement of lines and tabs.

At this point you are ready to translate the source file, so you will exit the editor, saving the source file.

► **Assembling the Source File (Creating the .OBJ File)**

Once the .ASM file is created, it can be translated using either MASM or TASM. We will give instructions for both.

First enter

C> **masm first;**↵   or   C> **tasm first**↵

which is short for

> C> **masm first.asm;**↵   or   C> **tasm first.asm**↵

Things you type are shown in boldface. The ↵ character represents the Enter or carriage return key, and doesn't appear on the screen. If you forget the ';' at the end of the line with masm, you will be asked a series of questions, all of which can be answered by hitting the Enter (carriage return) key.) If the assembler gives error messages, see the end of this section for hints on possible problems.

These and following commands can be entered as shown from a DOS prompt or in a MSDOS command window while running Windows, or by using the Run command under the File menu in the Windows Program Manager.

▶   **Creating the Executable (.EXE) File**

Your next task is to convert the object file into an executable file called FIRST.EXE using the LINK utility program supplied with MASM (the LINK program that comes with DOS won't work) or the TLINK program that comes with TASM. The command is

> C> **link first;**↵   or   C> **tlink first**↵

which is short for

> C> **link first.obj;**↵   or   C> **tlink first.obj**↵

A common beginner's error is to type

> C> link *or* tlink first.**ASM**...

You will get an error message telling you that you have an **illegal object file**. Indeed you do.

The *object file* is first.OBJ!

Again, if you forget the ';' with link, answer all questions with Enter. Finally, if the link was successful, you **execute** your program as follows:

```
C> first↵
Hello, my name is Bill Jones

C>
```

If you get an error anywhere along the way, follow the usual programming procedure of determining where it is and correcting the error by re-editing the source file, FIRST.ASM, and assembling and linking again.

In MASM 6.0 and later there is also a simpler combined command ml (Masm-and-Link) which will do the entire job:

```
C> ml first.asm↵          (masm 6.0 and later)

C> first↵
Hello, my name is Bill Jones
```

The .ASM extension is *crucial* as ml can also be used to process other types of files (such as .OBJ files) and needs the extension to decide how to process the file. Make sure you see the line

> Assembling: *(whatever the file name is)*

after the ml command is given.

As mentioned before, ed and WinEdit allow some shortcuts in these procedures. See Appendix C for details.

A few hints may help if you have difficulties:

- Follow the arrangement of my program exactly, changing only the part of the Message line within quotes. Alignment in columns is produced by using tabs. Fields which line up under the "First column" designation must start in column 1.
- Upper and lower case aren't distinguished (except within quotes) in assembly language. We will use particular conventions of capitalization to make programs easier to read.
- The particular name chosen for the PROC, Hello in FIRST.ASM, is unimportant, but the three occurrences of Hello must match exactly:

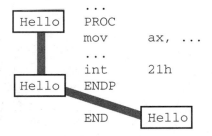

```
         . . .
Hello    PROC
         mov      ax, . . .
         . . .
         int      21h
Hello    ENDP
         END      Hello
```

- I purposely chose a different name (Hello) for the PROC than for the source file (FIRST). The commands used to edit, assemble, link, and execute a program are based *only* on the .ASM file name (FIRST), *not* on the PROC name (Hello).
- Anything following a semicolon on a line is a **comment** and is ignored by all but human readers.
- Note carefully the periods (.) in front of .MODEL, .STACK, .DATA, and .CODE.

The working part of the program does only two things: it displays the message given on the line Message and it returns to the operating system to process the next command.

2.2 • Structure of an IBM PC Assembly Language Program

This section is a discussion of the structure of simple assembly language programs, using our first program as motivation and prime example.

Generally each line of an assembly language program is of the form

Program Line		
Label	*Operation*	*Operands* ; *Comment*

where each field may be omitted, depending on the purpose of the line. Once a semicolon (;) not in quotes occurs on a line, the remainder of the line is ignored by the assembler and can be used by the programmer as a **comment**. An entire line can be treated as a comment by putting a semicolon at the beginning of the line. Blank lines can be used freely to improve readability. Comments in the first program are highlighted below.

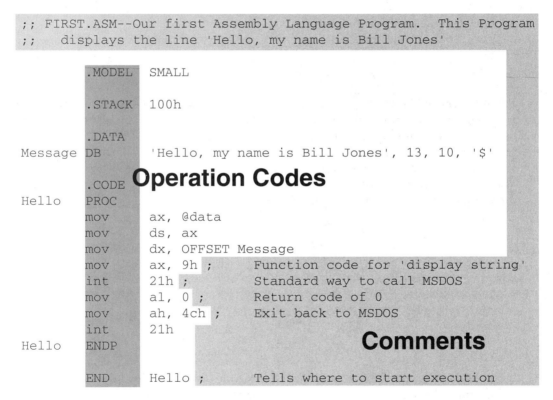

```
;; FIRST.ASM--Our first Assembly Language Program.  This Program
;;   displays the line 'Hello, my name is Bill Jones'

          .MODEL   SMALL

          .STACK   100h

          .DATA
Message   DB       'Hello, my name is Bill Jones', 13, 10, '$'

          .CODE
Hello     PROC
          mov      ax, @data
          mov      ds, ax
          mov      dx, OFFSET Message
          mov      ax, 9h  ;      Function code for 'display string'
          int      21h ;          Standard way to call MSDOS
          mov      al, 0 ;        Return code of 0
          mov      ah, 4ch ;      Exit back to MSDOS
          int      21h
Hello     ENDP

          END      Hello ;        Tells where to start execution
```

The most important part of each line is the *operation* field. There are two kinds of operations in our first program: those representing an actual (executable) single machine instructions, such as mov, a data movement instruction, and those such as .DATA and DB, representing (non-executable) instructions to the assembler. The latter are called **pseudo-operations**. Both types of operations are specified using a symbolic code called an **operation code**, or **op-code** for short. There is one op-code per line (except for empty and comment lines) and they are normally written aligned one tab stop in. I will generally distinguish between actual machine instructions and pseudo-operations by showing the former in all lowercase and the latter in all uppercase. (Again, the assembler ignores case except within quotes.) The op-code fields in our first program are also highlighted above.

Labels, which are optional, are an example of **symbolic names**, which are strings of characters that the programmer invents. To be precise, a symbolic name is a string of up to 31 characters consisting of letters, digits, and special characters '@', '$', '_', and '?', the first of which must not be a digit (to distinguish symbols from numbers.) Upper and lower case are normally equivalent. You should avoid using the special characters as initial characters except for special system uses. It's easiest to remember that anything you think would be a legal symbolic name is.

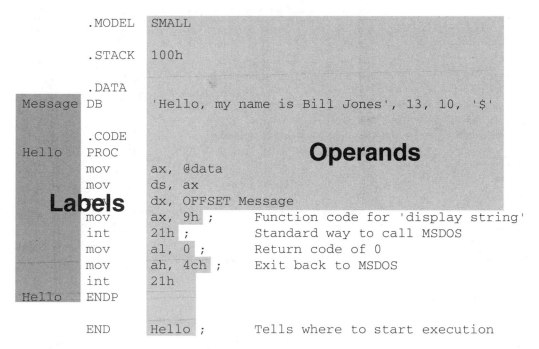

```
;; FIRST.ASM--Our first Assembly Language Program.  This Program
;;   displays the line 'Hello, my name is Bill Jones'

          .MODEL  SMALL

          .STACK  100h

          .DATA
Message   DB      'Hello, my name is Bill Jones', 13, 10, '$'

          .CODE
Hello     PROC
          mov     ax, @data
          mov     ds, ax
          mov     dx, OFFSET Message
          mov     ax, 9h  ;    Function code for 'display string'
          int     21h  ;       Standard way to call MSDOS
          mov     al, 0  ;     Return code of 0
          mov     ah, 4ch  ;   Exit back to MSDOS
          int     21h
Hello     ENDP

          END     Hello  ;     Tells where to start execution
```

Operands

Labels

Each op-code can have zero or more **operands**. "Real" machine instructions usually have one or two.

The labels and operands in our first program are highlighted in the diagram above.

2.2.1 • Global Program Structure

A simple IBM PC assembly language program is divided into three sections, called **segments**. They are introduced by the pseudo-operations .STACK, .DATA, and .CODE (see the diagram on the following page). The .STACK segment is used to reserve space for the stack. All programs must use a stack, but we will postpone the description of its use until later, most notably in Chapters 6, 13, and 15. The .DATA segment is used to declare variables and data storage, with or without initialization, while the .CODE segment is used for the executable program code.

```
;; FIRST.ASM--Our first Assembly Language Program.  This Program
;;   displays the line 'Hello, my name is Bill Jones'

        .MODEL  SMALL
```

```
        .STACK  100h          Stack Segment
```

```
        .DATA                 Data Segment
Message DB      'Hello, my name is Bill Jones', 13, 10, '$'
```

```
        .CODE
Hello   PROC
        mov     ax, @data     Code Segment
        mov     ds, ax
        mov     dx, OFFSET Message
        mov     ax, 9h ;      Function code for 'display string'
        int     21h ;         Standard way to call MSDOS
        mov     al, 0 ;       Return code of 0
        mov     ah, 4ch ;     Exit back to MSDOS
        int     21h
Hello   ENDP

        END     Hello ;       Tells where to start execution
```

Within the .CODE segment the code is divided into PROCedures, much like C/C++ functions, by the PROC/ENDP pseudo-operation pair:

```
Name        PROC    ;   Start of PROC; Name chosen by programmer

;           Code for Name

Name        ENDP    ;   Same Name; PROC/ENDP match in pairs
```

The last line of an assembly program is always an END pseudo-operation. Its operand is the *Name* of the main program (the one that's executed first):

```
        END     Name
```

Compare the above way of specifying the main program to C/C++—in which the main program can occur anywhere but must be called main. In assembly language, the main program can be anywhere and have any name. (Later we will have programs made up of multiple source files, also as in C/C++. All will have END statements but only the one containing the main program will also have the label of the first PROC to be executed, as above.)

In addition, each program will have a preamble which, for now, consists of

```
; Comments explaining purpose, giving author, etc., of program

        .MODEL SMALL ;        To be explained in Chapter 12
```

and the main PROCedure (also for now) must start with the two instructions

```
        mov     ax, @data
        mov     ds, ax ;        Also to be explained in Chapter 12
```

The various code fragments above are collected into the following standard **boilerplate** which is a basis for all simple programs:

```
; Comments explaining purpose, giving author, etc., of program

        .MODEL SMALL
        .STACK 100h

        .DATA
```

                            Data Definitions go here

```
        .CODE
Name    PROC ;                Choose your own Name
        mov     ax, @data
        mov     ds, ax
```

                        Executable program code goes here

```
Name    ENDP
        END     Name
```

2.2.2 • The .STACK Segment

The .STACK segment is declared with the statement

```
        .STACK n
```

where n is the number of bytes reserved for the stack. We shall use $n = 100h$ (= 256) throughout, which is sufficient for our purposes.

2.2.3 • The .DATA Segment

The .DATA segment is used to define variables, with or without initial values. In our first program, the statement

```
Message    DB      'Hello, my name is Bill Jones', 13, 10, '$'
```

uses the DB (define byte) pseudo-operation to define a string of bytes, which is the message to be displayed on the screen.

In general, the two most commonly used types of data on the PC are byte and word variables. These are declared with the DB and DW pseudo-operations, respectively. These pseudo-operations also allow us to specify initial values for the variables. For instance, the code

```
Abc        DB       14
Def        DW       -299
```

declares Abc to be a byte variable with initial value 14 and Def to be a word variable with initial value –299. A byte can contain any unsigned number from 0 to 255 or any signed number from –128 to 127. (The signed numbers –128 to –1 correspond to the unsigned numbers 128 to 255 in a byte. For an explanation, see Section 1.3 and Exercise 1.3—4). Trying to initialize with a value outside these ranges will cause an assembler error.

A *sequence* of values can be specified, which causes one variable to be declared for each value. The label, if any, is the name of the *first* variable declared. Thus

```
AByte      DB       12, 99, 20
```

declares three consecutive variables with initial values 12, 99, and 20 respectively. AByte is the name of the variable whose initial value is 12. (The byte containing 99 is an 'anonymous' variable, and can be referred to as [AByte+1]. The variable containing 20 can be referred to as [AByte+2]. We will start using this notation systematically in Chapter 10.) The code above is completely equivalent to

```
AByte      DB       12
           DB       99
           DB       20
```

or

```
AByte      DB       12, 99
           DB       20
```

If the actual contents of the word or byte are unimportant, that is, if a value will be stored in the word or byte before its contents are used, then the value can be given as **?**, as in

```
ByteVar    DB       ? ; ByteVar is a byte with NO initial value
WordVar    DW       ? ; WordVar is a word with NO initial value
```

(Of course these variables will have *some* initial values. The programmer is merely claiming the initial values will never be used.)

The assembler keeps track of how much memory it has filled so far with a **location counter**, one of its own internal variables which is initially 0. The location counter gives the address of the next memory location to be filled. Thus if the location counter is 100 and the line of code

```
           DB       12, 99, 20
```

is encountered, the assembler arranges that address 100 contains 12, address 101 contains 99, and address 102 contains 20. The location counter is then set to 103. We can show the relationship of memory and location counter as

```
100:  101:  102:  103:   ...
```

12	99	20		

where each rectangle represents a byte of memory. If we label the declaration

```
AByte       DB      12, 99, 20
```

as above, we can picture these bytes as

```
AByte:
```

12	99	20	

with `AByte` referring only to the memory byte containing 12.

Bytes containing the ASCII representation of characters can be defined by enclosing the characters in paired single (') or double (") quotes:

```
Hi          DB      'H', 'e', 'l', 'l', 'o'
```

The declaration of `Hi` above is equivalent to

```
Hi          DB      'H'
            DB      'e'
            DB      'l'
            DB      'l'
            DB      'o'
```

and to

```
Hi          DB      'Hello'
```

and

```
Hi          DB      "Hello"
```

Each of these would produce

```
Hi:
```

'H'	'e'	'l'	'l'	'o'

All of these cause the symbol `Hi` to refer to a byte of memory containing the ASCII character `'H'` (*not* to the whole string of ASCII characters). Also, the actual contents of memory would be the numerical representations of these characters:

```
Hi:
     | 72 | 101 | 108 | 108 | 111 |
```

We in fact don't have to use the quoted form at all—the assembler would produce exactly the same results with

```
Hi       DB      72, 101, 108, 108, 111 ;  BAD style
```

because 72 is the ASCII representation of `'H'`, etc. (The numeric form should not be used, though, as it is unnecessarily mysterious.)

For some non-printing characters such as carriage return and line feed (whose ASCII values are 13 and 10, respectively), the only way to get them with a DB instruction is to include them numerically, as in

```
Message  DB      'Hello, my name is Bill Jones', 13, 10, '$'
```

from our simple introductory program. (Note that as our discussion above indicates, the variable `Message` is actually the name of a single byte location containing the character `'H'`.

Data definitions can be repeated by using the DUP operation. For instance

```
Ones     DB      100 DUP (1)
```

defines 100 consecutive bytes containing the number 1 (the first of which is called 'Ones'), and

```
         DB      10 DUP (2, 3, ?)
```

defines 30 bytes which are, consecutively, 2, 3, ?, 2, 3, ?, … ? .

DW operates similarly except that it defines *words* of storage. We can represent the result of

```
AWord    DW      1234h
```

as occupying two consecutive bytes of memory as follows:

```
AWord:
     |   1234h   |
```

(The diagram is not intended to indicate the location of particular hex digits within the word, a tricky question which will be addressed in Chapter 10.)

Exercises 2.2

1. Make a diagram showing successive bytes of memory like those above to show the memory layout produced by the following data declarations:

```
Letters    DB      'ABC'
Digits     DB      1, 2, 3
Numbers    DW      6767h, 0ababh ; 'h' indicates hex
More       DB      'e', 10, 'fg'
Hush       DB      5 DUP ('S'), 'H!'
Two3       DB      3 DUP (2, 3, ?)
Recurse    DB      2 DUP ('X', 3 DUP (0))
```

(Hint: the '0' in 0abcdh is merely there to indicate to the assembler that a number follows. See Section 1.2.)

2. Give a single DB statement which has the same effect as each of the following groups:

a)
```
X          DB      5
           DB      'H'
           DB      'i'
```

b) ✓
```
Y          DB      5
           DB      10, 5, 10, 5
           DB      10, 5, 10
           DB      5, 10
```

(Recall that the ✓ mark on an exercise indicates that there is an answer or hint for it in the answers section at the back of the book.)

2.2.4 • The .CODE Segment

Before reading this section, you may wish to review some of the terminology introduced in Section 1.1. The overall structure of the 80X86 CPU can be represented in the diagram at the left.

	high byte	low byte
AX	AH	AL
BX	BH	BL
CX	CH	CL
DX	DH	DL

The 80X86 ALU has several registers, among which are four word (16-bit) registers, called AX, BX, CX, and DX, which are used for most computations. Each of these registers is divided into two byte (8-bit) registers—a **high byte** and a **low byte**. The high byte is the left-most 8 bits and is called 'high' because it is the high-order (most significant) bits of the register. The low byte is the right-most, or least significant, 8 bits. The high and low parts of AX are called AH and AL, respectively, with

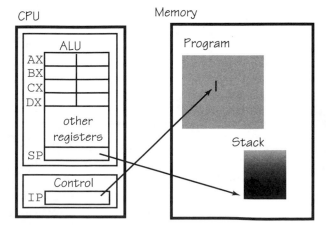

similar nomenclature for the other four registers. Each of these registers—in fact, all 80X86 registers—has a special purpose that only it serves, so the 80X86 does not have general registers in the sense of Section 1.1.

The executable part of the first program does three things, as follows:

```
mov     ax, @data      Standard Boilerplate
mov     ds, ax
```

```
mov     dx, OFFSET Message      DOS Display String Call
mov     ax, 9h
int     21h
```

```
mov     al, 0          DOS Return to DOS Call
mov     ah, 4ch
int     21h
```

Two instructions are used: the mov instruction which moves data from place to place and the int 21h instruction which causes the operating system to perform various functions. (Most, but not all, 80X86 operations are written with three letters.)

▶   **The mov Instruction**

The mov instruction is written

```
mov destination, source ; destination := source
```

Mov is really a *copy* operation since the previous contents of the source are unchanged. Thus if ax = 1234 and bx = 9876 and the instruction mov ax, bx is executed, we will have *both* ax and bx equal to 9876.

There are various possibilities for the source and destination operands:

```
mov     memory or register, memory or register or constant
```

which we abbreviate

mov instruction
mov   *mem/reg, mem/reg/constant*

Note:

mov copies FROM the right TO the left-hand operand.

Instead of reading mov ax, bx as 'move ax to bx' (incorrect), read it as 'move to ax, bx.' Right-to-left order may seem unnatural to you and, indeed, some CPUs use the reverse order, but it is the same order as assignment statements in high-level language and you will get used to it.

Moving from one memory location (variable) to another is illegal; use two movs, one from memory to a register and the second from the register back to memory. Thus

```
mov     ax, A ;         OK
mov     A, ax ;         OK
mov     ax, bx ;        OK
mov     A, 345 ;        OK
mov     ax, 345 ;       OK
mov     A, B ;          ILLEGAL--memory to memory
mov     345, A ;        ILLEGAL--can't move TO constant
```

The mov instruction can be used with either word or byte operands, but **both operands must have the same size**.

A constant in the range 128–255, which can fit into a byte, can be considered either a byte or a word constant. Thus any character can be considered either a byte or a word. Constants outside this range are necessarily words. Therefore we have

```
mov     ax, 24 ;        OK
mov     al, 24 ;        OK
mov     ax, 345 ;       OK
mov     al, 345 ;       ILLEGAL--word to byte move
```

Because of the many possible combinations of operands, there are in fact 28 different numeric operation codes representing mov instructions. Our first program already uses five of them, and the various mov instructions there have lengths of two or three bytes, so you can see that having an assembler to sort these things out is a practical necessity!

▶ **The int 21h Instruction**

Operating system functions on the IBM PC are called **DOS calls**, after the PC's operating system MSDOS. DOS stands for Disk Operating System. Using DOS calls is much like using standard procedures such as puts() in C/C++. DOS calls have the form

DOS Call
Load parameters to DOS call into registers
mov   ah, *function code*
int   21h   ; Call DOS
Returned values (if any) are in registers

The int instruction (to be explained in Chapter 15) is a special method of calling DOS. The '21h' as well as the function code in ah are traditionally written in hex. Each DOS call has its own function code number and pattern of registers used for sending and receiving values. The most important functions will be discussed in this text and are summarized in Appendix D.

We will now explain the two DOS calls in our first program.

▶ **The DOS Display String Call**

The DOS call with function code 9h is used to display a string of characters on the CRT screen. The 'h' isn't really necessary in the function code but I put it there to help remind us that it is the function code for a DOS call.) The 9h function displays a string of ASCII characters whose address is in the dx register, *up to but not including the first dollar sign character '$' encountered.* [*] The form of the call is

```
mov     dx, OFFSET Message
mov     ah, 9h
int     21h
```

The mov instruction is used to load the address of the ASCII string into DX. (The mysterious OFFSET will be explained in the Chapter 12.) The line in the data region

```
Message     DB      'Hello, my name is Bill Jones', 13, 10, '$'
```

is used to define the string to be displayed. The numbers 13 and 10 are the ASCII values for carriage return and line feed, respectively. Together, they cause the cursor—the place where the next character will be typed—to move to the beginning of the next line on the display. If we used only the carriage return (13), the cursor (shown as an underscore '_' below) would go to the beginning of the line we had just displayed

```
Hello, my name is Bill Jones
```

and if we used only the line feed (10), the cursor would go down one line, but not back to the beginning of that line:

```
    Hello, my name is Bill Jones
                                _
```

▶ **The Exit to DOS Call**

In assembly language you can't end a program by simply "falling out the bottom" as you can in C or Pascal. An explicit return to the operating system is required, and if you *do* fall through the bottom of your program, the computer will continue trying to execute whatever garbage lies in memory beyond the end of your program. To end execution of your program, you must execute the return to DOS call, which is

```
mov     al, 0h ;      Return code
mov     ah, 4ch ;     Exit to DOS function code
int     21h
```

The two mov instructions could also be written as the single instruction

---

[*] In section 1.1 we seemed to indicate that sending messages to the screen was easy, so you may wonder why we need a DOS call. There are several reasons, among them: (1) It really isn't that easy. It would require programming techniques we won't cover until Chapter 12 and requires a lot of work keeping track of the cursor, scrolling at the bottom of the screen, etc. (2) If you move characters directly to video memory, then you can't use DOS to redirect output.

```
        mov     ax, 4c00h
```

DOS call 4ch has one parameter, the **return code** in the al register. The return code is traditionally 0 for a normal return, nonzero for an error return. Other programs can test the returned value to determine whether or not to continue processing. (The return code is seldom used in DOS, but you should make a habit of supplying it anyway.)

Exercises 2.2 (concluded)

3.   Given the following data definitions,

```
W           DW      1234
A           DB      23
B           DB      -12
```

which of the following mov instructions are illegal, and why?

```
        mov     W, 74
        mov     W, 'J'   ✓
        mov     74, W    ✓
        mov     A, 74
        mov     A, ah
        mov     W, ah    ✓
        mov     A, B     ✓
```

4.   Fill in the contents of the specified registers as four hex digits, given the specified data definitions.

```
AWord       DW      5432h
AByte       DB      9ah
Another     DB      0bch
            . . .
            mov     ax, 1234h ;             ax = 1234h

            mov     ax, AWord ;             ax = _____
            mov     ax, 1234h
            mov     ah, AByte ;             ax = _____
            mov     ah, AByte
            mov     al, Another ;           ax = _____  ✓
            mov     ax, 1234h
            mov     al, ah ;                ax = _____
            mov     ax, 1234h
            mov     ah, 'A' ;               ax = _____
        ;           (HINT: 'A' = 65 = 41h)
            mov     ax, 1234h
            mov     ax, 'A' ;               ax = _____  ✓
            mov     ah, 1
            mov     al, 2 ;                 ax = _____  ✓
```

5.   What is displayed by the DOS display string call

```
mov     dx, OFFSET Msg
mov     ah, 9h
int     21h
```

for each of the following definitions of `Msg`? Assume that the cursor is at the left side of the screen before each display and show the final position of the cursor with an underline.

```
a) ✓
Msg         DB      'All '
            DB      'on one'
            DB      ' line', 13, 10, '$'
b)
Msg         DB      'One if by land,', 13, 10
            DB      'Two if by sea.', 13, 10, '$'
c)
Msg         DB      'One',13,10, 'Two', 13, 10, 'Three', 13, 10, '$'
d) ✓
Msg         DB      'One $',13,10,'Two', 13, 10, 'Three', 13, 10, '$'
e)
Msg         DB      'S', 10 DUP ('h'), '!', 13, 10, '$'
f) ✓
Msg         DB      4 DUP (5 DUP ('*'), 13, 10), '$'
g) ✓
Msg         DB      10 DUP ('*'), 13, 10
            DB      3 DUP ('*', 8 DUP (' '), '*'), 13, 10
            DB      10 DUP ('*'), 13, 10, '$'
```

6.   What is displayed by the following two DOS display string calls

```
mov     dx, OFFSET Msg1
mov     ah, 9h
int     21h
mov     dx, OFFSET Msg2
mov     ah, 9h
int     21h
```

for each of the following definitions of `Msg1` and `Msg2`? Assume that the cursor is at the left side of the screen before each display and show the final position of the cursor with an underline.

```
a)
Msg1        DB      'One if by land, $', 13, 10, '$'
Msg2        DB      'Two if by sea.', 13, 10, '$'

b)
Msg1        DB      'One if by land, ', 13, 10, '$'
```

```
Msg2        DB          'Two if by sea.', 13, 10, '$'
```

c) ✓
```
Msg1        DB          'One if by land, ', 13, 10
Msg2        DB          'Two if by sea.', 13, 10, '$'
```

7. Write data definitions for Msg so that the DOS display string call

```
mov     dx, OFFSET Msg
mov     ah, 9h
int     21h
```

will produce the following output:

a) Eat
    Neat

b) ✓down
        down
            down

SUMMARY

The assembly language programmer creates a program in a **source file** with extension .ASM. The source file PROG.ASM is translated into the **object file** PROG.OBJ by the command

```
masm prog;                      or                  tasm prog
```

Note the semicolon for MASM. An extension of .ASM is assumed. The object file is converted to an executable file PROG.EXE by the command

```
link prog;                      or                  tlink prog
```

Note again the semicolon on LINK but not TLINK. An extension of .OBJ is assumed. Link/tlink prog.**asm**; must **not** be used. MASM has the following substitute for these two commands:

```
ml prog.asm                 (.ASM extension required!)
```

The executable program is executed by entering the command

```
prog
```

Assembly language is heavily dependent on the structure of the CPU. Machines having the 80X86 CPU but running different operating systems such as UNIX, MSDOS, and OS/2 will nonetheless have very similar assembly languages (generally differing only in the operating system calls). Machines with very different CPUs, such as the 680X0 and the 80X86 will have very different assembly languages even if they are running the same operating system, such as UNIX. Even IBM mainframe computers have a different assembly language from IBM PCs. On the other hand, learning one assembly language makes all the others relatively easy to learn, just as knowing one high-level language makes any of the others easier to learn.

The following instructions were introduced:

```
mov     reg/mem, reg/mem/constant ; destination on left

int     21h ;           call DOS (function code in ah)
```

The following **pseudo-operations** were introduced:

```
        .MODEL SMALL
        .STACK size ;           declare stack segment
        .DATA  ;                start data segment
        DW     val1, val2... ; Define Word variables
        DB     val1, val2... ; Define Byte variables
        .CODE  ;                start code segment
Name    PROC   ;                start procedure Name
Name    ENDP   ;                end procedure Name
        END    Name ;           end assembly program—
               ;                start execution at Name
```

When a label is used with DW or DB, it refers to the first word or byte variable defined and is given a size of word or byte, respectively. Uninitialized variables can be defined by using **?** as the initial value. A list of values can be repeated by using the form *RepeatCount* DUP (*ListToRepeat*) in place of a single value in a DW or DB statement. A string of characters can be represented as its individual characters surrounded by quotes—'a', 'S', 't', 'r', 'i', 'n', 'g'—or as an entire string of characters surrounded by quotes—'aString'.

Chapter **3**

More on I/O

This chapter is chiefly concerned with showing how to simplify DOS calls by using macros, and how to do numeric I/O using procedures supplied on the disk that comes with this book. Methods for writing macros will be discussed in chapters 8 and 16, and the actual code for the numeric I/O procedures will be explained in chapters 7 and 11. The chapter also introduces a DOS call for single-character output. DOS calls for keyboard input will be discussed in chapters 5 (single character) and 10 (whole line).

3.1 • Macros

As you perhaps have noticed, writing DOS calls can become tedious. Much of the code is repetitive, and each call has its own function code and register usage. And there are perhaps twenty DOS calls in common use, not to mention the eighty or so that are used less commonly.

You are probably used to dealing with complexity by making the repeated code a procedure or function. The DOS display string call is only three instructions though, and if we made it into a procedure, the overhead for executing the procedure and passing the parameter (the message location) would be as long as the DOS call itself! A better facility would simply insert the necessary display string code each place you want it.

Assembly languages allow you to use a single invented name to represent a frequently used sequence of instructions. This name is used just like an ordinary machine instruction, and is called a **macro instruction**, or **macro** for short. *Macro* means "large" and is intended to suggest grouping several instructions into a single large instruction. This group can contain ordinary machine operations, pseudo-operations, or even other macro instructions.

When the assembler encounters the name of a macro, it replaces it with the sequence of instructions the macro consists of. The replacement process is called

---

3.1–2 Macros
op INCLUDE;
macros
_PutStr,
_PutCh,
_Exit;
macro library
PCMAC.INC

3.3 Magic Numbers
op EQU

3.4 Numeric I/O
op call,
EXTRN;
link library
UTIL.LIB
containing
routines
PutDec,
PutHex,
GetDec

macro
_GetDate

45

expanding the macro. A macro can have operands, just like ordinary operations, and these operands are substituted into the group of instructions making up the macro. If you are familiar with the C language, the C **#define** statement is in fact a macro facility. (The C++ inline function is not exactly a macro since the compiler is not *required* to insert the code where the function is invoked. In fact, for recursive inline functions, it can *not* be so inserted.)

We will eventually learn how to write our own macros (chapters 8 and 16) but for now we will use a package of macros called PCMAC.INC that is on the disk that comes with this book. Any source program which uses PCMAC.INC must contain the following line before using any of its macros:

```
INCLUDE PCMAC.INC
```

The statement above assumes that the PCMAC.INC file is in the current directory. If not, you will have to give a full path name of the file, such as

```
INCLUDE C:\ASMSTUFF\PCMAC.INC ; if PCMAC.INC is in C:\ASMSTUFF
```

Macro files are just ordinary text files which can be created and read like .ASM files (though you will find PCMAC.INC rather mysterious at this point).

The first two macros we will be using are _PutStr, which is a substitute for the DOS 9h call, and _Exit, which is a substitute for the DOS 4ch call. They are of the form

```
        _PutStr label-of-'$'-terminated-string
```
and
```
        _Exit  program-return-value
```

Program-return-value is optional and if omitted, 0 will be used. Note that I capitalize the first letter of macro names to distinguish them from machine operations and pseudo-ops for the human reader, and all macros in PCMAC.INC start with an underscore character _ to help distinguish them from other macros we might write.

FIRST.ASM can be rewritten using _PutStr and _Exit as follows (changed code shown in **boldface**):

```
;; FIRST.ASM—Our first Assembly Language Program. This program
;;    displays the line 'Hello, my name is Bill Jones' on the CRT
screen.

INCLUDE PCMAC.INC
           .MODEL SMALL
           .STACK 100h

           .DATA
Message    DB      'Hello, my name is Bill Jones', CR, LF, '$'

           .CODE
Hello      PROC
           mov     ax, @data
```

```
          mov    ds, ax
          _PutStr Message
          _Exit  0 ;     Return to DOS with (normal) return code 0
Hello     ENDP
          END    Hello ;        Tells where to start execution
```

It is very important to understand that the final executable program will be *identical* to our first version. Macros don't change the code that is executed; they merely make it easier to read and write! In particular, the registers that get altered in the first version also get altered here, but you can get yourself into trouble because it isn't evident which registers the macro changes. Thus

```
          mov    dx, 14
          _PutStr Message
          mov    A, dx ;      Does NOT set A to 14!
```

It would of course be safer if the macros saved and restored any register values they used, but standard assembly practice is to opt for the more efficient (and more dangerous) practice of not having them do so.

There are several ways to avoiding trouble with destroyed registers:

•   When in doubt, either don't depend on the contents of registers after macro uses, or look up the DOS call in Appendix D or some other reference to see which registers it uses.

•   PCMAC.INC includes 'safe' versions of all its calls which save and restore the registers ax, bx, cx, and dx unless they are used to return values from DOS. The safe version is indicated by replacing the initial '_' with an 's'. Thus the safe version of _PutStr is sPutStr. When in doubt, use the safe version.

•   Use another version of PCMAC.INC called PCMAC.SAF, in which all of the '_' macros are safe versions. You can either INCLUDE PCMAC.SAF instead of PCMAC.INC or simply copy PCMAC.SAF to your working area and rename it PCMAC.INC. With the .SAF set of macros, the _PutStr example above would set A to 14.

Exercises 3.1

1.   In the following code fragments character strings will be defined and _PutStr macro calls are given to display them. Determine what appears on the CRT screen when the DOS calls have all been completed. You should assume that the cursor is at the left side of the screen at the beginning of each _PutStr, and you should use an underscore (_) as in the examples in Section 2.2.4 to show where the cursor ends up.

```
Ex1Msg    DB     'Ex1 shows', 13, 10, 'two lines', 13, 10, '$'
          . . .
          _PutStr Ex1Msg

Ex2Msg1   DB     'Does Ex2 show', 13, 10
Ex2Msg2   DB     'two lines too?', 13, 10, '$'
          . . .
          _PutStr Ex2Msg1
```

```
Ex3Msg      DB      'What does Ex3', 13, 10, 10, 'do?$'
            . . .
            _PutStr Ex3Msg

Ex4Msg      DB      'Ex4 is also', 13, 'strange$'
            . . .
            _PutStr Ex4Msg ✓

Ex5Msg      DB      'Ex5 is too', 8, 8, 8, 'not', 13, 10, '$'
            . . .
            _PutStr Ex5Msg ✓
```

It will help you on the last two fragments above to know that when you display a character in a position that already contains one, the new character replaces the old one. Also, 8 is the ASCII **backspace** character, which moves the cursor back one character without erasing the character previously there.

```
Ex6Msg      DB      'The 64 $ question', 13, 10, '$'
            . . .
            _PutStr Ex6Msg

Ex7Msg      DB      'The 64 ', 36, ' question', 13, 10, '$'
            . . .
            _PutStr Ex7Msg ✓
```

Hint: 36 is the ASCII value of '$'.

2. Suppose we have declared

```
Message     DB      'Boo'
Char        DB      'k'
Ending      DB      '$', 13, 10
```

a) What is displayed by the code below?

```
            _PutStr Message
```

b) What is displayed by the code below?

```
            mov     Char, 'm'
            _PutStr Message
```

c) What is displayed by the code below?

```
            mov     Char, '$'
            _PutStr Message
```

3. ✓ Suppose you wanted to do a "destructive" backspace, that is, you wanted to erase the character on the screen that you were backspacing into. In other words, if the on-screen image is

```
ABCX_
```

(_ is the cursor), you want it to end up looking like

```
ABC_
```

What byte string should you display with the DOS 9h function to do the erase? (Remember that 8 is the ASCII code for a nondestructive backspace; that is, displaying a backspace alone in the example above would give you ABCX. Hint: you must display **three** characters.)

4.   Write assembly language code to print the following poem using _PutStr:

```
Roses are red,
Violets are blue,
Sugar is sweet,
And so am I.
```

3.2 • The DOS Display Character Call

You may have been wondering how you go about displaying the '$' character, since _PutStr stops when it sees a '$' and doesn't display it. In fact there is *no way* to display a '$' with _PutStr. (Ex6Msg and Ex7Msg in Exercise 3.1.1 print exactly the same thing, and neither prints the whole message.) The easiest way to display '$' is to use another DOS call, number 2h, which displays the single character it finds in register dl. Thus we could display a '$' by executing

```
mov    dl, '$'
mov    ah, 2h
int    21h
```

Using the corresponding macro, _PutCh, the code is

```
_PutCh '$'
```

The _PutCh macro can be used to display one or more characters by listing them in the operand position. For instance, we could display a carriage return/line feed pair by coding

```
_PutCh 13, 10
```

which generates two DOS 2h calls. (Note that _Put**Str** Message1, Message2 is not allowed.)

Exercises 3.2

1. What is displayed by the following sets of DOS calls?

    a)   `_PutCh 'B', 'i', 'l', 'l', 13, 10`

    b)   `_PutCh 66, 105, 108, 108, 13, 10`
    (Hint: The code here displays the same thing as the code in a) above. Which would you rather read or write?)

    c)   `_PutCh ' ', ' ', 'C', 13, ' ', 'B', 13`
                `_PutCh 'A', 13, 10`

    d)   `_PutCh 'x', 'y', 'C', 8, 8, 'B', 8, 8`
                `_PutCh 'A', 13, 10`

    (Hint 1: 8 is the ASCII backspace character. See Exercise 3.1—3. Hint 2: This exercise produces the same output as in part c).)

    e)   `_PutCh '\', 10, '\', 10, '\', 13, 10`

2. ✓ Write data declarations (DBs) and DOS calls to display the line

    `The 64 $ question`

3. Neither of the following pieces of code does what the programmer probably intended. Fix them.

    a) `Dol    DB     '$' ;`   in the .DATA segment
            `. . .`
            `_PutCh Dol ;`   in the .CODE segment

    b)   `_PutStr 'Bill$'`

3.3 • Magic Numbers

It is generally poor programming practice to use **magic numbers** in a program. Magic numbers are constants (usually other than 0 or 1) that have some significance in the program. Examples of magic numbers in our first program are 13, 10, 9h, and 4ch. It is better to give such numbers a symbolic name. C does it by using **#define**s, and our assembler does it with the EQU (short for EQUate) pseudo-op. We could code

```
CR          EQU     13
LF          EQU     10
Message     DB      'Hello, my name is Bill Jones', CR, LF, '$'
```

You might even want to set up an equate for '$':

```
MsgEnd      EQU      '$'
```

The code

```
A           EQU      B
```

is roughly equivalent to the C code

```
#define A B
```

B can be replaced by an expression. Thus

```
A            EQU    10
B            EQU    A + 1 ;        is LEGAL; sets B to 11
```

Forward references are allowed

```
A            EQU    B + 11 ;       is LEGAL; A eventually becomes 11
B            EQU    10
```

but uses of A can't occur before B is defined, and of course circular EQUates are forbidden
Once a symbol has been defined with the EQU pseudo-operation, it cannot be redefined.

There are several advantages to using EQUates:

- They make the program easier to read by documenting the meaning of constants.
- They make the program easier to change correctly, as the change only needs to be made in one place.
- Different versions of a program can be specified by the values of one or more EQUates, set at the beginning of the program.
- The points above are even more important in programs where a single constant has two different meanings.

As an example of the last point, suppose our program also used the number 13 as an unlucky number and we also declared

```
Unlucky   EQU     13
```

Then if at some later date we decided to change the unlucky 13's (but not the carriage return 13's), it would be easy to do.

You should use as few magic numbers as possible in your programs. What you should *not* do is give a constant a symbolic name which is just another name for its value. For instance, the statement

```
Thirteen EQU     13 ;           VERY BAD CODING PRACTICE
```

is worthless. If the value of `Thirteen` ever *does* change, the label becomes misleading. It is also usually pointless to give 0 and 1 symbolic names.

Writing a character in quotes also constitutes naming a magic number. You should *always* use 'A' to represent the character A in preference to 65, the magic number it equals. See for example Exercise 3.2—1 b).

3.4 • Numeric I/O

Programming I/O of numbers in assembly language turns out to be much more difficult than beginners expect it to be. In fact that's one of the reasons we use high languages whenever we can. It is only in Chapter 7 that we will be able to construct routines to get numbers from the keyboard and display numbers on the CRT, and even then those routines will be rather primitive. Since reading and displaying numbers is done repeatedly, a **library** called `UTIL.LIB`, on the disk included with this book, contains sub-procedures to do numeric I/O (and various other useful things that will be introduced as needed). The complete source code for the library procedures is contained in the subdirectory `UTILSRC` of that disk, but it will probably be pretty mysterious to you until further along in the book. This section describes the use of three simple numeric I/O procedures from that library:

GetDec   reads a decimal integer (with optional '–' sign) from the keyboard and returns with its value (as a binary number, of course) in `ax`. `GetDec` reads characters until it encounters one which cannot belong to the number.

PutDec   displays the (binary) number in `ax` as a decimal number (with – sign if negative) on the CRT screen.

PutHex   displays the (binary) number in `ax` as a hexadecimal number on the CRT screen (in exactly four characters, with no trailing 'h' or extra leading '0').

A program which uses these procedures must include the following `EXTRN` pseudo-operation line immediately after the `.CODE` pseudo-operation:

Accessing Library Procedures
`.CODE`
`EXTRN GetDec : NEAR, PutDec : NEAR, PutHex : NEAR`
`ProcName PROC etc.`

`EXTRN` stands for EXTeRNal, indicating that these procedures are defined elsewhere. The `EXTRN` statement only needs to list the procedures you are actually using. `NEAR` will be explained in Chapter 12.

The difference between `EXTRN` and `INCLUDE` is that `INCLUDE` causes the *assembler* to insert a *file* of *source text* into the program while assembling it, while `EXTRN` tells the assembler that the *linker* will find an *already assembled* `PROC` of this name in another of the *object files* it is told to link. More implications of this difference will be investigated in Chapter 13.

All of these procedures are executed by using the `call` instruction. To display a number on the CRT:

<table>
<tr><td colspan="2">Displaying Numbers</td></tr>
</table>

```
; Display a number in decimal
        mov     ax, number-to-be-displayed
        call    PutDec ;        Display number in decimal
; Display a number in hexadecimal
        mov     ax, number-to-be-displayed
        call    PutHex ;        Display number in hexadecimal
```

To input a decimal number from the keyboard, code

<table>
<tr><td>Inputting Numbers</td></tr>
</table>

```
        call    GetDec
;       Typed number is now in ax (in binary)
```

Note that GetDec doesn't display any prompt, so you should probably use _PutStr to inform the user that the program is waiting for a number. Possible code might be

```
Prompt  DB      'Type in X: $' ;        Note: No CR-LF
        . . .
        _PutStr Prompt
        call    GetDec
        mov     X, ax
```

Since the CR-LF is omitted in Prompt, the typed input will be beside the prompt. For example (user typing shown in bold face):

```
Type in X: 1234↵
```

Assembling a program using GetDec, PutDec, and PutHex is the same as before, but when LINKing the program, the linker must be told where to find GetDec, etc. The appropriate command is

```
link or tlink MyProgFileName,,,util;
```

Note: *exactly* three commas! The commas indicate that default values are to be used for two omitted parameters. Util appears by itself under the assumption that the file UTIL.LIB is in the current directory. If for instance it is in the directory C:\ASMSTUFF, then we would enter

```
link or tlink MyProgFileName,,,c:\asmstuff\util;
```

With masm 6.0 and later you can assemble and link in one step:

```
ml MyProgFileName.asm util.lib
```

Notice that, as before, the extensions .asm and .lib are essential to tell ML what to do with the various files. If util.lib is not in the current directory, its actual directory must be specified as above. Note that *the ML command contains no commas*.

▶ **Rueful Note**: (The reader may skip this note as it is embarrassing to the author.) I once did programming consulting for a man whose simple dictum was

If you haven't tested it, it doesn't work!

I have tried to live by the above rule and instill it in my students. When I first gave them GetDec to use, it failed. I had checked it out, but not as a separately compiled procedure. I fixed it and gave them the new version. It now worked, but it didn't echo ends of lines properly. I looked back at my test program and it had indeed uncovered this problem, *but I had fixed it by altering the test program!*

Example 3.4—1. Write an assembly language program DecToHex which reads in a decimal number from the keyboard and displays its representation in hex.

The .CODE part of a simpleminded program to do the conversion is

```
            .CODE
            EXTRN   GetDec : NEAR, PutHex : NEAR
DecToHex    PROC
            mov     ax, @data
            mov     ds, ax
            call    GetDec ;      ax := decimal number from keyboard
            call    PutHex ;      Display contents of ax in hex
            _Exit   0 ;           Return to DOS
DecToHex    ENDP
            END     DecToHex
```

The program above works, but it isn't very user-friendly. It really should contain a prompt telling the user what to enter and a message describing the output. But if we write

```
Prompt  DB      'Enter decimal number: $'
OutMsg  DB      'The hex equivalent is $'
        . . .
        _PutStr Prompt
        call    GetDec
        _PutStr OutMsg ;     WRONG!!!
        call    PutHex
```

the hex value displayed is garbage. The reason is that _PutStr destroys ah, and thus ax. Therefore we need to save ax before the second _PutStr call and restore it after. The best way we now know to save and restore a register is to set up a word variable in which to save it, as follows (changed parts shown in boldface):

```
Prompt  DB      'Enter decimal number: $'
OutMsg  DB      'The hex equivalent is $'
```

```
SaveAX     DW      ?
           . . .
           _PutStr Prompt
           call    GetDec
           mov     SaveAX, ax ; Save ax in variable SaveAX
           _PutStr OutMsg
           mov     ax, SaveAX ; Restore value of AX from SaveAX
           call    PutHex
```

We could also have used another register instead of SaveAX, say bx or cx *but not dx*. We have to know that the register is not otherwise in use and not altered by the DOS call.

The complete program is below. Note that we explicitly add the trailing 'H' that PutHex doesn't add.

```
;; DECTOHEX.ASM—A program which requests input of a decimal number
;;    from the keyboard and then prints its hex representation
;;
;;
;; Must be linked using
;;         link (or tlink) DECTOHEX,,,UTIL
;;
INCLUDE    PCMAC.INC
           .MODEL SMALL
           .STACK 100h

           .DATA
Prompt     DB      'Enter decimal number: $'
OutMsg     DB      'The hex equivalent is $'
SaveAX     DW      ?

           .CODE
           EXTRN   GetDec : NEAR, PutHex : NEAR
DecToHex   PROC
           mov     ax, @data
           mov     ds, ax

           _PutStr Prompt
           call    GetDec ;     ax := decimal number from keyboard
           mov     SaveAX, ax ; Save ax in variable AX
           _PutStr OutMsg
           mov     ax, SaveAX ; Restore value of AX from SaveAX
           call    PutHex ;     Display typed number in hexadecimal
           _PutCh 'H', 13, 10 ; Display trailing H (for hex)
;                              and carriage return/line feed
           _Exit  0 ;          Return to DOS
DecToHex   ENDP
           END     DecToHex
```

Typical executions might be (user's entries shown in boldface):

```
C> DECTOHEX↵
Enter decimal number: 1234↵
The hex equivalent is 04D2H

C> DECTOHEX↵
Enter decimal number: 111↵
The hex equivalent is 006FH


C>
```

Programming Problem 3.1

Write a program `Today` using `PutDec` which displays today's date in the form

```
Today is mm/dd/yyyy
```

with the month, day, and year filled in. The date is returned by the DOS Get Date call

```
        _GetDate ;         from PCMAC.INC
;        after the call    dh = month (1 to 12)
;                          dl = day (1 to 31)
;                          cx = year (e.g., 1984)
;                          (al is also the weekday (0 to 6)
```

To display the value of a *byte,* such as the month, use the code

```
        mov    al, dh
        mov    ah, 0 ;     Extend to word
        call   PutDec ;    Display month number
```

Don't try to display leading zeroes in the month or the day. Hints: `_PutCh` and `_PutStr` destroy the contents of `dl`. Do not call your program `DATE` since `DATE` is a DOS command.

Summary

Numeric constants can (and generally should) be given symbolic names with the `EQU` pseudo-operation:

```
DeckSize EQU    52
CPU      EQU    86
```

Four **macros** have been introduced from the `PCMAC.INC` file:

```
        _PutStr Label ;    Display string at label terminated
;                             by the '$' character (decimal 36)
;                          DESTROYS AX and DX
```

```
        _PutCh '>', 9 ;        Display a sequence of characters
;                              DESTROYS AX and DX

        _Exit  code ;          Return to DOS with return code.
;                                code = 0 is normal exit

        _GetDate ;         after the call:
;                              al = weekday (0 to 6)
;                              dh = month (1 to 12)
;                              dl = day (1 to 31)
;                              cx = year (e.g., 1984)
```

Before using any of these macros, the line

```
INCLUDE PCMAC.INC ;  or INCLUDE directory\PCMAC.INC
```

must be inserted in the source file.

Three **subprocedures** for doing numeric I/O are included in the library util.lib that comes with this book:

A decimal number can be read from the keyboard by executing the subprocedure **GetDec**:

```
        call   GetDec
;       GetDec waits for the user to type a decimal number
;          with optional - sign in at the keyboard. The number
;          translated to a 16-bit signed binary number which is
;          returned to the caller in ax
```

A number can be displayed in decimal on the CRT by executing the subprocedure **PutDec**:

```
;       Place signed binary number in ax
        call   PutDec
;       Decimal version of the number is displayed on the CRT
```

and in hex by executing the subprocedure **PutHex**:

```
;       Put unsigned (or signed) binary number in ax
        call   PutHex
;       Hex version of the number is displayed in four digits,
;          without sign or trailing H
```

Before use of any of these procedures, the program must contain the line

```
        EXTRN  GetDec : NEAR, PutDec : NEAR, PutHex : NEAR
```

The program must be linked using the command

```
link or tlink FileName,,,util;            (Note: exactly three commas!)
```

where `util` must be preceded by a directory name if it isn't in the current directory. The three commas indicate two deleted parameters. In order, they are the .EXE file name, which defaults to *FileName*, and a storage map file, which defaults to "none." The final semicolon is optional with `tlink`. We can also use

```
ml FileName.asm util.lib                    (MASM 6.0 and later)
```

Chapter 4

Arithmetic

It is essential to understand signed (2's complement) arithmetic in this chapter, so you should review Section 1.3 if necessary.

4.1 • Addition and Subtraction

The addition and subtraction operations are called `add` and `sub`. They have the same types of operands as the `mov` instruction:

```
add/sub       reg/mem, reg/mem/constant
```

and the functionality is

```
add       dest, source ;      dest := dest + source
sub       dest, source ;      dest := dest - source
```

The operands must be of the same size (both word or both byte), and at least one operand must not be from memory. The ax, bx, cx, and dx registers can be used for these operations with words and the ah, al, bh, ..., dl registers can be used for byte operations.

Example 4.1—1. Write assembly code for the statement A := B – C + 3, assuming word variables. Usually it is best to do all but the simplest computations in one or more of the CPU registers and then move the result to its final destination:

```
mov       ax, B
sub       ax, C
add       ax, 3
mov       A, ax
```

4.1 Add and Subtract
  ops add, sub, inc, dec, neg

4.2 Multiply and Divide
  ops imul, mul, idiv, div, cwd, cbw

4.3 Comments

Optional:

4.4 Instruction Format

4.5 Instruction Timing

59

Example 4.1—2. Write assembly code for the statement A := A + B. This code is about the most complicated situation where you might "do the arithmetic in memory":

```
mov    ax, B
add    A, ax
```

Note that

```
add    A, B  ;            ILLEGAL—two memory operands
```

is not allowed. A second method of adding B to A which does the arithmetic in a register *appears* to be longer:

```
mov    ax, A
add    ax, B
mov    A, ax
```

In fact though it's probably not worth worrying about such minor differences. In the first solution, the addition still has to take place by fetching A into the CPU, doing the addition, and then storing the result. The only real difference is the time needed in the second example to fetch the extra instruction. For a more extensive discussion on such micro-optimization, see the optional Section 4.4.

Example 4.1—3. Write assembly code for the statement A := A − 3. This code is a situation where "arithmetic in memory" should definitely be used, it can be accomplished in a single assembly language instruction:

```
sub    A, 3
```

The statements A := A + 1 and A := A − 1 occur so frequently that most computers have special instructions for them. (As a result, some languages such as C and C++ have special forms built in for these operations.) The 80X86 instructions are

```
inc/dec        reg/mem
```

Inc stands for increment and dec for decrement. Their functionality is

```
inc    dest            ;        dest := dest + 1
dec    dest            ;        dest := dest - 1
```

The *dest* operand can be either a byte or a word.

There is another instruction in the mold of inc/dec which is often useful:

```
neg            reg/mem
```

which negates its byte or word operand:

```
        neg     dest            ;       dest := - dest
```

Example 4.1—4. Suppose that `Char` is a byte variable containing a lowercase letter. Write assembly code to convert it to the corresponding uppercase letter.

We use the fact that

$$\text{Upper-case-letter} + \text{'a'} - \text{'A'} = \text{corresponding lower-case-letter}$$

for example, that 'w' = 'W' + 'a' – 'A'. Then the code would be

```
        sub     Char, 'a' - 'A'
```

Exercises 4.1

1. ✓ Fill in the blanks with the values resulting from the following code. Use exactly four hex digits for each value.

```
        mov     ax, 0FFFFh ;  = -1; ax = FFFFh

        inc     ax ;            ax = _____
        mov     ax, 0FFFFh
        inc     al ;            ax = _____
        mov     ax, 0FFFFh
        inc     ah ;            ax = _____
        mov     ax, 1234h
        sub     ax, 35h ;       ax = _____
;   Hint: negate and add
        mov     ax, 1234h
        sub     al, 35h ;       ax = _____
;   Same hint
        mov     ax, 1234h
        neg     ax ;            ax = _____
        mov     ax, 1234h
        neg     al ;            ax = _____
        mov     ax, 1234h
        mov     al, -1 ;        ax = 12FFh

        inc     AX ;            ax = _____
        mov     ax, 12FFh;
        inc     AL ;            ax = _____
        mov     ax, 1200h
        dec     AX ;            ax = _____
        mov     ax, 1200h;
        dec     AL ;            ax = _____
        mov     ax, 1234h
        sub     ax, ax ;        ax = _____
        mov     ax, 1234h
        sub     al, al ;        ax = _____
```

2. ✓ Suppose that we have defined the character string

```
    Alpha       DB      'a', 13, 10, '$'
```

What is displayed by the following code?

```
_PutStr Alpha
add     Alpha, 3
_PutStr Alpha
```

3. Translate the following pseudocode assignment statements into IBM PC assembly language. Assume that all variables are **signed words**.

   a) X := A + 19 – B
   b) X := X + 1

4. Suppose that `Digit` is a byte variable containing a digit character (e.g., '3'). Write assembly code to convert `Digit` to its numeric value and store it in the **word** variable `Value`. (Hint: to get the value from the character digit, subtract '0'.)

4.2 • Multiplication and Division

Multiplication and division are always more complex in computers than addition and subtraction, and it's obvious why they must be: multiplying two n-digit numbers will in general produce a $2n$ digit number, and to make division an inverse operation, we should be able to divide a $2n$ digit number by an n digit number. Also we want to be able to produce the remainder as well as the quotient on division.

Addition and subtraction are very fast operations—generally taking little more than the time necessary to fetch the instructions and operands from memory. (See Section 4.4.) On the other hand, multiplication is accomplished by repeated addition and division by repeated subtraction (the ALU in the CPU actually executes small loops). Also the problems of positive and negative numbers must be dealt with—there is no simple trick like 2's complement to save the day. In fact, early mini- and microcomputers didn't even have built-in multiplication and division instructions. They had instructions to help, but the user had to construct his or her own subroutines to do the operations.

In the 80X86 CPU, multiplication and division always take place in a special set of registers. When you multiply two 16-bit numbers, the product may require 32 bits to represent it, and similarly the product of two 8-bit numbers may require 16 bits. Because of the increase in length, the register (pair) containing the product is twice as long as the register containing the multiplicand:

Operand Size	Multiplicand	Multiplier	Product
BYTE	AL	Reg or Memory	AX
WORD	AX	Reg or Memory	AX(low) and DX(high)

To make division the inverse of multiplication, the register (pair) containing the number to be divided is twice as long as the divisor and the result. Also, division has *two* results, the quotient and the remainder:

Operand Size	Dividend	Divisor	Quotient	Remainder
BYTE	AX	Reg or Memory	AL	AH
WORD	AX and DX	Reg or Memory	AX	DX

(Notice that a *constant* operand is **not** allowed in either multiplication or division.)

Addition is the same operation whether the operands are assumed to be signed or unsigned, as is subtraction. Multiplication and division, however, require different operations for signed and unsigned operands. For instance, multiplication by –3 and by its 2's complement representation, 0FFFDh, considered as an unsigned number (65,533), are two very different operations! The 80X86 has two sets of operations—mul and div for *unsigned* operations and imul and idiv for *signed* operations.

There is one final problem to be considered. If we are processing 16-bit numbers, we expect to combine two words and get a word. How do we deal with the fact that multiplication will produce a 32-bit result and division requires a 32-bit operand?

Multiplication is easy. As we saw in Section 1.3, if we have a 32 bit number, either signed or unsigned, which actually fits in 16 bits, all we have to do is use the low-order 16 bits (ax here). Thus we could code the statement A := B * C (A, B, and C signed word variables) by writing

```
mov    ax, B
imul   C ;        ax not written; it is always assumed.
mov    A, ax ;    dx ignored—better be sure it can be!!
```

If the product is small enough, the high order bits in dx will be all sign bits, or in case of unsigned multiplication, all zeroes.

Division is a little trickier. In the word case, we would normally have a *16-bit* number which we wish to divide by another 16 bit number. In the computer, we need to convert the dividend (= numerator) into a 32 bit number. That's easy enough in case of unsigned numbers—just tack on 16 zeroes on the left. In case of signed numbers, though, we have to add on 16 zero bits if the number is positive, 16 one bits if it's negative. Sign extension comes up so often that the 80X86 has special instructions to accomplish it:

Sign Extension
cwd   ; Convert the signed **word** in ax to a **double**   ; **word** in dx, ax (high order in dx;   ;   ax unchanged)
cbw   ; Convert the signed **byte** in al to a **word**   ;   in ax

In both cases the conversion is done by extending the sign bit.

The code for the statement A := B / C (integer division with integer result; see Section 1.5) for signed word variables is

```
mov    ax, B
cwd
idiv   C
mov    A, ax ;        The remainder is in dx, if needed
```

The code for the statement X := Y **mod** 5 (remainder) for signed byte variables is

```
mov    al, Y
cbw
```

```
mov     bl, 5
idiv    bl ;            idiv 5 won't work
mov     X, ah ;         The quotient is in al
```

When you want to do division of unsigned numbers, all you have to do to extend the dividend is zero the high-order bits. For instance, to do A := B / C assuming the variables are unsigned words, do

```
mov     ax, B
mov     dx, 0 ;         extend unsigned B to 32 bits
div     C
mov     A, ax
```

(Sub dx, dx is a better way to set dx to 0. It will seem a little mysterious at first, but will become a common programming idiom.)

Certain facts seem to be have a very short life span, so I advise frequent rereading of the following

Very Important Reminders

- Multiplication and division can take place **only** in the ax/dx registers in **exactly** the form described in the tables above.
- You **cannot** multiply or divide directly by a **constant**. Move the constant to a register first and then multiply or divide.
- You **must** convert 8-bit dividends to 16-bit and 16-bit dividends to 32-bit. Use cbw/cwd for signed numbers, sub ah, ah/sub dx, dx for unsigned numbers

In the examples below we will assume that all variables are signed words.

Example 4.2—1. Code A := (B + C) / (X + 1)

```
mov     ax, B
add     ax, C ;         ax := B + C
mov     bx, X
inc     bx ;            bx := X + 1
cwd     ;               dx,ax := B + C
idiv    bx
mov     A, ax
```

Note that the code inc X ... idiv X would be **wrong**. The statement of the problem doesn't give us any right to change X; only A. Stick to the program specifications!!

Example 4.2—2. A := 3 * C – 14 * B (Note: we are using the usual high-level language order of precedence for operations; see Section 1.5.)

```
mov     ax, 3
imul    C
mov     bx, ax ;        Save 3 * C temporarily in bx
mov     ax, -14
```

```
imul    B ;             ax := -14 * B
add     ax, bx ;        adding -14 * B same as subtracting
mov     A, ax ;           14 * B
```

If you have a term which contains both multiplication and division, you can sometimes rearrange the operations so that sign extension isn't required.

Example 4.2—3. Code A := (B / C) * (D + 1). We will actually first compute B*(D + 1), which will leave the product in dx and ax, and then divide by C.

```
mov     ax, D
inc     ax
imul    B
idiv    C
mov     A, ax
```

Note that although multiplication never overflows, since there is always room for the product, division can overflow. For instance, in Example 4.2—3 above, if B = 1000, C = 2, and D = 999, the correct result would be 1,000,000 / 2 = 500,000, which is much too large to fit into a single word.

Exercises 4.2

1. ✓ Fill in the blanks with the values resulting from the following code. Use exactly four hex digits for each value.

```
            mov     al, -1
            mov     bl, -1
            mul     bl ;            ax = _____
;   Hint: Numbers above will be treated as unsigned although
;       written signed
            mov     al, -1
            mov     bl, -1
            imul    bl ;            ax = _____
            mov     ax, -1
            mov     bx, -1
            imul    bx ;            ax = _____
;                                   dx = _____
            mov     ax, -1
            mov     bx, 2
            imul    bx ;            ax = _____
;                                   dx = _____
            mov     ax, 0FF80h ;    = -128
            mov     bl, 2
            idiv    bl ;            al = _____, ah = _____
            mov     ax, 0FF80h
            mov     bl, 2
            div     bl ;            Gives divide overflow. Why?
```

2. Translate the following pseudocode assignment statements into IBM PC assembly language. Assume that all variables are **signed words**.

   a) Time := (Hours * 60 + Minutes) * 60 + Secs

b) ✓ `A := -B * (D - 1)`
c) `Digit := Num` **mod** `10`
d) `X := A / (L + M)`
e) `Tomorrow := (Today + 1)` **mod** `7`
f) ✓ `Hours := Minutes / 60;`
   `Minutes := Minutes` **mod** `60;` (Only one division operation!)
g) ✓ `Area := 22 * R * R / 7` (Note: cwd is **not** required. Why?)

3. Suppose that the word variable COL contains the current position of the cursor on the current line (starting at 1) and that tab stops are to be every 8 places, i.e., at 1, 9, 17, ... Thus when a tab is hit, we must ultimately do `COL := (((COL + 7) / 8) * 8) + 1`. Write assembly language code to reset COL in this way. (Exercise 9.1—4 has a much better method of doing it.)

4. A standard way to generate (pseudo-)random numbers on a computer is to obtain the next 'random' number from the last by the formula `newrand := (a * oldrand + c)` **mod** m, where a, c, and m are suitably chosen. The value of m can be chosen as 2^w where w is the number of bits in a machine word, in which case, the division isn't necessary! Write code to perform

$$X := (A * X + C) \bmod 2^{16}$$

where A = 31413, C = 3619H, and X is considered to be a random unsigned integer between 0 and 65,535. (A real production random number generator should use much larger numbers. The method above repeats at least every 65,536 numbers, which is insufficient for real applications. See Section 14.2 for implementation of a good *usable* generator.)

4.3 • Comments on Comments

Writing comments is an art form. In my experience, seasoned programmers often do it badly and beginners are much worse. There are no good hard-and-fast rules for commenting, but the following are some rules of thumb that I consider important:

- You are the main user of your comments. Comment as though you expect to come back in six months and modify or debug the program, remembering nothing about how it works. In particular, **your comments are intended for someone who knows how individual instructions work**. Comments such as

  ```
  inc    ax ;          Add 1 to ax  <== VERY BAD STYLE
  ```

  are almost always worthless!
- The next main user of your comments is the poor sap who must maintain your code when you have been promoted to a more exalted position. **When in doubt, over-comment**.
- Do comments as you write the code. The usual student practice of writing a "bare" program first and then adding the comments when it's debugged is counterproductive. In the first place, you lose the main utility of the comments: debugging your code. In the second, adding the comments often introduces bugs (such as omitting the ';').
- **Do not try to comment every line**. Textbook authors have often tried to make a comment-per-line rule in assembly language, but I don't believe in it. Many program lines are so

straightforward that a comment would hide more than it reveals, and other lines require several lines of comments to fully explain them. The comment-per-line rule is a way of avoiding consideration of what really constitutes useful commenting.

- On the other hand, one (excellent) text I have read advocates *never* having a comment that applied only to a single line of code. This rule is worth keeping in mind but not following slavishly.
- **When you change your program, change the comments**. If there is anything worse than a program without comments, it is a program in which the comments don't agree with the code! When you add new code, add appropriate comments with it.
- A well-known higher-level language such as C/C++ (or some pseudo-language which is similar; see Section 1.5) is often useful for comments.
- In complicated computations, comments which keep running track of the contents of registers are useful (particularly when you come back to debug the code later). For instance:

```
mov    ax, A ;        ax := A
add    ax, B ;        ax := A + B
cwd
idiv   C ;            ax := (A + B) / C
```

- Start programs with general comments concerning name, programmer, copyright notice, if any, etc. Most shops have a standard heading. You should also include a description of how the program is used (e.g., calling sequence if it is a subprocedure)
- Programs which are going to be used for any length of time should have a **revision history** somewhere in their standard heading. After the preliminary debugging is completed (i.e., when the original programmer thinks he or she is done), further changes should be described at the beginning of the program with date of change and the name or initials of the programmer making the change. Each programming shop has its own format, but one possible form is

```
;          REVISION HISTORY
;
; 2/14/96 Handle negative argument correctly     WBJ
; 3/24/96 Fix bug introduced by neg arg fix      LIV
; 5/9/96  REALLY fix neg arg problem this time   WBJ
```

4.4 • Internal Format of Instructions

The assemblers translate each instruction into a sequence of one or more bytes. This section gives a brief overview of the possibilities for the instructions we have encountered so far. It is necessary to have only a vague idea of the internal format of instructions, so this section can be skipped entirely on first reading or skimmed. Its main use will be in sections on instruction timing, such as the one that follows this one.

Every instruction has an **op-code** (operation code) byte. It is virtually always the first byte of the instruction. (In some special circumstances, it may be preceded by one or more prefix bytes.)

A few instructions such as cbw and cwd can be contained in a single byte. The int instruction has one byte for the op-code and one byte for the interrupt number.

Most other instructions have one (inc, dec, neg, mul, div, push, pop) or two (add, sub, mov)

operands, which so far can be a register, a memory location, or a literal constant. Such instructions generally have (and there are special cases here too) a second byte called the **mod r/m byte**, which specifies the type(s) of the operand(s). If one or both operands is a register, the actual register(s) is (are) specified by the mod r/m byte itself. If an operand is a memory location, the mod r/m byte is followed by the two-byte memory address of the operand. In a two-operand instruction, if the second operand is literal constant, the instruction is then followed by the one or two-byte constant operand. Thus one-operand instructions can be two or four bytes long, and two-operand instructions can be two, three, four, five, or six bytes long. The discussion above is a little oversimplified, in that there are short forms for several instructions. In particular, several two-operand instructions have forms without a mod r/m byte for the case where one of the operands is `ax` or `al`.

To summarize:

`cwd`
`cbw`

op-code

`inc/dec/neg/mul/div` *register*
`mov/add/sub` *register, register*

op-code	mod r/m

`inc/dec/neg/mul/div` *memory*
`mov/add/sub` *memory, register*
`mov/add/sub` *register memory*

op-code	mod r/m	address

`mov/add/sub` *register, byte constant*

op-code	mod r/m	const

`mov/add/sub` *register, word constant*

op-code	mod r/m	const

`mov/add/sub` *memory, byte constant*

op-code	mod r/m	address	const

`mov/add/sub` *memory, word constant*

op-code	mod r/m	address	const

To see the actual values of these fields, an **assembly listing** file can be created when the program is assembled. The assembly listing file is just another text file which can be viewed with an editor or printed on a printer. To create the listing file PROG.LST for the source file PROG.ASM, execute one of the following three instructions:

```
masm prog,,prog;
tasm prog,,prog
ml /Fl prog.asm
```

The right side of the assembly listing shows the source code, and the left side shows relative instruction locations and the translated instructions in hex. The listing formats of the two assemblers differ only slightly. The following diagram shows three lines from an assembly listing and how they are interpreted:

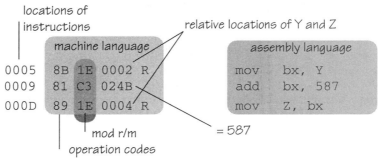

The Rs following the addresses indicate that the preceding operand is **relocatable**. A relocatable item may be changed (relocated) by the linker when multiple .OBJ files are linked (see Chapter 6).

4.5 • Timing of Instructions

This section is optional. It makes use of the optional Section 4.4.

In this section we are going to discuss some ways of estimating the relative execution times of various instructions. Armed with this information, you can hope to make your programs more efficient by reducing their execution times. Optimization as we will discuss it, by looking at just one or a very few instructions, is called **local optimization**, or sometimes **peephole optimization**. On the other end of the scale is more global optimization that looks at everything from whole loops up to the basic algorithm used to solve the problem.

Local optimization sounds like important stuff, so why have I labeled this section optional? The worth of local optimization is questionable for several reasons:

- On a 100 MHz Pentium, a good local optimization might save as much as 1/10,000,000 of a second. You have to execute such code many millions of times to realize even a tiny savings in time.
- It's hard to figure out where optimization is useful. Donald Knuth ("An Empirical Study of FORTRAN Programs," see the bibliography) found that in most of the programs he studied, four per cent of the program code accounted for more than half the execution time, and the location of that four per cent was not necessarily evident.
- Usually global optimization is *much* more useful. My favorite example of the effect of the algorithm used is a study of various strategies for symbol tables in a compiler by William

McKeeman ("Symbol Table Access", see the bibliography). The XPL language is a language for writing compilers, and as such, can be used to compile its own compiler. The original version used a linear search for the symbol table. The time for the compiler to compile *itself* was reduced 25 per cent (!!!) by changing from the linear search to the hashing technique. (Do not worry if you don't understand these terms.) This figure implies not just that a fourth of the compiler's time is spent searching the symbol table. It implies that a fourth can be *saved* by improving the search algorithm!

OK, so if local optimization is such a questionable undertaking, why bother to talk about it at all? Because it may be just as easy, or even easier, to write more efficient than less efficient code!

So let's take a look at the factors involved in instruction execution time. Most manuals and texts on assembly language list number of clock cycles required for each instruction, one for each of the members of the 80X86 CPU family. If you look at my instruction listings in Appendix B, you will find no such timing information. The reason is that, as I will explain in this section, it is *virtually impossible to predict execution times of sections of code*, even if you know how long it takes to execute each individual instruction in the section. Therefore rather than deluding ourselves with exact timings, we will make do with a few rules of thumb.

ad hoc rule 1 for local optimization

Except for certain slow instructions, such as `mul` and `div`, the execution time of an instruction is roughly proportional to the number of bytes in the instruction and the number of bytes of operands that must be fetched from or stored into memory

In other words, most of the variation in instruction execution time depends on the amount of time necessary to fetch the instruction and fetch or store its operands.

As a corollary to rule 1, since some instructions have shorter versions for `ax` and `al`,

ad hoc rule 2 for local optimization

When using registers, it may be faster to use `ax` or `al`.

Finally, as we have seen, the gains are limited and fairly unpredictable, so I advocate

ad hoc rule 3 for local optimization

Don't worry a lot about it.

If you are still with me, the rest of this section will show just how complicated it is to figure out instruction timings. We will assume for the basis of discussion an 80486 66 MHz CPU, which, at the time of this writing was on its last legs commercially, but still faster than many existing PCs. At 66 MHz (MegaHerz; the clock time is 66 million cycles per second), the CPU instruction clock ticks about every 15 nanoseconds (1 nanosecond = 1 billionth of a second). Typical fast instructions on such a CPU (`mov`, `add`, `sub`, `inc`, `dec`, etc.) take 1–3 clock cycles, or 15–45 nanoseconds. *In addition they need the time necessary for fetching and storing* of the instructions themselves and their operands..

To look at fetch and store time, let us start with a fairly simple model of memory. Typical computer memory as I am writing takes 60-70 nsec (nanoseconds) for a fetch or a store. Let's assume 60. With the 486, memory is fetched or stored in four–byte chunks, starting on an address divisible by four. Thus, depending on how it is situated in memory, a two-byte instruction could be contained in one or two such chunks and a six–byte instruction in two or three of them. Things are not as complicated as they seem, though, since instructions are usually executed in sequence and what is left over from the current instruction will probably be used in the next. Therefore it is reasonable to postulate the fetch time of an instruction as

$$\text{instruction fetch time} = (\text{number of bytes}/4) * 60 \text{ nsec}$$

Thus a two–byte instruction takes about 30 nsec to fetch and a six–byte instruction, about 90 nsec to fetch.

In addition, if an operand is fetched from or stored into memory, that will require another memory access, taking at least another 60 nsec. Thus the fetching of an instruction and its operand may well take several times as long as its execution.

Let's pause a moment to see how we can use the ideas above to improve our programming.

Example 4.5—1. Write code to perform A := B – 333 where A, and B are word variables. One version of the code, with assembly listing (see Section 4.4), is

```
0005 8B 16 012E R           mov   dx, B ;      Bad code
0009 89 16 00C8 R           mov   A, dx
000D 81 2E 00C8 R 014D      sub   A, 333
```

which requires a total of 14 bytes of instructions, a fetch of B, a store in A, followed by a fetch of A (to perform the addition) and another store of A. These instructions might take roughly 210 nsec for instruction fetch, 240 nsec for operand fetch and store, and only 90 nsec to actually execute the instructions. On the other hand, the code

```
0005 8B 16 012E R           mov   dx, B ;      Better code
0009 81 EA 014D             sub   dx, 333
000D 89 16 00C8 R           mov   A, dx
```

is only 12 bytes long and does only one fetch and one store. Thus total fetch and store time goes down from 450 to 300 nsec, while the execution time of 90 nsec stays the same.

Unfortunately, I have greatly oversimplified the description of fetching and storing. The biggest complicating factor with the 486 and later CPUs is **cache memory**. *The use of cache is automatic and entirely invisible to the programmer*. However, it can greatly speed up memory accesses.

The 486 chip has 8 KBytes (8,196 bytes) of cache on the chip itself, and typical 486 computers come with enough external cache to make up 256 KBytes of cache memory. Typical cache memory has 15–25 nsec access time, and so is 2–4 times faster than ordinary memory.

Roughly, cache memory works in the following way. When an item is fetched from memory, it is placed in the cache as well as manipulated by the CPU. If that item is needed again at a later time and is still in the cache (we say a **hit** has occurred) then only fetching from the cache is necessary. A similar technique is used for storing. Thus for a good sized loop, (or even a fairly large program) the entire program may need to be fetched into cache only once, after which fetch time is reduced to perhaps a fourth of its original value. In example 4.4—1 above, the total fetch and store time thus might be reduced to 75 nsec, compared to an execution time of 90 nsec. Notice though, that doesn't invalidate our argument in that example!

The situation with cache memory is complicated by the fact that interrupts (to be discussed in detail in Chapter 15) can occur at any time, which can cause large parts of cache to be overwritten and thus have to be reloaded. Also, more and more machines running under various versions of Microsoft Windows do some type of multitasking, which can also cause the cache to be overwritten and invalidated.

Another memory speedup technique used by the 486 is a 16-byte **prefetch buffer**, which allows the 486 to fetch instructions ahead of where it is executing if memory isn't being used for anything else at the time. Prefetching is overlapped with instruction execution, thus in some instances, execution time may depend totally on instruction fetching time. (The prefetch buffer has a long history. Even the lowly 8088 had a four-byte prefetch buffer.)

The paragraphs above constitute a very brief and imprecise discussion of some of the issues affecting memory access. I have not even considered such things as **wait states** and **DMA access**, which can also slow down memory access. I hope though that I have convinced you of the efficacy of my ad hoc rules above.

Programming Problem 4.1

Write an assembly language program FORMULA which computes

$$X := (N - 5 * R) / K \quad (/= \text{integer division})$$

where X, N, R, and K are signed word variables. Your program should use GetDec to input N, R, and K and PutDec to display X (see Section 3.4). A run with test data N = 14, R = 7, and K = 5 would appear as follows (user's responses in boldface):

```
C:> formula
N = 14
R = 7
K = 5
X = -4
```

Test data that you should try, with the corresponding values of X, are

N =	14	20	14	−20	14
R =	7	1	−7	1	7
K =	5	5	5	5	−5
X =	−4	3	9	−3	4

Style Note: even though it may seem tedious writing essentially the same code three times for input, it is probably better not to attempt a loop, even if you have read ahead. The non-loop is cleaner, more readable, and more maintainable. Also don't try to be super efficient and keep all the variables in registers. The code becomes hard to read, and if the formula computed is modified, the program will have to be completely rewritten.

(Reminder: You can use **Ctrl-P** to get a transcript of your results on an attached printer.)

SUMMARY

We introduced a variety of instructions involved with arithmetic. The instructions, separated into similar classes, are

```
add    dest, source ;           add
sub    dest, source ;           subtract
```

(*dest* can be a register or a memory location; *source* can be a register, memory location, or constant; At least one of the operands must *not* be a memory location; operands must be the same size.)

```
inc    dest ;                   increment
dec    dest ;                   decrement
neg    dest ;                   negate
```

(*dest* can be a register or a memory location.)

```
mul    source ;                 unsigned multiply
imul   source ;                 signed multiply
```

(byte operation: ax := al * *source*; word operation: dx, ax := ax * *source*)

```
div    source ;                 unsigned divide
idiv   source ;                 signed divide
```

(byte operation: al := ax / *source*; ah := ax **mod** *source*;
word operation: ax := dx, ax / *source*; dx := dx, ax **mod** *source*;)

(*source* can be a register or memory location.)

```
cbw ;                           convert byte to word
```

(ax := al **via sign extension**)

```
cwd ;                           convert word to double word
```

(dx, ax := ax **via sign extension**)

(These instructions are used in preparation for idiv.)

The operand in mul, imul, div, and idiv can't be a constant. Move the constant to a register first.

NOTE: The add, sub, inc, dec, and neg instructions can also be used—with word operands only—with the word registers sp, bp, si, and di. (Sp will be discussed in chapter 6 and the latter three will be discussed chapter 10.)

Debug Workshop I

Introduction to Debuggers

The classic way to debug a program is to plant code at various places in the program which displays what you hope are crucial values. Unfortunately the values displayed often turn out not to be the ones you really need, or so many values are displayed that the program takes a long time to execute and it is difficult to extract the important values from the mass of output. Also, any time debugging code is added to or removed from a program, there is a very real danger that bugs will be added *or removed*.

It is particularly difficult to use the method described above to debug assembly language programs because I/O is so complicated, and tends to destroy values in registers that we need to know or which need to be used later.

With the advent of interactive computer systems came more powerful tools—interactive debuggers—which allow us to actually observe the program as it executes.

An **interactive debugger** is itself a program. It runs under interactive control by the user at the keyboard and, in turn, controls the execution of the program being debugged. The user, through the agency of the debugger, can execute the program a statement at a time, looking at values in registers and memory as they are computed. In addition, the debugger can set markers called **breakpoints** (to be discussed in detail in Debug Workshop II after Chapter 5) at interesting places in the program. The program being debugged can then be run from the start or restarted from wherever it last stopped, stopping at the first breakpoint it encounters. At the breakpoint, values can again be examined and the user can make decisions as to where to set further breakpoints.

A debugger must take over some resources of the computer and in effect 'fake' an environment for the program it is testing so that the program will think it is operating alone. Early interactive debuggers attempted to be as small as possible, with the result that all values and addresses were in octal (base 8) or hex and the human user could communicate using symbols only in very limited ways. Many versions of DOS come with such a basic debugger, a program called DEBUG, which still is sometimes useful in debugging very large programs or in special circumstances. With a debugger like DEBUG, the user must compute actual addresses in memory of the desired code or data, which can be very timeconsuming (and error prone). It also requires that the user have a detailed knowledge of assembly language. MASM version 4.0 came with a program called SYMDEB which included the functions of DEBUG and was still fairly small but also had the ability to reference code labels and variables by their symbolic names.

The two debuggers we'll discuss here, Microsoft's CodeView (CV), which has been supplied with Microsoft's MASM assembler from version 5.0 on, and Borland's Turbo Debugger (TD), which is supplied with Borland's TASM assembler, have greatly enhanced symbolic capabilities. Both allow the user to display several lines of the *original source code* in a window, execute it line by line, stop at various points in it, and display values of variables *or expressions* written in the syntax of the original source code. Both debuggers are very large, complex programs in their own right, often much larger than the programs they are debugging! Specific versions discussed are TD, from assembler version 2.0 on, and CV, from assembler version 6.11. Discussing CV is something of a problem since it has gone through three major versions since I started the first edition of this book using MASM 5.1. With each succeeding version Microsoft has added more standard windowing functionality comparable to those TD has had since version 2.0. Why does this story have a familiar ring to it? To paraphrase the immortal Fred Allen, "Imitation is the sincerest form of Microsoft." Anyway, I will discuss CV version 4.01 which came with MASM 6.11, but acknowledge that I am shooting at a moving target.

I.1 • Common Points in CV and TD

Both CV and TD have many common points of operation. If you're used to using Windows, there is little that is new in this section and you need only scan it briefly. The CV and TD interfaces are similar to Windows, but they operate in text mode so the graphics aren't as elaborate. To get the maximum use of each debugger, your program must be assembled with debugging information using special assemble and link commands. If you don't use them, you can still debug your program but you won't see your variable and label names and other symbolic information.

The most convenient way to use the debuggers is with a **mouse**, and I will give most prominence to mouse instructions. All operations can also be performed without a mouse too.

▶ **Using a Mouse**

Mice for the PC come with two or three buttons. When you move the mouse on a surface, a corresponding rectangle (the **mouse cursor**) moves on the screen. Virtually everything is done with the left button (if you are a sinister person, it may be possible to reconfigure your mouse so that the right button serves that function instead). The center button, if any, is never used and is gradually becoming extinct. There are three basic actions with a mouse:

- **Clicking** a button with the mouse cursor at a particular position. I will use **click left** and **click right** to indicate which button is to be clicked. Clicking is generally used to select the thing the mouse cursor points to.
- Holding the (left) mouse button and **dragging** with the mouse cursor. Dragging is typically used to move or change the size of a window on the screen.
- **Double-clicking** a button—clicking the button twice in fairly rapid succession without

moving the mouse cursor in between. Double-clicking usually indicates click left with some shortcut selection action, and doesn't occur much with our debuggers. For instance, a single click in a file list highlights the file while a double-click may open it.

We will start our lesson on each debugger withan exercise in using the mouse to rearrange the windows on the video screen.

▶   **Using Menus**

The top line of the screen is the **menu bar**. Each word in the menu bar is the title of a list of related commands called a **menu**.

- To cause a menu to drop down from the menu bar, either click on the menu name or hold down the **Alt** key and type the first letter of the menu name.

Click left or click and drag to pull down Edit menu (or Alt-E)

In the following illustration, we have dropped the Edit menu by one of these means.

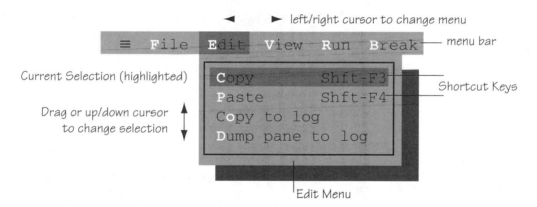

- To pick a particular item in a menu do *one* of the following:
    1) Click left on the desired selection, or
    2) Use up and down cursor arrows to highlight the selection you want, then hit the Enter key, or
    3) Type the highlighted letter (usually the first) of the chosen menu item.
- **Mouse Shortcut:** Click left on the menu title on the menu bar, causing the menu to drop down, then click left on the desired menu item.
- **Keyboard Shortcut:** Many menu selections have keyboard shortcuts which can be used without pulling down menus at all. They are shown at the right end of the menu selection (so you can try to remember them to use *next* time.) For instance, Shift-F3 (the function key F3, not 'F' followed by '3') can be used as a substitute for the copy menu

action above.

- **Closing a menu** without using it: Click left somewhere outside the menu or hit the Esc key.

Some menu choices will be followed by three dots: **...** . Choosing such an entry will cause the display of another window (a **dialog box**) in which further choices must be made. Click left with the mouse to select fields or use the Tab key to move between fields in the dialog box and the Enter key to accept the information in the window.

To shorten the descriptions of the keyboard versions of menu commands, we will write things like

Alt-F(ile **L**(oad *other things to type, if any*

meaning, in the example above, pull down the File menu with **Alt-F**, then choose the load function with **L** and do whatever else is specified.

▶ **Using Windows**

Each debugger uses the full screen, which is divided up into various **windows**, each containing a collection of information about the running program. For instance the **source** or **code window** contains the original source program, which you can follow line by line, and the **register window** shows the current contents of the registers. One window is always designated as the **active window**—which one is shown by a special highlighted border. Cursor keys, etc., always operate on the active window (unless a menu or dialog box is open).

- To **change the active window**, click on any visible portion of the desired window. The new active window is moved in front of all the other windows. You can also cycle through the various windows to make the one you want active by hitting **F6** repeatedly. Also, each window has a **window number** given on its upper border, and a window can be made active by typing **Alt-window number**.

Some windows won't be large enough to display their entire contents—in case of the code window, an entire source file. When such a window is *active*, it is possible to use it to view different parts of its contents, a process called **scrolling**.

- To **scroll a window** up or down, use the **scroll bar** on the right-hand edge of the window.

Somewhere between the arrows on the scroll bar is a box called the **thumb**, which shows the approximate position of the current window among all the data it can view. Scroll one line up or down by clicking left on the up or down arrow at the ends of the scroll bar. Scroll a whole window-full by clicking above or below the thumb. Drag the thumb for more substantial scrolling. The **PgUp** and **PgDn** keys are the equivalent of clicking above and below the thumb, respectively.

Some active windows also have horizontal scroll bars, whose use is similar.

- Windows have three forms: **maximized** (occupying the whole screen), **normal** (occupying part of the screen), and **iconized** (a small symbolic representation of the window). One can switch between these versions of the window by clicking left on appropriate symbols in the upper right-hand corner of the border of the window.
- Ordinary and iconized windows can be **moved** by dragging them by their upper border, and ordinary windows can be **resized** by dragging their lower right-hand corner.
- Windows can be **opened** (made visible and active) and **closed** (cleared from the screen).

▶ **Tracing, Stepping, and Running**

Tracing a program means executing it one line at a time, stopping before each line is executed to allow the user to examine the current state of registers and memory. There are two forms of tracing, called **tracing** and **stepping**, which are identical except when applied to a `call` instruction (and a few others). When the **trace** command is applied to a `call` instruction, the sub-procedure being called is then also traced line by line *if it has debugging information* (that is, if it was assembled with the special switch discussed further on). If the **step** command is applied, tracing is suspended until the program reaches the line immediately below the `call`. Stepping is invaluable when the sub-procedure being `called` is already debugged, at least in the current situation under test. Since the only subprocedures we will be using for a while are those assembled without debugging information, we won't really see a difference between step and trace until Debug Workshop III, which follows Chapter 6. To summarize the terms:

- **Step**   Execute line by line, but step *over* calls.
- **Trace**   Execute line by line, but trace *into* called subprocedures that have debugging information.

In addition there is

- **Run** or **Go**   Execute until the program terminates for some reason.

It may help in remembering these terms that their initials, **RST**, are consecutive letters in the alphabet and each successive command generally executes a *shorter* distance before stopping than its predecessor. Each debugger has function keys and mouse actions for each of these commands.

▶ **Getting Help**

Click on 'Help' towards the right end of the menu bar or hit **F1**. Both debuggers also have Help lines at the bottom of the screen which give keystrokes for useful commands in the current (changing) situation. Clicking left on one of the help messages at the bottom of the screen is equivalent to striking the key.

At this point, the two debuggers diverge, so they will be treated separately in the next two sections. You only need to read the section for the debugger you are using—CodeView with MASM and Turbo Debugger with TASM. For each debugger, we will cover the following information for a source program PROG.ASM:

- Use PROG.ASM to make a special PROG.EXE for use with the debugger.
- Start the debugger on PROG.EXE.
- Manipulate windows: open and close; switching between maximized, iconized, and ordinary; moving and resizing.
- Exit the debugger.
- Use the window manipulation techniques introduced above to configure the debugger for convenient use. Save the configuration for automatic reuse later.
- Execute a program line by line, observing as you go
  a) contents of registers,
  b) values of variables, and
  c) output of the program.

I.2 • CodeView Introduction

Following the outline from the end of the last section:

- To prepare an assembly program called PROG.ASM for use with CodeView, assemble and link it with the commands

  ```
  C:\> masm /zi prog;↵
  C:\> link /co prog;↵ (or link /co prog,,,util;↵)
  ```

  (↵ represents the Enter key) or the all-in-one command

  ```
  C:\> ml /Zi prog.asm util.lib↵
  ```
  (upper case 'Z' and lower case 'i' *required*.!)

CV Exercise 1

Make a CodeView-ready version of the program DBGEX1.ASM in the DEBUG directory on the disk that comes with this book. You will need the resulting .EXE file for later exercises in this section.

- To execute CodeView on PROG.EXE, type

  ```
  C:\> cv prog↵
  ```

Note: If you are running in **Windows**, CV must be run from a **DOS** window, that is, start 'MSDOS Prompt' from the 'Main' folder. Exiting windows and running in DOS doesn't seem to work, as CV thinks it is being run in the wrong mode and refuses to execute.

If you have a monitor which is VGA or beyond (as almost everyone does now) you can cause CodeView to put 50 lines on the screen instead of 25 by executing

```
C:\> cv /50 prog↵
```

and thus get more information in your windows or more windows on the screen. You only have to use the /50 switch once—whenever CodeView is invoked, it remembers the settings in force when it was last exited. To get back to the standard 25-line screen, use the **/25** switch (once).

The first time it is executed, CodeView shows three windows—from top to bottom, the **locals window** showing local variables and their values, the **source window** showing source code with the next line to be executed highlighted, and the **command window**. The command window is used to type commands to CV, which are relics of the older line-oriented debuggers.

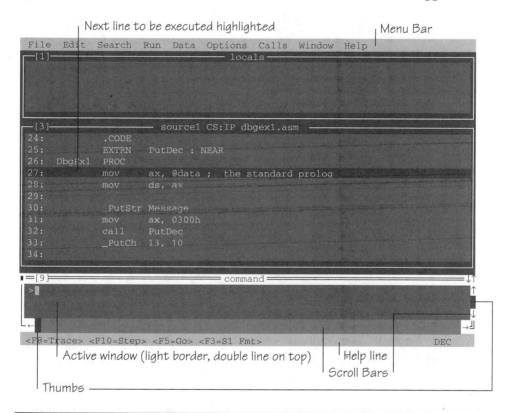

Note: If the command window contains the message

```
Warning: no CodeView information for …
```

then you have not assembled and linked your program correctly according to the instructions. Exit CodeView (see below), reassemble and link properly as at the beginning of this section, and reenter CodeView.

- The **active window** has a light border and a double upper line in the border. The following are examples of active and inactive windows:

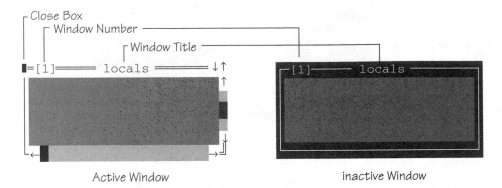

Active Window   inactive Window

To **open** a window, choose it from the Window menu or press **Alt-W**(indows **#** or **Alt-#** where '#' is the single digit window number. The active window can be **closed** (removed from the screen) by clicking left on its close box in the upper left-hand corner of the window border or using **Alt-W**(indows **C**(lose. Recall that a window can be made **active** either by clicking on it, typing **F6** until it is the active window, or typing **Alt-#**, replacing # with the window number.

The active window can be moved and resized as follows:

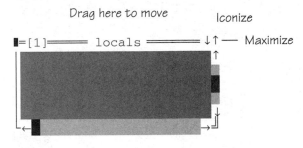

Drag here to resize

By dragging on any part of the upper border other than the ends, the window can be **moved**. Also, **Alt-W**(indows **M**(ove or **Ctrl-F7**, then move with the cursor keys, **Enter** key to end.

By dragging on the lower right-hand corner, the window can be **resized**. Also, **Alt-W**(indows **S**(ize or **Ctrl-F8**, then resize with the cursor keys, **Enter** key to end.

Can be omitted on first reading:

By clicking on the down-pointing arrow at the right of the upper border, **Alt-W**(indow miN(imize or **Ctrl-F9** the window can be **iconized**:

Icon, Active

Icon, inactive

To return an iconized window to its ordinary form, double-click left on the icon or make it active and choose **Alt-W**(indows **R**(estore or **Ctrl-F5**.

To **maximize** a window, click on the up-arrow in the upper right-hand corner of the border or type **Alt-W**(indow maX(imize (**Ctrl-F10**). A maximized window fills all of the screen excepting the menu bar and the help line. The upper right-hand corner of the maximized window offers two clickable options:

Return to normal
Iconize

- To **Exit** CodeView, choose exit from the File menu or use **Alt-F**(ile eX(it or **Alt-F4**.

- CV is initially configured for high-level languages such as C/C++. The locals window doesn't show anything useful in assembly and the registers window, which is very useful, is closed.

CV Exercise 2

Reconfigure your CodeView screen (if necessary) using techniques learned above so that it always opens looking like the picture on the next page. (If you or someone else has been messing with your copy of CodeView, you can return to the default initial screen for the purposes of this exercise by executing CodeView changing the number of lines per screen. For instance, if the number of lines per screen is presently 50 and you want it to stay that way. Execute cv /25 ..., exit CodeView, and then execute cv /50 ....)

1) Execute CodeView on the program DBGEX1 (.EXE) created in CV Exercise 1.
2) Close the locals window.
3) Open the registers window and move it to the top right side of the screen. If you are using a 50-line screen, shorten the registers window so it doesn't overlap the command window.
4) Move the source1 (code) window to the top of the screen, just below the menu bar. Resize

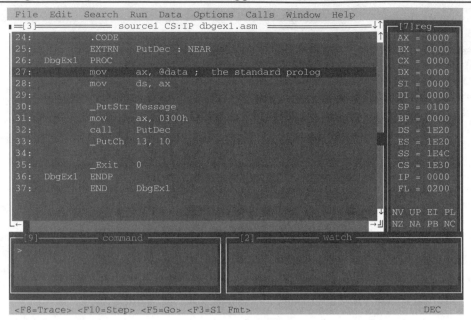

```
 File  Edit  Search  Run  Data  Options  Calls  Window  Help
 ■═[3]════════════ source1 CS:IP dbgex1.asm ══════════════↓↑  ─[7]reg──
  24:            .CODE                                        ↑  AX = 0000
  25:            EXTRN   PutDec : NEAR                           BX = 0000
  26:  DbgEx1    PROC                                            CX = 0000
  27:            mov     ax, @data ;  the standard prolog        DX = 0000
  28:            mov     ds, ax                                  SI = 0000
  29:                                                            DI = 0000
  30:            _PutStr Message                                 SP = 0100
  31:            mov     ax, 0300h                               BP = 0000
  32:            call    PutDec                                  DS = 1E20
  33:            _PutCh  13, 10                                  ES = 1E20
  34:                                                            SS = 1E4C
  35:            _Exit   0                                       CS = 1E30
  36:  DbgEx1    ENDP                                            IP = 0000
  37:            END     DbgEx1                                  FL = 0200

                                                                NV UP EI PL
 └←                                                        →↓   NZ NA PB NC

  ┌[9]─────────── command ───────┐  ┌─[2]──────── watch ──────┐
  │ >                            │  │                         │
  │                              │  │                         │
  │                              │  │                         │
  └──────────────────────────────┘  └─────────────────────────┘
 <F8=Trace> <F10=Step> <F5=Go> <F3=S1 Fmt>                   DEC
```

the source1 window so that it touches but does not overlap the command and register windows.

5) Make the command window active and make it narrower, so it covers roughly the left half of the screen.

6) Open the **watch window** with **Alt-W**(indow **2**(. Watch or **Alt-2** and move and resize it so that it sits at the bottom right-hand corner of the screen. The use of the watch window will be described in ❻ b) below.

7) Exit CodeView. The state of the CodeView screen on exit is always saved and restored the next time CodeView is entered.

- To **execute** your program within the debugger, the CodeView keys for Run, Step, and Trace are

  F5 **Run** (CV calls this operation **Go**).
  F10 **Step** (*over* calls).
  F8 **Trace** (step-by-step, every instruction for which there is debugging information).

They are given on the help line at the bottom of the screen. You can also accomplish the function by clicking left on the appropriate help message. When you have executed through the _Exit statement, the format of the source1 window will change (you will lose most source code information). To **rerun** your program from the beginning, choose restart from the run menu or press **Alt-R**(un **R**(estart.

a) The contents of various CPU **registers** appear in hex in the register window on the right of the screen. The value of ah is of course the left two hex digits of ax and al is the right two, etc. As each instruction is executed, the changed registers are highlighted in the registers window. The strange letters at the bottom of the window are the **flags**, the discussion of which will start in Chapter 5.

b) You can cause the current values of particular **variables** to be displayed and updated continuously in the **watch window** as your program executes. Choose Add Watch from the Data menu using **Alt-D**(ata **A**(dd Watch or **Ctrl-W** and enter the name of the variable you want to watch. If the blinking block cursor is on a variable in the source window when you choose Add Watch, that variable will appear as the default choice of the variable you want to watch, and you can accept that variable name or type in another. Move the cursor to a variable by clicking left on it with the mouse or by making the code window current with F6 and moving to the variable with the arrow keys.

You can watch a whole collection of values in a **memory window**. Choose **Alt-W**(indows **5**(. Memory 1 or **Alt-5** for the first memory window, **Alt-6** for the second. The memory windows start displaying from the beginning of your .DATA, can be scrolled up and down, and are updated continuously. To start at a different location or display a different format, activate the window and choose Memory Window from the Options menu.

As previously mentioned, line oriented commands can be entered in the **command window**. For instance, the command ?*variable-name*↵ causes the value of *variable-name* to be displayed. (But the display isn't updated if the variable's value changes.) Normally the command window must be active to enter commands, but if the source window is active, typing a command makes the command window the active window *temporarily*.

Values displayed in the watch window and by the ? command are in the **current number base**, which is shown at the right-hand end of the help line at the bottom of the screen (initially DEC = decimal). You can change the current number base by typing the following commands into the command window:

n16↵	Change current number base to hex.
n10↵	Change current number base to decimal.

CodeView 'remembers' the chosen current number base from session to session. Values in the register window are always displayed in hex.

One mildly annoying feature of CodeView is that it uses the C/C++ language notation to display hex numbers—the prefix 0x instead of the suffix h. Thus the assembly hex number 3afh appears as 0x3af in CodeView.

You can change the display method used for a particular variable in either the watch or command window by entering its name as *variable-name*,***letter***. Possible values of ***letter*** are **d** (decimal), **x** (hex) and **c** (char).

Note: Remember that '?' is *required* in the command window, *forbidden* in the watch window.

c) To view the normal **output screen** produced by your program, chooseView Output from the Windows menu, or enter **Alt-W**(indows **V**(iew Output or **F4**. Hit any key to return to the CodeView screen.

I.3 • Turbo Debugger Introduction

In this section, we will cover the outline at the end of Section I.1 for the Turbo Debugger.

- To prepare an assembly program called PROG.ASM for use with Turbo Debugger, assemble with the command

      C:\> **tasm /zi prog**↵

(↵ represents the Enter key) and link it with the command

      C:\> **tlink /v prog**↵   (or **tlink /v prog,,,util**↵)

The /zi and /v are *switches* which cause TASM and TLINK to save source-code information for use by the debugger.

TD Exercise 1

Make a Turbo Debugger-ready version of the program DBGEX1.ASM in the DEBUG directory on the disk that comes with this book. You will need the resulting .EXE file for later exercises in this section.

- To execute Turbo Debugger on PROG.EXE, type

      C:\> **td prog**↵

line containing cursor (flashing underline)

Triangle points to next line to be executed

Menu Bar

```
 ≡  File  Edit  View  Run  Breakpoints  Data  Options  Window  Help        READY
┌[■]=Module: dbgex1 File: dbgex1.asm 27 ════════════════════════════1=[↑][↓]═┐
          EXTRN    PutDec : NEAR                                              ▲
  DbgEx1  PROC
►         mov      ax, @data ;  the standard prolog
 ·        mov      ds, ax

 ·        _PutStr Message
 ·        mov      ax, 0300h
 ·        call     PutDec
 ·        _PutCh  13, 10

 ·        _Exit    0
  DbgEx1  ENDP
          END      DbgEx1



                                                                             ▼
└◄■                                                                          ►┘
┌─Watches───────────────────────────────────────────────────2─┐

 F1=Help F2=Bkpt F3=Mod F4=Here F5=Zoom F6=Next F7=Trace F8=Step F9=Run F10=Menu
```

Active window (double white outline)   Scroll Bars   Help Line

Thumbs

Note: If you get a window containing the message

Program has no symbol table

then you have not assembled and linked your program correctly according to the instructions above. Use the Esc or Enter key to exit the error window, exit TD (see below), reassemble and link properly as at the start of this section, and reenter TD.

If you have a monitor which is VGA or beyond (as almost everyone does now) you can cause Turbo Debugger to put 50 lines on the screen instead of 25 by executing **Alt-O**(ptions **D**(isplay options… **4**(3/50. The 50-line option gives you room for more information in your windows or more windows on the screen. You only have to specify the number of lines once in each directory you are working in—it will be remembered in future executions of TD.

The first time it is executed, Turbo Debugger starts up showing two windows, from top to bottom, the **module window** showing source code with a triangle in the left margin indicating the next line to be executed, and the **watch window** (see the previous page). Variables or expressions can be inserted in the watch window (see below), which then constantly displays their current values.

The **Help Line** at the bottom of the screen shows some current meanings of function and other keys. Holding down the Ctrl or Alt keys for a short period of time shows the meanings of keys shifted with the Ctrl or Alt key. In addition to striking the key combination, you can also perform the function by clicking left or right on that part of the help line.

- The **active window** has a light double line in the border. The following are examples of active and inactive windows, respectively:

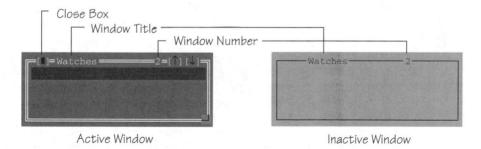

Active Window   Inactive Window

To **open** a window, choose it from the View menu or pressing **Alt-V**(iew **W**(*indow name* where 'W' is replaced by the appropriate letter in the window name. For instance, to open the registers window, use **Alt-V**(iew **R**(egisters. The active window can be **closed** (removed from the screen) by clicking left on its close box in the upper left-hand corner of the window border or using **Alt-W**(indow **C**(lose or **Alt-F3**. A window can be made **active** either by clicking on it, typing **F6** until it is the active window, or typing **Alt-#**, replacing **#** with the window number.

The active window can be moved and reshaped as follows (see the following page for a diagram): By dragging on any part of the upper border that doesn't have another meaning, the window can be **moved**. By dragging on the lower right-hand corner, the window can be **resized**. You can also use **Alt-W**(indow **S**(ize/Move or **Ctrl-F5**, then use the cursor keys to move the window,

Shift-cursors to resize it, then the Enter key to end.)

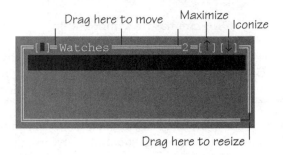

Drag here to move   Maximize   Iconize

Drag here to resize

Can be omitted on first reading:

By clicking on the down-pointing arrow at the right of the upper border or **Alt-W**(indow **I**(conize / restore, the window can be **iconized**:

Icon, active   Icon, inactive

To return an iconized window to its ordinary form, click left on the icon or make it active and click on the up arrow or choose **Alt-W**(indow **I**(conize / restore. Double-click on the icon to maximize it.

To **maximize** (**Zoom**) an ordinary window, click on the up-arrow in the upper right-hand corner of the border or type **Alt-W**(indow **Z**(oom) or **F5**. The resulting window fills most of the screen. Click left on the double arrow in the upper right-hand corner or **Alt-W**(indow **I**(conize / restore to return to the ordinary window.

return to normal

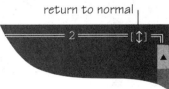

- To Exit TD, choose exit from the File menu or use **Alt-F**(ile **Q**(uit or **Alt-X**.

- TD needs to be reconfigured for maximum usefulness.

TD Exercise 2

Reconfigure your Turbo debugger screen (if necessary) using techniques learned above so that it always opens with the window configuration on the next page.

1) Execute TD on the program DBGEX1 (.EXE) created in Exercise TD 1. If you or someone else has been messing with TD and it doesn't look like the initial configuration on p. 86, for the

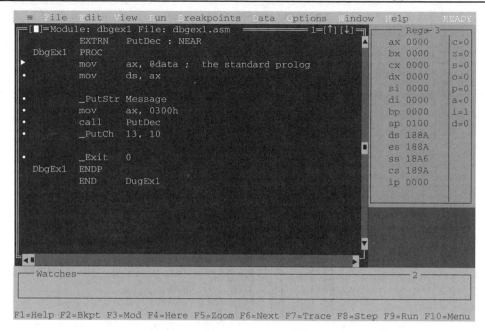

```
 ≡  File  Edit  View  Run  Breakpoints  Data  Options  Window  Help        READY
┌[■]═Module: dbgex1 File: dbgex1.asm ══════════════1=[↑][↓]┐ ┌─Regs─3─┐
│         EXTRN    PutDec : NEAR                          ▲ │ ax 0000 │c=0
│  DbgEx1 PROC                                              │ bx 0000 │z=0
│►        mov      ax, @data ;  the standard prolog         │ cx 0000 │s=0
│  •      mov      ds, ax                                   │ dx 0000 │o=0
│                                                           │ si 0000 │p=0
│  •      _PutStr  Message                                  │ di 0000 │a=0
│  •      mov      ax, 0300h                                │ bp 0000 │i=1
│  •      call     PutDec                                   │ sp 0100 │d=0
│  •      _PutCh   13, 10                                   │ ds 188A │
│                                                         ■ │ es 188A │
│  •      _Exit    0                                        │ ss 18A6 │
│  DbgEx1 ENDP                                              │ cs 189A │
│         END      DugEx1                                   │ ip 0000 │
│                                                           └────────┘
│                                                         ▼
│◄■                                                       ►
┌─Watches───────────────────────────────────────────────2─┐
│                                                          │
└──────────────────────────────────────────────────────────┘
F1=Help F2=Bkpt F3=Mod F4=Here F5=Zoom F6=Next F7=Trace F8=Step F9=Run F10=Menu
```

purposes of this exercise, exit TD, delete the file TDCONFIG.TD from the current directory, and restart TD.

2) Open the registers window and move it to the top right side of the screen.

3) Resize the module (code) window so that it touches but does not overlap the register window. (Otherwise the register window will disappear when the module window is active.)

4) To cause the window layout to be saved automatically each time TD is exited, choose Save from the Options menu by mousing or pressing **Alt-O**(ptions **S**(ave… . Turn on the 'X' in front of **L**ayout entry, either by clicking on the box or typing the 'L'. There should also be an 'X' in the **O**ptions box. Now each time you restart TD *in the current directory,* it will use the same window layout it had when you last exited the debugger. Each directory that you work in will have its own saved configuration file.

5) Exit Turbo Debugger.

- To **execute** your program within the debugger, the Turbo Debugger keys for Run, Step, and Trace are

F9	**Run** (until a breakpoint or end of program).
F8	**Step** (*over* calls).
F7	**Trace** (step-by-step, every instruction).

Note: The larger the function key number, the further in general we execute. These keys are given on the help line at the bottom of the screen. You can also accomplish the function by clicking left on the appropriate help message. The line about to be executed has a 'triangle pointer' in the left margin of the code. To **rerun** your program from the beginning, choose program reset from the run menu or **Alt-R**(un **P**(rogram reset or **Ctrl-F2**.

a) The contents of various CPU **registers** appear in hex in the register window on the right of the screen. The value of ah is, of course, the left two hex digits of ax and al the right two, etc. As each instruction is executed, the changed registers are highlighted in the registers window. The strange letters at the right of the window are the **flags**, discussed starting in Chapter 5.

b) You can cause the current values of particular **variables** to be displayed and updated continuously as your program executes in the **watch window**. For instance if the variables

```
Message    DB     'I am a message$'
Vbl        DW     29
```

are watched, the contents of the watch window are

```
Message            byte[15]    "I am a message$"
Vbl                word    29  (1Dh)
```

Numbers are displayed as unsigned numbers. Thus –24 would be displayed as 65512 (ffe8h).

There are a variety of ways of adding a variable to the watch window. The most straightforward, if klunkiest method, is to choose Add Watch from the Data menu or **Ctrl-F7**. A dialog box appears, in which you enter the name of the variable to watch, then click OK or hit Enter. If the blinking underline cursor was on a variable in the module (source) window when you chose Add Watch, that variable will appear as the default choice of the variable to be watched, and you can use that name or change it. Move the cursor to a variable by clicking left on it with the mouse or by making the code window current with F6 and moving the underline cursor to the variable with the arrow keys.

a SpeedMenu

In addition, there are various quick methods using what TD calls SpeedMenus. Each TD window (and each pane in a window divided into pieces) has a **SpeedMenu** of commonly performed tasks associated with it which can be popped up by **clicking right** in the window or hitting **Alt-F10** (which operates on the active window). A task can be chosen by clicking left or right on it or cursoring to it and hitting Enter. Each entry in a SpeedMenu has a highlighted letter, which can be used to choose the entry. Also, when the corresponding window is active, **Ctrl-*letter*** can be used to perform the SpeedMenu function without opening the SpeedMenu first. You may recall that if you hold down the Ctrl key, the help line shows some functions available with the Ctrl key. They are in fact SpeedMenu functions, and vary depending on which window is active:

Ctrl: W-Watch E-Edit R-Remove D-Delete all I-Inspect C-Change

help line for SpeedMenu commands

Thus the SpeedMenu **W**(atch command can also be initiated by **Ctrl-W**. In the module (source) window, if the flashing underline cursor is on a variable, the SpeedMenu **W**(atch (**Ctrl-W**) immediately inserts that variable in the watch window. If no variable is indicated, the command brings up the same dialog box as the menu command. In the watch window, the SpeedMenu **W**(atch (**Ctrl-W**) command brings up the same dialog box as the menu command. You can also **remove a watch** by highlighting the line with the variable to be removed and choosing SpeedMenu **R**(emove (**Ctrl-R**). You can exit the SpeedMenu without using it by clicking right or left outside of it, hitting **Alt-F10** again, or hitting the Esc key.

To display the values of **all variables** in a window, choose Variables from the View menu, **Alt-V**(iew **V**(ariables. Switch between the panes of the resulting window with the mouse or the Tab key and scroll up and down through the window.

c) To view the normal **output screen** produced by your program, the user screen, choose User Screen from the Window menu, **Alt-W**(indow useR(Screen or **Alt-F5**. Return to the TD screen by striking any key.

Note: Each time you run TD, it saves restart information so that if you rerun TD on the same .EXE file, it will start with the same watches set, etc. If you have reassembled TD since the restart information was saved, on restarting TD you will get a window with the dialog

Restart info is old, use anyhow?

Simply click on **No** or type N to continue.

I.4 • Debugger Exercises

At various times throughout the book, we will present exercises designed to familiarize you with your debugger. The source code for these exercises is in the subdirectory DEBUG on the disk that comes with this book. You should assemble and link each exercise as it occurs using the instructions in Section I.2 or I.3 (or in the file itself) and then follow instructions here or (more briefly) in the file.

Debug Example 1: Start your debugger on the DBGEX1.EXE file created in CV 1 or TD 1. The code is as follows:

```
;; DbgEx1—Trace, step, run, and viewing output

INCLUDE   PCMAC.INC
          .MODEL SMALL
          .STACK 100h

          .DATA
Message   DB     'The magic number is $'

          .CODE
          EXTRN  PutDec : NEAR
DbgEx1    PROC
          mov    ax, @data ;   The standard prolog
          mov    ds, ax

          _PutStr Message
          mov    ax, 8888h
          call   PutDec
          _PutCh 13, 10
```

```
            _Exit   0
DbgEx1      ENDP
            END     DbgEx1
```

Procedure:

1) Execute the program first by **Step**ping through it (CV: F10 or click left on <F10=Step> on the bottom help line. TD: F8 or click left on F8-Step on the bottom help line.) Note that the line about to be executed is highlighted in CV, indicated by a triangle at the beginning in TD, and that any registers changed by the last executed instruction are highlighted in the register window. Note also that you don't actually see the code for PutDec executed.

   You will note that if you step (or trace) through the _Exit macro the two debuggers will exhibit different behaviors. CV will switch the source code screen to a machine language format and you will find yourself about to execute the mov ah, 4ch and int 21h instructions. When you have executed those instructions, CV will give you a termination message in the command window. TD will give you a dialog with the message **Terminated, exit code 0**, or whatever number you specified in the _Exit macro.

2) Restart the program using **Alt-R**(un R(estart in CV, **Alt-R**(un P(rogram reset or **Ctrl-F2** in TD.

3) Trace through the program using **F8** or click *left* on <F8=Trace> in CV, **F7** or click left on F7-Trace in TD. The results should be identical to step 1). PutDec will not be traced, as it was assembled without debugging information. We will see how to trace into such a procedure anyway in Debug Workshop III. You might want to trace a procedure without debugging information because you don't want to bother to reassemble and relink, or you might not have the source code to the procedure. You might be looking for a bug in someone else's code, for instance, or you might just be curious. It is even possible to trace DOS calls with sufficient trickery. Chapter 15 gives enough information for you to do that.

4) Restart again and Run to get to the end of the program using F5 or click left on <F5=Run> in CV, F9 or click left on F9-Run in TD.

5) View the output using F4 or **Alt-V**(iew O(utput in CV, Alt-F5 or **Alt-W**(indow useR(Screen in TD.

Debug Example 2: Trace a program, viewing the results of arithmetic operations.

Assemble and link DBGEX2.ASM with debug information. (UTIL.LIB not required.)

```
;;   DbgEx2—looking at arithmetic with the debugger

INCLUDE   PCMAC.INC
          .MODEL SMALL
          .STACK 100h

          .DATA
```

```
A         DW      3
B         DW      -3


          .CODE
DbgEx2 PROC
          mov     ax, @data ;  The standard prolog
          mov     ds, ax

;    add WORD
          mov     ax, 8888h
          add     ax, 99h
  ??? 1   ;                     ax = _____
;    add BYTE
          mov     ax, 8888h
          add     AL, 99h
  ??? 2   ;                     ax = _____
;    decrement WORD
          mov     ax, 0
          dec     ax
  ??? 3   ;                     ax = _____
;    decrement BYTE
          mov     ax, 0
          dec     AL
  ??? 4   ;                     ax = _____
;    multiply UNSIGNED
          mov     ax, -3 ;   = 0FFFdh unsigned
          mul     A
  ??? 5   ;                     dx = _____, ax = _____
;    multiply SIGNED
          mov     ax, -3
          imul    A
  ??? 6   ;                     dx = _____, ax = _____
;    divide UNSIGNED
          mov     ax, 7
          sub     dx, dx
          div     B
  ??? 7   ;                     dx = _____, ax = _____
;    divide SIGNED
          mov     ax, 7
          sub     dx, dx
          idiv    B
  ??? 8   ;                     dx = _____, ax = _____
;    another divide
          mov     ax, -10
          idiv    A
  ??? 9                         dx = _____, ax = _____
          _Exit   0
```

```
DbgEx1    ENDP
          END     DbgEx1
```

Procedure:

1) Trace (**F7** in TD, **F8** in CV) (or step, **F8** in TD, **F10** in CV) through the program, noting the values requested in the comments. Note that the code line is highlighted (CV) or pointed to (TD) *before* it is executed, so you have to record the values when you have traced or stepped to the *next* line. ??? is a trivial do-nothing macro defined in PCMAC.INC whose sole purpose is to provide a line that tracing will stop on, so you can record the values.

2) You will note that there is a **bug** near the end of the program. Both debuggers give you minimal information about the problem.

   CV: In the command window, the message 'Error: Illegal Instuction,' which is not exactly a correct description of the situation.

   TD: A window with the message 'Terminated, exit code 256.' You know that this termination isn't normal since normal exit codes given by the _Exit macro return a byte, which is, at most, 255. However, it is up to you to guess what the error is.

3) Exit from the debugger, fix the error, reassemble and relink, and verify that your correction works.

I.5 • Automating Assembly

In order to simplify assembling and linking for use with a debugger, you might want to create one of the following three files and call it, say, ASSEM.BAT:

```
masm /zi %1;
link /co %1,,,util;
        or                          (MASM)
ml /Zi %1.asm util.lib

tasm /zi %1                         (TASM)
tlink /v %1,,,util
```

(Use the full path name of util.lib if necessary. It does no harm to include the UTIL library even if it isn't needed. If the main program makes no use of any of its procedures, none will be linked in.) ASSEM.BAT should be placed in the current directory or in one of the directories specified by your PATH variable. Then in order to assemble and link a program ABC.ASM for debugging you need only enter

```
assem abc
```

Execution of the above will cause execution of the lines of ASSEM.BAT as if you had typed them as commands with (in this case) abc replacing the '%1' wherever it occurs.

SUMMARY

Programs are prepared for the CV or TD symbolic debugger as follows:

CV	TD

```
        CV                          TD

  masm /zi prog;              tasm /zi prog
  link /co prog,,,util;       tlink /v prog,,,util
  cv prog                     td prog
```

For MASM, the first two lines can be replaced by

```
  ml /Zi prog.asm util.lib
```
                                    (note case of /Zi!)

Menus can be pulled down by hitting Alt and the first letter of the menu name. Then use up or down cursor keys followed by Enter to choose an option, or strike the highlighted letter. With a mouse, click left on the menu bar item and click on the desired menu item. Type Esc to exit a menu without making a choice.

Various useful commands are listed in the table below. A complete summary of the debugger commands used in this book is found in Appendix E.

command	CV	TD
run	**F5**	**F7**
step *over* calls	**F10**	**F8**
trace *into* calls	**F8**	**F9**
exit	**Alt-F**(ile e**X**(it or **Ctrl-F4**	**Alt-X**
watch variable name	**Alt-W**(atch **A**(dd	**Alt-D**(ata **W**(atch *or* use submenus (**Alt-F10** or click right)
display variable value	**?** *variable*	**Alt-V**(iew **V**(ariables
view program output	**F4**	**Alt-F5**
open a window	**Alt-V**(iew…	
close current window	Click left on close box (left end of top line) *or*	
	Ctrl-F4	**Alt-F3** *or* **Alt-W**(indow **C**(lose
change current window	Click left in window, **Alt**-new window number, *or* **F6**	
restart program	**Alt-R**(un **R**(estart	**Alt-R**(un **P**(rogram reset or **Ctrl-F2**
move window	click left on upper window border and drag, *or*	
	Alt-W(indow **M**(ove *or* **Ctrl-F7**	**Alt-W**(indow **S**(ize/Move *or* **Ctrl-F5**
resize window	click left on lower right hand corner and drag, *or*	
	Alt-W(indow **S**(ize *or* **Ctrl-F8**	**Alt-W**(indow **S**(ize/Move *or* **Ctrl-F5**

Chapter 5

Comparing and Branching

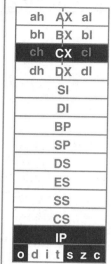

registers discussed

ah	AX	al
bh	BX	bl
ch	CX	cl
dh	DX	dl
	SI	
	DI	
	BP	
	SP	
	DS	
	ES	
	SS	
	CS	
	IP	

o d i t s z c

5.1 • Decision-Making in Assembly Language

Computer programs are of no particular worth unless decisions can be made in them. In IBM PC assembly language (and that of most modern computers) decision-making is a two step process:

1) Two numbers are compared, using cmp, the **compare** instruction, which sets several bits in a 16-bit register of the CPU called the **flags** register, and

2) A **conditional jump** instruction is executed which does or does not go to a new location based on the values of those flags.

The cmp instruction has two operands just like the mov instruction:

        cmp   reg/mem, reg/mem/constant

with the usual limitation of at most one *memory* operand per instruction. The operands can be either bytes or words, but as usual must be the same size.
    The instruction

        cmp   op1, op2

performs the subtraction *op1 – op2*, sets the flags according to the result, and discards the result. The flags set by the cmp instruction are as follows

Bit Number: 11   7 6   0

| | O | | S | Z | | C |

O = Overflow Flag (OF)   S = Sign Flag (SF)

Z = Zero Flag (ZF)   C = Carry Flag (CF)

(The S flag is set to the sign of the result, the Z flag is set to 1 if the result is zero, and the O and C flags are set to the Overflow and Carry status of the result.[*] The shaded portion of the flags register represents other flags and unused bits.)

For each one of these flags there are two **conditional jumps**. For instance, jc jumps if the carry flag is set, i.e., is equal to 1, and jnc jumps on no carry flag, that is, CF = 0. The usual >, <=, etc. conditions require a complicated combination of these jumps (see Exercise 5.1—6), so the 80X86 also provides a number of conditional jumps to take care of the most commonly occurring situations. The actual flag settings can pretty much be ignored.

We will start with the jumps based on **signed** numbers.

For SIGNED numbers, after cmp op1, op2			
je	address;	Jump if equal	(op1 = op2)
jne	address;	Jump if not equal	(op1 ≠ op2)
jg	address;	Jump if greater	(op1 > op2)
jge	address;	Jump if greater or equal	(op1 ≥ op2)
jl	address;	Jump if less	(op1 < op2)
jle	address;	Jump if less or equal	(op1 ≤ op2)

You can think of the relation in the conditional jump instruction as sitting between the operands of the cmp instruction. For example,

```
cmp  op1,    op2

jl    address
```

If the condition in a conditional jump is true, then the jump is taken, that is, the next instruction executed is at *address*. If the condition is false, then we fall through to the instruction following the conditional jump. Recalling from Section 1.1.1 that the IP register contains the address of the next instruction to be executed, the instruction

       jcondition   *address*

is equivalent to executing

---

[*] The overflow flag is set for addition and subtraction depending on whether overflow has occurred, as explained in Section 1.3. The carry flag is set on addition and subtraction by the carry out the left end. Although the carry is ignored for signed arithmetic, it can be quite useful in other situations.

$$\textbf{if } condition \textbf{ then } IP := address$$

In addition, there is often the need for an **unconditional jump**, one which is taken in all circumstances:

```
jmp    address;    jump unconditionally
```

which is equivalent to executing

$$IP := address$$

Addresses are of course just locations in memory, that is, they are numbers. As with data locations though, it is much easier to use labels to represent them symbolically. Still, an annoying inconsistency is that *code labels must be followed by a colon (:)*. The rule is

Labels of pseudo-instructions must *not* have colons. All other labels *must* be followed by a colon.

Typical pseudo-instructions we have labeled are DW, DB, EQU, PROC, and ENDP.
For example, consider the following program fragment:

```
        cmp    ax, bx
        jl     axLess ;    go to label 'axLess' if ax < bx
        mov    X, 1
        jmp    Both ;      go to label 'Both'
axLess: mov    X, -1
Both:
```

Here, axLess and Both are labels. A code label can be written on a line with an instruction or on a line by itself (perhaps with a comment). Writing a label on a line by itself tends to make important parts of the code stand out, and also makes it easier to add or delete code after the label. Thus the fragment above could read

```
        cmp    ax, bx
        jl     axLess ;    go to 'axLess' if ax < bx
        mov    X, 1
        jmp    Both
axLess:        ;           Better Style, sometimes
        mov    X, -1
Both:
```

The code above could be rewritten in a pseudocode as

$$\textbf{if } (ax < bx) \textbf{ then } X := -1 \textbf{ else } X := 1 \textbf{ end if}$$

Translating **if** conditions to assembly language can get rather complicated. For instance, even in the simple statement above, the **else** part appears before the **then** part in assembly language. I find the following procedure helps in translating pseudocode **if** statements into assembly language. First of all, I assume that the assembly language code will actually appear in the same order as the pseudocode is written (**then** before **else**). Of course, depending on the **if** condition, certain parts of the code will have to be skipped. I show that by drawing arrows above and below the line of the code, at appropriate places:

```
if (ax < bx) then X := -1 else X := 1 end if
```

false

Jumps on the condition being *true* and unconditional jumps will be written above the line, and jumps on the condition being *false* will be written below the line. This convention makes the diagrams easier to read.

After you have drawn the diagram, you can then translate the various parts of it into assembly language, leaving a blank corresponding to each start of an arrow and inserting a label for each arrow head:

```
        cmp     ax, bx ;        if ax < bx then ...

        mov     X, -1 ;           X := -1

Lab1:           ;               else
        mov     X, 1 ;            X := 1
Lab2:           ;               end if
```

Then you go back and fill in the blank lines with the appropriate jumps. One thing which can be very helpful in inserting *false* jumps is that for every instruction JXX to jump on condition XX true, there is a corresponding JNXX instruction, for 'Jump on Not XX' which is taken when condition is false. (Of course `jnle` is the same instruction as `jg`, etc.) Thus our code becomes

```
        cmp     ax, bx ;        if ax < bx then ...
        jnl     Lab1 ;                  (Jump on Not Less)
        mov     X, -1 ;           X := -1
        jmp     Lab2
Lab1:           ;               else
        mov     X, 1 ;            X := 1
Lab2:           ;               end if
```

Note the importance of the '`jmp Lab2`' instruction. Without it, you are in fact translating the code

```
if (ax < bx) then X := -1 end if
X := 1
```

which is just a clumsy and inefficient way of saying

```
X := 1
```

That is, X will always get set to 1, no matter what `ax` and `bx` are! Omitting this 'jump around the else' is one of the most frequent sources of errors in beginners' assembly language programs. (It is also one reason for the popularity of if-then-else in high-level languages.)

Example 5.1—1. Write a program fragment which sets the word X to 0 if it is greater than XMAX.

We start with the high-level statement

$$\textbf{if} \ (X > XMAX) \ \textbf{then} \ X := 0 \ \textbf{end if}$$

which we can 'decorate' with arrows as follows:

$$\textbf{if} \ (X > XMAX) \ \textbf{then} \ X := 0 \ \textbf{end if}$$
false

When we do the first stage of translating into assembly language, we have to avoid an immediate error: if we write `cmp X, XMAX` we have an illegal instruction, as we can't have both operands of `cmp` in memory. The solution is to move one of them to a register:

```
        mov     ax, X
        cmp     ax, XMAX ;      if (X > XMAX) then...

        mov     X, 0 ;          X := 0
Lab:            ;               end if
```

Notice that the comparison is done so that the order of the numbers being compared is the same as the order in the high-level code. The choice of order means that if X *is* greater than XMAX, the greater-than flags will be set. If you switch around the order of the comparands, you also have to remember to switch the jump condition, and confusion tends to take over. Now we can add the jump:

```
        mov     ax, X
        cmp     ax, XMAX ;      if (X > XMAX) then...
        jng     Lab
        mov     X, 0 ;          X := 0
Lab:            ;               end if
```

Notice that an unconditional jump is not required here as we don't have an **else** clause.

The "decoration" technique is particularly useful with complicated **if** statements containing **and** and **or** operations in their conditions. With ands and ors we use **short circuit evaluation**, in which we stop evaluating the condition as soon as we find that it must be true or false no matter what the rest of the evaluation could give. [*] For instance in evaluating `(A >= 5) or (B <> 1)` if we discover that `(A >= 5)` is true, then we don't have to test `(B <> 1)`. Of course if we found that

---

[*] Some high-level languages, such as C/C++ and Fortran, *require* short-circuit evaluation as part of the language definition. One can then write a statement like `if (A <> 0) and (X/A < 0.005)then` … . The Pascal language definition makes short-circuit evaluation *optional*, but in most Pascals, it is *not* used.

(A >= 5) is false, we would have to go ahead and test (B <> 1).

Example 5.1—2. Apply the technique of short circuit evaluation to:

if (A < B) **and** (B >= 14) **then** X := A **else** X := B **end if**

Since if (A < B) is false, we know the whole condition fails, we can decorate the statement above as follows:[*]

if (A < B) **and** (B >= 14) **then** X := A **else** X := B **end if**

false

First write the code with the usual spaces and labels:

```
          mov     ax, A
          cmp     ax, B ;        if (A < B) and ...

          cmp     B, 14 ;          (B >= 14) then ...

          mov     ax, A
          mov     X, ax ;            X := A

Lab1:             ;                else
          mov     ax, B
          mov     X, ax ;            X := B
Lab2:             ;              end if
```

and we can fill in the blanks with the appropriate jumps:

```
          mov     ax, A
          cmp     ax, B ;        if (A < B) and ...
          jnl     Lab1
          cmp     B, 14 ;          (B >= 14) then ...
          jnge    Lab1
          mov     ax, A
          mov     X, ax ;            X := A
          jmp     Lab2
Lab1:             ;                else
          mov     ax, B
```

---

[*] Compare the decorated statement if **and** is replaced by **or**:

true

if (A < B) **or** (B >= 14) **then** X := A **else** X := B **end if**

false

```
        mov    X, ax ;          X := B
Lab2:          ;                end if
```

Here we can make use of an important simplification technique which might be called **factoring**. We notice that both halves of the **if** branch end on the same instruction, mov X, ax. We can replace these instructions with a single occurrence outside the end of the two branches by deleting the first occurrence of mov X, ax and moving the Lab2: label to before the second occurrence:

```
        mov    ax, A
        cmp    ax, B ;          if (A < B) and ...
        jnl    Lab1
        cmp    B, 14 ;            (B >= 14) then ...
        jnge   Lab1
        mov    ax, A ;          X := A
        mov    X, ax
        jmp    Lab2
Lab1:          ;                else
        mov    ax, B ;          X := B
Lab2:
 ↑      mov    X, ax
Lab2:          ;                endif
```

We also recognize that the second mov ax, A instruction is superfluous since A is already in ax, so our code now becomes

```
        mov    ax, A
        cmp    ax, B ;          if (A < B) and ...
        jnl    Lab1
        cmp    B, 14 ;            (B >= 14) then ...
        jnge   Lab1
        mov    ax, A ;
        jmp    Lab2 ;           X := A
Lab1:          ;                else
        mov    ax, B ;          X := B
Lab2:
        mov    X, ax
               ;                endif
```

Notice the two boldface jump instructions. With the deletion of the mov instruction, they now constitute an example of a **jump around a jump**—a conditional jump followed immediately by an unconditional jump followed *immediately* by the destination of the conditional jump. The code

can almost always be replaced by the simpler code

> J**not**_condition_ SomewhereElse

Thus our final solution to Example 5.1—2 is:

```
            mov     ax, A
            cmp     ax, B ;        if (A < B) and ...
            jnl     Lab1
            cmp     B, 14 ;          (B >= 14) then ...
            jge     Lab2 ;             X := A
    Lab1:           ;               else
            mov     ax, B ;            X := B
    Lab2:
            mov     X, ax
```

Note that if the compound condition is true, only the instruction following Lab2 is executed, while if it is false, *both* the instruction following Lab1 and that following Lab2 are executed, just as in the original version.

The kind of optimization we performed above is very common in assembly language programming. It is related to the local or peephole optimization we discussed in optional Section 4.5 and will discuss in optional Sections 5.7 and 5.8. It is relatively simple to write compilers to do this optimization automatically.

For the optimization to be possible though, we have to make the right choices for the registers in which to hold variables and intermediate results. The same problem crops up in arithmetic too, as only certain registers can be used for multiplication and division and we may need to plan ahead to get our results in the right registers without moving them. Problems of register optimization are more than a local phenomenon, and are one of the more difficult problems for compilers to solve automatically.

Exercises 5.1

In these exercises, all variables are assumed to be signed words unless otherwise specified. Recall (Section 1.5) that in our pseudocode, **begin-end** or { } brackets aren't required to group statements. Proper bracketing follows from the use of **end if**. Also, I will always show the correct grouping via indentation.

1. Translate the following high-level code fragments into assembly language program fragments.

    a) ✓ X := |A|, i.e., X := A if A ≥ 0, −A if A < 0.
    b) **if** (A <= B) **then** Max := B **else** Max := A **end if**
    c) **if** (Minute = 59) **then**
    >   Minute := 0
    >   Hour := Hour + 1
    else
    >   Minute := Minute + 1
    end if

d) **if** (C = ' ') **or** (C = 9) **then** WhiteSpace := 1 **end if**
(The ASCII tab character is the number 9.)

e) **if** (C >= 'A') **and** (C <= 'Z') **then** UpperCase := 1
else UpperCase := 0 **end if**

f)✓ **if** (X > 0) **then** SgnX := 1
else

       if X < 0 **then** SgnX := −1 **else** SgnX := 0 **end if**
end if
(Only one comparison is necessary.)

g) OrdTime := MilTime;
if (MilTime < 1200) **then**
       AMPM := 'A'
       if (MilTime < 100) **then**
          OrdTime := OrdTime + 1200
       end if
else
       AMPM := 'P'
       if (MilTime >= 1300) **then**
          OrdTime := OrdTime − 1200
       end if
end if

2. a) Translate the following decorated pseudocode statement into assembly language:

if ((A >= 14) **or** (B = 17)) **and** (C <> −5) **then** X := X + 1 **end if**

b)✓ Translate the following pseudocode statement into assembly language:

if ((X > 5) **and** (Y < 0)) **or** (Z <= 13) **then** A := 10 **else** A := 2 **end if**

3. Each of the following assembly language fragments corresponds to a single high-level language if statement. Give such a statement in pseudocode or the high-level language of your choice. (Note that you shouldn't use register names in the high-level language version, where they would be meaningless.)

```
a)        cmp    A, 1
          jnl    A1
          mov    A, 1
A1:

b)        mov    ax, A
          cmp    ax, B
          jng    B1
          sub    B, ax
```

```
            jmp     B2
B1:         mov     ax, B
            sub     A, ax

B2:


c) ✓        mov     ax, A
            cmp     ax, 100
            jnle    C1
            cmp     ax, 10
            jnge    C1
            cwd
            idiv    B
            mov     A, ax

C1:


d)          cmp     A, 1
            je      D1
            cmp     A, 2
            jne     D2
D1:         inc     A
            jmp     D3
D2:         dec     A
D3:
```

4. Eliminate jumps around jumps in the following code fragments:

```
a)          cmp     A, 14
            jge     S1
            jmp     S2
S1:         mov     X, 21
S2:


b)          cmp     X, ax
            jne     L1
            jmp     L2
L1:         neg     X
            inc     X

L2:


c) ✓        cmp     ax, 0
            jg      around
            jmp     over
around:     inc     ax
            jmp     through
over:       dec     ax
through:
```

5. ✓ Write an assembly program fragment which converts a *number* in the word variable D, $0 \leq D \leq 15$ to an ASCII character in the byte variable HEXD which is its hex value. For instance, if D = 3 then HEXD = '3' and if D = 14 then HEXD = 'E'. (Hint: Don't use fifteen comparisons!)

6. a) The actual test performed by the jg instruction is 'jump if ZF = 0 and SF = OF.' It should be clear that the condition ZF = 0 is necessary—it means that *op1* ≠ *op2*. Also, SF = OF = 0 means that there was no overflow on the subtraction and the sign was positive, so *op1* ≥ *op2*. But what is the meaning of SF = OF = 1, and why is it necessary to include it as one of the conditions under which *op1* > *op2*? (Hint: what if *op1* = 32,000 and *op2* = – 32,000?)

 b) ✓ Write code using only the j[n]z, j[n]s, j[n]o, and jmp instructions which mimics the instruction jg Lab.

 c) What is the actual test performed on the flags by the jl instruction?

5.2 • Unsigned Conditional Jumps

It is sometimes necessary to use unsigned forms of conditional jumps. Subtraction is the same whether the numbers are signed or unsigned; we just need to test different combinations of the flags. The necessary instructions are

For UNSIGNED numbers, after cmp op1, op2		
ja address; Jump if above		(op1 > op2)
jae address; Jump if above or equal		(op1 ≥ op2)
jb address; Jump if below		(op1 < op2)
jbe address; Jump if below or equal		(op1 ≤ op2)

and their corresponding negated forms (jna, etc.). For instance,

Always use an unsigned jump when comparing addresses.

When we compare addresses, we think of the larger address occurring *after* the smaller in memory. 1111h < 2222h, of course, but how about comparing 7777h and 8888h? If we used a signed jump, we would get 7777h > 8888h, as 8888h is negative! This bug is particularly insidious because we often check out programs in small test cases, where all of the addresses will be 'positive.' Then some time later when our 'well-debugged' code becomes part of a larger program, the larger program may start failing.

The following example gives a concrete situation in which it is crucial to compare addresses. It is fairly complex and you may wish to skip it for now, but it addresses an important problem and should be returned to.

Example 5.2—1. We wish to write a program which moves a block of bytes starting at an address in ax to a block starting at an address in bx. The size of the block will be in cx. We won't know how to do the move until Chapter 10, but let's isolate the problem of determining the direction of the move—from the bottom of the block to the top or from top to bottom.

If the source and destination blocks don't overlap, either top-down or bottom-up moving works, but if they do overlap, the proper direction depends on which block has the lower memory address. You should move top down (high addresses first) and if the destination is *higher*, bottom up (low addresses first) if it is lower. (To see what goes wrong if the move is in the wrong direction, consider the following situation in which the destination block is *higher* than the source block:

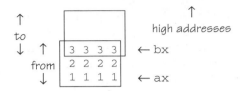

If the move proceeds **top-down**, as is shown in stages below, the move is **successful**.

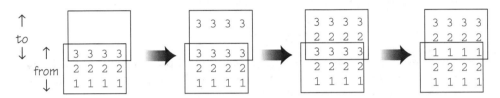

moving top to bottom

If you do it **bottom-up**, though, you get the following **incorrect** result:

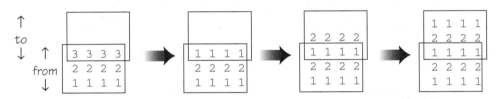

moving bottom to top (WRONG!)

The most obvious code to compare the addresses is

```
;; Example 5.2—1 Bad solution
;;
            cmp     ax, bx
            jl      MoveTopDown ; BAD conditional jump!!
MoveBottomUp:
```

The bug occurs when one address is so large as to appear negative. If for instance ax = 7fffh and bx = 8000h, then the source (ax) certainly comes before the destination, but is greater since bx is negative! The correct solution is

```
;; Example 5.2—1 CORRECT solution
;;
            cmp     ax, bx
            jb      MoveTopDown ; UNSIGNED conditional jump!!
MoveBottomUp:
```

Note also that characters whose ASCII value is 128 and above will appear to be negative. For instance, the following code to test for control characters is wrong

```
cmp    al, ' '
jl     CtrlChar ;    WRONG!
```

because the jump will also be taken for extended ASCII characters 128 and greater. The correct form is

```
cmp    al, ' '
jb     CtrlChar
```

Therefore it pays to

Use an unsigned jump when comparing characters

Exercises 5.2

1. ✓ DOS stores some times-of-day internally as a word, where the leftmost 5 bits are the hour, the next 6 bits are the minute, and the final 5 bits are the second divided by 2. Suppose that `Time1`, `Time2`, and `Late` are word variables with `Time1` and `Time2` containing times. Write assembly code to set `Late` equal to the later of the two times. (**Note:** a 24 hour clock is used so the hour can be 16 or greater, in which case a time will appear to be negative.)

2. In the first solution to Example 5.2—1, will the signed comparison be correct if *both* addresses are 'negative'?

3. ✓ In addition to the characters from 'A' to 'Z' and 'a' to 'z', the extended ASCII characters 128–154 and 160–167 are letters in various foreign languages. Write code which jumps to the label `Letter` if `al` contains a character in any of these ranges.

4. ✓ What condition on the four flag bits will cause the `ja` instruction to execute the jump?

5. In many cases it doesn't really matter which kind of jump you use when comparing characters. One example is when you are testing for characters in a range. For instance, consider the following code which tests to see if al contains an ASCII digit:

```
        cmp    al, '0'
        jl or jb notDigit
        cmp    al, '9'
        jle or jbe isDigit
notDigit:
```

What would happen though if you mixed jump instructions, using one signed and one unsigned jump? Try both possibilities.

5.3 • Loops

Loops are just special cases of compare and branch (though see Section 5.5 for examples of how they can be optimized). There are however instructions which aid in the construction of certain standard types of loops.

The **counting loop**, a loop which simply executes its body a fixed number of times, is so common that most machines have a special instruction for handling it. On the 80X86 that instruction is `loop`. It uses the `cx` register as a counter of the number of times remaining to execute the loop body. The code to execute '*body*' N > 0 times is

Execute "body" N>0 times		
	mov	cx, N ; Perform loop N times for N > 0
theLoop:		
	body	
	loop	theLoop

The instruction

```
        loop    aLabel
```

is equivalent to the pseudocode

```
cx := cx - 1; if cx ≠ 0 then goto aLabel
```

Note: the `loop` instruction *always* uses `cx` as its counter, but that `cx` is *never* mentioned in the instruction! The operand label of the `loop` instruction must occur physically before the `loop` instruction itself.

Example 5.3—1. As a quasi-religious exercise, display the message 'I will write bug–free programs!' 100 times.

A solution without the `loop` instruction is

```
;; Example 5.3-1 — Solution 1—without the loop instruction
;;
        . . .
        .DATA
BugMsg  DB      'I will write bug-free programs!', 13, 10, '$'
        . . .
        mov     bx, 1 ;  bx is counter; unaffected by _PutStr
BugLoop:
        _PutStr BugMsg
        inc     bx
        cmp     bx, 100
        jle     BugLoop
```

Compare the program above to

```
;; Example 5.3-1 — Solution 2—using the loop instruction
;;
            . . .
        .DATA
BugMsg  DB      'I will write bug-free programs!', 13, 10, '$'
            . . .
        mov     cx, 100 ; cx is counter; unaffected by _PutStr
BugLoop:
        _PutStr BugMsg
        loop    BugLoop
```

We have already seen that ax and dx have special purposes in multiplication and division, and now we see that cx has the special purpose of *counting*, in loop and other instructions to be introduced later.

Note that

```
        mov     cx, N ;         Perform loop N times for N > 0
theLoop:
            body
        loop    theLoop
```

performs the loop exactly N times if **N > 0**. Note that loop doesn't terminate on cx < 0. In effect, cx is treated as being unsigned. The case where N = 0 is even trickier, because although it isn't reasonable to execute a loop a negative number of times, it is reasonable to do it 0 times. However the cx register is counted down *before* the first test is done, so if N were initially 0, the loop would be executed 65,536 times! Since the 0 special case occurs so frequently, the 80X86 also has the instruction

```
        jcxz    Dest ;          Jump if CX register Zero
```

Note: the cx register is the *only* register with its own command to test for zero, and there is **no** jcxnz instruction.

Execute *"body"* N times where N $\geq$ 0		
mov cx, N ;	Perform loop N times for N >= 0	
jcxz Done		
theLoop:		
body		
loop theLoop		
Done:		

Example 5.3—2: Compute N! using the loop instruction as in Example 5.3—1.

```
;; Example 5.3-2—N! = N(N-1)(N-2)...3 2 1 for N >= 0
;;
        mov     cx, N ;         counter and multiplier
        mov     ax, 1 ;         accumulator for N!
```

```
                  jcxz   Done ;           0! = 1
       NFact:
                  mul    cx ;             for numbers ≥ 0, imul = mul
                  loop   NFact
       Done:      ;                       At this point, N! is in ax
```

Example 5.3—3. Display the outline of a box WDTH characters wide (WIDTH is a reserved word) and HEIGHT characters high, where WDTH and HEIGHT are word integers. The sides are constructed from the box-drawing characters in the IBM extended ASCII character set (see Appendix A). Each corner is a single character, and WDTH is the number of horizontal bars on top and bottom and HEIGHT the number of vertical bars on the sides, both excluding the corner characters.

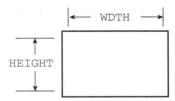

Drawing boxes as above around parts of the screen is a common way of dressing up user-screens and making them more readable. The graphics characters can't be typed directly into most editors, but we can use the ASCII equivalents which are given by the following EQUates:

```
       VERT      EQU    179 ;            Vertical Bar
       HORIZ     EQU    196 ;            Horizontal Bar
       ULCORNER  EQU    218 ;            Upper Left Corner
       LLCORNER  EQU    192 ;            Lower Left Corner
       URCORNER  EQU    191 ;            Upper Right Corner
       LRCORNER  EQU    217 ;            Lower Right Corner
```

The top and bottom borders of the box are easy enough, being counting loops to display HORIZes preceded and followed by the display of the corners. The middle of the box is trickier though, because it requires a counting loop within a counting loop, and there is only one cx register. One solution is to keep the row count in another register (we choose bx because _PutCh doesn't interfere with it) and move the row count into cx just before we use the loop instruction on it. Our solution is

```
       ;; Example 5.3-3—Solution
       ;;
                  _PutCh ULCORNER ;      Display top of box
                  mov    cx, WDTH
       TopLoop:
                  _PutCh HORIZ
                  loop   TopLoop
                  _PutCh URCORNER, 13, 10
       ;
                  mov    cx, HEIGHT ;  Number of rows of middle
       MidLoop:
```

```
           mov     bx, cx ;        save number of rows to do
           _PutCh VERT
           mov     cx, WDTH
MidRow:

           _PutCh ' '
           loop    MidRow
           _PutCh VERT, 13, 10
           mov     cx, bx ;        Restore number of rows to do
           loop    MidLoop
;
           _PutCh LLCORNER ;    Display bottom row
           mov     cx, WDTH
BotLoop:

           _PutCh HORIZ
           loop    BotLoop
           _PutCh LRCORNER, 13, 10
```

Our last example in this section makes use of the fact that the version of GetDec in UTIL.LIB returns with the carry flag set (= 1) if the number read was illegal and clear (= 0) if the number was legal.

Example 5.3—4. After GetDec has read a number, test that a legal number was typed in and if not, request up to 10 times that the user try again.

The code makes use of a loop which can terminated either by the loop instruction (error exit) or the jnc instruction (successful exit).

```
           ;; Example 5.3-4
           ;;
                   .DATA
BadNum     DB      'Invalid number; please retype: $'
ErrExit    DB      'Too many errors; ending program', 13, 10, '$'
RETRIES    EQU     10
                   ...
                   .CODE
                   ...
           mov     cx, RETRIES+1 ;    + 1 for initial try
GetLoop:
           call    GetDec
           jnc     GoodNum ;     If carry clear, valid number
           _PutStr BadNum
           loop    GetLoop
           _PutStr ErrExit ;     When we get here, too many retries
           _Exit 1 ;             Non-zero usually used for error
GoodNum:
```

Exercises 5.3

1. Write assembly language code to do the following:

a) ✓ Set $ax := 1^2 + 2^2 + 3^2 + ... + N^2$, where N is a nonnegative word variable.

b) ✓ Display the US flag star pattern:

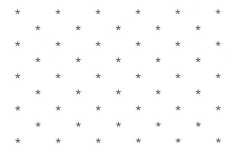

c) Display your name, surrounded by a box as in Example 5.3—3. For instance, the output of my program would be

```
┌─────────────────┐
│  Bill Jones     │
└─────────────────┘
```

5.4 • Arithmetic and the Flags

Cmp isn't the only instruction that sets the flags. In fact, most arithmetic instructions do so, and we can often use that fact to simplify code. The important things we need to know are:

- **add**, **sub**, **inc**, **dec**, and **neg** set the flags based on the result of the operation. It is as though each of these instructions was followed by an instruction cmp *Result*, 0, except that cmp *Result*, 0 would never set OF or CF. Note that inc and dec do not affect the carry flag, a fact which is occasionally useful (see Example 14.1—2).
- **mul** and **imul** set OF and CF to 1 if there are any significant bits of the product in dx (word operation) or ah (byte operation) and are cleared otherwise. Thus you can use OF to determine if the product of two 16-bit numbers is a 16-bit number.
- **div** and **idiv** leave the flags in an unpredictable state.

Note:

mov NEVER alters the flags!

After an arithmetic instruction that sets the flags, a jge instruction for instance would be interpreted as "jump on result greater than or equal **to 0**" and a je as "jump on equal **to 0**". Je and jne are in fact identical to the instructions jz and jnz (jump on zero and nonzero, respectively), and the latter may make the code read a little better in some situations.

We can use the fact that arithmetic alters flags to get a slightly different solution to Example 5.3—3. Instead of writing

```
        mov     cx, HEIGHT
        . . .
        mov     bx, cx
        . . .
        mov     cx, bx
        loop    MidLoop
```

we could write

```
        mov     bx, HEIGHT
        . . .
        mov     bx, cx
        . . .
        mov     cx, bx
        dec     bx
        jne     MidLoop ;       'loop' using bx, as cx is in use
```

that is, two mov instructions would be deleted.

Since many instructions (such as jumps) do not change the flags, one can sometimes separate the comparison from the jump (as in Exercise 5.1—1 f)). When in doubt, consult Appendix B, which contains a list of the 80X86 instructions with the flags they modify. If you don't have such a reference handy, the simplest thing to do is always do the conditional jump immediately after a cmp instruction and don't depend on arithmetic to set the flags. Your programs may be slightly less efficient, but will be safer.

Exercises 5.4

1. Rewrite the following assembly code segments without using the cmp instruction:

```
    a)          sub     al, 'a'
                cmp     al, 0
                jl      notLc

    b) ✓       dec     ax
                cmp     ax, 0
                jge     NonNeg

    c)          add     bx, 100
                cmp     bx, 0
                jne     NotM100
```

2. ✓ Assume that al contains an ASCII character. If this character is a decimal digit (i.e., '0' ≤ al ≤ '9') then convert it to its numerical equivalent. Otherwise, jump to NotDigit. You are allowed to destroy the contents of al, which means that you can use a subtract and a compare rather than two compares and a subtract.

5.5 • Reading Single Characters

For the case studies in the next section, we here introduce the DOS and BIOS operations for reading single characters from the keyboard. This section is optional if you want to also skip the next section (for now), but these operations will also be needed at various other times in the future.

Keyboard input is a prime example of the layering of hardware, the BIOS (see Section 1.1.2), and DOS.

As far as the hardware is concerned, each key on the keyboard has a **scan code**, a number from 0 to 127 unrelated to ASCII. When a key is pressed, its scan code is sent to the computer, and when the key is released, the scan code + 128 is sent.

The BIOS processes key presses and releases as they come in, translating the scan codes of ASCII keys into their ASCII codes and using the scan codes from shift keys to keep track of whether the shifts are up or down. When a non-shift key has been pressed, the BIOS saves its scan code and ASCII value, if any, in a **keyboard buffer** which can contain up to 15 keystrokes. If the buffer is full, any further non-shift key presses cause the BIOS to emit a beep and ignore the character. For further details on the keystroke queue and its uses, see Chapter 15.

The cooperating actions of the BIOS and hardware happen independently of what any user program is doing. When the program wants to read a character from the keyboard it uses a call to the ROM BIOS or a DOS call layered on top of the BIOS call. If there are characters in the keyboard buffer, the BIOS call returns the ASCII value, if any, and scan code of the first waiting character and deletes the character from the buffer. If no keystrokes are waiting, the BIOS waits for one. Characters are returned in the order in which they were typed in.

DOS calls add functionality to the BIOS call by allowing an **echo** of the keystroke to the screen, collecting a whole line of input, or redirecting input from a file. The echo consists of displaying the typed character. DOS waits to echo a typed character until a program asks for it so that DOS can be told (by the type of DOS call) whether or not to echo the character. (Reading without echoing can be useful for such things as passwords, or when you want to 'massage' the data before you echo it.)

The PCMAC.INC macro _BIOSCh implements the BIOS call to read a keystroke as follows:

```
        _BIOSCh ;              Read from keyboard WITH NO ECHO
;    returns with
;        al = ASCII key value or 0
;        ah = scan code of key
;    equivalent to the code
;        mov    ah, 0h ;    Function 0
;        int    16h ;       Note 16h, not 21h
```

A program using _BIOSCh must do its own echoing to the screen, if any, of characters typed. To get automatic echoing, use the _GetCh DOS call described further down.

Tables of scan codes can be found in many references (for instance, the book by Norton and Wilton in the bibliography) or by using a program like the following:

Example 5.5—1. Use _BIOSCh to get scan codes and ASCII values, if any, of a keystroke.

```
;; BIOSKEY.ASM—Use the BIOS keyboard read function to determine
;;   scan codes. To use, enter
```

```
;;
;;              BIOSKey
;;
;;      and strike any key when requested.

                .MODEL SMALL
                .STACK 100h
INCLUDE         PCMAC.INC
                .DATA
Prompt          DB      'Strike a key: $'
ScanMsg         DB      13, 10, 'The scan code was $'
ASCIIMsg        DB      ' and the ASCII value was $'

                .CODE
                EXTRN   PutDec : NEAR
BIOSKey         PROC
                mov     ax, @data
                mov     ds, ax

                _PutStr Prompt
                _BIOSCh
                mov     bx, ax ;        _PutStr destroys ax
                _PutStr ScanMsg
                mov     al, bh ;        Scan code was in ah
                mov     ah, 0 ;         Unsigned extend to word
                call    PutDec
                _PutStr ASCIIMsg
                mov     al, bl ;        ASCII Value (or 0) was in al
                mov     ah, 0 ;         Unsigned extend to word
                call    PutDec
                _PutCh '.', 13, 10

                _Exit  0
BIOSKey         ENDP
                END     BIOSKey
```

Note that the two values we wanted to display were *byte* values, and since PutDec displays the value of the *word* in ax, we had to extend the byte in al to a word by filling ah with zeroes using mov ah, 0. (We could also have used sub ah, ah.) Note also that we preserved the contents of ax around the _PutStr call by saving it in bx. The method above uses the fact that _PutStr doesn't alter bx.

The program is assembled and linked as usual with UTIL.LIB.

The following are sample executions of BIOSKey (user's typing in boldface; key descriptions (which don't echo), are surrounded by <...>; the Enter key is indicated by ↵):

```
c:> bioskey↵
Strike a key: <F5>                    (No Enter required)
The scan code was 63 and the ASCII value was 0.


c:> bioskey↵
Strike a key: <top-row +>
The scan code was 13 and the ASCII value was 43.


c:> bioskey↵
Strike a key: <numeric keypad +>
The scan code was 63 and the ASCII value was 43.


c:>
```

The discussion of scan codes contained an over simplification. The IBM **extended keyboard**—with which virtually all PCs are now equipped—has an extra dedicated set of cursor movement keys between the regular keyboard and the numeric keypad on the right, as well as an extra Ctrl and Alt key. Hitting one of these new keys causes _BIOSCh to appear to read *two* characters, the first with scan code 0E0h and the second with the same scan code as is generated by the corresponding key on the old keyboards. Thus if down arrow key (2) on the numeric keypad is hit, _BIOSCh returns the scan code 80, and if the down arrow on the extended keypad is hit, two calls to _BIOSCh produce, successively, scan codes of 0E0h and 80. Exercise 5.5—1 suggests altering BIOSKey to deal with this fact.

There are several DOS keyboard input functions. The _GetCh macro gathers two of these functions into a single macro with an optional parameter:

```
_GetCh ;              Read and echo to the display
_GetCh noEcho ;       Read and don't echo to the display
```

In either case, DOS returns with the ASCII code of the character read in al. If the key has no ASCII value, the call returns al = 0 and a second call to _GetCh returns the key's scan code. _GetCh has the following advantages over _BIOSCh:

- Keyboard input can be redirected from a file using the <*filename* construct on the command line.
- Echo can be taken care of automatically (and is automatically copied to the printer when the Ctrl-P printing toggle is on).
- _GetCh is guaranteed to work on any computer running DOS, even if it isn't very PC compatible.

_BIOSCh has the following advantages over _GetCh:

- Each keystroke corresponds to precisely one call to _BIOSCh (except for a few characters on the extended keyboard).
- Different keys such as the two '+' keys can be distinguished even if they correspond to the same ASCII code.
- _BIOSCh guarantees that input comes from the keyboard even if input was redirected.

Thus the user can be required to enter password from the keyboard rather than using the riskier expedient of storing it in a file.

• _BIOSCh is slightly faster.

The Enter key sends **only** a carriage return character, ASCII 13. In order to echo an end-of-line properly, even with _GetCh, you must test for the occurrence of a carriage return and when found, **explicitly** echo a line feed (10) character.

Note that with both _GetCh and _BIOSCh, the keystroke is returned immediately without waiting for an Enter or Return to be typed, and that as a result, none of the usual editing, such as backspace to erase, etc., is done. If you wish the usual keyboard editing, use the _GetStr function described in Section 10.3.

Exercise 5.5

1.   As was pointed out above, the IBM Extended Keyboard has extra copies of some keys, and hitting one of these keys produces the effect of *two* keystrokes, the first with the scan code 0E0h and the second with the same scan code as the duplicated key. Modify the BIOSKey program so that when such a key is struck, the output line starts with

```
        Extended keyboard key;   the scan code was...
```

2.   Write code to read and echo a character using _GetCh, sending an additional line feed (10) character if a return (13) was read. In any case, leave the character read in al. (The code is easy since _PutCh destroys only ah and dl.)

5.6 • Loop Case Studies

This optional section discusses techniques for optimizing loops in assembly language that don't exist in high-level languages. You need to have read Section 5.5 to understand the first example.

First we have a rather straightforward example showing how keyboard input can be processed.

Example 5.6—1. Write assembly code to read a line of input from the keyboard and echo it to the display, converting all lowercase letters to uppercase letters. Use the _GetCh macro introduced in Section 5.5.

An end of line is indicated when a carriage return character (ASCII 13) is read. Thus we can set up the following decorated pseudocode loop:

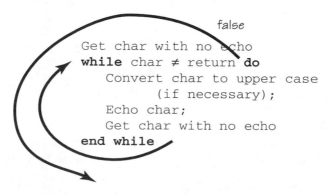

```
                                    false
        Get char with no echo
        while char ≠ return do
            Convert char to upper case
                    (if necessary);
            Echo char;
            Get char with no echo
        end while
```

Notice that 'Get char with no echo' occurs twice. That is a common situation that arises in high-level languages when you have to read and process *n* items and read one extra piece of data to terminate the loop that isn't processed. By altering one of the arrows a little though, we can get rid of one of the 'Get char...' statements:

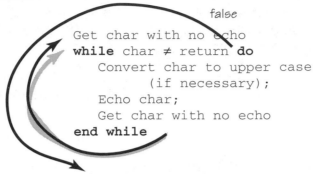

```
                                           false
        Get char with no echo
        while char ≠ return do
            Convert char to upper case
                    (if necessary);
            Echo char;
            Get char with no echo
        end while
```

Recalling that _GetCh puts the keystroke in al, the code for this loop becomes

```
GetLoop:
            _GetCh noEcho ;      Get without echo
            cmp    al, 13 ;      End of Line?
            je     Done
    Convert char to upper case (if necessary)
    Echo char
            jmp    GetLoop
    Done:
```

One of the recurring themes in this book is conversion of lowercase to uppercase characters. (It wouldn't seem that the following simple method could be improved upon, but it can!) A character is lowercase if it is between 'a' and 'z', so a decorated if statement for 'Convert char...' is

if (char ≥ 'a') **and** (char ≤ 'z') **then** add 'A' – 'a' to char **end if**

$$false$$

(For the conversion to uppercase, see Section 1.4.) The final consideration is that when the end of line is reached, we must not only echo the carriage return but also a line feed (ASCII 10). Putting everything together, the solution is

```
        ;; Example 5.6-1—Read a line and convert lc to uc on echo
        ;;
        GetLoop:
                _GetCh noEcho ;      Get without echo
                cmp    al, 13 ;      End of Line?
                je     Done
                cmp    al, 'a' ;     Is character lower case
                jnae   EchoIt ;        no   (unsigned jump)
```

```
            cmp     al, 'z'
            jnbe    EchoIt ;        no    (unsigned jump)
            add     al, 'A'-'a' ;  yes, convert to upper case
EchoIt:
            _PutCh al ;            Do the echo
            jmp     GetLoop
Done:
            _PutCh 13, 10 ;    Display End of Line (no 10 on input!)
```

Note that we have used unsigned comparison for characters, which isn't really necessary here. But see Exercise 5.6—3 below.

Example 5.6—2. Suppose that N is a word variable, N > 0, and we wish to set the signed word K equal to the largest number such that $2^K \le N$.

Note: K is the integer part of $\log_2 N$, which is a very useful number in computer science. It is the number of times you must do N := N / 2 in order to get N = 1. Thus if you use a 'divide-and-conquer' algorithm on N data items, K (or K + 1) is the number of times it must be done. For instance, it is the approximate number of key comparisons in the Binary Search. You can ignore these facts though and simply consider the example as an abstract programming problem, one which will allow us to demonstrate several loop optimization techniques.

Pseudocode to solve Example 5.6—2 is easy:

```
K := 0;
while (2^K ≤ N) do K := K + 1;
K := K - 1   { we exited the loop because K was 1 too big }
```

Rather than recompute 2^K each time through the loop, we will keep K and 2^K in two registers that change in step with each other, say have K in ax and 2^K in bx. (This programming technique is called **strength reduction**. We are 'reducing' an expensive operation, exponentiation, to a cheaper operation, multiplication.) A decorated high-level program could be

```
                                     false
     ax := 0; bx := 1           // bx = 2^ax
     while bx ≤ N do
         ax := ax + 1
         bx := 2 * bx
     end while
     K := ax - 1
```

We can actually make a further strength reduction, replacing bx := 2 * bx with bx := bx + bx!

```
;; Example 5.6-2—First Solution
;;
            mov     ax, 0 ;        ax := 0
```

```
          mov     bx, 1 ;         bx := 2**ax (** = "to the power")
LogLoop:
          cmp     bx, N ;         while 2**ax <= N do ...
          jnle    Done
          inc     ax ;                ax := ax + 1
          add     bx, bx ;            bx := 2 * bx (= 2**ax again)
;                                         (better than multiplying)
          jmp     LogLoop
Done:     ;                       end while
          dec     ax ;            as 2**ax > N
          mov     K, ax
```

(In the comments, ** is used to represent the 'to the power of' operator, as in Fortran. Comments like 'ax := 0' and 'ax := ax + 1' would seem to be the sort of comments I warned you against in Chapter 4, but I think they are useful in situations when one is keeping track of computations in several registers. Also, they help tie the assembly to the original high-level code and keep you from having to flip back and forth between reading comments and reading assembly code. As I said, there are no hard and fast rules for writing comments.)

Simple as the loop above seems, there are several ways it can be improved. We can avoid the final decrement by letting bx = 2**(ax + 1). Also it is faster to do a comparison between two registers than between a register and memory, so we will keep N in a register. The improved portion would be (new code in boldface):

```
;; Example 5.6-2—Second Solution
;;
          mov     ax, -1 ;        ax := -1
          mov     bx, 1 ;         bx := 2**(ax + 1)
          mov     cx, N ;         cx := N
LogLoop:
          cmp     bx, cx ;        while 2**(ax + 1) <= N do ...
          jnle    Done
          inc     ax ;                ax := ax + 1
          add     bx, bx ;            bx := 2 bx (= 2**(ax + 1) again)
          jmp     LogLoop
Done:     ;                       end while
          dec     ax
          mov     K, ax
```

If the comparison isn't in a loop, there's no point in moving the other comparand to a register first as the mov takes as long as the comparison to memory. If the comparison is in a loop, however, a savings can occur. This technique of moving an invariant operation outside a loop—in this case, fetching N into the CPU—is called **code motion** (the moving of **loop-invariant operations**, that is, operations which do the same thing in every execution of the loop, outside the loop). It is similar to the technique of factoring discussed earlier in this chapter. (And is related to the information in the optional Section 4.5, where it is seen that cmp bx, cx is about three times as fast as cmp bx, N.) The operation mov cx, N is a loop invariant because the value of N does not change during execution of the loop.

A second small but useful optimization is to put the loop termination test at the *end* of the loop rather than the beginning. There will still be two jump instructions, but only one of them is executed *inside* the loop, shortening loop execution time. Once again, we show the new solution with changed parts in boldface:

```
;; Example 5.6-2—Third Solution
;;
        mov     ax, -1 ;        ax := -1
        mov     bx, 1 ;         bx := 2**(ax + 1)
        mov     cx, N ;         cx := N
        jmp     LoopTest
LogLoop:
        inc     ax ;            ax := ax + 1
        add     bx, bx ;        bx := 2 * bx (= 2**(ax + 1))
LoopTest:
        cmp     bx, cx ;        if 2**(ax + 1) <= N then ...
        jLE     LogLoop ;          ... continue looping
Done:
        mov     K, ax
```

Notice that the jump condition is reversed (and the label Done is no longer required). The technique of putting loop tests at the end is sometimes called using **trailing decisions** and often speeds up assembly language code.

You may well ask: is it really necessary to go to all this trouble? The answer is in fact *no*, virtually all the time. It is much better to have one technique you are comfortable with (and that works!) than four or five rattling around in your head that may or may not work. On the other hand, one of the pleasures of assembly language is the ability to tinker with code and get it just right.

One more thing: the dictum in any programming language of not using magic numbers might be extended in assembly language to not using magic *registers*. The program above is rather difficult to read even with the comments because of all the registers used. Our friend the EQU operator can come to our assistance here and allow us to give symbolic names to registers. We can therefore give one final version of the program:

```
;; Example 5.6-2—Fourth and Final Solution
;;
Kreg    EQU     ax
Exp2K   EQU     bx ;                    2**(K + 1)
Nreg    EQU     cx
        mov     Kreg, -1 ;              K := -1
        mov     Exp2K, 1 ;             Exp2K := 2**(K + 1)
        mov     Nreg, N ;              cx := N
        jmp     LoopTest
LogLoop:
        inc     Kreg ;                 K := K + 1
        add     Exp2K, Exp2K ;         Exp2K := 2 * Exp2K !!
LoopTest:
        cmp     Exp2K, Nreg ; if 2**K <= N then ...
```

```
jle     LogLoop ;           ... continue looping
mov     K, Kreg
```

Note that even the most fastidious assembly language programmer will usually be satisfied with solution 1 or 2.

Exercises 5.6

1. Write assembly code to read a password from the keyboard. Display the message 'Enter Password: ' and echo each character that the user types as an asterisk ('*'). If the user types a backspace character (which enters as the number 8), erase the last character typed by displaying a backspace, a space, and another backspace. You shouldn't erase beyond the beginning of the password so you need to keep a count of the asterisks on the screen.

2. Write assembly code to read a line of input typed at the keyboard, echoing all printable characters (ASCII representation between 32 and 126) as the characters themselves, and echoing all the control characters (ASCII 1 through 26) in the following way: 1 = Ctrl-A is displayed as the two characters ^A, 2 = Ctrl-B as ^B, ..., 26 = Ctrl-Z as ^Z. That is, if Char contains the control character read, the character to be displayed is Char + 'A' - 1. The carriage return terminating the line will echo as ^M and the program then terminates. (Note that Ctrl-C will terminate the program before it gets a chance to echo.)

3. ✓ Suppose in Example 5.6—1 we wanted to convert *all* lower case letters to upper case, even the foreign ones (see Exercise 5.2—3). Why is an approach that starts

```
cmp     al, 'a' ;      Is character lower case
jnge    EchoIt ;         no
```

doomed to failure?

4. Find and store in the word variable K the largest integer whose square is <= N, a nonnegative word variable; that is, K is the integer part of the square root of N.

5.7 • Some Technical Details on Compares and Jumps

This section can be omitted on first reading, but be sure to come back to it because it's **important**. It is also a continuation of the optional Section 4.4 on internal representations of instructions. In order to use compare and jump instructions efficiently, it is occasionally necessary to know a few more details. This section might be subtitled "jumps around jumps revisited."

Most jumps go to nearby places in the code, so the 80X86 encodes all conditional jumps as two bytes, the numeric op-code of the jump and the **displacement** to the jump destination.

op-code	displ

For the purposes of this discussion, I will call such jumps **two-byte jumps**. A two-byte jump such as (jl opcode) (disp) is processed by the CPU's fetch-execute cycle (see Section 1.1.1) as follows:

1) The instruction is fetched and the IP updated to point to the following instruction.
2) The flags are checked, and if the 'less than' condition holds, the CPU *sign-extends disp* to a word and does IP := IP + *disp*. (Because displacements are treated as 2's complement numbers, both forward and backward jumps are possible.)

The CPU is now ready to fetch the correct next instruction, whether or not the jump was taken. The assembler computes the displacements for you (a major aid) and most of the time, you need not be aware of the actual internal representation of jumps.

It is clear, though, that a two-byte jump has a range at most 127 bytes forward and 128 bytes backward, and conditions may arise when a program needs to jump further than that. The unconditional jump instruction `jmp` provides the needed escape hatch. In *addition* to a two-byte unconditional jump, the 80X86 also has a **three-byte** unconditional **jump** in which the displacement is a word, allowing a jump forward of 32,767 bytes and backward of 32,768 bytes. The three-byte jump is virtually always sufficient.

op-code	displ

The assembler does its best to decide which form of `jmp` to use. When jumping backwards, it is easy because it knows how far back the destination is, but when jumping forward it must guess. It guesses that a three-byte jump will be needed, and if it later finds that two bytes will suffice, it changes the three-byte jump to a two-byte jump followed by a `nop` (no-operation instruction, which does nothing), a single byte. It can't simply replace three bytes in the code two two as that would change all of the following addresses (but see the end of this section and Appendix F). If you think that a forward jump can be handled by a two-byte jump, you can write

```
jmp     SHORT Label ; <= 127 bytes forward
```

Guessing for jumps fairly far away is chancy, but if you guess wrong, the assembler will inform you and you can remove the 'SHORT.'

When you write a *conditional* jump which attempts to jump too far, the assembler will give you an error message such as **jump out of range**, and you can fix it and reassemble by replacing an instruction like

```
jcond  aLabel ;      out-of-range jump
```

with the pair of instructions

```
jNcond JAJ1 ;      Jump around jump necessary here...
jmp    aLabel ;       ...because of long distance
JAJ1:
```

I will call the code above a **five-byte jump**, for obvious reasons. It has the internal format

op-code	3	jmp	displ

Note that the displacement of 3 on the conditional jump is precisely what we need to get around the unconditional one.

Of course the five-byte jump is just a 'jump around a jump' which I previously warned you against. Because of its greater size and consequent slower execution, it should be used *only* in a situation where the range of the jump is too great for a two-byte jump.

TASM and MASM optimize jump sizes for you automatically, though TASM requires a little interference from the user.

If TASM assembles a program which has the pseudo-operation JUMPS at its start, TASM replaces all backwards conditional jumps which are out of range with five-byte jumps, and replaces *all* forward conditional jumps with five-byte jumps. If the forward five-byte jump is subsequently discovered to be unnecessary, the five bytes are replaced by the original two-byte jump and three nop instructions. If, in addition, the user specifies the /m (multiple passes) switch on the TASM command line, TASM will squeeze out all of the extra nop instructions in three- and five-byte jumps.

MASM does all the above work for you—no extra pseudo-instructions or switches are required.

I feel that the jump optimization described above is a solution in search of a problem. Two-byte jumps virtually never fail and when they do, they are easily fixed manually. Unnecessary use of three-byte jumps instead of two also seems a minor inefficiency. Nonetheless, I suppose the facility is worth using if you have it. For a description of how it might be implemented, see Appendix F.

The loop instruction is encoded just like a twobyte jump, except that the displacement is treated as an *unsigned* number and always *subtracted* from the IP. Thus the loop instruction can be used for jumps back at most 255 bytes.

The cmp instruction uses the same internal formats as add/sub/mov. (See Section 4..4)

Exercises 5.7

1. Assume that each of the following conditional jumps is further than 128 bytes forward or backwards, and therefore do the necessary conversion to jumps around jumps

```
jge    FarAway  ✓

Jne    FurtherAway

jl     ReallyFar

jae    OuterSpace
```

5.8 • Timing of Instructions, Continued

This section is a continuation of Section 4.5, and is also optional.

The cmp instruction is essentially a sub instruction that doesn't store its result, and can be treated just like sub in terms of timing.

The conditional and unconditional jump instructions and the loop instruction are very fast, taking essentially the time necessary to retrieve them from memory. One delicate point is that when a conditional or unconditional jump is actually *taken*, the prefetch buffer on the 80X86 is drained and reloaded from scratch (see Section 4.5 for a description of the prefetch buffer). Thus if you have a choice, it might be slightly more efficient to try to arrange it so that conditional jumps were usually *not* taken. This strategy doesn't seem to be particularly useful, though. In the following loop, the jump is usually taken (that is, all but once):

```
aLoop:      . . .
            . . .
            . . .
            cmp     A, ax
            jl      aLoop
```

However, if we put the test at the start of the loop so that the jump is normally not taken:

```
aLoop:      cmp     A, ax
            jnl     Done
   . . .

            . . .
            . . .
            jmp     aLoop
   Done:
```

we get an extra jump instruction at the end of the loop which is *always* taken.

Programming Problem 5.1

Write a program which appears to display a vertical bar character ' | ' moving left to right in 79 positions across the screen, then back right to left across the screen. (Hint: If you have just displayed a ' | ', the cursor will be just to the right of it. To 'move' the character one space to the right, you must display the characters Backspace (8), ' ' (a space, to erase the old ' | '), and a new ' | '. If you display the ' | ' in the last, or 80th, position in the screen, the cursor will go to the next line and you won't be able to get it back to the previous line (with what you know).

Programming Problem 5.2

Many 'user-friendly' programs assist users by validating input as it is typed. Write a program which models this behavior by reading a line of input which must consist of digits only. Any digit character typed is echoed, and a carriage return character causes termination of the program after a carriage return/line feed pair are echoed. When any character other than a digit or carriage return is typed, echo a 'beep' character (ASCII 7).

Programming Problem 5.3

Write a program Triangle which uses GetDec to read three numbers, which are to be interpreted as the lengths of the three sides of a possible triangle. Your program should display 'Sides form a triangle' or 'Sides do not form a triangle' according to which is true. The three sides form a triangle if the sum of every pair of sides is greater than the third remaining side. (**Note:** three tests are necessary to show that a triangle is formed. The test given also *automatically* handles the case where a side is 0 or negative.) Be sure to test your program sufficiently. Your test cases for sides *not* forming a triangle should include, but not be limited to, 10, 25, 15; 25, 15, 10; and 10, 15, 25.

Programming Problem 5.4

Write a program which reads numbers (using GetDec) until –9999 has been entered and then displays (using PutDec) the largest number and the smallest number which have been entered. At the very least, you should test your program in the situations when no data is entered (that is, –9999 is entered first), when all the numbers entered are negative, and when all the numbers entered are positive.

SUMMARY

New instructions:

```
cmp    reg/mem, reg/mem/constant
```

Operands must be the same size (both words or both bytes). At least one operand must not be a memory address. The cmp instruction sets flags in the flags register of the CPU, which can then be tested by various conditional jumps. The flags of interest are CF, carry, SF, sign, OF, overflow, and ZF, zero. Add, sub, inc, dec, and neg also set the flags. (Inc and dec don't set CF).

Signed or unsigned conditional jumps:

je = jz	jump on equal or on zero
jne = jnz	jump on not equal or not zero

Signed conditional jumps:

jg = jnle	jump on greater, or not less than or equal to
jge = jnl	jump on greater than or equal to, or not less
jl = jnge	jump on less, or not greater than or equal to
jle = jng	jump on less than or equal to, or not greater

Unsigned conditional jumps:

ja = jnbe	jump if above, or not below or equal
jae = jnb	jump if above or equal, or not below
jb = jnae	jump if below, or not above or equal
jbe = jna	jump if below or equal, or not above

Jumps based directly on flags:

jz = je	jump on Zero Flag set (= 1)
jo	jump on Overflow Flag set (= 1)
jc	jump on Carry Flag set (= 1)
js	jump on Sign Flag set (=1)

There are also the corresponding instructions jnz, jno, jnc, and jns which jump if the corresponding flag is cleared (= 0).

Unconditional jump:

```
jmp            ; always jump
```

Conditional jumps are limited to a range of 128 bytes before and 127 bytes after themselves.

Jmp has no such limitation.

In addition there is a special conditional jump

```
jcxz            ; jump if the cx register is 0
```

A special conditional instruction is useful for counting loops:

```
loop    label
```

is equivalent to the code

```
cx := cx - 1; if cx ≠ 0 then goto label;
```

NOTE: The cmp instruction can also be used—with word operands only—with the word registers sp, bp, si, and di. (Sp is duscussed in chapter 6 and the latter three are discussed in chapter 10.)

Two new macros were introduced:

```
        _BIOSCh ;           Keyboard scan code -> ah; ASCII
;                               equiv (if any) to al; No echo
;                           DESTROYS AX

        _GetCh [noEcho] ;   Keyboard character -> al; if the
;                               optional parameter noEcho (without
;                               []s) is present, char is not
;                               echoed. If input is 0, next input
;                               is scan code
;                           DESTROYS AX
```

Debug Workshop II

Debugging with Breakpoints

Debugging programs that execute many instructions—for example, programs with loops that execute many times—is extremely tedious with just the trace operation. For this reason, debuggers have a **breakpoint** capability, which allows the user to mark one or more places in the program (**set** one or more **breaks**). The program can then be executed at full speed until it encounters one of the breakpoints, causing reentry of the debugger just *before* the marked instruction is executed. This workshop will show how to set two kinds of breakpoints in our two debuggers, and give an example of their use.

Each debugger has two types of breakpoints:

- **Permanent breakpoints** remain set until the user explicitly removes (*clears*) them. It is possible to set permanent breakpoints in several places, which can be very handy if you're not quite sure where your program is going! Breakpoints can be set or cleared any time your program is stopped in the debugger—at its beginning, at a trace or step, or at another breakpoint. Striking the Run key then executes until the next breakpoint occurs, or until the end of the program.

    Lines with permanent breakpoints are highlighted in the source window.

    It is possible to add conditions of various kinds to permanent breakpoints, such as passing through the point a certain number of times or doing so until an expression is true. Such **conditional breakpoints** are very powerful, but beyond the scope of this book.

- **Temporary breakpoints** are automatically cleared the next time any break occurs. Setting a temporary breakpoint also automatically executes the Run command, so it is faster to use (but there can be only one temporary breakpoint). A temporary breakpoint can also be thought of as "go to cursor line" or (as it is called by the Turbo debugger) the "here" command.

With either type of breakpoint, the break occurs just *before* the breakpoint line is executed.

II.1 • CodeView Breakpoints.

As always, you must assemble and link with the switches which save debugger information (/Zi and /co, respectively).

▶ **Preliminaries for Setting *or* Clearing any Breakpoint**

1) Make the source window the active window (if it isn't already) by clicking left on it, using **F6**, or hitting **Alt-3**.
2) Scroll the window so that the line where you want to set or clear the break is visible using the mouse and the right-hand scroll bar, the cursor keys, or **PgUp** or **PgDn**

▶ **Set a Permanent Breakpoint**

3) Setting and clearing *can* use the same method, which toggles the breakpoint on and off. *Either*
   a) Double-Click left on the line you want,
   or
   b) Move the flashing box cursor to the line (click on it with the mouse or use the cursor keys) and hit the **F9** key.

You can get more control by moving the flashing box cursor to the line as in 3 b) above, then *set* a breakpoint by choosing Set Breakpoint from the Data menu using **Alt-D**(ata **S**(et Breakpoint... and clicking left on OK (or hit Enter). You can also *clear* a breakpoint by choosing Edit Breakpoints from the Data menu, clicking left on the appropriate breakpoint or cursoring to it (notice the scroll bar to the right) and clicking on Remove or type **R**(emove or tab to the Remove button and hit Enter.

You can also *set* a breakpoint at any *label* by typing bp *label* in the command window and hitting **Enter**.

▶ **Set a Temporary Breakpoint (Go to Cursor) and Start Executing**

3) *Either*
   a) Click *right* on the line, *or*
   b) Move the flashing underline cursor to the line (click on it with the mouse or use the cursor keys) and hit **F7**.

You must set a breakpoint on a line with actual code (an instruction or macro) on it.

II.2 • Turbo Debugger Breakpoints.

As always, you must assemble and link with the switches which save debugger information (`/zi` and `/v`, respectively).

▶ **Preliminaries for Setting *or* Clearing any Breakpoint**

1) Make the module window (with source code) the active window (if it isn't already) by clicking left on it, using **F6**, or hitting **Alt-#**, where **#** is the number of the window.
2) Scroll the window so that the line where you want to set or clear the break is visible using the mouse and the right-hand scroll bar or the cursor keys or **PgUp** or **PgDn**.

▶ **Set or Clear a Permanent Breakpoint**

3) Setting and clearing use the same method, which toggles the breakpoint on and off. *Either*
   a) Move the mouse cursor (the rectangle) to one of the first two columns in the line (an asterisk (*) shows in the mouse cursor when you are in the correct columns) and click left,
   or
   b) Move the flashing underline cursor to the line (click on it with the mouse or use the cursor keys) and hit **F2,** or choose Toggle from the Breakpoint menu or **Alt-B**(reakpoint **T**(oggle.

   You can also *set* a breakpoint at any *label* by choosing At… from the Breakpoint menu (**Alt-B**(reakpoint **A**(t…), entering the label in the dialog box, and clicking OK or hitting **Enter**.

▶ **Set a Temporary Breakpoint ("Here") and Start Executing**

3) Move the flashing underline cursor to the line (click on it with the mouse or use the cursor keys).
4) Hit **F4**.

II.3 • Two Debugging Exercises

For the first exercise, assemble and link DBGEX3.ASM (found on the disk accompanying this book) for use with the appropriate debugger. UTIL.LIB is not required.

```
;; DbgEx3—Breakpoints and loops

INCLUDE    PCMAC.INC
           .MODEL SMALL
           .STACK 100h

           .DATA

           .CODE
DbgEx3     PROC
```

```
        mov     ax, @data ;   The standard prolog
        mov     ds, ax

        mov     ax, 0
        mov     bx, 1
        mov     cx, 100
Squares:
        add     ax, bx
        add     bx, 2
; (1) Trace, filling in ax and bx at the loop instruction
;    below the first four times through:
;                   ax = _____, bx = _____
;                   ax = _____, bx = _____
;                   ax = _____, bx = _____
;                   ax = _____, bx = _____
        loop    Squares
; (2) Set a breakpoint on _Exit 0 line and Run
EndSquares:
;                   ax = _____, bx = _____
        _Exit   0
DbgEx3  ENDP
        END     DbgEx3
```

Procedure

1) Trace (click left on `Trace` on the help line or hit **F7** in TD, **F8** in CV) through the loop once or twice, filling in the contents of `ax` and `bx` at (1). The easiest way is to put `ax` and `bx` in the watch window. Make the source window active, click on an occurrence of `ax` in the program, enter **Ctrl-W** in either debugger, then do the same for `bx`. In CV, you may also wish to set the default display mode to decimal by entering **N10** and **Enter** in the command window.

2) You may quickly tire of tracing through each statement in the loop individually and simply skip to the `loop Squares` statement:

   a) See to it that the window containing the source code is the active window. (**F6** in both debuggers. The current window contains the flashing underline cursor.)

   b) Execute up to but not including the `loop Squares` line: In either debugger, move the cursor (flashing box) to the `loop Squares` line and hit **F7** in CV (go to cursor line) or **F4** in TD (Here). In CV you can shortcut this whole procedure by clicking right on the `loop Squares` line. In any case, the program starts execution automatically and stops as it is about to execute the `loop Squares` line.

   c) Finish filling in the four values of `ax` and `bx` for various times through the loop.

3) Set a breakpoint at the `_Exit 0` line. (You could also get there with the go-to-cursor command, but then you wouldn't have practiced setting breakpoints.) .

   CV: Double-click left on the line or move the cursor to the line and hit **F9**. The break line is shown in high intensity. Repeating the action turns the breakpoint off. Finally, you can also set the breakpoint by entering `bp EndSquares↵` in the command window.

   TD: Make the module window current with F6, move the flashing underline cursor to the

EndSquares line, and enter **Alt-B**(reakpoint **T**(oggle or **F2**. The breakpoint line will be highlighted. (Repeating the command would turn the breakpoint off.) Another way without moving the cursor is to enter **Alt-B**(reakpoint **A**(t... EndSquares↵

4) Run (click on Run on the help line or hit **F5** (CV) or **F9** (TD)) the program from this point. At the breakpoint, examine the values in ax and bx. The result should be $10000 = 100^2$.

5) The observed value of ax in the watch window should be $10000 = 100^2$.

For the second exercise, we are going to debug a program DbgEx4 whose purpose is to read a number and then display its factorization into primes. (Recall that a **prime number** is a number divisible only by itself and 1.)

The idea behind the program is quite simple: we keep the not-yet-factored part of the number in bx and the next possible factor in cx. Bx starts as the number originally entered and cx starts at 2. Each time through the main loop, we check to see if cx divides bx. If it does, we output cx and remove the factor in cx from bx. If it doesn't divide bx, we increment cx by 1 and try again.

For example, suppose we wanted to factor 15. At the start, bx = 15, cx = 2. Cx doesn't divide bx so increment cx to 3. 3 does divide 15 so output 3, remove the factor of 3 from 15, so bx = 5, cx = 4. Of course 4 isn't prime but we don't have to worry about 4 dividing bx since we already know that 2 doesn't. When 4 doesn't divide bx, increment cx to 5. 5 does divide bx, and we're done.

A couple of questions remain to be answered: how do we decide if cx divides bx evenly and how do we terminate the loop? For the first question, we divide bx by cx and check for 0 remainder. For the second there are many possibilities. I decided to terminate on cx > bx because that condition seemed the surest way to avoid an infinite loop in case there were bugs. The (nearly debugged) program is as follows:

```
;; DbgEx4.ASM—Program which inputs a number and displays its
;;   prime factorization. NOT COMPLETELY DEBUGGED!
;;
INCLUDE    PCMAC.INC
           .MODEL SMALL
           .STACK 100h

           .DATA
Prompt     DB      'Enter a number greater than 1: $'
TweenMsg DB        ' ' ;    _PutStr TweenMsg displays ' x ' where
TweenChar DB       ? ;         x = TweenChar
Blank      DB      ' $'

           .CODE
           EXTRN   GetDec : NEAR, PutDec : NEAR
DbgEx4     PROC
           mov     ax, @data
           mov     ds, ax
GetNumber:
           mov     TweenChar, '='
           _PutStr                 Prompt
           call    GetDec
           cmp     ax, 1
```

```
            jle     GetNumber

            mov     bx, ax ;        Save input
            call    PutDec
            mov     cx, 2 ;         cx = current possible prime factor
PrimeLoop:
            mov     ax, bx ;        test number divisible by cx
            sub     dx, dx
            div     cx
            cmp     dx, 0 ;         If remainder = 0, we have a factor
            jne     NextPrime

            mov     bx, ax
            _PutStr TweenMsg
            mov     TweenChar, '*' ;    Change to '*'
            mov     ax, cx ;        Output prime factor
            call    PutDec
NextPrime:
            inc     cx ;            Not necessarily a prime, but won't
;                                    divide until it is
DoneTest:
            cmp     bx, cx
            jge     PrimeLoop
            _PutCh 13, 10
            _Exit  0
DbgEx4      ENDP
            END     DbgEx4
```

Procedure

1) Make a copy of the program as, say, factors.asm and use that copy for your work. Then if you foul the program up badly you can easily start over again from the original.
2) Assemble and link with debugger information for your debugger, including util.lib.
3) Note that the program doesn't quite work by trying the following test cases:

```
C:\> factors
Enter a number greater than 1: 15
15 = 3 * 5                          (OK)
C:\> factors
Enter a number greater than 1: 12
12 = 2 * 3                          (Wrong; missing factor of 2)
C:\> factors
Enter a number greater than 1: 24
24 = 2 * 3 * 4                      (Wrong; should be 2 * 2 * 2 * 3)
```

4) Debug the program by setting breakpoints at one or two key locations (for example, PrimeLoop and/or DoneTest) and checking the values of bx, and cx there. You might

want to put watches on bx and cx. Look at both the 12 and 24 test cases. Hint: The fix requires adding, deleting, or modifying exactly one instruction.

Summary

Breakpoints allow sections of program code to be executed at full speed, stopping execution and reentering the debugger only at predetermined points (the breakpoints). Permanent breakpoints stay in the code until explicitly removed, and you can set many of them at one time. Only one temporary breakpoint can be set at a time, and setting such a breakpoint starts execution. Stopping at any breakpoint (or at the end of the program) removes the temporary breakpoint.

Breakpoints can be manipulated as follows:

Breakpoint		CV	TD
Permanent	Toggle*	Double-click left on line	Click left in first two cols (on an *)
		or move the cursor to the desired line of code *and*	
		F9	**F2** *or* **Alt-B**(reakpoint **T**(oggle
	Set	**Alt-D**(ata **S**(et Breakpoint..., enter *label* and click left on OK, *or* **bp** *label* in command window	**Alt-B**(reakpoint **A**(t..., enter *label* and click left on OK
	Clear	**Alt-D**(ata **E**(dit Breakpoints..., cursor to breakpoint, and **R**(emove	**Alt-B**(reakpoint **A**(t..., enter *label*, Di(sabled, and click left on OK
Temporary		Click right on line	(no mouse command)
		or move the cursor to the desired line of code *and*	
		F7	**F4**

---

* Toggle: set breakpoint if off, clear if on.

Chapter 6

Subprograms

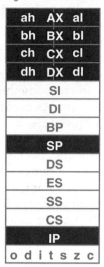

registers discussed

ah	AX	al
bh	BX	bl
ch	CX	cl
dh	DX	dl
	SI	
	DI	
	BP	
	SP	
	DS	
	ES	
	SS	
	CS	
	IP	
o d i t s z c		

One of the most important structuring devices for a program is its division into subprograms. Subprograms also provide a simple interface for allowing pieces of code to be reused in the same or different programs, with perhaps different sets of input data. We have *used* subprograms before (GetDec, PutDec, etc.). In this chapter we learn how to write such procedures. (Another way of organizing repeated code is to use macros.)

6.1 • Writing Subprograms

A **subprogram** is like a main program in form:

```
SubProg   PROC
          . . .
          code to accomplish the purpose
           of the subprogram
          . . .
          ret
SubProg   ENDP
```

where any name can be substituted for *SubProg*. This subprogram is invoked by executing the statement

```
          call SubProg
```

in some executing program. Paired with the call instruction is the ret instruction in *SubProg* which returns us to the statement immediately following the call instruction. (We will discuss the exact mechanism in Section 6.3.)
High-level languages usually separate subprograms into two classes ac-

cording to how they are executed. **Procedures** are executed as a complete statement by themselves and **functions** are executed as part of evaluating an expression—the function returns a value which is used in the expression. Even C and C++, which officially term all of their subprograms 'functions' make such a distinction in usage. Assembly language PROCs are much like functions in the early C programming language: the only programming difference between something that acts like a function and something that acts like a procedure is that the function returns a value and the procedure doesn't. As in early C, an assembly subprogram which is written like a function can also be used as a procedure, by merely ignoring the returned value. In the case of assembly language PROCs, the value returned is usually in ax if it's small enough. (Modern C and C++ require that a C/C++ function declare a return type. If the return type is void, the 'function' acts like a procedure and doesn't return a value.)

Assembly language PROCs can be in the same source file as the program that calls them or can be in different files. We'll consider the same-file case in this section. We might have a single file PROG.ASM as follows:

```
;; PROG.ASM
INCLUDE   PCMAC.INC
          .MODEL SMALL
          .STACK 100h
          .DATA
          ...
          .CODE
Main      PROC
          mov   ax, @data
          mov   ds, ax
          ...
          call  SubProg
          ...
          call  SubProg
          ...
          _Exit
Main      ENDP

SubProg   PROC
          mov   ax, @data ;  needed only in
          mov   ds, ax ;      main program
          ...
          ret
SubProg   ENDP

          END   Main
```

Notes:

- The ordering and naming of the PROCs is immaterial. The main program is determined by the final END statement, which determines the PROC to be executed first. Unlike C/C++, the main PROC doesn't have a special name

- Subprograms don't need the code initializing ds, as that code has already been executed in the main program.

- For readability, data which is used only by SubProg should be physically associated with it. You can temporarily reenter the .DATA area, give the data for SubProg, and then use .CODE to reenter the code area.

```
         . . .
Main     ENDP

         .DATA
         . . .
         data for SubProg
         . . .
         .CODE
SubProg  PROC
         . . .
```

- In MASM (version 6.0 and later), labels defined inside a PROC are local to the PROC and cannot be referenced outside the PROC, unless 'published' with a PUBLIC statement (see Section 6.4 below). That is,

```
Aproc       PROC
            . . .
            jmp    insideBproc ; Can't see insideBproc from here!
            . . .
Aproc       ENDP
Bproc       PROC
            . . .
insideBproc:      ;              Not visible from Aproc in MASM
```

is illegal in MASM. High-level languages such as C/C++ and Pascal work the same way, in that variables and labels defined inside a subprogram aren't visible outside it. Code like the above is probably a bad practice anyway. In TASM, all labels are visible throughout a single source file, which agrees with traditional practice of assembly languages.

6.2 • The Stack

The hardware stack and stack pointer sp (see Section 1.1.1) are intimately related to subprograms, and it is time for us to talk more about the stack and the instructions that manipulate it.

A **stack** is a list of data items which can be altered by adding or removing items at one end only. The stack concept is very powerful and widely used in programming, being essential to the implementation of such high-level languages as Pascal, C, and C++. Most modern computers have a **hardware stack**, that is, a stack known to the CPU, which supplies special instructions for its manipulation. On the 80X86, the CPU's sp (stack pointer) register is used to point to the end of the stack at which things are added or removed. That is, sp points to the *newest* item on the stack, the one most recently added but not yet removed. [*]

The operation of adding a new item to the stack is called **pushing** it onto the stack, and the operation of removing the newest item from the stack—the one pointed to by sp—is called **popping** the item from the stack. The 80X86 has instructions for pushing and popping the stack:

```
push   mem/reg          and          pop   mem/reg
```

The operand for push and pop must always be a **word**. The operation push X is roughly equivalent to the pseudo-code

```
sp := sp - 2 { down 2 as a WORD is always pushed }
(Word at location sp) := X
     { if we think of sp as a pointer, the code to set the word}
     { would be *sp = X in C/C++, sp^ := X in Pascal }
```

and the instruction pop X is roughly equivalent to

```
X := (Word at location sp)  { X = *sp in C/C++, X := sp^ in Pascal }
sp := sp + 2
```

To see how the stack works, suppose we start in the situation

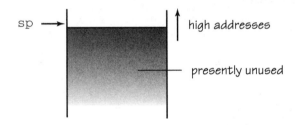

and have memory defined by

```
X          DW          1111
Y          DW          2222
Z          DW          ?
```

If we execute

```
push   X
```

the stack looks like

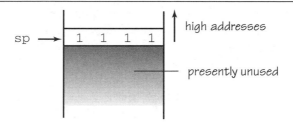

Then if we execute

```
push    Y
```

we get

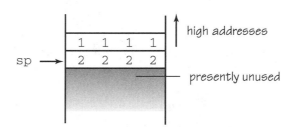

Note that the pop instruction not only removes the newest item on the stack, but also stores that item in the argument of the pop instruction. Thus if we execute

```
pop     Z
```

Z is set to 2222 and a stack that looks like

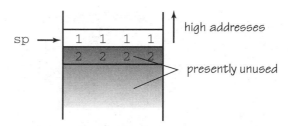

The word containing 2222 is not actually removed from memory. We are only *modeling* the behavior of the abstract stack idea, and we can simply ignore any extra information which doesn't come from the original stack concept. (You can't count on items popped from the stack remaining in unused stack memory, though, because the operating system also uses the stack.)

The push instruction can't be used to push a constant directly. That is, the instruction push 5 is illegal. It can be replaced with the code

```
mov     ax, 5
push    ax ;   equivalent to the ILLEGAL push 5
```

The hardware stack is implemented as a block of memory, the amount specified by the .STACK pseudo-operation. For instance, the statement .STACK 100h specifies a stack with 100h (= 256) byte or 80h (=100h/2 = 128) word entries. The stack starts at high memory addresses and grows downwards. A snapshot at a particular moment of program execution might show the stack as follows:

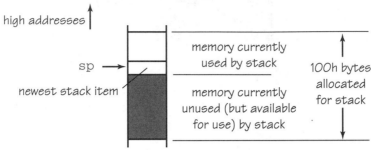

Sp, which is shown as a pointer here, actually contains the *address* of the newest item on the stack. At program startup, DOS initializes sp to point to the word just beyond stack memory:

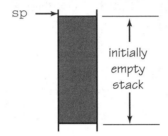

Notice that if you do 'push X' followed by 'pop X', the stack and X are unchanged. Thus

Preserve *Something*
push   *Something*
; *operations which either don't use the stack, or whose net*
; *effect is to leave the stack unchanged; i. e., same*
; *number of pushes and pops*
pop   *Something*

saves *Something* before executing the italicized code and restores the value of *Something* afterwards.

Saving and restoring *registers* is particularly important in subprogram calls. Typically, the caller has important information in registers and doesn't know which registers are altered by the subprogram. We could either require that the caller save and restore all registers it is using, just in case, or we could require that the subprogram do it. Since the subprogram only needs one copy of the save and restore code, and since it better knows what registers it uses, we make the rule that

Subprograms should save and restore any registers they use

Of course, if a subprogram is a function returning a value in a register—for instance, GetDec returning the number read in ax—that register isn't saved and restored. In addition, some high-level languages have conventions that only some registers are to be preserved. (Since ax, cx, and dx are commonly used for computations, they often aren't required to be saved and restored.) We however will make it a practice to save and restore all registers that aren't used to return a value.

The standard way to save and restore registers is to use the stack. Thus if SubProg alters ax, bx, and cx, and wants to save and restore them, we could code

```
Subprog    PROC
           push    ax
           push    bx
           push    cx
           . . .
           pop     cx ;          Note: pop in REVERSE order
           pop     bx
           pop     ax
           ret
SubProg    ENDP
```

Of course for saving and restoring by pushing and popping to work properly, the stack has to be in the same condition just before pop cx that it was in just after push cx. It is all right to use the stack in between, but it is very important to follow the second rule that

Subprograms should pop all items and only those items that they push on the stack

We have already seen other examples in which the stack could have been used for temporary storage. For instance in Example 3.4—1, instead of the following code to save and restore ax:

```
call    GetDec
mov     SaveAX, ax ;  Save ax in variable SaveAX
_PutStr OutMsg
mov     ax, SaveAX ;  Restore value of ax from SaveAX
```

we could have used

```
call    GetDec
push    ax ;          Save ax on the stack
_PutStr OutMsg
pop     ax ;          Restore value of ax from the stack
```

leaving the stack in the same position it was in when we started.

In Example 5.5—1, instead of the code

```
_BIOSCh
mov     bx, ax ;      _PutStr destroys ax
_PutStr ScanMsg
```

```
        mov     al, bh ;        Scan code was in ah
        mov     ah, 0 ;         Extend to word
        call    PutDec
        _PutStr ASCIIMsg
        mov     al, bl ;        ASCII Value (or 0) was in al
        mov     ah, 0 ;         Extend to word
        call    PutDec
```

we could have written

```
        _BIOSCh
        push    ax ;            _PutStr destroys ax
        push    ax ;              (need two copies)
        _PutStr ScanMsg
        pop     ax ;            Can't just pop a byte
        mov     al, ah ;        Scan code was in ah
        mov     ah, 0 ;         Extend al to word
        call    PutDec
        _PutStr ASCIIMsg
        pop     ax ;            ASCII Value (or 0) was in al
        mov     ah, 0 ;         Extend al to word
        call    PutDec
```

Exercises 6.2

1. Fill in the values the specified registers and memory locations will have as the following code fragment is executed:

```
    A       DW      1111h
    B       DW      2222h

            . . .
            push    A
            mov     ax, 3333h
            push    ax
            push    B
            pop     ax ;        ax = _____ ✓

            pop     B ;         B  = _____ ✓
            mov     bx, 4444h
            push    bx
            pop     ax          ax = _____

            pop     bx          bx = _____
```

2. What is the effect of the code

```
            push    ax
```

```
push    bx
pop     ax
pop     bx
```

3. ✓ Why can't we save and restore `sp` in a subprogram using

```
push    sp
. . .
pop     sp
```

6.3 • The Stack, `call`, and `ret`

`Call` and `ret` cooperate ingeniously through use of the stack and IP, the instruction pointer.

Recall from Section 1.1.1 that the IP register in the CPU contains the address of the next instruction to be executed. In the fetch-execute cycle discussed there, as an instruction is fetched to be executed, IP is incremented so that when the fetch is completed, IP is the address of the instruction *following* the current one.

The effect of the instruction "call subProc" is "push the IP register and jump to subProc," that is, push IP and replace it with the address of subProc. By the time the push happens, the IP has already been updated so it is the address of the instruction following `call subProc`. Thus what is pushed is the address we want to come back to, the **return address**.

Assuming that the return address is still (or again) on top of the stack, `ret` is the reverse of the `call` instruction. It simply pops the stack into the IP register, so that the next instruction executed is the instruction following the `call`.

After a `call` instruction the stack looks like

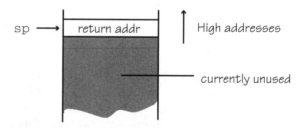

After executing the corresponding `ret` instruction, the stack looks as follows:

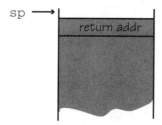

While executing `subProc`, the stack can be used for local storage, such as for temporary storage for the contents of registers.

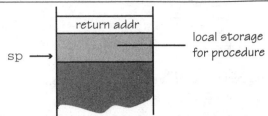

One of the most ingenious temporary uses of the stack is to **call other subprocedures!** In fact a procedure can call itself recursively, arbitrarily many times. The only thing to remember is the second rule from Section 6.2, that a procedure must pop off everything, and *only* those things, that it puts on the stack. Thus the return address will be available in the right position when the `ret` instruction is executed. When a subprocedure is called within a subprocedure, the `call` and corresponding `ret` take care of keeping the stack tidy automatically.

Exercises 6.3

1. ✓ Suppose you are given the following code:

```
                call    procA
        ;                   order of execution of this line _____
                . . .
        procA   PROC
                call    procB
        ;                   order of execution of this line _____
                ret
        procA   ENDP
        procB   PROC
        ;                   order of execution of this line _____
                ret
        procB   ENDP
```

By inserting numbers 1–3, indicate the order in which the comment lines are executed assuming we start at the statement `call procA`.

2. ✓ What would result from executing the following (incorrect) pieces of code?

```
a)              call    procA
                . . .
        procA   PROC
                call    procB
                ret
        procA   ENDP
        procB   PROC
                pop     ax
                ret
        procB   ENDP

b)              call    procP
```

```
                . . .
    procP       PROC
                push    ax
                ret
    procP       ENDP

c)              jmp     procX
                . . .
    procX       PROC
                ret
    procX       ENDP
```

6.4 • Separately Translated Subprograms

Moving the subprogram to a separate file, so that it can be separately assembled and (perhaps) used by many different programs requires a few extra statements. Let us suppose we wish to separate PROG.ASM into two separate files, MAIN.ASM containing Main and SUB.ASM containing SubProg.

```
;; MAIN.ASM
INCLUDE   PCMAC.INC
          .MODEL  SMALL
          .STACK  100h
          .DATA
          . . .
          .CODE
          EXTRN     SubProg : NEAR
Main      PROC
          mov     ax, @data
          mov     ds, ax
          . . .
          call    SubProg
          . . .
          call    SubProg
          . . .
          _Exit
Main      ENDP
          END     Main
```

```
;; SUB.ASM
INCLUDE   PCMAC.INC ; if necessary
          .MODEL  SMALL
          .STACK  100h
          .DATA
          data for SubProg
          .CODE
          PUBLIC  SubProg
SubProg   PROC
          same as before
;    mov ax, @data/mov ds, ax
;       still not needed
          ret
SubProg   ENDP
          END        ; NO LABEL!!!
```

The two programs must be assembled separately (or see ML below). Using LINK or TLINK (or ML), the two programs are linked together, and the actual address of SubProg is inserted in the two call SubProg instructions:

TASM link:	tlink main + sub,,,util.lib (if needed)
MASM link:	link main + sub,,,util.lib; (if needed)
ML assembly and link:	ml main.asm sub.asm util.lib (if needed)

When using ML, if a program doesn't need to be reassembled, you can include its .OBJ file instead of its `.ASM` file in the file list. For instance, if you don't need to reassemble `MAIN.ASM`, the command can be

```
ml main.obj sub.asm util.lib
```

In all cases above, a file `MAIN.EXE` is created as a result.

Notes:

- Assembly is entirely separate and independent for the two source files. Therefore if you want to use macros in `SubProg`, you have to include the macro file there. By the same token, if you want to call external subprograms in `SubProg`, you need `EXTRN` statements for them there as well.
- Normally, no `.STACK` statement is necessary in the subprogram. If stack space is specified, it is added to that specified by the main program.
- Part of the work of an assembler is creating a **symbol table**, which is used to record programmer-defined symbols and information about them, such as location in storage, etc. This information is thrown away when the assembler is done, so the link program can't know how to fill in the addresses in the call instructions, or even where such instructions are. The `EXTRN` statement causes the assembler to save each location at which the `EXTRN` symbol is used so that the linker can later fill in that location. Correspondingly, the `PUBLIC` statement causes the assembler to save the location of the `PUBLIC` symbol for use by the linker. That information is saved in special records in the respective `.OBJ` files.
- `.DATA` used by the two programs must be separated into that used by the main program, which goes into `MAIN.ASM`, and that used by the subprogram, which goes into `SUBPROG.ASM`. If you have data which is used both places, then an `EXTRN`/`PUBLIC` combo must be used. For instance:

```
;; MAIN.ASM
        . . .
        .DATA
        PUBLIC  COMN
COMN    DW      ?
        . . .
        .CODE
        EXTRN   SubProg : NEAR
        . . .
```

```
;; SUB.ASM
        . . .
        .DATA
        EXTRN   COMN:WORD
        . . .
        .CODE
        PUBLIC  SubProg
SubProg PROC
        . . .
        reference to COMN
```

`EXTRN` statements for `.DATA` must appear in the `.DATA` section and those for `.CODE` must appear in the `.CODE` section. Note that we have created a **global variable** `COMN` here, that is, any program can manipulate `COMN` as long as it has the correct `EXTRN` statement. Using the method above for communicating values in programs intended for general use is not a particularly good idea, as it requires you to set up the correct type of `EXTRN`/`PUBLIC` handshaking to find the variable, and if something goes wrong in its use, you may be faced with tracking the problem down over many source files..

- The `END` statement in the main program still contains the label where the program starts (here, `Main`). The END statement in *subprograms* does not contain a label (the program can start executing only in one place).

Example 6.4—1. For this example, we'll construct a simple modification of `PutHex`. This version displays a zero ahead of a hex number if it starts with a letter (A–F) and appends the letter 'h' to the end. Since the procedure we are constructing here is more elegant than `PutHex`, we will call it `PutHexxe`. The number to be displayed (which will be in `ax`, as in `PutHex`) will start with a letter if it is above or equal (unsigned jump!) to 0A000h. Therefore the code will be:

```
;; PUTHEXXE.ASM—Like PutHex, but prefixes a number starting with a
;;    letter with '0' and suffixes all numbers with 'h'
;;
;;       Input:   ax = number to display
;;       Output:  None
;;
;;  All Registers are Preserved
INCLUDE   PCMAC.INC
          .MODEL SMALL
          .CODE
          PUBLIC PutHexxe
          EXTRN  PutHex : NEAR
PutHexxe  PROC
          push   dx
          push   ax ;          Preserve registers used by _PutCh!!!
          cmp    ax, 0a000h
          jb     NoZero ;    unsigned compare
          push   ax ;        Make a second copy of ax
          _PutCh '0'
          pop    ax ;        recall second copy of ax...
NoZero:
          call   PutHex ;      ...and display it
          _PutCh 'h'
          pop    ax
          pop    dx
          ret
PutHexxe  ENDP
          END
```

Notes:

- We see here an example of a subprocedure calling another subprocedure, as `PutHexxe` calls `PutHex`.
- A main program calling `PutHexxe` needs the following statements

```
          .CODE
          ...
          EXTRN  PutHexxe : NEAR
```

```
      . . .
mov    ax, whatever
call   PutHexxe
```

If the main program does not call `PutHex` itself, then *it* does not need an `EXTRN PutHex` statement. If the program containing these statements is called `MAIN.ASM`, then the program can be linked via

TASM link:	`tlink main + puthexxe,,,util.lib`
MASM link:	`link main + puthexxe,,,util.lib;`
ML assembly and link:	`ml main.asm puthexxe.asm util.lib`

Exercise 6.4

1. ✓ Write a complete separately translatable subprocedure `Space` which takes as input an integer in `ax` and displays that number of blanks. What is a reasonable reaction of the `Space` program to negative input? To input of zero?

6.5 • Creating Program Libraries (Optional)

This section will never be used again, but will be useful if you want to know how to create and maintain program libraries such as `UTIL.LIB`.

The general command for manipulating a program library is

MASM:	`lib library-file-name commands ;`	(note the ';')
TASM:	`tlib library-file-name commands`	

The *library-file-name* is just a file name, with or without `.LIB` extension. If the library file does not already exist, it is created. The *commands* are a list of `.OBJ` file names (the `.OBJ` extension is optional) prefixed by characters indicating what is to be done with those files:

Prefixes	Actions
+	add file to library
−	delete file from library
− +	replace file in library with new version

Thus, to create a new library `NLIB.LIB` containing files `A.OBJ`, `B.OBJ`, and `C.OBJ`, execute

```
lib (or tlib) nlib +a +b +c
```

To delete `B.OBJ` from `nlib`, execute

```
lib (or tlib) nlib -b
```

To replace `A.OBJ` and `C.OBJ` in `nlib` with new versions, execute

```
lib (or tlib) nlib -+a -+c
```

6.6 • How the Linker Works (Optional)

The information in this section is of a fairly advanced nature and will not be used later in the book.

When one of the assemblers translates a source file into its corresponding object file, it creates a symbol table containing all the names and attributes of symbols defined in the source. It uses that table in its translation, then discards it when it is done. Since PUBLIC symbols may be defined in one file and referenced in another, they require special treatment so that the necessary symbolic information is preserved for the linker. In fact, the assembler saves two tables in the .OBJ file—a table of EXTRN symbols and a list of places (there can be many for each symbol) where the symbol is *referenced*, and a table of PUBLIC symbols and the (unique) place each is *defined*.

For instance, consider

```
;; EXAMPLE.ASM
          . . .
          .CODE
          EXTRN  A : NEAR, B : NEAR
          PUBLIC X, Y
X         PROC
          . . .
          call   A
          . . .
          call   B
          . . .
          call   A
          . . .
X         ENDP
Y         PROC
          . . .
          call   A
          . . .
          call   B
          . . .
Y         ENDP
          END
```

In MASM 6.0 and later, PROC names such as X and Y are PUBLIC by default. The calls to A and B above are called **unresolved external references** and must be filled in by the linking program (which is its main purpose). The assembler does its part by creating a file EXAMPLE.OBJ which has the following schematic form:

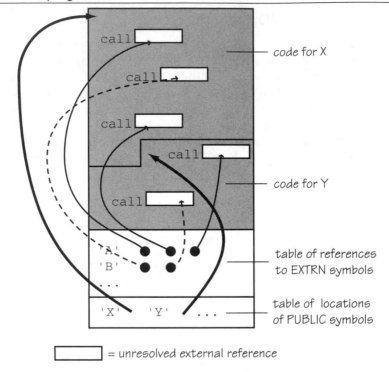

= unresolved external reference

Notes:

- The actual character string representing the label must be saved so that cross-references between files can be resolved. On the other hand, the `call` operation code will of course have been saved in its numeric form.
- There are different types of locations and different ways that they need to be filled. (Symbols can be `.CODE` or `.DATA`, and if `.DATA`, `WORD` or `BYTE`.) The tables of `PUBLIC` and `EXTRN` symbols must also contain this information.
- If for instance `X` contains a call to `Y`, the assembler can resolve it just as it resolves forward jumps.

The linking process of attaching calls to their destinations is called **resolving external references**. That process is now straightforward, if a little messy. Suppose we have the command

```
link/tlink P1+P2+...+Pn,,,L1+L2+...+Lm;
```

The command above links together the files `P1.OBJ`, `P2.OBJ`, ... `Pn.OBJ`, resolving external references between them and using the libraries `L1.LIB`, `L2.LIB`, ... `Lm.LIB` to resolve any further external references. It performs the following steps:

1) Read each `Pi.OBJ` file in turn and merge it into three objects: a file `OC` of object code, a table `XSR` of `EXTRN` symbol references, and a table `PSD` of `PUBLIC` symbol definitions.
   a) If `OC` contained *n* bytes of code before `Pi` was read in, `Pi`'s code will start offset *n* bytes from 0.

b) For each EXTRN symbol in Pi.OBJ, add it and its references in Pi.OBJ to the end of XSR even if it is already there. (Multiple entries for a symbol may result, but these entries are of variable length and the end of the table is the only place we can be sure to have room.) Add *n* to each of Pi's reference locations.

c) For each PUBLIC symbol, check to see if it is already in PSD. If so, it is multiply defined and an error has occurred. Otherwise add it to the end of PSD, and add *n* to its definition location.

2) For each symbol in XSR, look it up in PSD. If it is there, resolve all references for that symbol and delete the symbol and its external references from the XSR.

3) If the XSR is now empty, **all references are resolved** and we are done!

4) If not, for each library Li.LIB, read through each .OBJ file and see if it has any PUBLIC symbols that are symbols in the XSR. If so, read in that .OBJ file as in step 1) above.

5) If no new .OBJ files were added in step 4), then there are external references that cannot be resolved, and **linking fails**! Otherwise, go back to step 2).

Example 6.6—1. The following simple example may help to solidify the above process. Suppose we wish to test the procedure PutHexxe using a test program TestHex. The linking statement will be

```
link/tlink testhex + puthexxe,,,util.lib;
```

Let the files have the following information:

TESTHEX.OBJ:
>   Code Length: 34 bytes
>   EXTRNs: 'PutHexxe', one reference at relative location 14
>   PUBLICs: none

PUTHEXXE.OBJ:
>   Code Length: 56 bytes
>   EXTRNs: 'PutHex', one reference at relative location 27
>   PUBLICs: 'PutHexxe', defined to be relative location 0

in UTIL.LIB, PUTHEX.OBJ:
>   Code Length: 71 bytes
>   EXTRNs: none
>   PUBLICs: 'PutHex', defined to be relative location 0

The link steps are as follows:

1) Read TESTHEX.OBJ. Code file has 34 bytes. Contents of tables are
>   XSR: 'PutHexxe', one reference at location 14
>   PSD: empty

Read PUTHEXXE.OBJ. add 34 (previous code file size) to locations in its tables. Size of code is now 90 bytes (= 34 + 56). Contents of tables are updated to be
>   XSR: 'PutHexxe', one reference at location 14
>   'PutHex', one reference at location 61 (= 27 + 34)
>   PSD: 'PutHexxe', defined to be location 34 (= 0 + 34)

2) Look up `'PutHexxe'` in the PSD. It's there, defined at location 34. Insert '34' at location 14 of the code file. Delete `'PutHexxe'` entry from the XSR.

Look up `'PutHex'` in the PSD. It isn't there.

At the end of step 2), the tables now are

    XSR: `'PutHex'`, one reference at location 61

    PSD: `'PutHexxe'`, defined to be location 34

3) Not done as XSR still contains entries.

4) Read UTIL.LIB, finding `'PutHex'` in PUTHEX.OBJ. Read in PUTHEX.OBJ, adding 90 (previous code file size) to locations in its tables. Size of code is now 161 bytes. Contents of tables are updated to be

    XSR: `'PutHex'`, one reference at location 61

    PSD: `'PutHexxe'`, defined to be location 34

              `'PutHex'`, defined to be location 90 (= 0 + 90)

5) A file was added, so go back to step 2).

2) Look up `'PutHex'` in the PSD. It's there, defined at location 90. Insert '90' at location 61 of the code file. Delete `'PutHex'` entry from the XSR.

At the end of step 2), the tables now are

    XSR: empty

    PSD: `'PutHexxe'`, defined to be location 34

              `'PutHex'`, defined to be location 90

3) The XSR is empty so we're done.

Notes:

- The linking process must terminate. For the loop 2) through 5) to continue, at least one new .OBJ file must have been added—that is, at least one new PUBLIC symbol definition that didn't previously exist. There are only finitely many such symbols.

- We may search through each library several times (though it is unlikely to be more than once or twice).

- When we get through with step 4) the first time, we must have gotten all of the EXTRN symbol references from the original Pi.OBJs, or we will never get them. However .OBJ files from the library, may have their own EXTRN symbol references that must be resolved. (Example: on the disk supplied with this book, the procedure PutDec in UTIL.LIB calls a subprocedure Bin2Dec which is also in UTIL.LIB, so UTIL.LIB must be scanned twice.

- Subprograms in libraries can reference PUBLIC symbols in the Pi.OBJs. For instance in the example in the item just above, the command

```
link/tlink test+bin2dec,,,util.lib
```

would link a test program and new version of Bin2Dec with the version of PutDec in UTIL.LIB.

- To simplify the description above, we have ignored the .DATA part of the object files. To include it would have required a second object file, OD, independent of OC, to contain the .DATA parts of the programs and a table of relocatable address locations in OD that the linker would also have to fill in. (See the end of Section 4.4.)

Exercise 6.6

1. Work through an example similar to example 6.6—1 involving the statement

```
link/tlink test,,,util;
```

Let each of the following files have the following information:

TEST.OBJ:
> Code Length: 80 bytes
> EXTRNs: 'PutDec', two references at relative locations 30 and 45
> PUBLICs: none

in UTIL.LIB, PUTDEC.OBJ:
> Code Length: 42 bytes
> EXTRNs: 'Bin2Dec', one reference at relative location 31
> PUBLICs: 'PutDec', defined to be relative location 10

in UTIL.LIB, BIN2DEC.OBJ:
> Code Length: 123 bytes
> EXTRNs: none
> PUBLICs: 'Bin2Dec', defined to be relative location 24

Programming Problem 6.1

Write a separately assembled function procedure YesNo which displays the message

```
(Y or N)?
```

and waits for an answering character on the same line. When the character is typed, echo it and a carriage return/line feed (the user doesn't enter the line feed). If an upper- or lowercase Y is typed, the function returns 1 in ax. If an upper- or lowercase N is typed, it returns 0. If any other character is typed, redisplay the message and start all over again. (Each new display of the message will be on a separate line because of the carriage return/line feed.) Test your program with a main program TestYes which can cause the following dialogue:

```
C:> TestYes↵
Do you want to continue (Y or N)? Y↵
Do you want to continue (Y or N)? y↵
Do you want to continue (Y or N)? Q↵
(Y or N)? n↵
Really Stop (Y or N)? Y↵
Done
C:>
```

The messages 'Do you want to continue,' 'Really Stop,' and 'Done' are generated by TestYes.

Programming Problem 6.2

The **greatest common divisor** (GCD) of two integers is the largest positive integer which divides both evenly. Thus GCD(100, 240) = 20, GCD(34, 27) = 1, and GCD(0, 14) = 14. A standard elementary programming exercise computes the GCD of M and N (both > 0) without using division (which is slow) by the following method:

```
while (M <> N) do
        if (N > M) then N := N - M else M := M - N end if
end while
GCD := N // = M, too
```

Justification of the method (optional): Since M and N start out positive, they remain positive (why?), and every time through the loop, the larger one gets smaller. Therefore either the loop terminates or they both reach 1, in which case the loop also terminates. It should also be easy to see that the GCD of M and N after the loop is the same as before the loop, and that GCD(N, N) = N.

Write a separately assembled function GCD to find the GCD of the integers in ax and bx using this algorithm and return the value in ax. Treat the cases M or N = 0 or negative as special cases: GCD(–M, N) = GCD(M, N); GCD(–32768, –32768) = –32768, GCD(–32768, N) = GCD(16384, N) if N ≠ –32768. GCD(0, 0) really should be ∞, but return 0. Test your program with at least the set of examples given at the start of the problem. (See also Programming Problem 9.3.)

SUMMARY

The instruction

```
        call          routine
```

executes *routine* as a procedure or function by pushing the address of the instruction following the call, the return address, onto the stack, and jumping to label *routine*.

Routine returns to its caller by executing the instruction

```
        ret
```

which pops the word pointed to by sp off the stack and places it in IP. The procedure or function *routine* must pop from the stack exactly the number of words it pushes on so that the item placed in IP is the return address that was pushed by the call instruction. *Routine* should also save and restore any registers that its caller expects it to preserve. *Which* ones it saves is determined by externally specified conventions. Each high-level language has its own conventions.

The stack instructions are

```
    push   source ;              push (word only!)
    pop    dest ;                pop (word only!)
```

Reminder: *source* in push can't be a constant. Move the constant to a register first.

In order to write procedures as separately translated linkable routines, the calling program must include the statement

        EXTRN *routine* : NEAR

and the file containing *routine* must include the statement

        PUBLIC   *routine*

The LINK/TLINK statement is

    link/tlink P1+P2+...+Pn,,,util;

links files `P1.OBJ`, `P2.OBJ`, ... `Pn.OBJ` to produce an executable file called `P1.EXE`.

Debug Workshop III

Procedures

This workshop discusses methods of debugging with procedures. We will get our first meaningful look at the difference between Trace and Step, and will see techniques for dealing with separately translated subprograms, even those without debugging information. Finally, we will get some information on viewing the stack.

III.1 • CodeView

▶ **Viewing Source Code in Another Code File (= Module)**

The source code of any file which was assembled with debugging information (/Zi switch) can be viewed in the Source1 window by making that window active and using **Alt-F**(ile Open **M**(odule..., then picking from the list of available source files. You can also view source code in two different modules simultaneously by opening the Source2 window, **Alt-W**(indow 4(. Source 2 or **Alt-4**. Either window can be reset at will as above to show the source code of any module compiled with debugging information.

▶ **Setting Breakpoints in Another Module**

Three easy methods of setting a breakpoint in a module not displayed are (1) trace into the module, then set the breakpoint, (2) open the module in a window as above and set the breakpoint, and (3) (for setting a breakpoint at a PUBLIC label) enter the command bp *label* in the command window.

▶ **Tracing into Modules Without Debugger Information**

If you try to trace from a call instruction in code with debugger information into code without it, you will execute the called procedure without stopping, finally stopping at the instruction following the `call`, just as if you had done a Step command. To trace *into* the call, you have to change the format of the Source window.

There are three formats for the Source window: **Source** looks like your `.ASM` file, with line numbers:

```
20:             mov     ax, @data ;    the standard prolog
```

Assembly shows the numeric form of the translated code on the left and a minimally symbolic form on the right. Macro expansions are shown:

```
Hello:
24C5:0000 B8CF24         MOV     AX, 24CF
```

Mixed shows Source and Assembly format interleaved:

```
20:             mov     ax, @data ;    the standard prolog
24C5:0000 B8CF24         MOV     AX, 24CF
```

You can cycle among these formats by making the Source1 window active and hitting **F3** or clicking left on `<F3=S1 Fmt>` on the help line, or choosing **Alt-O**(ptions **S**(ource1 Window... **S**(ource, **M**(ixed Source and Assembly, or **A**(ssembly. As the Source window format is "remembered" by CodeView, you will probably want to set it back later with **Alt-O**(ptions **S**(ource1 Window... **S**(ource.

You can also set a breakpoint at the called routine name, which is a PUBLIC symbol, using the **bp** *label* command.

Once you have gotten inside a module without debugging information, either with a breakpoint or tracing, you can set further breakpoints in the usual ways, or by using **bp** *HexAddress* in the command window, where *HexAddress* is found after the colon near the start of the line on which you wish to break: xxxx: *HexAddress*.

▶ **Viewing the Stack**.

There really is no good way in CodeView. The command

```
DW SS:SP L n
```

(**D**ump **W**ords starting at **SS:SP** of **L**ength *n*) in the command window displays the top *n* words on the stack, top-of-stack first. Unfortunately, though, whenever SP changes, you have to reenter the DW command. The meaning of the "SS:" part of the command should become evident in Chapter 12.

III.2 • Turbo Debugger

▶ **Viewing Source Code in Another Module**

Either enter **Alt-V**(iew **M**(odule... or **F3**. You will be presented with a list of modules with debugging information. Cursor through to the one you want and hit Enter.

▶ **Setting Breakpoints in Another Module**

The easiest method is to view the module as above and then use any of the previously described methods. You can also set a breakpoint in one module while viewing another with the command **Alt-B**(reakpoint **A**(t... *Label* if *Label* is PUBLIC, *SourceFile#Label* otherwise.

▶ **Tracing into a Module without Debugging Information**

If you try to trace from a call instruction in code with debugger information into code without it using the module window, you will skip to the end of the call, just as if you had done a Step command. To trace *into* the call, open the CPU window with **Alt-V**(iew **C**(PU or make it the active window if it is already open. The upper left pane of the CPU window shows the translated code on the left and a symbolic form on the right. If the symbolic form is preceded by a diamond, it is your original source code. The translated form of macro expansions is shown. Tracing in the CPU window jumps *into* calls, even if they have no debugger information. You can set breakpoints in the CPU window just as in the Module window.

You can also set a breakpoint at any PUBLIC symbol (such as the procedure's name) with the **Alt-B**(reakpoint **A**(t... *Symbol* command. If your program breaks at such a location and there is no debugger information, the CPU window is automatically opened.

Once you have gotten inside a module without debugging information, either with a breakpoint or tracing, you can set further breakpoints in the usual ways, or by using **Alt-B**(reakpoint **A**(t... *HexAddress*, where *HexAddress* is found after 'cs:' near the start of the line on which you wish to break.

▶ **Viewing the Stack**.

The best way to view the stack is with **Alt-V**(iew **C**(PU. The pane in the lower right-hand corner of the CPU window is (part of) the stack. The actual top of the stack is shown by the entry ss:*xxxx*▸*yyyy*, where *xxxx* is the current value of sp and *yyyy* is the current value on the stack. The top will normally be the bottom entry in the stack pane, and as much of the stack as fits in the pane will rise above the current value. By resizing the CPU window, you can arrange to show more stack entries (drag the lower right-hand corner of the CPU window or use **Alt-W**(indow **S**(ize/Move). By clicking left on the stack pane or tabbing to it you can get a scroll bar and scroll the pane up or down to view more of the stack. (The stack pointer will return to the bottom on the pane on the next trace/step/run.) At the left we see a stack pane of reasonable size, with eight entries. Assuming that we specified .STACK 100h, the entries 0100, 0102, 0104, and 0106 shown here would not actually be in the stack. Sp started out at 0100 and the first item pushed onto the stack, 0001, is stored at 00FE. The illustration shows that five words have been pushed onto the stack, culminating in the most recent, 0B324h at sp = 00F6.

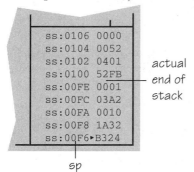

```
ss:0106  0000
ss:0104  0052
ss:0102  0401      actual
ss:0100  52FB  ──  end of
ss:00FE  0001      stack
ss:00FC  03A2
ss:00FA  0010
ss:00F6▸B324
```

sp

To view the stack pane and the source code window at the same time, move the CPU window so that it is on the right-hand side of the screen, and cycle to the following window stacking order:

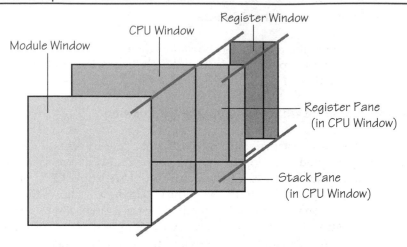

You can bring a particular window to the front by entering **Alt-#** where # is the window number in the upper right-hand corner. If you resized the module window to show the register window, it will now show the register and stack panes of the CPU window.

III.3 • Debugger Example 5: Tracing and Stepping

The following program implements a function much loved by teachers of elementary programming courses. For any positive integer n, $f(n)$ is defined as $n/2$ if n is even, $3n+1$ if n is odd. The question is what happens if we repeatedly replace n by $f(n)$? For instance, if we start with $n = 3$, we get successively $n = f(3) = 10$, $n = f(10) = 5$, $n = f(5) = 16$, $n = f(16) = 8$, $n = f(8) = 4$, $n = f(4) = 2$, and $n = f(2) = 1$. When the sequence reaches 1, it starts cycling 4, 2, 1, 4, 2, 1… In every known example, the sequence eventually reaches this 4, 2, 1 cycle (though as far as I know there is no proof that the sequence always gets to this point). The DBGEX5.ASM file contains three PROCs:

Fun   which computes f(n). ax = n on entry; ax = f(n) on exit.

SeqLen   which computes the number of steps $n = f(n)$ that are necessary to reach $n = 1$. ax = n on entry and ax = SeqLen(n) on exit. Note that SeqLen(1) = 0, SeqLen(2) = 1, and SeqLen(3) = 7.

Main   which tests SeqLen. It takes as input lower and upper limits and computes the maximum SeqLen over all numbers within those limits.

The program code, *which contains bugs*, is

```
;; DbgEx5.ASM—Test the following function of positive integers:
;;
;;     f(n) = n/2 if n is even; = 3n+1 if n is odd
;;
;;  The program includes two subprograms, Fun which computes f(ax)
;;    and returns the value in ax, and SeqLen which takes a
;;    positive number in ax and finds out how many iterations of ax
;;    := Fun(ax) are necessary to reach 1, returning that number in
;;    ax. Both functions preserve all registers except ax.
```

```
;;
;;   The main program takes as input two integers and computes
;;    the maximum SeqLen for all integers in that range
;;
;; Assemble with debug information and link with util.lib
;;
INCLUDE    PCMAC.INC
           .MODEL SMALL
           .STACK 100h


           .DATA
LLP        DB     'Lower Limit: $'
ULP        DB     'Upper Limit: $'
OutMsg     DB     'The maximum sequence length is $'
ForMsg     DB     ' for $'
XwithLargest DW ? ;            Number with max SeqLen so far


           .CODE
Main       PROC
           EXTRN  GetDec : NEAR, PutDec : NEAR
           mov    ax, @data
           mov    ds, ax

           _PutStr LLP
           call   GetDec
           mov    bx, ax ;    Lower Limit = current test case in bx
           cmp    ax, 0
           jle    BadLim
           _PutStr ULP
           call   GetDec
           mov    cx, ax ;    cx will equal count of numbers to test
           sub    cx, bx
           jge    OK
BadLim:
           _Exit  1 ;            Exit if LL > UL or LL <= 0
OK:
           inc    cx ;         Number of tests = UL - LL + 1
           mov    dx, -1 ;     Largest SeqLen so far
TestLoop:
           mov    ax, bx
           call   SeqLen ;     ax := SeqLen(n)
           cmp    ax, dx ;     if SeqLen > largestSeq then
           jle    NextAX
           mov    dx, ax ;           largestSeq := ax
           mov    XwithLargest, bx ; XwithLargest := n
NextAX:
           inc    bx ;            n := n + 1
```

```
              loop    TestLoop

              _PutStr OutMsg
              call    PutDec
              _PutStr ForMsg
              mov     ax, XwithLargest
              call    PutDec
              _PutCh 13, 10

              _Exit   0
Main          ENDP

SeqLen        PROC
              push    cx ;        Preserve cx, use for SeqLen value
              sub     cx, cx ;    Initialize SeqLen to 0
EndTest:
              cmp     ax, 1
              je      SeqDone
              call    Fun ;       ax := Fun(ax)
              inc     cx
              jmp     EndTest
SeqDone:
              mov     ax, cx
              pop     cx
              ret
SeqLen        ENDP

Fun           PROC
              push    cx
              push    dx ;        Preserve registers for later use
              sub     dx, dx ;    Extend ax to dx,ax unsigned
              mov     cx, 2
              div     cx ;        Now, ax := orig ax / 2
              cmp     dx, 0 ;      and dx = remainder
              je      FunDone ;   Ax was even; result is in ax

              mov     cx, 3
              mul     cx
              inc     ax
FunDone:
              pop     dx
              pop     cx
              pop     bx
              ret
Fun           ENDP

              END     Main
```

Procedure:

Since we are going to change DbgEx5, make a copy to work with, calling it perhaps FUNNY.ASM. We are going to debug the program inside-out: first debugging Fun, then SeqLen, then Main. First though we have to work our way in to Fun to make sure it is getting the correct data. Assemble FUNNY.ASM with debugging information (/Zi) and link (/co for link, /v for tlink) with util.lib.

1) Main reads the lower limit and stores it in bx, then reads the upper limit and uses it and bx to compute the count in cx of the number of integers to test. The count is *upper limit – lower limit + 1*. To test if these numbers are getting set correctly, set a breakpoint two lines after OK:, the instruction mov dx, -1 (boldface in the code above). (To set the breakpoint, double-click left on the line in CV, click left in the first two columns in TD.) Run the program (**F5** in CV, **F9** in TD). Enter 3 for both lower and upper limits. When you reach the breakpoint, bx, the lower limit, should be 3 and cx, the count should be 1.

2) *Trace* the program step by step until Fun is entered (**F8** in CV, **F7** in TD). As you go, note that on entry to SeqLen and on entry to Fun, ax = 3 as it should be.

3) Trace through the computation of Fun(3), which should return with ax = Fun(3) = 10. Then trace through the computation of Fun(10), which should exit with ax = 5. Somewhere along the line you should discover a bug in Fun. Exit the debugger, use your editor to fix the bug, reassemble with debugging information, then trace the computations of Fun(3) and Fun(10) again. Repeat this step until the results are correct. You may then wish to trace the computation of a few more values of Fun, just to be certain. When you are satisfied that Fun is working, go on to the next step.

4) Finish tracing the computation of SeqLen(3), which should return with ax = 7 as the sequence of values for 3 is 3, 10, 5, 16, 8, 4, 2, 1. Use Step (**F10** in CV, **F8** in TD) instead of Trace to avoid tracing Fun over and over again. SeqLen shouldn't have any bugs (unless you inadvertently inserted some).

5) Go to the end of the program, where the output should be

```
The maximum sequence length is 7 for 3
```

If you have used the standard PCMAC.INC, there will be a bug in Main. Fix it, reassemble and relink, and verify that the output is as stated above. Since you have reasonable confidence that SeqLen works, step when you get to the call SeqLen instruction.

6) Restart the program (**Alt-R**(un **R**(estart in CV, **Alt-R**(un **P**(rogram reset in TD) and test it again, this time for lower limit 7 and upper limit 9. Set a breakpoint at cmp ax, dx, just after call SeqLen in Main. Run to execute SeqLen three times and examine the values returned in ax, which should be 16, 3, and 19. Each time, trace through the next few instructions to make sure that dx, the maximum, is getting set correctly. Check that the final output is

```
The maximum sequence length is 19 for 9
```

7) Finally, test the program with lower limit 1 and upper limit 100. You should get the output

```
The maximum sequence length is 118 for 97
```

If any of these outputs is incorrect, fix bugs and try again.

Exercise III.3

1. Turn the debugged version of DbgEx5 into three separately translated procedures and debug the result.

III.4 • Debugger Example 6

We will finish this workshop with two debugger examples using DbgEx6. In this section we will show how to view and set breakpoints in separately compiled modules, and follow changes in the stack as the program is executed. In particular, we will show that an item popped off the stack can have its location on the stack overwritten even though the program has taken no such specific action. Because the two debuggers do things so differently here, we will give the source code once and treat the debugger procedures separately. The main program of DbgEx6 is

```
;; DbgEx6—The Stack and Separately Compiled Procedures
;;
INCLUDE   PCMAC.INC
          .MODEL SMALL
          .STACK 100h

          .CODE
DbgEx6    PROC
          EXTRN   PutDec : NEAR, EndL : NEAR
          mov     ax, @data ;   The standard prolog
          mov     ds, ax

          mov     ax, 1 ;       Numbers to be pushed in ax
          mov     cx, 5 ;       Number of numbers to push initially
PushLoop:
          push    ax
          add     ax, ax ;      Pushing 1, 2, 4, 8, 16
          loop    PushLoop
BP1:      pop     ax
          call    PutDec ;      Display 16
          call    EndL
          mov     cx, 3 ;       Number of numbers to pop
PopLoop:
          pop     ax
          call    PutDec ;      Display 8, 4, and 2
          call    EndL
          loop    PopLoop

BP2:      _Exit   0
DbgEx6    ENDP
          END     DbgEx6
```

Our pretty trivial separate subprocedure is the function EndL, which mimics the function of the C++ stream I/O operand endl and outputs a carriage return and line feed. It preserves the registers it uses, ax and dx:

```
;; ENDL.ASM—Output carriage return-line feed
;;
              .MODEL  SMALL
CR            EQU     13
LF            EQU     10
              .CODE
              PUBLIC  EndL
EndL          PROC
              push    ax
              push    dx
              _PutCh  CR, LF
              pop     dx
              pop     ax
              ret
EndL          ENDP
              END
```

Assemble each of these programs with the /Zi switch, and link with the command

```
link /co debugex6+Endl,,,util; or tlink /v debugex6+Endl,,,util
```

and enter the appropriate debugger via td or cv debugex6.

CodeView Procedure

1) Check the initial contents of the stack by entering **dw ss:sp L 2** in the command window. Note that sp = 0100, the stack is empty, and the entry at 0100 is garbage above the actual end of the stack.

2) Set breakpoints at BP1 and BP2 (double click left just below BP*n*, enter **bp** BP*n* in the command window, or move cursor to code window line just below BP*n* and hit **F9**). Set a breakpoint at the ret instruction EndL, **Alt-F**(ile Open **M**(odule **EndL** and set the breakpoint in one of the previous ways.

3) Go = Run (**F5**) to BP1 and observe the contents of the stack (**dw ss:sp L 5** in the command window). Note that there are five word entries on the stack now and that sp = 0100h − 2 × 5 = 00F6h.

4) Trace (**F8**) the pop instruction (highlight on call PutDec) and observe contents of the stack and ax. Is 0010h (= 16) still one word below sp (**dw ss:sp-2 L 10**)? The mysterious disappearance of 0010h will be (partially) explained at the end of this section.

5) Trace again on call PutDec. Note that we don't enter PutDec even though we used trace because PutDec (in util.lib) was translated without debugging information.

6) Trace through push dx in EndL and observe the contents of the stack, noting that 8, 4, 2, and 1 are still there. Recall from Section 6.3 that the call instruction pushes the address of the instruction following it onto the stack before jumping to the procedure. Write down the

current value of sp and the first few stack entries. Although EndL does several pushes and pops, it should be the same again after the next step

7) Run (**F5**) to the ret operation. Note the value of sp, which should be the same as it was at the end of Step 6. The stack contents should also be the same (**dw ss:sp L 4**). Delete the breakpoint at ret so the remaining calls to EndL will execute at full speed. (**F9** or click left twice on the highlighted line.)

8) Trace through the ret instruction and observe the stack (**dw ss:sp L 2** just before and **dw ss:sp L 1** just after ret). Note that just before the ret instruction, the current stack entry is the return address you identified in Step 6, and that ret pops it off the stack and into IP.

9) Run to BP2 and observe the output (**F4**) and the contents of the stack which should now be empty (sp = 0100h) again.

Turbo Debugger Procedure

1) As in Section III.2, arrange it so that the stack pane of the CPU window shows behind and to the right of the Module window. You should be showing about eight stack entries. Note that the stack entry indicating sp will be sp = 0100 and the value shown for it will be garbage above the actual end of the stack.

2) Set breakpoints at BP1 and BP2 (click left in the first two spaces on the line or **Alt-B**(reakpoint A(t... BP*n* or move cursor to line and hit **Alt-B**(reakpoint T(oggle or **F2**) and at the ret instruction in EndL (**Alt-V**(iew **M**(odule **EndL** and use one of the three previous methods).

3) Run (**F9**) to BP1 (note that the code window changes back to DbgEx6) observe the contents of the stack in the stack pane of the CPU window (see Section III.2 and step 1) above). Note that there are five word entries on the stack now and that sp = 0100h – 2 × 5 = 00F6h.

4) Trace (**F7**) the pop instruction and observe contents of stack and ax. Is 0010h (= 16) still in the 00F6h entry, one below sp? You may have to scroll the stack pane to see it. Activate the CPU window, TAB to the stack pane, and use the scroll bar or **PgDn** key. The mysterious disappearance of 0010h will be (partially) explained at the end of this section.

5) Trace again on call PutDec. Note that we don't enter PutDec even though we used trace because PutDec (in util.lib) was translated without debugging information.

6) Trace through push dx in EndL and observe the contents of the stack, noting that 8, 4, 2, and 1 are still there. Where is the *return address* for the call instruction that called PutDec? Recall from Section 6.3 that the call instruction pushes the address of the instruction following it onto the stack before jumping to the procedure) Write down the current value of sp and the first few stack entries. Although EndL does several pushes and pops, it should be the same again after the next step.

7) Run (**F9**) to the ret operation. Note the value of sp, which should be the same as it was at the end of Step 6. The stack contents should also be the same (CPU window). Delete the breakpoint at ret so the remaining calls to EndL will execute at full speed. Use **Alt-B**(reakpoint T(oggle or **F2**.

8) Trace through the ret instruction and observe the stack (CPU Window). Note that just before the ret instruction, the current stack entry is the return address you identified in step 5), and that ret pops it off the stack and into IP.

9) Run to BP2 and observe the output (**Alt-F5**) and the contents of the stack which should now be empty (sp = 0100h) again.

Why 0010h vanishes: (Actually, you may first ask "why doesn't it vanish?" since it has been popped from the top of the stack. Remember though that the pop instruction doesn't actually remove anything from memory. It merely *copies the* item and adds 2 to sp. Something in addition to the pop instruction is going on here.) Your program isn't the only thing that uses the stack. Every time an **interrupt** occurs, information gets pushed onto the stack, overwriting items previously popped from it. Therefore it isn't *surprising* that 0010h has disappeared, since interrupts are happening all the time (a pun, since the time clock causes interrupts). How could I be so *sure* that 0010h would be gone, though? Because the breakpoint mechanism is in fact an interrupt, so it's guaranteed that 0010h is gone! (For more details, see Chapter 15.)

III.5 • More on Debugger Example 6

This example uses DbgEx6 to demonstrate how to trace into code with no debugging information. We will trace into a call of PutDec in UTIL.LIB. Use the same DbgEx6.EXE file that you created in Section III.4, still with debugging information.

CodeView Procedure

1) Set breakpoints at BP1 and BP2 as in Section III.4.
2) Make sure you are viewing DbgEx6 in Source mode, **Alt-O**(ption **S**(ource1 Window... **S**(ource or hit **F3** until the Source1 window looks like your source code, with line numbers.
3) Recall from Section III.4 that if you Go (**F5**) to BP1 and Trace (**F8**) through the call PutDec instruction, you don't go into PutDec because it has no debugging information. You can check this fact again if you wish, then restart you program with **Alt-R**(un **R**(estart.
4) Change to assembly viewing mode, **Alt-O**(ption **S**(ource1 Window... **A**(ssembly or **F3** to a format with much less symbolic information. Run to BP1 and Trace. This time you will go *into* the PutDec procedure.
5) Restart the program (see Step 3). You will probably want to return the Source window to Source mode (**Alt-O**(ption **S**(ource1 Window... **S**(ource) or **F3**.
6) Set a breakpoint at PutDec (**bp** putdec in the command window). Hit Go (**F5**) twice, noticing the mode of the Source1 window.
7) Delete the breakpoint at PutDec by double-clicking on the highlighted line or moving the cursor to the highlighted line and hitting **F9**. Run again to breakpoint at BP2. What mode is the screen in now?

Turbo Debugger Procedure

1) Set breakpoints at BP1 and BP2 as in Section III.4. Make sure the Module window is active.
2) Recall from Section III.4 that if you Run (**F9**) to BP1 and Trace (**F7**) through the call PutDec instruction, you don't go into PutDec because it has no debugging information. You can check this fact again if you wish, then restart you program with **Alt-R**(un **P**(rogram Reset or **Ctrl-F2**.
3) Open the CPU Window using **Alt-V**(iew **C**(PU and make it the active window. Run to BP1 and Trace. This time you will go *into* the PutDec procedure. Notice that in the CPU window, much less symbolic information is shown for PutDec than for DbgEx6.
4) Restart the program (see Step 2) and close the CPU windowusing (**Alt-W**(indow **C**(lose or **Alt-F3**.
5) Set a breakpoint at PutDec using **Alt-B**(reakpoint **A**(t... PutDec. Hit Run (**F9**) twice and

note that a CPU window opens automatically at `PutDec`.

SUMMARY

When a program is made up of multiple source files, each can be assembled with debugging information and the various different source code files shown in the code window of the debugger for viewing and setting and clearing of breakpoints.

Tracing on a `call` instruction to a subprogram with debugger information causes the debugger to stop on the first statement of the subprogram. Stepping on a `call` instruction to a subprogram with debugger information reenters the debugger after returning from the `call`. If the subprogram has no debugger information, Trace and Step are identical in the Source1 window in Source format (CV) and in the Module window (TD)

If viewing from the Source1 window in Mixed or Assembly format (CV) or the CPU window (TD), Trace stops at the first instruction of the called subprogram whether or not there is debugger information for it. (In CV, change the Source window format to Assembly using **F3** repeatedly or **Alt-O**(ption **S**(ource1 Window... **S**(ource, **M**(ixed, or **A**(ssembly. In TD, **Alt-V**(iew **C**(PU.) Breakpoints can also be set at `PUBLIC` labels with bp (CV) or **Alt-B**(reakpoint **A**(t... (TD).

To view the stack in CV, use the command **dw ss:sp L n**, where **n** is the number of words from sp up that you wish to view. In TD, use the lower right-hand pane of the CPU window.

Chapter 7

Applying Assembly I: Numeric I/O

I/O of numbers turns out to be surprisingly difficult, because of the necessity of base conversion. (At the very lowest level, recall from Section 1.4 that '5' ≠ 5.) Numeric I/O is one of several ongoing themes in the book which we use to motivate and demonstrate various assembly language techniques. In this chapter we will develop simple versions of `GetDec` and `PutDec`. When we learn how to use arrays (Chapter 10), we will be able to improve on our techniques (Chapter 11). This chapter can be delayed until after Chapter 10, but should not be entirely omitted.

7.1 • PutDec I: Displaying Unsigned Numbers

We wish to convert from internal, binary representation, to external, decimal ASCII character representation. Since the computer is doing the computations in binary, we will use the method of **repeated division by 10**. One difficulty is that the digits appear in reverse order. Here, we will push all the digits as we compute them, then pop and display them one by one to get them in the correct order.

As a first pass, we are going to develop code to display an unsigned (binary) number in decimal. The resulting code will eventually become the procedure `PutUDec`, which is available in `UTIL.LIB`. Lest there be confusion, let us again emphasize that

> ## There is no detectable difference internally between signed and unsigned numbers.

A number is signed if it is treated as signed (for example, displayed with `PutDec`) and unsigned if it is treated as unsigned (for example, displayed with

PutUDec). A program can switch at will between these two interpretations (perhaps with disastrous results).

To help fix our ideas, let's look at an example. We will show how to display the binary number 1111011B as a decimal number. All of our numbers will be binary so the trailing Bs will be omitted. Long division in binary is the same as long division in decimal, except that the subtraction is in binary. Finally, to convert to displayable digits we recall from Section 1.4 that

$$\textbf{'n' = n + '0'} \qquad \textbf{for any digit n}$$

For example, '7' = 7 + '0'. We start of dividing by 1010B = 10 to find the last digit, '3':

```
              1100
      1010 ) 1111011
             1010
             ----
             1010
             1010
             ----
               011 + '0' = '3'
```

To find the remaining two digits we will divide twice more by 1010B, obtaining

```
            1                          0
   1010 ) 1100               1010 ) 1
          1010                       0
          ----                       -
            10 + '0' = '2'           1 + '0' = '1'
```

Thus if we display the digits in reverse order, we get '123', which is the decimal representation of 1111011B.

We will assume that at the start of the code the number to be displayed is in ax, placed there by the calling program. For unsigned numbers, all of the bits are numeric digits, so $0 \le ax \le 2^{16} - 1 = 65{,}535$. Therefore the number can be displayed using, at most, five decimal digits. For now we'll display exactly five digits, including any leading zeroes. The overall model of our program is

```
          mov   cx, 5 ;        Number of digits to compute
PushDigs:
          Get and push one digit
          loop  PushDigs

          mov   cx, 5 ;        Number of digits to display
PopDigs:
          Pop and display one digit
          loop  PopDigs
```

As we mentioned, 'Get and push...' will involve repeated division by 10, as follows:

```
ax, dx := ax / 10, ax mod 10
convert the digit in dl to ASCII
push    dx
```

The first line represents the simultaneous computation of the quotient and the remainder by the `div` instruction (which we use since the number is unsigned). We must push dx since only words can be pushed on the stack. We will ignore the `dh` half.

To convert the numeric value of a digit to its ASCII representation, we use n + '0' = 'n', that is,

```
add     dl, '0' ;      convert the digit in dl to ASCII
```

The code for *'Pop and display one digit'* is straightforward:

```
pop     dx
_PutCh dl
```

Adding the code above to the correct division code, we get

```
;; PUTUDEC.ASM—Display an unsigned number
;;    First version: display 5 digits
;;
        .MODEL SMALL
INCLUDE  PCMAC.INC
        PUBLIC PutUDec
PutUDec   PROC
;  save registers here
        mov     cx, 5 ;        Compute digits backwards
PushDigs:
        sub     dx, dx ;       Convert ax to unsigned double-word
        mov     bx, 10
        div     bx ;           ax, dx := ax div 10, ax mod 10
        add     dl, '0' ;      convert to ASCII
        push    dx
        loop    PushDigs

        mov     cx, 5 ;        Display digits in correct order
PopDigs:
        pop     dx
        _PutCh dl
        loop    PopDigs
;  restore registers here
        ret
PutUDec   ENDP
        END
```

We can create a simple test program TESTPUTU.ASM as follows:

```
              .MODEL SMALL
INCLUDE       PCMAC.INC
              .STACK 100h
              .DATA
              .CODE
              EXTRN    PutUDec : NEAR
TestPutU      PROC
              mov      ax, @data ;   (Not necessary as .DATA not used)
              mov      ds, ax
              mov      ax, 1234 ;    test case;
              call     PutUDec
              _Exit    0
TestPutU      ENDP
              END      TestPutU
```

If we start with ax = 1234, at successive executions of loop PushDigs we have

1.	ax = 123 dx = 4	cx = 5	Stack:	sp → '4'	↑ high addresses

2.	ax = 12 dx = 3	cx = 4	Stack:	'4' sp → '3'	↑ high addresses

3.	ax = 1 dx = 2	cx = 3	Stack:	'4' '3' sp → '2'	↑ high addresses

4.	ax = 0 dx = 1	cx = 2	Stack:	'4' '3' '2' sp → '1'	↑ high addresses

5.	ax = 0 dx = 0	cx = 1	Stack:	'4' '3' '2' '1' sp → '0'	↑ high addresses

Then at the successive executions of _PutCh we will have

1.	dx = '0'	cx = 5	Stack:	'4' '3' '2' sp → '1' '0'	↑ high addresses

2.   dx = '1'   cx =4   Stack: '4'
                                                          '3'
                                          sp →   '2'   ↑ high addresses
                                                          '1'
                                                          '0'

etc., and the digits will print in the correct order.

Note that we can improve the efficiency of the program by moving 10 into bx *before* the PushDigs loop, thus doing the mov only once.

Now that we have a program that works, let's try to generate output without the leading zeroes. That's fairly easy—we simply stop when ax becomes zero. The only tricky thing to worry about is that if ax was originally 0, we must print a leading zero (the only digit). Therefore we must always go through the push loop at least once, so it is a loop with the test at the end (like **repeat** … **until** in Pascal and **do … while** in C).

In the new version, instead of stopping the push loop by using a counter, we stop when ax = 0 and use cx to count the number of digits pushed. That way, in the second loop we can display only the digits we computed.

```
;;   Second attempt: no leading zeroes
;;
            . . .
            mov     cx, 0 ;         Count digits pushed
            mov     bx, 10
PushDigs:
            sub     dx, dx ;        Convert ax to unsigned double-word
            mov     bx, 10
            div     bx
            add     dl, '0'
            push    dx ;            (can push words only)
            inc     cx
            cmp     ax, 0
            jne     PushDigs
;
            mov     cx, 5
PopDigs:
            pop     dx
            _PutCh dl
            loop    PopDigs
```

As suggested in the comments in the original version, we need to save and restore the registers we use, which are now determined to be ax, bx, cx, and dx, so we add code as follows:

```
PutUDec     PROC
            push    ax ;            Save registers to be used
            push    bx
            push    cx
            push    dx
```

```
        mov     cx, 0 ;         Count digits pushed
        mov     bx, 10
PushDigs:
        ...                     etc.
        loop    PopDigs
        pop     dx ;            Restore saved registers
        pop     cx
        pop     bx
        pop     ax
        ret
PuUtDec ENDP
```

Notice that the PutUDec code itself also uses the stack, but that everything pushed onto the stack is popped off. By the time the ret instruction is executed, sp is back pointing at the return address.

The final version is

```
;; PUTUDEC.ASM—a procedure to display the contents of ax as an
;;  unsigned number in decimal
;;
INCLUDE     PCMAC.INC
            .MODEL SMALL
            .CODE
            PUBLIC PutUDec
PutUDec     PROC
            push    ax ;        Save Registers
            push    bx
            push    cx
            push    dx
            mov     cx, 0 ;     Initialize digit count
            mov     bx, 10 ;    Base of displayed number
PushDigs:
            sub     dx, dx ;    Convert ax to unsigned double-word
            div     bx
            add     dl, '0' ;   Compute the ASCII digit...
            push    dx ;        ...push it (can push words only)...
            inc     cx ;        ...and count it
            cmp     ax, 0 ;     Don't display leading zeroes
            jne     PushDigs
;
PopDigs:    ;                   Loop to display the digits
            pop     dx ;         (in reverse of the order computed)
            _PutCh dl
            loop    PopDigs

            pop     dx ;        Restore registers
```

```
                pop     cx
                pop     bx
                pop     ax
                ret
PutUDec         ENDP
                END
```

Reviewing the material of Chapter 6, to translate, link, and test PutUDec we would execute the statements

```
masm testputu;
masm putudec;
link testputu+putudec;
testputu
```

or

```
tasm testputu+putudec
tlink testputu+putudec
testputu
```

or

```
ml testputu.asm putudec.asm
testputu
```

7.2 • PutDec II: Turning `PutUDec` into `PutDec`

PutDec displays binary numbers interpreted as *signed* numbers. PutUDec gives us a good start on PutDec because the positive signed 16-bit numbers are the numbers in the range $0\ldots32{,}767 = 2^{15} - 1$, and numbers in this range are the same whether considered to be signed or unsigned. (They are simply the words whose leftmost bit is 0.) Therefore we could code PutDec as follows, using PutUDec to display positive signed numbers:

```
if (ax < 0) then
      Display('-')
      ax := -ax
end if
PutUDec(ax)
```

The difficulty is our old friend –32,768 the negative number which has no corresponding positive number—that is, –(–32,768) = –32,768 in 16-bit 2's complement. The simplest thing to do is just to treat –32,768 as a special case:

```
if (ax = -32768) then Display('-32768')
else
      if (ax < 0) then
            Display('-')
            ax := -ax
      end if
      PutUDec(ax)
```

```
end if
```

Putting the code above together with the PutUDec code, PutDec is

```
;; PUTDEC.ASM — a procedure PutDec which displays the contents of
;;   ax as a signed decimal number on the CRT.
;;
;;   call via:
;;          EXTRN   PutDec: NEAR
;;          mov     ax, theNumber
;;          call    PutDec
;;
                .MODEL SMALL
INCLUDE     PCMAC.INC
                .DATA
M32768      db          '-32768$'
                .CODE
                PUBLIC PutDec
PutDec      PROC
                push    ax
                push    bx
                push    cx
                push    dx
                cmp     ax, -32768 ; -32768 is a special case as there
                jne     TryNeg ;       is no representation of +32768
                _PutStr M32768
                jmp     Done
TryNeg:
                cmp     ax, 0 ;         If number is negative ...
                jge     NotNeg
                mov     bx, ax ;         save it from _PutCh
                neg     bx ;            make it positive and...
                _PutCh '-' ;            display a '-' character
                mov     ax, bx ;        To prepare for PushDigs
NotNeg:
                mov     cx, 0 ;         Initialize digit count
                mov     bx, 10 ;        Base of displayed number
PushDigs:
                sub     dx, dx ;        Convert ax to unsigned double-word
                div     bx
                add     dl, '0' ;       Compute the ASCII digit...
                push    dx ;            ...push it (can push words only)...
                inc     cx ;            ...and count it
                cmp     ax, 0 ;         Don't display leading zeroes
                jne     PushDigs
;
PopDigs: ;                              Loop to display the digits
```

```
                pop     dx ;                (in reverse of the order computed)
                _PutCh dl
                loop    PopDigs
    Done:
                pop     dx ;            Restore registers
                pop     cx
                pop     bx
                pop     ax
                ret
    PutDec      ENDP
                END
```

Exercises 7.2

1.   One push and one pop can be saved in PutDec by putting cmp ax, 0/jne PushDigs *before* push dx and displaying the first digit without popping. Such a change is tricky though because there might only be one digit and if we went into the PopDigs loop anyway, with cx = 0, we would loop 65,536 times or until something disastrous happened. Show how the change could be made *correctly*.

2.   How could PutDec be modified to display the input number in hex rather than decimal. (Hint: part of the problem is solved in Exercise 5.1—5. A better method will be introduced in Chapter 9.)

3.   Assuming you have the Space procedure from Exercise 6.4—1, show how PutDec could be modified to become a procedure PutRDec which takes as input a number in ax to be displayed and a number of columns in bx to display it in. The number is to be displayed right justified in the specified number of columns, with the full number being printed anyway even if bx isn't big enough. (Hint: you are going to want to insert a call to Space between PushDigs and PopDigs.)

4.   PutDec still works properly if the five lines of code from 'cmp ax, -32768' to 'TryNeg:' are omitted. Why? (Students find omitting the code confusing, and as a result I prefer to leave the lines in.)

7.3 • GetDec I: Reading a Number from the Keyboard

Next we will develop a version of GetDec, which reads in a decimal number typed at the keyboard and returns the binary version of that number in ax as its value; that is, GetDec acts like a **function**. As we mentioned earlier, in assembly language, a function is just a sub-procedure that returns a value (in ax if the value is small enough).

  We will read the digit characters one at a time using the _GetCh DOS call introduced in Section 5.5, which reads and echoes the character, leaving the resulting ASCII in al. We keep reading until a character which isn't a digit occurs. This character will be discarded.

  Translating an ASCII character into its numerical value is just the inverse of what we did in PutDec:

```
            _GetCh
    Check that al is a digit character
            sub     al, '0' ;      Value of digit read ==> al
```

```
mov     ah, 0 ;         Convert to a full word
```

Here we are doing a base conversion from decimal to binary, and the computer will be doing the arithmetic in binary, the destination base of the conversion. As we mentioned in Section 1.2, when we want to do a base conversion with arithmetic in the destination base, we use the multiplication method. Suppose we have read the digits '5', '2', and '4' so far, and have computed their value, which is, of course, 524. If we read another digit '3', the number we are trying to construct has the value 5243 = 524 * 10 + 3. Thus our pseudocode for each digit is

Read next digit and get its value;
new NumberValue := *old* NumberValue * 10 + *new digit value*

We can put our ideas together into the following pseudo-code loop:

```
NumberValue := 0
Read(character)
while character is a digit do
        Convert character to DigitValue
        NumberValue := NumberValue * 10 + DigitValue
        Read(next character)
end while
```

As is usual in loops like the one above, we need an extra Read(character) *outside* the loop because we read one more character than we use (but note that the unused character is the *last* one read, not the first).

It will turn out in the code that it is useful to be able to swap the contents of two registers, for which we can make use of the **exch**ange instruction:

```
xchg    reg/mem, reg/mem
```

As usual, the operands must be the same size—byte or word—and only one memory operand is allowed. For instance, if ax = 5 and bx = –14 and the instruction xchg ax, bx is executed, the result will be ax = –14 and bx = 5. It is not possible to exchange the contents of two memory locations directly, but it can be done with one xchg and two movs.

Exchanging memory locations A and B		
mov	ax, A ;	ax := old A
xchg	ax, B ;	B := old A, ax := old B
mov	A, ax ;	A := old B

The pseudocode above can be translated into the following assembly language:

```
;                       NumberValue   in bx
;                       character     in al
;                       DigitValue    in ax
;
        mov     bx, 0 ;         NumberValue := 0
```

```
                _GetCh ;                Read(character) (and echo)
ReadLoop:
                cmp     al, '0' ;       Is character a digit?
                jb      Done ;          No
                cmp     al, '9'
                ja      Done ;          No
                sub     al, '0' ;       Yes, convert to DigitValue & extend
                mov     ah, 0 ;           to word (to add it to NumberValue)
                xchg    ax, bx ;        Save DigitValue and get NumberValue
                mov     cx, 10 ;         in position to be multiplied by 10
                mul     cx ;            NumberValue * 10 ...
                add     bx, ax ;          ...+ DigitValue ==> NumberValue
                _GetCh
                jmp     ReadLoop
Done:
```

As we saw in Example 5.6—1, we can coalesce the two _GetCh macros calls, and we can also move the loop-invariant operation mov cx, 10 outside the loop. Now we have

```
                mov     bx, 0 ;         accumulated NumberValue in bx := 0
                mov     cx, 10
ReadLoop:
                _GetCh ;                Read character ==> al
~~ReadLoop:~~
                cmp     al, '0' ;       Is character a digit?

                        ...as before

                ~~mov     cx, 10~~

                        ...as before

                add     bx, ax ;                ...+ DigitValue ==> NumberValue
                ~~_GetCh~~
                jmp     ReadLoop
Done:
```

One minor problem with the program is that when _GetCh echoes a carriage return, it echoes *only* the carriage return, and doesn't add a line feed. To avoid overtyping the previous line, we add the following code after the label Done:

```
Done:
                cmp     al, 13 ;        If last char read was a RETURN...
                jne     NoLF
                _PutCh 10 ;             ...echo a matching line feed
NoLF:
```

We now have everything we want except the ability to read negative numbers. All we have to add is

```
Read(character)
if (character = '-') then
      remember that sign is -
      Read(character)
end if
process digits as before
if sign was negative then NumberValue := -NumberValue
```

Note that we don't allow an optional '+' sign. See Exercise 7.3—5.

Putting the code all together with the necessary boilerplate to make a separately compiled function, we get

```
;; GETDEC.ASM — a function to read a decimal number (with optional
;;  minus sign) from the keyboard and return the binary value in
;;  ax. There is no error checking
;;
;;        calling sequence:
;;        EXTRN  GetDec: NEAR
;;        call   GetDec ;      On return, number read is in ax
;;
          .MODEL SMALL
INCLUDE   PCMAC.INC
          .DATA
Sign      DB     ?
          .CODE
          PUBLIC GetDec
GetDec    PROC
          push   bx ;          Don't need to save ax, but bx,
          push   cx ;           cx, dx must be saved and restored
          push   dx
          mov    bx, 0 ;       accumulated NumberValue in bx := 0
          mov    cx, 10
          mov    Sign, 0 ;     Guess there will be no sign
          _GetCh ;             Read character ==> al
          cmp    al, '-' ;     Is first character a minus sign?
          jne    AfterRead
          mov    Sign, '-' ;   yes
ReadLoop:
          _GetCh
AfterRead:
          cmp    al, '0' ;     Is character a digit?
          jb     Done ;        No
          cmp    al, '9'
          ja     Done ;        No
```

```
              sub    al, '0' ; Yes, cvt to DigitValue and extend to a
              mov    ah, 0 ;     word (so we can add it to NumberValue)
              xchg   ax, bx ;      Save DigitValue
                     ;               and set up NumberValue for mul
              mul    cx ;        NumberValue * 10 ...
              add    bx, ax ;    ... + DigitValue ==> NumberValue
              jmp    ReadLoop
Done:
              cmp    al, 13 ;    If last char read was a RETURN...
              jne    NoLF
              _PutCh 10 ;        ...echo a matching line feed
NoLF:
              cmp    Sign, '-'
              jne    Positive
              neg    bx ;        Final result is in bx
Positive:
              mov    ax, bx ;    Returned value —> ax
              pop    dx ;        restore registers
              pop    cx
              pop    bx
              ret
GetDec        ENDP
              END
```

Note that the beginning of ReadLoop is a little intricate as we may jump into the loop after its beginning if the first character read isn't a minus sign. Jumping into the middle of a loop is usually prohibited in high-level languages, and we can see why given the murkiness of the above code.

Exercises 7.3

1. Fill in the contents of the specified registers in the following code as four hex-digit numbers:

```
              mov    ax, 1234h
              xchg   ah, al ;    ax = _____
              mov    ax, 1234h
              mov    bx, 5678h
              xchg   ax, bx ;    ax = _____
       ;                         bx = _____
              mov    ax, 1234h
              mov    bx, 5678h
              xchg   ah, bl ;    ax = _____ ✓
       ;                         bx = _____ ✓
              mov    ax, 1111h
              mov    bx, 2222h
              mov    cx, 3333h
              xchg   ax, bx
```

```
        xchg    ax, cx ;        ax = _____,
    ;                           bx = _____
    ;                           cx = _____
```

2. Write assembly code to exchange the values of ax and bx using only
    a) the mov instruction and another register, say dx,
    b) the push and pop instructions and no extra registers.

3. Write a test program for GetDec which asks the user for a number, reads the number with GetDec, and displays the result with PutDec, then loops back up and repeats the process. You can terminate the program with Ctrl-C, which isn't elegant but is effective.

4. Why can't we declare

```
    Sign    DB    0
```

and omit the line mov Sign, 0 from the program?

5. Show how GetDec could be modified to also allow an optional '+' sign before a (positive) number.

6. Show how to alter GetDec so that it skips over initial blank and tab (= 9) characters before reading the number.

7. Show how to alter GetDec so that you don't have to jump inside ReadLoop after either possibility for the sign test. (Hint: move _GetCh to the end of the loop.)

8. ✓ (Hard, but valuable) There is no error checking in the version of GetDec given here. For instance, you can type in '923653487' or 'x' (no digits) or '–x' (sign but no digits) and GetDec will present you with some sort of answer. As was mentioned in Example 5.3—4, the sophisticated version of GetDec in util.lib returns with the carry flag set (= 1) if there was an error, clear (= 0) if not. Alter the version of GetDec developed above so that it too returns with the carry flag set or cleared in that way. The instructions for clearing and setting the carry flag are, respectively, clc and stc (no operands). Example 5.3—4 shows how the caller tests the carry flag with jc or jnc.
    (Hint: when you multiply by 10, the answer will be entirely in ax if there is no overflow—that is, OF = 0. When you add a digit value, you should never get a carry. Before setting the sign, the result should be positive, except when it equals 8000h (= –32768), in which case the Sign byte should indicate a negative number. Count digits as you go and indicate an error if no digits occurred.)

Programming Problem 7.1

Write a program MilTime which displays the time of day in the form

```
    The time is hhmm hours
```

using the military (24-hour) clock. To display pairs of digits, write a separately assembled procedure `TwoDigit` which takes as input a number between 0 and 99 in `al` and displays it as exactly two digits at the current cursor position. Thus if the input is 0, 5, or 14, the characters displayed will be 00, 05, and 14, respectively. ***Do not use `PutDec` to construct `TwoDigit`.*** `TwoDigit` doesn't even require a loop.

The time is returned by the DOS get time call (function 2ch, `PCMAC.INC` macro `_GetTime` with no parameters) as follows: `ch` = hour (0 to 23), `cl` = minute (0 to 59), `dh` = second (0 to 59), `dl` = hundredth of second (0 to 99).

An alternate problem is a program `RegTime` which displays the time in the form

```
The time is hh:mm AM or PM
```

`PutDec` is used to print hours and `TwoDigit` to print minutes. 12 must be subtracted from hours greater than 13, hour 0 must be changed to 12 AM, etc.

In either case, test your function by comparing its results with the DOS `TIME` command. (Type Enter after invoking `TIME` to avoid changing the time.)

Programming Problem 7.2

Write a program `RevLine` which reads and echoes one line of input from the keyboard and then displays the line, reversed, on the line following. A sample execution is

```
C> revline
Enter a line: backward
Reversed: drawkcab
```

Hint: Push each character as it is read and echoed. When you've read the whole line, pop and `_PutCh` each character from the stack. How do you know when you're done? One easy way is to save the initial value of `sp` before you start pushing characters.

SUMMARY

Digits are converted between binary and ASCII using the formula

$$'n' = n + '0'$$

`PutDec` and `PutUDec` use the division method of base conversion to convert from binary to decimal, and use the stack to reverse the order of the digits.

`GetDec` uses the multiplication method to convert from decimal to binary.

We introduced the new instruction

```
xchg  dest1, dest2 ;  exchange operands
```

`dest1` and `dest2` can be register or memory; at least one must be a register. Both operands must be the same size.

In Exercise 7.3—7 we also introduced

```
stc    ;              Set carry flag (to 1)
clc    ;              Clear carry flag
```

In Programming Problem 7.1 we introduced the DOS macro

```
_GetTime
```

which returns the time as follows: ch = hour(0-23), cl = minute, dh = second, and dl = hundredth of second.

Chapter **8**

Writing Macros and Program Testing

In this chapter we will learn how to define macros such as _PutStr and _PutCh. This chapter could have occurred much earlier, could be delayed much later, or could be skipped entirely. The material here is used only for occasional discrete uses. Chapter 16, which extends the material discussed here can be skipped too. The reason I've placed this chapter here is that we are going to use the testing of PutDec, whose code was developed in the last chapter, as an extended example of macro techniques. You don't need to have worked through that code to understand this example.

On the other hand, writing and using macros is a powerful way to make programs easier to write, easier to read, and more accurate.

8.1 • Writing Simple Macros

Every macro has a single **macro declaration**, and zero or more **macro invocations**. The invocations must occur physically after the declaration. (The file PCMAC.INC is essentially just a list of macro declarations.) The diagram at the top of the next page shows the declaration of a single macro MacDef and three invocations of MacDef.

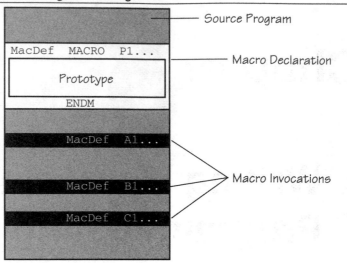

8.1.1 • Macro Declarations

The general form of a macro declaration is

```
MacroName MACRO    Macro Parameter List
          . . .
          Prototype of the macro
          . . .
          ENDM
```

The **prototype** of the macro is a sequence of 'real' machine instructions (or other macro invocations!) which will replace every invocation of `MacroName`.

Example 8.1—1. A simple form of the `_PutStr` macro could be declared as follows:

```
_PutStr    MACRO  aString
           mov    dx, OFFSET aString
           mov    ah, 09h
           int    21h
           ENDM
```

The two `mov` and one `int` instruction form the prototype. The character '_' is just another character in the macro name and could be used in any macro. However we will reserve the initial '_' for DOS and BIOS call macros, to make it easier to recognize them.

A macro invocation has the form

```
MacroName    Actual Parameters to the Macro
```

In effect, in the first phase of assembling a source program, all macro *declarations* in the program are removed from the program (and placed, temporarily, in a table of macros used by the assembler). At each macro *invocation*, the prototype text replaces the invocation text, with `Actual Parameters to the Macro` replacing the parameters in `Macro Parameter List`, as we see symbolically represented in the diagram below. The legend 'Prototype(P1 ← X)' represents the result of textual substitution of X for P1 in 'Prototype' and is called **macro expansion**. It is performed by the assembler as one of its first acts.

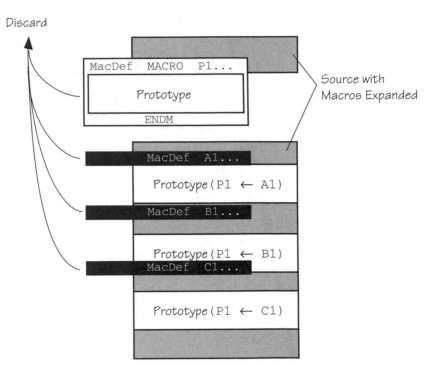

Macro declarations can appear almost anywhere before they are used, but it is probably best to put them at the beginning of the program, before .STACK and .DATA.

8.1.2 • Macro Expansion

As a trivial example, suppose we define the macro AddUp as follows:

```
AddUp       MACRO    A, B, SUM
            mov      ax, A
            add      ax, B
            mov      SUM, ax
            ENDM
```

Then an invocation of the form

```
            AddUp    3, bx, Total
```

would assemble exactly as if we had written

```
mov     ax, 3
add     ax, bx
mov     Total, ax
```

Notice that if AddUp is invoked, say, 20 times in the program, it will generate exactly 60 machine instructions in the final program.

Actual parameters in a macro invocation are normally separated by commas, but blanks and tabs can also be used.

If a macro invocation has more parameters than the declaration, the extra parameters are ignored. If it has fewer parameters, the extra parameters in the declaration are set to the empty string.

MASM issues a *warning* if too many actual parameters are used.

For instance if we declare

```
DecBytes MACRO  A, B, Symbol
Symbol   DB     A DUP (B) ; A copies of B
         ENDM
```

the invocation

```
DecBytes 100, ?, Stuff, MoreStuff
```

expands to the code

```
Stuff    DB     100 DUP (?)
```

while the invocation

```
DecBytes 100, 'ABCDE'
```

expands to the code

```
DB     100 DUP ('ABCDE')
```

8.1.3 • Parameter Parentheses

Blanks, tabs, and commas act as parameter separators, so if you want to include them within a single parameter, you must enclose the parameter in **parameter parentheses**, a matched set of < … > parentheses. Thus 10 DUP(3, 5) is three parameters, '10', 'DUP(3', and '5)', while <10 DUP(3, 5)> is the single parameter '10 DUP(3, 5)'. Note that one outer set of parameter parentheses is removed before the parameter is actually passed to the macro.

For instance the invocation

```
DecBytes 100, 5 DUP (3)
```

would produce the code

```
DUP       DB       100 DUP (5)
```

which probably is not what was intended. If we use

```
DecBytes 100, <5 DUP (3)>
```

we get

```
DB       100 DUP (5 DUP (3))
```

The invocation

```
DecBytes <13, 10, 5>, <'a Line', 13, 10>, Stuff
```

expands to the code

```
Stuff     DB       13, 10, 5 DUP ('a Line', 13, 10)
```

Having blanks act as parameter separators can be very confusing. For instance,

```
10 DUP(5)            is two parameters
10 DUP (5)           is three parameters
10 DUP ( 5 )         is five parameters
```

and 10DUP(5) is one parameter, but will probably generate illegal code. In the interest of safety, follow the general rule:

Surround complicated macro parameters with < > parentheses.

<10 DUP(5)>, <10 DUP (5)>, and <10 DUP (5)> all constitute a single parameter, and will probably all translate as the programmer intended.

The rest of this section involves a subtle point concerning macros calling macros, and can be skipped for now.

Suppose that bMac is a macro which invokes the macro aMac using one of its (bMac's) parameters:

```
bMac      MACRO aPar
          ...
          aMac    aPar ;          DANGEROUS
          ...
          ENDM
```

The aMac call is dangerous because you have no way of telling if aPar is complicated. For instance, the statement bMac <10 DUP(5)> invokes bMac with a *single* parameter, 10 DUP(5) (the assembler strips off the outermost set of statement parentheses). Then in the aMac invocation, aPar becomes *two* parameters, because of the embedded blank! If the bMac user knew about the internal usage of the parameter, he or she could use the statement bMac <<10 DUP(5)>>, but there isn't much point in using macros if you have to know detailed contents of their code. A safer solution is

---

Whenever a macro parameter is passed as a parameter to an inner macro, it should be enclosed in < > parentheses.

A safe version of bMac is

```
bMac      MACRO  aPar
          . . .
          aMac   <aPar> ;       Safe--Note <>
          . . .
          ENDM
```

The code

```
          bmac   <10 DUP(5)>
```

will generate the code

```
          . . .
          aMac   <10 DUP(5)>
          . . .
```

At this point worrying about blanks in parameters may seem inconsequential, but as we go on, parameters will tend to get more and more complicated, and blanks may well creep in.

8.1.4 • Local Symbols

When a label is defined within a macro, problems arise. For example if we define the macro

```
Max       MACRO  A, B
          mov    ax, A
          cmp    ax, B
          jge    noChange
          mov    ax, B
noChange:
          ENDM
```

and if Max is invoked twice in the same file,

```
          Max    X, 100
          . . .
          Max    Y, 0
```

the following code is generated:

```
                mov     ax, X
                cmp     ax, 100
                jge     noChange
                mov     ax, 100
      noChange:
                . . .
                mov     ax, Y
                cmp     ax, 0
                jge     noChange
                mov     ax, 0
      noChange:
```

That is, the label noChange is multiply defined, which is an error. Most macro languages have a mechanism for generating unique labels to take care of this problem. In MASM and TASM, this mechanism is the LOCAL pseudo-operation used immediately after the MACRO statement. If we write

```
Max           MACRO   A, B
              LOCAL   noChange
              mov     ax, A
              cmp     ax, B
              jge     noChange
              mov     ax, B
    noChange:
              ENDM
```

Each time the Max macro is invoked, noChange is replaced by a unique symbol which is constant throughout that one macro invocation, but different for every other local symbol and in every other macro invocation. (The actual symbol chosen is of the form ??nnnn where nnnn is a four digit decimal number starting at 0.) It is possible to have multiple local symbols in a single macro, as in the macro Clip that constrains its first parameter to lie between its second and third:

```
Clip          MACRO   A, LOW, HIGH
              LOCAL   changeIt, Done
              mov     ax, LOW
              cmp     ax, A
              jg      changeIt
              mov     ax, High
              cmp     A, ax
              jle     Done
    changeIt:
              mov     A, ax
    Done:
              ENDM
```

The first time Clip is invoked, changeIt will be replaced by ??0000 and Done by ??0001. The second time, changeIt will be replaced by ??0002 and Done by ??0003. If then Max is invoked, noChange will be replaced by ??0004, and so forth.

Example 8.1—2. Recall the PutHexxe subprogram of Chapter 6. It is an example of reused code, so it is reasonable to ask if it can be done with a macro, and if so, *whether the subprogram or macro method is superior.* As with most such questions in computer science, the answer will be 'it all depends.' (The question is a loaded one because there wouldn't be two common methods to do the same thing if there weren't strong reasons for doing each on different occasions!)

Recall that PutHexxe is like PutHex except that it displays a leading '0' if the hex number would start with a letter (A–F) and always displays a trailing 'h'. Testing for the leading zero, we have the code

```
        cmp     ax, 0A000h
        jb      noZero ;        Note unsigned compare
        _PutCh '0' ;            Add leading zero
        . . .
noZero:
```

which could cause noZero to be multiply defined. Therefore we should make noZero a LOCAL symbol and define the macro as follows:

```
;; PutHexxe as a macro.
PutHexxe  MACRO   theNumber
          LOCAL   noZero
          mov     ax, theNumber
          cmp     ax, 0A000h
          jb      noZero ;        Note unsigned compare
          push    ax
          _PutCh '0'
          pop     ax ;            _PutCh destroyed ax
noZero:
          EXTRN   PutHex : NEAR ; just in case
          call    PutHex
          _PutCh 'h'
          ENDM
```

Notes:

- We have used a macro (_PutCh) within a macro. Thus the user has to know to INCLUDE PCMAC.INC. The safest way to get around that requirement would be to replace internal macro calls with the actual code.
- The macro destroys ax and dx, the latter via _PutCh, which is not evident on its surface. Perhaps it should push and pop these registers just as the subprogram PutHexxe did.

These remarks point up a general problem with macros:

Macros are more dangerous than subprograms.

In a macro, we have neither the degree of isolation nor the degree of control that we have in subprograms.

8.1.5 • Parameter Separator (&)

The parameter separator is in some sense the opposite of parameter parentheses <>. Parameter parentheses allow us to combine into a single parameter things that would normally be separate parameters—blanks, commas, etc.—when we invoke a macro. The parameter separator '&' allows us to separate parts of text in a macro prototype in order to recognize parameters that normally wouldn't be seen by the assembler. One use of the parameter separator is to allow the insertion of parameters in character strings. For instance if we declare

```
DolStr    MACRO  lab, par      ; BAD DEFINITION
lab       DB     'par', '$'
          ENDM
```

and invoke the macro with the statement 'DolStr A, <A String>', the code generated is

```
A         DB     'par', '$'
```

which clearly isn't what was intended. The problem is that the macro expander doesn't look inside quote marks for parameters. By using the parameter separator '&' though, we can inform the assembler that we are beginning or ending a parameter. A correct definition of DolStr would be

```
DolStr    MACRO  lab, par      ; GOOD DEFINITION
lab       DB     '&par&', '$'
          ENDM
```

Now the same invocation as before produces

```
A         DB     'A String', '$'
```

Whenever the slightest doubt arises, it is a good idea to surround parameters in prototypes with '&' symbols.

8.1.6 • Assembly Listings

If you want to see what code is actually produced by macros, you can look at the **assembly listing**. As I mentioned in Section 4.4, the command

```
masm or tasm afile,,afile;
```

(note two consecutive commas) will assemble a file AFILE.ASM and produce a listing file AFILE.LST, which will include the final lines of macro expansions. In MASM (6.0 and later) we can get the same result by entering

```
ml /Fl afile.asm
```

The resulting .LST file can be printed with the DOS PRINT command or viewed with your text editor.

Exercises 8.1

1. Suppose that we have declared

    ```
    MoreBytes MACRO  A, B, C, D
    A         DB     B, C, D
              ENDM
    ```

    What code is produced by the following macro invocations?

    ```
                MoreBytes ABC, 12, 'x', 13

                MoreBytes DEF, 10 DUP (?), Y, Z  ✔

                MoreBytes DEF, <10 DUP (?)>, Y, Z  ✔

                MoreBytes GHI, 1, 2, 3, 4, 5, 6

                MoreBytes , 'A', 'B', 'C'  ✔
    ```

2. ✔ Suppose that we have declared

    ```
    Display    MACRO  A
               mov    dl, A
               int    21h
               ENDM
    Display2   MACRO  C1, C2
               mov    ah, 02h
               Display <C1>
               Display <C2>
               ENDM
    ```

    What code is produced by the following macro invocation?

    ```
                Display2 13, 10
    ```

    Note that Display will be expanded also.

3. a) ✔ The macro Abs aValue defined below generates code to replace aValue by its absolute value. What is wrong with the definition and how should it be fixed? (Hint: try part b) with the uncorrected version.)

```
Abs        MACRO  aValue
           cmp    aValue, 0
           jge    valPos
           neg    aValue
valPos:
           ENDM
```

b) ✓ Show how the corrected `Abs` macro will cause the following code to be expanded:

```
Abs    ax
Abs    dl
Abs    MemLoc
```

c) Write a macro `Sign aValue` which replaces `aValue` with its sign: 1 if `aValue` > 0, 0 if `aValue` = 0, and −1 if `aValue` < 0.

4. Write a macro `BoxRow LeftEnd, Middle, NumMid, Rightend` which displays the character `LeftEnd`, then `NumMid` copies of the character `Middle`, and finally the character `RightEnd` followed by a carriage return and line feed. Use `BoxRow` to provide a simplified version of Example 5.3—3.

5. '&'s are also useful when one wants to concatenate parameters with each other or other text. Rewrite the macro

```
IfTest     MACRO  A, Rel, B, TrueDest
           cmp    A, B
           jRel   TrueDest ;    INCORRECT!
           ENDM
```

so that the invocation

```
IfTest XYZ, ge, 100, XYZBig
```

produces the code

```
cmp    XYZ, 100
jge    XYZBig
```

8.2 • An Extended Example: Program Testing

Program testing is a somewhat controversial subject in the academic community. Edsger Dijkstra, perhaps the most prominent computer scientist of our time, has said that testing can only show the presence of bugs, not their absence. Consider for instance a program which simply multiplies two 16-bit numbers. There are $2^{16} \times 2^{16} \approx 4{,}000{,}000{,}000$ possible sets of data to be tested. Even if we do a million test cases, we have still tested only a statistically insignificant 0.025% of the possibilities. Clearly something more than just brute testing is required to construct correct programs, and therefore various methods of reliable program construction (such as structured programming) and theoretical proof of program correctness have been proposed.

On the other hand, all but the most doctrinaire would probably agree that some testing is essential. After all, no matter how carefully programs are constructed and their validity proven, humans make errors too, and *proving* even fairly simple programs correct is an incredibly complex undertaking. Also, programs often treat many different sets of data with the same code, so testing can increase our confidence in the code much more than the actual number of test cases would indicate, even though that confidence should never be complete.

In this section we will discuss a reasonable *minimum* plan for program testing, and show how it can be applied to testing `PutDec` from Chapter 7.

We should choose sets of data for testing a program which at least satisfy the following conditions:

- Every instruction in the program should be executed in at least one test. (See Section 3.4: If you haven't tested it, it doesn't work.)
- Test boundary values—largest and smallest values and values on either side of a place where the treatment of the data changes. These values are places where 'off by one' errors commonly occur.
- Test some 'random' values between the boundaries. Often a programmer's preconceived notions of how a program is supposed to work or how it is 'normally' used causes important test conditions to be omitted.

There can of course be some overlap in values chosen to meet these criteria.

Trying these values doesn't by any stretch of the imagination guarantee that the program is bug-free, but it will increase our confidence in the program. Such tests are often described as **stupid not to**, since if the program eventually fails in such simple ways, the programmer looks like a real idiot!

Once the test cases are chosen, they should be kept as a suite of tests to be performed *in its entirety* every time the program is changed. Complete retesting in this way is known as **regression testing**. Almost every programmer has experienced the situation where fixing one problem causes another, and has said at least once 'but the change I made here couldn't possibly have affected that problem over there.' When a bug is uncovered and fixed, code to test whether the bug is present should be added to the test suite so that future regression testing will detect if a future change unfixes the bug.

Ideally, the test suite should itself check that its tests are correct. Such automation helps to eliminate human error, simplifies the testing process, and makes it more likely that regression testing will actually be applied.

Example 8.2—1. Design a test suite for `PutDec`.

Unfortunately, a program like `PutDec` can't be entirely self-testing, because some human has to look at the output. (We could presumably write the results to a file and then read the file and check that the numbers were written correctly, but we would end up with a test program that was more complicated than the program it was testing!) From the conditions above, we can choose test values to be displayed as follows:

- To exercise every instruction, we need to include –32768, some other negative value, and a positive value.

- To check boundaries, we need to check –32767 and –1 (the boundary values of the negative numbers) and 0 and 32767 (the boundary values of the nonnegative numbers). I would also test 1, as displaying 0 is often something of a special case and we want to make sure we can display the smallest positive number without leading zeroes.
- For random values, I would pick in-between values with all possible numbers of digits and each digit occurring at least once: –12345, –864, –9, 10, 1057. Note that with these five values I will also be testing that non-leading zeroes can be printed. I haven't tested all possible lengths in both positive and negative numbers on the (hopeful) assumption that once we have handled the sign, positive and negative intermediate values are handled the same.

Thus our set of test data is –32768, –32767, –12345, –864, –9, –1, 0, 1, 10, 1057, 32767, and our testing program `TestProg` will consist of the sequence

```
mov ax, aNumber
call PutDec
_PutCh 13, 10
```

for each *aNumber* to be tested. (We inserted a carriage return/line feed pair to be able to separate consecutive test outputs.) Copying these three lines eleven times, inserting the appropriate numbers, would require writing 33 lines of uninteresting code. Even if we made a procedure of the common part (the second and third lines), we would have to write 22 repetitive lines of the form `mov ax, aNumber`/`call theProcedure`. Writing our own macro can cut down the dog-work to writing eleven, mostly non-repetitive, lines.

Example 8.2—2: A simple test program for `PutDec`.

```
;; TESTPROG.ASM — Example 8.2-2, a test suite for the
;;  PutDec procedure
INCLUDE    PCMAC.INC

DispNum    MACRO  aNumber
           mov    ax, aNumber
           call   PutDec
           _PutCh 13, 10
           ENDM

           .MODEL SMALL
           .STACK 100h
           .DATA
           .CODE
           EXTRN  PutDec: NEAR
TestProg   PROC
           mov    ax, @data
           mov    ds, ax
           DispNum -32768
           DispNum -32767
           DispNum -12345
```

```
                DispNum -864
                DispNum -9
                DispNum -1
                DispNum 0
                DispNum 1
                DispNum 10
                DispNum 1057
                DispNum 32767
                _Exit  0
     TestProg   ENDP
                END    TestProg
```

When `TestProg` is run, the output will consist of eleven lines of numbers, and it will require reference back to the source code to determine if the program is working correctly. It might be helpful if each test could display the number as it was *supposed* to appear as well as the way `PutDec` displayed it:

```
        supposed-to-print=actually-printed
        . . .
```

thus making it easy to check the results without reference to the source code of `TestProg`.

Example 8.2—3. Alter `DispNum` macro so that the 'num = num' form above is displayed. The altered macro is

```
     DispNum    MACRO  aNumber ;; second version
                LOCAL  NumMsg
                .DATA ; Switch temporarily back to the .DATA section
     NumMsg     DB     '&aNumber& = $'
                .CODE ; Switch back to the .CODE section
                _PutStr NumMsg
                mov    ax, &aNumber&
                call   PutDec
                _PutCh 13, 10
                ENDM
```

A version of the test program using this macro is in `TESTPRG2.ASM` in `CHAP08` on the disk that comes with this book. Now the statement

```
        DispNum 123
```

displays the line

```
        123 = 123
```

Notes:

- The label `NumMsg` must be declared `LOCAL` or it will be multiply defined (eleven times in `TestProg`).
- As was mentioned in Chapter 6, one can switch back and forth between `.CODE` and `.DATA` segments of the program at will. Schematically, repeated use of the `DispNum` macro will generate the following code

```
.DATA
aaaa
.CODE
AAAA
.DATA
bbbb
.CODE
BBBB
.DATA
cccc
.CODE
CCCC
. . . .
```

The assembler collects the `.DATA` pieces and the `.CODE` pieces and assembles them as though they had been written

```
.DATA
aaaa
bbbb
cccc
. . . .
.CODE
AAAA
BBBB
CCCC
. . . .
```

- The parameter separator '&' is used so that the assembler can 'see' the parameter `aNumber` inside quotes. If we had written

```
NumMsg    DB      'aNumber = $'
```

instead, the invocation

```
DispNum 123
```

would produce the line

```
aNumber = 123
```

Exercises 8.2

1. Write a macro Mesg which can be invoked by the line

$$\textit{Mesg} \quad \textit{<any old thing, whatever>}$$

and when executed will print the line

$$\textit{any old thing, whatever}$$

Mesg will have to switch to the .DATA region and use DB to declare storage containing the message '*any old thing, whatever*.' (Note the use of < > parentheses to allow the use of blanks, etc., in a single parameter.)

2. ✓ Write a macro ErrMsg errNo, returnVal which displays the message

$$\textit{*** ERROR errNo ***}$$

and _Exit s with a returned value of returnVal. (errNo is of course replaced by the actual value used in the macro call.)

8.3 • Pseudo-Macros for Repetition

Our assemblers have three **pseudo-macros** which expand a prototype repeatedly at the position in the code where the pseudo-macro occurs. They constitute a sort of an immediate macro definition. The three operations are

```
REPT   n      REPeaT n times
IRP           Indefinite RePeat.
IRPC          Indefinite RePeat Characters
```

Each has the general form of usage

```
        OP Parameters
...prototype...
        ENDM
```

where *OP* is one of IRP, IRPC, and REPT, and *prototype* is to be expanded repeatedly *at this position in the source file*. Note that the three pseudo-macros cause code to be generated at the place (and only at the place) where they occur, while a macro definition *never* causes code to be generated at the place where it occurs.

The simplest of the pseudo-macros is REPT which merely repeats the prototype *n* times

```
        REPT    n
...prototype...
        ENDM
```

with no parameter substitution. For instance,

```
DB      20 DUP (5, 3, ?, 18, 10)
```

can also be generated by the instructions

```
REPT    20
DB      5, 3, ?, 18, 10
ENDM
```

Using REPT instead of DUP can be convenient for a long data sequence. However REPT is even more useful in conjunction with the '=' pseudo-operation, which we now introduce.

The '=' pseudo-operation is written in a form similar to the EQUate pseudo-operation:

label = *expression* (must evaluate to a constant at assembly time)

As with EQU, a *label* defined with '=' needs no other declaration, and the value exists and is known only while the program is being assembled, not while the program is being run (unless the value is explicitly saved for run-time by being used in code or data definition.) The differences between = and EQU are that

- A *label* defined with the '=' pseudo-operation can be redefined arbitrarily often, whereas EQUates cannot be redefined. Among other things,

  ```
  label = label + 1 ;              is legal
  ```

  (and increments the current value of *label* during assembly by 1) but

  ```
  label      EQU     label + 1;    is ILLEGAL
  ```

  If *label* isn't previously defined, it is undefined here, and if it is previously defined, it is now multiply defined. When assigned by '=', the current value of *label* is the one most recently assigned as the source is processed line by line.

- EQUates can be used to give symbolic names to character strings, while '=' can be used only for numeric values. Thus

  ```
  aThing    EQU    BYTE PTR B ; is legal
  ```

  but

  ```
  aThing = BYTE PTR B ;            is ILLEGAL!!!
  ```

Example 8.3—1. Use '=' and REPT to generate the lowercase alphabet in 26 consecutive bytes of memory.

```
Letter = 'a'
          REPT    26
          DB      Letter
Letter = Letter + 1
          ENDM
```

The code above works as follows: The first line assigns the *number* 97 (the ASCII value of 'a') to Letter, and therefore the lines of code

```
          DB      97
          DB      98
          DB      99
    ...etc.
          DB      122
```

are generated.

The other two pseudo-macros allow for more flexibility. For instance, writing

```
          IRP     param, <x1, x2, ... xn>
    ...prototype containing &param&...
          ENDM
```

causes the prototype to be expanded here *n* times, first with param set to *x1*, then with it set to *x2*, ..., then *xn*. Each *xi* can be any character string legal as a macro parameter—in particular, any string not containing a blank, comma, or tab. It is as if we had declared

```
TempMacro MACRO param
    ...prototype containing &param&...
          ENDM
```

and then coded

```
          TempMacro x1
          TempMacro x2
          ...
          TempMacro xn
```

Example 8.3—2. Entry to and exit from procedures often requires saving and restoring of multiple registers, which can be done easily using IRP. For instance,

```
          IRP     aReg, <ax, bx, cx, dx>
          push    &aReg&
          ENDM
```

generates the code

```
                push    ax
                push    bx
                push    cx
                push    dx
```

Example 8.3—3. We can use `IRP` to output a sequence of decimal numbers. The code

```
aNumb       DW      123
aNother     DW      -5
            . . .
            mov     bx, 884
            IRP     DecNum, <aNumb, aNother, bx, -222>
            mov     ax, &DecNum&
            call    PutDec
            _PutCh  ' '
            ENDM
            . . .
```

would produce the output

```
123 -5 884 -222
```

Example 8.3—4. We can use `IRP` to automate test generation in `TestProg` in Example 8.2—2:

```
        IRP     num, <-32768,-32767,-12345,-864,-9,-1,0,1,10,...>
        DispNum &num&
        ENDM
```

(The actual numbers must be supplied in place of the dots, of course.)

In cases where each value to be substituted is a single character, the shorter form `IRPC` can be used. It is of the form

```
        IRPC    param, string-of-characters
    ...prototype containing &param&...
        ENDM
```

`IRPC` works like `IRP` except that each character in *string-of-characters* is treated as a separate value for `param`. *String-of-characters* is not surrounded by quotes, but if it contains blanks or commas it must be surrounded by < >.

Example 8.3—2 (revisited). The `IRP` statement in the first part of this example can be rewritten

```
        IRPC    regLet, abcd
        push    &regLet&x
        ENDM
```

Note that the '&' character between `regLet` and `x` is necessary as otherwise 'regLetx' will appear to be a single identifier, and that the `IRPC` form of the macro wouldn't work if we wanted to push `sp`.

Exercises 8.3

1. ✓ What code is generated by each of the following program fragments?

```
            IRP     x, <2, 3, 5, 7, 11, 13, 17>
            DB      &x&
            ENDM


            IRPC    n, 123456789
Number&n&   DB      &n&
            ENDM


Counter = 0ah
            REPT    10
            DB      Counter
Counter = Counter + 10h
            ENDM


Outside = 10h
            REPT    5
Inside = 1
            REPT    3
            DB      Outside+Inside
Inside = Inside + 1
            ENDM
Outside = Outside + 10h
            ENDM
```

2. Use '=' and `REPT` to generate 100 consecutive bytes of memory containing the numbers 1, 2, 3, … 100.

3. Use '=' and `REPT` to generate 52 bytes of memory containing upper and lower case letters of the alphabet alternating in order. That is, memory will contain 'A', 'a', 'B', 'b', … . Note that only one counter is necessary if you use the fact that lower-case-letter = corresponding-upper-case-letter + 'a' − 'A'.

4. Use `IRP` to write two *macros*, `PushX <Reg1,  ...>` and `PopX <Reg1,  ...>` which, respectively, push and pop a list of registers. Note that for instance `PushX` must start out something like

```
PushX     MACRO   RegList
          IRP     aReg, <&RegList&>
          . . .
```

because the call to PushX will strip off the < > from RegList and it must be reestablished for use by IRP. Note also that there will be two ENDMs.

5. Show that Example 8.3—1 can be rewritten using either IRP or IRPC.

SUMMARY

Macros are declared (before use) with the code

```
MacroName MACRO  parameter list
        ...prototype...
           ENDM
```

Within prototypes, macro parameters can be distinguished by surrounding them with '&' characters.

Such macro definitions produce no code in and of themselves, but are expanded into code by invocations of the form

```
MacroName   actual parameter list
```

Parameters in the actual parameter list are normally separated by commas, but can also be separated by blanks and tabs. Extra parameters are ignored and missing parameters are assumed to be the empty string. Text including commas, blanks, and tabs can be combined into a single parameter by surrounding it with <> parentheses.

The LOCAL pseudo-op can be used at the beginning of a macro definition to declare labels which will be replaced uniformly by unique labels each time the macro is invoked. The form is

```
MacName    MACRO  parameters
           LOCAL  label1, label2, ...
           ...
label1:
           ...
label2:
           ...
           ENDM
```

The '=' pseudo-operation is similar to EQU except that the label values it defines can be redefined using it and it can only be used with numeric values.

The pseudo-macro

```
           REPT    n
        ...prototype...
           ENDM
```

causes prototype to be copied n times.

The pseudo-macro

```
IRP     P, <P1, ... Pn>
...prototype containing P...
        ENDM
```

causes *prototype* to be copied *n* times, first with *P1* substituted for *P*, then *P2* for *P*, etc.
The pseudo-macro

```
IRPC    P, character-string
...prototype containing P...
        ENDM
```

causes *prototype* to be copied n = (length of *character-string*) times, first with the first character of *character-string* substituted for *P*, then the second, etc.

Chapter 9

Bit Operations

registers discussed

ah	AX	al
bh	BX	bl
ch	CX	**cl**
dh	DX	dl
	SI	
	DI	
	BP	
	SP	
	DS	
	ES	
	SS	
	CS	
	IP	

o d i t s z **c**

Computer hardware often requires that several pieces of information be packed in a single word or byte, and programs sometimes also pack information as a space-saving device. For instance

- The default for color displays is CGA. For each character on the CGA screen there is an associated byte called the **attribute byte** which determines how the character is displayed. Three bits of the byte determine the mixture of red, green, and blue in the character, three more determine the color of the background, one bit determines whether the character is high or low intensity, and one whether it is blinking. (We will discuss attribute bytes in more detail in Chapter 19.)
- Graphics programming often requires turning on or off individual or small groups of bits representing a single dot, or *pixel* on the screen.
- The PC keyboard has several shift keys (two regular, Ctrl, Alt, Num Lock, Insert mode, etc.) The status of each key is recorded as a single bit in a byte in the BIOS Data section of memory, and individual bits must be set or interrogated by the BIOS as keys are pressed.
- Part of the directory information about each file on the disk is the date and time of last modification. To save space, each of the two is packed into a single word.
- Information controlling serial (COM) ports such as Baud rate, parity, and data and stop bits is packed in a single word.
- File allocation on disks is controlled by the File Allocation Table, or FAT. On floppy disks, each entry in the table is 12 bits long—one byte and the first four bits of the next or the last four bits of one byte and all of the next one.

9.1 Boolean Operations
ops and, or, xor, not, test

9.2 Shift Operations
ops shl/r, sal/r, rol/r

9.3 PutHex Implementation

Optional:

9.4 High-Level Languages
9.5 RECORD Structures
op RECORD

One of the major purposes of bit operations is extracting or altering parts of such packed information.

There are two types of bit operations on a digital computer—bit by bit Boolean operations and shifts.

9.1 • Boolean Operations

Boolean operations, like arithmetic operations, can be applied to either bytes or words. In order to avoid endless repetition of 'words or bytes', we will, for the moment, only talk about words, but the corresponding operations also take place on bytes.

The 80X86 CPU (and most others) implements the logical operations AND, OR, and XOR (eXclusive OR), which are applied between corresponding bits of two words, and the logical operation NOT which is applied to the individual bits of a single word. These operations treat the 16 bits of a word as 16 boolean variables, 0 signifying **false** and 1 signifying **true**. The results of performing the various logical operations on individual bits can be shown by a **truth table**:

A	B	A **and** B	A	B	A **or** B	A	B	A **xor** B	A	**not** A
0	0	0	0	0	0	0	0	0	0	1
0	1	0	0	1	1	0	1	1	1	0
1	0	0	1	0	1	1	0	1		
1	1	1	1	1	1	1	1	0		

Intuitively, A **and** B is true only if **both** A and B are true. In English, the meaning of the word 'or' is vague, implying sometimes that "or both" is possible (as in "Joanna or Ben can do it") and sometimes that 'or both' is impossible (as in "That will work or I'm a monkey's uncle"). In programming we separate these meanings into two separate ors, an **inclusive or**—usually written just **or**— in which A **or** B is true if **either** A or B is true (**or both**) and an **exclusive or**—usually written **xor** for computers—in which A **xor** B is true if either A or B is true, but **not** both. **Not** A is true precisely when A is false.

And, or, and xor are instructions using exactly the same format as add, sub, and mov, while the not instruction uses the same format as inc or dec. That is, their operands are

```
and/or/xor   reg/mem, reg/mem/constant
not                   reg/mem
```

with no more than one of the operands a memory reference. Their functionality is

```
and    dest, source ;      dest := dest AND source
or     dest, source ;      dest := dest OR source
xor    dest, source ;      dest := dest XOR source
not    dest ;              dest := NOT dest
```

where the operations are applied bit by bit. The operands are either both bytes or both words.

If for instance we apply and to two words, the logical AND operation is applied to each corresponding pair of bits, one from each operand. The result of each AND sets the corresponding bit of the result word. Thus if we have

```
AX = 0001 0010 0011 0100 B
BX = 1111 1110 1101 0011 B
```

and execute the instruction 'and ax, bx', the result is

```
AX = 0001 0010 0001 0000 B
BX = 1111 1110 1101 0011 B
```

(BX is unchanged; the bits are shown in groups of four for ease of reading). If we start with the same register values, the result for 'or ax, bx' is

```
AX = 1111 1110 1111 0111 B
BX = 1111 1110 1101 0011 B
```

The result for 'xor ax, bx' is

```
AX = 1110 1100 1110 0111 B
BX = 1111 1110 1101 0011 B
```

and the result for 'not ax' is

```
AX = 1110 1101 1100 1011 B
```

The not operation is actually the 1's complement, usually simply called the *complement*.

It is probably more useful to think of the and, or, and xor instructions in terms of their usual function in a computer program. And is used to selectively clear (set to 0) bits of a word, or to selectively turn them on, and xor to selectively toggle them (that is, change 1s to 0s and 0s to 1s. In each case we are going to do A := A *OP* B where we think of B as performing a **masking operation** on A. In this interpretation, B is called a **mask**. A graphical representation may be helpful. A and B are represented as

where

☐ = 0s, ■ = 1s, ▦ = random 0s and 1s, and ■ = complement of ▦

The standard operations are as follows:

- **Use AND to clear parts of an item**; i.e., clear A to 0 wherever the mask is 0. This operation is sometimes called **masking out** part of A.

A AND B

- **Use OR to set parts of an item**; that is, set A to 1 wherever the mask is 1

A OR B

- **Use XOR to toggle parts of an item**; that is, interchange 1's and 0's

A XOR B

- **Use NOT to toggle *all* of an item**

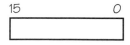

NOT A

And, or, and xor set sign and zero flags are set according to the result, and overflow and carry flags are cleared. The most common usage is to AND with a mask and do a jz to determine if any of the bits corresponding to the mask were 1. It is such a common operation that there is a separate instruction to accomplish it, the test instruction

```
test   reg/mem, reg/mem/constant
```

which has the same operands as and/or/xor. Test ANDs its operands and uses the result to set the flags, but *discards the result*. Typical usages are

```
test   ax, ax ;      A substitute for cmp ax, 0
```

and

```
test   ax, 1
jnz    AXisOdd ;    Test for ax odd
```

In all of the examples that follow, we will sometimes need to number the bits in a word (or byte). Different classes of CPUs adopt different schemes. The standard way of numbering bits on the 80X86 CPU is to start from the right, numbering from 0. Thus bits of a word are numbered

```
15              0
┌─────────────┐
│             │
└─────────────┘
```

and the bits of a byte are numbered similarly 0-7 from right to left. Bit n thus has the numerical value 2^n.

Example 9.1—1. The PC's keyboard hardware actually knows nothing about ASCII. Each key is numbered with a **scan code** (see Section 5.5). When a key is pressed, it sends its scan code and when released, its scan code + 128. It is up to the BIOS to do the necessary translation. Among other things, the BIOS maintains the shift status of the keyboard in a byte at location 417h. We don't know how to address such a byte yet (we will in Chapter 12) so let's simply assume that the byte is declared by

```
KbdStatus DB    ?
```

The meanings of 1-values in the various bits are

bit	mask	interpretation
7	10000000B	Insert mode on
6	01000000B	Caps lock on
5	00100000B	Num lock on
4	00010000B	Scroll lock on
3	00001000B	Alt key down (either one if more than one)
2	00000100B	Ctrl key down (either one if more than one)
1	00000010B	Left shift key down
0	00000001B	Right shift key down

When the various keys are pressed or released, the ROM BIOS executes code to keep these status bits corresponding to the actual keyboard status, which it has no other way of knowing. **Note:** the following exercises make extensive use of magic numbers. Later on in the chapter, we will show various ways in which that can be avoided.

- Process the 'Ctrl key down' action, which involves **setting** a bit

```
or      KbdStatus, 00000100B ;   Set Ctrl bit
```

- Process the 'Alt key up' action, which involves **clearing** a bit:

```
and     KbdStatus, 11110111B ;   Clear Alt bit
```

- Process the 'Num Lock key down' action, which involves **toggling** a bit; that is, setting it to 1 if it was 0 and to 0 if it was 1. (Hitting the Num Lock key toggles the number keys on the right of the keyboard between use as a numeric keypad and use as cursor keys.)

```
xor     KbdStatus, 00100000B ;   Toggle Num Lock bit
```

- Go to location `Shifted` if either shift key is down, which involves **testing** two bits:

```
test    KbdStatus, 00000011B ;   If a shift key is down
jnz     Shifted ;                go to Shifted
```

- Convert the lowercase letter in `al` to upper case if either shift key is down. If the Caps lock key is down, toggle the resulting case of the letter. (The PC keyboard BIOS actually works this way.) We use a new way of converting between upper- and lowercase letters, which depends on the fact that the codes for corresponding upper- and lowercase letters are identical except that **bit 5 is 0 for upper case, 1 for lower case**.

```
          test    KbdStatus, 00000011B ;  If either shift key down
          jz      TestCaps
          and     al, 11011111B ;              change to upper case
TestCaps:
          test    KbdStatus, 01000000B ;  If Caps Lock down...
          jz      Done
          xor     al, 00100000B ;              toggle case
Done:
```

Note: The ordinary programmer should not use or alter the bits in byte 417h directly. The ROM BIOS call int 16h, function code 02h, returns the keyboard status byte in al.

Example 9.1—2. The directory information for a disk file contains the date of last modification in a single word in the following format:

year – 1900   bits 9-15 (leftmost seven bits)
month   bits 5-8 (January is 1)
day   bits 0-4 (rightmost five bits)

The gray lines show separate hex digits. Suppose the word Date contains such a date. We will write code to set its month to October (= 10).

We must first mask out the old month value, so the code is

```
          and     Date,1111111000011111B ;  Clear previous bits 5-8
          or      Date,0000000101000000B ;   and insert 10 = 1010B
```

We could also have written the two constants as 0fe1fh and 0140h.

Example 9.1—3. DOS allocates memory in multiples of 16 bytes. Suppose that the word variable Size contains a number of bytes to be allocated, which may not be a multiple of 16, and round it up to the next higher multiple of 16.

The code is

```
          add     Size, 15 ;    make Size >= next multiple of 16
          and     Size, 0fff0h ; then cut it down to the multiple
```

(0fff0h = 1111111111110000B, of course.) A table of the results of the operations for various values of Size follows:

Size	after add	after and
64 = 0000000000100000B	0000000000101111B	0000000000100000B = 64
65 = 0000000000100001B	0000000000110000B	0000000000110000B = 80
...		
79 = 0000000000101111B	0000000000111110B	0000000000110000B = 80

Example 9.1—4. (This example is an application of the **xor** operation for those familiar with linked lists.) Set up a list which is linked both forwards and backwards, but uses only a single pointer field.

In the early days of computing, when computer memories were tiny and every bit counted, someone noticed that a list could be linked both forwards and backwards using only a single link field and a curious property of the **xor** operation: If X := A **xor** B, then A **xor** X = B and B **xor** X = A. (See Exercise 9.1—5 below.) If Prev is the address of the previous node, and Next the address of the next node, we set the link field of the current node to Prev **xor** Next. We can picture the situation as follows:

Here we are assuming that the link field is at the beginning of the node and the remaining contents spread out to the right. To move through the list from start to finish, we must keep two pointers, CURR to the current node and PREV to the previous node. To move to the next node, we set

```
new CURR := CURR link xor PREV; new PREV := old CURR;
```

To move CURR back one node, we set

```
new PREV := PREV link xor CURR; new CURR := old PREV;
```

Exercises 9.1

1. ✓ Fill in the contents of al where requested below:

```
        mov    al, 11010110B
        and    al, 01111000B ;        al = _____
        mov    al, 11010110B
        or     al, 01111000B ;        al = _____
        mov    al, 11010110B
        xor    al, 01111000B ;        al = _____
        mov    al, 11010110B
        not    al ;                   al = _____
        mov    al, 0C9H
        and    al, 1EH ;              al = _____
        mov    al, 0C9H
        and    al, 15 ;               al = _____
```

```
mov    al, 0C9H
or     al, 1EH ;                    al = _____
mov    al, 0C9H
xor    al, 1EH ;                    al = _____
mov    al, 0C9H
not    al ;                         al = _____
```

(Hint on the later ones: Convert to binary, mentally if possible.)

2. ✓ `SomeBits` is a word assumed to contain various subfields. Write assembly language code to use or modify the fields of `SomeBits` in the following ways. (Recall that bits are numbered from the right, starting at 0.)

    a) Set bits 5-9 to all 0's.
    b) Set bits 5-9 to all 1's.
    c) Set bits 5-9 to 11001B (whatever their previous contents).
    d) Toggle bit 12—that is, turn it off if it was on, on if it was off.
    e) If bit 3 is non-zero, jump to label `ItsOn`.

3. The Pascal `ODD` function returns true (1) if its integer (word) argument is odd, 0 otherwise. Write an assembly language macro `ODD    X` which sets $ax := ODD(X)$.

4. ✓ As mentioned in Exercise 4.2—3, a word variable COL recording the position of the display cursor can be updated to the next tab stop by the formula $COL := (((COL + 7) / 8) * 8) + 1$. Rewrite the code to evaluate the assignment statement, replacing the divide and multiply with a single masking operation. (Hint: see Example 9.1—3.)

5. ✓ Show that if A and B are single bits and X is set equal to A **xor** B, then A **xor** X = B and B **xor** X = A. Use a truth table which considers all the combinations of values of A and B, and the resulting values of X, A **xor** X, and B **xor** X (see Example 9.1—4 for an application).

9.2 • Shift Operations

Shifting the contents of a word or byte left or right can also be a useful operation. With decimal numbers, shifting to the right is equivalent to cutting digits off the right end; that is, dividing by 10. Shifting to the left means adding zeroes at the right end; i.e., multiplying by 10. With binary numbers, left shifts correspond to multiplication by 2 and right shifts to division by 2 (2 = 10B). Binary numbers on a computer are fixed length, and 2's complement adds complications, so we also have to decide what to do with the left end of shifted items. We are actually going to discuss three sets of shift instructions here which differ in what they do with the bits shifted out one end and into the other.

    The simplest type of shift instruction is to shift zeroes into the vacated positions and to throw away the bits shifted out the other end. These are the **logical shifts** `shl` (shift left) and `shr` (shift right). It is sometimes convenient to keep track of the last bit shifted out, so that bit gets put in the Carry Flag (CF). (See Section 5.1 for a description of the Flags register.) Pictorially we have[*]

---

[*] All our shift drawings and examples will show words. The situation for bytes is similar.

The operations are written

shl/shr *mem/reg, count*

Count is either 1 or the cl register. When the count is specified as cl, the shift is left or right by the number of bits specified by cl. Thus if we start with ax = 1101001011010001B and cl contains 3 then

shr	ax, 1 ;	would result in	ax = **0**110100101101000 and CF = 1
shl	ax, 1 ;	would result in	ax = 1010010110100010 and CF = 1
shr	ax, cl ;	would result in	ax = **000**1101001011010 and CF = 0
shl	ax, cl ;	would result in	ax = 1001011010001**000** and CF = 0

Shifting left adds zeroes to the right end of the word or byte, which is effectively multiplying by a power of 2. Shifting right effectively divides by a power of 2 *if the number is positive.* To allow right shifting to divide by 2 for negative numbers, the 80X86 defines a second type of shift, an **arithmetic shift**. These instructions have the same form as the logical shifts

sal/sar *mem/register, count*

Sal is actually the same instruction as shl, but sar and shr are different. Sar and shr do the same thing with the bits shifted out the right end, but the new bits shifted in on the left end by sar are always the same as the previous sign bit—we say the shift *propagates the sign bit.* We can picture the arithmetic shifts as

Thus if ax and cl are as before

| sar | ax, 1 ; | would result in | ax = **1**110100101101000 and CF = 1 |
| sar | ax, cl ; | would result in | ax = **111**1101001011010 and CF = 0 |

The last shifts to be considered here are the **rotates** rol (rotate left) and ror (rotate right).[*] With these instructions, the bits shifted out one end are shifted back in the other, with the final bit shifted out also going to the C Flag as usual. These can be pictured as

---

[*] There is another type of rotate, RCL and RCR, which is used for multiple-precision arithmetic operations (see Exercise 14.1—2).

The operations are written

rol/ror mem/reg, count

and if ax and cl are as before, then

```
ror      ax, 1 ;      would result in ax = 1110100101101000 and CF = 1
rol      ax, 1 ;      would result in ax = 1010010110100011 and CF = 1
ror      ax, cl ;     would result in ax = 0011101001011010 and CF = 0
rol      ax, cl ;     would result in ax = 1001011010001110 and CF = 0
```

Example 9.2—1. Date is a word containing the date of last modification of a file as in Example 9.1—2 in the last section. Write code to extract the month field from a word Date of that format and store it as a number between 1 and 12 in a word Month.

```
;; Example 9.2-1: Solution 1
;;
         mov     ax, Date
         mov     cl, 5
         shr     ax, cl ;        Month to low-order position
         and     ax, 0000000000011111h ; Mask out year
         mov     Month, ax
;;
;; Example 9.2-1: Solution 2
;;
         mov     ax, Date
         and     ax, 0000000111100000h ;   Mask out Year and Day
         mov     cl, 5
         shr     ax, cl ;        Month to low-order position
         mov     Month, ax
```

Example 9.2—2. With Month and Date in the same form as the previous example, write code to store Month in its proper place in Date.

```
;; Example 9.2-2: Solution 1
;;
         mov     ax, Date
         and     ax, 1111111000011111h ;   Clear any previous month
         mov     bx, Month
         and     bx, 0000000000001111h ;   Make new month fit
;                                                     just in case
         mov     cl, 5
         shl     bx, cl
```

```
            or      ax, bx ;        Insert new month
            mov     Date, ax
```

MASM and TASM also have operators AND, OR, XOR, NOT, SHL, and SHR which can be used like + and – to form constant expressions for instruction operands. The shift operators SHL and SHR are used by writing *item-to-shift* SHL/R *number-of-bits*. For instance, Solution 2 to Example 9.2—1 could be written more safely as follows:

```
;; Example 9.2-1: Revised Solution 2
;;
MONTH_OFFSET EQU 5 ;            Number of bits from right of word
            mov     ax, Date
            and     ax, 1111B SHL MONTH_OFFSET ; Clear Year and Day
            mov     cl, MONTH_OFFSET
            shr     ax, cl ;            Month to low-order position
            mov     Month, ax
```

and the solution to Example 9.2—2 as

```
;; Solution 2 to Example 9.2-2
;;
MONTH_OFFSET EQU 5 ;            Number of bits from right of word
MOMASK      EQU     1111B SHL MONTH_OFFSET ; MASK is a reserved word
            mov     ax, Date
            and     ax, NOT MOMASK ; Mask out any previous month
            mov     bx, Month
            mov     cl, MONTH_OFFSET
            shl     bx, cl ;        Shift month into position
            and     bx, MOMASK ;  Make new month fit, just in case
            or      ax, bx ;        Insert new month
            mov     Date, ax
```

Example 9.2—3. Write assembly code to compute $P := X^n$ where X, n, and P are word variables, $n \geq 0$, using the following algorithm:

```
P := 1
D := X
while (n <> 0)
        if (n is odd) then P := P * D end if
        D := D * D
        n := n / 2
end while
```

The method above for computing powers is much more efficient for large n than the brute force method of multiplying X by itself n–1 times.) We can make use of the new instructions in this chapter as follows (*note that we are not using the* `loop` *instruction*):

```
            mov     ax, 1 ;       ax is P := 1
            mov     bx, X ;       bx is D := X
            mov     cx, N ;       cx is n
PowLoop:
            jcxz    Done ;         while (n <> 0)
            shr     cx, 1 ;          n := n / 2
            jnc     NotOdd ;       was old n odd?
            imul    bx ;                Yes; P := P * D;
NotOdd:
            xchg    ax, bx ;       D
            imul    ax ;                   :=
            xchg    ax, bx ;              D * D
            jmp     PowLoop
Done:
            mov     P, ax
```

Exercises 9.2

1. ✓ Fill in the contents of `al` where requested below:

```
            mov     cl, 3
            mov     al, 11010110B
            shl     al, 1 ;                  al = _____
            mov     al, 11010110B
            shr     al, 1 ;                  al = _____
            mov     al, 11010110B
            shl     al, cl ;                 al = _____
            mov     al, 11010110B
            shr     al, cl ;                 al = _____
            mov     al, 11010110B
            sal     al, 1 ;                  al = _____
            mov     al, 11010110B
            sar     al, 1 ;                  al = _____
            mov     al, 11010110B
            sal     al, cl ;                 al = _____
            mov     al, 11010110B
            sar     al, cl ;                 al = _____
            mov     al, 11010110B
            rol     al, 1 ;                  al = _____
            mov     al, 11010110B
            ror     al, 1 ;                  al = _____
            mov     al, 11010110B
            rol     al, cl ;                 al = _____
            mov     al, 11010110B
            ror     al, cl ;                 al = _____
            mov     al, 3Ch
            shl     al, 1 ;                  al = _____
```

```
mov     al, 3Ch
shr     al, 1 ;                    al = _____
mov     al, 24
shl     al, 1 ;                    al = _____
mov     al, 24
shr     al, 1 ;                    al = _____
mov     al, 99h
rol     al, 1 ;                    al = _____
```

2. ✓ The following sequences of code have the effect of multiplying or dividing ax by a constant. What is the constant?

```
sal     ax, 1 ;        ax := ax * ____

sar     ax, 1 ;        ax := ax / ____

mov     cl, 3
sal     ax, cl ;       ax := ax * ____

sar     ax, cl ;       ax := ax / ____

mov     bx, ax
sal     bx, 1
add     ax, bx ;       ax := ax * ____

mov     bx, ax
sal     bx, 1
sal     bx, 1
add     ax, bx
sal     ax, 1 ;        ax := ax * ____

mov     bx, ax
sal     bx, 1
add     ax, bx
saR     ax, 1 ;        ax := ax * ____
```

3. ✓ Suppose that X is a word variable. Write code to go to location NBitOn if bit N of the word X is 1 assuming that $0 \le N \le 15$ and that
   a) N is a word variable.
   b) N is a symbolic constant defined by an EQUate.
Recall that bits are numbered right to left, from 0.

4. Pseudocode to implement the binary search usually contains a line of the form

```
mid := (lo + hi) / 2    { / is integer division }
```

Write PC assembly code to find mid assuming hi, lo, and mid are word variables.

5. ✓ The time of last alteration of a disk file is stored in the directory information about the file in a single word of the following form:

hour	bits 11-15 (in the range 0–23)
minute	bits 5-10
second/2	bits 0-4 (we can only store second/2 because only 5 bits are left)

a) Suppose that `Time` is a variable containing a time in the format above. Write assembly code to extract the minutes and store it as a number between 0 and 59 in a word variable `Minute`.

b) Suppose that `Time` and `Minute` are word variables as above. Write code to replace the minute field in `Time` with the contents of `Minute`.

6. As mentioned at the beginning of this chapter, each byte of information on the CGA (Color Graphics Adapter) display screen on the IBM PC has attached to it an *attribute byte* which tells how that byte will be displayed. The format of the attribute byte is

Blink	bit 7 (1 = blink on)
Background Color	bits 4-6
Intensity of Foreground	bit 3 (1 = high)
Foreground Color	bits 0-2

The foreground color is the color of the character being displayed. Colors are specified as three bits representing Red, Green, and Blue, left to right. For more details, see Chapter 19. Suppose `Attr` is a byte containing a display attribute.

a) Write assembler code to set the background color to Red (= 100B).

b) Write assembler code to toggle Blink (that is, turn it off if it's on, on if it's off).

c) Write assembler code to set the background color to the complement (NOT) of the foreground color.

d) Write assembler code to extract the background color and store it as an integer between 0 and 7 in the byte `Back`.

e) Store bits 0-2 of the byte `Back` as the background color field in the byte `Attr`.

7. `DbgEx5` in Debug Workshop III makes use of the function `Fun`, which takes its input and returns its output in `ax` and whose value is given by $Fun(ax) = ax/2$ if `ax` was even, $= 3\,ax + 1$ if `ax` was odd. Write a version of `Fun` which uses no division or multiplication instructions.

9.3 • An Application—Code to Implement `PutHex`

As a complete example we will develop code for a separately compiled `callable` procedure `PutHex` as described in Section 3.4. We can use essentially the same method we used for `PutDec`, dividing repeatedly by 16 instead of 10. Because 16 is a power of 2, dividing by it is easy: just shift right 4. By modifying the method slightly, it is also possible to avoid the problem of getting the digits in reverse order. Symbolically, suppose the four hex digits are α, β, γ, and δ, as in

α	β	γ	δ

For the first digit, we shift right 12 bits, mask out all but the rightmost 4 bits (not necessary for the first digit, but we're in a loop), and convert to hex:

For the next digit, we shift right 8 bits and mask:

Repeating the above process, we get the four hex digits in order. The skeleton of our loop is

```
            mov     cl, 12
HexLoop:
            compute and display hex digit cl bits from the right
            sub     cl, 4 ;         Sets flags
            jge     HexLoop
```

The only remaining thing to worry about is converting a number between 0 and 15 to the corresponding ASCII hex digit. If it is less than 10, we just add '0' as we have done before. Noting that 10 becomes 'A', 11 becomes 'B', etc, we can convert numbers 10 and above by adding 'A' – 10. (We will develop a better method in Section 10.3.) The program is

```
;; PUTHEX.ASM—procedure to display the contents of ax in hex
;;
INCLUDE     PCMAC.INC
            .MODEL SMALL
            .CODE
            PUBLIC PutHex
PutHex      PROC
            push    ax ;            Work register
            push    bx ;            Used to save AX
            push    cx ;            Used for shift counter
            push    dx ;            Used by _PutCh
            mov     cl, 12 ;        current right shift amount
            mov     bx, ax ;        preserve for later use
HexLoop:
            mov     ax, bx ;        Get next digit into position...
            shr     ax, cl ;          ...(shifting by 0 works!)
            and     al, 000fh ;       ...and clear other bits
            cmp     al, 10 ;        Convert digit to ASCII character
```

```
                jl      DecDigit
                add     al, 'A'-10 ; 10 ==> 'A', 11 ==> 'B', etc.
                jmp     PutCh
        DecDigit:
                add     al, '0'
        PutCh:
                _PutCh al
                sub     cl, 4 ;         Sets flags
                jge     HexLoop
                pop     dx ;            Restore registers
                pop     cx
                pop     bx
                pop     ax
                ret
        PutHex  ENDP
                END
```

Exercises 9.3

1. ✓ Write a procedure `PutHexB` which displays `al` as two hex bytes. Note that the only bit operations that are required are two shift instructions.

2. Rewrite `PutHex` to find the successive hex digits by repeatedly *rotating* left 4 bits instead of shifting right 12, 8, 4, and 0 bits. You will need a separate counter to terminate the loop.

9.4 • A Little Something Extra: Bit Instructions in High-Level Languages

This section is optional—intended for those wishing information on how higher-level languages are translated. It assumes a somewhat more detailed knowledge of C/C++ and Pascal than I usually do in this book.

Some confusion may naturally arise between the assembly operations and, or, and not and operations with the same or similar names in high-level languages. In Chapter 5 we evaluated **and**s and **or**s in high-level language conditional statements in an entirely different manner than we are doing here. In essence, we were interested in only a single truth value in Chapter 5, whereas the bit instructions here are dealing simultaneously with 8 or 16 truth values.

Consider the if statement

if (Grade = 'F') **or** ((Grade = 'D') **and** Status = 1) **then**
        Status := 2

In Chapter 5 we would have translated this **if** statement as follows, using compare and branch and short-circuit evaluation:

```
                cmp     Grade, 'F' ; if (Grade = 'F') ...
                je      UpStatus ;      ... or
                cmp     Grade, 'D' ;    ... ((Grade = 'D') ...
                jne     NoUp ;          ... and
```

```
            cmp    Status, 1 ;    ... (Status = 1)) ...
            jne    NoUp
UpStatus: ;                              ... then
            mov    Status, 2
NoUp:
```

The method we have used might be called the **position method**, as whether you have determined truth or falsehood is determined by your current position executing the code.

A different method is to treat a relation like Grade = 'D' as the Boolean it really is and convert the its truth value to 0 or 1. One way to do the conversion is

```
            mov    ax, 0
            cmp    Grade, 'D'
            jne    F1
            inc    ax
F1:
```

The Booleans thus created can then be combined using the CPU's AND and OR instructions. The example above becomes

```
            mov    ax, 0
            cmp    Grade, 'F'
            jne    F1
            inc    al ;          al := (Grade = 'F')
F1:
            cmp    Grade, 'D'
            jne    F2
            inc    ah ;          ah := (Grade = 'D')
F2:
            mov    bl, 0
            cmp    Status, 1
            jne    F3
            inc    bl ;          bl := (Status = 1))
F3:
            and    ah, bl ;      ah := (Grade = 'D') and (Status = 1)
            or     ah, al ;      ah := ah or (Grade = 'F')
            jz     NoUp ;        jump if ah false
            mov    Status, 2
NoUp:
```

Our second method might be called the **expression method**, as truth or falsehood is determined by whether an expression is 1 or 0.

The method that the compiler of a high-level language uses may depend on the specifications of the language. The Pascal standard says you can use either method, but *traditionally Pascal uses the expression method*, even though it takes more space and more execution time. There are two reasons for the usual Pascal choice:

- The expression method of evaluation is necessary, at least in part, when assigning to Boolean variables, so if it is always done, only one evaluation method is required
- There are theoretical advantages in terms of proof of program correctness in evaluating all parts of a condition, no matter what (for instance, if one part involves evaluating a function with a side-effect).

The expression method has the *dis*advantage that statements like **if** (x <> 0) **and** (a / x < 10)... do not work as intended. In this case, if the first condition is false, the second condition will be evaluated anyway and result in a fatal error.

The C/C++ languages, on the other hand, meet the issue of choice of evaluation method head-on, at the expense of making the language more complicated and error prone. C and C++ have *two* sets of logical operators

&, |, ^, ~   *Bit*wise and, or, xor, and not, respectively; expression method
&&, ||, !=, !   *Logical* and, or, xor, and not, respectively; position method

The bitwise operations use the CPU's and, or, xor, and not instructions and *must* evaluate fully. The logical operations are *required* by the language standard to evaluate left-to-right and use short circuit evaluation. Therefore in order to get the position method translation of the '**if** (Grade....' statement, the C programmer would write

```
if ((Grade=='F') || ((Grade=='D') && (Status==1))) Status = 2;
```

and to get the expression method translation, he or she would write

```
if ((Grade=='F') | ((Grade=='D') & (Status==1))) Status = 2;
```

C/C++ has two different 'equals'. The C/C++ = and == correspond to the Pascal and pseudocode := (assignment) and = (comparison), respectively. C/C++ dispenses with the keyword **then** and the entire condition being tested must be surrounded by parentheses. Actually, a C/C++ programmer would write the above code with fewer parentheses as

```
if (Grade=='F' || (Grade=='D' && Status==1)) Status = 2
```

because C/C++ (unlike Pascal) uses the *correct* order of evaluation of logical expressions)

C/C++ also includes shift-left and shift-right operations << and >>. On the C's I have examined, the compiler attempts to decide whether the item being shifted is signed or unsigned, using sal and sar in the former case and shl and shr in the latter. Some Pascals such as Turbo Pascal also implement shift operations as the (nonstandard) operators **shl** and **shr**.

Exercises 9.4

1. Let A and B be word variables. Write assembly language code to implement either of the following (equivalent) statements:

```
A := B = 10 ; { Pascal }          A = B == C; /* C */
```

(equivalent to **if** (B = 10) **then** A := 1 { = true } **else** A := 0)

2. ✓ Let A and B be word variables. Write assembly language code to implement the following C statements:
   a) if (A > 10 && B <= 14) ++A; (here ++A = inc A)
   b) if (A > 10 & B <= 14) ++A;

9.5 • Assembler RECORD Structures (Optional)

This section covers a more elegant method of specifying packed subfields of words and bytes. It is entirely optional.

Our assemblers for the IBM PC have special data definition pseudo-operations which simplify access to parts of words or bytes. These operations don't come up very often, and we won't use them again in the book.

Declaring a RECORD in our assemblers is rather like declaring a **record** in Pascal or a **struct** in C. The main difference is that an assembler record must fit entirely in a byte or word. The form of the declaration is

```
RecName    RECORD field₁:size₁, ... fieldₙ:sizeₙ
```

The sizes are in bits and must add up to 16 or less. If the sizes add up to 8 or less, a byte is used for the record; if not, a word is used. Fields are allocated left to right, but if the record size doesn't fill up its byte or word, the whole group of fields are right-justified. That is, the record declaration

```
XmplRec    RECORD A:4, B:6, C:1
```

declares a record of the following format

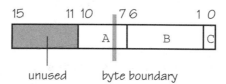

Once XmplRec is declared, we can define words using XmplRec just as if it were DW, except that we initialize fields by enclosing them in pointy brackets <,,,> (not to be confused with parameter parentheses). For example

```
Example    XmplRec <5,3,0>
```

Declares Example to be a field of the format XmplRec with initial values of A = 5, B = 3 and C = 0. An equivalent definition would be

```
Example    DW      (5 SHL 7) + (3 SHL 1) + 0
```

or

```
Example    DW      0286h
```

Using RECORDs doesn't make it any easier to pack and unpack words and bytes. The main advantages are documentation and the fact that defining a RECORD automatically gives symbolic names to various other quantities which are used in packing and unpacking information in the record. For instance, if *Field* is a field in a record declaration, then in any operand expression,

Field	is the number of bits that *Field* is from the right end of the word or byte,
WIDTH *Field*	is the number of bits in *Field*,
MASK *Field*	is a bit mask which can be used to extract *Field* from its word or byte, that is, it has 1's exactly in the bit positions occupied by *Field*.

Thus when Xmp1Rec is declared as above,

A = 7	WIDTH A = 4	MASK A = 0000011110000000B
B = 1	WIDTH B = 6	MASK B = 0000000001111110B
C = 0	WIDTH C = 1	MASK C = 0000000000000001B

Example 9.5—1. Redo Example 9.1—1 using the techniques in this section.

```
KbdRec      RECORD Ins:1,Caps:1,Num:1,Scroll:1,Alt:1,Ctl:1,Shifts:2
KbdStatus KbdRec <> ;          Or simply KbdStatus     DB ?
          . . .
          or     KbdStatus, MASK Ctl ;      Set Ctl Bit
          . . .
          and    KbdStatus, NOT MASK Alt ; Clear Alt bit
          . . .
          xor    KbdStatus, MASK Num ;      Toggle Num Lock bit
          . . .
          test   KbdStatus, MASK Shifts ; If a shift key
          jnz    Shifted ;      is down, go to Shifted
          . . .
ASCIIChar RECORD Case:1, Rest:5
          test   KbdStatus, MASK Shifts ; If either shift key down
          jz     TestCaps
          and    al, NOT MASK Case ;        Change to upper case
TestCaps:
          test   KbdStatus, MASK Caps ;   If Caps Lock down...
          jz     Done
          xor    al, MASK Case ;                Toggle case
Done:
```

Example 9.5—2. Redo Example 9.1—2 using the techniques in this section. That is, set the month to October in a date of the following format:

```
DateRec     RECORD Year:7, Mon:4, Day:5
Date        DateRec <>
          . . .
          and    Date, NOT MASK Mon
```

```
or      Date, 10 SHL Mon
```

Example 9.5—3. Redo Example 9.2—1 using the techniques in this section. That is, with. `Date` and `DateRec` defined as above, extract `Month` from `Date`.

```
mov     ax, Date
and     ax, MASK Mon
mov     cl, Mon
shr     ax, cl
mov     Month, ax
```

Example 9.5—4. Redo Example 9.2—2 using the techniques in this section. That is, pack `Month` into the `Mon` field in `Date`.

```
mov     ax, Date
and     ax, NOT MASK Mon ; Zero out any previous month
mov     bx, Month
mov     cl, Mon
shl     bx, cl
and     bx, MASK Mon ;      Make it fit, just in case
or      ax, bx
mov     Date, ax
```

Exercises 9.5

1. ✓ Redo Exercises 5 and 6 of Section 9.2 declaring the appropriate `RECORD` data types and using `MASK` and the field names as we have done in this section.

Programming Problem 9.1

Write and debug a separately compiled assembly procedure `PutBin` which takes as input a number in `ax` and displays the number in binary on the CRT screen as 16 ASCII 0's and 1's. Test your procedure with –32768, –1, 0, 1, and 32767. (Hint: Let `PutHex` be your guide.)

Programming Problem 9.2

Write and debug a separately translated assembly language function `GetHex` which reads and echoes hex digits from the keyboard and converts them into a word, which it returns as its value in `ax`. `GetHex` should accept upper- or lowercase A-F as hex digits, but need not accept a leading sign. It should stop reading digits when a character which isn't a hex digit is encountered. When that character is a carriage return, `GetHex` should also echo a line feed. Follow the general model of `GetDec` in Section 7.3, but shift instead of multiplying. Write a main program which thoroughly tests `GetHex`.

Programming Problem 9.3

The **greatest common divisor** algorithm presented in Programming Problem 6.2 can be improved by using shifts to take care of division by 2. The new algorithm for M, N > 0 is

```
pow := 0
while (M is even) and (N is even)
        pow := pow + 1
        M := M shr 1
        N := N shr 1
end while
        { Now GCD(orig M, orig N) = GCD(M, N) * 2^pow }
        { and now M or N is odd, so GCD(M, N) is odd }
while (M is even) M := M shr 1 end while
while (N is even) N := N shr 1 end while
        { There are no further factors of 2 in the GCD so }
        { we can get rid of such factors whenever they occur }
while (M <> N)    { M and N are odd and non-zero }
        if (M > N) then
                M := M - N  { Making M even and <> 0 }
                while (M is even) M := M shr 1 end while
        else
                N := N - M; { Making N even and <> 0 }
                while (N is even) N := N shr 1 end while
        end if
end while
GCD := N shl pow { = N * 2^pow }
```

As in Programming Problem 6.2, write and test a separately assembled procedure to compute the GCD of ax and bx, returning the value in ax. Also handle the cases other than M, N > 0 as described there. The code above seems long and complicated but the assembly language version is scarcely longer than the pseudocode.

SUMMARY

In this chapter we have introduced the following new logical instructions:

```
and    dest, source ;       dest := dest AND source
or     dest, source ;       dest := dest OR source
xor    dest, source ;       dest := dest XOR source
test   source1, source2 ;   source1 AND source2 set flags
not    dest                 dest := NOT dest
```

and shift instructions

```
         shl    dest, count ; dest := dest shifted left count
     ;                                 bits logically
         shr    dest, count ; dest := dest shifted right count
     ;                                 bits logically
         sal    dest, count ; dest := dest shifted left count
     ;                                 bits arithmetically
```

```
          sar     dest, count ; dest := dest shifted right count
    ;                                   bits arithmetically
          rol     dest, count ; dest := dest rotated left count
    ;                                   bits
          ror     dest, count ; dest := dest rotated right count
    ;                                   bits
```

Count is either the literal number 1 or `cl`. In the latter case, the number of bits to be shifted is in the `cl` register.

Corresponding to these operations we introduced the following operators on constants in operand expressions: AND, OR, XOR, NOT, SHL, and SHR.

The RECORD pseudo-operation was introduced to make bit-field processing more readable and reliable.

Chapter *10*

Arrays

This chapter is perhaps the most crucial in the book for understanding the particular flavor of assembly language. Its importance can't be overestimated, and its careful study will be repaid many times over.

This chapter can be read after chapter 5, with only occasional use of the `shr` and `test` instructions from chapter 9. One example in Section 10.3.2 uses the `REPT` and `=` pseudo-operations from Section 8.3.

10.1 • Addressing

There are various issues involving the operands of instructions that we either haven't discussed at all or have only glossed over briefly. It is finally necessary to discuss them in detail. If you are familiar with C/C++ pointers and pointer arithmetic, you will notice many things here that look familiar. (In fact, C/C++ pointers were designed to mimic assembly language in order to make them efficient to implement.) However, things are not exactly the same, and I will try to point out the important places at which C/C++ pointers and assembly addressing diverge.

10.1.1 • Memory Address *versus* Memory Contents

In high-level languages, an identifier usually refers to the *contents* of a memory location. Thus if A is a variable in C, using A in an expression refers to the value stored in the memory location named A. If you would like to refer instead to the *address* of the variable A, in C you would use the expression &A. Thus in C,

    x = A;   gives x the value stored in variable A
    p = &A;   gives the pointer p the value of the address of the variable A

Looked at differently, A is something which changes in the course of the program; &A does not. (All right, that's an oversimplification.)

In assembly language, things aren't nearly as simple. When we associate a name with a memory location, as we do for A and B below:

```
A         DB     24
B         DW     1234
```

and use A and B in instructions, we have been in the habit of thinking of them as representing the *contents* of their respective memory locations. Assemblers allow us to represent contents by name because that is what we want most often. As we shall see though, in assembly variable names are often best understood as referring to the *address* of the variable, and referral to *contents* by the name alone is allowed only as a matter of convenience.

Thus in the instructions

```
mov    al, A
mov    bx, B
```

A and B are taken to be the contents of their memory locations. As we have seen, briefly, in the DOS call corresponding to the _PutStr macro discussed in Chapters 2 and 3, if we want to refer to the *address* of a memory location in an instruction, we can use the keyword OFFSET. Thus

```
mov    bx, B ;          moves the contents of B to bx
mov    bx, OFFSET B ;   moves the address of B to bx
```

Thus we can think of OFFSET in masm/tasm as being the equivalent of the & operator in C/C++: it converts a variable into its address.

10.1.2 • Address Arithmetic

In high-level languages, arrays allow us to refer to a collection of similar data by a single name and individual items in the collection with the name and a numeric subscript. Thus the array A might have individual items A[3], A[14], etc.

In assembly language, an array A of 8 bytes might be declared by

```
A         DB     0Ah, 1Ah, 2Ah, 3Ah, 4Ah, 5Ah, 6Ah, 7Ah
```

Equivalently, the array could also have been declared

```
A         DB     0Ah
          DB     1Ah
          DB     2Ah
          etc.
```

(The numbers are chosen just to make each array entry identifiable by its contents. Any other values, or '?', could also have been chosen.) A itself refers only to the first byte in the array, the one containing 0Ah. The other bytes are *anonymous* locations without a specific name. We can refer to these anonymous locations by using A modified with **address arithmetic**. As we shall see, A+3 refers to the byte containing 3Ah and A+7 refers to the byte containing 7Ah. In fact, if we think of A as being the *address* of the byte containing 0Ah, then A+3 is the address of the byte containing 3Ah, and so on.

To try to make it clear what is going on, let's introduce a fairly standard notation. If α is an address in memory, then [α] is the **contents of memory at address** α. If p is a pointer variable in a high-level language, then [p] would correspond to *p in C/C++ and to p^ in Pascal. We have chosen to use the [ ] notation instead of one from a high-level language because masm and tasm support the [ ] notation.

Now, if I write mov al, A + 3 and we apply our experience from high-level languages, we would expect to load al with the value of the variable A, + 3; that is, with [A] + 3 = 0Dh. That is not the way assembly language works.

```
mov     al, A+3 ;     sets al to [A+3] = 3Ah, NOT [A]+3!!!
```

For emphasis, if X is the name of a memory location,

- In a high-level language, X + 1 is [X] + 1
- **In assembly language X + 1 is [X + 1]**, i.e., the contents of memory location (X + 1).

To make referring to contents clearer, we will use the notation allowed in masm/tasm of

```
mov     al, [A+3] ;   same as mov al, A+3
```

The two possible choices for a meaning for mov al, A+3 could be represented as al := [A+3] (the one chosen) and al := [A]+3 (the rejected option). There are two good reasons why the second choice is unacceptable in assembly language.

First, the *address* A+3 can be computed at assembly time (or at least at link time) so the mov instruction can be completely translated before the program is run if al := [A+3] is the interpretation. To represent al := [A]+3, [A] can only be known at run-time (and may be different each time the mov instruction is executed), so the second option would have to be translated into the *sequence* mov al, A / add al, 3. Conversion to two instructions simply requires more sophistication than assemblers are supposed to possess.

Second, if mov al, A+3 means set al := [A]+3, what does mov A+3, al mean? [A]+3 := al is nonsensical while [A+3] := al is meaningful.

Thus mov al, A+3 is the same as mov al, [A+3]. If we want to move the address A+3 (it would have to be to a word registers since addresses are words) we use the longer form mov ax, OFFSET A+3 because we need to move addresses much less often.

Example 10.1—1. The following definitions of the three arrays

```
A       DB      0Ah, 1Ah, 2Ah, 3Ah, 4Ah, 5Ah, 6Ah, 7Ah
B       DB      0Bh, 1Bh, 2Bh, 3Bh
C       DB      0Ch, 1Ch, 2Ch, 3Ch, 4Ch, 5Ch
```

cause the following arrangement of bytes in memory

```
A:                           B:              C:
 0A 1A 2A 3A 4A 5A 6A 7A 0B 1B 2B 3B 0C 1C 2C 3C 4C 5C
```

Then the following references have the results given:

```
mov    al, [B + 3] ;       sets al := 3Bh
mov    al, [B + 4] ;       sets al := 0Ch = [C]!!!
mov    al, [A + 10] ;      sets al := 2Bh = [B + 2]
mov    al, [A + 15] ;      sets al := 3Ch = [C + 3]
mov    al, [B - 3] ;       sets al := 5Ah = [A + 5]!!!
mov    al, [C - 10] ;      sets al := 2Ah = [A + 2]
```

For instance, the bytes in the B array can be counted as follows:

```
                          ... B-4  B-3  B-2  B-1
A      DB     0Ah, 1Ah, 2Ah, 3Ah, 4Ah, 5Ah, 6Ah, 7Ah

              B    B+1  B+2  B+3
B      DB     0Bh, 1Bh, 2Bh, 3Bh

              B+4  B+5  B+6 ...
C      DB     0Ch, 1Ch, 2Ch, 3Ch, 4Ch, 5Ch
```

In other words, the assembler treats memory as a large array with subscripts extending arbitrarily far in either the positive or negative direction! If you think about it, this free-form array is an obvious consequence of the fact that by the time the program is run, all information about how memory was defined is long since lost and all the program has to go on is what is actually in memory. B-2 is the address of the byte containing 6Ah, whether or not that byte was originally considered part of the B array. Languages like Pascal which enforce subscript bounds do so by adding *extra* code to the program to do the checking.

To summarize,

Address Arithmetic
mov   a**x**, OFFSET A+3 ;   ax := A+3 (the ***address***)
mov   al, [A+3] ;   al := ***contents*** at addr
;   (A+3); same as mov al, A+3
mov   al, [A]+3 ;   **ILLEGAL**

(We have to use ax for the OFFSET since an offset is always a word.)

It is best *always* to think of an address expression as representing an address, rather than the contents of memory at the address. For instance, if B is the name of a word array, the two instructions

```
mov    ax, OFFSET B + 3
mov    ax, [B + 3] ;       = mov ax, B + 3
```

translate with *identical* operand fields, both being the *address* B + 3. The only difference in the two instructions is in the mov opcode: the first says "move my literal operand into ax," and is the same opcode as would be used with the instruction mov ax, 1234; the other says "move the contents of memory at the address specified by my operand into ax." Note that no parentheses are necessary in OFFSET B + 3—(OFFSET B) + 3 would mean the same thing as OFFSET (B + 3) and OFFSET B + 3.

10.1.3 • Types of Address Expressions

I have so far glossed over an important point, which must now be discussed. We can declare *word* as well as *byte* arrays:

```
A           DB      0Ah, 1Ah, 2Ah ;             Byte array
B           DW      0Bh, 1Bh, 2Bh, 3Bh ;        Word array
```

We know that mov al, A moves the contents of the *byte* in memory at A to al, and mov ax, B moves the contents of the *word* in memory at B into ax. In terms of our [ ] notation, if A is byte variable, [A] is the byte at address A, and if B is a word variable, [B] is the word at address B. This typing of addresses as to word or byte also carries over into address expressions. A $\pm$ n is a *byte* address and [A $\pm$ n] is the byte at that address. B $\pm$ n is a *word* address and [B $\pm$ n] is the word at that address. Thus

```
mov     ax, [B + 2] ; sets ax := 1Bh
mov     ax, [B + 6] ; sets ax := 3Bh
```

If you are familiar with C/C++ pointers, getting words from [B $\pm$ n] should not be too surprising. C/C++ allows one to add and subtract integers from pointers, giving new pointers *of the same type*. **There is a crucial difference though.** Suppose that p were a C/C++ pointer. In C/C++, to simplify the programmer's job and make the code more machine independent, when the expression p + 3 is used, C/C++ automatically multiplies the 3 by the size of whatever it is that p points to. That is, p + 3 points to the third item after p *no matter how big the items are.* Hence if p is a word pointer with value the address B, p + 3 would be the address B + 6! If on the other hand, p were a pointer to characters and set to A, p + 3 would be the address A + 3.

Example 10.1—2. If we declare the three arrays AW, BW, and CW of words by

```
AW          DW      000Ah, 010Ah, 020Ah, 030Ah, 040Ah
BW          DW      000Bh, 010Bh, 020Bh, 030Bh
CW          DW      000Ch, 010Ch, 020Ch, 030Ch, 040Ch, 050Ch
```

then we can count elements of the BW array as follows:

```
                            ... BW-6  BW-4   BW-2
AW          DW      000Ah, 010Ah, 020Ah, 030Ah, 040Ah

                    BW     BW+2   BW+4   BW+6
BW          DW      000Bh, 010Bh, 020Bh, 030Bh
```

```
                      BW+8    BW+10    BW+12   ...
   CW         DW      000Ch, 010Ch, 020Ch, 030Ch, 040Ch, 050Ch
```

The following array references have the results given:

```
   mov      ax, [BW + 2] ;      sets ax := 010Bh
   mov      ax, [BW + 10] ;     sets ax := 010Ch
   mov      ax, [AW + 10] ;     sets ax := 000Bh
   mov      ax, [AW + 20] ;     sets ax := 010Ch
   mov      ax, [BW - 4] ;      sets ax := 030Ah
```

10.1.4 • Rules for Address Expressions

At this point, it is worthwhile to discuss what constitutes legal address arithmetic. Just as it would be meaningless to add inches and pounds, there are address expressions which are meaningless, and therefore prohibited.

An address and a number are really two different kinds of objects. An address refers to a place in computer memory, but a number is unitless. We could think of an address as being a street address, like <512 Pine> and a number as being the number of houses away that another address is. <512 Pine> + 3 would be three houses beyond <512 Pine>. Certainly <512 Pine> + 3 would not necessarily be <515 Pine>; it might well be <520 Pine>. Similarly, <512 Pine> − 2 would be two houses before <512 Pine>. We also might say that <534 Pine> − <512 Pine> = 5 if <534 Pine> is the fifth house after <512 Pine>. It would be meaningless to speak of <512 Pine> + <534 Pine> or 3 × <512 Pine>.

The same kind of reasoning holds for addresses in memory. The fundamental difference between addresses and ordinary numbers is that if the program is loaded into a different place in memory, *addresses change but ordinary numbers do not.*

In most situations, your intuition is probably sufficient to determine whether or not an address expression is legal, but in complicated situations you may have to appeal to the following definition:

Legal Address Arithmetic

Symbols are addresses if they label memory locations, e.g. if they appears in the label field of a DW or DB or in the code segment followed by a colon. Symbols EQUated to addresses are addresses. Symbols EQUated to constant numbers are ordinary numbers.

If α and β are addresses and n is an ordinary number then

$\alpha \pm n$ is legal, and is another address
$\alpha - \beta$ is legal, and is an ordinary number
(α) is legal, and is an address

Any expression involving only ordinary numbers is legal, and its value is an ordinary number.

The *only* expressions which form legal addresses are those built up as above.

Every address α has a particular type, and $\alpha \pm n$ is of the same type

---

Whether an address expression is an address or an ordinary number is important. For instance, if α is an address and *n* an ordinary number, we have seen that mov ax, α moves the *contents* of memory location α to ax while mov ax, *n* moves the *number n* itself to ax. Thus mov ax, B - A for B and A addresses moves the number B - A to ax. In the instruction mov ax, OFFSET α, OFFSET in effect converts α from an address to an ordinary number.

Example 10.1—3. Using the array declarations in Examples 10.1—1 and 2, we can form the address expressions

A + 14	an *address*, of the form α + *n*
B - A	a *number*, of the form α – β, and in fact = 8 (Count bytes)
CW - AW	a *number*, = 18
AW + (B - A)	an *address*, the address of the word at AW + 8

The following shows an application of address arithmetic.

Example 10.1—4. Display a name centered in a line on the CRT screen.

The biggest part of the problem is displaying the large constant number *n* of blanks that appear before the name. Assuming $n \le 80$ (or any other fixed constant) as it is here, we can get 80 consecutive blanks followed by a '$' by declaring

```
          DB      80 DUP (' ')
BlankEnd  DB      '$'
```

and can display *n* blanks by executing

```
          _PutStr <BlankEnd - n>
```

(The <> brackets are used because otherwise the internal blanks in the address expression would make it appear that there were *three* parameters to _PutStr. (See Section 8.1.3.)) Using BlankEnd - *n* works because _PutStr displays characters starting at the address which is its argument and continuing until it encounters a '$' character.

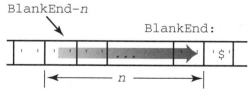

BlankEnd - *n* is the address of a string of exactly *n* blanks, followed by a '$' character (if $n \le 80$).

If the name to be displayed has *n* characters, then to center it, we must first display $40 - n/2$ blanks:

```
          _PutStr <BlankEnd - (40 - n / 2)>
```

In order to avoid having to count characters and treating *n* as a magic number (subject to change if the name changes, for instance), we could declare

```
MyName    DB      'Bill Jones'
EndName   DB      13, 10, '$'
```

then n = EndName − MyName. Using this expression for n, the following code displays the centered name:

```
_PutStr <BlankEnd - (40 - (EndName - MyName) / 2)>
_PutStr MyName
```

Notice that the expression in the first _PutStr is a perfectly legal address expression. EndName − MyName is an ordinary number (here, 10), hence so is (40 − (EndName − MyName) / 2), so Blanks + this number is indeed a legal address.

All assembly languages use some symbol ($ on our assemblers) to represent the *location counter*, the next location into which code will be assembled. Instead of defining EndName as above, we might have made things a bit more transparent by writing

```
MyName    DB      'Bill Jones'
NameLen   EQU     $ - MyName ;  the difference of two addresses
          DB      13, 10, '$'
```

Making a few more alterations in the definitions we could write

```
ScreenWidth EQU 80
          DB      ScreenWidth DUP (' ')
BlankEnd  DB      '$'
          . . .
          _PutStr <BlankEnd - (ScreenWidth - NameLen) / 2>
          _PutStr MyName
```

Note that the *position* of the NameLen declaration is crucial. If it were placed *after* the DB 13, 10, '$' line, it would be three bytes too big (though NameLen EQU $ − MyName − 3 would work in *that* position). Note also the **difference between the character '$' and the location counter $** (without quotes). '$' is the constant 36 while $ is an address which varies depending on the location at which it is used within the program.

Exercises 10.1

1. ✓ Suppose we have declared

```
A       DW      0A00h, 1A01h, 2A02h
B       DW      0B00h, 1B01h, 2B02h, 3B03h
C       DB      0Ch, 1Ch, 2Ch, 3Ch, 4Ch, 5Ch
D       DB      0Dh, 1Dh, 2Dh
```

a) What will the contents of ax or al be after execution of each of the following instructions?

```
mov     ax, A ;                 ax = _____
mov     ax, [A] ;               ax = _____
mov     ax, [A + 4] ;           ax = _____
mov     ax, [B + 4] ;           ax = _____
mov     ax, [A + 10] ;          ax = _____
mov     ax, [B - 4] ;           ax = _____
mov     al, [C + 2] ;           al = _____
mov     al, [C + 7] ;           al = _____
mov     al, [D] ;               al = _____
mov     al, [D - 3] ;           al = _____
```

b) What is B – A? C – A? D – C? A – B?

2. ✓ Suppose we have declared

```
E       DB      'Error', 13, 10, '$'
F       DB      'OK$'
```

What are the contents of al after executing each of the following instructions?

```
mov     al, [E + 3] ; al = _____
mov     al, [E + 5] ; al = _____
mov     al, [F + 2] ; al = _____
mov     al, [E + 9] ; al = _____
mov     al, [F - 2] ; al = _____
```

3. ✓ Assuming the following definitions in the .DATA segment

```
Msg     DB      'Ground$'
CRLF    DB      13, 10, '$'
```

What is displayed by the following code?

```
_PutStr Msg
mov     Msg, ' ' ;    a single blank character
_PutStr Msg
_PutStr CRLF
```

4. ✓ Suppose that we have defined the character string

```
Alpha       DB      'abcdefghijkl', 13, 10, '$'
```

What is displayed by the following code?

```
_PutStr Alpha
add     Alpha, 3
_PutStr Alpha
```

```
add     Alpha + 4, 6 ;        Alpha + 4 = [Alpha + 4] here
_PutStr Alpha
```

5. a) ✓ What are the contents of `al` in the two following cases?

```
Case1   EQU     27
        . . .
        mov     al, Case1 + 2
Case2   DB      27, 44, 18
        . . .
        mov     al, [Case2 + 2]
```

b) ✓ The code fragment

```
A       EQU     486
        . . .
        add     al, A - 444
```

adds the number 42 to `ax`, while

```
A       DB      486
        . . .
        add     al, [A - 444]
```

probably does not. Why? Under what circumstances would the second piece of code also add 42 to `al`?

6. If we have defined

```
Msg     DB      'Hello, friends!', 13, 10, '$'
```

what is displayed by

```
_PutStr Msg
_PutStr Msg+7 ; Hint: Msg+7 is the address of the 'f'
mov     Msg, 'M'
mov     Msg + 5, 'w'
_PutStr Msg ✓
```

7. ✓ If we have defined

```
Number  DB      '321'
Dumber  EQU     '3'
CRLF    DB      13, 10, '$'
```

what is displayed by

```
mov     al, Number
_PutCh al
mov     al, Number+2
_PutCh al
mov     al, Dumber
_PutCh al
mov     al, Dumber+2
PutCh al
_PutStr CRLF
```

10.1.5 • Byte Swapping

Suppose we have declared

```
A       DB      0Ah, 1Ah, 2Ah, 3Ah
BW      DW      000Bh, 010Bh, 020Bh, 030Bh
C       DB      0Ch, 1Ch, 2Ch, 3Ch, 4Ch
```

We know what happens when we use [BW+ n] where n is even—a multiple of the item size of the array—and small. What happens though if n is odd or negative or large, and ranges into the byte arrays A and C? *Something* must happen, because BW $\pm$ n is still a legal address. Just exactly *what* is one of those picky details that doesn't come up often, but nonetheless is one that you really need to understand. It is based on the way that the 80X86 assembles bytes in memory into words.

If we declare

```
AWord       DW      1234h
```

there are two possible ways of storing the two bytes making up AWord in memory: high order byte first or low order byte first. The 80X86 CPU is said to be **byte swapped** because it stores the low order byte first (i.e., in the lower address). In this example, 34h goes into the first byte, labeled AWord, and 12h goes into the second:

AWord:

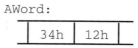

It is almost as if we had written

```
AWord       DB      34h, 12h ;      (almost) equivalent to DW 1234h
```

(It isn't completely equivalent because the first method defines AWord as a *word* and the second defines it as a *byte*.)

In this method of storing words, the low-*order* byte (the 34h here) is stored in the byte with the lower *address*. Computers which do byte swapping are also called **little-endian**, presumably because the front end of the item in memory is the low-order byte of the number. CPUs that do it the other way, such as the 680X0 CPU, are called **big-endian**. If two consecutive bytes of memory contain, say, 01h 02h, the value of those bytes as a 16 bit integer is 0201h = $(2 \times 16 + 0) \times 16 + 1 = 513$ in an IBM PC and 0102h = $(1 \times 16 + 0) \times 16 + 2 = 258$ in an Apple Macintosh! The difference in byte order in words is one of the things that makes trading files between the two machines tricky. (Arabic is written from right to left, but Arabic numbers are written just like ours, high-order digits to the left. Thus English is big-endian and Arabic is little-endian.)

The 80X86's way of putting the right byte in a word first is consistent with the way it numbers bits of bytes and words: also going from right to left, starting from 0.

Numbering of Bits in Words and Bytes

In turn, this method of numbering bits is reasonable because then the nth bit has value 2^n.

Byte swapping can be confusing, so it may be helpful to remember

---

**Words in Assembly Language programs and words in registers have bytes in their normal order.
Words in memory have their bytes swapped.**

The set of instructions

```
aWord     DW      1234h
          . . .
          mov     ax, aWord
```

and the instruction

```
          mov     ax, 1234h
```

do just what we would expect—they place 1234h in ax with 12h in ah and 34h in al.

$$ax \quad \boxed{12 \;\mid\; 34}$$

As every occurrence here of 1234h is either a word in assembly language or a word in a register, the bytes are always in the same order.

On the other hand,

Moving a word to or from memory swaps bytes.

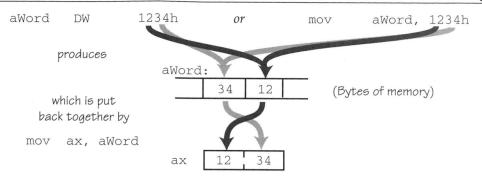

```
aWord      DW       1234h          or        mov      aWord, 1234h
```

The net result of this discussion is that if everything is written as words, you get just what you expect:

```
aWord      DW       1234h
           . . .
           mov      ax, aWord ;    sets ax = 1234h (ah = 12h, al = 34h)
```

The only time you have to be careful is when you have to look at pairs of bytes as words, or *vice versa*.

▸ **Variable Sizes Can Be Changed**: prefixing a variable with WORD PTR forces it to be interpreted as a word and prefixing with BYTE PTR causes it to be interpreted as a byte. Changing types in this way is called a type **override** or **cast** or **coercion**.

Thus we could write

```
A          DW       14
B          DB       100
C          DB       'Hello'
           . . .
           mov      ax, WORD PTR B ;    sets al to 100, ah to 'H' = 72
           mov      al, BYTE PTR A ;    Sets al := 14
```

Note that WORD PTR B is the word consisting of the byte B and the byte following it in memory. BYTE PTR A is the first byte making up A, the low order byte containing 14.

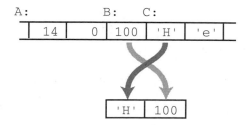

We can also use WORD or BYTE PTR in an EQUate. If we define

```
WPB          EQU      WORD PTR B
```

we can write

```
         mov     ax, WPB
```

instead of

```
         mov     ax, WORD PTR B
```

Exercises 10.1 (continued)

8. a) Show the contents of bytes of memory defined by the following

```
B          DB       12h, 34h
W          DW       1234h
```

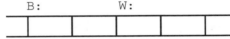

(Each byte contains exactly two hex digits.)

   b) Fill in the contents of ax as exactly four hex digits after each of the indicated mov instructions.

```
         mov     ax, 1234h ;            ax = 1234h

         mov     ax, WORD PTR B ;       ax = _____
         mov     ax, W ;                ax = _____
         mov     ax, 1234h
         mov     al, BYTE PTR W ;       ax = _____
```

   c) ✓ If we have declared

```
Alpha      DB       'ABCDEFG'
```

   what are the contents of ax as exactly four hex digits after executing the instructions

```
         mov     ax, WORD PTR Alpha ;     ax = _____

         mov     ax, WORD PTR Alpha+1 ;   ax = _____
```

   (Hint: 'A' = 41h, 'B' = 42h, etc.)

9. Show the contents of the two consecutive *bytes* of memory produced by

```
X          DW       1234 ;          Note: NO TRAILING H!
```

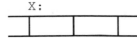

(Hint: Convert 1234 to hex.)

10.1.6 • Byte Swapping and Address Arithmetic (Optional)

In this section we will apply our knowledge of byte swapping to perverse situations involving address arithmetic. I hesitantly label it 'optional,' because I think you can probably skip it, at least for now, but I feel that this material is really essential to a full understanding of the 80X86.

Example 10.1—5. (Optional and harder) Suppose we have made the declarations

```
D           DB      -7, 14, 22
E           DW      434, -18, 26
```

Then the following array references have the results given. Look further on for an explanation of how the results were obtained:

```
mov     al, D + 4 ;          sets al := 01h
mov     ax, E + 3 ;          sets ax := 1AFFh
mov     ax, E - 2 ;          sets ax := 160Eh
mov     al, BYTE PTR E+3 ;   sets al = 0FFh = -1
mov     ax, WORD PTR D+2 ;   sets ax = 0B216h
```

The easiest way to figure these out is to compute the contents of memory byte by byte, and the easiest way to do that is to convert everything to hex. $-7 = 0F9h$, $434 = 01B2h$, and $-18 = 0FFEEh$, etc., so, taking into account byte swapping when a word goes into memory, the contents are

```
D:          E:
┌──┬──┬──┬──┬──┬──┬──┬──┬──┐
│F9│0E│16│B2│01│EE│FF│1A│00│
└──┴──┴──┴──┴──┴──┴──┴──┴──┘
          │ 434 │ -18 │ 26 │
```

The result of `mov al, D+4` then follows from

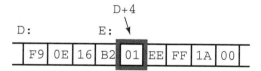

The result of `mov ax, E+3` follows from

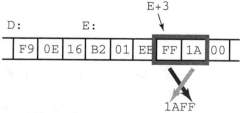

and the result of `mov ax, E-2` follows from

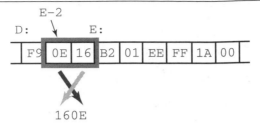

The result of `mov al, BYTE PTR E+3` should now be obvious from the diagrams, and the result of `mov ax, WORD PTR D+2` follows from

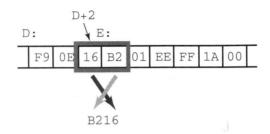

Exercises 10.1 (concluded)

10. ✓ Suppose we have declared

```
A       DW      0A00h, 1A01h, 2A02h
B       DW      0B00h, 1B01h, 2B02h, 3B03h
C       DB      0Ch, 1Ch, 2Ch, 3Ch, 4Ch, 5Ch
D       DB      0Dh, 1Dh, 2Dh
```

What will the contents of `ax` or `al` be after execution of each of the following instructions?

```
mov     ax, [A + (C - B)] ;        ax = _____
mov     al, [D + (A - B)] ;        al = _____
mov     ax, [A + 3] ;              ax = _____
mov     ax, [B - 3] ;              ax = _____
mov     al, [C - 2] ;              al = _____
mov     al, [C - 11] ;             al = _____
mov     al, BYTE PTR [A + 3] ;     al = _____
mov     ax, WORD PTR [C - 11] ;    ax = _____
```

10.2 • Arrays

10.2.1 • Arrays in General

In assembly language, a (one-dimensional) **array** is a collection of **entries**, each of the same length and placed one after the other in computer memory with no gaps. For instance an array of *n* entries, each of which is *s* bytes long, will occupy $n \times s$ contiguous bytes of storage.

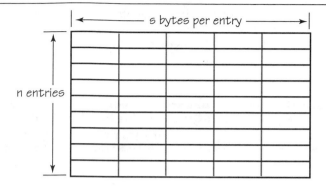

The reason for requiring that all entries be the same length and that there be no gaps in data storage is that then it is very easy to locate the ith entry in the array: if the array starts at location *ArAddr*, then the location of the ith entry (starting from 0) is *ArAddr* + $i \times s$. For instance, the fourth entry of the array would be found as follows:

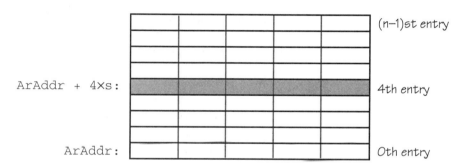

As you can see, in assembly language, the most natural place for subscripts to start is at 0, so that an array of n entries is indexed from 0 to $n - 1$. Starting at 0 is called **0-origin indexing** and is also used by C/C++ (for the same reason). We will show in Section 10.4 below how to simulate other index origins.

We have already seen examples of arrays of bytes and words. To declare an uninitialized array A of N items of S entries each, as above, we could use

```
N       EQU    . . .
S       EQU    . . .
A       DB     N DUP (S DUP (?))
```

with the nested DUPs being used to emphasize that we are declaring N copies of items of size S.

Elements of arrays of bytes or words can be manipulated directly by instructions using the [A + n] notation. With the 80386 and higher CPUs, it is also possible to manipulate arrays of double words (four bytes per entry) and in some cases, quad words (eight bytes per entry). Array items of other sizes can be used, but the machine doesn't do the work for you.

Our assemblers allow A[i] as an alternative notation to [A + i]. However I will not use the former notation in instructions because I think it confusing. In an array of words, for instance, A[4] refers to the fourth entry in the array in high-level languages, but to refer to the fourth entry in assembly, we must use [A + 8]!

I will reserve the notation A[*i*] for use in comments and program descriptions, where it will represent the *i*th entry in the high-level language sense. Thus in the array above, we could use the notation A[4] to represent the whole fourth entry consisting of bytes ArAddr+4×S to ArAddr + 5×S − 1.

To emphasize, in this book

A[*i*] is the high-level *i*th array entry.
[A+*i*] is the array entry starting at byte A+*i*.

You are of course allowed to confuse the distinction, to your own peril.

Higher-dimensional arrays can be considered to be arrays of arrays. For instance, a two-dimensional array can be considered to be a one-dimensional array, each of whose entries is a one-dimensional array. We will consider multidimensional arrays only in Exercise 10.2—8 below.

10.2.2 • Using Arrays

We already know how to manipulate array elements with constant subscript. For instance

Example 10.2—1. Let B be an array of bytes. Write code to set B[5] := 27.

```
mov    [B+5], 27 ;   B[5]  := 27
```

Example 10.2—2. Let W be an array of words. Write code to set W[5] := 27.

```
        mov    [W + 2*5], 27 ; W[5]  :=  27
; =     mov    [W + 10], 27
```

Variable subscripts are more complicated. If N is a variable containing a subscript for an array Ar, what we actually need to compute is something like [Ar + [N]]. We cannot write such an address in general, but we can use an equivalent form when N is one of four particular CPU registers:

bx and bp   The **base registers**. We are already familiar with bx as a general purpose register. Bp is called the **base pointer** and is used only in stack operations (to be described in Chapter 13). Bp is introduced here for completeness and because it works much like bx, but

---

Use bp in the stack only, NEVER for general-purpose indexing.*

---

si and di   The **index registers**. Si is called the **source index** and di is called the **destination index** from their usage in special string-processing instructions (to be discussed in Chapter 18). However, their use in ordinary subscripting is not limited to being a source or a destination, respectively.

---

* This rule above isn't just some whim on my part. Trying to use bp in other places will almost certainly get you into deep trouble.

Bp, si and di are similar to the registers ax, bx, cx, and dx that we have already seen, except that they are exclusively *word* registers. All of the arithmetic, logical, and shift instructions (except for multiplication and division) can be performed in the new registers, just as they can in ax, bx, cx, and dx. Bx and bp have much the same properties as si and di for subscripting, and all four registers will often be termed index registers.

Operands involving index registers are written in PC assembly language in the form

$$\left[\; address\text{-}expression + \left\{ \begin{array}{l} \text{bx} \\ \text{bp} \\ \text{si} \\ \text{di} \end{array} \right\} \; \right] \; \text{or} \; \left[\; \left\{ \begin{array}{l} \text{bx} \\ \text{bp} \\ \text{si} \\ \text{di} \end{array} \right\} \; \right]$$

The braces {} indicate a choice of register. The second form is equivalent to the first form with an *address-expression* of 0. Examples of such addresses are [Ar + bx], [Ar - 5 + si], [2+si], and [bp]. The address [*address-expression* + *index-register*] actually represents [*address-expression* + [*index-register*]], that is, the contents of the memory location equal to *address-expression* + contents of *index-register*. Note though that **the inner set of brackets isn't written in assembly language.**

Example 10.2—3. Let B be an array of bytes and N a word variable. Write code to set B[N] := 27.

```
; Example 10.2-3: Solution
;
        mov     di, N
        mov     [B + di], 27 ;      B[N] := 27
```

We could just as well have used bx or si instead of di. However we cannot write mov [B + N], 27, or use, say, ax in place of di.

> **ONLY bx, bp, si, and di can be used as index registers in assembly instructions.**

Example 10.2—4. With B and N as above, write code to set B[N+3] := 27

```
; Example 10.2-4: Solution 1
;
        mov     di, N
        add     di, 3
        mov     [B + di], 27 ;      B[N+3] := 27
```

We are actually moving to [B + ([N] + 3)] = [B + 3 + [N]], and we can rewrite the code in such a way that the add instruction is not needed:

```
; Example 10.2-4: Solution 2
;
        mov     di, N
        mov     [B + 3 + di], 27 ; B[N + 3] := 27
```

In the first solution, the add instruction is done each time the instruction sequence is executed. In the second, it is done only once, when the program is assembled. Thus the second solution is (slightly) faster, as well as shorter.

Example 10.2—5. Let W be an array of words and N a subscript in a word variable. Write assembly code to set W[N + 3] := 27.

W[N+3] starts at location W + ([N] + 3) × 2 (each entry in the array is two bytes long). We can compute ([N] + 3) × 2 in an index register, doing the multiplication by 2 the fast way—using a shift instruction (see Section 9.2):

```
; Example 10.2-5: Solution 1
;
        mov     bx, N
        add     bx, 3
        shl     bx, 1 ;         bx := 2 * (N + 3)
        mov     [W + bx], 27 ; W[N + 3] := 27
```

As before we can use the fact that (W + ([N] + 3) × 2) = (W + 6 + 2 × [N]) to simplify the code:

```
; Example 10.2-5: Solution 2
;
        mov     bx, N
        shl     bx, 1 ;         bx := 2 * N
        mov     [W + 6 + bx], 27 ; W[N + 3]  := 27
```

Reminder: The notation A[*i*] is legal in our assembly language, but is usually **different from** A[*i*] in a high-level language. We will use the A[*i*] notation only in the high-level language sense.

The next sequence of examples will involve loops. A typical loop processing an array W of 100 words in a high-level language looks like

```
for N := 0 to 99 do
      process W[N]
end for
```

which does *process* W[N] for N = 0, 1, 2, ... 99 in that order. In assembly language we can often optimize such a loop (as a good compiler might) to avoid the use of a variable N in memory:

```
        mov     cx, 100 ;       cx = number of items left to process
        mov     si, 0 ;         si := 2 * N
Process:
        process W[N]  = [W + si]
        add     si, 2 ;         2 * (N + 1) = 2 * N + 2
        loop    Process
```

A loop to process a byte array would inc the index each time through instead of adding 2. Once again, there is nothing profound about using si—bx or di would have done as well.

Example 10.2—6. Let W be an array of 100 words. Write code to set W[N] := 0 for N = 0...99.

```
; Example 10.2-6: Solution 1 (subscript method)
;
          mov    cx, 100
          mov    di, 0 ;       N := 0
ZeroLoop:
          mov    [W + di], 0 ; W[N] := 0
          add    di, 2 ;       N := N + 1
          loop   ZeroLoop
```

There's actually a more efficient way to implement the loop, a way which should look familiar to C/C++ programmers:

```
; Example 10.2-6: Solution 2 (pointer method)
;
          mov    cx, 100
          mov    di, OFFSET W ; WP := pointer to W = address of W
ZeroLoop:
          mov    [di], 0 ;          [WP] := 0
          add    di, 2 ;            WP := WP + 2
          loop   ZeroLoop
```

Recall that [di] is like [0 + di] except that the former instruction needs less space in memory. Therefore 'mov [di], 0' is a shorter instruction than 'mov [W + di], 0', so it takes less time to fetch it from memory and therefore the loop runs faster. We will call methods like Solution 1 the **subscript method** and those like Solution 2 the **pointer method**.

If you translated the two programs above into C or C++, the first would use arrays and the second would use pointers. The greater efficiency of the second version is why fluent speakers of C/C++ tend to use pointers instead of arrays. As we have seen, C/C++ also makes the pointer form as machine-independent as subscripts by having the statement WP = WP + 1 cause WP to be incremented not by 1 but by the size of the array element WP points to (in this example, 2).

The forms of indexing we have developed so far are just special cases of the most general form of indexing expression in which both a base and an index register can be used. The form is

$$[\text{ address-expression} + \left\{ \begin{matrix} \text{bx} \\ \text{bp} \end{matrix} \right\} + \left\{ \begin{matrix} \text{si} \\ \text{di} \end{matrix} \right\}]$$

As before, the braces {} indicate a choice, and any one or two of the three terms above can be omitted, giving us all of the forms of indexing we used previously. The type of addressing which uses *both* a base and an index register is called **based indexing**, or double indexing. Intuitively, the base register acts as the address of the array and the index register acts as the subscript, though the roles are often reversed.

In based indexing:
  1) the base and index registers can only be ADDED, and
  2) EXACTLY ONE of the three items: base register, index register, and *address-expression* must contain (be) an ADDRESS.

The reason for the second limitation above is that a based indexing expression must be an address in memory, and the only way to get such a thing when adding three items is to have one of them be an actual address and the others be 'displacements' from that address. (We have also called displacements 'ordinary numbers.')

Based indexing is only occasionally useful, generally when manipulating more than one array at the same time. We will see a sample usage in Example 10.2—7 below.

With the introduction of the various forms of indexing we now have seen all forms of instruction operands that work on all PCs. (For further modes on 80386 and above, see Chapter 21.) The forms are constant, register, memory address, and any of the various indexing forms discussed above. All but constant and register constitute a memory reference, so any two-operand instruction (like mov, add, or cmp) must have at least one of its operands a constant or register.

Example 10.2—7. W and X are arrays of 100 words. Write code to copy the W array into the X array.

For the first solution, use a single index register as a subscript for both arrays:

```
; Example 10.2-7: Solution 1
;
        mov     cx, 100
        mov     bx, 0 ;                 N := 0
Copy:
        mov     ax, [W + bx] ;          ax := W[N]
        mov     [X + bx], ax ;          X[N] := ax
        add     bx, 2 ;                 N := N + 1
        loop    Copy
```

Note that we could not have written 'mov [X + bx], [W + bx]' as that would involve two memory references in a single instruction, which is prohibited.

We could also solve the problem by using two index registers as pointers, one into each array:

```
; Example 10.2-7: Solution 2
;
        mov     cx, 100
        mov     si, OFFSET W ;          WP := address of W
        mov     di, OFFSET X ;          XP := address of X
Copy:
        mov     ax, [si] ;              ax := [WP]
        mov     [di], ax ;              [XP] := ax
        add     si, 2 ;                 WP := WP + 2
```

```
          add    di, 2 ;                  XP := XP + 2
          loop   Copy
```

Using the pointer method shortens the mov instructions inside the loop, but requires a second add instruction. A third solution uses only a single pointer register and address arithmetic:

```
; Example 10.2-7: Solution 3
;
          mov    cx, 100
          mov    si, OFFSET W
Copy:
          mov    ax, [si]
          mov    [X - W + si], ax
          add    si, 2
          loop   Copy
```

Recall that X - W is an ordinary number, and so can be added into the address in si to get another address. Even more elegant is to use bx as the difference between X and W and use based indexing:

```
; Example 10.2-7: Solution 4
;
          mov    cx, 100
          mov    si, OFFSET W
          mov    bx, X - W
Copy:
          mov    ax, [si]
          mov    [bx + si], ax
          add    si, 2
          loop   Copy
```

Example 10.2—8. The array C of 100 bytes is assumed to contain a string of ASCII characters. Check it to see if it contains the '$' character and go to location HasDollar if it does.

```
; Example 10.2-8: Solution
;
          mov    cx, 100
          mov    si, OFFSET C ;    CP := address of C array
Check:
          cmp    BYTE PTR [si], '$' ; if [CP] = '$'
          je     HasDollar ;              then go to HasDollar
          inc    si ;               CP := CP + 1
          loop   Check
```

The specification BYTE PTR is necessary because [si] has no size attached to it, and the constant '$' doesn't either.

Example 10.2—9. B is assumed to be an array of 100 ASCII characters. Convert all lowercase letters in the array to the corresponding uppercase letter.

```
; Example 10.2-9: Solution
;
            mov     cx, 100
            mov     si, OFFSET B
UpCase:
            mov     al, [si]
            cmp     al, 'a'
            jl      NotLC ;          if char >= 'a'
            cmp     al, 'z'
            jg      NotLC ;                   and char <= 'z' then
            add     BYTE PTR [si], 'A'-'a' ;  convert char to uc
NotLC:
            inc     si
            loop    UpCase
```

(Example 10.3—3 has a more elegant solution to this problem.)

We close this section with code which uses an array with larger element size.

Example 10.2—10. Write assembly code which displays the current day of the week.

Recall from Programming Problem 3.1 the DOS call 2ah (PCMAC.INC macro _GetDate) which returns the date information in registers as follows:

cx = Year
dh = Month   (1–12)
dl = Day   (1–31)

In addition, the call also returns

al = Day of Week   (0–6)

AL (converted to a word) can be used as an index into the array DayName defined as follows:

```
DayName     DB      'Sunday$   '
            DB      'Monday$   '
            DB      'Tuesday$  '
            DB      'Wednesday$'
            DB      'Thursday$ '
            DB      'Friday$   '
            DB      'Saturday$ '
```

In order that DayName be an array, all entries have to be the same length, so we have padded each entry with blanks to make them all 10 bytes long, the length of longest entry. Therefore the address of the name of the nth day is DayName + 10 * n. The code to print out the day of the week would be

```
; Example 10.2-10: Solution
;
        _GetDate ;          sets al := day number
        mov    bl, 10 ;     can't imul 10
        imul   bl ;         ax = 10 * weekday
        add    ax, OFFSET DayName
        _PutStr ax
```

Note: the 80X86 has a group of string manipulation instructions which will simplify or speed up many of the loop operations on arrays. They don't always apply to a particular problem though, and the methods discussed here do. The string manipulation instructions will be discussed in Chapter 18.

Exercises 10.2

1. ✓ Suppose we have declared

```
N         DW     5
CArray    DB     'Intel 80X86'
WArray    DW     4, -15, 33, 87, 2, -11
```

What will the contents of `ax` or `al` be after executing each of the following code groups?

```
        mov    bx, 3
        mov    al, [CArray + bx] ;      al = _____

        mov    bx, N
        mov    al, [CArray + bx] ;      al = _____
        mov    al, [CArray + 2 + bx] ;  al = _____

        mov    bx, N
        shl    bx, 1
        mov    ax, [WArray + bx] ;       ax = _____
        mov    ax, [WArray - 2 + bx] ;   ax = _____

        mov    bx, OFFSET Carray
        mov    al, [bx] ;                al = _____
        mov    al, [3 + bx] ;            al = _____

        mov    bx, OFFSET WArray
        mov    ax, [bx] ;                ax = _____
        mov    ax, [8 + bx] ;            ax = _____

        mov    bx, OFFSET Carray
        mov    si, 3
        mov    al, [bx + si] ;           al = _____
```

```
        mov     al, [3 + bx + si] ;      al = _____

        mov     bx, OFFSET WArray
        mov     si, 6
        mov     ax, [bx + si] ;          ax = _____
        mov     ax, [4 + bx + si] ;      ax = _____
```

2. Figure out what each of the following code fragments does. You can trace each fragment using the data definitions in Exercise 1, but you should give a general description of what is being accomplished, not what is happening to the particular data above.

```
(a)         sub     ax, ax          ; One way of setting ax := 0
            mov     bx, 10
Mystery1:
            add     ax, [WArray + bx]
            sub     bx, 2
            jge     Mystery1


(b) ✓       mov     ax, [WArray]
            mov     bx, 2
            mov     cx, 5
Mystery2:
            cmp     ax, [WArray + bx]
            jge     M2
            mov     ax, [WArray + bx]
M2:         add     bx, 2
            loop    Mystery2


(c)         mov     ax, 1
            mov     bx, 0
            mov     cx, 6
Mystery3:
            mov     [WArray + bx], ax
            add     bx, 2
            inc     ax
            loop    Mystery3


(d)         mov     bx, 0
            mov     cx, 11
Mystery4:
            cmp     [CArray + bx], '0'
            jl      M4
            cmp     [CArray + bx], '9'
            jle     Done
M4:         inc     bx
            loop    Mystery4
Done:
```

3. ✓ Rewrite each of the mystery programs in Exercise 2 using the pointer method (`[bx]` indexing) instead of the subscript method (`[WArray + bx]` or `[CArray + bx]` indexing).

4. Suppose that A, B, and C are arrays of 100 words.
   (a) Write code to place in `ax` the smallest integer in A. Use the pointer method (`[bx]` indexing) as opposed to the subscript method.
   (b) Write code to set all entries in A to 1. Use the pointer method.
   (c) ✓ Write code to set `A[i] := B[i] + C[i]` for i = 0, 1, ...

5. Suppose that we have recorded the tab stops we wish to use in a byte array `TabStop`, with the property that `TabStop[0] < TabStop[1] < ... TabStop[N]`, which is the highest set tab stop (N a word variable). If COL is the byte variable containing the current position of the cursor and a tab is entered, the new value of COL is the smallest `TabStop[I]` which is greater than COL. If no such value exists, the new value of COL is `COL + 1`. Write assembler code to compute this new value of COL.

6. The '10' in Example 10.2—10 above is a 'magic number'. Show how we can define a symbolic constant `DayLen` to be used in place of '10' which is the correct value no matter what (constant) length `DayName` entries are.

7. ✓ Redo Example 10.2—10 using an **address table** of pointers, which allows you to use variable-length day names:

```
Monday      DB      'Monday$'
Tuesday     DB      'Tuesday$'
Wednesday   DB      'Wednesday$'
                . . .
Days        DW      Monday, Tuesday, Wednesday, Thursday, ...
; These are pointers to the start of each day name string
```

8. ✓ M is a 3 × 5 array of bytes, defined as follows

```
M           DB      00h, 01h, 02h, 03h, 04h
            DB      10h, 11h, 12h, 13h, 14h
            DB      20h, 21h, 22h, 23h, 24h
```

We can think of M as a one-dimensional array of five-byte entries, each of which is an array of five bytes. Find an address expression for the address of the entry M[i, j] assuming i and j are constants, the address of M[0, 0] = M, and the contents of M[i, j] are ijh.

10.3 • Array Applications

10.3.1 • Reading a Whole Line from the Keyboard

Up until now, when reading from the keyboard, we have used _GetCh or _BIOSCh to read a single character at a time. Characters come in as keys are hit, with no chance for the usual keyboard editing with the backspace key. Now that we can process characters a whole array at a time though, we can use the _GetStr DOS call, which reads a whole line of characters using the usual keyboard editing.

The form of the call is

```
_GetStr GetStruct
```

where GetStruct is the following rather complicated data structure:

Byte 1   Maximum number of bytes in the Buffer (programmer-defined)
Byte 2   Number of bytes actually read, not including Enter (This number inserted by the
             DOS call)
Bytes 3...   The buffer, where DOS places the bytes read.

If Byte 1 = n, then _GetStr will accept at most n bytes of input, *including the Enter key*. If the person entering the data tries to type more than $n-1$ bytes before pressing Enter, the computer will beep and refuse to accept them. The carriage return character is inserted in the buffer after the other bytes read, *but is not included in the count* in Byte 2. Thus the length in Byte 2 will be at most $n-1$.

A sample of the _GetStr data structure can be declared in the .DATA area as follows:

```
MAXCHAR    EQU    100 ;          Or whatever; avoid magic numbers
GetStruct  DB     MAXCHAR ;      A byte containing the number
           DB     ? ;            The byte to store actual number read
Buffer     DB     MAXCHAR DUP (?) ; Allocate MAXCHAR bytes but
;                 don't initialize them (DUPlicate ? MAXCHAR times)
```

The declarations above allocate 102 bytes of storage. If we type Stuff⏎ in response to an _GetStr call using GetStruct, the resulting bytes in memory are

rest of Buffer
→

GetStruct: Buffer:

100	5	'S'	't'	'u'	'f'	'f'	13	

Note that _GetStr always echoes its input line, but echoes only the *carriage return* at the end of the line. That is, in the above example, the flashing cursor will end up at the beginning of the input line, under the 'S'.

```
Stuff
```

The *program* using _GetStr must output a line feed with _PutCh to get the cursor to the next line. The typical code will be

```
_GetStr GetStruct
_PutCh 10
```

which will produce

```
        Stuff

        _
```

Example 10.3—1. Read a line of characters from the keyboard and display them in reverse order.

We first saw the reversing problem in Programming Problem 7.2, where we used a stack to solve it, but it turns out that using an array is a more natural method. Now that we know how to manipulate arrays, it is worthwhile to use the _GetStr macro call. The reading part is

```
; Example 10.3-1: Part 1 (Read a string from the keyboard)
;
            .DATA
MAXBUF      EQU     100
GetBuf      DB      MAXBUF ;        maximum number of chars to read
GetCnt      DB      ? ;             number of chars actually read
CharStr     DB      MAXBUF DUP (?) ;    The chars read
            ...
            .CODE
            ...
            _GetStr GetBuf
            _PutCh 10 ;             _GetStr echoes the carriage return
;                                   at the end of the line but not a
;                                   line feed
```

To display the characters in reverse order, we need to get an index register pointing to the last character in the array:

```
; Example 10.3-1: Part 2 (Make bx point to the last char read)
;
            mov     bl, GetCnt ; Actual number of chars read
            mov     bh, 0 ;        Convert it to a word
            add     bx, OFFSET CharStr-1
```

How do we know we want to add OFFSET CharStr-1 to get it to point to the last character read? As usual, the best way to solve such problems is to look at a trivial case. When only one character is read, GetCnt = 1, the first character is also the last character, and we want to point at CharStr = GetCnt + CharStr − 1.

Now all we need is to display the characters, decrementing bx for each. Since we need a count in cx for the loop instruction and we should also test for an empty line entered, we will make a slight modification to Part 2:

```
; Example 10.3-1: Part 2, modified
;
            mov     cl, GetCnt ; Actual number of chars read
            mov     ch, 0 ;        Convert it to a word
            jcxz    Done
            mov     bx, OFFSET CharStr-1
```

```
        add     bx, cx ;        bx --> last character read
;
;              Part 3 (Display the reverse of the string just read)
;
Reverse:
        _PutCh [bx]
        dec     bx
        loop    Reverse
Done:
```

Another way of doing parts 2 and 3, which has the advantage of using only one register, is

```
; Example 10.3-1: parts 2 and 3 revisited
;
        mov     bl, GetCnt
        mov     bh, 0
        test    bx, bx ;        Equivalent to cmp bx, 0 but shorter
        je      Done
Reverse:
        _PutCh [CharStr - 1 + bx]
        dec     bx
        jne     Reverse
Done:
```

Exercises 10.3

1. ✓ Write a code fragment which displays the message 'Enter your name: ', reads in the line typed using _GetStr, places a '$' character at the end of the line entered, and uses (two executions of) _PutStr to display 'Hello, *whatever-you-entered*.'

10.3.2 • Conversion Tables

One extremely important application of arrays is in code conversions. For example, IBM mainframe computers use a character code called EBCDIC which is entirely different from ASCII, and we might wish to convert between the two. Also the IBM PC and Apple Macintosh both use ASCII, but have different extended character sets and we might want to convert between them.

Typically, we will have a range lo..hi of values to be converted and we will use an array Converter with subscripts in the range lo..hi to perform the conversion. If lo ≤ X ≤ hi, then its converted value is Converter[X]. The Converter array can also be thought of as a sort of function.

Example 10.3—2. Convert a number between 0 and 15 in al to its ASCII representation as a hex digit. (The technique here allows us to simplify the code for PutHex developed in Section 9.3).

Using arrays, the conversion is simple:

```
;; Example 10.3-2: Solution 1
```

```
HexDigit   DB        '0123456789ABCDEF'
           ...
           mov     bl, al ;       Get al into an index register...
           sub     bh, bh ;       ... and convert it to a word
           mov     al, [HexDigit + bx]
```

There is also a rather curious instruction designed specifically for code conversions:

```
xlat ;             Translate--replace al by the entry corresponding
;                      to it in the table pointed to by bx
```

That is, xlat sets al := [bx + al] (which is not a legal address in assembly language, of course). The translation above can be rewritten

```
;; Example 10.3-2: Solution 2

HexDigit   DB        '0123456789ABCDEF'
           ...
           mov     bx, OFFSET HexDigit
           xlat
```

In the PutHex routine, we could use si instead of bx to save the original input to PutHex and load bx with OFFSET HexDigit only once.

Example 10.3—3. Convert all lowe case characters in a string to uppe case.

If we set an array up properly, the conversion can be almost automatic. We want an array UpIt such that for any character C not a lower case letter, UpIt[C] = C, and for any lower case letter, UpIt[C] = C + 'A' - 'a', the corresponding uppercase letter.

If for instance si points to the string, whose length is in cx, then the code to convert the string could be

```
;; Example 10.3-3: Solution 1

cvLoop:
           mov     bl, [si] ;     get next character
           sub     bh, bh ;       convert it to a word
           mov     bl, [UpIt + bx]
           mov     [si], bl ;     can't move memory to memory
           inc     si
           loop    cvLoop
```

A version using xlat would be

```
;; Example 10.3-3: Solution 2

           mov     bx, OFFSET UpIt
```

```
cvLoop:
            mov     al, [si] ;      get next character
            xlat
            mov     [si], al
            inc     si
            loop    cvLoop
```

Defining the `UpIt` data structure is trivial but tedious. We could declare

```
UpIt        DB      0,1,2,3,4,5, ...
            ...
            DB      90,91,92,93,94,95,96,65,66,... ; 97 = 'a'
            etc.
```

To find ways to avoid this amount of work, we are about to launch into an extended discussion of techniques developed in Section 8.3 for generation of large tables. If you would prefer to take these techniques on faith, you can skip to the final definition of `UpIt` near the end of this section.

We could of course declare the array to be uninitialized

```
UpIt        DB      256 DUP (?)
```

and then initialize it in the program with two loops:

```
            mov     cx, 256
            mov     bx, 0 ;         bx will be used for the subscript
Init1:
            mov     [UpIt + bx], bl
            inc     bx
            loop    Init1 ;    After this loop, UpIt[C] = C for all Cs
            mov     cx, 26 ;   Now initialize the lower case letters
            mov     al, 'A'
            mov     bx, 'a' ; al will be the upper case version of bx
Init2:
            mov     [UpIt + bx], al
            inc     bx
            inc     al
            loop    Init2
```

A better way is to use the REPT pseudo-macro and = pseudo-operation introduced in Section 8.3. Recall that REPT *n* repeats *n* times the lines after it up to the corresponding ENDM and '=' is similar to EQUate except that values can be redefined. We could define our conversion array as follows:

```
Counter = 0
            REPT    97 ;            Do all characters before lower case
            DB      Counter
Counter = Counter + 1
```

```
            ENDM
            REPT    26 ;           Do lower case characters
            DB      Counter+'A'-'a'
Counter = Counter + 1
            ENDM
            REPT    256-97-26 ;    Do rest of chars. Expr OK as long as
;                                  it's constant
            DB      Counter
Counter = Counter + 1
            ENDM
```

We still haven't labeled this array as UpIt, though. We can't put UpIt inside a REPT/ENDM pair as then UpIt would be defined more than once. We could break out the 0 case separately and write

```
UpIt        DB      0
Counter = 1
            REPT    96 ;           etc.
```

It would be nicer if we could just put UpIt on a line by itself, as we can with labels in the .CODE section. That doesn't work in the .DATA section since the assembler wouldn't know whether the label was of a BYTE or a WORD. We can however use the new pseudo-operation LABEL to perform a similar function. The code

> *Name*   LABEL BYTE *or* WORD

assigns to *Name* the current location counter value ($) with the BYTE or WORD attribute, but reserves no storage.

The code

```
UpIt        LABEL   BYTE
Counter = 0
            REPT    97             ; etc.
```

solves our problem neatly without making the 0 entry a special case.

Just a couple of other fine points and we can give a final version. First, if you get an output listing (.LST file) of your assembly, you will end up with about five pages of very uninteresting code—all of the DB instructions. That can be avoided by preceding the first REPT pseudo-op by the .SALL pseudo-op which Suppresses the listing of ALL code generated by macros (REPT is considered a macro for this purpose). To restore listing, use the pseudo-op .LALL. Also, we can make our code a little more reliable and readable if we use expressions for some of our 'magic numbers.' Finally, UpIt is an array which might be used in many different places (in Exercise 10.3—4 below, for example), so it would be worthwhile to place it in a separate file to be linked in where needed. As before, UpIt would have to be declared to be PUBLIC. The corresponding EXTRN would be a little different than we are used to. Always before, the EXTRN was a code location. Here it is a data location, and we have to tell the assembler what type of data it is. Specifying data type is done with

```
            EXTRN   UpIt:BYTE ;    or WORD, if it were a WORD label
```

which should be placed in the `.DATA` region of the program using `UpIt`.

The complete code for `UpIt`, which is in `util.lib`, is

```
;; UPIT.ASM--Array for lower-to-upper case conversion in Example
;; 10.3-3.
;;
;;  To use this array, insert the statement EXTRN UpIt:BYTE in the
;;  .DATA region of your program and link with your program. Then
;;  for any character c, UpIt[c] = c if c is not a lowercase
;;  character, and if c is lowercase, UpIt[c] is the corresponding
;;  uppercase character.
;;
            .MODEL SMALL

            .DATA
            PUBLIC UpIt
UpIt        LABEL  BYTE
Counter = 0
            .SALL
            REPT   'a' ;          Counter goes from 0 to 'a' - 1
            DB     Counter
Counter = Counter + 1
            ENDM
            REPT   'z'-'a'+1 ;   Do lowercase letters
            DB     Counter-'a'+'A'
Counter = Counter + 1
            ENDM
            REPT   255 - 'z'
            DB     Counter
Counter = Counter + 1
            ENDM
            .LALL
            END
```

Note that we have indeed defined values for 255 - 'z' + 'z' – 'a' + 1 + 'a' = 256 characters.

Exercises 10.3 (concluded)

2. ✓ There are two simple ways to determine if a character is a vowel. One is to search for it in the array 'aeiouyAEIOUY' and the other is to use an array like `UpIt` whose value is 1 at a vowel, 0 otherwise. Write code fragments to jump to label `aVowel` if `al` contains a vowel using each of these methods, and compare them in terms of space and time trade-offs.

3. Write `.DATA` declarations of an array `CharType` of 256 characters such that `CharType[C]` is 0 if C is unprintable (< ' ' or ≥ 127), = 2 if C is a digit, = 3 if C is an upper or lower case letter, and = 1 if C is any other printable character.

4. a) Write .DATA declarations of an array Secret of 256 bytes which can be used as in this section to convert all upper and lower case letters to the uppercase letter following ('A' and 'a' go to 'B', ... 'Z' and 'z' go to 'A') and all other characters to 0.

    b) Write assembly code to take as input an array Message of N characters, to convert each character using the array Secret, and to display the resulting nonzero characters, (thus creating a secret code).

10.4 • Arrays in High-Level Languages

This section discusses techniques which occur frequently in high-level language programs using arrays.

Programs in high-level languages often use subscripts of the form *variable ± constant*. When translated to assembly language, we have seen that it is not necessary to add or subtract the *constant* with an instruction. For instance, if A is an array of items, each of them *s* bytes long, and N is a variable and *c* a constant, then

$$\text{address of A}[N \pm c] = A + s \times ([N] \pm c)$$
$$= (A \pm s \times c) + s \times [N]$$

(A ± s * c) is a valid address expression which can be computed once and for all at assembly time, and s * [N] is often already lying around in a register. Even if it isn't, it is no more difficult to index by N + c than it is to index by N.

Exercise 10.4—1. W is an array of 100 words. Determine whether W is sorted into increasing order, jumping to location NotSorted if not.

```
; Example 10.4-1: Solution 1--Subscript method
;
            mov     si, 0 ;             N := 0
            mov     cx, 99 ;            Loop count
IsSortedLoop:
            mov     ax, [W + si] ;      ax := W[N]
            cmp     ax, [W + 2 + si] ;  compare to W[N+1]
            jg      NotSorted ;         if W[N] > W[N+1]
            add     si, 2 ;             N := N + 1
            loop    InsertedLoop


; Example 10.4-1: Solution 2--Pointer Method
;
            mov     si, OFFSET W ;      WP := address of W[0]
            mov     cx, 99 ;            Loop count
IsSortedLoop:
            mov     ax, [si] ;          ax := W[N]
            cmp     ax, [2 + si] ;      compare to W[N+1]
            jg      NotSorted ;         if W[N] > W[N+1]
            add     si, 2 ;             N := N + 1
            loop    InsertedLoop
```

As we have seen, it is most natural in assembly language for an array of n elements to have subscripts varying from 0 to $n - 1$, **0-origin indexing**. C and C++ follow assembly closely in that respect. For instance, int anArray[100] declares anArray to be an array of 100 words with subscripts varying from 0 to 99. As in assembly language, anArray is considered to be a memory address (pointer) in C/C++ when used by itself. In C/C++, rather than requiring the programmer to write address expressions like anArray + s * i for the address of anArray[i], the programmer writes anArray + i and C/C++ does the multiplication of i by the array item size s automatically. The C/C++ method of address arithmetic simplifies programming and increases machine independence. (A given type may have different sizes on different machines).

In other high-level languages, things get a bit more complex. Many algorithms are expressed more naturally in arrays whose subscripts run from 1 to n (**1-origin indexing**) and a few work best with some other subscripting origin altogether. The original Fortran used 1-origin indexing exclusively, and modern Fortran, as well as Pascal, Ada, etc., allows arbitrary lower and upper limits for subscripts.

For instance, consider the Pascal declaration

```
var A : array [lo .. hi] of SomeType;
```

which declares an array of $hi - lo + 1$ elements. (The +1 comes from the fact that both subscript limits are included. To implement such arrays, the compiler in essence creates a related array A0 of $hi - lo + 1$ elements:

```
var A0 : array [0 .. hi - lo] of SomeType;
            { actual storage for array A }
```

Then every array reference A[N] in the high-level language is translated into a reference to A0[N − lo]. That is

$$
\begin{aligned}
\text{address of A[N]} \quad &= \text{A0} + s \times (\text{[N]} - lo) \\
&= (\text{A0} - lo \times s) + s \times \text{[N]}
\end{aligned}
$$

As before, there is no more run-time overhead in referencing A0[N − lo] than there is in referencing A0[N], so there is no penalty in allowing arbitrary origins for subscripts.

In addition, the technique for A[N ± constant] still works.

$$
\begin{aligned}
\text{address of A[N ± c]} \quad &= \text{A0} + s \times (\text{[N]} - lo \pm c) \\
&= (\text{A0} - (lo \pm c) \times s) + s \times \text{[N]}
\end{aligned}
$$

as (A0 − (lo ± c) * s) is again an address expression computable at translation time.

In assembly language, it is normal to declare the storage for the array A with the name A rather than A0 and make the mental transition to 0-origin indexing.

Example 10.4—2 Suppose we want to simulate an array which would be declared by the Pascal declaration

```
var W : array [7..83] of integer;
```

a) Declare storage for W with the statement

```
W           DW      (83 - 7 + 1) DUP (?)        ; 77 words
```

b) Write assembly code for the statement W[20] := 42;

```
        mov     [W - 2*7 + 2*20], 42
```

c) Write assembly code for the statement W[N] := 42; where N is a word variable.

```
        mov     bx, N
        shl     bx, 2 ;         bx := 2 * N
        mov     [W - 2*7 + bx], 42
```

d) Write assembly code for the statement

```
for N := 30 to 40 do
     W[N] := 0
end for
```

Since N never appears in the code in an essential way, we can write

```
            mov     bx, OFFSET W + 2 * (30 - 7)
            mov     cx, 40 - 30 + 1
ZeroLoop:
            mov     WORD PTR [bx], 0
            add     bx, 2
            loop    ZeroLoop
```

Example 10.4—3. Suppose we have an array CharBuf of characters whose length sits in a byte variable CharLen. (These variables might be the third and second fields in the _GetStr data structure, respectively. See Section 10.3.1.) We want to count the number of occurrences of each printable ASCII character in CharBuff. For our purposes, printable characters will be those whose ASCII value lies in the range 32 = ' ' through 126. (127 corresponds to the delete key.) We will use an array of words Count for the counts since we might want to count lines repeatedly and the counts might therefore get large.

We first need to declare the Count array. In Pascal, this declaration would be

```
var Count : array [32..126] of integer;
```

and in assembly language it would be

```
Count       DW      (126 - 32 + 1) DUP (?)
```

We may as well assume that CharBuff has 0-origin indexing, so the following pseudocode would do the counts:

```
for i := 0 to CharLen - 1 do
    if (CharBuff[i] ≥ 32) and (CharBuff[i] ≤ 126) then
        Count[CharBuff[i]] := Count[CharBuff[i]] + 1
    end if
end for
```

The only tricky part is the statement which increments a Count. CharBuff[i] is a byte and must be converted to a word, and because we are indexing a word array, must be multiplied by 2. If we assume that CharBuff[i] is in bl, the code would be

```
sub    bh, bh ;       convert CharBuff[i] to word
shl    bx, 1 ;         and multiply by 2
inc    [Count - 2*32 + bx]
```

In general, it's easy to get confused when one has to keep track of array element size and subscript lower limit.

The whole code fragment is

```
; Example 10.4-3: Solution
;
        mov    cl, CharLen
        sub    ch, ch ;       cx := CharLen converted to word
        jcxz   Done ;         Always a good safety measure
        mov    si, OFFSET CharBuff ;    Use pointer method
CountLoop:
        mov    bl, [si] ;     bl := CharBuff[i]
        cmp    bl, 32
        jb     NextChar
        cmp    bl, 126
        ja     NextChar
        sub    bh, bh ;       convert CharBuff[i] to word
        shl    bx, 1 ;         and multiply by 2
        inc    [Count - 2*32 + bx]
NextChar:
        inc    si
        loop   CountLoop
Done:
```

Exercises 10.4

1. Suppose that we have implemented the Pascal-style array

    var A : **array** [1..100] **of** integer;

in assembly language with the declaration

```
A0         DW     100 DUP (?)
```

Also assume that N is a word variable and that $bx = 2 \times N$.

a) Write assembly language code to do the following:

```
A[5] := 27; A[N] := 27; A[N + 3] := 27; ✓
```

b) What high-level language array elements are represented by the following address expressions?

```
[A0 + 24]          [A0 + bx]          [A0 + 32 + bx] ✓
```

c) Write assembly language code to check if N is a legal subscript for the A array by checking the value of bx. Go to location SubError if the value is not legal.

d) ✓ Write assembly language code to perform the function of the following loop:

```
for i := 1 to 100 do
    A[i] := i
end for
```

(Hint: It is probably best to use three registers, one for i, one for subscripting with 2*i, and one for the loop count (originally 100) if that many registers are available.)

2. ✓ Declare an array MoName of three-character names of months ('Jan', 'Feb', etc.) Each entry should have a terminating '$' character and thus will be four bytes long. Write a code fragment using _GetDate to print today's date in the form Mmm dd, yyyy using your array and PutDec. (See Example 10.2—10. This exercise is an example of 1-origin indexing which occurs naturally in assembly language.)

3. Recall that in Exercise 10.2—5, we used an array TabStop[0..N] to compute the next tab stop after column COL (which starts at 1) by finding the smallest i for which TabStop[i] > COL. It would be faster to compute the tabbed-to position if we had a byte array TabTo such that TabTo[COL] is the next tab stop after COL. Thus if TabStop[0] = 5, TabStop[1] = 7, TabStop[2] = 12, etc., TabTo[1] = ... = TabTo[4] = 5, TabTo[5], TabTo[6] = 7, TabTo[7] = ... = TabTo[11] = 12, ...

a) Write assembly code to compute the TabTo array from the TabStop array and N. Assume that the TabTo array has 120 elements.

b) Write assembly code to compute NewCol := TabTo[COL].

4. This exercise makes use of the array Count declared in Example 10.4—3.

a) Write assembly language code to set all entries of the Count array to 0.

b) Write assembly language code to display the count array, as follows: only nonzero entries are displayed, one per line. The first character on the line is the character being counted,

followed by three spaces, followed by the number of times the character occurred. (Use
`PutDec`.)

c) ✓ Suppose that the necessary counts have been made and that we do not wish to distinguish
between upper and lower case letters. Write assembly language code which is equivalent to
the pseudo-Pascal code

```
for c := 'A' to 'Z' do
      Count[c] := Count[c] + Count[c + 'a' - 'A']
                             { Combine uc and lc counts }
      Count[c+32] := 0       { don't print lc counts }
end for
```

Programming Problem 10.1

Write a program `HISTOGRM` which reads a series of nonnegative integers from the keyboard, terminated by a negative number. The program then prints one line for each number, consisting of a
sequence of asterisks representing its value. The number of asterisks is determined as follows: Find
the largest of the numbers, N. If N is less than 80, each asterisk represents 1 unit, and if N is greater
than or equal to 80, each asterisk represents (N + 79) / 80 units. Your program should start by
printing 'Each * represents *nnn* units', followed by one row of asterisks for each number. Thus if the
input numbers are 3, 14, 7, –1, the output is

```
Each * represents 1 unit

***
**************
*******
```

Use `GetDec` to read the numbers and `PutDec` to print the number of asterisks per unit. (Note that
with `GetDec`, you can enter more than one number per line.)

Programming Problem 10.2

Write a program `REVNAME` which reads a name from the keyboard (using `_GetStr`) in normal 'first
[middle name]... last' order, where [middle name}... indicates 0 or more middle names, and displays the name in order 'last, first [middle name]...' (Hint: start at the right end of the input line and
search backwards for a blank. This algorithm would be unsatisfactory to physicist Robert Van de
Graff and composer Ralph Vaughn Williams, as well as all Jr.s and IIIs, etc.)

Test your program with an empty input string, a string with a single name, a string with two
names, and a string with four or five. (The first two cases may or may not be considered errors, but
they shouldn't crash your program.)

Programming Problem 10.3

(Harder) Write a program `PIGLATIN` which reads a line of text from the keyboard and displays its
translation into Pig Latin. Thus the line 'Gypsy music is thrilling but square' should produce the
output 'ypsyGay usicmay isway illingthray utbay aresquay.' The algorithm is as follows:

1) Read the line of input using _GetStr, mark its end (somehow), and put its starting address into si.
2) Increment si until it points to a non-blank character. If this character is the end of string mark, quit. Otherwise, save the value of si in di.
3) Increment si until it points to a vowel. If si ≠ di (i.e., we aren't at the start of the word) and si points to a 'u' and si–1 points to a 'q' or a 'Q', increment si again. (The 'u' in 'qu' is not a vowel for our purposes.)
4) Save si in bx. Display the character pointed to by si and increment si, repeating the process until si points to a blank or the end of the input line.
5) If bx = di, display a 'w'.
6) Display the character pointed to by di and increment di, repeating as long as di < bx (Note: Be sure to use unsigned jump as you are comparing addresses)
7) Go back to Step 2.

You may assume that your input is reasonably correct, for example., that 'qu' will actually be followed by a vowel, and that there is no punctuation.

SUMMARY

New Instruction

```
xlat ;        Replaces al with [bx + al]
```

New Pseudo-Operation

To declare a name in the .DATA section without reserving any storage, use

```
Name        LABEL    datatype
```

where *datatype* can be WORD or BYTE (or others we haven't covered).

To suppress listing of macro (and REPT and IRP) expansions in the .LST file, use the pseudo-operation .SALL. To restore listing of such expansions, use .LALL.

To declare that a label *Label* declared in the current file is to be visible to other files declaring it in an EXTRN *Label*:*type* statement, use the statement

```
PUBLIC Label
```

The following is a complete table of methods of addressing memory on the 8086-80286. *Addr* stands for an address, constant, or expression involving these.

simple	indexed		based indexed	
	[bx]	[*Addr*+bx]	[bx+si]	[*Addr*+bx+si]
Addr	[bp]	[*Addr*+bp]	[bx+di]	[*Addr*+bx+di]
(or [*Addr*])	[si]	[*Addr*+si]	[bp+si]	[*Addr*+bp+si]
	[di]	[*Addr*+si]	[bp+di]	[*Addr*+bp+di]

The notation *reg*/*mem* includes all of these possibilities as well as the eight byte registers al, ah, bl, bh, cl, ch, dl, dh and the eight word registers ax, bx, cx, dx, si, di, sp, bp. **Note:** *bytes* in si, di, sp, and bp cannot be directly specified.

For the purposes of arithmetic, a variable name in assembly language is understood to represent the *address* of the variable. The following operations on addresses, with their corresponding results, are legitimate:

address ± integer constant	(produces another address)
address – address	(produces an integer constant)

Parentheses can be used for grouping. Any arithmetic or logical operation can be used on integer constants to produce another constant.

The dollar sign ($) represents the current value of the location counter in address expression.

Arrays can be declared by listing their elements. Array items are accessed using address arithmetic or by one of the four indexing registers: bx, si, di, and bp (bp is used only for indexing in the stack and will be explained in Chapter 13). Bx and bp are also called *base registers*.

If A is an array, [A + n] stands for the element of the array at address A + n. The notation A[n] is used here only to represent subscripting in a high-level language. If A in the high-level language has subscripts in the range *lo*..*hi* and each entry in the array contains *size* bytes, then

$$\text{the address of entry } A[n] = A + size \times (n - lo)$$

Typical usage has *size* × n in an index register *reg*, allowing use of the instruction address [A – size × lo + *reg*] can be written in the address field of an assembly language statement.

The standard code for the loop

```
for n := lo to hi do
     process A[n]
end for
```

using the subscripting method is

Subscripting Method
| ```
          mov     n, lo
          mov     indexreg, 0
          mov     cx, hi - lo + 1 ;   number of items in array
ProcLoop:
          process [A + indexreg]
          inc     n
          add     indexreg, size
          loop    ProcLoop
``` |

Using the pointer method, the code is

Pointer M ethod
| ```
          mov     n, lo
          mov     indexreg, OFFSET A - size * lo
          mov     cx, hi - lo + 1 ;   number of items in array
ProcLoop:
          process [indexreg]
          inc     n
          add     indexreg, size
          loop    ProcLoop
``` |

If the actual value of n isn't needed in the loop, the two instructions referring to n can be omitted.

The DOS call macro _GetStr reads a line from the keyboard, with the usual editing. It is of the form

```
          _GetStr GetStruct ; Where GetStruct is a data
;                             structure as described below
;                             DESTROYS AX and DX.
; GetStruct DB    MAXLEN
;           DB    ?
;           DB    MAXLEN DUP (?)
```

_GetStr reads $n \le$ MAXLEN bytes from the keyboard up to and including a carriage return, echoes those bytes, including the carriage return (but no line feed), sets [GetStruct+1] to $n-1$, and places the keyboard characters, including the carriage return, in bytes 2 through $n+1$ of GetStruct.

The byte array UpIt is available in util.lib. For any character C, UpIt[C] = C if C is not a lower case letter. For any lower case leter C, UpIt[C] is the corresponding upper case letter.

Debug Workshop IV

Arrays and Byte Swapping

Neither debugger gives much useful help in debugging arrays in assembly language and CodeView is even confusing in places. However, we will discuss what procedures there are and also demonstrate byte swapping, as discussed in Section 10.1.5.

We will be using as our example the do-nothing program DbgEx7 listed below, which is in the DEBUG sub-directory of the disk that comes with this book. The use of the two debuggers on this program will be described in separate sections.

IV.1 CodeView
IV.2 Turbo Debugger

```
;; DBGEX7.ASM--Arrays and byte swapping
;;
INCLUDE     PCMAC.INC
            .MODEL SMALL
            .STACK 100h
            .DATA
A           DB      1, 2, 3, 4, 5
AW          DW      1006, 1005, 1004, 1003, 1002, 1001

            .CODE
DbgEx7      PROC
            mov     ax, @data
            mov     ds, ax

            mov     ax, [AW + 2]
            mov     ax, OFFSET AW + 2
            mov     cx, 234h
            mov     ax, [AW + 1]
            add     2, bx
```

```
           _Exit   0
DbgEx7     ENDP
           END     DbgEx7
```

IV.1 • CodeView

Procedure

Assemble DBGEX7.ASM (/Zi) and link (/co) with debugging information. Execute DbgEx7 with CV.

1) Hit **F3** until the Source1 window is in mixed source and assembly mode (hex versions of the instructions interleaved with the original source code).

2) *Trace* (**F8**) until you get to the line with MOV AX, WORD PTR [0011]. The source and assembly lines will look something like

```
15:              mov      ax, [AW + 2]
xxxx:0005 A11100         MOV       AX, WORD PTR [0011]
```

(*xxxx* is a hex number which will vary from computer to computer.) Note that the address is shown as 0011, its actual hex value, in the assembly to the right of the line, and byte swapped as 1100 to the left of the line, as it is actually stored byte by byte in memory. (A1 is the operation code for this mov instruction.)

3) There are a variety of ways of viewing the contents of the AW array. Perhaps the simplest is with the command dw AW L 6 in the command window (dump words starting at AW for length 6). This dw command produces output of the sort

```
yyyy:000F  03EE 03ED ...        (03EEh = 1006)
```

If you dump by bytes (db AW L 12), you can once again see the byte swapping:

```
yyyy:000F  EE 03 ED 03 ...
```

4) Using the command window has the disadvantage that you must reenter the command if you want to view further changes. Viewing the Memory1 (or 2) window shows the data updated as the program progresses. Open the Memory1 window, **Alt-W**(indows **5**(. Memory1 or **Alt-5**. Choose the area to be displayed with **Alt-O**(ptions M(emory1... A(ddress expression and enter AW in the window. Choose the display format with **Alt-O**(ptions M(emory1... D(isplay format: and choose integer. With a mouse, both options can be accomplished at once. Click OK or hit Enter when you are done. The Memory1 window should start with the (decimal) contents of the AW array 1006 1005 ...

5) Trace (**F8**) one line. Note that ax now contains 03ED. The translation of the mov ax, OFFSET AW + 2 instruction is B81100. Note that the operand part of this instruction, 1100, is the same as for mov ax, [AW + 2], and that the only difference is in the operation code, B8 versus A1.

6) Trace again, noting that ax now contains 0011, and that the mov instruction has swapped the bytes back. Trace through the mov cx, 234h instruction to verify that it does the same

thing.

7) Trace the mov ax, [AW + 1] instruction to verify that the kinds of horrible things I described in Section 10.1.6 do take place. Ax should end up with the value ED03.

8) We are now going to try to display a subscripted value. This attempt won't be very successful because CodeView doesn't have a MASM expression evaluator. It evaluates all expressions as C/C++ expressions, and among other things automatically multiplies subscript by item length, which would be right for C/C++ but gives the wrong result for MASM. For instance we are going to set a watch on [AW + bx], as best we can. Enter **Ctrl-W** and each of the following three expression to be watched: &AW+bx. ('&' is the C equivalent of OFFSET), *(&AW+bx) ('*' is the C equivalent of [ ]), and AW+bx. You will note initially (with bx still 0) that AW + bx = *(&AW+bx) = 1006 and &AW+bx = 0x*yyyy*:0x000F as expected. (0x... is the C/C++ notation for hex.) After tracing the add bx, 2 instruction though, note that &AW+bx = 0x*yyyy*:0x0013, *(&AW+bx) = 1004 and AW + bx = 1008. We see that &AW+bx = OFFSET AW + 2[bx], *(&AW+bx) = [AW+2[bx]], and AW+bx = [AW]+[bx].

IV.2 • Turbo Debugger

Procedure

Assemble DBGEX7.ASM (/zi) and link (/v) with debugging information. Execute DbgEx7 with TD.

1) Open the CPU window (**Alt-V**(iew **C**(PU) to view assembled versions of the instructions interleaved with the original source code.

2) *Trace* (**F7**) until you get to the line with MOV AX, [0007]. The source and assembly lines will look like

```
#dbgex7#15:  mov ax, [AW + 2]
  cs:0005 A10700        MOV      AX, [0007]
```

Note that the address is shown as 0007, its actual hex value, in the assembly to the right of the line, and byte swapped as 0700 to the left of the line, as it is actually stored byte by byte in memory. (A1 is the operation code for this mov instruction.)

3) To view the AW array, one can either use the dump pane, which is the lower lefthand corner of the CPU window (TAB to it or click left in it to make it active) or use the Dump window, **Alt-V**(iew **D**(ump, which has the same format. Use the SpeedMenu for the dump pane or window to display (go to) AW (click right in the pane or **Alt-F10** and choose **G**(o to… or hit **Ctrl-G**) and enter AW. The default is to display by bytes, and the pane now starts ds:0005 EE 03 ED 03 …. .

4) Change format by again using the SpeedMenu **D**(isplay as… or **Ctrl-D** and choose 'word.' You will now see the array in the form ds:0005 03EE 03ED …, and you can see that in the byte form, the bytes were swapped.

5) Trace (**F8**) one line. Note that ax now contains 03ED. The translation of the mov ax, OFFSET AW + 2 instruction is B80700. Note that the operand part of this instruction, 0700, is the same as for mov ax, [AW + 2], and that the only difference is in the operation code, B8 versus A1.

6) Trace again, noting that ax now contains 0007, and that the mov instruction has swapped

the bytes back. Trace through the `mov cx, 234h` instruction to verify that it does the same thing.

7) Trace the `mov ax, [AW + 1]` instruction to verify that the kinds of horrible things I described in Section 10.1.6 do take place. `Ax` should end up with the value EE03.

8) We are now going to display a subscripted value. Set a watch (**Ctrl-F7**) on `[AW+bx]`. You will note initially (with `bx` still 0) that the value is given as `word 1006(3EEh)`. After tracing the `add bx, 2` instruction the watch window will show that the value of `[AW+bx]` is `word 1005 (3EDh)`, as expected.

SUMMARY

Arrays can be debugged using the Memory 1 or 2 windows (CV) or the Dump pane of the CPU window (TD). In either case, the display can be started at the beginning of the array and the format changed to match (more or less) that of the actual array items. TD allows one to watch subscripted expressions such as `[A + bx + di]`. CV has a somewhat similar mechanism which is unsatisfactory for debugging assembly language.

Chapter 11

Applying Assembly II: Using Arrays

This chapter is optional but its study should give a deeper understanding of arrays and programming in assembly language and array techniques used in higher level languages. All sections are more or less independent of each other.

11.1 • PutDec III: `Bin2Dec`

This section assumes a knowledge of Chapter 7, particularly Sections 7.1 and 7.2.

In programming `PutDec`, the problem we faced in converting a binary number to its external decimal representation was that if we find our digits by repeatedly dividing by 10, they come out in reverse order. In our original solution to the problem in Chapter 7, we reversed the order by pushing the digits onto the stack as they were computed and then popping them off and displaying them. Now that we know about arrays, there are other possibilities.

The simplest method is to compute the digits in reverse order and use an array to get them in the correct order. Omitting the leading zeroes becomes virtually automatic, and we also don't have to count digits any more. (As before, the number is assumed to be in `ax`. Changes from the final version of `PutUDec` are shown in **boldface**.)

```
OutArray  DB      5 DUP (?)
Stopper   DB      '$'
          ...
          mov     si, OFFSET Stopper ; Start at
;                                       right end
          mov     bx, 10
PushDigs:
          sub     dx, dx
          div     bx
```

```
        add     dl, '0' ;       Convert next digit to ASCII
        dec     si ;            si points to current first digit
        mov     [si], dl
        push    dx
        cmp     ax, 0
        jne     DigLoop
        _PutStr si
restore register and return
```

Note that the test for ax = 0 is placed at the *end* of the loop, so that at least one digit is always displayed.

With arrays, a more useful generalization of PutDec is possible. Instead of constructing a procedure to display a decimal number, we will construct a procedure which converts a binary to a decimal number as a string of characters at a specified place in memory. The procedure, which we call Bin2Dec, will take as input a binary number in ax and an address in di of a place in memory where the decimal conversion is to be stored. On exit, di will point to the first memory location following the translated decimal number. This routine will make it possible to translate numbers for output to arbitrary files, not just to the terminal screen. An example call is as follows:

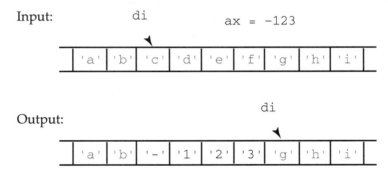

Input: di   ax = −123

| 'a' | 'b' | 'c' | 'd' | 'e' | 'f' | 'g' | 'h' | 'i' |

Output: di

| 'a' | 'b' | '−' | '1' | '2' | '3' | 'g' | 'h' | 'i' |

Once again we have the problem of generating the digits in reverse order. In the solution above, we generated the digits right to left with the last digit going into a fixed location. The output of Bin2Dec must *start* at a fixed location, however, so the program isn't as neat as the one above for PutUDec. As in the first version of PutDec, we will use a two-stage process, now storing the digits as they are computed in an array and then copying them in reverse order to the place pointed to by di. The overall plan is

```
handle the case ax < 0;
n := 5
repeat                  { compute digits }
      n := n - 1; compute Digit[n]
      ax := ax / 10
until ax = 0
for i := n to 5 do output Digit[i] end for
```

The code to output a character is

```
        mov     BYTE PTR [di], character
        inc     di
```

Note: BYTE PTR is necessary if *character* could be either word or byte, as [di] could also be either. The complete procedure is

```
;; BIN2DEC.ASM--Procedure to take a binary number in ax and
;;    convert it to decimal, storing the ASCII characters in memory
;;    starting at di. On output, di contains the address of the
;;    first character after the last digit of the converted number.
;;
;; Calling Sequence:
;;        EXTRN   Bin2Dec:NEAR
;;        mov     ax, theNumber
;;        mov     di, OFFSET thePlace
;;        call    Bin2Dec
;;
;; All registers except di are preserved
;;
        .MODEL SMALL

        .DATA
M32768  DB      '32768'
Digit   DB      5 DUP (?) ;   Array of digits computed

        .CODE
        PUBLIC Bin2Dec
Bin2Dec PROC
        push    ax
        push    bx ;        Holds divisor (10)
        push    cx ;        Count of digits generated
        push    dx
        push    si
        test    ax, ax ;    Is number negative?
        jge     Positive
        mov     BYTE PTR [di], '-' ;     yes, output - sign
        inc     di
        cmp     ax, -32768 ; Does ax = -ax?
        jne     NotM32768
        mov     si, OFFSET M32768 ; Address of digits
        mov     cx, 5 ;        Number of digits (sign already set)
        jmp     Transfer
NotM32768:
        neg     ax
Positive:
        mov     si, OFFSET Digit + 5 ; One beyond end
        sub     cx, cx ;      Count := 0
```

```
              mov     bx, 10
DigLoop:
              sub     dx, dx
              div     bx
              add     dl, '0'
              dec     si ;          Point to next digit position
              inc     cx ;             and count digit
              mov     [si], dl ;      and save digit
              test    ax, ax ;      is ax 0?
              jne     DigLoop ;     if not, more digits to process
Transfer:
              mov     al, [si] ;    Digit[i]
              mov     [di], al
              inc     si
              inc     di
              loop    Transfer

              pop     si
              pop     dx
              pop     cx
              pop     bx
              pop     ax
              ret
Bin2Dec       ENDP
              END
```

Now it is easy to rewrite PutDec making use of Bin2Dec:

```
;; PUTDEC.ASM--New version using Bin2Dec. Procedure to display
;;   a binary number in ax in decimal on the CRT screen.
;;
;;  Calling Sequence:
;;       EXTRN   PutDec:NEAR
;;       mov     ax, theNumber
;;       call    PutDec      *
;;
;;  All registers are preserved
;;
INCLUDE   PCMAC.INC

          .MODEL SMALL

          .DATA
Digits    DB      7 DUP (?) ;   Leave room for number and '$'

          .CODE
          PUBLIC PutDec
```

```
             EXTRN   Bin2Dec : NEAR
PutDec       PROC
             push    ax
             push    dx
             push    di
             mov     di, OFFSET Digits
             call    Bin2Dec ;     number already in ax
             mov     BYTE PTR [di], '$'
             _PutStr Digits
             pop     di
             pop     dx
             pop     ax
             ret
PutDec       ENDP
             END
```

Dec2Bin is roughly the reverse of Bin2Dec. Dec2Bin takes as input the address of a character array (presumably containing a decimal number) in si and returns with the binary version of that number in ax and si pointing to the first character *after* the decimal number. For example,

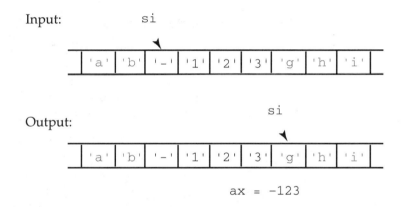

With Dec2Bin we could rewrite GetDec as follows:

```
Buffer       DB      20 DUP (?) ;  or however big it needs to be
             . . .
GetDec       PROC
             Save Regs
             push    si
             code to read characters into Buffer
             and terminate the string with a non-digit character.
             mov     si, OFFSET Buffer
             call    Dec2Bin
             pop     si
             restore other registers
             ret ;       value read is already in ax from Dec2Bin
```

```
GetDec      ENDP
```

Character reading can best be accomplished by using the `_GetStr` DOS call introduced in Section 10.3.1.

Exercises 11.1

1. ✓ Write an assembly language function `PrintLen` which takes as its input a number in `ax` and returns as its value, also in `ax`, the number of characters required to display the number. (Hint: for a positive number, compare the number to the successive elements of an array whose elements are 10000, 1000, 100, 10, and 1. For a negative number, add 1 to the result you'd get for the corresponding positive number. Note: if you use an unsigned conditional jump, you don't have to treat –32768 as a special case.)

2. Use `PrintLen` from the previous exercise and `PutDec` to write another version of the procedure `PutDecR` from Exercise 7.2—3. `PutDecR` takes a number in `ax` and a minimum print-width in `bx`, and writes out blanks ahead of the number so that `ax` is displayed right-justified in at least the number `bx` of spaces.

3. Write an assembly language function `Dec2Bin` and corresponding `GetDec`, as described above.

11.2 • C/C++ Type Variable Length Character Strings

(This section will be more intelligible to those with some knowledge of the C or C++ programming languages.)

In the C/C++ programming languages, character strings can be of any length. They are specified by the address of their first character, and are terminated by a **null character**—all zero bits, **not** '0'. The null character is not included as part of the string for the purposes of computing its length. Thus if we declare

```
String1     DB      'A short string', 0
String2     DB      'This is a longer string containing the digit 0'
            DB      ', but terminated only by a 0 byte', 0
String3     DB      100 DUP (?)
```

then `String1` contains 14 characters and `String2` contains 79 characters and ends with the four characters 'byte'. `String3` can contain any C-type string whose length is 99 characters or less. (Storage is also required for the terminating null byte.)

C has a wide variety of built-in functions and procedures for manipulating such strings. We will give versions of a few of them here, and leave two others to the reader as exercises.* We will treat these characters strings as arrays whose length isn't known, and therefore for which counting with `cx` can't be used as a loop terminator.

---

* We have inverted the names of the standard C functions here because our calling protocol is different—C normally passes parameters on the stack while we are passing them in registers. Thus our `LenStr` corresponds to C's `strlen,` our `CpyStr` to C's `strcpy,` etc.

Example 11.2—1. Write a function LenStr which takes as input the address of the first byte of a C-type string in si and returns the number of characters in the string in ax. As a bonus, LenStr will also leave si pointing to the terminating 0 byte of the string.

```
;; LENSTR.ASM--return length of C string pointed to on entry by si
;;
;;    Calling Sequence:
;;          EXTRN   LenStr:NEAR
;;          mov     si, OFFSET theString
;;          call    LenStr
;;
;;    On exit, ax contains the string's length (excluding the
;;      terminating null byte) and si points to that byte. All
;;      other registers are preserved.
;;
            .MODEL SMALL

            .CODE
            PUBLIC LenStr
LenStr      PROC
            mov     ax, si ;      save si to subtract at end
LenLoop:
            cmp     BYTE PTR [si], 0
            je      Done
            inc     si
            jmp     LenLoop
Done:
            neg     ax
            add     ax, si ;      ax := loc of null byte - start
            ret
LenStr      ENDP
            END
```

Example 11.2—2. Write a procedure CpyStr which copies a C-type string whose starting address is in si into a sequence of bytes whose starting address is in di. The null-byte terminating the string at si is also copied.

```
;; CPYSTR.ASM--copy C string from si to di
;;
;;    Calling Sequence:
;;          EXTRN   CpyStr:NEAR
;;          mov     si, OFFSET sourceString
;;          mov     di, OFFSET destinationString
;;          call    CpyStr
;;
;;    On exit, si points to the null byte terminating the source
;;      string, di to the null byte terminating the copied string,
```

```
;;      and all other registers are preserved.
;;
            .MODEL SMALL

            .CODE
            PUBLIC CpyStr
CpyStr      PROC
            push    ax ;          We will use al for moving bytes
CpyLoop:
            mov     al, [si]
            mov     [di], al ;    mov doesn't set flags!
            cmp     al, 0 ;       Compare after move so null byte gets
            je      Done;          moved, too
            inc     si
            inc     di
            jmp     CpyLoop
Done:
            pop     ax
            ret
CpyStr      ENDP
            END
```

Example 11.2—3. Write a function CpyStr which takes as input pointers to C strings in si and di and returns with ax > 0, < 0, or = 0 depending on whether the si string is lexicographically greater than, less than, or equal to the di string.

Lexicographic order (dictionary order) is determined as follows: compare the two strings, character by character, left to right, until an unequal pair of characters is found. The ordering of the strings is then the ordering of those two characters. If no unequal pair is found, then of course the strings are equal. Thus 'abcdxxx' < 'abce'. When CmpStr compares two strings, one of which is a prefix of the other (as in 'pre' and 'prefix'), the longer string turns out to be larger. Getting the correct order in this way is a direct result of using a null (all zero) byte as the string terminator character. Because of the way ASCII represents upper and lower case letters, every upper case letter is less than every lower case letter, so 'Zzyqb' < 'aaa'.

The code is a little tricky because of the various different ways the loop can terminate. An outline is as follows:

```
while ([si] = [di]) and ([si] ≠ 0) do
     si := si + 1; di := di + 1
end while
return [si] − [di]
```

Note that we don't have to test for [di] ≠ 0 because [si] = [di] and [si] ≠ 0 guarantee that [di] ≠ 0. We analyze the situation at the end of the loop as follows:

1) If [si] = 0, we have reached the end of the si string. If [di] also equals 0 the strings are equal. If [di] ≠ 0, the si string is a prefix of the di string, and so is less than it.

2) if [di] = 0, a similar analysis to 1) holds.

3) if neither [si] = 0 nor [di] = 0, then [si] and [di] correspond to 'real' characters in their respective strings and the loop must have terminated because [si] and [di] are the first corresponding characters which are unequal.

The argument above is valid if we assume that characters are always positive. That isn't true if characters in the extended ASCII character set are considered as signed bytes. In order to make the comparison work for such characters, we must convert the two characters to words first as *unsigned* numbers, then subtract. If we subtract bytes first and then do the *signed* conversion (which we must do, since a negative result is possible), we may get the wrong answer.

The program is

```asm
;; CMPSTR.ASM--return ax < 0, = 0, > 0 according as string at si
;;    is <, =, or > string at di
;;
;;    Calling Sequence:
;;        EXTRN   CmpStr:NEAR
;;        mov     si, OFFSET leftString
;;        mov     di, OFFSET rightString
;;        call    CmpStr
;;
;;    On exit, ax contains the result and all other registers are
;;      preserved
;;
            .MODEL SMALL

            .CODE
            PUBLIC CmpStr
CmpStr      PROC
            push    bx
            push    si
            push    di
CharLoop:
            mov     al, [si]
            mov     bl, [di]
            cmp     al, bl ;    Are current bytes equal?
            jne     Done ;         no
            cmp     al, 0 ;     yes; are the strings terminated?
            je      Done ;         yes
            inc     si
            inc     di
            jmp     CharLoop
Done:
            sub     ah, ah ;    Must do unsigned convert BEFORE
            sub     bh, bh ;       subtracting the two characters
            sub     ax, bx ;    ax := [si] - [di]
            pop     di
```

```
                pop     si
                pop     bx
                ret
    CmpStr      ENDP
                END
```

There are various ways these string processing routines can be improved, but the best way is to use the special string processing instructions on the 80X86, which we will discuss in Chapter 18.

Using Debuggers with C strings Both CV and TD allow you to display C style strings in human-readable form. Suppose we have declared

```
    CString     DB      'This is a string', 0
```

CV: To watch CString, enter '&CString, s' in the Watch window. To dump the current value, type '?&CString, s' in the command window. (The ampersand is a C operator which returns a pointer to its argument.)

TD: To watch CString, enter 'CString, s' in the Watch window. If TD can recognize the argument as a C string, as it can in this example, the ', s' be omitted.

Exercises 11.2

1. Write a procedure CatStr which concatenates the C-string starting at si onto the end of the C-string starting at di. Thus if we declared

```
    Str1        DB      'A String', 0, 20 DUP (?)
    Str2        DB      ' and a half', 0
```

and executed

```
                mov     si, OFFSET Str2
                mov     di, OFFSET Str1
                call    CatStr
```

The result would be as if we had declared

```
    Str1        DB      'A String and a half', 0, 9 DUP (?)
    Str2        DB      ' and a half',0
```

(Hint: use LenStr, in particular its side effect on si, but otherwise generally follow the model of CpyStr.)

2. Write a procedure SPut which displays on the CRT screen a C-type string whose starting address is in si.

3. Standard Pascal doesn't include variable length strings and as a result there are various ways of

implementing them. The most common way is as an array of bytes, the first byte of which is the (current) length of the string. Thus the Pascal version of `Str2` in Exercise 1 would be

```
Str2      DB      11, ' and a half'
```

(As you can see, the maximum length of such strings in 255 bytes, so a few Pascals use a whole 16-bit word for the length.) Write versions of the `LenStr` (much easier than the C version), `CpyStr` (easier) and `CmpStr` (harder) procedures for Pascal-type strings.

4. ✓ Using the array `UpIt` from Section 10.3.2, write a new version `CmpStrI` (CoMPare STRing and Ignore case) of `CmpStr` from Example 11.2—3 which compares two strings lexicographically, considering corresponding upper and lower case letters equal. Thus 'Z' would compare greater than 'a'. (Hint: as the two characters are loaded to be compared, convert them to upper case if necessary.)

5. Assume that `Roman` is a C-type string containing a Roman numeral, in all upper case. For instance, `Roman` might be defined by

```
Roman     DB      'CCLIX',0 ;    259
```

Write a program fragment using a translation array like `UpIt` in Example 10.3—2 to multiply Roman by 10; that is, I → X, V → L, etc.

11.3 • Sets

You will need to read Chapter 9 before reading this section. Some knowledge of Pascal may also help.

The Pascal language has a **set** data type, which is actually implemented as an array of bits. Such a set is always arranged in some fashion to be a set of numbers in the range 0-n. To simplify matters, we will consider a set of numbers in the range 0-255, which is one of the most common cases, including as it does, sets of characters. Such a set will be represented by an array of 256 bits, where the number i is in the set only if the ith bit is 1 (numbering from 0). In order to represent such an array, we use the bits of a byte to represent 8 consecutive elements of the array. Thus our 256 bit array will require $256/8 = 32$ bytes. The ith bit of the array will reside in the $i/8$ th byte, at position $i \bmod 8$. (Recall that / is integer division, with no remainder, and **mod** is the remainder from integer division.)

Example 11.3—1. Give the data definition of the 32 byte set of all upper and lower case letters. Recalling that 'A' = 65, 'Z' = 90, 'a' = 97, 'z' = 122, and recalling that bits are numbered from the right end of bytes and words, we can write

```
Letters   DB      8 DUP (0), 2 DUP (0FEh, 0FFh, 0FFh, 07h)
          DB      16 DUP (0)
```

Example 11.3—2. Write an assembly language function `InSet` (the Pascal operator `in` is a reserved word in assembler) which takes as input a number in `al` and a pointer to a 'set' of integers in the range 0-255 in `si` and returns 1 if the number in `ax` is in the set, 0 otherwise.

We use bit operations to extract al / 8 and al **mod** 8:

```
;; INSET.ASM--Solution to Example 11.3-2
;;
;;  Calling Sequence:
;;        EXTRN  InSet:NEAR
;;        mov    al, possibleElement
;;        mov    si, OFFSET theSet
;;        call   InSet
;;
;;   On exit, ax is 1 if possibleElement is in theSet, 0
;;     otherwise. All other registers are preserved.
;;
            .MODEL SMALL

            .CODE
            PUBLIC InSet
InSet       PROC
            push   bx
            push   cx
            push   si
            mov    bx, 00f8h ;   = 0000 0000 1111 1000B
            and    bx, ax ;      convert to word, last 3 bits 0'd
            mov    cl, 3
            shr    bx, cl ;      bx := al div 8 = relative word
            mov    cl, 7
            and    cl, al ;      cl := al mod 8 = bit in word
            mov    al, [bx + si] ;    Get correct byte
            shr    al, cl ;      Get bit in right position
            and    ax, 1 ;          ...and zero out everything else
            pop    si
            pop    cx
            pop    bx
            ret
InSet       ENDP
            END
```

Example 11.3—3. Write a procedure SetUnion whose input is pointers to two sets, in si and di, and a pointer in bx to a 32 byte array which is to contain their union. (Union is a reserved word in MASM 6.0 and above.)

The **union** of two sets is the set of items which are in one set or the other (or both). The OR operation is just what we need. Base/Displacement (double) indexing can also be used with effect:

```
;; SETUNION.ASM--Solution to Example 11.3-3
;;
;;   Calling Sequence:
```

```
;;              EXTRN   SetUnion:NEAR
;;              mov     si, OFFSET Set1
;;              mov     di, OFFSET Set2
;;              mov     bx, OFFSET resultSet
;;              call    SetUnion
;;
;;      On exit, resultSet will contain the union of Set1 and Set2.
;;        All registers are preserved
;;
                .MODEL SMALL

SETSIZE    EQU     32


                .CODE
                PUBLIC SetUnion
SetUnion   PROC
                push    ax ;            To be used for working register
                push    bx
                push    cx ;            To be used for count
                push    si
                push    di

                mov     cx, SETSIZE ; Number of bytes to process
                sub     si, bx ;      si := Set1 address - result address
                sub     di, bx ;      di := Set2 address - result address
UnionLoop:
                mov     al, [bx + si]
                or      al, [bx + di]
                mov     [bx], al
                inc     bx
                loop    UnionLoop

                pop     di
                pop     si
                pop     ax
                pop     bx
                pop     cx
                ret
SetUnion   ENDP
                END
```

Exercises 11.3

1.   The **intersection** of two sets is the set of all items which are in both sets. Write a procedure Intersect similar to the SetUnion procedure in Example 11.3—3 which computes the intersection of two sets pointed to by si and di and places it in the set pointed to by bx.

2. The set **difference** A – B of two sets A and B is the set of all items which are in A but not in B. Write a procedure SetDif similar to the SetUnion procedure in Example 11.3—3 which computes the set difference <set pointed to by si> – <set pointed to by di> and places it in the set pointed to by bx. (Hint: A – B corresponds to the logical operation A AND (NOT B).)

3. A set A is said to be a **subset** of B if every element of A is an element of B. Write a function Subset which takes as input two sets A pointed to by si and B pointed to by di and returns 1 if A is a subset of B, 0 otherwise. (Hint: A is a subset of B if and only if A – B is empty.)

4. The **cardinality** of a set is the number of elements in the set. Write a function Card which takes as input a set pointed to by si and returns the number of elements in the set in ax.

Note: Set intersection, union, difference, and the relations **in** and subset are all part of standard Pascal, expressed as A * B, A + B, A – B, A **in** B, and A <= B, respectively.

11.4 • Multiway Branching; C/C++ `switch` and Pascal `case` Statements

Some knowledge of Pascal and/or C is useful later on in this section.

Arrays also provide a powerful way to accomplish multiway branching. The simplest multiway branch statements to implement are the BASIC ON...GOTO statement and the Fortran computed GOTO. The statements are similar so we will only discuss the former. One common variant has the form

```
ON expression GOTO #1, #2, ... #N
```

where #1, ..., #N are statement numbers. When the statement is executed, *expression* is evaluated, control is transferred to statement #1 if *expression* is 1, to #2 if it is 2, ... to #N if it is N, and otherwise we drop through to the statement following the ON statement. For example the statement

```
30      . . .

        ON X GOTO 80, 30, 100
50      . . .

80      . . .

100     . . .
```

causes control to be passed to line 80 if X = 1, line 30 if X = 2, line 100 if X = 3, and line 50 if X is any other value.

The ON ... GOTO statement could be implemented as a sequence of IF THEN ELSEs as follows:

```
I = expression
IF I = 1 THEN GOTO #1
ELSE IF I = 2 THEN GOTO #2
   . . .
ELSE IF I = N THEN GOTO #N
```

The difficulty with the method above is that it is in fact a linear search for the right statement and if there are more than four or five alternatives, it is slower than necessary.

A better approach is to create an array of labels and treat *expression* as an index into that array. The array is created much as we usually do:

```
OnGoLab    DW     L#1, L#2, ..., L#N
```

where we have added the letter L in front of each line number to convert it into a legal assembly label. The executable part of the code is

```
            mov    bx, expression ; i.e., compute expression into bx
            cmp    bx, 1
            jl     NextStmt
            cmp    bx, N
            jg     NextStmt
            shl    bx, 1 ;                bx := bx * 2 for indexing
            jmp    [OnGoLab - 2 + bx] ;       Base subscript is 1
NextStmt:
```

with the Ls scattered through the program in their normal format:

```
    L#3:
```

Note: In order for the code to work as written in both masm and tasm, the jump table must be in the same PROC as the indexed jump and physically occur *before* it. There are various ways of making it work with the jump table in the .DATA area or after the indexed jump, but they vary from assembler to assembler and we won't go into them.

For our specific example, the code would look like

```
            . . .
L30:
            . . .
            jmp    AfterGoLab
OnGoLab    DW     L80, L30, L100
AfterGoLab:
            mov    bx, X
            cmp    bx, 1
            jl     L50
            cmp    bx, 3
            jg     L50
            shl    bx, 1
            jmp    [OnGoLab - 2 + bx]
L50:
            . . .
L80:
            . . .
L100:
            . . .
```

The syntax of the C/C++ **switch** and Pascal **case** statements are quite different but in fact they are performing the same function as ON ... GOTO. We will only look at the C/C++ **switch** statement—the Pascal **case** statement is similar. ON *expression* GOTO... is easier to process than switch (*expression*)... as in the latter, values of *expression* need not occur contiguously in a range 1-N. Consider for instance

```
switch (aChar) {
  case '+': handle addition; break;
  case '-': handle subtraction; break;
  case '*': handle multiplication; break;
  case '/': handle division; break;
default:
        illegal operation;
};
```

Here the legal values of aChar, the *expression*, are '+' = 43, '−' = 45, '*' = 42, and '/' = 47. We will translate the code above into something like the code for ON aChar-41 GOTO .... We must sort the case labels into increasing order and insert labels into the gaps in order to define the label array:

```
          . . .
          jmp     SwitchJump
CaseLabs  DW      mulLabel, addLabel, defaultLabel, subLabel
          DW      defaultLabel, divLabel
SwitchJump:
          mov     bl, aChar
          cmp     bl, '*'
          jb      defaultLabel
          cmp     bl, '/'
          ja      defaultLabel
          sub     bh, bh ;            convert to word
          shl     bx, 1
          jmp     [CaseLabs - 2 * '*' + bx]
addLabel:
          handle addition
          jmp     EndOfSwitch ; (translates 'break')
subLabel:
          etc.
          . . .
defaultLabel:
          illegal operation
EndOfSwitch:
```

There are several difficulties with the solution given above. First of all, there are several magic numbers floating around the code which are all the more insidious because it isn't evident that there are any magic numbers at all! The particular relationship of the ASCII character values is crucial to the correctness of CaseLabs, as is the determination of largest and smallest character—it could be quite tricky to add a new operator, for instance. Translating the original switch statement is the sort of thing that a compiler can do easily and correctly, but which can be very tricky for a human programmer.

The second problem is that by the time we have set up the array form of the case (the lines `mov bl, aChar` through `shl bx, 1` in the example above), the computer has probably done as much work as it would do if we had translated the case statement with repeated **if then else**s. As an extreme example, consider the code

```
switch (i) {
    case -1000: ...
    case 1000: ...
}
```

A properly constructed compiler for **switch** statements should gather the case labels and compute their range. If there are relatively few cases, say under 5, or if the number of cases is **sparse** in the range, say *range / number-of-cases* > 10, one should probably use repeated **if then else**s instead of an array of labels.

Exercises 11.4

1. ✓ Programmers often use **finite state machines** as a model for programs that must determine whether or not character strings satisfy certain properties. For instance, suppose we must read a line of a's and b's and determine if there are an odd number of a's and an even number of b's. We 'build' a machine with four states, OO, OE, EO, and EE. The first letter determines if the number of a's seen so far is odd or even and the second letter does the same for the number of b's. The machine starts in the state EE and the string is correct if we end in the state OE. A pseudo-code version of the program is

```
c := _GetCh
state := EE
while c <> 13
   switch state
      case EE:   if c = 'a' then state := OE
                 else state := EO end if
      case OE:   etc.
   end switch
   c := _GetCh
 end while
if state = OE then goto Good
else goto Bad end if
```

Write an assembly language fragment to realize the code above. It may be convenient to define the four states as the numbers 0, 2, 4, and 6 to make the switch statement easy to implement.

Programming Problem 11.1

`_GetCh` returns characters as they are entered at the keyboard, with none of the usual keyboard editing (backspace, etc.) handled. Write a separately translated program `GetChar` which returns the next character typed at the keyboard in `al`, and which takes care of keyboard editing. Use the

_GetStr macro (see Section 10.3.1) to read a whole line at a time, then return the characters one at a time, including the carriage return indicating end-of-line. Write a main program to test GetChar which allows input of several lines, including empty ones. Suggested method: Keep a word in memory containing the address of the next character to return. Use the count field (second byte in the _GetStr buffer area) to indicate how many 'real' characters are left in the buffer to be returned. Initialize this count to –1. When GetChar is entered, check the count field and if it is negative, do a _GetStr *GetStruct* and _PutCh 10, and initialize the pointer variable to OFFSET *GetStruct*+2. Then in any case, output the character indicated by the pointer variable, increment that variable and decrement the count.

Programming Problem 11.2

(Hard) Write a program Romanize which takes as input an ordinary decimal number and as output displays the number in Roman numerals. For instance, input of 1357 would produce output of MCCCLVII. You should make use of the C string manipulation functions in Section 11.2 and the multiply-by-10 array in exercise 11.2—5. The basic procedure is the same as GetDec. Instead of starting with 0, start with an empty string. When a digit is read, multiply the string which is the conversion of the previous digits by 'X'. Using an array such as

```
RomanDig   DB      0, 0, 0, 0, 0 ;     empty string for 0 digit
           DB      'I', 0, 0, 0, 0 ;   extra 0s to make every entry
           DB      'II', 0, 0, 0 ;       the same length
           DB      'III', 0, 0
           etc.
```

convert the newly read digit into a string which is its Roman numeral equivalent, and concatenate it onto the end of the previous string (now multiplied by 'X'). When you get to a non-digit, display the string you computed. For example, if the number 496 were entered, the string computed would be, successively, '', 'IV', 'XL', 'XLIX', 'CDXC', 'CDXCVI'.

SUMMARY

The reversing of the digits in binary-to-decimal conversion can be done by storing them in an array, or the digits can be produced in the correct order by dividing by elements of an array of powers of 10.

C/C++-style variable length strings consist of an array of characters, terminated by a 0 byte. Codeview and the Turbo debugger can display C/C++ strings, the former via &*stringname*, s and the latter via *stringname*, s.

Pascal-style variable length strings consist of a length byte (or word) followed by a fixed-length array of characters large enough to hold the maximum-length string.

Pascal sets are implemented as an array of bits.

C/C++ **switch** and Pascal **case** statements can be implemented as an indexed jump into an array of labels.

Chapter 12

Segments

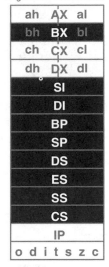
Actual addresses on the IBM PC are given as a *pair* of 16 bit numbers, the *segment* and the *offset*, written in the form segment:offset. We have been able to ignore the segment part before because it is for the most part constant. It is contained in one of four *segment registers*, to be introduced in this chapter. Usually only the offset part is contained in individual instructions.

The material of this chapter will seem difficult, partly because of the amount of picky detail and partly because it's not initially evident how important this information is. Understanding it is really essential, though, both in assembly language and in many programs in high-level languages. Specific places where these concepts are important are

- Real-world application programs usually allow (or require) users to specify some or all of their parameters on the **command line** (e.g., ml /Zi progfile.asm). Access to this information in assembly language (here, the switch /Zi and the file name progfile.asm) requires use of a segment we have not yet dealt with, the **Program Segment Prefix (PSP)**.
- **Environment variables** such as the PATH are in another segment, whose address is found in the Program Segment Prefix.
- Output to the CRT screen is ultimately performed by moving characters into **video memory**, which is in yet another segment. Normally the character movement is done by DOS or BIOS calls, but for the fastest I/O, many programs must do it directly (see Chapter 19). Also, if you want to save part of the screen so that it can be temporarily replaced by a pop-up window or menu, direct access to video memory is required.
- The BIOS Data area (from address 400h) stores information (such as location of the cursor, keyboard input queue, etc.) in tables in low-addressed RAM memory, yet another segment. Most of the time, this

information can be accessed using DOS or BIOS calls, but some applications require direct access to this memory (e.g., Example 15.5—1, which requires direct access to the keyboard input queue).

- **Terminate and Stay Resident (TSR)** programs and other interrupt handlers (see Chapter 15) grab control of the CPU from another running program, which is normally using different segments. Thus the TSR or handler must be able to save the running programs segment registers, set up its own, and restore the running program's segment registers when it is done.

- The programs we have written so far have been limited to three segments, which limits their code and data areas to about 130 KBytes, roughly one fourth of the available PC memory. Many modern applications such as word processors and spread sheets require much more memory.

Everything in this chapter through the first part of Section 12.4 can be read pretty much any time after chapter 2. From then on, a knowledge of chapter 10 is presupposed.

12.1 • Segments and Offsets

The natural size for an address on the 80X86 is a word, 16 bits. Unfortunately a word is only enough to address 2^{16} = 65,536 bytes, and it was evident when the 8086 was designed that more memory was needed. The designers decided to go with 2^{20} (çirca one million) bytes (which wasn't enough either, as it turned out). Since the required 20 bit address doesn't fit naturally into the world of eight bit bytes, some finagling is required.

We will refer to memory addresses in two ways, as a five hex digit (20 bit) number or more commonly, as the computer does: as a *pair* of 16 bit words. This pair is called the **segment** and the **offset** parts of the address, and written as the two numbers (usually hex) separated by a colon, **segment:offset**. The two methods of representing addresses are related as follows:

segment:offset represents the 20 bit address $16 \times segment + offset$.

As $16 = 2^4$, segment:offset pairs can represent addresses up to $2^4 \times 2^{16} = 2^{4+16} = 2^{20}$, as desired. The multiplication is simple: append four binary zeroes (or one hex zero) to the end of the segment and add the offset. Thus the address 13a5h:3327h corresponds to the memory address 16d77h computed by

$$
\begin{array}{lr}
\textit{segment} & 1\ 3\ a\ 5\ \boxed{0} \\
\textit{offset} & +\ \ 3\ 3\ 2\ 7 \\
\hline
\textit{address} & 1\ 6\ d\ 7\ 7
\end{array}
$$

80X86 memory is divided into **paragraphs**, which are 16 byte blocks of memory starting on addresses divisible by 16. Thus a paragraph always starts at an address wxyzh:0 = wxyz0h (w, x, y, and z represent arbitrary hex digits). The segment part of an address is really the address of a paragraph of memory.

A **segment** is a contiguous block of paragraphs which is addressed by the (fixed) segment address of its first paragraph and a varying offset. As only the offset part of the address varies within a segment, a segment can contain at most 2^{16} = 65,536 bytes, and thus at most $2^{16} / 2^4 = 2^{12}$

= 4096 paragraphs. The smallest segment is a single paragraph.

An 80X86 program is organized as a number of these segments, so that the segment part of program addresses tends to remain relatively constant. The programs we have created so far have three segments—the **code**, **stack**, and **data segments**, declared with the .CODE, .STACK, and .DATA directives, respectively. The linker gathers together all pieces of .CODE into a single segment, and does likewise with all pieces of .STACK and .DATA. In this chapter we will see that it is also possible to write programs with many code and data segments. In order to declare segments other than the standard ones, we will need the SEGMENT pseudo-operation to be introduced in the Section 12.3.

Notice that many different segment:offset pairs can give the same memory address: 16d77h is also given by 16d7h:0007h, 1000h:6d77h, 1116h:5c17h, and many others. The relationship of various segment:offset addresses to each other is not always evident either. The addresses 162dh:0007h, 1400h:236ah, 1234h:4033h are in the order lower to higher memory address, as they represent the actual locations 162d0h + 7h = 162d7h, 14000h + 236ah = 1636ah, and 12340h + 4033h = 16373h, respectively. [*]

Any symbolic memory address *label* defined in a segment can have two operators applied to it:

SEG *label*	The (16 bit) segment address at which the segment containing *label* is loaded, *and*
OFFSET *label*	The (16 bit) offset from the beginning of that segment of *label*.

The OFFSET part of the address is determined by the linker but the SEG part can only be determined when the program is finally loaded. Most of the work is done by the assembler, but it is possible to have parts of the same segment assembled in two or more source code files. One of the functions of the DOS program loader is to fill in the segment locations where necessary. As we will see, the only such place where a segment location is needed in our programs so far is in mov ax, @data, as @data is the SEG of the .DATA segment.

There are in theory many different possibilities for SEG and OFFSET. The SEG value actually chosen by the assembler is the beginning segment address of the segment in which the variable is defined, and the SEG value in turn determines the OFFSET uniquely.

SEG/OFFSET are in some sense operations inverse to the ':' operation for combining segment:offset pairs:

$$SEG \; label : OFFSET \; label = label \; \text{(more or less)}$$

The **address arithmetic** discussed in Section 10.1 takes place only with addresses in the same segment, and only involves the offset part of the address. Thus

$$\text{address} \pm \text{constant} = (\text{segment:offset}) \pm \text{constant} = \text{segment:(offset} \pm \text{constant)}$$

and

$$(\text{segment:offset}_1) - (\text{segment:offset}_2) = \text{segment:(offset}_1 - \text{offset}_2)$$

---

[*] The 8086/88 has only 20 address bits A0, …, A19 so any carry out the left end is ignored—that is, addresses **wrap**. For instance 0FFFFh:21h = 0:11h. The 80286 and higher CPUs have more address bits, but when running in DOS mode, the twenty first bit A20 is permanently set to 0 for compatibility with the 8086/88.

(Segment$_1$:offset$_1$) – (segment$_2$:offset$_2$) is undefined if segment$_1 \neq$ segment$_2$ because the assembler has no way of knowing where segment$_1$ and segment$_2$ will be loaded when the program is executed (or even what their relationship will be when the program is linked). Both assemblers will give you an error if you try to subtract addresses from different segments.

Exercises 12.1

1. ✓ What actual (20 bit) memory addresses correspond to the segment:offset pairs 1035h:3a22h, 0a355h:9211h, and 3133h:0c3a4h?

2. ✓ Find three different segment:offset pairs which correspond to the 20 bit address 7b3cfh.

3. ✓ Arrange the following segment:offset addresses in increasing order by memory location: 023ah:2130h, 044bh:0002h, and 033ah:1137h.

4. ✓ The normal IBM PC memory has a maximum size of 640K. What is the segment:offset form of 640K? That is, what is the segment:offset form of the first address which is *not* an ordinary address?

12.2 • Segment Registers

The 'address' that sits in an instruction is actually the *offset* part of the address. Whether OFFSET *label* or simply *label* appears in an instruction in assembly language, it is the offset that is stored with the instruction in memory.

The segment part of the address changes much less often and resides in one of four sixteen bit **segment registers**:

Segment Registers	
cs	Code Segment
ds	Data Segment
ss	Stack Segment
es	Extra Segment

We now know all the CPU registers we have to deal with: the ordinary registers ax, bx, cx, dx, si, di, bp, sp, the four segment registers, and the IP and flags registers (which must be referenced indirectly). (There are more in the 80386 and above and in math co-processor chips; see Chapters 20 and 21.).

The operations which can be performed on segment registers are very limited: mov to or from memory or an ordinary word register, and push or pop. Thus

Segment Register Operations

```
        mov    ax, @data
        mov    ds, ax ; mov segreg, constant is illegal

        mov    ax, ds
        mov    es, ax
;or ...
```

```
;            push    ds
;            pop     es ; Because mov segreg, segreg is illegal
```

In normal operation, segment registers are seldom referenced explicitly. Each machine instruction chooses the most likely segment register automatically:

Default Segment Registers	
Use...	...for addresses in...
cs	call and jmp instructions, and instruction fetches (using ip)
ss	instructions involving indexing by bp. used implicitly in push, pop, and call and ret instructions for the return address
ds	all other instructions.

Es is used in situations where more than the standard three segments are being manipulated.

As we saw in Debug Workshop IV, in *both* of the instructions "mov ax, A," and "mov ax, OFFSET A", the offset part of the address of A is what is stored in memory with the instruction. The keyword 'OFFSET' in the second instruction is only used as a signal to the assembler to use a different numerical operation code in translating it! The instruction "mov ax, A" (op code 0A1h) means "move the contents of the word at memory location ds:OFFSET A into ax," while "mov ax, OFFSET A" (op code 0B8h) means "move the *number* OFFSET A into ax."

The default segments can be overridden by preceding the instruction by a **segment override** byte. With proper declarations, the assembler will usually supply the override for you automatically (though the program must still manage the contents of the segment registers). Occasionally though, an explicit segment override is required. To force the use of segment register 'xs', write the form 'xs:' in front of the address to be overridden, as in mov WORD PTR es:[bx+8], 100. (See Examples 12.4—3, 12.5—2, and 12.7—1)

When calling a PROC in a different segment (which is termed a **far call**), *both* the cs and IP register must be changed, which means that both the original cs and IP must be saved and restored. There are in fact separate call and ret instructions for far calls. (There are far jumps as well; see Section 12.7 for more information. We will make little use of far calls and jumps).

You may have wondered how segment registers get their initial values. When DOS loads a program, it gets the initial values of ss:sp and cs:IP from a short header record in the .EXE file, where they were placed by the linker. The stack starts at the first paragraph after the code and data and its length (= the initial sp) is the sum of all declared stack segment sizes.[*] The linker gets the initial value of cs:IP from the END *Label* directive in one of the source programs. The program might have multiple data segments and there is no reason to prefer one over the other, so DOS starts

---

[*] The fact that the stack is at the end of the program makes it possible to change its size easily in the .EXE file. Changing stack size is one of the minor functions of the DOS utility EXEPACK See also Programming Problem 17.2.

ds (and es) pointing to the PSP, to be described in Section 12.5. We have been setting ds at the beginning of our programs with the code

```
mov     ax, @data
mov     ds, ax
```

which loads ds with the segment address @data of the standard .DATA segment. We couldn't write 'mov ds, @data' because there is no version of the mov instruction for moving a *constant* to a segment register.

12.3 • Defining Segments

Before MASM version 5.0, declaration of program segments was a rather complex affair. MASM 5.0 introduced the simplified declarations .STACK, .DATA, and .CODE for the three most commonly used segments, and TASM also uses this notation. To declare other segments we need the full-blown declarations, which we will introduce in this section.

The unsimplified way of declaring a segment is

Segment Declaration
SegName   SEGMENT *SegmentOption*, ...
...declarations, code, etc.
SegName   ENDS

The declaration of segments is similar in appearance to declaration of PROCs: the name of the segment must appear on both the SEGMENT and the ENDS statement.

We will discuss only three basic types of full segment declarations, **public**, **at**, and **private** (rarely used). (These are called the **combine type** of the segment and relate to how the linker puts together segments of the same name from different files.) We will discuss two public segment types, code and data, whose only distinction is the kind of information saved for the debugger. The segment declarations are

```
SegName     SEGMENT PUBLIC ;          Defines shared DATA segments

SegName     SEGMENT PUBLIC 'CODE' ;   Defines shared CODE segments
;                 'CODE' is needed only when assembled for debugging so
;                 that the programmer can view source code in the
;                 debugger's source code window

SegName     SEGMENT AT address ;      Defines a segment outside the
;                 program, at a fixed memory location address:0

SegName     SEGMENT ;                 Defines private (non-
;                 shared) segments
```

PUBLIC segments with the same name appearing in separately compiled procedures are linked, one after the other, into a single segment in the final program. The .CODE and .DATA segments are PUBLIC. In fact, .DATA is approximately equivalent to

```
@data      SEGMENT PUBLIC
           ...data declarations...
@data      ENDS
```

and .CODE is approximately equivalent to

```
@code      SEGMENT PUBLIC 'CODE'
           ...data declarations...
@code      ENDS
```

AT segments are used chiefly to reference parts of memory at fixed absolute addresses. Most of these are locations that have meanings to the hardware. For instance, the memory for the Color Graphics Adaptor (CGA) display starts at location 0b800:0h, so we could declare

```
Video      SEGMENT AT 0B800h
           ...declarations
Video      ENDS
```

Another useful segment is the BIOS Data, which is a SEGMENT AT 40h.

Note that

AT segments don't generate any code or data of their own.

They simply give you a symbolic means to reference things that already exist at particular locations in memory.

Private segments don't combine with any segment defined in any other file, even if the segments have the same name. We will make use of such a segment only once, in the library program GetMem in Example 12.6—2, where we define a private segment of maximum size, 64 K bytes to hold blocks of allocated memory. Other programs don't *need* to know the segment's name, and if another segment accidently combined with it, the resulting segment would be too big

12.4 • The ASSUME Statement

One reason for the use of SEGMENT declarations is to allow the assembler to do most of the work of deciding whether to use the default segment register or to provide a segment override. In order for the assembler to decide on the segment register, though, the programmer must inform the assembler of the contents of the segment registers with the ASSUME pseudo-operation, which is of the form

```
ASSUME SegReg : SegName [, SegReg : SegName...]
```

where *SegReg* is one of the four segment registers cs, ds, es, or ss and *SegName* is either the name of a segment or the keyword NOTHING, indicating that the contents of the segment register are unknown. (For instance, the segment register may point to some unknown place defined in another source program or in DOS.)

We have not had to use the ASSUME statement before because when we use simplified segment directives, our assemblers start using the **default ASSUME**:

```
ASSUME cs : @code, ds : @data, es : NOTHING
```

(MASM 6.0 and beyond more properly assumes that cs is the segment of whatever code segment we are currently in.)

An ASSUME for a particular register applies to all the program text which follows it in line-by-line order, not execution order, up until the next ASSUME statement that affects that register.

Loading segment registers and ASSUMEing their contents are two entirely independent operations, and *both* are required when a segment register changes.

The typical code is

Loading a Segment Register
```mov   xs, SegName ; xs is some segment register```
```ASSUME xs : SegName```

You should develop the discipline of doing a new ASSUME for each segment register immediately after you change it. The only exception is when you load ds with @data at the beginning of a program, since the assembler is already making the correct assumption for you.

To reemphasize the statement in the box above:

---

1. ASSUME *never* changes segment registers.
2. Changing segment registers *never* changes ASSUMES.

If you are willing to accept the contents of the two boxes above without further explanation, skip ahead to Example 12.4—1. If not, the following discussion will attempt to convince you of their necessity.

Rule 1 is merely a matter of efficiency. We will often ASSUME the contents of a particular register because we know that some other program (or DOS) has loaded it, and it would be inefficient for us to load it again. When we introduce the PSP segment in the next section, we will often ASSUME es : PSP (because DOS loads es for us) and there is *no* straightforward way of having the assembler generate the code to do it for us.

Rule 2 is a little harder to understand for it appears that the assembler could usually tell what is in the segment registers. For instance, consider the code

```
        mov     ax, SegA
        mov     es, ax
;               Assembler canNOT assume es contains SegA here!!!!
```

The code above appears unequivocally to set es to SegA. Suppose, however, it was embedded in the larger code

```
          cmp     X, 100
          jg      L1
          mov     ax, SegB
          jmp     L1+3
          . . .
L1:
          mov     ax, SegA
          mov     es, ax ; L1+3 is the address of this very
;                          instruction; es could contain SegA or SegB
```

Note: The first part of the code could even be in another .ASM file if L1 were PUBLIC, and L1 could be considerably farther away from the code that loads es. Moreover, it isn't difficult to concoct examples which are even more arcane (see the exercises). The upshot of the preceding discussion is that there is *no* foolproof way for the assembler to determine what's in the segment registers, so the assemblers don't even try.

Once the assembler is told what is in each segment register, and also knows from the position of label declarations which segment each label is in, the assembler provides the correct addressing if it can, or indicates an error.

Example 12.4–1 This example shows how the assembler constructs addresses and decides on segment overrides.

Suppose that we have the following situation

```
ASeg      SEGMENT PUBLIC
          . . .
A         DW      ?
          . . .
ASeg      ENDS

BSeg      SEGMENT PUBLIC
          . . .
B         DW      ?
          . . .
BSeg      ENDS

CSeg      SEGMENT PUBLIC
          . . .
C         DW      20 DUP (?)
          . . .
CSeg      ENDS

          .CODE
```

```
           . . .
X          DW      ?
           . . .
           ASSUME ds : ASeg, es : BSeg ;    and cs -> code segment
```

1) The instruction

```
           mov    A, ax
```

uses OFFSET A for its address part and needs SEG A in a segment register. As SEG A = ASeg is assumed in ds, and ds is the default segment for the instruction above, the assembled address will be OFFSET A, with no segment override.

2) For the instruction

```
           mov    B, ax
```

the assembler uses OFFSET B for its address part and needs SEG B = BSeg in a segment register, and here it is in es. As es is not the default for the mov instruction, the assembler generates a segment override, giving the address es:OFFSET B.

3) For the instruction sequence

```
           mov    bx, CSeg
           mov    ds, bx
           mov    C, ax ;       Assembler signals (false) ERROR!!!!
```

the assembler needs SEG C = CSeg in a segment register, and *even though CSeg is actually in ds*, the assembler hasn't been told it is (with an ASSUME statement) so the assembler signals an error!

4) For the instruction

```
           mov    X, ax
```

the assembler uses the address cs:OFFSET X.

5) In the instruction sequence

```
           mov    bx, 0
           mov    [B + bx], ax
```

the assembler knows that B is in BSeg, that BSeg is in es, and that therefore it should assemble the address es:[OFFSET B + bx]. On the other hand, consider the code

```
           mov    bx, OFFSET B
           mov    [bx], ax ; Assembler doesn't detect real ERROR!!!
```

The code above contains a particularly ghastly programmer error. As with segment registers, the assembler has no way of knowing that bx contains something which requires an es override, and therefore it uses the default ds segment. Ax will get moved into some strange location in ASeg. A **splatter bug** like the code above can be very difficult to find. A program may work fine when run with a debugger and crash when run alone, or *vice versa,* because running with the debugger moves the program in memory, and in one location it may clobber something inessential while in the other it might clobber something crucial.

The correct way to write the code is

```
mov    bx, OFFSET B
mov    es:[bx], ax ; Explicit override necessary!!!
```

(End of Example 12.4—1.)

We can access any known, fixed location in memory using the SEGMENT AT option. For instance, to access a word variable WordVar at segment:offset address m:n, where m and n are constants, we declare

```
SegName    SEGMENT AT m
           ORG     n
WordVar    DW      ?
SegName    ENDS
```

The (new) ORG pseudo-operation is a reliable way of making sure that data occurs at a particular offset within a segment. The instruction

```
ORG      n
```

sets the assembler's location counter in the current segment ($) to n.

ORG can be used to move back and forth within a segment. Thus if we also wished to define other variables A1, A2, … in *SegName* at offsets $n1$, $n2$, …, we could write

```
SegName    SEGMENT AT m
           ORG     n
WordVar    DW      ?
           ORG     n1
A1         DW      ? ;           or DB
           ORG     n2
A2         DW      ?
           . . .
SegName    ENDS
```

even if n, n1, n2, … are out of order.

In order to access WordVar, we would use the code

```
mov    ax, SegName
mov    es, ax
ASSUME es : SegName
access WordVar
```

Es was designed for situations like the above—when we need short temporary use of a segment register. If we already had something in es that we wished to preserve, we could push es before the code above and pop it after.

Example 12.4—2: Data for the ROM BIOS is in a segment starting at memory address 400h (segment address 40h). For instance, location 410h is an equipment list. Bits 4 and 5 specify whether the CRT is color (10B) or monochrome (11B). Write code jumping to location Color if the CRT is color.

```
BIOSData   SEGMENT AT 40h
           ORG     10h
EquipList DW       ?
BIOSData   ENDS
           . . .
           mov     ax, BIOSData ;      See footnote below
           mov     es, ax
           ASSUME es:BIOSData
           test    EquipList, 10000B ; Assem supplies es: override
           jz      Color ;             Color CRT installed
```

(The BIOS int 11h call which returns the equipment list in ax is a much safer and more machine-independent method of getting the equipment list. For a partial list of BIOSData storage, see Section 5 of Appendix D.)

SEGMENT AT 40h and ORG 10h put EquipList at address 40h:10h = 40h * 16 + 10h = 410h. We could also have used segment:offset addresses 0:410h, 41h:0, or even 25h:1C0h, but it is better to use the pair chosen because it corresponds to the natural segment structure.

The *address* in

```
SegName   SEGMENT AT address
```

is mostly for documentation, and matters only if we code something like mov ax, *SegName*, which is equivalent to mov ax, *address*.* However, if we declare

```
aSeg      SEGMENT AT 100h
A         DW      ?
aSeg      ENDS
```

---

* There is a bug in TASM 4.0 which was not there in earlier versions and may not be in later versions. It causes mov ax, *SegName* not to work properly for AT segments. To make the BIOSData code above work for TASM 4.0 (and everything else I've tested), you can use the less esthetic code below:

```
BIOSDataSeg EQU   40h
BIOSData    SEGMENT AT BIOSDataSeg
            . . .
            mov   ax, BIOSDataSeg ;    INSTEAD of mov ax, 40h
            mov   es, ax
            ASSUME es : BIOSData ;      NOT BIOSDataSeg
```

and execute the code

```
mov     ax, 222h
mov     ds, ax
ASSUME ds : aSeg
mov     A, 1234
```

then the address used in the mov instruction will be ds:OFFSET A = 222h:OFFSET A!

Example 12.4—3: Moving data between segments.

Suppose that ds:si and es:di are the starting addresses of two word arrays containing cx words, and we wish to copy the array at ds:si into the array at es:di. In this example, no ASSUME statement is needed, and even if there was one, it wouldn't tell us what overrides to use (see the last part of Example 12.4—1). Assuming the blocks don't overlap, one version is

```
CopyLoop:
        mov     ax, [si] ;      default ds used for source
        mov     es : [di], ax ;  explicit override required
        add     si, 2
        add     di, 2
        loop    CopyLoop
```

(mov es:[di], [si] is a mov instruction with two memory operands, and thus is illegal.)
If bx is available, we can make the loop more efficient by using based indexing:

```
        mov     bx, 0
CopyLoop:
        mov     ax, [bx + si]
        mov     es : [bx + di], ax
        add     bx, 2
        loop    CopyLoop
```

Here we have inverted the usual roles of bx and si/di: si and di are used as bases and bx is used as an index.

Example 12.4—4: _PutStr can also cause subtle segmenting bugs.

Consider the code

```
Data2       SEGMENT PUBLIC
Message1    DB      'Hide $'
Data2       ENDS

            .DATA
Message2    DB      'and seek', 13, 10, '$'
```

```
          .CODE
BadSeg    PROC
          mov     ax, @data
          mov     ds, ax
          mov     ax, Data2
          mov     es, ax
          ASSUME es:Data2
          _PutStr Message1 ;          DOES NOT WORK!
          _PutStr Message2
```

When executed, it gives results something like

```
| %*æ ^çand seek
and seek
```

The reason is that the DOS function assumes that the message to be displayed is at location **DS**:dx. In the code above, ds is set wrong for Message1 and it's another of those situations where the assembler has no way of knowing it's wrong. If the macro were executing mov al, Message1, the assembler would be able to supply the correct segment. But as you perhaps remember from chapter 2, the instruction being executed is mov dx, **OFFSET** Message1, which makes no use of a segment register. The segment register isn't actually *used* until we get into DOS, and by then it is too late to set it properly.

In fact, the _PutStr macro has an optional second parameter that we haven't been using, a *segment*. If we replace the first _PutStr with

```
_PutStr Message1, es
```

and reassemble and re-execute the program, we get

```
hide hide
```

which is also wrong! Of course now the *second* _PutStr call is using ds, which is now the same as es, and is wrong for Message2. A solution, with appropriate ASSUMEs, is

```
push    ds ;                    Save ds
_PutStr Message1, es
ASSUME ds : Data2 ; for documentation
pop     ds
ASSUME ds : @data ; Restore ds
_PutStr Message2
```

Now is as good a time as any to bring up a nasty surprise that the assemblers have in store for us. For reasons to be discussed in Section 12.7, the assemblers ASSUME that ss as well as ds is set to @data when abbreviated segment directives are used. Resetting ss (and sp) so ss = ds doesn't happen, though, unless the program goes through some fairly complicated code to make it true. (See Exercise 15.3—2c.) In the code

. . .

```
        ASSUME ds:NOTHING
        mov    ax, A ;        A is a variable in the .DATA segment
```

both assemblers would silently and cheerfully assemble the mov instruction *with an ss segment override!* Even if we wrote

```
        . . .
        ASSUME ds:NOTHING, es:@data
        mov    ax, A ;        A is a variable in the .DATA segment
```

both assemblers will choose the ss override in preference to es!

I will suggest two solutions to the problem, one to avoid the difficulty and the other to help the assembler catch you if you forget to avoid the difficulty. You can avoid the difficulty if you make sure that ds always contains @data whenever you refer to a variable in the .DATA segment, and you can make sure that the assembler always catches you if you get the segments wrong by doing the following:

When using multiple data segments, insert the following statement immediately after .MODEL

ASSUME SS : NOTHING

If you include the above ASSUME statement religiously, you will avoid a great deal of debugging pain. (For other approaches to the problem, see Section 12.7.)

We note in closing this section that the ORG pseudo-operation also has other uses. For instance

Example 12.4—5. Use ORG to get a cleaner definition of the array UpIt from Example 10.3—3. (This example is one in a continuing series of methods of converting lowercase to uppercase letters.)

UpIt is an array of 256 bytes such that for any byte C, UpIt[C] = C if C is not a lowercase letter and is the corresponding uppercase letter if C is a lowercase letter. Using ORG, the definition is simple. (The use of REPT and = are discussed in Section 8.3 and LABEL is discussed in Section 10.3.2.)

```
UpIt      LABEL  BYTE
Counter = 0
          REPT   256
          DB     Counter
Counter = Counter + 1
          ENDM
Counter = 'A'
          ORG    UpIt + 'a'
          REPT   26
          DB     Counter
Counter = Counter + 1
          ENDM
          ORG    UpIt + 256
```

Note:

- If the *contents* of a particular memory location are defined more than once in an assembly program (as they are here), the definition which comes last physically is the one used.
- In Example 12.4—2 we were able to use ORG `constant` because we knew our location from the beginning of the segment. Here we must use ORG UpIt+`constant` because we don't have an absolute location in the segment. The linker might combine this declaration with other .DATA in such a way that UpIt didn't start at offset 0! Therefore the ORG must be specified relative to the beginning of UpIt.
- The location counter $ is reset to the end of the UpIt array via ORG UpIt + 256 as otherwise if any further data definitions were added, they would wipe out the latter part of UpIt. There are no further definitions in this source file and definitions in other source files wouldn't pose a problem, but we have used **defensive programming** here. We might add something else later. If you can conceive of a possible error and can defend against it, do it!

Exercises 12.4

1. (This problem uses operations from Section 9.1.) Memory location 40h:17h contains the current status of the keyboard shift keys (see Example 9.1—1). Write assembler code to
   a) Put the shift status byte in al. (Int 16h, function 2 is a safer method, but use segments here.)
   b) Turn NumLock (bit 5) on.
   c) Turn Alt shift (bit 4) off.

2. ✓ Write code to set the array C

```
CSeg        SEGMENT PUBLIC
            . . .
C           DW      20 DUP (?)
            . . .
CSeg        ENDS
```

to all 0s. Make no assumptions about the segment registers, loading es with CSeg. Do the problem two ways, using the subscript method and the pointer method.

3. ✓ Given the declarations

```
Seg1        SEGMENT PUBLIC
            . . .
U           DW      123
Seg1        ENDS

Seg2        SEGMENT PUBLIC
            . . .
X           DW      -555
Seg2        ENDS

            .CODE
```

```
            . . .
P           DW     ? ; DW in the .CODE seg is rare, but can happen!
            . . .
            ASSUME ds : Seg1, es : Seg2
```

Fill in the segment overrides, *if any*, that the assembler will generate for the following instructions:

```
            mov     ax, X ;                 override:
            mov     ax, U ;                 override:
            mov     ax, P ;                 override:
            mov     ax, [X + bx] ;          override:
            mov     ax, [U + bx] ;          override:
            mov     bx, OFFSET X
            mov     ax, [bx] ;              override:
            mov     bx, OFFSET U
            mov     ax, [bx] ;              override:
```

4. Suppose we have declared

```
    atSeg       SEGMENT AT 123h
    aVar        DW     ?
    atSeg       ENDS
```

What is used as the segment:offset address of aVar in each of the following sequences of instructions?

```
            mov     ax, atSeg
            mov     es, ax
            ASSUME es : atSeg
            mov     aVar, ax


            mov     ax, 8000h
            mov     es, ax
            ASSUME es : atSeg
            mov     aVar, ax
```

5. a) Show why ds *never* needs to be *loaded* at the ASSUME statements marked (*) and (**) below, even though the ASSUME statement are necessary:

```
            mov     ax, aSeg
            mov     ds, aSeg
            ASSUME ds : aSeg
            cmp     x, 100 ;      x is in aSeg
            jl      xOK
            _PutStr ErrMsg, @data
            ASSUME ds : @data ; (*)
            mov     ax, y ;       y is in .DATA
```

```
            call    PutDec
            _Exit   1
    xOK:

            ASSUME ds : aSeg ;    (**)
```

b) Explain why the assembler can't conclude what the contents of es are after the move into es:

```
    aSeg        SEGMENT PUBLIC
                . . .
    aSeg        ENDS

                .DATA
                PUBLIC theSeg
    theSeg      DW      aSeg
                . . .
                mov     es, theSeg
```

6. The programs PutDec and Bin2Dec developed in Section 11.1 make the implicit assumption that ds contains @data. Show how to fix these programs so that they work no matter what ds contains when they are called.

The versions of PutDec and Bin2Dec—as well as the versions of GetDec and Dec2Bin—supplied on disk make no assumptions about the value of ds on entry.

7. Use the ORG pseudo-operation as in Example 12.4—5 to give a cleaner definition of the CharType array specified in Exercise 10.3—3.

12.5 • The Program Segment Prefix (PSP)

The **Program Segment Prefix (PSP)** is the most important segment other than the three standard ones. It is a 256 byte segment attached by DOS to the beginning of *all* programs. Much of what it contains is not officially documented and quite a bit of what's left is archaic and no longer of much use. However, of great importance is the fact that the last 128 bytes of the PSP are initialized with the command line that was used to invoke the program.

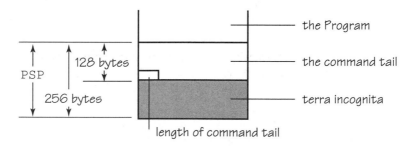

Bytes 129-255 contain the **command tail**, the command that was typed at the keyboard with the name of the program itself removed, and byte 128 contains the length of the command tail.

When a program is executed from the keyboard, the tail as stored in the PSP is followed by a carriage return character, which isn't included in the count. (There is room for the carriage return because the maximum length of a typed command line is 127 characters, and when the command name itself is removed, the command stored in the PSP is at most 126 characters long.) Thus if we execute some program DOIT by typing

```
DOIT Par1 Par2
```

the bytes of the PSP from byte 128 on will be as follows:

10	' '	'P'	'a'	'r'	'1'	' '	' '	'P'	'a'	'r'	'2'	13	...

The 10 is the number of characters in the line and the 13 is the carriage return at the end of the line, which is not included in the 10 count.

When a program is executed by another program (see Section 17.4) the last 128 characters of the PSP can be of any form (including lengths > 127) so it does not pay to depend on the carriage return character.

There isn't an entirely appropriate way to declare the PSP in a program. Any segment other than an AT segment would reserve memory *after* the beginning of your program, which doesn't correspond to the PSP and which would never be used. But the PSP isn't a normal AT segment either because it doesn't occur at a fixed location in memory; it is always the 256 bytes before the beginning of your program. We will take the path of least harm and call it an AT segment, slightly abusing the notation.

We need to choose some conventional address at which to start the PSP segment—the author uses 0–256 (even though 0–16, the relative *paragraph* might be more appropriate). *The 0–256 has no meaning other than to signal the reader that something special is happening.* We will use the following declaration to access the command line:

<table>
<tr><td colspan="3" align="center">To Declare the PSP</td></tr>
<tr><td>PSP</td><td>SEGMENT AT</td><td>0-256</td></tr>
<tr><td></td><td>ORG</td><td>128</td></tr>
<tr><td>CmdLen</td><td>DB</td><td>?</td></tr>
<tr><td>Command</td><td>DB</td><td>127 DUP (?)</td></tr>
<tr><td>PSP</td><td>ENDS</td><td></td></tr>
</table>

If we wish to make use of the PSP, at the beginning of our program, we can write

<table>
<tr><td colspan="3" align="center">To Use the PSP</td></tr>
<tr><td></td><td>.CODE</td><td></td></tr>
<tr><td>Name</td><td>PROC</td><td></td></tr>
<tr><td></td><td>mov</td><td>ax, @data</td></tr>
<tr><td></td><td>mov</td><td>ds, ax</td></tr>
<tr><td></td><td>ASSUME</td><td>es:PSP</td></tr>
<tr><td></td><td>. . .</td><td></td></tr>
</table>

Note once again that the ASSUME statement doesn't correspond to what is explicitly loaded because as previously mentioned, DOS initializes ds and es with the PSP segment address, and because the assembler automatically assumes @data is in ds.

Example 12.5—1. Write a program `CmdTail` which displays the command tail of its command line in the form

```
My command tail is | whatever-it-is|
```

This example gives a simple application using the PSP. To this end, we will put a '$' character at the end of the command tail and use `_PutStr` to display it. (Of course `_PutStr` won't display all of it if the command tail happens to contain a '$' character.)

Assuming that we have declared the PSP by

```
PSP        SEGMENT AT 0-256
           ORG     80h
CmdLen     DB      ?
Command    DB      127 DUP (?)
PSP        ENDS
```

and have left `es` containing PSP as above, then in order to insert the '$' character, we have to get an index register pointing to the first character beyond the end of the command tail. The '$' character goes at location `Command + [CmdLen]` (Command + contents of `CmdLen`). In order to use the byte `CmdLen` as an index, it must be converted to a word which can be done by setting its high-order byte to zero. The code for inserting the '$' is

```
        mov    bl, CmdLen
        sub    bh, bh ;            bx := command length
        mov    [Command + bx], '$' ;    replace CR with '$'
```

The assembler supplies the `es` segment override on the first and last instructions automatically.

The code above is somewhat dangerous, though, since as previously mentioned, it is possible that `CmdLen` is greater than 126, in which case the `mov ... '$'` command could clobber your code! Therefore it is prudent to add code to check `CmdLen`, and if it is too big, cut it down to size:

```
             mov    bl, CmdLen
             sub    bh, bh ;               bx := command length
             cmp    bx, 126 ;              if command length > 126 then
             jle    LengthOK
             mov    bx, 126 ;                  command length := 126
LengthOK:
             mov    [Command + bx], '$' ;     replace CR with '$'
```

The rest of the program is straightforward. The complete code is:

```
;; CMDTAIL.ASM—Displays the command tail used to execute this
;;  program. The command line
;;
;;        cmdtail stuff and more stuff
;; displays
;;        My command tail is | stuff and more stuff|
```

```
          ;;
          INCLUDE   PCMAC.INC
                    .MODEL SMALL
                    ASSUME SS:NOTHING ; Safety measure! See Section 12.4
                    .STACK 100h

          PSP       SEGMENT AT 0-256
                    ORG    80h
          CmdLen    DB     ?
          Command   DB     127 DUP (?)
          PSP       ENDS


                    .DATA
          Msg       DB     'My command tail is |$'

                    .CODE
          CmdTail   PROC
                    mov    ax, @data
                    mov    ds, ax
                    ASSUME es:PSP

                    _PutStr Msg

                    mov    bl, CmdLen
                    sub    bh, bh ;              bx := command length

                    cmp    bx, 126 ;            if command length > 126 then
                    jle    LengthOK
                    mov    bx, 126 ;                command length := 126
          LengthOK:
                    mov    [Command + bx], '$' ;   replace CR with '$'

                    _PutStr Command, es ;      Command not in .DATA segment
                    ASSUME ds : PSP ;          For documentation purposes
                    _PutCh '|', 13, 10
                    _Exit  0
          CmdTail   ENDP
                    END    CmdTail
```

Example 12.5—2 Write a program UPPER which displays the command tail with all lower case letters converted to upper case. Thus

```
    UPPER Now is the time
```

produces the display

```
    NOW IS THE TIME
```

We will use the array UpIt introduced in Example 10.3—3, which has the property that for any character C, UpIt[C] = C unless C is a lower case letter, in which case UpIt[C] is the corresponding uppercase letter. UpIt is in util.lib.

UPPER is somewhat similar to CmdTail in the last example, but as we must process each command character individually to do the conversion, we will also display each character individually. The program is

```
;; UPPER.ASM—displays its command line with all lower case letters
;;   converted to upper case. Thus
;;
;;   upper William B. Jones
;;
;; produces the output
;;
;;   WILLIAM B. JONES

        INCLUDE  PCMAC.INC
                 .MODEL SMALL
                 ASSUME SS:NOTHING ;  Important! See Section 12.4
                 .STACK 100h

PSP      SEGMENT AT 0-256
                 ORG    128
CmdLen   DB      ?
Command  DB      127 DUP (?)
PSP      ENDS

                 .DATA
                 EXTRN  UpIt : BYTE ; Informs assembler that UpIt
;                                     needs @data in seg register
                 .CODE
Upper    PROC
                 mov    ax, @data
                 mov    ds, ax
                 ASSUME es : PSP
                 mov    cl, CmdLen
                 mov    ch, 0 ;       cx := command length
                 jcxz   Done;         Guarantee at least one character
                 cmp    cx, 126 ;     if command length > 126 then
                 jle    LengthOK
                 mov    cx, 126 ;         command length := 126
LengthOK:
                 mov    si, OFFSET Command
DispLoop:
                 mov    bl, ES:[si] ; EXPLICIT seg override required!
                 sub    bh, bh
                 _PutCh <[UpIt + bx]> ; —> upper case (if necessary)
```

```
              inc    si
              loop   DispLoop
Done:

              _PutCh 13, 10          ; CR, LF
              _Exit  0
Upper         ENDP
              END    Upper
```

Notice that the explicit segment override **ES**:[si] is required since the assembler does not know that [si] contains something in the PSP segment, and therefore would use the default ds segment if left to its own devices. The EXTRN declaration for UpIt occurs in the .DATA segment so the assembler assumes UpIt will actually be in that segment, whose segment address is in ds. Thus no segment override is required for [UpIt+bx].

EXTRN symbols must be declared in the same segment (name) in which the symbol is actually defined.

Finally, note that we enclosed the argument of a macro _PutCh, [UpIt + bx], in pointy brackets as otherwise the blanks could cause the argument to be treated as *three* parameters.

We could also have used the xlat instruction to do the translation. We need to exercise some caution here, too, as xlat assumes that the table address is **ds**:bx. Ds is correct here, so the altered code would be

```
              . . .
              mov    bx, OFFSET UpIt
DispLoop:

              mov    al, es:[si] ; EXPLICIT seg override required!
              xlat ;                -> upper case (if necessary)
              _PutCh al
              . . .
```

Example 12.5—3. Write a program AddUp which takes as input a sequence of positive or negative numbers on the command line and produces their sum as output.

We will use the function Dec2Bin introduced in Section 11.1 and Exercise 11.1—3 and also included in UTIL.LIB on the disk accompanying this book. Dec2Bin takes as input the address in **ds**:si of a string of characters. It then scans off a decimal integer, leaving ds:si pointing to the first character after the number and the number scanned in ax in binary form. Writing this procedure presents us with two problems:

- Since Dec2Bin uses ds:si to scan the string, **ds must point to the PSP**, where the command line resides. Therefore, Dec2Bin had better not expect ds to point to the .DATA segment. (The one in UTIL.LIB doesn't.)
- Dec2Bin requires a non-digit character to terminate its scan. Normally the command line will be terminated by a carriage return in the PSP, but to be sure, we will cut it down to, at most, 126 characters and insert one at the end.

The overall program structure is

```
set ds:si to PSP:offset of command line in PSP
initialize Sum to 0
while ds:si doesn't point to a carriage return do
      call Dec2Bin
      Sum := Sum + ax
end for
display Sum with an appropriate message
```

The code is

```
;; ADDUP--a procedure to add up positive and negative numbers on
;;  command line and display their sum. Uses Dec2Bin and PutDec
;;
;; The command line
;;
;;        addup 123 -331 42 187
;;
;; produces the output
;;
;;        The sum is 21

        INCLUDE    PCMAC.INC
                   .MODEL SMALL
                   ASSUME SS:NOTHING
                   .STACK 100h

PSP                SEGMENT AT 0-256
                   ORG     128
CmdLen             DB      ?
Command            DB      127 DUP (?)
PSP                ENDS


                   .DATA
CR                 EQU     13
LF                 EQU     10
RsltMsg            DB      'The Sum is $'

                   .CODE
                   EXTRN   Dec2Bin: NEAR, PutDec: NEAR
AddUp              PROC
                   ASSUME ds : PSP, es : PSP ; Bin2Dec needs ptr in ds:si!

                   mov     bl, CmdLen
                   mov     bh, 0 ;            Point to character after last
                   cmp     bx, 126 ;          if command length > 126 then
```

```
                 jle     LengthOK
                 mov     bx, 126 ;                command length := 126
      LengthOK:
                 mov     [Command+bx], CR ;   end it with carriage return

                 mov     bx, 0 ;          Use bx to accumulate sum
                 mov     si, OFFSET Command
      ScanLoop:
                 cmp     BYTE PTR [si], CR ; default ds (PSP) OK here!
                 je      Done
                 call    Dec2Bin
                 add     bx, ax
                 jmp     ScanLoop
      Done:
                 _PutStr RsltMsg, @data ;   Sets ds := @data
                 ASSUME ds:@data ;            ...so inform the assembler
                 mov     ax, bx
                 call    PutDec
                 _PutCh CR, LF

                 _Exit  0
      AddUp      ENDP
                 END     AddUp
```

There are a couple of useful lessons we can draw from the AddUp program.

- You should keep the assembler informed of what is in the segment registers even if you aren't using the contents. It is a useful reminder to you and, once again, a safety feature if the program is ever modified.
- Utility routines that need local storage should either use the stack (preferably) or set ds themselves (saving and restoring ds, of course). In fact, PutDec uses the .DATA area (for the string '–32768'). We're safe in AddUp because by the time we use PutDec, ds is loaded properly. But we should make sure PutDec handles ds correctly in *all* cases. The version included with UTIL.LIB handles ds correctly.

Exercises 12.5

1. DOS allows one to use UNIX-like I/O redirection. (For instance '< *filename*' on the command line causes input to be taken from *filename* instead of the keyboard and '> *filename*' causes screen output to go to *filename* instead. The DOS command line interpreter program COMMAND.COM removes the redirection information from the command line automatically before the program is executed. What would you expect the command line part of the PSP to look like after entering the command

```
DOIT Par1 /S < AFile Par2 > Another.Fil
```

(For further information about I/O redirection, see Chapter 17.)

2. ✓ When we wish to reference the command line, why can't we simply ignore the first 128 bytes of the PSP and declare

```
PSP2        SEGMENT AT 0-128
CmdLen      DB      ?
Command     DB      127 DUP (?)
PSP2        ENDS
```

3. ✓ The word starting at offset 32h in the PSP contains the **maximum number of open files** for the program being run. Write assembly code to make the necessary declarations for the PSP segment and a .CODE segment which displays this number with PutDec.

4. Why is it that when testing for command length, we can use a signed conditional jump when testing in a register

```
mov     bl, CmdLen
sub     bh, bh
cmp     bx, 126
jle     LenOK
```

but must use an *unsigned* conditional jump

```
cmp     CmdLen, 126
jbe     LenOK
```

when testing in the CmdLen byte itself?

12.6 • Pointers (Optional)

Pointers in high-level languages are just memory addresses. In order to be able to specify any location in memory, the segment:offset form is used, which takes a double word. In 80X86 parlance, they are called **far pointers**, to distinguish them from single word pointers called **near pointers** that contain the offset part of the address only. Near pointers can be used only in a single segment, where the segment part of the pointer is understood. All the pointers considered in this section are far pointers.

Pointer variables can be declared using the DD (Define Double word) pseudo-operation. When the value field contains an address, it is interpreted as the segment:offset form of that address.

```
X          DW      ? ;        an integer variable
PX         DD      X ;        a far pointer initially pointing at X
PP         DD      ? ;        an unitialized far pointer
LongInt    DD      123456 ;   a 32-bit integer
```

The null pointer (**NULL** in C/C++, **nil** in Pascal) which points to nothing and is used to terminate lists, etc., is assigned some conventional value in assembly language which can't otherwise occur—0:0 in Turbo Pascal, for instance.

To make it easier to deal with pointers, the 80X86 has two instructions for loading a segment:offset pair into `ds` or `es` and a general purpose register.

```
lds    reg, DWordVbl ; sets ds:reg := DWordVbl
les    reg, DWordVbl ; sets es:reg := DWordVbl
```

`Lds`/`les` assume that the offset part of the address comes first in memory, and `DD` sets it up that way. This ordering is consistent with the least-significant-first ordering of bytes within a word.

There is no single instruction for storing a double word pointer. Storing requires two word instructions, and the two one-word pieces of the double word variable must be cast to type `WORD`. Thus to store `es:bx` in PP, the code is

```
mov    WORD PTR PP, bx ;   set PP := es:bx
mov    WORD PTR PP + 2, es
```

Example 12.6—1. Traverse a linked list.

Suppose that the double word pointer `First` points to the first element of a linked list, each of whose nodes has a pointer to the next node at relative location NEXT (`EQU` some constant) in the node. For instance, a node containing a single word of information might be six bytes long, the first two for the information and the last four for the NEXT pointer. In that case, NEXT = 2, the relative location of a node's pointer.

The loop to process each node in some way (e.g., print the contents) would be

```
          les      bx, First ;           es:bx points to current node
          ASSUME es : NOTHING ;          we don't know es's segment
ListLoop:
          test     bx, bx ;              is es:bx null?
          jnz      GoOn
          mov      ax, es
          test     ax, ax ;              (Can't use test on seg reg)
          jz       Done ;                yes

          process es:bx

          les      bx, es:[NEXT + bx] ;     link to next node
          jmp      ListLoop
Done:
```

Example 12.6—2. Write a function `GetMem` which takes as input a number of bytes in `ax` and returns a pointer to a newly allocated piece of storage of that size pointed to by `es:bx`. Return the null pointer (`es = bx = 0`) if there is insufficient room.

`GetMem` is equivalent to the `malloc` function in C and (roughly) the `New` procedure in Pascal and the `new` operation in C++. Done right, memory allocation can be quite a complex problem. Normally, a block of memory called a **heap** is used and pieces carved off of it as needed. When the heap is exhausted, it can be enlarged if any memory is left in the machine. Pascal also has a `Dispose` procedure, C a `free` function, and C++ a `delete` operation to return allocated memory to the heap. To simplify matters, we will use only a fixed block of memory for the heap, which cannot be increased, and won't implement the equivalent of `free` or `Dispose`.

Since no program but `GetMem` need know anything about the internals of the heap, we will allocate it as a **private segment**, one with no parameters after the `SEGMENT` pseudo-op. Recall that such segments are visible only in the source program in which they are declared. Of course, other programs will be able to use the memory allocated in this private segment since they will be passed a segment:address in it; they just won't know its segment name. The structure of the heap is

```
HeapSeg     SEGMENT
MAXHEAP     EQU     0FFFEh ;      make the heap one full segment
NextHeap    DW      HeapStart ;   offset of next block to allocate
HeapStart   DB      MAXHEAP DUP (?) ;   the heap
HeapSeg     ENDS
```

Each time `GetMem` is called, it will return es:bx = HeapSeg:*old* NextHeap and will increment `NextHeap` by the number of bytes allocated (assuming there was enough room). The following diagram gives before and after snapshots of `HeapSeg` for a typical call:

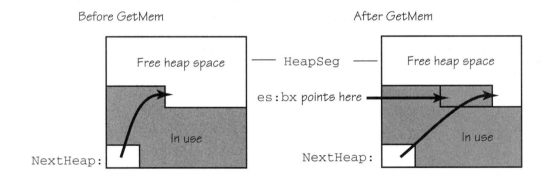

Note that because of the location of `NextHeap`, we will **never** allocate a pointer with offset part 0. The complete code for `GetMem` itself is[*]

```
;; GETMEM.ASM—program to take as input a requested size in bytes
;;  and return as output a pointer to a block of that size. If
;;  such a block is unavailable, return the null pointer.
;;
;; Calling Sequence:
;;      EXTRN   GetMem : NEAR
;;      mov     ax, numberOfBytesRequested
;;      call    GetMem
;;
;;  The program returns with es:bx pointing to the allocated
```

---

[*] TASM produces two warnings on this file, one incorrect and both immaterial.

```
;;   memory, or null, All regs except ax, bx, and es are preserved.
;;
            .MODEL SMALL
            ASSUME SS:NOTHING ; Safety first!

HeapSeg   SEGMENT
MAXHEAP   EQU    0FFFEh ;     make the heap one full segment
NextHeap  DW     HeapStart ; offset of next block to allocate
HeapStart DB     MAXHEAP DUP (?) ;  the heap
HeapSeg   ENDS

            .CODE
            PUBLIC GetMem
GetMem    PROC
            mov    bx, HeapSeg
            mov    es, bx
            ASSUME es : HeapSeg
            mov    bx, MAXHEAP + 2;    Is there enough room?
            sub    bx, NextHeap ;      bx = amt of heap available
            cmp    bx, ax
            jae    OK ;      must be unsigned compare; amount of
;                           heap available will initially appear
;                           to be negative
            mov    bx, 0 ;        Indicate not enough memory
            mov    es, bx ;       (Pascal simply dies in this case)
            ret
OK:
            mov    bx, NextHeap ;      es:bx now properly set
            add    NextHeap, ax ;       and NextHeap properly updated
            ret
GetMem    ENDP
            END
```

The program is a little tricky, particularly in the determination of whether there is enough room to allocate the request. Note that MAXHEAP+2 = 0. In fact, the first time through, NextHeap will be 2 and at the comparison, bx will be MAXHEAP + 2 - 2, which is indeed the amount of memory available. If we have allocated n bytes of memory, then NextHeap will be 2 + n and bx will be MAXHEAP + 2 - (2+n) = MAXHEAP - n, which is again correct. However, doing the comparison in the following way is incorrect:

```
            add    ax, NextHeap
            cmp    ax, MAXHEAP + 2 ;  Bad comparison!
            jbe    OK
```

There is a version of GetMem in UTIL.LIB.

12.7 • Memory Models (Optional)

(This section can be omitted on first reading.) We are going to close out this chapter by describing the meaning of the .MODEL pseudo-operation, as well as the NEAR modifiers in the EXTRN statement. We will also describe the arrangement of standard segments in memory and give a more extensive discussion related to the ASSUME SS:NOTHING statement.

There are two types of call and jmp instructions: **near** instructions which jump to the same segment and **far** instructions which (perhaps) go to a different segment. Near instructions need only contain the *offset* part of their destination and a near call needs only push the IP, which is the offset part of its return address.

Far calls and jmps must contain the complete segment:offset address of their destination, and call must push the segment (CS) *and* offset (IP) of its return address.

Since there are two different calls with different size return addresses on the stack, there must also be two different ret instructions, a near one which pops only into IP and a far one which pops into both IP and CS.

EXTRN *label*:NEAR   is used to indicate that any call or jmp to this label is to be assembled as a *near* call.

EXTRN *label*:FAR   is used to indicate that any call or jmp to this label is to be assembled as a *far* call.

In addition, we may refer to data which is always in the same segment (**near** data) using only the offset of the data, or to data which is in several segments (**far** data) and which therefore requires both segment and offset to refer to the data. In particular, a pointer can be classified as a **near pointer** (one word, containing the offset only) or a **far pointer** (two words, containing both the segment and the offset). Far pointers were discussed in the previous section.

Determining what kind of calls and what kind of pointers to use can get quite chaotic, particularly in high-level languages, so six **memory models** are defined to categorize the type of memory access that a program will use. They are shown in the table on the facing page.

The .MODEL statement is used in assembly language to specify the memory model. You need not memorize the table. Normally, one starts writing a program in small model and changes to a larger model as that becomes necessary. In assembly language, the main purpose of the model is to tell the assembler how procedures will be called, and hence whether to assemble a near or a far return.

.MODEL SMALL, COMPACT, or TINY   states that all declared PROCs in this source file are to return with *near* ret instructions and should be declared in other source files via EXTRN *label*:NEAR.

	Code Segments	Data Segments
tiny	One segment contains PSP, code, data, and stack; used for .COM programs (not discussed in this text)	
small	one (near calls)	one (near pointers)
compact	one (near calls)	multiple (FAR pointers)
medium	muliple (FAR calls)	one (near pointers)
large	multiple (FAR calls)	multiple (FAR pointers)
huge	multiple (FAR calls)	multiple (FAR pointers), segments larger than 64K, requiring special treatment

.MODEL MEDIUM, LARGE, or HUGE   states that all declared PROCs in this source file are to return with *far* ret instructions and should be referenced in other source files via EXTRN *label*:FAR.

In addition, individual PROCs in a source file can override the .MODEL statement via

Name   PROC   NEAR   *or*   Name   PROC   FAR

and a far return can be *forced* using the retf instruction. The .MODEL statement is required in all programs with simplified segment directives, even where its information is not needed (such as files containing only a .DATA segment).

The two assemblers have methods of making PROCedure declarations that resemble those in high-level languages—declaring parameters and local variables with data types, etc.—that we will discuss in Section 13.2. If you use one of these methods, the .MODEL chosen can be used by the assembler to determine for you where parameters are on the stack and the order in which they are pushed (see Section 13.1), and if you declare variables or parameters to have pointer type, the .MODEL will also determine whether the pointer is near or far.

As a general rule, if you are combining assembly programs with those of a high-level language, you should use the same model in assembly as you are using in the high-level language (where the model is generally much more important).

In order to allow a *true* small model program, the assemblers automatically group .DATA and .STACK segments into a single segment. Since the stack must come at the end of the program, the segments always occur in the order PSP, .CODE, .DATA, and stack.

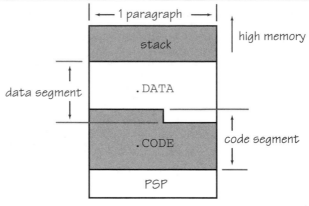

Segment Order
with Simplified Segment Directives

Note that the stack segment always starts at a paragraph boundary, but that the .CODE and .DATA segments can share a paragraph if the .CODE segment doesn't fill up its last paragraph.

The *actual* initial settings of the segment, sp, and IP registers when execution commences are

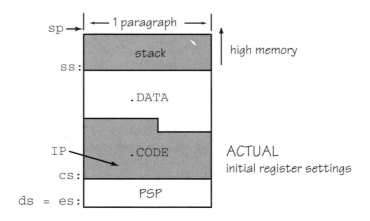

where sp and IP are byte offsets from the settings of ss and cs, respectively. But in order to be able to assume a single segment for data, the assemblers *assume* that the register settings are as in the diagram at the top of the next page. This assumption is made *even in COMPACT and LARGE models.* We of course have been doing the code from the very beginning to set up ds, but setting up ss is much more complicated. (sp, being the offset from ss, must be changed also, and the whole process must be done carefully, lest an interrupt occur while it is happening. See Exercise 15.3—2c.)

As long as we never change ds, the assembler's assumption about ss isn't a problem, as the default ds will be used in preference to ss anyway. However as we saw in Section 12.4, if we change the contents of ds, the assembler will be perfectly happy to use ss: as a segment override to get addresses in the .DATA area. Even if we put @data in es, both assemblers will use ss in preference to es! There are several possible solutions to this invalid ss problem:

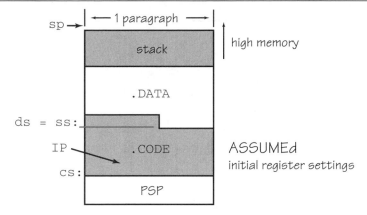

1) Use the necessary startup code to change ss (and with it sp) to the value the assembler expects. MASM and TASM both have a built-in macro, .STARTUP, which generates this code. The two assemblers exhibit slightly different behavior when using this macro.

2) Tell the assembler not to combine .DATA with the stack with the .MODEL statements

```
      .MODEL SMALL, FARSTACK ;          MASM 6.0 and above
```

or

```
      .MODEL SMALL, NOLANGUAGE, FARSTACK ;   TASM
```

Actually, to be precise, we should use COMPACT instead of SMALL here.

3) Disable the assembler's assumption about ss. I have suggested the statement

```
      ASSUME SS:NOTHING
```

This statement above is somewhat misleading, since it doesn't assume that ss is empty or its contents invalid. A better terminology would be 'UNKNOWN' instead of 'NOTHING.' Even better would be to use ASSUME SS:STACK, but that statement doesn't have the desired effect in TASM.

None of these solutions is entirely satisfactory in a book such as this, which attempts to cover both assemblers and to take a pedagogical approach. I have chosen 3) as being the easiest and the most universally applicable. What it does is obvious, though why it is doing it is certainly mysterious. With solution 3), the fact that ss is 'wrong' isn't a problem because when ss is used as a segment register, it is always used with addresses based eventually on sp, and ss and sp are correct *relative to each other*. As for the other solutions, 1) is complex and mysterious and, I think, violates one of the basic reasons for teaching assembly language—trying to get the student close to the machine—and 2), which is in many ways the best solution, has no single universally available form.

Exercises 12.7

1. ✓ Many PC assembly language books tell you that you should start out your main program with the code

```
Name        PROC    FAR
            push    ds
            mov     ax, 0
            push    ax
```

and return to DOS with the instruction

```
            ret    ;                  Which gives a FAR return.
```

What is going on here? (Hint: The first two bytes of the PSP always contain 0cdh, 20h which is the instruction `int 20h`. The `int 20h` instruction is a long-obsolete (though still available) way of returning to DOS.)

2. ✓ If a program has a stack segment using 256 bytes, a `.DATA` segment using 26 bytes, and a `.CODE` segment using 436 bytes, how many paragraphs of memory does the program use, including the PSP segment?

Programming Problem 12.1

Write an assembly language program `PAL` which looks at the rest of its command line and determines whether or not it's a palindrome. A palindrome is a phrase which reads the same forwards and backwards if punctuation, space, and capitalization are ignored. For instance, sample output of your program should be

```
c:> pal A man, a plan, a canal: Panama!
Palindrome
c:> pal Otto ought to
Not a palindrome
c:> pal foof
Palindrome
```

The last test is to make sure your program handles palindromes with an even number of characters. Suggested method: Do the processing in two stages. In the first stage, copy the command line from the PSP to a storage area in your `.DATA` segment, omitting anything but letters of the alphabet and converting all lower case letters to upper case (or vice versa). In the second stage, check for palindromedness.

Programming Problem 12.2

Another feature DOS has in common with UNIX is the idea of **environment variables**. The values of these variables can be obtained by programs and used to alter the programs' execution. Two environment variables which usually exist are COMSPEC, which tells DOS where to find its command line interpreter (normally COMMAND.COM), and PATH, which gives COMMAND.COM a list of directories to search for programs to be executed. Other variables can be defined by executing the SET command:

```
SET variable=character-string-value
```

This statement most often appears in the AUTOEXEC.BAT file, which is executed upon startup of the computer. For instance, MASM uses the environment variable INCLUDE (if it is defined) to tell it standard places to look for INCLUDE files. If we had assembly include files in c:\asm\incl and C include files in c:\c\incl, we might add the following line to our AUTOEXEC.BAT file:

```
SET INCLUDE=C:\ASM\INCL;C:\C\INCL
```

Each program has its own environment stored at EnvSeg:0, where EnvSeg is the contents of the word at offset 2Ch in the PSP. The environment consists of a sequence of C-strings of the form *variable=character-string-value*—that is, a string of ASCII characters followed by a 0 byte. (See Section 12.2.) The whole set of environment strings is terminated by another 0 byte, that is, by an empty string. In DOS 3.0 and above, the second 0 byte is followed by a 1 byte, followed by a 0 byte, followed by the full path name of the program being executed, once again terminated by a 0 byte.

The problem (finally!): Write an assembly language program DISPENV which displays all its environment variables, one variable and value per line. Then skip a line and display the complete name of the program being executed. For instance, the result of such a display might be

```
COMSPEC=C:\COMMAND.COM
PATH=C:\DOS;C:\ASSEM

C:\WORK\DISPENV.EXE
```

Note to CodeView users: CodeView adds an extra environment variable at the end containing funny characters, so you will get a slightly different result running in CodeView than standalone. (See also Debug Workshop V following, Section V.3, Step 5.)

Programming Problem 12.3

(For those who are familiar with pointers and who have read Section 12.6.) Write a program which reads a string of integers from the keyboard using GetDec, terminating on some conventional value such as −9999. For each number read, create a node to contain the number and a 'next node' pointer (6 bytes total in a node) using GetMem. Insert the node in a linked list (initially empty) in increasing order of numerical value. When the terminating value has been encountered, display the numbers in the list in order, using PutDec. (For the really valorous, use a binary search tree—10 bytes per node—instead of a linear list.)

SUMMARY

Every IBM PC address is made up of two 16-bit words, the *segment* and the *offset*, written segment:offset. The actual memory address such a pair represents is 16 × segment + offset. Each segment contains a certain number of *paragraphs*, which are 16 byte blocks starting on an address divisible by 16. Generally instructions contain the offset part of the address and the segment part of the address is contained in one of four *segment registers,* cs, ds, ss, and es (the code, data, stack, and extra segment registers). Instructions normally choose a default segment register—cs for program addresses, ds for data addresses, ss for stack operations. The default segment can be overridden with a *segment override prefix* of the form xs:, where xs is one of the four segment registers. The assembler is informed of the contents of the segment registers using the ASSUME pseudo-op and the assembler determines when segment overrides are needed and applies them. Initially the default is

```
ASSUME cs : @code, ds : @data
```

Contrary to the above assumption, ds and es point to the PSP (Program Segment Prefix) at the start of execution, and ds must be explicitly loaded with @data or the assumptions changed with a new ASSUME. Also, ss is ASSUMEd to contain @data and if multiple segments are used, this (false) assumption should be canceled with the statement

```
ASSUME SS : NOTHING ;      Safety measure
```

Segments other than the standard three can be declared with full segment directives of the form

```
Name        SEGMENT options
    segment contents
Name        ENDS
```

The three most important options of full segment declarations are PUBLIC, PUBLIC 'CODE', and AT *segment-address*. AT *segment-address* segments generate no code or data but specify names and addressing for known locations in memory.

The PSP is specified as an AT segment (at the conventional location 0–256), even though it isn't at a fixed address. The most important parts of the PSP, for our purposes, are byte 128, which contains the number of bytes in the command tail (the command line with the program name itself removed), and bytes 129-255, which contain the actual command tail.

The location counter (offset) in a segment can be set by the pseudo-operation

```
ORG    address ;   Set location counter to address
```

Pointers are generally represented as segment:offset pairs and can be defined with the DD (Define Double word) pseudo-operation. A pointer can be loaded into xs:reg with the instruction lxs reg, *pointer,* where xs is ds or es.

A code address is NEAR relative to the current segment if it is in the same segment; otherwise it is FAR. Call and jmp instructions have different forms depending on whether they refer to NEAR or FAR addresses, hence the requirement in EXTRN statements to specify NEAR or FAR. The ret instruction also varies depending on whether the PROC was called from a NEAR or FAR address. Pointers can also be NEAR or FAR—NEAR if they use a single word containing only the offset part of the address and FAR if they use a double-word containing both segment and offset. The .MODEL statement determines whether a NEAR or FAR ret is used and whether pointers should be NEAR or FAR.

Debug Workshop V

Segments

In this workshop we will discuss how the debuggers can be used to view data in any segment in memory.

V.1 • CodeView and Segments

Note that we now have an explanation for the mysterious numbers before the colons in the Source1 and Memory1 windows. When in mixed source and assembly or assembly mode, hex addresses of instructions in the Source1 window are shown in segment:offset form, with the segment part generally being the same as the contents of the `cs` register. Similarly the addresses in the Memory1 window are in segment:offset form, with the most common segment being the contents of `ds`.

To display memory in any segment, you can open the Memory1 (or 2) window, pull down the Options menu, and choose Memory1 to change the origin and format of the Memory1 window. If a variable is declared in the current Source1 window as being in a particular segment, specifying its name to the Memory1 window will set both segment and offset correctly. Otherwise, you can give the segment:offset form of the address explicitly. For instance, use `es:80` to display the command line (assuming that `es` still points to the PSP and the current number base is hex; if the current number base is decimal (as it starts out in MASM), use `es:128` or change the base to hex with the command n16).

You can also use **db** or **dw** commands in the command window to dump bytes or words, with or without an explicit segment part of the address. If only a numeric offset is given, `ds` will be used as the segment part of the address. If no address is given, the dump will begin from the end of the previous dump. If you use **d** alone as the command, the new dump will also be in the same format as the previous dump. To dump the stack, you can use **dw ss:sp** and to dump the command line part of the PSP, you can use **db es:80**. As before, the amount of information displayed can be limited by following the command with **L** *n*, which displays *n* items of the specified type (*n* is in the current number base).

V.2 • Turbo Debugger and Segments

Any part of memory can be viewed using the data Pane of the CPU window (open the CPU window using **Alt-V**(iew **C**(PU). Note that in the CPU window (and the dump window) addresses are shown in segment:offset form, and if the segment value is actually in a segment register, the register name is shown instead of its value. Make the Data Pane (in the lower-left corner) active by TABbing to it or clicking left in it. You can move around short distances within memory by using the cursor keys and **PgUp** and **PgDn**. To move by great leaps, use the SpeedMenu.

The SpeedMenu of the active window or pane is pulled down by hitting **Alt-F10** or clicking on the pane or window with the *right* mouse button. If *X* is the first letter of a SpeedMenu command, it can be accessed via either **Alt-F10** *X* or **Ctrl-X**. Holding down the Ctrl key prompts for some SpeedMenu commands on the help line.

The **Ctrl-G** *address* SpeedMenu command allows us to view any portion of memory. *Address* can be a variable name or a segment:offset address. For instance, to view the command line assuming that the PSP segment is in es, *address* would be es:80h.

Rather than using the CPU window, you might prefer to use the dump window, **Alt-V**(iew **D**(ump, which is similar to the lower left-hand pane of the CPU window.

The easiest way to look at the stack is to use the lower right pane of the CPU window. See Debug Workshop Section III.2 for a complete description.

V.3 • Debug Example 8

The code of DBGEX8.ASM might better be called WhereAmI, as it displays the location of its PSP. The code is

```
;; DBGEX8.ASM--Display the location of my PSP
;;
;;        assemble as usual and link with UTIL.LIB
;;
INCLUDE    PCMAC.INC
           .MODEL SMALL
           .STACK 100h
           .DATA
Message    DB     'My PSP is located at $'

           .CODE
           EXTRN   PutHex : NEAR
DbgEx8     PROC
           _PutStr Message, @data ;   loads ds for us
           mov    ax, es ;      still contains SEG PSP
           call   PutHex
           _PutCh 'h', 13, 10
           _Exit  0
DbgEx8     ENDP
```

```
END     DbgEx8
```

Assemble and link your program for use with your debugger. Then do as follows:

1) Run the program without a debugger and note its output; call this number PSP1.
2) Run it with a debugger and note its output now; call this number PSP2. Your *debugger* will be loaded at PSP1. The debugger then occupies PSP2 – PSP1 paragraphs. If your computer has extended memory (see Section 1.1.3), that is memory above the 1 MByte limit, most of the debugger should be in extended memory and the space between PSP1 and PSP2 is occupied by a rather small part of the debugger necessary to communicate with the extended memory part.
3) Reload the program with your debugger and examine the command line area at PSP2:80h. The number found there is not the 'real' PSP. It was faked for you by your debugger. The 'real' PSP is the debugger's PSP, at PSP1:80h. Compare the two command lines.
4) The word at offset 2h in the PSP contains the **memory allocation** for the program, that is, it is the segment address of the first paragraph not allocated to this program. Look at PSP1:2, which should equal PSP2, and look at PSP2:2, which should show that your program is allocated the rest of available memory; that is, PSP2:2 will probably be 0A000h.
5) The word at PSP:2ch is the segment address of the segment containing the **environment variables** (the PATH, etc.) for the current program. That is, if E is the word at PSP:2cH, then the environment variables start at address E:0. Take a look at your environment variables with your debugger and try to determine their structure. (See Programming Problem 12.2 for more information.)
6) The word at PSP:32h is the **maximum number of open files**. Compare the value of this word in PSP1 and PSP2.

Exercise V.3

1. Use a debugger and DbgEx8 instead of DOIT to verify the solution to Exercise 12.5—1.

Summary

Viewing arbitrary data memory:

CV: Use **db** or **dw** *address* in the command window, or use the Memory1 window and set its contents using the dialog window produced by the Alt-O(ptions M(emory1… command.

TD: Use the dump window or the data pane of the CPU window, opened from the View Menu. Use the Goto command in the SpeedMenu (equivalent to **Ctrl-G**) to choose the address at which data display is to start.

Useful words in the PSP:

2h	first segment not used by the program
2ch	segment containing environment variables
32h	maximum number of open files.

Chapter 13

Procedures and High-Level Languages

registers discussed

ah	AX	al
bh	BX	bl
ch	CX	cl
dh	DX	dl
	SI	
	DI	
	BP	
	SP	
	DS	
	ES	
	SS	
	CS	
	IP	

o d i t s z c

Up to now, the procedures and functions we have been writing have been very simple. They have not required any substantial amount of storage for parameters or local variables, and recursion and reentrancy (defined below) have not been required. In this chapter we will develop a framework which will encompass the most general requirements for procedures. With it we will be able to see how high-level languages compile procedures and how assembly language procedures can be called by high-level language procedures.

Thie chapter presupposed Sections 12.1–4.

13.1 • Procedures and the Stack

To simplify terminology, whenever we say 'procedure' in this chapter, we mean both procedures and functions.

The stack has a much greater role in the implementation of procedures in high-level languages than just the call and return operations. Consider for instance the other problems that must be solved in order to get a full implementation:

- How are parameters passed? Passing them in registers, as we have done up to now, is useful only for procedures with a few short parameters. Also, how do we pass reference parameters (Pascal **var** parameters, C++ reference variable parameters, and *all* Fortran parameters)?
- How do we handle storage for local variables, temporaries, etc.? Fortran used permanent global storage for everything, which wastes space when the variables are only needed while the procedure is actually executing.
- Having a single permanent storage location for each local variable also makes it difficult to implement **recursion** (a procedure which calls itself, either directly or indirectly, is said to be recursive), as each active

call requires its own set of the local variables.

- Some procedures, particularly those in operating systems need to be **reentrant**, that is they must be usable by several different programs simultaneously. (What happens for instance if a program is performing Disk I/O when a 'hot key' is pressed, activating a Terminate and Stay Resident program, which also wants to do disk I/O? Non-reentrancy in DOS causes problems. See Chapter 15 for more information.)

One simple concept provides the basis for the solution of all of these problems. Each procedure in execution is assigned a **stack frame**, a fixed-sized block of memory on the stack for parameters, return address, local variables, and register storage, etc. In essence, when a procedure is called, its stack frame is pushed onto the stack. The routine itself may then push and pop temporary storage on the stack. If it calls other procedures (causing their frames to be pushed onto the stack) its own stack frame remains on the stack while the other procedures are executing. Only when the procedure finally exits is its stack frame (and any temporary storage it is using) popped off of the stack.

Note: As we will see in Section 13.2.3, our assemblers have methods of declaring procedures and their parameters and local variables in a manner similar to high-level languages. If you use one of these methods, it will allow you to ignore some or all of the material in this section. However I recommend that you avoid using the high-level methods until you thoroughly understand how the stack frame works as detailed here.

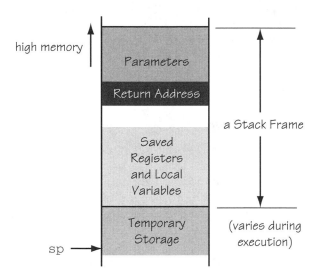

The bp (**base pointer**) register which was introduced but not explained in Chapter 10 points to a fixed position in the middle of the stack frame of the currently executing procedure, and the stack pointer sp points to the end of the procedure's temporary storage.

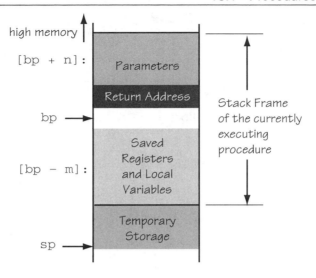

Because bp is an index register (actually a base register), various parts of the stack frame can be referenced relative to bp—positive displacements for parameters and negative displacements for local variables. The displacements from bp will be the same for every execution of the procedure, so that once bp is set, the actual location of the stack frame in memory is immaterial. **Any memory address which makes use of bp uses ss, the stack segment register**, by default. The addresses using bp are of the form [*displacement*+bp], [*displacement*+bp+si], or [*displacement*+bp+di].

The responsibility for setting up the stack frame is divided between the caller and the callee. Also, bp **must be saved and restored**, which is done in the stack location pointed to by bp.

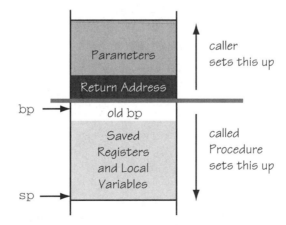

The caller does its work by pushing parameter values onto the stack (which at that time are part of the caller's temporary storage) and then executes the call instruction, which has the effect of pushing the return address onto the stack.

The called procedure does its part first by saving and resetting bp with the code

Start of Procedure
`Callee    PROC`
`          push    bp`
`          mov     bp, sp`
`          . . .`

Then space for local parameters (if any) is allocated on the stack and registers that must be saved are pushed, with the code

Set Up Stack
`. . .      ;         (Start of Procedure code)`
`sub     sp, n ; Reserve n bytes of local storage`
`push    reg1 ;         (n must be even)`
`push    reg2`
`. . .`

The setup code above results in the following stack structure, in which parameters are referred to by [bp + 4], [bp + 6], ... (assuming small model, that is, the normal situation in which call pushes only the IP register onto the stack) and local variables are referred to by [bp - 2], [bp - 4], ...* (The saved registers never need to be referred to directly; they need only be popped at the end of the procedure.)

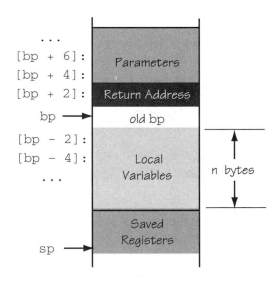

At the end of the procedure, assuming that all temporary storage has been popped off the stack, sp will be pointing to the last saved register value and we can exit the procedure by executing

---

* In medium and large model programs, (see Section 12.7)a *far* call is used, which pushes two words, and the parameters are at [bp + 6] [bp + 8] ... .

Exit Procedure
. . .
pop   *reg2*
pop   *reg1*
mov   sp, bp ;   Two-instruction sequence to
pop   bp ;   restore bp
ret

The code to set and restore bp should always be used exactly as we have given it, to avoid errors.*

Example 13.1—1. Trace the following pseudo-program, showing a snapshot of the stack at the indicated place. Local variables y and b are indicated by the declarations **word** y and **word** b.

Using the 'labels' in comments such as { L1: } to indicate return addresses

```
procedure p(x)
   word y

   y := 2 * x
   { take stack snapshot here }
end p

procedure q(a)
   word b

   b := a + 1
   if (a < 0) then q(b + 1) { L1: }
             else p(b + 2) { L2: }
   endif
end q

{ main program }
   q(-1) { L3: }
end main program
```

If we assume that initially, bp = sp, we get the diagram at the top of the next page. Note that the location labeled a in q's second stack frame is also a temporary location in the first execution of q (for the parameter to q), and that the location labeled x in p's stack frame is a temporary location in the second execution of q (for the parameter to p).

---

* High-level languages like Pascal and Ada, which allow nested procedures and functions, require an additional structure in the stack frame such as a **display**. For a description of how such a display can be set up using the 80286 and above enterinstruction, see the end of Section 21.1.

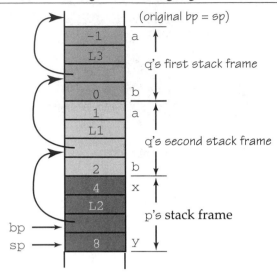

There are only two more decisions to be made:

- In what order are parameters pushed? That is, if we make the procedure call p(a, b, c), which code should we generate

push a			push c	
push b		*or*	push b	?
push c			push a	

- Who should pop the parameters off of the stack, the caller or the callee?

The answer to both questions depends on whether the language requires that a procedure always be called with the same fixed number of parameters. There is one set of choices for Pascal (and most other languages that require a fixed number of parameters) and another for C and C++.

Pascal parameter conventions: Parameters are pushed in the order encountered. For the procedure call P(a1, ... an) with *n* one-word parameters, the parameters are pushed in the order encountered, resulting in the stack-frame shown at the top of the next page (small model assumed). Because *n* is a known constant at translation time, the location of parameter *i* relative to bp is also.

Since the called procedure knows how many parameters it has, it can pop them off itself, which would be more efficient than requiring each individual call to do it. The only problem is that if the called procedure pops before doing its ret, then the return address will be lost, and if it does the ret first, control will be returned to the caller before the pop can take place. To simplify the process of pop-with-return, the 80X86 has another form of the ret instruction

```
          ret     n ;      Pop return address from stack into IP and
    ;                         then pop n more bytes off the stack
```

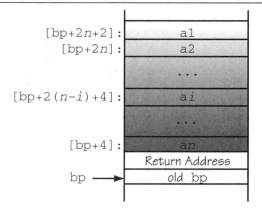

$[bp+2n+2]$: a1

$[bp+2n]$: a2

. . .

$[bp+2(n-i)+4]$: ai

. . .

$[bp+4]$: an

Return Address

bp ⟶ old bp

Pascal Parameter Conventions

If before the `ret n` instruction, we had

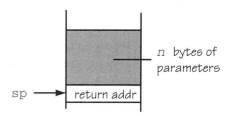

n bytes of parameters

sp ⟶ return addr

then afterwards we would have

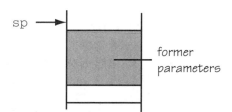

sp ⟶

former parameters

C/C++ parameter conventions: Some C and C++ functions (e.g., `printf`) can be passed a different number of parameters with each call. If parameters were pushed in the order encountered, there would be no way of telling where the first parameter was. (In `printf`, the first parameter is a formatting string, which in turn determines the (variable) number of remaining parameters.) Therefore in C and C++, parameters are pushed in the reverse of the order encountered. For the procedure call P(a1, ... an) with n one-word parameters, the parameters are pushed in the order an, ... a1, resulting in the following stack-frame for P:

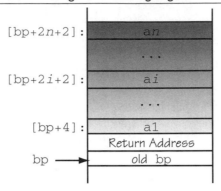

C/C++ Parameter Conventions

Also because of the possibility of a varying number of parameters, the called procedure uses `ret` (without an operand) to return and the caller, who knows how many parameters were passed, pops the parameters with an instruction such as

```
add     sp, n ;         pop n bytes from the stack
```

Example 13.1—2. Develop a function `Pow(X, n)` returning X^n for $n \geq 0$ using Pascal conventions.

We will use a variant of the algorithm developed in Example 9.2—3 where local variables are used instead of registers to hold P and D. The new version of the code is

```
            mov     P, 1 ;          P := 1
            mov     ax, X
            mov     D, ax ;         D := X
PowLoop:
            cmp     n, 0 ;          while (n > 0) do
            jle     Done
            shr     n, 1 ;            Set n := n div 2
            jnc     NotOdd ;          if original n was odd (CF=1) then
            mov     ax, P
            imul    ax, D
            mov     P, ax ;               P := P * D
NotOdd:
            mov     ax, D
            mul     ax, D
            mov     D, ax ;           D := D * D
            jmp     PowLoop ;       end while
Done:
```

The parameters will be pushed in the order encountered:

```
            push    value of X
            push    value of n
```

```
            call    Pow
```

This calling sequence means that when Pow is entered, the stack looks as follows:

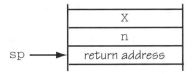

After Pow has been entered, the standard preamble executed to save and reset bp, and four bytes added to the stack (subtracted from sp) for storage for the local variables D and P, the stack looks as follows:

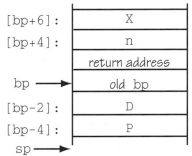

assuming small model. In order to avoid a lot of mysterious magic numbers, we can define all of these numbers with EQUates, and use our original code for Pow unchanged!

```
X           EQU     WORD PTR [BP+6]
n           EQU     WORD PTR [BP+4]
D           EQU     WORD PTR [BP-2]
P           EQU     WORD PTR [BP-4]
```

The complete subprogram, with the necessary saving and restoring of dx, is as follows:

```
;; Pow(X, n)--computes and returns X**n in ax. Calling sequence:
;;
;;          EXTRN   Pow:NEAR
;;          push    X
;;          push    n
;;          call    Pow
;;
            .MODEL SMALL

X           EQU     WORD PTR [BP+6]
n           EQU     WORD PTR [BP+4]
D           EQU     WORD PTR [BP-2]
P           EQU     WORD PTR [BP-4]
```

```
                  PUBLIC  Pow
Pow               PROC
                  push    bp
                  mov     bp, sp
                  sub     sp, 4 ;      Allocate 4 bytes of local storage
                  push    dx
                  mov     P, 1 ;       Start of original Pow code
                  . . .
Done:             ;                    End of original Pow code
                  mov     ax, P ;      Return value in ax
                  pop     dx
                  mov     sp, bp
                  pop     bp
                  ret     4 ;          Return, popping four bytes of params
Pow               ENDP
                  END
```

Example 13.1—3. Rewrite the Pow function using C/C++ conventions.

Most of the program is unchanged. The changed parts are given below in boldface:

```
;; Pow(X, n)--computes and returns X**n in ax. Calling sequence:
;;
;;          EXTRN  Pow:NEAR
;;          push   n
;;          push   X
;;          call   Pow
;;          add    sp, 4 ;      pop parameters

            .MODEL SMALL

X           EQU    WORD PTR [BP+4]
Y           EQU    WORD PTR [BP+6]
D           EQU    WORD PTR [BP-2]
            . . .
            mov    sp, bp
            pop    bp
            ret
Pow         ENDP
            END
```

Note that as before, we are returning the function value in ax. However, if the function value requires a lot of memory, the caller may be required to push storage for the function value onto the stack before the parameters are pushed.

In the two examples above, we are using **value parameters**. The actual value of the parameter is pushed onto the stack. Value parameters are the default in Pascal, and in C are used for *all* parameters except arrays. It is usually the easiest method to implement, but makes it more difficult to pass values back to the calling program through parameters. We will discuss the alternative, **reference parameters** (Pascal **var** parameters, C++ reference variable parameters, and all Fortran parameters) in Section 13.4.

Note that we have now taken care of the problems of implementing both recursion and reentrancy. **Recursion** is handled by having a different stack frame for each active instance of the procedure. **Reentrancy** is handled in the same way, where now it is possible for different callers to have different stacks. When switching between different simultaneous users of a procedure, we will switch register sets (including IP). Switching from one user's bp, sp, and ss to the other's will have the effect of switching between variable storage for the two users.

IMPORTANT NOTE: For reasons that escape the author, many people seem to feel that every program gets its input from the keyboard and displays its output on the CRT. Thus in the Pow function such a person would read *X* and *n* at the beginning of the function (perhaps destroying parameter values that were passed) and then display the result at the end. Doing I/O in the function like this makes it *useless* for general purpose inclusion in larger programs.

Never, NEVER, NEVER do I/O in a procedure or function unless the program specification explicitly calls for it.

Exercises 13.1

1. ✓ Suppose we execute the code

```
            .MODEL SMALL
            . . .
            mov    ax, 104
            push   ax
            mov    ax, -86
            push   ax
            call TestProc;
            . . .
TestProc    PROC
            push   bp
            mov    bp, sp
            sub    sp, 2
            mov    [bp - 2], 77
  ;         ...you are here
```

starting with the stack as given below. Fill in the values you can determine or their descriptions as well as the new bp and sp.

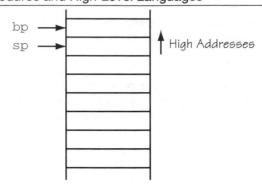

2. ✓ Consider the following pseudocode:

```
procedure p(a)
   word b

   b := a + 2
   if (a < 20) then q(b + 1) { L1 }
              else {take stack snapshot here }
   end if
end p

procedure q(c)
   word d

   d := c + 3
   p(2 * d) { L2 }
end q

{ main program }
   p(0) { L3 }
end main program
```

With the same conventions as in Example 13.1—1, draw a snapshot of the stack at the indicated place.

3. Consider the following pseudocode:

```
word function fact(n) { a function returning a word value (in ax) }
   if (n <= 1) then
      { take stack snapshot here }
      return fact := 1
   else
      return fact := n * fact(n - 1) { L1 }
   end if
end fact
```

```
{ main program }
  x := fact(3) { L2 }
end main program
```

With the same conventions as in Example 13.1—1, draw a snapshot of the stack at the indicated place.

4. ✓ Assume small model in each of the following exercises.

a) Write an assembly language version of the following function using Pascal procedure conventions:

```
word function absdiff(x, y)

  if x > y then return absdiff := x - y
  else return absdiff := y - x
  end if
end absdiff
```

b) Write an assembly language code fragment for the code

```
z := absdif(x+3, 14)
```

using Pascal conventions.

c) How would the solutions to parts a) and b) differ if they were written to C/C++ conventions? An equivalent C program would be

```
int absdif(x, y)
int x, y;
{
  if (x > y) return x - y;
  else return y - x;
}
```

5. Assume small model in each of the following exercises.

a) Write an assembly language version of the following function using Pascal procedure conventions:

```
word function smallest(x, y, z)
  word s

  if x < y then s := x else s := y end if
  if s > z then s := z end if
  return smallest := s
end smallest
```

b) How would the solution to part a) differ if it were written to C/C++ conventions?

6. Most high-level languages allow procedures and functions to be passed as parameters. For instance, procedural parameters can be very useful in general purpose sorting routines (where the method of key comparison can be passed as a procedure), in numerical routines (in which a function to be integrated or plotted is passed as a parameter), or in systems programs (where a procedure to be executed in case of error is passed). Show how we might implement the following pseudocode in assembly language:

```
procedure p(procedure q) { i.e., q is passed as a parameter to p }

    . . .
    q { call the procedure passed as a parameter }
    . . .
end p

procedure r{ this is the procedure that will actually be passed }
    . . .
end r

{ main program }
    . . .
    p(r)
    . . .
end main program
```

(Hint: if you code the instruction `call X` and X is a variable of type `DWORD PTR` (or declared with the `DD` pseudo-operation), X is interpreted as a memory location containing the segment:offset address of the routine to be called. If X is of type `WORD PTR` or declared with a `DW` pseudo-op, X is interpreted as the offset of the routine. A similar convention holds for `jmps`.) (The method hinted at here is only satisfactory in a language like C and C++ in which procedures aren't nested and one need not pass a whole environment. For the complete solution, see Exercise 21.1—2.)

13.2 • A Little Something Extra: Communicating with High-Level Languages

As you have seen, the interface between assembly language and high-level languages depends on the language (and sometimes on the particular implementation of the language. In Section 13.2.1 we discuss Turbo Pascal (versions 4.0 and later) and in Section 13.2.2, Microsoft Visual C++/Borland C++. We will show how to write assembly language programs which can be called by programs in these languages. In Section 13.2.3 we will show how new features of the `.MODEL`, `PROC`, and `LOCAL` pseudo-operations and the `ret` (no operand) instruction can be used to streamline the process of creating assembly programs callable from C/C++ and Pascal.

This section represents a minimum introduction to the subject. For further details, see the documentation of the language you want to interface with.

13.2.1 • Turbo Pascal

To call an assembly language procedure from Turbo Pascal (version 4.0 and later), the assembly language procedure must have the following general form:

```
          .MODEL small or large
          .DATA
          . . .
    global variables defined here.
    Use EXTRN to reference global variables defined in Turbo.
    Turbo cannot reference variables defined here.

          .CODE
          PUBLIC procedure-name
procedure-name PROC
          push    bp ;         ds will be @data on entry
          mov     bp, sp
          sub     sp, number of bytes of local storage
          push    ds ;         if ds is altered
          . . .
   code for the procedure
          . . .
          pop     ds ;         if ds is altered
          mov     sp, bp
          pop     bp
          ret     n ;          n is number of bytes of parameters
procedure-name ENDP
          END
```

Parameters are pushed in the order encountered, so the first parameter is the furthest from bp. Returned function values are in ax if small enough, in dx and ax if they fit in two words. Otherwise, Turbo Pascal passes a far (two-word segment:offset) pointer to the place to store the result as a zeroth parameter to the function.

All Pascal global variables (that is, variables declared outside of any procedure or function) reside in the segment named .DATA, and it is assumed by all Pascal programs that ds points to that segment. Ds is the only register (other than the stack registers sp, bp, and ss) which must be preserved by subprograms.

To call such a procedure or function from a Pascal program, the following two declarations are needed:

```
{$L procedure or function file name}

procedure procedure-name ( parameters ); external;
 or
function procedure-name ( parameters ): return-type; external;
```

Note that there must be no space between '{' and '$.' The comment beginning {$L... is called a **pseudo-comment**. Traditionally such comments are *not* ignored by the compiler, and in fact are used to transmit special information to it.

Normally Turbo Pascal uses the small model for procedure calls, but uses the large model for procedures and functions declared in the interface section of a unit.

Example 13.2—1. Write an assembly function MaskWd(nBits, off) to be called from Turbo Pascal which takes as input a number of bits nBits an an offset off and produces as output a word containing nBits contiguous 1s, shifted left by off bits.

Thus MaskWd(7, 5) = 0000111111100000B. The first version of the assembly code is

```
;; MASKWDP1.ASM--Turbo Pascal version; MaskWd(nBits, off) produces
;; a word with nBits 1's, offset off from the right end
            .MODEL SMALL

            .CODE
            PUBLIC MaskWd
nBits       EQU     WORD PTR [bp+6] ;   Parameters pushed in the
off         EQU     WORD PTR [bp+4] ;    order encountered
MaskWd      PROC
            push    bp
            mov     bp, sp ;       Needn't push ds as it isn't changed
            mov     ax, 8000h ;    Get one 1 bit in sign position
            mov     cx, nBits
            dec     cl
            jl      ReturnZero
            sar     ax, cl ;       Propagate sign bit
            add     cx, off
            inc     cl
            rol     ax, cl
Done:
            pop     bp
            ret     4
ReturnZero:
            sub     ax, ax
            jmp     Done
MaskWd      ENDP
            END
```

To use MaskWd in a Turbo Pascal program, assemble it in the usual way with MASM or TASM. Then enter the following declarations in the program that uses it:

```
{$L maskwdp1}

function MaskWd(nBits, off : integer) : integer; external;
```

Then to use the function, simply invoke MaskWd(m, n) anywhere in any expression.

13.2.2 • Microsoft Visual C++/Borland C++

The general idea of linking with C++ (and C) is similar to that for Pascal, with a few modifications due to the peculiarities of C/C++. The general outline of a C or C++ callable procedure is

```
            .MODEL model of C or C++ caller
            .DATA
            . . .
   global variables defined here.
   Use EXTRN to reference global variables defined in C/C++.
   C/C++ can reference PUBLIC variables defined here.

            .CODE
            PUBLIC _procedure-name
_procedure-name PROC
            push    bp ;            ds will be @data on entry
            mov     bp, sp
            sub     sp, number of bytes of local storage
            push ds, si, di if altered
            . . .
    code for the procedure
            . . .
            pop di, si, ds if altered
            mov     sp, bp
            pop     bp
            ret
_procedure-name ENDP
            END
```

C and C++ use si and di for register variables, if any, so si and di have to be preserved by a function that uses them.

C/C++ automatically prefixes its PUBLIC (global variable and non-static function) names with a '_' character. Parameters are pushed in the *reverse* of the order encountered, so the first parameter is the nearest to bp. Returned function values are in ax if small enough, in dx and ax if they require two words. C and C++ are case sensitive as far as identifiers are concerned, so the assembler must be told to be **case sensitive** for PUBLIC symbols also, as follows:

```
masm /mx ... or ml /Cx ...
tasm /mx ...
```

To call such a procedure or function from a C++ program, the following prototype is needed:

```
extern "C" return-type procedure-name ( parameters );
```

The "C" part of the prefix is needed because C and C++ use a different calling method. Omit the "C" part if calling from a C program.

Example 13.2—2. Write a version of the MaskWd function described in Example 13.2—1 to be called from C or C++ .

Our first version of the assembly code is

```
;; MASKWDC1.ASM--Microsoft Visual C/C++ or Borland C/C++ version;
;;  MaskWd(nBits, off) produces a word with nBits 1s, offset
;;   off from the right end
;; Assemble with /Cx switch (ML) or /mx switch (MASM and TASM)
            .MODEL SMALL

            .CODE
            PUBLIC _MaskWd
nBits       EQU    WORD PTR [bp+4] ;   Parameters pushed in the
off         EQU    WORD PTR [bp+6] ;    reverse of order encountered
_MaskWd     PROC
            push   bp
            mov    bp, sp ;       Needn't push ds, si, or di
            mov    ax, 8000h ;  Get one 1 bit in sign position
            mov    cx, nBits
            dec    cl
            jl     ReturnZero
            sar    ax, cl ;     Propagate sign bit
            add    cx, off
            inc    cl
            rol    ax, cl
Done:
            pop    bp
            ret    ;             Don't pop parameters
ReturnZero:
            sub    ax, ax
            jmp    Done
_MaskWd     ENDP
            END
```

To use `MaskWd` in a C or C++ program, assemble it with

```
ml /c /Cx maskwdc1.asm
      or
masm /mx maskwdc1;
      or
tasm /mx maskwdc1
```

(The `/c` parameter in the `ml` command causes assembly to stop with the `.OBJ` file.) Enter the following prototype in the C++ program that uses it:

```
extern "C" int MaskWd(int, int);    /* omit "C" in C */
```

Then to use the function, simply invoke `MaskWd(m, n)` anywhere in any expression.

The easiest way to link the program with C or C++ programs is to use the `cl` (Visual C++) or `bcc` (Borland C++) command. If we wish to create a program `testmsk` from `maskwdc1.obj` and a C++ program `testmsk.cpp`, we would use

```
cl testmsk.cpp maskwdc1.obj
        or
bcc testmskcpp maskwdc1.obj
```

13.2.3 • Assembler Help with High-Level Languages

Masm and tasm offer quite a bit of help in communicating with high-level languages. The fundamental tool involves adding a second parameter to the .MODEL statement, a language name:

$$.MODEL\ size,\ PASCAL$$

or

$$.MODEL\ size,\ C$$

(There is no C++ specification; use C instead.) Specifying the language as above has the following consequences for the PUBLIC, EXTRN, and PROC pseudo-operations and the ret instruction, *the version with no operand*:

- If the C language is specified, all symbols declared PUBLIC or EXTRN have a leading '_' added to them.
- Code to save and set up the bp register is added immediately after any PROC statement, and code to restore the bp register is added immediately before any ret statement.
- The PROC statement can specify USES R1 R2 ... Rn where each Ri is one of the 80X86 machine registers. The USES clause causes the specified registers be pushed onto the stack immediately after the PROC statement and to be popped from the stack in reverse order just before each ret in the PROC. (Note that there are no commas between the registers.)
- The PROC statement can specify the parameters which are used to call it after the optional USES statement. The assembler will then equate each parameter name to [bp + n] where n is the appropriate amount. Account is taken as to whether the program is large or small in model. For the Pascal language type, parameters are assumed to be pushed in the order encountered, and for C, in the reverse of the order encountered.
- When parameters are specified in the PROC statement and the language type is Pascal, the ret instruction is automatically changed to ret m, where m is the number of bytes of parameters specified in the PROC statement.

Because the ret with no operand has become so powerful, we will start writing it as RET when a language is specified in the .MODEL statement, even though the assemblers don't distinguish between ret and RET.

In the presence of the statement .MODEL SMALL, C, the declaration

```
Stuff     PROC    USES SI DI, A : WORD, B : DWORD, C : WORD
```

(note: no comma between SI and DI!) produces the code

```
push    bp
mov     bp, sp
push    si
push    di
```

```
A          EQU    WORD PTR [bp + 4]
B          EQU    DWORD PTR [bp + 6]
C          EQU    WORD PTR [bp + 10]
```

and the RET instruction produces the code

```
pop    di
pop    si
mov    sp, bp
pop    bp
ret
```

In the presence of the statement .MODEL LARGE, PASCAL, the PROC declaration above produces the code

```
           push   bp
           mov    bp, sp
           push   si
           push   di
A          EQU    WORD PTR [bp + 12]
B          EQU    DWORD PTR [bp + 8]
C          EQU    WORD PTR [bp + 6]
```

and the RET instruction produces the code

```
pop    di
pop    si
mov    sp, bp
pop    bp
ret    8
```

In addition, the LOCAL pseudo-operation can be used to declare local variables immediately after the PROC statement. The format for local variables is similar to that for parameters in the PROC statement itself. The LOCAL pseudo-operation results in decrementing sp sufficiently to leave room for the locals and EQUating the local variable names to the proper type of [bp - n]. For instance, the declarations

```
           .MODEL whatever, PASCAL or C
           ...
aProc      PROC   USES SI DI
           LOCAL  A : WORD, B : DWORD
```

is equivalent to the code

```
aProc      PROC
           sub    sp, 6
A          EQU    WORD PTR [bp - 2]
```

```
B               EQU     DWORD PTR [bp - 6]
                push    si
                push    di
```

and the RET instruction produces the code

```
                pop     di
                pop     si
                mov     sp, bp
                pop     bp
                ret     whatever
```

Example 13.2—3. Let's redo examples 13.2—1 and 13.2—2. We can write the Pascal case as follows:

```
;; MASKWDP2.ASM--Turbo Pascal version; MaskWd(nBits, off) produces
;; a word with nBits 1's, offset off from the right end
                .MODEL SMALL, PASCAL

                .CODE
                PUBLIC MaskWd
MaskWd          PROC    nBits : WORD, off : WORD
                mov     ax, 8000h ;   Get one 1 bit in sign position
                mov     cx, nBits
                dec     cl
                jl      ReturnZero
                sar     ax, cl ;      Propagate sign bit
                add     cx, off
                inc     cl
                rol     ax, cl
Done:
                RET
ReturnZero:
                sub     ax, ax
                jmp     Done
MaskWd          ENDP
                END
```

The really fascinating thing is that the only thing we have to do to change to the C/C++ version is change the comments and the .MODEL statement!

```
;; MASKWDC2.ASM--C/C++ version; MaskWd(nBits, off) produces
;;  a word with nBits 1's, offset off from the right end.
;;  Assemble using /Cx switch (ML) or /mx switch (TASM and MASM)
                .MODEL SMALL, C
                ...
```

Exercises 13.2

1.   What does `MaskWd` produce in the 'pathological' cases like `off < 0`, `nBits + off > 16`, etc.?

2.   Write code for each of the following procedures and procedure calls using either Turbo Pascal or the C/C++ conventions, or both.

   a) ✓ Write a function `Card(s)` with integer (word) parameter `s` returning an integer equal to the number of 1 bits in `s`. For instance, `Card(18)` = 2 and `Card(-1)` = 16.

   b)   Write a fragment of assembly code to translate

```
a := b + Card(c)
```

   c)   Write a function `Peek(segm, offs : integer) : integer;` which takes as input two integers `segm` and `offs` and returns as output the word at memory location `segm:offs`.

   d)   Write a fragment of assembly code to translate the call

```
ShiftStatus := Peek(40h, 17h)
```

   (The arguments would actually be $40, $17 in Turbo Pascal, 0x40, 0x17 in C/C++.)

   e)   Write a procedure `Poke(val, segm, offs : integer);` which stores the word `val` at memory location `segm:offs`. (In C, a procedure is coded just like a function. It just doesn't bother to return a value.)

   f)   Write a fragment of assembly code to translate the call

```
Poke(5h, 40h, 17h)
```

3.   Rewrite the code for `Pow` in Example 13.1—2 and 3 using the techniques in Section 13.2.3. The code in the two programs should be identical except for the `.MODEL` statement.

13.3 • A Little Something Extra: Inline Assembly Language

This section isn't related to the others in this chapter, in the sense that it doesn't make any direct use of the stack frame, but because of its similarity to the material in the last section, this chapter seems like the most logical place for it.

In the early days of high-level languages (the late 50s and early 60s), a few compilers allowed the programmer to drop into assembly language as a way of dealing with the limitations of the high-level language. Such inline assembly code was relatively easy to implement. The high-level language compilers translated into assembly language anyway, and all they had to do was copy the programmer-supplied assembly language. The practice was soon abandoned, though, for a variety of reasons: it was recognized that including assembly language made programs non-portable; compilers started translating directly to machine language; and high-level languages became more capable.

However, the PC high-level language market is highly competitive and everybody seems to want to be a hacker, so things have come full circle. The current versions of several popular compilers for the PC allow the programmer to drop into assembly language. We will discuss briefly the capabilities of three: Turbo Pascal, Borland C++ and Microsoft Visual C ++. As an example, we will rewrite our `MaskWd` function from Examples 13.2—1 and 2 in each setting.

Turbo Pascal allows the inclusion of assembly language between **asm**/**end** brackets. One can refer there to variables, parameters, etc. declared in the Pascal part of the code. If a function returns a one-word value, assembly code sets that value by moving it to a variable called **@Result**. The Pascal code for MaskWd is:

```
{ maskwdtp.pas -- maskwd in turbo Pascal with inline assembly }

function MaskWd(nBits, off : integer) : integer;
  begin
    if (nBits <= 0) then
      MaskWd := 0
    else
      asm
        mov  ax, 8000h
        mov  cx, nBits
        dec  cl
        sar  ax, cl
        add  cx, off
        inc  cl
        rol  ax, cl
        mov  @Result, ax{ returned value }
      end
  end; { MaskWd }
```

Microsoft Visual C++ works somewhat similarly, except that the assembly code is marked by _asm (note leading underscore) and the assembly itself is a single instruction on the same line following _asm or is enclosed in C/C++ statement parentheses { }. There is no special place to store the function result. Move the value to a local variable in the _asm part, then return the local variable in the C/C++ code. (Visual C insists on an explicit return in a function.) The code for MaskWd is

```
/* maskwdmc.cpp -- maskwd in Visual C++ with inline assembly */

int MaskWd(int nBits, int off)
{
  int value;
    _asm {
         mov cx, nBits
         dec cx
         jl  Return0
         mov ax, 8000h
         sar ax, cl
         add cx, off
         inc cl
         rol ax, cl
         mov value, ax
    }
```

```
    return value;    /* can't return without a value */
}
```

The Borland C++ syntax is similar to Visual C++ except that asm (no _) is used as the keyword. Borland C++ also has the extremely useful feature of allowing you to refer to registers in the C/C++ code itself. Note for instance, the references to _CX and _AX in the following code:

```
/* maskwdbc.cpp -- maskwd written in Borland C++ */
/*  with inline assembly */

int MaskWd(int nBits, int off)
{
  if ((_CX = nBits - 1) < 0)
    return 0;
  _AX = 0x8000; /* Get one 1 bit in the sign position */
  asm {
          sar  ax, cl
          add  cx, off
          inc  cl
          rol  ax, cl
  }
  return _AX;    /* for documentation; it will do this anyway */
}
```

Use of these register pseudo-variables can be dangerous, though. In the original version of this code, I put the statement _AX = 0x8000 before the beginning of the if statement and the program didn't work because Borland C++ used ax to compute nBits - 1 before moving it to the cx register.

Exercises 13.3

1.   Redo Exercise 13.2—2 using the high-level language of your choice and dropping into assembly language where necessary.

13.4 • A Little Something Extra: Reference Parameters

The information in Section 12.6 on pointers is necessary for understanding this section.

At this point, the only way we know of passing results back from a procedure is via function values (or changing PUBLIC variables).

Example 13.4—1. Write a procedure to swap two values.

Consider for instance the following version, in an unspecified language:

```
procedure Swap(x, y)
  word temp
  temp := x
  x := y
```

```
            y := temp
        end Swap
```

If we implement this code in assembly language as we have been doing, we would come up with something like

```
;; BAD CODE for Swap!!
;;
x               EQU     WORD PTR [bp+6]
y               EQU     WORD PTR [bp+4]
                PUBLIC Swap
Swap            PROC
                push    bp
                mov     bp, sp
                mov     ax, x
                xchg    ax, y
                mov     x, ax
                pop     bp
                ret     4
Swap            ENDP
```

The trouble with this procedure is that if we execute Swap(a, b), the *values* of a and b will get interchanged *on the stack*, then popped and lost forever, and a and b will be unchanged.

Example 13.4—2. Implementing Swap C-style.

The C programming language has only value parameters of most types, and changes the values of parameters by passing pointer to them rather than the parameters themselves. Thus in C, the procedure Swap would be

```
void Swap(int *xp, int *yp)  /* void indicates it's a procedure */
/* xp and yp are pointers to integers */
{
  int temp;

  temp = *xp; /* *xp = what xp points to, i.e., x */
  *xp = *yp;
  *yp = temp;
}
```

Int *xp says that the variable xp is a pointer to an integer, and is equivalent to Pascal's **var** xp : ^integer; . *xp is the integer that xp points to, and is equivalent to Pascal's xp^. Recalling the treatment of pointers in Section 12.6 (and assuming two-word pointers), we could write code for the C version of Swap as follows:

```
;; SWAP--procedure to swap two integer values using C conventions
;;
                .MODEL SMALL
                ASSUME SS:NOTHING ;  Safety measure; see Section 12.4

                .CODE
xp              EQU     DWORD PTR [bp+4] ;  C parameters are reversed
yp              EQU     DWORD PTR [bp+8]
                PUBLIC Swap
Swap            PROC
                push    bp
                mov     bp, sp
                push    ds
                push    si
                push    di ;            save registers
                lds     si, xp ;        ds:si --> x
                les     di, yp ;        es:di --> y
                mov     ax, ds:[si]
                xchg    ax, es:[di]
                mov     ds:[si], ax
                pop     di
                pop     si
                pop     ds
                pop     bp
                ret ;                   the caller pops params in C
Swap            ENDP
                END
```

When we wish to swap a and b in C, we would execute Swap(&a, &b) ('&' is the *address of* operator in C). The assembly code would be

```
                mov     ax, SEG b
                push    ax
                mov     ax, OFFSET b
                push    ax
                mov     ax, SEG a
                push    ax
                mov     ax, OFFSET a
                push    ax
                EXTRN   Swap : NEAR
                call    Swap
                add     sp, 8
```

Example 13.4—3. Implementing Swap Pascal or C++ style.

You can use identical code in C++ or mimic the C code in Pascal, but Pascal and C++ give you a more structured and safer method—**var** parameters in Pascal and reference variable parameters in C++, which are in fact different notations for the same thing. The Pascal version of Swap would be written

```
procedure Swap(var x, y : integer);
  var temp : integer;
  begin
    temp := x;
    x := y;
    y := temp
  end;
```

and the C++ version would be

```
void Swap(int &x, int &y)       /* makes x and y var parameters */
{
  int temp;

  temp = x;
  x = y;
  y = temp;
}
```

In both languages the call would be Swap(a, b). The interesting thing is that *the assembly language code generated would be essentially identical* in all three versions. The only differences would come from parameter order, who pops the parameters, and what registers must be preserved. That is, the only differences are implementation differences between C/C++ and Pascal on *all* procedures, not just this one.

Exercises 13.4

1. ✓ Fill in the blanks in the following complete assembly language procedure, whose purpose is to implement the following Pascal procedure:

```
procedure SetIt(var x: integer; y: integer);
begin
  x := y
end;
```

```
            .MODEL  SMALL
            .CODE
x           EQU     DWORD PTR _____

y           EQU     WORD PTR _____
SetIt       PROC
            push    bp
            mov     bp, sp
            push    ds
```

```
              push    si

              _____   si, x

              mov     ax, _____

              mov     _____, ax

              pop     _____

              pop     _____

              ret     _____
      SetIt   ENDP
              END
```

2. a) ✓ Write C/C++-style assembly code to implement the following procedure (the keyword void just means it doesn't return a value):

```
      void SumDiff(int x, in  y, int &sum, int &diff)
      {
          sum = x + y;
          diff = x - y;
      }
```

b) Write a code fragment to perform the call

```
      SumDiff(14, a - 22, M, N);
```

c) What declaration would be necessary in a C++ program to make the call in part b) to the assembly program written in part a)?

3. ✓ When an array reference such as a[i] is passed as a parameter, it is necessary to pass the *address* of a[i]. If a is a word array whose subscripts start at 1, this address is OFFSET $a - 2 + 2 * i$. To make it easier to compute such an address, we can use the **new instruction lea**.

Load Address		
lea	*reg, memory ref* ;	Load Effective Address

which loads the address of *memory ref* rather than its contents. The instruction

```
      lea reg, Variable
```

is equivalent to

```
      mov reg, OFFSET Variable
```

while the instruction

```
lea     reg, [n + indexreg]
```

is equivalent to

```
mov     reg, indexreg
add     reg, n
```

Thus we can obtain the address of the `a[i]` above by writing

```
mov     bx, i
shl     bx, 1
lea     reg, [a - 2 + bx]
```

Write assembly code, assuming `a` is a word array in the .DATA segment with subscripts starting at 1, to perform the C++ or Pascal procedure calls

```
Swap(a[3], a[18]);   and   Swap(a[i], a[i+1]);
```

4.   C normally passes arrays by reference; i.e., it passes a pointer to the first entry in the array. Write assembly language versions of the standard C functions `strlen`, `strcpy`, and `strcmp`. Non-standard (in that they don't pass parameters on the stack) forms of these functions are given in Examples 12.2—1-3, respectively. Each of these functions will have (one or two) parameters which will be pointers to the starts of strings pushed onto the stack.

Programming Problem 13.1

Write an assembly language function `Fib` which takes as input the integer n and produces as output the nth Fibonacci number. The nth Fibonacci number is defined recursively as follows:

$$\text{Fib}(0) = 0; \text{Fib}(1) = 1, \text{ and } \text{Fib}(n) = \text{Fib}(n–1) + \text{Fib}(n–2) \text{ for } n \geq 2$$

In fact it would be very poor practice to implement Fib directly from the recursive definition. For instance, to compute Fib(10) we would have to compute Fib(9) once, Fib(8) twice, Fib(7) three times, Fib(6) five times, etc. You should implement one of the following functions in assembly language:

```
word function Fib (n)
  word sum, this, prev, i

  if n <= 0 then Fib := 0
  else
    prev := 0
    this := 1
    for i := 2 to n do
      sum := this + prev
```

```
        prev := this
        this := sum
      end for
      return Fib := this
    end if
end Fib
```

or

```
word function Fib (n)
  word function FibHelp (n, prev, this)

    if n = 1 then FibHelp := this
    else FibHelp := FibHelp(n - 1, this, this + prev)
    end if
  end FibHelp

  {Fib code here}
  if n < 1 then Fib := 0
  else Fib := FibHelp(n, 0, 1)
  end if
end Fib
```

Be sure that parameters are passed properly on the stack, that local variables, if any, are saved on the stack, and that correct use is made of bp. Test your function by writing a main program which prints out Fib(1), ..., Fib(10) on successive lines.

Programming Problem 13.2

Ackerman's function $A(x, y)$ is defined by

$$A(x, y) = \quad \begin{array}{ll} 0 & \text{if } y = 0 \\ 2y & \text{if } x = 0 \\ 2 & \text{if } y = 1, \text{ and} \\ A(x - 1, A(x, y - 1)) & \text{otherwise} \end{array}$$

It isn't good for much, but it is much loved by computer scientists as an example of a *very* recursive function. Write an assembly language program such that the command line

```
ackerman x y
```

where x and y are actual integers, will display the value of $A(x, y)$. Use Dec2Bin in UTIL.LIB to do the input conversion (see Exercise 11.1—3 for a description of how the function is used).

Note: $A(x, y)$ grows *very* rapidly with x. $A(0, y) = 2y$, $A(1,y) = 2^y$, and $A(2, y) = {}_2 2^{2^{\cdots^2}}$ (y times).

Programming Problem 13.3

Requires Section 13.4. Write an assembly language function `Biggest(x, y, z)` which returns the largest of its three arguments. The code should use the `Swap` procedure developed in Section 13.4 as follows:

```
word function Biggest( x, y, z)

    if (x < y) then Swap( x, y )end if
    if (x < z) then Swap( x, z )end if
    return Biggest := x
end Biggest
```

Note: The parameters to `Swap` must be reference parameters and that x, y, and z must NOT be reference parameters to `Biggest`. You need to push the segment:offset address of parameters to `Swap`. In this example of course, the segment will be `ss`. The easiest way to push complicated offsets onto the stack is to use the `lea` instruction introduced in Exercise 13.4—3.

Test your two procedures by writing a main program which calls `Biggest` at least three times to test the three possibilities for largest element, and prints out the result each time.

SUMMARY

Parameters are passed to subprograms by pushing them onto the stack. In Pascal style they are pushed in the order encountered, in C/C++ style, they are pushed in the reverse order. For value parameters, the actual value is pushed onto the stack and for reference parameters, a pointer to the value is pushed.

The initialization code to a subprogram contains

```
Name        PROC
            push    bp
            mov     bp, sp
            sub     sp, n ;      n = # of bytes of local parameters
```

The code above results in bp pointing to the storage for the old bp, with parameters starting at bp + 4 (bp + 6 in medium and large models where far calls are used) and local variables starting at bp − 2. Function values are normally returned in ax if one word, dx and ax if two words. The standard exit code for a procedure with *m* bytes of parameters is

```
            mov     sp, bp
            pop     bp
            ret ;                C version; caller pops params with
    ;                              add sp, m
```

or

```
            mov     sp, bp
            pop     bp
            ret     m ;          Pascal version; pop params here
```

Bp can be used for based indexing with si and di, but normally its value is *changed* only in the two ways listed above.

New Instructions:

```
ret    n ;              pops the return address off the stack
;                       like ret, and then pops n bytes off
;                       the stack

lea    reg, operand ;   loads register reg with the address of
;                       operand in memory rather than the
;                       contents of that address.
```

Extensions to Pseudo-Instructions:

```
.MODEL   size, language ;        language = C or PASCAL
PROC     USES R1 ... Rn, variable:type, variable:type, ...
LOCAL    variable:type, variable:type, ...
RET
```

Use of all of these instructions in concert greatly simplifies the process of writing assembly procedures and functions callable from Pascal or C/C++. The PROC and immediately following LOCAL statements above automatically generate the code necessary to set up the stack frame, allocate space for the listed local variables, and push registers R1, ..., Rn onto the stack. EQUates are set up for the parameters specified in PROC, in the proper order according to *language* and the proper distance above bp according to *size*. For the local variables declared by LOCAL, RET restores the saved registers R1, ..., Rn and bp and generates the correct type of ret instruction according to *language*.

Chapter 14

Applying Assembly III: Multiple Precision and Decimal Arithmetic

registers discussed

ah	AX	al
bh	BX	bl
ch	CX	cl
dh	DX	dl
	SI	
	DI	
	BP	
	SP	
	DS	
	ES	
	SS	
	CS	
	IP	

o d i t s z **c**

Up to now we haven't given any really essential uses of assembly language (with the exception of replacing time-critical high-level programs with hand-optimized assembly language). Even DOS calls and low-level BIOS calls are available in virtually every high-level package that pretends applicability as a systems programming tool. In this chapter we will finally discuss some applications that can be done satisfactorily *only* in assembly language: multiple precision and decimal arithmetic and the use of multiple precision arithmetic to code a good pseudorandom number generator. The only parts of this chapter which will be used again are the library routines MPPutDec and Random and the very first part of Section 14.1.

14.1 • Multiple Precision Arithmetic

Because of the limited word length on the 8086-88 and 80286 (16 bits) it isn't possible to do integer arithmetic directly on large integers. The 80X86, like most machines with short word length, has instructions to assist in extending operations to integers represented by multiple words or bytes. We have already seen two such instructions: cwd and cbw. Here are two more, adc (add with carry) and sbb (subtract with borrow):

```
adc     dest, source ;     dest:=dest+source+CarryFlag
sbb     dest, source ;     dest:=dest-source-CarryFlag
```

In fact, subtraction is not *exactly* the same as adding the 2's complement. The *results* are the same but in adding the 2's complement, the carry flag would be set to the carry out the left end. In subtraction, the carry flag is set to the *complement* of the carry. In effect, in subtraction, the carry flag is set to represent the amount that would have to be *borrowed* to perform the subtraction. Don't worry about the details of this, though. It is enough to know that sub works in such a way that sbb works. Adc and sbb take operands in the same format as add and sub, and they have word and byte versions.

These new instructions make it easy for us to represent large integers in multiple words and do the arithmetic just as we learned in elementary school, in effect treating them as base 2^{16} representations instead of base 10. Symbolically, we will represent an n word multiple precision number as $An-1 \mid An-2 \mid \ldots \mid A1 \mid A0$, where $An-1$ is the high-order word and is stored last in memory. This low-order first convention agrees with the ordering of bytes in words. We can treat multiple precision numbers as being signed, using the 2's complement for negation (take 1's complement and multiple-precision-add 1.) Thus the left-most bit of the last word would be the sign bit.

Suppose for instance we have two double-word integers $A1 \mid A0$ and $B1 \mid B0$ which we want to add, getting $C1 \mid C0$. If we think of these as though they were two digit numbers, we would set $C0 = A0+B0$ (separating out the carry) and $C1 = A1 + B1 + $ (carry from the last step).

$$
\begin{array}{r r}
\text{carry} & \\
A1 & A0 \\
+\ B1 & B0 \\
\hline
C1 & C0 \\
\end{array}
$$

(We are ignoring the possibility of a carry out the left end, which would be a third digit to the left of C1.) The assembly code is

```
;   Double Precision addition C1|C0 := A1|A0 + B1|B0
        mov     ax, A0
        add     ax, B0
        mov     C0, ax ;      Doesn't alter carry flag
        mov     ax, A1 ;      Ditto
        adc     ax, B1
        mov     C1, ax
```

In order to fit the code into a loop more easily, we can change the add to an adc instruction—as long as we see to it that the carry flag is initially 0. To zero the carry flag, we use:

```
clc   ;     Clear Carry flag (i.e., set it to 0)
```

The new version (changed code in boldface) is

```
;   Double Precision addition C1|C0 := A1|A0 + B1|B0
        clc
        mov     ax, A0
        adc     ax, B0
        mov     C0, ax ;      Doesn't alter carry flag
        mov     ax, A1 ;      Ditto
        adc     ax, B1
        mov     C1, ax
```

The code for double-precision subtraction is:

```
;  Double Precision subtraction C1|C0 := A1|A0 - B1|B0
            clc     ;               no borrow from rightmost digit
            mov     ax, A0
            sbb     ax, B0
            mov     C0, ax ;        Doesn't alter carry (= borrow) flag
            mov     ax, A1 ;        Ditto
            sbb     ax, B1
            mov     C1, ax
```

For communication with high-level languages, we will now construct a package of multiple-precision routines. To simplify the programs, we will assume that the pair of operands in any particular call are the same length (but see Programming Problem 14.3). We specify the routines

```
MPAdd(A, B, Len);        { A := A + B; A and B have Len words }
MPSub(A, B, Len);        { A := A - B; A and B have Len words }
MPInc(A, Len);           { A := A + 1; A has Len words }
MPDec(A, Len);           { A := A - 1; A has Len words }
MPNeg(A, Len);           { A := -A; A has Len words }
MPPutDec(A, Len);        { Display the (unsigned) value of A }
```

A and B will be double-word pointers containing the segment:offset address of integers which are Len words long. For the arithmetic routines, we will exit with the carry bit set as it would be for single word operations.

Example 14.1—1. Construct the code to *call* MPAdd(A, B, Len).

The offset (low-order) part of the address must come first in memory and since pushing something on the stack *reduces* the stack pointer, the segment part of the address must be pushed *first*. Pushing the parameters in left-to-right (Pascal) order, one version of the code is

```
            mov     ax, SEG A ;     Pascal Parameter Sequence
            push    ax ;            can't push constant
            mov     ax, OFFSET A
            push    ax
            mov     ax, SEG B
            push    ax
            mov     ax, OFFSET B
            push    ax
            mov     ax, n ;         length of A and B
            push    ax
            call    MPAdd
```

As in Section 12.6, we could have a pointer to one of the integers, say A, declared as follows

```
A           DW      n DUP (?)
APtr        DD      A ;             sets APtr = seg A:offset A, offset
;                                   in first word
```

and push `APtr` as follows:

```
push    WORD PTR [APtr + 2] ;    Note reverse order,
push    WORD PTR [Aptr] ;   to get order in stack right
```

We must use the WORD PTR cast or the assembler will signal an error since `APtr` is a double word and `push` handles only single words.

Note that if C calling conventions were used, we would push the parameters in reverse order but that *seg:offset are still pushed in the same order.* That is, the C parameter sequence using pointers would be would be

```
mov     ax, n ;                 C parameter sequence
push    ax ;                        Pass length
push    WORD PTR [BPtr + 2]
push    WORD PTR [Bptr] ;       Pass B
push    WORD PTR [APtr + 2]
push    WORD PTR [Aptr] ;       Pass A
call    MPAdd
```

Example 14.1—2. Construct the code for `MPAdd`.

Looking at our code for double-precision add, we see that it can be turned into a loop for A := A + B for integers of arbitrary size with the pseudo-code

Multiple Precision Add
clc
for $i := 0$ to $n - 1$ do
mov   ax, B[i]
adc   A[i], ax
end for

We can put the pointer to A in ds:si and the pointer to B in es:di using the instructions `lds si, APtr` and `les di, BPtr`, respectively. `Lds` and `les` were introduced in Section 12.6. We can put *n* in cx and use the `loop` instruction to control the loop:

```
set up ds:si --> A and es:di --> B
        mov     cx, n
        clc
AddLoop:
add B[i] = es:[di] to A[i] = [si] as above
add 2 to si and di
        loop    AddLoop
return carry flag
```

We can make the usual optimization of going to based indexing so we only need to increment one index register

```
        set up ds:si --> A and es:di --> B
                sub     bx, bx ;        bx := 0
                mov     cx, n
                clc
AddLoop:
        add B[i] = es:[bx+di] to A[i] = [bx+si] as above
        add 2 to bx
                loop    AddLoop
        return carry flag
```

The next problem is what to do about the fact that adding 2 to si will mess up the carry flag. We preserve the flag by using two inc si's instead of add si, 2. Inc works where add doesn't because

inc and dec don't alter the carry flag!

Presumably that is precisely to make code like this work. The complete procedure is

```
;; MPADD.ASM--Multiple precision A := A + B
;;
;; Calling Sequence:
;;      push pointer to A
;;      push pointer to B
;;      push number of words in A and B
;;      EXTRN  MPAdd: NEAR
;;      call   MPAdd
;; Returns carry flag = carry out the left end. Only ds preserved
;;
;; Multiple precision quantities are stored low order word first.
;; On exit, carry bit is set to carry out the left end.
;;
                .MODEL SMALL
                ASSUME SS:NOTHING ; Safety move; See Section 12.4

                .CODE
                PUBLIC MPAdd
APtr    EQU     DWORD PTR [bp+10]
BPtr    EQU     DWORD PTR [bp+6]
Len     EQU     WORD PTR [bp+4]
MPAdd   PROC
                push    bp
                mov     bp, sp
                push    ds
                lds     si, APtr ;    ds:si --> A
                les     di, BPtr ;    es:di --> B
                ASSUME DS:NOTHING, ES:NOTHING ; Defensive programming
```

```
            sub     bx, bx ;        bx := OFFSET B - OFFSET A
            mov     cx, Len
            clc
AddLoop:
            mov     ax, es:[bx + di] ; ax := B[i]
            adc     [bx + si], ax ;    A[i] := A[i] + B[i]
            inc     si ;               avoid destroying C Flag!
            inc     si
            loop    AddLoop
Done:
            pop     ds
            pop     bp
            ret     10 ;            Pop parameters from stack
MPAdd       ENDP
            END
```

MPSub is, of course, quite similar. MPInc and MPDec require a slightly different technique because when we increment or decrement the low-order word, we might get a carry or borrow which we need to propagate leftward. The problem is that inc and dec don't set the carry flag.

Example 14.1—3. Develop the code for MPInc.

We propagate a possible carry leftward by using adc A[i], 0. As mentioned above, we can't use inc to get the ball rolling, so we use adc A[0], 0 at the first stage too, arranging it so that the carry bit is initially 1 by using the instruction

```
    stc   ; Set Carry flag (i.e., set it to 1)
```

The pseudocode is

```
        stc
    for i := 0 to n - 1 do
        adc    A[i], 0
    end for
```

Another technique is to note that we can jump out of the loop when there is no further carry, giving us a loop like

```
        stc
    for i := 0 to n - 1 do
        adc    A[i], 0
        jnc    Done
    end for
Done:
```

Now however we see that we will *always* be adding 1, so we don't need adc, in which case, we also don't need to initialize the carry bit. The final version is

Multiple Precision Increment		
for i := 0 **to** n - 1 **do**		
add	A[i], **1** ;	Still can't use inc!
jnc	Done	
end for		
Done:		

Note that we still need the counting loop because we could still have a carry out the left end.

To make MPInc have the same behavior with the carry flag as inc does, we must save and restore the carry flag. We can save it in al with the following code:

```
mov     al, 0 ;       can't sub al, al as that destroys
adc     al, 0 ;          the carry flag
```

Then at the end of the procedure, we merely shift al right 1 to restore the carry flag.

```
;; MPINC.ASM--Multiple precision A := A + 1
;;
;; Calling Sequence:
;;        push pointer to A
;;        push number of words in A
;;        EXTRN  MPInc: NEAR
;;        call   MPInc
;; Preserve carry flag, ds and bp
;;
;; Multiple precision quantities are stored low order word first.
;; On exit, carry bit is set to carry out the left end.
;;
           .MODEL SMALL
           ASSUME SS:NOTHING

           .CODE
           PUBLIC MPInc
APtr       EQU    DWORD PTR [bp+6]
Len        EQU    WORD PTR [bp+4]
MPInc      PROC
           push   bp
           mov    bp, sp
           mov    al, 0 ;      save carry flag as right
           adc    al, 0 ;         bit of al
           les    si, APtr ;    es:si --> A
           mov    cx, Len
IncLoop:
           add    WORD PTR es:[si], 1
           jnc    Done
           inc    si
           inc    si
```

```
            loop    IncLoop
Done:
            pop     bp
            shr     al ;            restore carry bit
            ret     6
MPInc       ENDP
            END
```

Note that we have used es as the segment register, as it doesn't need to be saved and restored. Using a nonstandard segment register could turn out to be somewhat inefficient, as we must therefore add an extra byte, the es: segment override, inside the loop. Most of the time though, the loop body will be executed only once.

Example 14.1—4. Develop the code for MPNeg.

We can't accomplish MPNeg simply by negating each word. That should be fairly clear, because 2's complement involves doing 1's complement and adding 1. The carry from adding 1 could propagate into higher-order words. Thus the final value of any 'digit' depends on the values of the 'digit's to the right of it. The simplest program seems to result from doing the 2's complement using brute force, complementing with the not instruction and adding 1. Luckily the not instruction doesn't affect any of the flags, in particular the carry flag, so we can do the 'not' and increment in the same loop. The pseudocode is

Multiple Precision Negation

```
            stc
for i := 0 to n - 1 do
            not     A[i]
            adc     A[i], 0
end for
```

For MPNeg we must go completely through the loop and if we used es for A's segment, we would use two segment overrides each time through. Therefore it seems better to use ds and accept the overhead of pushing and popping it. At the end, the carry flag is set as in the simple neg instruction—to the complement of the carry out the left end from adding 1. Note that our procedure for setting the carry flag doesn't require any conditional jumping. The procedure is

```
;; MPNEG.ASM--Multiple precision A := - A
;;
;; Calling Sequence:
;;      push pointer to A
;;      push number of words in A
;;      EXTRN  MPNeg: NEAR
;;      call   MPNeg
;; Only ds is preserved
;;
;; Multiple precision quantities are stored low order word first.
;;
```

```
                .MODEL SMALL
                ASSUME SS:NOTHING

                .CODE
                PUBLIC MPInc
APtr            EQU     DWORD PTR [bp+6]
Len             EQU     WORD PTR [bp+4]
MPInc           PROC
                push    bp
                mov     bp, sp
                push    ds
                lds     si, APtr ;    ds:si --> A
                ASSUME  ds:NOTHING
                mov     cx, Len
                stc     ;             add 1 to 1's complement
NegLoop:
                not     WORD PTR [si]
                adc     WORD PTR [si], 0
                inc     si
                inc     si
                loop    NegLoop
Done:
                mov     al, 0 ;       don't disturb carry bit
                adc     al, 0 ;       al := carry bit
                not     al ;          complement carry bit
                shr     al, 1 ;       ... and return it to c flag
                pop     ds
                pop     bp
                ret     6
MPNeg           ENDP
                END
```

Multiplication and division are a little harder. Multiple precision multiplication is a straightforward implementation of the hand method of developing partial products and adding them, but the bookkeeping gets complex. Division is much harder, even as it is by hand. The analogue of the hand method would require 'guessing' digits of the quotient and altering them if the guess proved wrong. Repeated multiple precision subtraction, with shifting, is another possibility.

It is rather easy to multiply or divide a multiple-precision number by a single-precision number, though. We will demonstrate division by writing a procedure MPPutDec(A, Len) which does repeated multiple-precision division by 10 and is (more or less) the multiple-precision analogue of PutDec. This example turns out to be quite an interesting exercise, and produces probably the most elaborate program we have discussed thus far.

First let's talk about dividing a multiple-precision number by 10. To simplify matters **we will assume that all our numbers are unsigned, or signed and positive** (but see Programming Problem 14.2). Let's say we want to divide A5 | A4 | A3 | A2 | A1 | A0 by 10, (A5 is the most significant word and A0 the least significant). Treating the An's as digits (base 65,536), we can proceed as we would by hand:

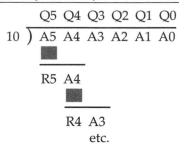

First we divide 10 into A5. As we need a 32 bit divisor, we divide 10 into $dx \mid ax = 0 \mid A5$, giving Q5 in ax and R5 in dx (the product Q5 * 10 doesn't appear and isn't needed in the machine algorithm). Then to find Q4, we divide $R5 \mid A4$ by 10, and R5 is already in dx! Thus the pseudocode to do A := A / 10, leaving the remainder in dx, is

```
        dx := 0 ;                   initial 'remainder digit'
   for i := n - 1 to 0 do
        mov    ax, A[i]
        div    10                   We will put 10 in a register
        mov    A[i], ax ;  dx now set up for next division
   end for
```

Notice that whereas the other algorithms went in the direction low- to high-order byte, the one above one goes from high to low.

Example 14.1—5. Develop code for the procedure MPPutDec for printing multiple precision (unsigned or positive) numbers. (This procedure is included in UTIL.LIB.)

Since we're writing a service routine, we can't simply destroy the number that the user only asked us to print, as the simple code above does. Therefore we must move the number into local storage and manipulate *that* version. Since we don't know how long the number might be, it is reasonable to use the stack as temporary storage. Therefore we will use the following general structure:

```
   for i := n - 1 to 0 do
        push A[i]    { puts A in same order on stack }
   end for
    { call the copy of A on the stack S }
   repeat
        S, dx := S / 10, S mod 10      { as above }
        push dx + '0'
   until S = 0       { so we don't print leading 0's }
   while there is still a digit on the stack
        pop and display it
```

The code inside the **repeat** loop is our division code from above, slightly augmented by the fact that we need to determine if S is 0 after the division (we set a variable NZD to 0 before the division starts and set it to 1 if a non-zero 'digit' occurs during the division process) and we keep a count $DigCt$ of the digits computed and pushed so we will know how many to pop off and display. A more detailed version of the **repeat** code is

```
repeat
   dx := 0
   NZD := 0
   for i := n - 1 to 0 do
      mov  ax, A[i]
      div  10
      mov  A[i], ax
      if ax ≠ 0 then NZD := 1 end if
      push dx + '0'
      inc  DigCt
   end for
until NZD = 0
```

We chose to push the A[i]s onto the stack in the order $n - 1$ down to 0 not because that preserves the order of the number in memory (which it does) but because of the following curious fact: we know where A *starts*, but have to compute a pointer to its last word ($A + 2 * (n - 1)$). That word will be the first word pushed onto the stack, so it will be at a *known* location on the stack, making it easy to code the inner loop for the division. Our plan for using the stack is

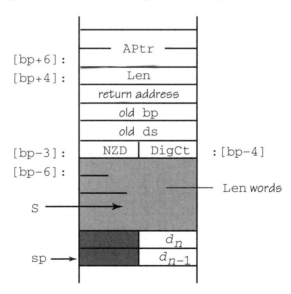

If we let $NumLeft$ be the displacement from bp of the first word below the fixed part of the stack frame (as it happens, $NumLeft = -6$), then the indexing in the division loop can work as follows:

$$si := NumLeft ; \quad i := n - 1$$
$$cx := n$$

```
MPDivideBy10:
                mov     ax, [bp + si] ;    default to ss segment
                div     10
                mov     [bp+si], ax
                ...
                sub     si, 2 ;            i := i - 1
                loop    MPDivideBy10
```

The complete procedure is

```
;; MPPUTDEC.ASM--Display a multiple-precision number on the CRT
;; in decimal. Number is assumed positive or unsigned.
;;
;; Calling Sequence:
;;
;;          push    pointer to number
;;          push    words in number
;;          EXTRN   MPPutDec : NEAR
;;          call    MPPutDec
;;
INCLUDE     PCMAC.INC
            .MODEL SMALL
            ASSUME SS:NOTHING

            .CODE
            PUBLIC MPPutDec
APtr        EQU     DWORD PTR [bp+6]
Len         EQU     WORD PTR [bp+4]
NZD         EQU     BYTE PTR [bp-3] ;   Has a non-zero digit occurred
DigCt       EQU     BYTE PTR [bp-4] ;   Number of digs pushed on stack
NumLeft     EQU     -6 ;            Offset to left word of number to put
MPPutDec    PROC
            push    bp
            mov     bp, sp
            push    ds
            sub     sp, 2 ;                 Storage for DigCt, NZD
;
; First--move the number to local storage, where it can be altered
;
            lds     si, APtr ;      ds:si --> A
            mov     ax, Len ;       n
            mov     cx, ax ;        Number of words to move
            dec     ax ;            ax = n - 1
            shl     ax, 1 ;         ax = 2 * (n - 1)
            add     si, ax ;        ds:si --> last entry in A

PushArg:
```

```
            push    [si] ;       push A[i]
            add     si, 2 ;      i := i - 1
            loop    MovIn

            mov     DigCt, 0
            mov     bx, 10 ;     The divisor
;
;                   repeat ... until NZD = 0
;
DigLoop:
            mov     NZD, 0 ; indicates no non-zero digits in quotient
;
;           compute S := S / 10; remainder --> dx
;
            mov     si, NumLeft ; Left end (high order) of S rel bp
            mov     cx, Len
            mov     dx, 0 ;         Initial high-order bits of dividend
MPDivideBy10:
            mov     ax, [bp+si] ; dx:ax := prev remdr:brought down
;                                               next digit
            div     bx
            mov     [bp+si], ax
            test    ax, ax
            jz      ZeroResult
            mov     NZD, 1 ;     Quotient nonzero; need another step
ZeroResult:
            sub     si, 2
            loop    MPDivideBy10 ;     End of divide by 10

            add     dl, '0' ;    Convert final remainder to ASCII
            push    dx
            inc     DigCt

            cmp     NZD, 0
            jne     DigLoop ;    End of repeat ... until
;
;                   All digits computed and pushed on the stack
;
            mov     cl, DigCt
            sub     ch, ch ;     cx := DigCt converted to word
PutLoop:
            pop     ax
            _PutCh  al
            loop    PutLoop

            mov     ds, [bp-2] ; Restore and quit
            mov     sp, bp
```

```
            pop    bp
            ret    6
MPPutDec    ENDP
            END
```

MPPutDec was tested with a main program that passed 32 bit integers to it. It was particularly easy to use 32 bit integers because the assembler does input conversions for double-precision numbers in the DD statement, so you know what you're supposed to get. That is, if you try to display

```
Num         DD     1234567
```

with MPPutDec, you should get 1234567. To be really sure, one should test with larger numbers, in which case determining whether you have the right answer can be tricky.

Exercises 14.1

1. ✓ Compilers for the 80X86 normally only allow arrays which can fit in a single segment, i.e., 65,536 bytes at most. This limitation is because index registers are 16 bits long and efficient indexing is important in processing arrays. Some compilers also allow **HUGE** arrays which exceed this limit. As part of implementing HUGE arrays, assume that you have a segment address in ds and a double-precision offset from that segment address in dx (high word) and ax. Write code which turns ds, dx, and ax into a segment address in es and an offset in si. Thus ds = 1234h, dx = 0001h, and ax = 5432h could produce es = 2777h, si = 0002h. Don't worry about error detection, but your code shouldn't destroy dx, ax, and ds.

2. ✓ There is a fourth type of shift instruction, rcl/rcr (Rotate with C Flag left/right) which is like rol/ror (see Chapter 9) except that the operand *together with the C Flag* is treated as a 9-bit (byte operand) or 17-bit (word operand) operand and rotated.

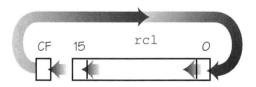

These instructions are very useful in multiple precision shifting. Write routines MPSAL(A, Len) and MPSAR(A, Len) to do arithmetic left and right shifts of a multiple-precision number by one bit.

3. ✓ The Boolean *not* operator in C/C++ is written '!'. By definition, !x is 1 if x is 0 and is 0 if x is nonzero (C interprets nonzero as true). Write assembly code to set ax := !X where X is a word variable *without using cmp or test and branch!* (Hint: neg sets the carry flag to 1 if the original number negated was *any nonzero value* and sets the carry flag to 0 if the number was 0 (that is, it sets it as if it were doing a subtract from 0).)

4. Harder: Write a routine MPCmp(A, B, Len) which does a multiple-precision signed compare of multiple-precision A and B of length Len which returns with the flags set so that jg succeeds exactly when A > B, je when A = B, etc. (Note that you must start at the high-order end of A and B

and work down. Compare A and B word for word until inequality is seen. If it happens in the first word compared of A and B, the flags will be correctly set and you can exit immediately. Otherwise the unequal 'digits' will be unsigned and the flags will have to be manipulated on that basis and also based on the sign of A (which is the same as the sign of B, since their first words are equal).

5.   Suppose that ds:si and es:di contain two segment:offset addresses. Write code to jump to dsBig if ds:si represents an address greater than es:di, to esBig if es:di represents the larger address, and to equal if they represent the same address. (Hint: add ds shifted left 4 to si, multiple precision, in bx|ax, and add es shifted left 4 to di in dx:cx. Then do a double-precision comparison.) This test is important if we wish to copy data from ds:si to es:di and the areas overlap. See Example 5.2—1. If ds:si '<' es:di then we should copy backwards, from the tops of the arrays down.

14.2 • The 'Minimal Standard' Random Number Generator

As an application of multiple-precision techniques, we will implement a 'good' **random number generator**. In Exercise 4.2—4 we implemented a very simple random number generator—one which is not satisfactory in real-world applications (which require millions of random numbers) because it repeats after at most 65,536 applications.

Stephen K. Park and Keith W. Miller (see the Bibliography) have proposed a **minimal standard** random number generator, which is acceptably good (most of those that were surveyed weren't), reasonably fast, and implementable on any computer. Their method is typical in that the next 'random' number is computed from the previous random number. In this case, the random numbers are 32 bit integers and the formula is

```
new Random Number := (A * old Random Number) mod (2^31 - 1)
```

Park and Miller's suggested value of A is 16,807, which is not as good as some possibilities but has the advantage of being single precision and simplifying the computations.

When this algorithm is implemented in a high-level language on a 16 bit machine, the arithmetic must generally be done with real numbers and it is very tricky and slow. The division in particular is quite slow. The interesting thing is that the algorithm can be implemented in assembly language without a division! The resulting improvement in speed can be very important when large quantities of random numbers are used.

To avoid the division, we merely note the fact (from elementary number theory; see the exercises at the end of this section) that for a number $d_k d_{k-1} \ldots d_0$ in base n, with digits $d_k, d_{k-1}, \ldots, d_0$

$$d_k d_{k-1} \ldots d_0 \bmod (n-1) = (d_k + d_{k-1} + \ldots + d_0) \bmod (n-1)$$

The formula shows that we can find $d_k d_{k-1} \ldots d_0$ **mod** $(n-1)$ by adding the digits in base n, then if the result has more than one digit, add the digits again, and keep adding until we get a single base n digit, which must be the remainder. (If $n = 10$, this procedure is just the familiar method of "casting out nines.") In our case, we must represent our number in base 2^{31}, which is relatively easy on a binary machine, even a 16 bit one.

The method is as follows (see the later paper of David G. Carta, listed in the bibliography.) We assume that the old (soon to be new) random number is in S1|S0. The following steps must be performed:

1) Compute P2 | P1 | P0 = A × S1 | S0

The multiplication can be done by mimicking the hand-procedure for multiplication:

$$
\begin{array}{rrr}
 & & A \\
\times\ S1 & & S0 \\
\hline
pp01 & pp00 & \quad (S0 \times A) \\
pp12\ \ pp11 & & \quad (S1 \times A) \\
\hline
P2\ \ \ \ P1 & P0 &
\end{array}
$$

The code is

```
mov     ax, S0
mov     bx, A
mul     bx
mov     si, dx ;      si := pp01 (pp = partial product)
mov     di, ax ;      di := pp00 = P0
mov     ax, S1
mul     bx ;          ax := pp11
add     ax, si ;      ax := pp11 + pp01 = P1
adc     dx, 0 ;       dx := pp12 + carry = P2
```

2) Represent P2 | P1 | P0 in base 2^{31}. That is, divide P2 | P1 | P0 by 2^{31}, writing P2 | P1 | P0 = 2^{31}p + q where $0 \le q < 2^{31}$. Then the base 2^{31} representation of P2 | P1 | P0 is p | q. The division is easily done on a binary computer:

```
p := (P2 SHL 1) + sign bit of P1; q := (P1 AND 7fffh) | P0
```

It is easy to compute the expression above by using the `rcl` instruction introduced in exercise 14.1—2. Rcl treats the combined first operand and C flag as a whole and rotates it.

```
shl     P1, 1 ;       Sign bit of P1 --> C Flag
rcl     P2, 1 ;       P2 := P2 SHL 1 + C Flag
shr     P1, 1 ;       Zero sign bit of P1
```

3) If p + q (double-precision addition!) is < 2^{31}, then it is the new random number. If not, turn off the sign bit (the left of the two base 2^{31} digits needed to represent p + q) and add 1 to get the correct value.

And that's all there is to it! Our program assumes that the **seed** of the random number generator, the starting value, is defined elsewhere as a PUBLIC.

```
;; RANDOM.ASM--implementation of minimal standard random number
;;  generator. See article by David G. Carta, CACM Jan 1990, p. 87
;;
```

```
;;   Calling Sequence:
;;
;;        EXTRN  Random: NEAR
;;        call   Random
;;   0 < value < 2**31 - 1 returned in dx|ax
;;
;;   Assumes ds set to @data.
             .MODEL SMALL
             .DATA
             EXTRN  Seed : DWORD ;        Defined elsewhere
A            EQU    16807
S0           EQU    WORD PTR Seed ;    Low order word of seed
S1           EQU    WORD PTR Seed+2 ;  High order word of seed

             .CODE
             PUBLIC Random
Random       PROC
;
;            P2|P1|P0 := (S1|S0) * A
;
             mov    ax, S0
             mov    bx, A
             mul    bx
             mov    si, dx ;      si := pp01 (pp = partial product)
             mov    di, ax ;      di := pp00 = P0
             mov    ax, S1
             mul    bx ;          ax := pp11
             add    ax, si ;      ax := pp11 + pp01 = P1
             adc    dx, 0 ;       dx := pp12 + carry = P2
;
;            P2|P1|P0 = p * 2**31 + q, 0 <= q < 2**31
;
;            p = P2 SHL 1 + sign bit of P1 --> dx
;                   (P2:P1:P0 < 2**46 so p fits in a single word)
;            q = (P1 AND 7FFFh)|P0 = (ax AND 7fffh)|di
;
             shl    ax, 1
             rcl    dx, 1
             shr    ax, 1
;
;            dx|ax := p + q
;
             add    dx, di ;      dx := p0 + q0
             adc    ax, 0 ;       ax := q1 + carry
             xchg   ax, dx
;
;            if p+q < 2**31 then p+q is the new seed; otherwise whack
```

```
;               off the sign bit and add 1 and THATs the new seed
;
            test    dx, 8000h
            jz      Store
            and     dx, 7fffh
            add     ax, 1
            adc     dx, 0 ;        Multiple precision add 1
Store:
            mov     S1, dx
            mov     S0, ax
            ret
Random      ENDP
            END
```

The `Random` function works as-is with Turbo Pascal. All you have to do to make it work with Visual or Borland C++ is change `Random` to `_Random`, `Seed` to `_Seed`, and save and restore `di` and `si`. (See Section 13.2.) The C/C++ version is on the disk accompanying this book under the name `RANDOMC.ASM`.

Testing the routine is simple. Park and Miller tell us that if you start with a seed of 1, the 10,000th random number should be 1,043,618,065.* Making `Seed` an external variable allows us to set it to anything we like in the testing program. (Many random number generators have an associated procedure called something like `Randomize` which gives the appearance of a random starting seed so that results are different each time the program is run. One way to initialize is to set `Seed` equal to the time clock using a routine like `GetTime` from Section 15.3.1. Since `Seed` really shouldn't be visible to everyone, as only `Random` and `Randomize` need to know about it, `Randomize` should probably be part of the same source file as `Random`, and `Seed` shouldn't be public. However the form I have given here allows me to demonstrate an assembly function reading a Pascal global below.) The following is a simple assembly test program:

```
;; RANDTEST.ASM--test Minimal Standard Random number generator for
;;   correctness by computing 10000 random numbers. Final number
;;   should be 1043618065
;;
INCLUDE     PCMAC.INC
            .MODEL SMALL
            .STACK 500h
            .DATA
            PUBLIC Seed
Seed        DD      1 ;            For test purposes
Counter     DW      10000 ;       Number of random nums to compute
```

---

* As it turns out, this is a lousy way to check this function. In the first edition of the book, I used inc (which doesn't set the carry flag) instead of add for the multiple precision add 1 at the end of the program. And it passed the test. I only noticed the error in the last proofreading of this edition. The corrected version also passes the test! Why? The only time it makes a difference is when the 'add 1' takes place *and* when ax is all 1's. The *latter*, on the average, happens once in 65,536 trials. And we had only 10,000 trials. This example presents a fine case study in the perils of program testing.

```
RN          DD      ? ;                 Saved final random num

            .CODE
RandTest    PROC
            EXTRN   MPPutDec:NEAR, Random:NEAR
            mov     ax, @data
            mov     ds, ax
RanLoop:
            call    RandLInt
            dec     Counter ;       cx is destroyed by RandLInt
            jnz     RanLoop
            mov     WORD PTR RN, ax
            mov     WORD PTR RN+2, dx
            mov     ax, SEG RN
            push    ax
            mov     ax, OFFSET RN
            push    ax
            mov     ax, 2
            push    ax
            call    MPPutDec ;      Proc developed in previous section
            _PutCh 13, 10
            _Exit  0
RandTest    ENDP
            END     RandTest
```

For instance we could write the following Pascal test program:

```
program RandTest;

const
   TestSeed = 1;
   NRands = 10000;
   ExpectedValue = 1043618065;

var
   Seed : LongInt;   { Double Word; automatically PUBLIC }
   Rand : LongInt;   { to save random numbers }
   i : integer;      { the loop counter }

{$L Random}
function Random : LongInt; external;

begin
  Seed := TestSeed;
  for i := 1 to NRands do
    Rand := Random;
```

```
      if (Rand = ExpectedValue) then WriteLn('Test passed.')
      else WriteLn('Test FAILED.');
   end.
```

The disk accompanying this book also has a C++ version.

The standard sort of random number generator returns a number x satisfying $0 \leq x < 1$. We can create such a function from Random and use it to replace Random, the random number generator supplied with Turbo Pascal. (According to Park and Miller, the version circa 1987 wasn't very good.) The code is as follows:

```
   var
      Seed : LongInt;

   {$L Random}
   function Random : LongInt; external;

   function Rand : real;
   begin
      Rand := Random / MaxLongInt { = 2**31 - 1 }
   end;
```

For an *assembly* method of dividing by $2^{31} - 1$ using a numeric coprocessor, see Example 20.4—1.

Note that the ideas discussed in this section are somewhat controversial. See the letters of Marsaglia and Sullivan concerning the papers of Park and Miller and Carta, and responses from Park, Miller, and Stockmeyer (listed under 'Marsaglia' in the bibliography).

Exercises 14.2

1. ✓ For the mathematically inclined:
   a) Show that $(an + b)$ **mod** $(n-1) = (a + b)$ **mod** $(n-1)$. (Use the fact that x **mod** y is the unique r such that $x = qy + r$ for some integer q, and $0 \leq r < y$.)
   b) Convince yourself that if number $d_k d_{k-1} \ldots d_0$ is a number in base n then

   $$d_k d_{k-1} \ldots d_0 \textbf{ mod } (n-1) = (d_k + d_{k-1} + \ldots + d_0) \textbf{ mod } (n-1)$$

   by showing that $((((an + b)n + c)n + d)n + e)$ **mod** $(n-1) = (a + b + c + d + d)$ **mod** $(n-1)$ by repeated application of part a).

14.3 • Decimal Arithmetic

Computers use binary computation as their primary mode because it is much faster than decimal. Bankers and the like though worry about things like the fact that \$.10 (ten cents) can't be represented exactly as a binary number. (\$.10 = .000110011001100… in base 2, a nonterminating number.) Also, business computations tend to do a lot of reading and writing of numbers (hence a lot of conversions to and from binary if on a binary machine) but relatively little computation.

Originally, there were two types of computers, business computers that did their arithmetic in decimal (for example, the IBM 1401) and scientific computers that did their arithmetic in binary (for example, the IBM 7090). To satisfy the needs of both types of users, binary computers appeared in the '60s which could also do arithmetic with decimal numbers in **Binary Coded Decimal** (**BCD**) form. In BCD, a byte is divided into two **nibbles** of four bits each. Each nibble can represent numbers from 0 to 15, and in particular from 0 to 9. Thus a byte can represent two decimal digits. Longer numbers are formed by stringing several bytes together. For instance

```
Numb        DB      45h, 23h, 01h
```

represents the decimal number 12345. We could reserve one nibble for the sign, but to simplify things, we will assume that BCD numbers are unsigned, and all nibbles represent real digits.

Example 14.3—1 Write a procedure DecPut(APtr, Len) which displays the BCD number at APtr (low-order byte first) of length Len bytes. To simplify things, do not bother to suppress leading zeroes.

We use the code for PutHexB from Exercise 9.3—1 since displaying BCD digits is the same as displaying hex digits if we don't have to suppress leading zeroes. The procedure is

```
;; DECPUT.ASM--Display BCD number with leading zeroes
;;
;; Calling Sequence:
;;        push pointer to BCD number A
;;        push number of bytes in A
;;        EXTRN  DECPut: NEAR
;;        call   DECPut
;;
;; Only ds is preserved

INCLUDE    PCMAC.INC

           .MODEL SMALL
           ASSUME SS:NOTHING

           .CODE
           PUBLIC DECPut
APtr       EQU    DWORD PTR [bp+6]
Len        EQU    WORD PTR [bp+4]
DecPut     PROC
           push   bp
           mov    bp, sp
           push   ds
           lds    si, APtr ;    ds:si --> A
           mov    DI, Len ;     cx must be used for shifting
           mov    cl, 4 ;       shift amount
           add    si, DI
           dec    si ;          ds:si --> left end of A
PutLoop:
```

```
            mov     bh, [si] ;    bx = xy??
            shr     bx, cl ;      bx = 0xy?
            shr     bl, cl ;      bx = 0x0y
            add     bx, '00'
            _PutCh  bh
            _PutCh  bl
            dec     si
            dec     DI
            jnz     PutLoop

            pop     ds
            pop     bp
            ret     6
    DecPut  ENDP
            END
```

Some larger computers include powerful instructions for doing decimal arithmetic on strings of bytes. Microcomputers though tend to have only 'help' instructions which aid the user in coding his or her own decimal arithmetic instructions.

Suppose for instance that we wished to add 32 and 45, decimally. As BCD bytes these would be the numbers 32h and 45h. Adding them, we get 77h, or 77, the right answer. When we try to add something like 79 and 47, however, we get 79h + 47h = c0h, which bears no resemblance to the actual result 126.

There are two new instructions which take care of the problem of carry from right nibble to left for us

```
    daa     ; Decimal Adjust Addition result in al
    das     ; Decimal Adjust Subtraction result in al
```

These instructions operate on al, use a flag we won't go into, and so should always immediately follow an add or subtract to that register:

```
            mov     al, 79h
            add     al, 47h ;     adc and inc also work properly
            daa     ;             sets al to 26h and Carry Flag to 1

            mov     al, 47h
            sub     al, 79h ;     sbb and dec also work properly
            das     ;             sets al to 68h and Carry
    ;                             (= Borrow) to 1
```

The actual mechanism of daa and das is rather intricate but you needn't know what it is as long as you follow the models above slavishly. For instance, suppose A and B are 10 decimal digit (= 5 byte) numbers, low order bytes first, and we wish to perform A := A + B. The code is

```
            mov     di, OFFSET A
            mov     si, OFFSET B
```

```
        mov     cx, 5
        clc     ;               start with carry bit clear
AddLoop:
        mov     al, [di]
        adc     al, [si]
        daa
        mov     [di], al
        inc     di ;            carefully preserving the c flag
        inc     si
        loop    AddLoop
```

The code for decimal A := A – B is similar, with the adc/daa lines replaced by

```
        sbb     al, [si]
        das
```

As you might expect, multiplication and division are much more difficult. We can reduce the problem to something similar to the multiple-precision binary multiplication we discussed in Section 14.1 if we can just come up with a means of multiplying two bytes, that is, two two-digit BCD numbers. Two methods suggest themselves. In both cases we find the product of the two numbers uvh and xyh by forming the sum of four separate products u * x * 100 + (u * y + v * x) * 10 + v * y. (The multiplications by 10 and 100 can be done by shifting 4 and 8 bits, respectively.)

In one case, I did the four multiplications using the binary hardware instructions and converted back to decimal using "the famous aam trick" (see Section 17.3.2). In the other, I did a table lookup on the two digits to get their decimal product. I timed both procedures on 10,000 iterations of all possible pairs of digit pairs (see Section 15.3.1) and came to the conclusion that the second method, the table-lookup method, was almost twice as fast. Here, for the record, is the faster method of these two. (There are other methods which may well be even faster.)

```
;; MUL2TABL.ASM--routine to multiply two pairs of BCD decimal
;;   digits using a multiplication table.
;;
;;
;; Calling Sequence
;;          mov     dl, multiplicand ;  (= wxH)
;;          mov     dh, multiplier ;    (= uvH)
;;          EXTRN   Mul2Tabl: NEAR
;;          call    Mul2Tabl
;;
;;
;;          On exit, the four digit product is in al, ah (low
;;          order digits in al). bx, cx, and dx are destroyed

        .MODEL SMALL
        .DATA
; The ith row of TimesTable is i * 0, i * 1, ..., i * 9 in decimal
;   plus six bytes of padding to make indexing easy.
; If i and j are decimal digits, their decimal product is at
;   [TimesTable + i SHL 4 + j]
```

```
TimesTable DB      10 DUP (00h), 6 DUP (?)
           DB      00h,01h,02h,03h,04h,05h,06h,07h,08h,09h
           DB      6 DUP (?)
           DB      00h,02h,04h,06h,08h,10h,12h,14h,16h,18h
           DB      6 DUP (?)
           DB      00h,03h,06h,09h,12h,15h,18h,21h,24h,27h
           DB      6 DUP (?)
           DB      00h,04h,08h,12h,16h,20h,24h,28h,32h,36h
           DB      6 DUP (?)
           DB      00h,05h,10h,15h,20h,25h,30h,35h,40h,45h
           DB      6 DUP (?)
           DB      00h,06h,12h,18h,24h,30h,36h,42h,48h,54h
           DB      6 DUP (?)
           DB      00h,07h,14h,21h,28h,35h,42h,49h,56h,63h
           DB      6 DUP (?)
           DB      00h,08h,24h,16h,32h,40h,48h,56h,64h,72h
           DB      6 DUP (?)
           DB      00h,09h,18h,27h,36h,45h,54h,63h,72h,81h
           DB      6 DUP (?)


           .CODE
           PUBLIC Mul2Tabl
Mul2Tabl PROC
           mov     cl, 4 ;        Commonly used shift amount
           mov     bx, dx ;       Assume dx = uvwxH; compute uv * wx
           and     bx, 0f0fh ;  bx = 0v0xH
           shl     bh, cl ;       bx = v00xH
           rol     bx, cl ;       bx = 00xvH

;  Compute the four products

           mov     al, [TimesTable + bx] ;   al = x * v
           mov     bx, dx
           and     bx, 0f0f0h ;  bx = u0w0H
           shr     bh, cl ;       bx = 0uw0H
           shr     bx, cl ;       bx = 00uwH
           mov     ah, [TimesTable + bx] ;   ah = u * w
;                                         ax = u * w * 100 + x * v
           mov     bx, dx
           and     bx, 0f00fh ;  bx = u00xH
           rol     bx, cl ;       bx = 00xuH
           mov     ch, [TimesTable + bx] ;   ch = u * x
           mov     bx, dx
           and     bx, 0ff0h ;    bx = 0vw0H
           shr     bx, cl
           mov     dl, [TimesTable + bx] ;   dl = v * w
;  Shift and add
```

```
                sub     dh, dh ; v * w and u * x must be multiplied by 10
                shl     dx, cl
                add     al, dl
                daa
                xchg    ah, al
                adc     al, dh
                daa
                xchg    ah, al ;        ax := ax + v * w * 10
                mov     dl, ch
                sub     dh, dh
                shl     dx, cl
                add     al, dl
                daa
                xchg    ah, al
                adc     al, dh
                daa
                xchg    ah, al ;        ax := ax + u * x * 10
                ret
    Mul2Tabl    ENDP
                END
```

Exercises 14.3

1. ✓ Alter the procedure in Example 14.3—1 so that it suppresses leading zeroes.

Programming Problem 14.1

In Programming Problem 13.1, we wrote a function Fib to compute the nth Fibonacci number. The problem with that program is that Fibonacci numbers grow very rapidly—like 2^n—and using 15 bit integers doesn't allow us to compute Fib(n) for n very large. Modify your solution to Problem 13.1 (or write one, if you haven't already) so that it continues to take a 15 bit argument, but produces a double-word result (in dx | ax). Using MPPutDec, write a main program which computes and prints Fib(n) for n = 1 to 30. (for reference, Fib(30) = 832,040.)

Programming Problem 14.2

Alter MPPutDec so that it displays signed numbers. Hint: use MPNeg. Add an extra high-order word, consisting of all sign bits, to the copy of the argument on the stack so that negation works correctly even in the case of the number which is its own negative.

Programming Problem 14.3

Write a function MPMove(D, DLen, S, SLen) which moves the signed multiple-precision word at S to D. S and D are double word pointers and SLen and DLen the lengths of the numbers they point to, in words. If DLen is greater than SLen, lengthen S by sign extension and if smaller, shorten S by removing high-order words. Return 0 if the move was successful, 1 if overflow occurred (which can happen only in a shortening operation.) Test your program using the version of MPPutDec developed in Programming Problem 14.2.

Programming Problem 14.4

Write a procedure MPGetDec which reads in a multiple precision decimal number from the keyboard. As with MPPutDec, it should take as input the segment:offset of the array in which the number is to be stored and the number of words in the array. Note that you will have to program a multiple precision multiply by 10. Test your program by writing a main program to get and then display (using MPPutDec) long decimal numbers. (This problem will given you a chance to do some testing of MPPutDec with longer numbers.)

Programming Problem 14.5

We could define *signed* decimal numbers by specifying that the rightmost nibble (the right nibble of the first byte) represents the sign—0–7 = +, 8–15 = –. Then every decimal number would have an *odd* number of digits. As with multiple precision binary arithmetic, such numbers can be passed around as a two word pointer and a length in bytes. Write and test routines to perform functions for decimal arithmetic similar to the binary routines in Section 14.1:

DecPutS(Aptr, Len)   Displays the signed decimal number (Note: you must work from the top (most significant digit) down. Don't display leading zeroes. Do this procedure first to check the others

DecAdd(APtr, BPtr, Len) Does A := A + B
DecSub(APtr, BPtr, Len) Does A := A – B

Note: All DecSub needs to do is change sign (but *not* in the originally passed number) and invoke DecAdd.

For example, if we define

```
A        DB     68h, 45h, 23h, 01h, 00h
APtr     DD     A
```

then the call DecPutS(Aptr, 5) should display –123456 .

SUMMARY

New Instructions:

```
adc    dest, source ;     dest := dest + source + CarryFlag
sbb    dest, source ;     dest := dest - source + CarryFlag

clc    ; Clear Carry flag (i.e., set it to 0)
stc    ; Set Carry flag (i.e., set it to 1)

daa    ; Decimal Adjust Addition result in al
das    ; Decimal Adjust Subtraction result in al

rcl    ; Rotate with Carry Left
rcr    ; Rotate with Carry Right
```

Chapter 15

Interrupts

The interrupt is a mechanism by which the CPU can take control of the machine from an executing program, and pass control to a different program. Normally, this second program does its work quickly and invisibly and passes control back to the original program, but interrupts can cause such things as error termination of programs and switching among users of time-shared computers. The use of interrupts is pervasive in modern computer architecture and its understanding is crucial.

15.1 • Generalities about Interrupts

An **interrupt** is an intervention by the CPU into the normal flow of program execution. The CPU saves the state of the interrupted program—enough information that the interrupted program can be resumed—and transfers control to another program in memory, called the **interrupt handler**. Usually, at the end of processing by the interrupt handler, control is returned to the originally executing program in such a way that that program is unaware it was interrupted, or at least, unaware of exactly where that it was interrupted. That is, we say that the interrupt is **transparent** to the interrupted program. Typical examples of interrupts are:

- Interrupts on completion of I/O, such as whenever a key is pressed or released at the keyboard. The ability of computers to do I/O and computation simultaneously, with interrupt handlers to record I/O completion and if necessary to start new operations, greatly increases *throughput*, the amount of work accomplished.
- Clock interrupts. Most computers have a **real-time clock** which 'ticks', that is, causes an interrupt, a fixed number of times per second. Its handler can then be used to maintain time-of-day in the operating sys-

tem. Many computers also have an **interval timer** (or the operating system may implement one using the real-time clock) which can be set to cause an interrupt when a certain amount of time has elapsed. For instance, on a time-shared computer, the interval timer may be set to the amount of time in the current user's **time slice** and its interrupt used to switch to another user.

- Error interrupts, such as divide by 0, illegal op code, illegal memory address, or machine (hardware) errors.
- Execution of instructions, whose specific purpose is to cause an interrupt (and therefore to cause a particular interrupt handler to be executed), such as the `int` instruction on the 80X86.

Each interrupt has an **interrupt number** which is communicated to the CPU in some way by the causer of the interrupt. The CPU either communicates the number to the interrupt handler so that the handler can choose the necessary function, or uses the number to select the appropriate handler from a table of handler addresses. The latter approach, called **vectored interrupts**, is the method of choice because it is faster.

Since an interrupt may have nothing to do with the executing program (on a time-shared computer, it may not even concern any program currently in memory), most modern computers have a protection mechanism which allows interrupt handlers to reside only in the operating system, though the operating system may then allow users to intercept certain interrupts, perhaps by simulation. One advantage (and danger) of the IBM PC is that the general user can handle interrupts.

Interrupts can be **enabled** or **disabled**. Usually there is a way of enabling and disabling *all* interrupts on the machine at once (a capability this powerful is usually restricted to the operating system). As we shall see, certain operations can take place reliably *only* when interrupts are disabled, but if interrupts stay disabled very long, some interrupts may be lost. (For instance, if several keys are struck while interrupts are disabled, all but the first or last keystroke will be lost.)

Often individual interrupts can be selectively disabled, which was originally done by setting a bit mask with one bit per interrupt. Thus interrupts which can be disabled are called **maskable interrupts**, and those which can't—generally serious conditions such as power failure or machine error— are called **non-maskable interrupts**.

All requests for interrupts which occur during the execution of an instruction are held until its completion. Then the CPU chooses one of the perhaps many requests to be honored, and holds the remaining ones until the next time an instruction is completed and interrupts are enabled. To give interrupt handlers a chance for a clean start, the CPU usually starts interrupt handlers with interrupts disabled. The fact that a program can wreak unholy havoc on the machine when interrupts are thus disabled is another reason that user programs are not normally allowed to handle interrupts.

It is helpful to classify interrupts in various ways. Many of these classifications overlap, some of the boundaries are vague, and a few interrupts may fit in different categories on different computers.

- **Hardware** *vs.* **software** interrupts. A hardware interrupt is caused by some physical occurrence in the computer, such as I/O completion or a clock tick, while software interrupts are due to the execution of some designated instruction or instructions whose purpose is to cause an interrupt. On the 80X86, the `int` instruction is the main software interrupt, and the only one we will discuss. An illegal instruction (bad opcode, protected memory violation, etc.) falls somewhere between these types but tends to be considered a hardware interrupt.

Hardware interrupts can in turn be divided into two overlapping classifications, internal vs. external and synchronous vs. asynchronous.

- **Internal** *vs.* **external** interrupts. An internal interrupt is one whose meaning is fixed within the CPU, such as divide by 0. External interrupts are those generated by signals sent to the CPU by other chips or boards, such as I/O controllers, clock devices, memory management hardware, etc. The interrupt number of external interrupts is chosen by the external device. Many boards which can be added to a computer—for example, network boards, mouse and tape controllers, etc.—come with switches on the board that allow the user to choose which interrupt the board will cause, and thus avoid conflicts with other boards. As more functionality is added to CPU chips, some external interrupts become internal.

- **Asynchronous** *vs.* **synchronous** interrupts. Synchronous interrupts (literally, *with time*) occur at exactly the same place every time the program is executed. Typical examples are error interrupts due to illegal op codes, illegal memory addresses, and division by 0. Software interrupts are, of course, also synchronous. Asynchronous interrupts happen at unpredictable times relative to program execution, and include such things as interrupts due to completion of I/O operations, machine errors, and even, oddly enough, interrupts due to the clock! * (Clock interrupts are asynchronous with respect to the program because the program starts at random times relative to the clock and suffers random delays due to keyboard and disk I/O, etc.) It is particularly important that asynchronous interrupt handlers be transparent. Some of the most difficult bugs to find are related to asynchronous interrupts, as the conditions aren't precisely repeatable.

One other less important, and less precise, way to classify interrupts are that they can indicate an **error condition** or a **normal condition**. The interrupt handler for an error condition usually doesn't return to the interrupted program. Some interrupts, such as the keyboard interrupt from a Ctrl-C, might be considered either normal or error (some programs ignore Ctrl-C or use it as some normal signal to the program).

15.2 • Interrupt Processing on the 80X86

The 80X86 has 256 interrupts, numbered 0 to 255. Although it isn't crucial, you may be interested to know that Intel, the designer of these CPUs, reserved interrupts 0–1Fh for internal hardware interrupts. IBM decided to use several unused interrupts in that range for communicating with the ROM BIOS, with the result that certain internal hardware interrupts which were introduced in later models of the 80X86 can't normally be used on IBM PCs. Microsoft has reserved interrupts 20h–3Fh for software interrupts used by DOS. The remaining interrupts are available for use as either external hardware or software interrupts.

---

* There are, in effect, two clocks in a computer, one which controls the timing of instruction execution and the **real-time clock**, which is the one that causes interrupts and which can be used to keep track of ordinary time (socalled *wall-clock* time). When a computer is said to have a 100 MHz (MegaHerz) CPU, this says that the former clock ticks at the rate of 100 million times per second. Each instruction execution requires one or more such ticks. If the 100 MHz clock caused interrupts, nothing would *ever* get done!

A powerful feature of the 80X86 architecture is that any interrupt, even those interpreted as hardware-related, can be caused by executing the instruction

```
int    n ;           cause interrupt n
```

The ability to simulate any interrupt can be very useful in debugging handlers for rarely occurring events such as machine errors.

On the 80X86, interrupt enabling is controlled by the **I flag**, bit 9 in the flag register, which is controlled by the instructions

```
sti ;  set I Flag to 1; that is, enable interrupts
cli ;  clear I Flag to 0; that is, disable interrupts
```

Most interrupts are maskable *as a group* by these instructions, but there is no method in the CPU of selectively enabling and disabling individual interrupts.

The 80X86 uses vectored interrupts. The memory locations 0-1023 contain the **interrupt vector table** with one four-byte entry for each interrupt number. Each entry is called an **interrupt vector**, and contains the segment:offset address of the interrupt handler for a particular interrupt. The entry for interrupt n is the four bytes in memory locations 0:4n ... 0:4n+3. Thus the interrupt vector for the DOS call interrupt 21h is in memory locations 0:84h ... 0:87h. (The BIOS data starts just after the interrupt vector table, at location 1024 = 40h:0.)

The 80X86 interruption mechanism operates in the following way.

1. When an external device (or the CPU itself) wishes to cause an interrupt, it makes an **interrupt request**, that is, it sends a signal to that effect to the CPU including the number of the interrupt it desires. All interrupt requests that come *during* execution of an instruction are held until execution of the instruction is completed.

2. At the end of each instruction execution, before the next instruction is fetched, the CPU checks to see if there are any interrupt requests from enabled interrupts waiting. If there are, the CPU chooses one among them for **interrupt service**. If more than one request was waiting, the remaining ones are held for the next available service opportunity.

3. The 80X86 CPU performs the following steps to service interrupt *n*:

    a) Push the flag register onto the stack.
    b) Disable interrupts. The T flag is also turned off. See Section 15.3.2.
    c) Push the code segment and offset of the next instruction in the interrupted program (cs and IP) and replace cs and IP with the interrupt vector for the chosen interrupt (for interrupt *n*, the segment:offset pair at location 4*n. Performance of this step is in effect a far call to the interrupt handler (see Section 12.7).

These operations are indivisible and cannot themselves be interrupted. The saved state of the interrupted program consists of cs, IP, and the flag register.

Once the above operations are completed, the automatic actions of the CPU are finished, and all further interrupt processing is under the explicit control of the interrupt handler.

Normally the interrupt handler will quickly reenable interrupts, which means that interrupt handlers can themselves be interrupted. Thus the use of the stack for storing information about the interrupt is crucial. The handler will also save and restore any registers it uses. When it is finished with its work and wishes to return to the interrupted program, it restores the registers it saved and executes the instruction

```
iret ; Return from Interrupt
```

which pops two stack items into IP and `cs` (in effect it does a far return) and then pops the next item back into the flag registers. Among other things, popping the flags restores the I flag to its previous status, that is, interrupts are reenabled if that wasn't done before (unless the bit was changed in the flag register saved on the stack).

Be sure to distinguish

- **interrupt request**, which can happen at any time during execution of an instruction. There may be several interrupt requests pending at the same time.
- **interrupt service**, which is initiated by the CPU between instruction executions when a request for an enabled interrupt is pending. Interrupt service consists of saving certain basic information about the state of the interrupted program and transferring control to the interrupt handler for one particular interrupt request.
- **interrupt handler**, a program which resides in memory. The handler is usually a part of the ROM BIOS or the operating system, but user programs may also include handlers for some interrupts.
- interrupt service is normally terminated by execution of the `iret` instruction in the interrupt handler.

The interrupt vector table is first set up by the boot-up procedure in the BIOS when the computer starts up, setting addresses of interrupt handlers for the interrupts the BIOS handles (interrupt 10h for the display and interrupts 9h and 16h for the keyboard, for instance), and setting all other interrupt vectors to the simplest possible handler, which is nothing but an `iret`. When DOS loads, it replaces some of these trivial handlers with its own handlers (for interrupt 21h, for instance). Various Terminate and Stay Resident (TSR) and user programs set up their own handlers for various interrupts—either permanently or temporarily, for the life of the program. A program may also replace a previously specified interrupt handler, either because it was incorrect or because some different functionality is required. Finally, a user-program may *add* functionality to an existing interrupt handler by the technique of **piggy-backing** on an interrupt, which will be discussed in detail in Section 15.4

The interrupt mechanism has two important consequences which should be mentioned. First, because interrupts save and restore the flags, it is all right for an interrupt to happen between a compare and its corresponding conditional jump. Second, interrupts may occur at almost any time, and when they do, they wipe out things previously popped from the stack which may still be in memory.

Exercises 15.2

1. What is the location of the interrupt vector for the BIOS call int 16h? What is found at that location?

2. ✓Our debuggers normally skip over DOS calls. How would you go about tracing into a DOS call?

15.3 • Applications: Timing Operations and Debuggers

In this section we will show how understanding interrupts is important when reading the clock, and how interrupts make debuggers possible.

15.3.1 • Reading the Clock and Timing Operations

The PC keeps time by generating an interrupt 8 approximately 18.2 times per second. The standard interrupt handler for this interrupt maintains a count of clock ticks since midnight in the double-word at 40h:6ch. When another midnight passes, that is, when the number of ticks reaches 1800B0h, the clock is reset to 0 and the byte at 40:70h is set to 1 to warn DOS's time-keeping procedures to reset to the next day (and reset 40:70h to 0). We can access clock information using the assembler's SEGMENT AT mechanism (see Chapter 12):

```
BIOSData  SEGMENT AT 40h
          ORG     6ch
Clock     DD      ? ; Ticks since midnight (18.2 ticks/second)
NextDay   DB      ? ; If non-zero, indicates midnight has
;                         passed and Clock reset to 0
Lo24Hours EQU     00B0h
Hi24Hours EQU     18h ;         1800B0h ticks/24 hours
BIOSData ENDS
```

Note that just as words are stored with the low-order byte first, double words are stored with the low-order word (and hence also the low-order byte) first.

We will construct a function GetTime (included in UTIL.LIB) with no arguments which returns the double precision number of ticks in dx and ax. Such a function can be used for timing programs and program parts by calling it before and after the code to be timed and doing a double-precision subtraction (see Section 14.1). In order to make relative timings work around midnight, we will add a day's worth of clock ticks to the function value when the NextDay flag is on. The function is

```
;; GETTIME.ASM--A function to read the time-of-day in
;;   ticks since midnight.
;;
;; Calling Sequence
;;
;;        EXTRN  GetTime : NEAR
;;        call   GetTime
```

```
          ;;
          ;; Time is returned as a double-word in dx, ax

                  .MODEL SMALL
                  ASSUME SS:NOTHING ; Safety measure

          ;                         BIOSData declarations as above

                  .CODE
                  PUBLIC GetTime
GetTime         PROC
                  mov    ax, BIOSData *
                  mov    es, ax
                  ASSUME es:BIOSData
                  cli    ;                  Disable interrupts
          ;                                 a clock interrupt
                  mov    ax, WORD PTR Clock ;   between these instructions
                  mov    dx, WORD PTR Clock+2 ; could give a VERY faulty
                  cmp    NextDay, 0 ;              result (carry from lo end)
                  sti    ;                  Enable interrupts
                  je     Done
                  add    ax, Lo24Hours ;      double-precision add
                  adc    dx, Hi24Hours
Done:
                  ret
GetTime         ENDP
                  END
```

Here we are following the Turbo Pascal/Visual C++/Borland C++ convention that es, dx, and ax need not be preserved.

The need to disable and reenable interrupts is an interesting facet of the program above. Suppose that Clock = 0FFFFh and Clock+2 = 0, and that a clock 'tick' occurs between the mov ax, WORD PTR Clock and mov dx, WORD PTR Clock+2 instructions. The first mov sets ax = 0FFFFh, then the interrupt causes the incrementing of the clock, resulting in dx = 1, and the second mov sets Clock+2 to 1. Now either 0FFFFh or 10000h would be a reasonable reading for the clock, but what we get is 1FFFFh! Disabling interrupts during the reading of the clock keeps such a wildly erroneous value from occurring. We must also include the cmp NextDay, 0 instruction in the region where interrupts are disabled or the same sort of thing could happen at midnight.

Using GetTime to time code is somewhat tricky because we are typically trying to time things that happen perhaps millions of time per second with a clock that only ticks 18 times per second. In order to get an accurate timing, we must repeat the operation enough that the clock ticks many times during the test. For instance, to repeat an operation 10,000,000 times, we could use the nested loop

---

* TASM users see the footnote on the bottom of page 312 in Section 12.4.

```
        mov     dx, 1000
BigLoop:
        mov     cx, 10000
SmallLoop:
        code to be timed
        loop    SmallLoop
        dec     dx
        jne     BigLoop
```

We of course have to account for the fact that there is some overhead in the loop, so first we time an empty loop, then the same loop containing the code to be timed. We still may not have an accurate timing, though. The 80386 and above machines generally have a cache memory, which holds recently used information in very fast memory. For a relatively small loop, much of the instruction fetching will take place into the cache only once, and so will contribute less to the total time over 10,000,000 iterations. Also, you should keep in mind that on any 80X86, the particular order in which instructions are executed can change the execution timing. (See Section 4.5, etc.)

15.3.2 • Interrupts and Debuggers

Two different interrupts, 1 and 3, are crucial for the construction of debuggers on the 80X86.

Normally the int instruction is two bytes long, one for the int operation code and one for the interrupt number. **Int 3** is a special case though, occupying only a single byte. This interrupt is used by debuggers for setting breakpoints. Since the shortest instructions on the 80X86 are a single byte, the int 3 instruction can be used to replace the first byte of any instruction. Debuggers such as CodeView and the Turbo Debugger set a **breakpoint** by replacing the byte at the break address with an int 3 instruction (keeping track of course of what used to be there so that they can show you what memory should look like and so that they can actually execute the instruction that was originally at that position). Normally usage of int 3 is hidden from the programmer by the debugger, but you can use int 3 to write an extremely simple procedure that can be invaluable in debugging. It is

```
        .MODEL SMALL ;          or whatever
        .CODE
        PUBLIC Int3 ;           or _Int3 in C/C++
Int3    PROC
        int     3
        ret
Int3    ENDP
        END
```

In situations where it is difficult to set breakpoints in the proper places (such as in a program which is executed by another program; for an example, see Section 17.4), simply drop in a call to Int3. When the int 3 is reached, simply Trace twice to get to the instruction following the Int3 call.

Interrupt 1 is the **single-step** interrupt. If the **T** (or **Trace**) **Flag** (bit 8 in the flags register) is set, an interrupt 1 is generated after each instruction is executed. The T flag is reset to 0 automatically at the same time that interrupts are disabled when processing an interrupt (and reset to its original value by `iret`). Interrupt 1 makes it easy for the debugger to single-step through a program. It also makes it easy for the debugger to execute the instruction at a breakpoint without losing the breakpoint:

1) The `int 3` in the first byte of the instruction is temporarily replaced with the original first byte of the instruction, and the T Flag is turned on.
2) The instruction is executed, after which the trace interrupt 1 handler returns control to the debugger.
3) The debugger now puts the `int 3` instruction back in place, turns the T Flag off, and returns to execution of the program being debugged.

It is important that the instruction actually be executed rather than simulated, as the amount of analysis required to simulate all the possibilities is tremendous. Also, different models of the 80X86 execute some instructions differently (`push sp`, for instance).

Turning the T Flag on and off is a little tricky, as there is no specific instruction to do it. The only way to access the entire flags register is to push and pop it with the special instructions `pushf` and `popf`. They are used as follows:

Turn the T Flag On		
`pushf`	`;`	Push flags register
`pop`	`ax ;`	and move it --> ax
`or`	`ax, 0100h ;`	T Flag := 1
`push`	`ax ;`	Reload flags register--
`popf`	`;`	all other flags unchanged

Exercises 15.3

1. ✓ Suppose that we first did `mov dx, WORD PTR Clock+2,` then `mov ax, WORD PTR Clock,` that `Clock` = 0FFFFh and `Clock+2` = 0, and that the clock 'ticks' between these two instructions. What will `dx`|`ax` equal?

2. ✓ a) On the 8086 and 8088, it was possible that an interrupt might occur between the two instructions `mov ss, something` and `mov sp, something else.` Why would such an interrupt be disastrous? How should the disaster be avoided?

   b) In the 80286 and later CPUs, the instruction `pop ss` and any instructions of the form `mov ss, something` automatically disable interrupts for exactly one instruction following them in order to avoid the problem in part a). Since `sp` could be loaded before or after `ss`, why not disable interrupts after any instruction that modifies `sp`, too?

   c) In Chapter 12 we saw that when simplified segment directives are used, the assemblers make the initial assumption that `ss = ds = @data`. Write startup code which resets the necessary registers to make this assumption true. It should work for all 80X86 models.

3. Explain how interrupts 1 and 3 might be used in the 'trace to the cursor' debugger instruction (F7 in CodeView, F4, the 'Here' command, in TD).

4. ✓ Explain how interrupts 1 and 3 might be used to implement the Step command in a debugger (which works like the trace command, except that it steps over calls to break again at the instruction following the call).

5. Suppose a debugger user set a breakpoint on a `cli` instruction. How would the debugger handle running from the `cli` instruction and maintaining the breakpoint? For that matter, how does a debugger handle the `cli` instruction?

15.4 • Interrupt Handlers

Suppose that we want to write an interrupt handler for interrupt n. In order to start using the interrupt handler we must change the segment:offset double word at location 0:4*n to the address of our code, and we often must also save the previous handler address. The simple-minded way to access this address is to define a `SEGMENT AT 0` to get at the interrupt vector table and modify parts of it directly. (Of course, we have to disable interrupts while modifying interrupt vectors!)

The problem is that a debugger or a multiprogramming environment like Microsoft Windows may be faking the processing of interrupts in order to maintain control of the machine. For that reason, one should only use special DOS calls to retrieve and modify interrupt vectors. There are two macros in `pcmac.inc` to use these calls:

> `_SetIntVec intno, Handler`

which sets interrupt `intno` to be handled by interrupt handler `Handler`. `Handler` can either be the actual (`NEAR` or `FAR`) label of the interrupt handler, or can be a double-word containing the seg:offset address of the interrupt handler.

> `_SaveIntVec intno, Location`

which stores the old interrupt vector for interrupt `intno` in the double-word at `Location`.

The underlying DOS call for `_SetIntVec` would destroys `ds`, but the `_SetIntVec` macro saves and restores it. `_SaveIntVec` destroys `es`, and informs the assembler via an `ASSUME` that it has done so.

There are two reasons we might want to get an old interrupt vector:

1) Often we don't want to rewrite a whole interrupt handler. The one for keyboard interrupts is extremely complex, needing to deal with scan codes and shift keys and special combinations like Ctrl-Alt-Del. We just want to add some functionality of our own, which we do by saving the location of the original handler and having the new handler call the old before or after its own processing. The process just described is called **piggy-backing** on the original handler.

2) If our program ever terminates, we must reset the interrupt vector to its original value. If it isn't reset, we have the worst sort of dangling pointer—a jump into code that no longer exists.

We might set up a handler using the code

Set Up an Interrupt Handler
| ```
OldIntVec DD      ?
          . . .
          _SaveIntVec  n, OldIntVec
          _SetIntVec   n, Handler
``` |
```

The code to return to the previous handler for interrupt *n* is

Restore OldIntVec
`_SetIntVec   n, OldIntVec`

The interrupt handler itself has the following form:

Interrupt Handler

`Handler  PROC`
`         push all registers used;`
`         process interrupt;`
`         pop all pushed registers;`
`         iret`
`Handler  ENDP`

We can piggy-back on the old interrupt at any time by executing the following code

Call old interrupt handler from new one

`SEG OldIntVec must be in a segment register`
`pushf  ;           push flags for other handler`
`cli    ;           if necessary`
`call   OldIntVec`

Since `OldIntVec` has the Double Word data type, the assembler knows that it is a variable containing the segment:offset address of the routine to be called.

Example 15.4—1. Simultaneous waiting for two different events (interrupts).

Some windows applications start a waiting process when the mouse cursor is moved over a button and if the button isn't clicked or the mouse moved within a short time, a help message is displayed. The problem here is in waiting for two or more events simultaneously. We will construct a simple example of such waiting in a program called SLEEP which waits roughly five seconds or until a key is pressed, and displays a message telling the user which happened. We will use our own interrupt handlers for the clock and the keyboard.

As we have seen, the clock performs an interrupt 8 roughly 18.2 times per second. The standard clock interrupt handler itself performs an `int 1ch` to allow others to process clock ticks. For the latter interrupt, we will insert our own handler which merely counts down a counter and sets a Done bit to 1 when the counter reaches 0. Normally, the handler for interrupt 1ch just does an `iret`, but since some other routine may already be using `int 1ch`, we should piggy-back onto it. We will do the same thing with the keyboard interrupt 9, which occurs whenever a key is pressed or released.

The overall plan for SLEEP is as follows:

```
Save old interrupt vectors for keyboard and clock;
Set those interrupt vectors to our handlers;
while not Done do { nothing! } ;
Cleanup: restore old interrupt vectors;
```

When SLEEP exits, pressing a key may have left a spurious keystroke in the queue, so just before we exit, we *test* for any characters in the keyboard input queue (int 16h, function 1 returns with flags indicating non-zero if there is a character waiting) and if so, remove it with _BIOSCh (int 16h, function 0; see Section 5.5). The loop to clean out the keyboard queue is

```
CleanQueue:        ;              Remove any keystrokes waiting
           mov     ah, 1 ;        Keystroke waiting?
           int     16h
           jz      toDos ;        No
           _BIOSCh ;              Yes, Read and ignore key
           jmp     CleanQueue
toDOS:
```

The main part of the program is straightforward:

```
ClockInt    EQU     1Ch
KbdInt      EQU     09h


            .DATA
WaitTicks EQU     100 ;              about 5 seconds
StartMsg  DB      'Sleeping...$'
StopMsg   DB      13, 'Sleep ended', 13, 10, '$'
Done      DB      ?
Counter   DW      ?
OldClockVect DD   ?
OldKbdVect DD     ?


            .CODE

;           Interrupt Handlers go here

Sleep       PROC
            mov     ax, @data
            mov     ds, ax

            _SaveIntVec ClockInt, OldClockVect
            _SaveIntVec KbdInt, OldKbdVect

            mov     Done, 0
            mov     Counter, WaitTicks

            _SetIntVec ClockInt, ClockHandler
            _SetIntVec KbdInt, KbdHandler

            _PutStr StartMsg

Idle:       test    Done, 1 ;      Wait for interrupt
```

```
                jz      Idle

                _SetIntVec ClockInt, OldClockVect
                _SetIntVec KbdInt, OldKbdVect

;               CleanQueue code goes here

                _PutStr StopMsg
                _Exit  0
Sleep           ENDP
                END    Sleep
```

The interrupt handlers must go physically *before* the invocations of _SetIntVec because _SetIntVec does some tricky fiddling with its second argument, and if the second argument hasn't occurred yet, you get fatal errors.

The clock handler is straightforward:

```
ClockHandler PROC
                push    ds ;            Save registers to be used
                push    ax
                mov     ax, @data
                mov     ds, ax
                pushf   ;                   to fake an interrupt
                call    OldClockVect ;      Piggy-Back
                dec     Counter
                jnz     NotDone
                mov     Done, 1 ;       Indicate time expired
NotDone:
                pop     ax ;            Restore registers used
                pop     ds
                iret
ClockHandler ENDP
```

You may well wonder why we bothered to load ds here since it would presumably be loaded correctly already by the idling main program. The trouble is, we can't really count on interrupting the main program! What if an interrupt happened during the first _PutStr in the main program? Ds would *probably* be right *but* ... And suppose some other interrupt that we know nothing about occurred and that it changed ds, and then a clock interrupt occurred.

When programming with interrupts, it pays to be pessimistic.

The keyboard handler would be even simpler if it weren't for the lines boldfaced below:

```
KbdHandler PROC
                push    ds
                push    ax
```

```
              mov    ax, @data
              mov    ds, ax
              pushf
              call   OldKbdVect
              cmp    Counter, WaitTicks - 5 ; Necessary for 386 (?)
              jge    KeepGoing
              mov    Done, 1
KeepGoing:
              pop    ax
              pop    ds
              iret
KbdHandler ENDP
```

The boldfaced lines have the effect of ignoring a keyboard interrupt that happens very soon after program execution starts. If the three bold-faced lines above are commented out, the program works just fine on 80286s. On an 80386 however, if the program is executed twice in succession, it works the first time but on each subsequent execution, a spurious interrupt 9 occurs within the first couple of clock ticks. Why? It is a mystery to me, but the code given above solves the problem.

15.5 • A Little Something Extra: A TSR Program (Optional)

Note: Writing successful TSR programs is an extremely complicated undertaking and is not for the faint of heart. The example TSR developed here is deceptively simple because it carefully avoids most (but probably not all) of the trouble one can get into in this type of program. Helpful references include Williams' *DOS 6: A Developer's Guide*, pp. 513-597, Hummel's *PC Magazine Assembly Language Lab Notes*, pp. 199-328, and Schulman's *Undocumented DOS*, 2nd ed., pp. 541-618 (see the Bibliography).

One powerful form for computer utility programs is as a resident program, that is, a program which is always in memory and therefore available on a moment's notice. Of course the ROM routines and much of the operating system are always resident, as are the interrupt handlers. Moreover the CONFIG.SYS file can cause the loading of device drivers, which are in many ways glorified interrupt handlers. They encapsulate a group of standard functions for I/O to a particular hardware device.

In addition to these resident programs, there are others which are not so standard. Often they are called up by striking a key or combination of keys called a **hot key**. One example of such a program is a screen capture program. When the hot key is hit, the mouse can be used to describe a rectangle on the screen that is saved to a file. In order for a program to have a hot key, it clearly must piggy-back on the keyboard interrupt 9.

These not-so-standard programs are loaded by being executed like ordinary programs. However instead of exiting to DOS in the usual way, the program performs a special DOS call called **Terminate and Stay Resident** (**TSR**) which leaves part of the program's code in memory.

In detail, the DOS program COMMAND.COM processes the command line from the keyboard and loads each new program to be executed at the lowest available address in memory (just above all previously resident code). Terminate and stay resident alters this lowest address so that it is above the part of the code to stay resident. Typically, in a TSR program, the first part of the program is devoted to the resident part and the last part to the setup code, which is no longer needed once the program becomes resident.

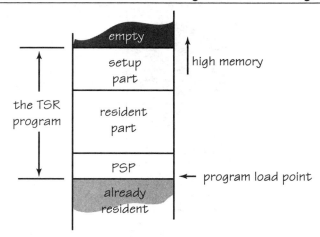

The amount of memory to be kept resident is specified in paragraphs (1 paragraph = 16 bytes), so we must compute N, a number of paragraphs just large enough to hold the required resident part of the code and the PSP:

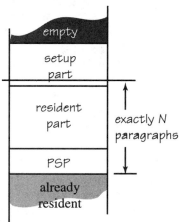

At this point in the code, the setup part executes the DOS Terminate and Stay Resident command:

```
mov    dx, N
mov    ah, 31h
mov    al, ReturnCode ;    as in the _Exit call
int    21h ;              Terminate and Stay Resident
```

This code results in the following situation:

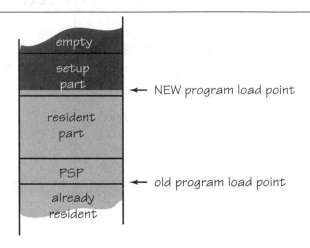

The overall plan of the usual TSR is as follows:

TSR Program
ResidentPart: ; various interrupt handlers;
SetupCode: ; Execution starts here
Perform initializations; that is, reset the
necessary interrupt vectors so that they point
to the handlers in the resident part;
Terminate and Stay Resident, telling DOS to keep
resident everything up to the first paragraph
boundary after 'SetupCode:'

It is also fairly standard for each TSR program to start with a data paragraph containing a **marker**, the name of the program in ASCII, and for the setup code to check to see if this marker already exists in memory so that the TSR program will only be loaded once. Some TSRs also can deinstall themselves, and the marker would be a way of finding the installed version.

Example 15.5—1. The IBM extended ASCII character set contains characters for '≤' (0f3h) and '≥' (0f2h). In order to be able to use these characters easily, we want to create a TSR INEQUAL which converts Alt-comma (< is Shift-comma) to ≤ and Alt-period (> is Shift-period) to ≥.

Our TSR will consist of an interrupt handler that piggy-backs on keyboard interrupt 9. In order to proceed, we must understand in more detail how DOS treats keystrokes.

Location 40h:17h is a byte containing the current status of the shift keys in the format discussed in Example 9.1—1. For now, we just need to know that the Alt key is represented by bit 3 (from the right, numbering from 0).

As we discussed in Section 5.5, each key on the keyboard has assigned to it a scan code from 0 to 127. (See Example 5.5—1 for a method of determining scan codes.) An interrupt 9 is generated each time a key is pressed or released. When pressed, the keyboard sends the scan code as input to the computer, and when released, it sends the scan code + 128.

The interrupt 9 handler turns each 'real' keystroke—that is, a key pressed other than a shift key—into a two-byte pair, the ASCII value of the key (or 0, if there isn't any) followed by the scan code for the key. These pairs are saved in a 16 entry **circular queue**, two bytes per entry, starting at 40h:1eh. The word at 40h:1ah is the **queue head**, that is, the offset to the character in the queue which will be retrieved next by _GetCh or _BIOSCh. 40h:1ch is the **queue tail**, which points one entry beyond the end of the characters already entered—the position at which the next character will be entered. The queue is said to be circular because when we get to the end of the 16 memory entries for the queue, we wrap around to the beginning. Suppose, for instance, that queue head = queue tail = 30h (that is, the queue is empty) and type 'Hello, world⏎'. The contents of the **keyboard queue** are

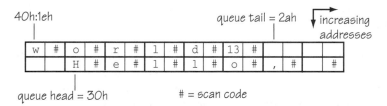

Notice that if the queue head equals the queue tail, the queue could either be empty or full. To avoid this ambiguity, the BIOS allows the queue to hold at most 15 entries (contrary to most documentation). One queue slot is always empty, and equal head and tail always indicates an empty queue.

The mechanism of our keyboard handler is simple. First we piggy-back on the normal handler and then check to see if the Alt shift is down and a keystroke has been newly added to the queue. If so, we check the scan code of the keystroke, and if it is of the comma or period key, replace the ASCII value with ≤ or ≥, respectively.

Since fewer than half of the keystrokes add to the queue (half of all keyboard interrupts are for letting a key *up*), an easy way is needed to tell if something has been added. One way is to compare the queue tail before and after doing the piggy-back call. Saving the old queue tail also has the advantage that if there is a new character, the old queue tail points directly to it, and we don't have to worry about manipulating the new queue tail, which may have wrapped around. The code is, roughly

```
; Our keyboard handler

        mov     bx, QueueTail
        pushf
        call    OldKbdVect ; piggy back on old keyboard handler
        cmp     bx, QueueTail
        je      Done
        if Alt key is down then
            if 40h:[1+bx] = comma scan code then 40h:[bx] := 0f3h
            else if it = period scan code then 40h:[bx] := 0f2h
```

The setup code is simple. We save the address of the old interrupt 9 handler for piggy-backing and reset the interrupt vector to point to our keyboard handler using the _SaveIntVec and _SetIntVec macros.

If we decide to call our program InEqual, the marker described above can be declared as the following 16 bytes at the beginning of the program:

```
Marker    DB       'InEqual
```

We don't have to search for it at *every* memory location, only at paragraph boundaries, which cuts our work by a factor of 16. (We are able to make this reduction, not because Marker is 16 bytes long but because programs must start at paragraph boundaries.) The code is something of a novelty because it involves using a *segment register* as a loop index, and goes something as follows:

```
for Segm := 41h to es do
    if 16 bytes at Segm:0 = 16 bytes at Marker
        then Display 'already loaded' and exit end if
end for
```

The limits on Segm are determined on the lower end by the location of the BIOS data (actually, we could safely start even a little higher) and the segment of our very own PSP, which is initially in es. We will put Segm in es, so we must save the initial value of es, say in dx. We can't compare or increment a segment register directly, so we'll also keep a copy of Segm in bx. The code could then be

```
                mov     bx, 41h ;            for Segm := 41h
                mov     dx, es ;                to es ( = Original PSP) do
                ASSUME ds : SEG Marker ;   previously set up
SrchLoop:
                mov     si, OFFSET Marker
                mov     cx, 8 ;             Number of words in marker
                mov     es, bx
CmpLoop:                ;                   if
                mov     ax, [si] ;        16 bytes in Marker =
                cmp     ax, es:[si] ;     16 bytes at es:OFFSET Marker
                jne     NotThisParagraph
                add     si, 2 ;             equal so far
                loop    CmpLoop
;                                           then Display 'already loaded'
;                                               and exit
NotThisParagraph:
                inc     bx ;              Not equal; try next seg
                cmp     bx, dx ;          Are we done?
                jb      SrchLoop ;         No, keep looking
;                                          Yes, not installed--install it
```

The most obvious overall structure for the program is:

```
              .DATA
Marker      DB       'InEqual     '
OldKbdVect  DD       ? ; WON'T WORK!
              . . .
              .CODE
KbdHandler PROC
```

```
;   code to piggy-back keyboard interrupt and convert Alt-, to
;   ≤ and Alt-. to ≥
KbdHandler ENDP


Setup     PROC
;   code to check for previous installation,
;   save old keyboard interrupt in OldKbdVect, and reset int 9
;    to KbdHandler. Then TSR so that new program load point is first
;    paragraph beyond Startup
Setup     ENDP


          .STACK 100h ; Last, because we'll ultimately use user's
;                          stack and don't want to waste memory
          END    Setup
```

The natural thing to do here is to put Marker and OldKbdVect in the .DATA region. I did, and got the program to work, except that if I tried to run another program after InEqual, the second program sometimes ran and then locked up, sometimes just locked up. I eventually realized that 1) the stack always comes last, no matter where it appears in the source code and 2) .DATA is always grouped with the stack, so it will come after the .CODE section too (see Sections 12.4 and 12.7). That meant that OldKbdVect was in the part of memory that was getting returned to the system for use, and when another program was loaded, OldKbdVect was getting clobbered. Therefore to insure that Marker and OldKbdVect were at the beginning of the code, I had to put them in the .CODE region. The new plan is as follows:

```
          .CODE
Data1     PROC
Marker    DB     'InEqual       '
OldKbdVect DD    ?
Data1     ENDP


KbdHandler PROC
;   code to piggy-back keyboard interrupt and convert Alt-, to
;   ≤ and Alt-. to ≥
KbdHandler ENDP


          .DATA
;   setup data to be discarded (Using this location in the source
;   code isn't too critical since it will be pushed to the end with
;   the stack after Setup anyway.


Setup     PROC
;   slightly modified marker checking code
;   code to save old keyboard interrupt in OldKbdVect and reset int
;    9 to KbdHandler. Then TSR so that new program load point is
;    first paragraph beyond Setup
Setup     ENDP
```

```
.STACK 100h ;        This is last anyway
END    Setup
```

Let us digress for a moment to talk about debugging a TSR. Debugging a TSR is agony, pure and simple. Turbo Debugger gives you some help—you can make it resident and set breakpoints in your TSR. (For a description of how this works, see the end of this section.) Unfortunately, debuggers seem to help only in finding the easy bugs in TSRs (this is perhaps true by definition). The hard bugs tend to lock up the machine, requiring that you reboot and lose any useful information that might be lying around. Even when you don't crash the machine, whenever you fix a bug you will have to reboot the machine to reinstall the corrected version.

There was one other bug in the program that was interesting (as opposed to tedious and/or embarrassing). I got the program to work fine with a debugger, but when I tried to run it without one, it refused to load, saying it was already loaded. This kind of behavior isn't too uncommon, as the debugger moves the program and fakes some of its environment. It wouldn't have been so surprising if the code running alone did *not* find something that was supposed to be there. Here, though, it was *finding* something that shouldn't be there.

I traced through the marker-checking code several times and convinced myself that it was working. I inserted a call to `PutHex` to display the segment at which `Marker` was supposedly found, and the program started working properly! At that point, I could only try brute force. I could make the program load properly by raising the initial segment tested from 41h to 2000h (so effectively, not checking the area where the program was failing). I then tried a lower segment of 1000h. The program loaded so I tried 1800h, which failed, etc. After a rather painful human binary search, I discovered that if I started searching at segment 1000h, I got the bad installation behavior, and if I started at 1020h, I got an actual installation.

When I looked at the memory between 1000h:0 and 1020h:0 with TD, it looked like part of a disk directory, including the entry 'TD   EXE' for TD. My first thought was that when I executed `INEQUAL`, this area would contain the directory entry for `INEQUAL`. Unfortunately, that is 'INEQUAL EXE', which certainly doesn't match 'InEqual   '. At this point, the light-bulb went on. Has it for you?

The area between 1000h and 1020h must be in a disk buffer area. If it could contain disk directory information, it might also contain the code of a program being loaded, in which case, it could contain `Marker`! The reason the program worked when I added `PutHex` was, presumably, that the program was longer, so another buffer full of information had been read in over `Marker`.

At this point, I remembered that *PC Magazine* often contains carefully written utilities in assembly language, and these are often TSRs. Perhaps they had a solution. I looked at one and it did. Just before comparing the program's marker area to other areas in memory, the first byte of the marker is complemented with a `not` instruction! Thus it will match the marker in a previously installed version of the program, but *not one lying around in a disk buffer*. If programs were annotated like chess games, this instruction would deserve three *ex*clamation points. I doubt I would ever have understood this trick without going through the previous suffering. The final code is

```
;; INEQUAL.ASM--A TSR whose raison d'etre is to turn Alt-,Shift-,
;; (or Alt-Shift-,) into <= and Alt-. (or Alt-Shift-.) into >=
;;
INCLUDE    PCMAC.INC
           .MODEL SMALL
           ASSUME SS:NOTHING
```

```
KbdInt      EQU     09h

ROMData     SEGMENT AT 40h
            ORG     17h
KbdStatus DB        ?
AltKey      EQU     00001000B
            ORG     1Ah
QueueHead DW        ? ;           --> next character pair to be read
QueueTail DW        ? ;           --> next slot to fill from keyboard
KbdQueue DB         16 DUP (?, ?) ; Scan code, ASCII value
ROMData     ENDS

CommaCode EQU       51 ;          Scan Codes
PeriodCode EQU      52
LessEq      EQU     0f3h ;        Extended ASCII character values
GrEq        EQU     0f2h

            .CODE
Data1       PROC    ;             *** Start of Resident Part ***
Marker      DB      'InEqual    ' ; to avoid double installation
OldKbdVect DD       ?
Data1       ENDP

KbdHandler PROC
            push    ds
            push    ax
            push    bx
            mov     ax, SEG ROMData *
            mov     ds, ax
            ASSUME ds : ROMData ;     cs already assumed at our SEG

            mov     bx, QueueTail ;   Was a character entered?
            pushf
            call    OldKbdVect ;      Piggy-back
            cmp     bx, QueueTail
            je      Done ;            No New Character

            test    KbdStatus, AltKey
            jz      Done
            mov     al, [1 + bx] ;    scan code of entered character
            cmp     al, CommaCode
            jne     CheckPeriod
            mov     BYTE PTR [bx], LessEq
            jmp     Done
CheckPeriod:
```

---

* TASM users see the footnote on the bottom of page 312, Section 12.4.

```
            cmp     al, PeriodCode
            jne     Done
            mov     BYTE PTR [bx], GrEq
Done:
            pop     bx
            pop     ax
            pop     ds
            iret
KbdHandler ENDP ;                    *** End of Resident Part ***

            .DATA
;; Startup Data--here so it will disappear on TSR
ErrMsg      DB      'InEqual already installed', 13, 10, '$'

            .CODE
Setup       PROC
            mov     dx, ds ;        Upper limit for search: current PSP
            mov     bx, 41h ;       Start Segment for Search
            not     Marker ;        To avoid getting false match (!!!)
SrchLoop:
            mov     si, OFFSET Marker
            mov     cx, 8
            mov     ds, bx
            ASSUME  ds:NOTHING ; ds is unknown in this loop
CmpLoop:
            mov     ax, cs:[si] ; Marker is in the code segment
            cmp     ax, [si]
            jne     NotThisParagraph
            add     si, 2
            loop    CmpLoop

            _PutStr ErrMsg, @data ;    Inequal already Loaded
            _Exit  1
NotThisParagraph:
            inc     bx
            cmp     bx, dx ;        Next seg to try, seg of  urrent PSP
            jb      SrchLoop

;                                 Not installed--install it
            _SaveIntVec KbdInt, OldKbdVect
            mov     es, dx ;        Save PSP segment in es
            _SetIntVec KbdInt, KbdHandler

            mov     dx, ((OFFSET Setup - Data1 + 15) SHR 4) + 16
;             = number of paragraphs to keep resident
;                (OFFSET Setup - Data1 + 15) SHR 4 rounds up to the
;                   whole number of paragraphs in the program
```

```
;               16 is added for the number of paragraphs in the PSP
;          (ErrMsg will come AFTER Setup in the final program)
        mov     ah, 31h
        mov     al, 0 ;        Return value of 0
        int     21h ;          Terminate and stay resident
Setup   ENDP

        .STACK 100h ;          We will ultimately use user's stack
        END     Setup
```

We end with the promised information on using Turbo Debugger to debug TSRs:

1) Assemble and link your program as usual for use with TD.
2) Start up TD, in the case above, with `TD INEQUAL`
3) Debug the startup code if necessary in the normal way. When the startup code does its TSR, TD will tell you this has happened.
4) **Very Important**, or you will 'lose' your code: Set a breakpoint in the resident part of your TSR.
5) Enter **Alt-F**(ile R(esident to make TD resident too. This returns you to the command line.
6) When you strike a key (or whatever) to enter your TSR and it gets to the breakpoint you set, you will reenter TD.

To find out where resident programs are in memory, you can use a command included in DOS 6.0 or later:

```
mem /c
```

or use, `tdmem`, a useful utility that comes with the Turbo Assembler. These programs tell you where resident programs are in memory, `tdmem` tells you which program controls which interrupts.

Exercise 15.5

1. `QueueTail` might also change because something has been removed from the queue; for example, because the Backspace or Escape key was hit. Convince yourself that the program works correctly (that is, is harmless) in such a situation. (The program will probably fail with keyboard macro programs, but if you have such a program, you don't need `InEqual`.)

15.6 • A Little Something Extra: Caveats for Interrupt Hackers (Optional)

This section contains a few remarks and points out some useful references for those hardy souls who wish to handle their own interrupts.

As we have said, if you redirect interrupts to use your code and your code goes away and the interrupt happens, you have the worst sort of dangling pointer disaster. This is not a problem with TSRs and so far we have saved and restored all altered interrupt vectors in programs which can go away. What if the program terminates abnormally, though? This could be caused by something as simple as the user hitting Ctrl-C or leaving a floppy drive door open. The example given in Section 15.4 was simple enough that it was unlikely to run into the problem.In more realistic programs, unexpected termination must be dealt with. Duncan's book *Advanced MSDOS Programming* (see the

Bibliography) spends substantial amounts of his Chapters 5 and 6 discussing the problem, and really just gives the surface a thorough scratching. Briefly, the key is that when DOS aborts program execution, it executes one of the interrupts 22h, 23h, or 24h, depending on the type of exit. Normally these interrupts do nothing, but you can grab them and use them to perform cleanup work. The locations of the original handlers for these interrupts are saved in the PSP, and automatically restored by DOS on exit from your program.

Another problem is that many of the crucial DOS calls and data structures aren't documented. A certain amount of folklore has grown up about them, but the main reason they are undocumented is that Microsoft reserves the right to change them! Schulman's book *Undocumented DOS* (see the Bibliography) has extensive information, examples, and advice on this subject, as well as an extensive bibliography of further information (though its title has the same validity as the statement 'This sentence is false.')

As an example, let us consider what is probably the best known 'undocumented' DOS call. DOS is not **reentrant**; that is to say, errors can happen if DOS is interrupted and the interrupt handler tries to call DOS. In order to avoid this problem, DOS sets a byte non-zero on entry and zeroes it on exit, and the undocumented DOS 34h call returns the address of that byte in es:bx.

A typical use of the 34h call would be a situation in which a TSR wishes to write a file. Rather than simply writing the file, it places the information to be written in a buffer and sets a byte in its own memory, called say IOPending, to 1. In addition the TSR has a piggy-back on the clock interrupt which executes the following code:

```
            cmp     IOPending, 0
            je      Done ;          Return from Interrupt
            push    bx
            push    es
            push    ax
            mov     ah, 34h
            int     21h ;           can we enter DOS?
            cmp     BYTE PTR es:[bx], 0
            jnz     OK
            pop     ax ;            DOS entry isn't safe
            pop     es
            pop     bx
            jmp     Done
OK:
            do the IO and set IOPending to 0, etc.
Done:
            iret
```

The 34h interrupt has been so widely used that it is unlikely that Microsoft would change it. In fact, it is described in the chapter on TSRs of the *MASM Programmer's Guide* (which has other useful and presumably authoritative information on the subject), and hence must at least be considered semi-documented.

15.7 • Something Extra: Simultaneously Executing Programs (Optional)

This section discusses 80X86 solutions to a problem involved with simultaneous execution of two or more programs, either in one CPU switching between programs by interrupts, or on multiple CPUs sharing the same memory. In Section 15.7.1, we will introduce the general problem. In 15.7.2-3, an abstract solution to the problem will be developed, and in 15.7.4 we will discuss implementations of this solution on the 80X86. The notions discussed here are crucial to the design of operating systems, networks, etc., but will not be used further in this book. However, careful study will deepen your understanding of interrupts. Our code fragments will use some fairly advanced Pascal or C concepts, but the explanations should prove sufficient so that a detailed knowledge of one of those languages will not be necessary.

15.7.1 • Race Conditions

One important difficulty with the design of operating systems is that several things may be happening simultaneously, or it may at least appear that this is the case. For instance, the processing of interrupts can sometimes best be understood if one assumes that the operating system (the interrupt handler) and the application program are operating simultaneously, since interrupts can cause their operation to be interleaved in quite arbitrary ways.

When two or more programs execute simultaneously (or nearly so) and access the same data, a **race condition** can develop. A race condition is a situation in which a program 'normally' operates correctly but under certain possible timings of the program (however unlikely they are to occur), the program operates incorrectly. * Unanticipated race conditions can be very difficult bugs to find and correct, because they occur only rarely and generally can't be repeated under controlled conditions.

We will now give an extended example of a race condition. If you are already familiar with the concept, skip to Section 15.7.2.

Operating systems often read and write files into arrays of bytes called buffers. Rather than permanently assigning a number of buffers to each program which needs them, thus wasting space when buffers aren't needed and perhaps running short when they are, the operating system may maintain a pool of buffers. A program which needs a buffer can request one, and when it is done, return it to the pool. The race condition occurs when application programs and the operating system compete for these buffers.

For a simple implementation, let's assume that the buffers can be strung together in lists using a word at the beginning called the Next field. The Next field contains the address (segment:offset or just offset) of the next buffer in sequence. We will be particularly interested in a list of available buffers pointed to by a variable Free. We assume the following declarations (Pascal or C/C++):

Pascal: C/C++:

```
type                                       struct Buffer {
    PointerToBuffer = ^Buffer;                 struct Buffer *Next;
```

---

* This is not quite a standard definition of race condition, but I think it captures the essence. What I call 'programs' here are more properly called 'processes' in the usual operating system terminology. For a more extended treatment of these and other questions raised in this section, see almost any text on operating systems theory, such as the one by Tannenbaum listed in the bibliography.

```
Buffer =                                    char contents[N];
   record                                   } *Free;
      Next : PointerToBuffer;
      contents : array [1..N] of char
   end;

var
   Free : PointerToBuffer;
```

The field `contents` is the actual storage (of N bytes) supplied by the buffer. We can picture the Free list as follows:

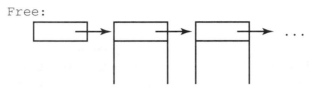

The operation of allocating a free buffer and setting some variable P to point to it (and removing the buffer from the `Free` list, of course) is given by the code

Pascal: C/C++:

```
P := Free;                                  P = Free;
Free := Free^.Next;                         Free = Free -> Next;
```

which results in the picture

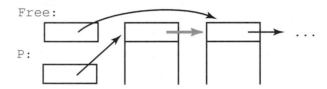

(For simplicity we are assuming that there is always something on the `Free` list.) We have grayed the pointer from the `Next` field of the assigned buffer because its old value will be changed or ignored.

The race condition arises if two different programs attempt more or less simultaneously to get a buffer. Suppose that program 1 attempts to set P1 pointing to a new buffer and program 2 to set P2 pointing to a new buffer, and that the following sequence occurs (Pascal code):

```
          { Program 1 is executing and requests a buffer }
P1 := Free;
          { Program 2 gets control, perhaps through an interrupt }
P2 := Free;
Free := Free^.Next;
   ...
          { Program 1 regains control before Program 2 finishes }
```

```
                { with the buffer it grabbed }
        Free := Free^.Next;
```

(Program 1 statements are shown in bold face, program 2 statements in normal type.) Then the following situations occur successively:

After **P1 := Free**:

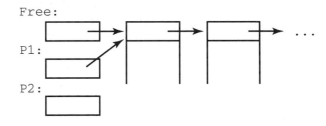

After P2 := Free:

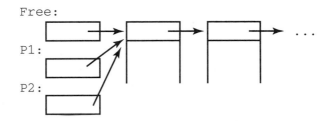

After Free := Free^.Next:

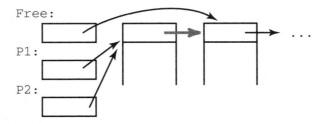

After **Free := Free^.Next**:

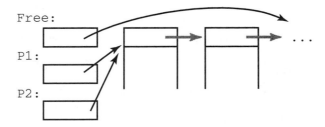

The result is that we have two different programs trying to use the same buffer at the same time, while a second buffer has been cast into the outer darkness.

15.7.2 • Semaphores: an Abstract Method of Synchronization

Perhaps the simplest method of avoiding this problem was proposed by Edsger Dijkstra. He hypothesized a new data type called the **semaphore** and two abstract operations on it, P and V, standing for Dutch words which we will translate as W (**Wait**) and S (**Signal**) respectively. If you are familiar with semaphores, you can skip ahead to Section 15.7.4.

The semaphore variable **s** has two possible values, 1 and 0. It is used to determine whether something of interest is available (1) or in use (0). The operation W(**s**) waits until **s** is 'available' (that is, **s** = 1), and sets **s** = 0, indicating that it is unavailable:

```
W(s):  if s = 1 then s := 0
       else goto W(s);
```

S(s) signals that s is again available:

```
S(s):  s := 1;
```

The reason that a semaphore must be a special data type is that the W(**s**) operation must be indivisible. That is, once one program has found **s** to be 1, it is allowed to set **s** to 0 before any other program is allowed to test **s**. If there are several programs waiting on **s** when S(**s**) sets **s** back to 1, only one is allowed to test it and set it to 0. The other programs will continue to wait.

If the testing and setting operations of W(**s**) were not indivisible, we could have a race condition, in which the sequence: program 1 finds **s** = 1, program 2 finds **s** = 1, program 2 sets **s** := 0, program 1 sets **s** := 0, would be possible.

We can think of a semaphore as being like a washroom with a single key. Anyone wanting to use the washroom waits for the key to be available (W(**s**)), takes the key along while using the washroom, and then returns the key (S(**s**)), guaranteeing that everyone will have privacy in the washroom. The indivisibility of the W operation guarantees that we can't have a situation where two potential users see the key simultaneously and both grab for it.

15.7.3 Using Semaphores to Solve Race Conditions

If we assume the existence of semaphores, then it is easy to solve race conditions such as the example in Section 15.7.1. In that case we use a semaphore to guarantee that only one program at a time can access the available buffer list Free. Any program wishing to get a buffer would execute the function

```
function GetBuffer : PointerToBuffer;
    { returned value points to a buffer taken from the Free list }
  begin
    W(GetBufSema);
    GetBuffer := Free;{ assign return value }
    Free := Free^.Next;
    S(GetBufSema)
  end;
```

Note that several programs might be executing `GetBuffer` at the same time, but all but one of them will be waiting on **`GetBufSema`** (a global semaphore variable) or about to exit `GetBuffer` after executing S(**`GetBufSema`**).

15.7.4 • Implementing Semaphores on the 80X86

Most modern computers have hardware instructions that make the job of implementing semaphores fairly easy. On the 80X86, the lowly `dec` instruction is almost all that is needed:

```
;; Code for W(s):
W:          dec     s
            jz      Available
            inc     s
            jmp     W
Available:
```

The code for S(s) is even easier, though there is a subtlety to be discussed later:

```
;; Code for S(s):
S:          inc     s
```

The code for W(**s**) is correct if all the programs using it are running on the same CPU. It works even though there could be an interrupt between `dec  s` and `jz Available`, during which another program could execute W(**s**). We would have the sequence of instructions

```
; s = 1
        dec     s ;            program 1; sets s = 0, Z flag = 1
; interrupt. Z flag is saved!!!
        . . .
        dec     s ;            program 2; sets s = -1, Z flag = 0
        jz      Available ;    program 2; jump not taken
        inc     s ;            program 2; sets s = 0
        jmp     W ;            program 2
        dec     s ;            program 2; sets s = -1, Z flag = 0
         etc. (program 2 continues to wait)
```

Here, in order to make things work, we have to assume that program 1 can resume execution to finish its use of **s**. To do this, W(**s**) would require more complicated code than mere **busy waiting**, as it now does. Perhaps it could do an `iret`, but continue to check each time a timer interrupt occurs. For the purposes of the example, we assume the sequence

```
        iret   ;           program 2; restores Z flag = 1!!
        jz     Available ;  program 1; jump taken!!
Available:
```

Note that the W(**s**) operation would also keep out other programs if an interrupt occurred during the program 2 wait and a program 3 also tried W(**s**). **s** would be either 0 or –1 at the start of program 3 so program 3 would dec it and find the result to be –1 or –2, but certainly not 0. (We assume that any value ≤ 0 for the concrete implementation of **s** represents a value of 0 for the abstract semaphore.)

It is important that S(**s**) use the code inc **s** instead of mov **s**, 1. The reason is that some other program may have done the dec **s** in W(**s**). If the program doing S(**s**) sets **s** to 1 and the one in W(**s**) then increments it, **s** will be 2, and the semaphore will no longer work properly. (This would be another race condition.)

The reason this implementation works is that *interrupts can't happen in the middle of executing an instruction*, so the inc and dec must be executed to completion before another program could gain control. If we could fetch and test **s**, but have an interrupt before storing the decremented value, we would again have a race condition. Unfortunately, just such a thing can happen if we have more than one CPU accessing the semaphore **s**. (The semaphore would have to be in some fixed memory location known to both CPUs.) Perhaps the most common place this can occur is in a **networking** situation, in which a computer will have one CPU to do its primary processing and another CPU on a **network interface card** (**NIC**) that uses the computer's memory (and perhaps file system), communicating with the main CPU when necessary by generating interrupts.

Our original semaphore solution doesn't work in the multiple CPU case because both CPUs are operating simultaneously. One doesn't have to wait till the other is between instructions to access the same piece of memory. We could have the sequence of operations

s	CPU1	CPU2	Comments
1	fetch **s**		get **s** = 1 as start of dec **s** operation
1	subtract 1		get 0 in CPU1; set ZF = 1
1		fetch **s**	get **s** = 1 as start of dec **s** operation
1	store in **s**		set **s** = 0; ZF still 1. use protected code in CPU1
0		subtract 1	get 0 in CPU2; set ZF = 1!
0		store in **s**	execute protected code in CPU2

The 80X86 CPU rescues us by supplying the lock instruction prefix. When lock is prefixed to an instruction, memory is locked for the duration of the single following instruction and no other CPU can access it. If memory is already locked, the CPU trying to lock waits until the previous lock is released before starting to execute its instruction. Thus we can repair W(**s**) as follows:

```
;; Code for multiple CPU version of W(s):
W:          lock    dec s
            jz      Available
            inc     s
            jmp     W
Available:
```

and the code for S(**s**) similarly:

```
;; Code for multiple CPU version of S(s)
S:          lock    inc s
```

The result in the CPU1/CPU2 example above is that the 'fetch **s**' in CPU2 cannot take place until after the 'store in **s**' operation is finished in CPU1.

Exercises 15.7

1. ✓ Show how W(**s**) and S(**s**) can be implemented using `lock xchg` **s**, `al`.

2. ✓ The semaphores discussed in this section are often called binary semaphores because they can only assume the values 0 and 1. The more general integer semaphores are allowed to have any non-negative value. The code for W and S for such a semaphore **s** is

```
W(s):  if n > 0 then n := n - 1      S(s): n := n + 1
       else goto W(s)
```

where the operation of W and S are indivisible. An integer semaphore can be thought of as controlling access to a resource of which there are several copies. Show how an integer semaphore could be implemented with an abstract binary semaphore and a global variable (together with a local variable in each program which uses the integer semaphore). **Note:** The `dec` implementation of semaphores works without change for integer semaphores, but the `xchg` implementation doesn't.

15.8 • A Little Something Extra: A Short History of Interrupts

Early computers were purely sequential. The CPU executed until I/O was required, and then came to a grinding halt until the I/O was completed. CPUs were very fast and very expensive, operating at electronic speeds, while I/O devices were relatively slow and inexpensive, operating at mechanical speed. About the mid 1950s, it was realized that the amount of control required by I/O devices was fairly simple, and these devices were therefore supplied with rather primitive control computers of their own, allowing the CPU and the I/O devices to proceed independently in parallel. The difficulty then was how to coordinate the CPU and one or more I/O devices. Since I/O devices are relatively slow, it is essential to lose as little time as possible between I/O operations. Therefore it is necessary to know immediately when an I/O operation is completed, so that the next one can be started. This led to the invention of the interrupt.

With the introduction of the interrupt, I/O programming became much more complicated. In addition, at about this time, computers started being used in batch mode, with one program job run after another. Time lost between these jobs became intolerable, not to mention the possibility that one job might destroy another. Therefore, machines started checking for more types of errors, and causing interrupts when they were detected rather than simply halting and waiting for a human operator to fix things up.

As we entered the third computer generation (Integrated Circuits) in the early 1960s, things became even more complex. Memory had become relatively inexpensive, so computers had enough that several programs could be in memory at once—generally one executing and the remainder waiting for I/O to complete. Mistakes became even more intolerable. Also, privacy and protection of files became another reason not to allow users to do their own hardware I/O.

As a result, certain operations, such as hardware I/O, were designated as **privileged**. The CPU could execute in one of two states—a **user state** for ordinary user programs and a **supervisor** or **kernel state**. Privileged instructions could be executed only in the supervisor state. Hardware and operating systems were designed so that the only way to enter the supervisor state also caused one to enter the operating system, where presumably the code was tested, true, and reliable. Attempting to execute privileged instructions in the user state caused an interrupt which would force the CPU into the supervisor state and into control by the operating system.

Of course, user programs still wanted to perform I/O, so there had to be some way to have it done through the mediation of the operating system. One could of course design various requests to the operating system to perform I/O operations, but when the time came to do them, the operating system would have to be in supervisor mode. Therefore, why not ask the operating system to do the function by executing an instruction which gets the machine into supervisor mode (and into the operating system, of course)? Initially this was often done with a specially chosen illegal instruction, but as it became evident that this was a useful operation, computer designers added software interrupts to their instruction sets for calling the operating system.

The original IBM PC (with the 8088 chip) had no supervisor mode and no privileged instructions. Only with the 80286 was a second mode of operation introduced, the **protected mode**, containing privileged instructions, etc. IBM PCs under DOS continued to operate under the so-called **real mode** which emulates the 8086-88. Although some PC software is still written to operate in real mode only, most of the newer stuff operates only on 80386 and above CPUs, and use protected mode and **extended memory**, which exists above the 1 MByte boundary.

Programming Problem 15.1

Write a TSR program DOSCount which piggy-backs on int 21h and counts the number of times that DOS has been called. The first time DOSCount is executed, it should install itself and initialize its count to zero. Each subsequent time it is executed, it should report the count-to-date and reset the count to zero.

Programming Problem 15.2

Many computer programs communicate information by 'beeping,' displaying the ASCII 7 character. This isn't very useful to the hearing impaired, so write a TSR which piggy-backs on the DOS 21h call. If the function code (ah) isn't 02h (_PutCh) or the character to be displayed (dl) isn't the beep (7), go ahead and execute the regular DOS call. Otherwise _PutCh 14, which is a pair of music notes, for roughly five seconds or until a key is struck, then erase the character with backspace, blank, backspace before piggy-backing. Do not flush the queue of key strokes.

SUMMARY

Interrupts are numbered 0 to 255. Interrupts can happen only between instructions. Interrupts can be classified as follows:

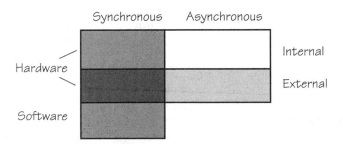

When interrupt *n* occurs, the CPU pushes the flag register, disables interrupts, and does a far call to the interrupt handler whose segment:offset address is given in the interrupt vector at 0:4*n. The sequence of interrupt vectors is collected into a segment of memory in locations 0 to 1023 called the *interrupt vector table*. The iret instruction is used at the end of an interrupt handler to do a far return and restore the saved flags.

Interrupt 3 and interrupt 1 have special uses in debugging—the debugger sets a breakpoint by replacing the byte at the breakpoint address with the single-byte int 3 instruction, and when the T flag (bit 8) is set in the flag register, the CPU generates an interrupt 1 after every instruction.

New Instructions

```
iret ;    Return from interrupt
sti ;     Enable interrupts
cli ;     Disable interrupts
pushf ;   Push Flags
popf ;    Pop Flags
lock ;    (prefix) Lock out other accesses to memory for the dura-
          tion of the following instruction
```

New DOS (int 21h) call

Terminate and Stay Resident, function 31h

Input: dx = number of paragraphs to keep resident
         al = return code
         ah = 31h
No return from DOS

New BIOS call

Is a keystroke waiting?

Input: ah = 1
         int 16h
Output: Zero flag indicated non-zero if a character is waiting.

New Macros

```
        _SaveIntVec intno, addr
```
where intno is the number of the interrupt to be saved and addr is a double-word storage location.
```
        _SetIntVec intno, handler
```
where intno is the number of the interrupt to be set and handler is either the actual near or far label of the interrupt handler or is a double-word containing the segment:offset address of the interrupt handler.

The UTIL.LIB routine GetTime (no parameters) returns the 32-bit number of clock ticks (at 18.2 ticks per second) since midnight in dx and ax.

Chapter **16**

Conditional Assembly and More on Macros

Conditional assembly is very useful in allowing a single source file to be tailored automatically into several object files for varied purposes (such as different models of 80X86 or different operating systems). The ability to custom-fit code is particularly useful in constructing a single macro to generate code for a wide variety of situations. In this chapter we will discuss conditional instructions with general areas of application, and those which are applicable only inside macros. At the end of the chapter, we give a complete review of macro and conditional assembly statements. This chapter can be skipped on first reading and returned to as needed. It presupposes the material of Chapter 8.

All programming languages allow the sequence of instructions *executed* when the program is *run* to be altered by testing various values known at runtime. Most assemblers and a very few high-level languages (C is the most notable example) allow you to affect the actual code generated by testing values known at *translation* time. Put another way, the cmp and various jump instructions allow one to change the sequence of instructions executed each time a section of code is *run*, while the IF pseudo-operations introduced here can produce a different object program each time the source program is *assembled*. Once the program is assembled, however, the object code is fixed and immutable, and all evidence of the IF pseudo-ops has disappeared. (*Execution* sequence of the program can still be changed by cmp and jumps, of course.)

IF pseudo-operations look a lot like **if** statements in high-level languages. The general form of such a conditional is

IF Pseudo-Operation
`IF condition`
`   ...lines assembled if 'condition'  true...`
`ELSE      (optional)`
`   ...lines assembled if 'condition'  false...`
`ENDIF`

The ELSE part of the IF is optional as usual. IFs can be nested, with a corresponding ENDIF required for each IF. A special form of nesting is allowed by replacing ELSE with ELSEIF, which gives a linear sequence of tests and requires only one ENDIF:

Sequence of IFs
`IF condition1`
`   ...lines assembled if 'condition1' is true...`
`ELSEIF condition2`
`   ...lines assembled if 'condition1' is false`
`      and 'condition2' is true...`
`ELSEIF condition3`
`   ...lines assembled if conditions 1 & 2 are false`
`      and 'condition3' is true...`
`ELSE      (optional)`
`   ...lines to be assembled if all conditions are false...`
`ENDIF`

As an example, suppose con is a constant (perhaps defined by an EQUate) and we wish to perform the instruction add ax, con, but wish to do it in the most efficient way possible, using special-case instructions such as inc where possible. The code is

```
IF con EQ 1
        inc     ax
ELSEIF con EQ -1
        dec     ax
ELSEIF con NE 0
        add     ax, con
ENDIF
```

When a program containing the sequence above is assembled, exactly one instruction is produced in the object program (except when con = 0, when no lines are generated.) Clearly using compare and jump to try to achieve the same purpose at *runtime* defeats the purpose—we would have to execute code like

```
        mov     bx, con
        cmp     bx, 1 ;         cmp con, 1 is illegal--two constants
        jne     L1
        inc     ax
        jmp     L3
```

```
L1:
            cmp     bx, -1
            ...     ;                       etc.
```

and *any* path through the code is going to be *much* less efficient than always simply executing `add ax, con`.

Of course the difference wrought by the `IF` code above isn't considerable, but we will give examples later where it is more substantial.

When would you use the `IF` code above? Presumably when you know `con` is a constant, but don't know what it is. The most common use for conditional assembly is in macros, where you may invoke the macro many different times in the course of executing a program and expect it to generate different code each time. For instance, the `_PutStr` macro generates different code depending on whether a segment for the message was given explicitly, and if it is given, what form it is in. (If it's `es`, it must be moved to `ds` via `ax`, for example.)

Also, `con` might be given different values for different versions of the program by changing an `EQU`ate at the beginning of the program or by defining a symbol in the command line with an assembly command like

```
masm or tasm /Dcon=whatever ...
```

Neither of these is a very good idea as it stands, as it is easy to forget to change all of the `EQU`ates manually or to forget to use the correct command line. However the `EQU`ates can be automated by putting them in an `INCLUDE` file and the command line defines can be automated by putting them in a `.BAT` file or by using the `make` utility that comes with both assemblers (which won't be discussed in this book).

There are many types of `IF`s in PC assembly language, and we will discuss only a few of the most commonly used. In all cases, for every `IF`*something-is-true* there is a corresponding `IF`*something-is-NOT-true*, so we will consider these `IF`s in pairs.

16.1 • Generally Applicable `IFs`

▶ `IF` *expression* and `IFE` *expression*

This form of the `IF` most nearly resembles those you are used to. In common with C/C++, '`IF` *expression*' is considered to be true if *expression* is nonzero, false of *expression* is zero. '`IFE` *expression*' is the contrapositive form, which is considered to be true if *expression* is Equal to zero. Various relational operators can be used to make such expressions look more familiar:

EQ	EQual
NE	Not Equal
LT	Less Than
LE	Less than or Equal to
GT	Greater Than
GE	Greater than or Equal to

An expression like '`A EQ B`' is given the value –1 = 0FFFFh if true, 0 if false. The usual bitwise `AND`, `OR`, and `NOT` operators are also available in such expressions.

Example 16.1—1. Redo Example 10.3.—2, the table for the conversion of lowercase to uppercase letters. The table, called UpIt, has the property that UpIt[c] = c if c is not a lowercase letter, UpIt[c] = c + 'A' - 'a', the corresponding uppercase letter, if c is a lowercase letter.

Using IF, =, and REPT (the latter was described in Section 8.4) we can write:

```
UpIt        LABEL   BYTE
Counter = 0
            REPT    256 ;           REPeaT 256 times
IF (Counter < 'a') OR (Counter > 'z')
            DB      Counter
ELSE
            DB      Counter + 'A' - 'a'
ENDIF
Counter = Counter + 1
            ENDM    ;               End of REPT
```

Example 16.1—2. Several versions of the same program may be kept in a single source file. (For instance, the standard version, the version with optional extra cost features, and the demo version we give away but which doesn't do windows, or versions for different machines, or versions for different assemblers or operating systems (DOS vs. OS/2 vs. UNIX), or the current version and the new version under test.) We can use an identifier, say Version and IF statements to choose the appropriate code. For instance:

```
IF Version EQ 100
    ...code for version 1.0...
ELSEIF Version EQ 102
    ...code for version 1.02...
ELSEIF Version EQ 200
    ...code for version 2.0...
ELSE
    ...code for Beta test version...
ENDIF
```

The value for Version can be set by one of the methods discussed at the end of the introduction to this chapter.

▶ **IFDEF** *identifier* and **IFNDEF** *identifier*

The first of these is true if *identifier* has been previously defined and the second is true if *identifier* was previously not defined. They have several uses.

Example 16.1—3. Give an identifier a default value if it hasn't been given one previously.

```
IFNDEF      identifier
identifier EQU    n
ENDIF
```

The code above might be part of an INCLUDE file. If the user of the include file gives *identifier* a value before the INCLUDE statement, it will have that value; otherwise it will have the value *n* given here.

Example 16.1—4. Do something only once. For example, to make sure that an include file ABC.INC was included only once, we might enclose it in the following code:

```
IFNDEF ABC_Included
      ... original ABC.INC code ...
ABC_Included EQU 0
ENDIF
```

Then a source file that tried to INCLUDE ABC.INC more than once would in effect get an *empty* file on all attempts after the first .

Example 16.1—5. Change assembly language instructions depending on the type of CPU you are using. For instance, the instruction 'push *constant*' is legal on an 80286 or higher but illegal on an 8086 or 8088.

First, we assume that the identifier CPU286 will be defined if the code is intended for the 80286. (It is of course possible to assemble code on any of the 80X86 CPUs for execution on any of the others.) Our assemblers won't assemble 'push *constant*' or any other non-8086-88 instruction unless we tell the assembler to permit the use of 80286 instructions by using the **.286 directive** at the beginning of the program. We could therefore code

```
IFDEF     CPU286
          .286
ENDIF
```

at the beginning of the program and then define a macro PushC to use whenever we want to push a constant:

```
PushC     MACRO   constant
IFDEF     CPU286
          push    &constant&
ELSE
          mov     ax, &constant&
          push    ax
ENDIF
          ENDM
```

On the other hand, one could define the *macro* PushC in one of two different ways, depending on CPU286:

```
IFDEF     CPU286
PushC     MACRO   constant
          push    &constant&
```

```
                ENDM
ELSE
PushC           MACRO   constant
                mov     ax, &constant&
                push    ax
                ENDM
ENDIF
```

Exercises 16.1

1. ✓ Suppose we have defined the macro

```
ShiftIt     MACRO   item, amount
IF          &amount& LT 0
            mov     cl, -&amount&
            shr     &item&, cl
ELSE
            mov     cl, &amount&
            shl     &item&, cl
ENDIF
            ENDM
```

then what code is generated by the following macro calls?

```
                ShiftIt ax, 3
                ShiftIt ABC, -5
```

2. Suppose we have defined the macro

```
ShiftL      MACRO   item, amount
IF          &amount& EQ 1
            shl     &item&, 1
ELSEIF      &amount& EQ 2
            shl     &item&, 1
            shl     &item&, 1
ELSE
            mov     cl, &amount&
            shl     &item&, cl
ENDIF
            ENDM
```

What code is generated by the macro calls

```
                ShiftL ax, 1
                ShiftL ABC, 2
                ShiftL [X + si], 8
```

3. Suppose we have defined the macro

```
CRLF      MACRO
IFNDEF    CR
CR        EQU      13
LF        EQU      10
ENDIF
          ENDM
```

What code is generated by the macro calls

```
          CRLF
          CRLF
```

4. ✓ Suppose we have defined the macro

```
Count     MACRO
IFDEF     ctr
ctr = ctr + 1
ELSE
ctr = 1
ENDIF
          ENDM
```

What lines of assembly are generated by the series of calls

```
          Count
          Count
          Count
```

5. What code is generated by the following lines? (See Section 8.4 for a description of REPT.)

```
          REPT     10
IFNDEF    lab
ctr = 1
lab       DW       ctr
ELSE
ctr = ctr + 1
          DW       ctr
ENDIF
          ENDM
```

6. Write code to declare an array HexVal of 256 bytes so that for any character c, if c is a hex digit ('0'…'9', 'A'…'Z', or 'a'…'z'), HexVal[c] is the numeric value of the hex digit and otherwise HexVal[c] is –1. For instance, HexVal['C'] = 12. Use REPT and IF as in the Example 16.1—1.

7. Write a macro EOSDef which EQUates EOS to '$' if it has not already been defined.

16.2 • IFs Usable Only in Macros

▶ **IFB** *<parameter>* and **IFNB** *<parameter>*

These IFs are used to determine whether or not a macro parameter is blank. The parameter *must* be surrounded with <> brackets. We have already made use of many macros that are written using IFB or IFNB.

Example 16.2—1. Write a version of the macro _PutStr with the segment of the string to be displayed as an optional second parameter.

We could define a simplified version of it as follows:

```
_PutStr   MACRO  StringOffset, StringSegment ;   Simplified version
IFNB <&StringSegment&>
          mov    dx, &StringSegment&
          mov    ds, dx
ENDIF
          mov    dx, OFFSET &StringOffset&
          mov    ah, 9
          int    21h
          ENDM
```

This code is a simplified version because the actual macro has to look at the types of the actual parameters StringOffset and StringSegment (using IF and some other things we won't go into) and generate different code accordingly.

Example 16.2—2. Improve the code of _PutCh.

An obvious implementation makes use of the IRP pseudo-macro (See Section 8.4). The code for _PutCh allowing one to display up to five characters is similar to the following:

```
_PutCh    MACRO  c1,c2,c3,c4,c5
          mov    ah, 2 ; DOS function code for display character
          IRP    c, <&c1&,&c2&,&c3&,&c4&,&c5&>
          mov    dl, &c&
          int    21h
          ENDM
          ENDM
```

One minor difficulty with the version above is that one often wants to display a single character that's already in dl (or that could be in dl with a little forethought). The only way to do it with the macro above is to code _PutCh dl, which generates the instruction mov dl,dl. Our improved version of _PutCh allows a call with no parameters to indicate that the character to display what is already in dl (unchanged parts in boldface):

```
_PutCh    MACRO  c1,c2,c3,c4,c5
```

```
            mov     ah, 2 ; DOS function code for display character
IFB <&c1&>
            int     21h
            _PutCh <&c2&>, <&c3&>, <&c4&>, <&c5&>
ELSE
            IRP     c, <&c1&,&c2&,&c3&,&c4&,&c5&>
            mov     dl, &c&
            int     21h
            ENDM
ENDIF
            ENDM
```

Note that the code

```
            mov     dl, 'a'
            _PutCh ,'b', 'c'
```

displays abc and the code

```
            _PutCh 'a',,,'x'
```

displays aaax.

▸ **IFIDNI** *<arg1>*, *<arg2>* and **IFDIFI** *<arg1>*, *<arg2>*

It is often the case that one wants to check a macro parameter for exact equality to a literal string. This check can be done with the pseudo-operations IFIDNI (if identical) and IFDIFI (if different). In both cases, the final "I" indicates "ignore case" of letters (DX = dx = Dx = dX). IFDIF and IFIDN are similar but don't ignore case. Once again, the <> brackets are required around the arguments.

Example 16.2—3. Let's construct a macro SegMove segReg, regMem which moves a register or memory operand regMem to the segment register segReg. The problem is that we can't do say a mov es, ds directly.

We need to check whether regMem is cs, ds, es, or ss. Unfortunately, there is no way to do something the equivalent to IF segReg IDNI cs OR segReg IDNI ds ... In this particular example, we can get around that by using the EXITM pseudo-operation which terminates macro expansion when it is encountered. The code is

```
SegMove    MACRO   segReg, regMem
IFDIFI <&regMem&>, <cs>
    IFDIFI <&regMem&>, <ds>
        IFDIFI <&regMem&>, <es>
            IFDIFI <&regMem&>, <ss>
            mov     &segReg&, &regMem&
            EXITM
```

```
                ENDIF
            ENDIF
        ENDIF
ENDIF
            push    &regMem&
            pop     &segReg&
            ENDM
```

Example 16.2—4. Symbolic representations of constants in macros.

For instance, in the Open File DOS command which will be introduced in the next chapter the file access method is specified by loading a number into al—0 for read only, 1 for write only, or 2 for read and write. In order to avoid having to remember these numbers, we can write a macro with a parameter called AccessMethod which is either the number itself or one of the strings RO, WO, or RW with the obvious interpretations. Then the macro code to load al could be as follows:

```
            . . .
IFIDNI <&AccessMethod&>, <RO>
            mov     al, 0
ELSEIFIDNI <&AccessMethod&>, <WO>
            mov     al, 1
ELSEIFIDNI <&AccessMethod&>, <RW>
            mov     al, 2
ELSE
            mov     al, &AccessMethod&
ENDIF
            . . .
```

Another solution is to use EQUates to define values for RO, WO, and RW and use IFDEF to make sure they are defined only once:

```
            . . .
IFNDEF      RO
RO          EQU     0
WO          EQU     1
RW          EQU     2
ENDIF
            mov     al, &AccessMethod&
            . . .
```

The second method has the disadvantage that it may interfere with some other usage of one of the labels RO, WO, or RW.

Exercises 16.2

1. ✓ Suppose that we have declared the macro

```
Def         MACRO  Lab, Count, Value
IFB <&Count&>
    IFB <&Value&>
&Lab&       DW      ?
    ELSE
&Lab&       DW      &Value&
    ENDIF
ELSE
    IFB <&Value&>
&Lab&       DW      &Count& DUP (?)
    ELSE
&Lab&       DW      &Count& DUP (&Value&)
    ENDIF
ENDIF
            ENDM
```

What code is generated by the following macro calls?

```
Def    A, 5, 18
Def    B,,24
Def    ,,-18
Def    C
Def    ,100
Def    D, 50, <20 DUP (1, 0)>
```

2. Suppose we have defined the macro

```
LoadC     MACRO  reg, con
IFIDNI <&reg&>, <ds>
          mov    ax, &con&
          mov    &reg&, ax
ELSEIFIDNI <&reg&>, <es>
          mov    ax, &con&
          mov    &reg&, ax
ELSE
          mov    &reg&, &con&
ENDIF
          ENDM
```

What code is generated by the following macro calls?

```
LoacC DS, 40h
LoadC ds, A
LoadC Es, B
LoadC ax, 1234h
```

3. Write a macro `MovRC reg, con` which does an optimized version of `mov reg, con` in the

sense that if the constant con is 0, it generates a sub reg, reg instruction.

4. Write a Macro PopBy const which pops const bytes off the stack by doing the necessary number of pop axs if const is 2 or 4 and otherwise adds const to sp.

5. Write a macro IMulC con[, reg] which multiplies ax by con using the imul instruction. Consider the special cases con = 1, 0, and –1, Otherwise, move con to the register reg (assumed to be bx if reg is blank), then do the multiplication.

Programming Problem 16.1

Each succeeding version of DOS added new DOS calls, with the result that some programs won't work with early versions of DOS. For instance, the _Exit call (function 4ch) and any calls involving the hierarchical file system (subdirectories) will not work with DOS versions 1.x. You can check the version number using the **get DOS version** call, function 30h, which returns the *major* version number in al and the *minor* version number in ah. For instance, DOS version 6.2 would return al = 6, ah = 20 (decimal). (DOS 1.x doesn't support this call, but returns ah = al = 0). Write a Macro CheckVer Major [, Minor] which takes as parameters the required major version number and (optionally) minor version number. If the actual DOS version in use is earlier than that specified by Major.Minor, then print the message 'Invalid DOS version' using the DOS 9h function call (as used by _PutStr) and exit to the operating system. As the 4ch function call isn't valid in DOS 1.x, the instruction int 20h must be used (which doesn't return an error code). If Minor is not specified, it is assumed to be 0.

   Checking your program out with various version of DOS will likely be difficult. (Unfortunately, the SETVER command available in later versions of DOS doesn't help.) Check it with at least one real one, trying at least three test cases (smaller, equal, and larger). Do test cases for other versions of DOS (particularly 1.0 and 1.1) by replacing int 21h in the get-version DOS call with a mov ax, *version*. (Without a real DOS 1.0 or 1.1 you don't really have a definitive test, but you'll probably have to make do with the mov.)

Programming Problem 16.2

This problem requires material from Chapter 9. Write a macros GetFld Wrd, nBits, Offs which extracts the nBits bits whose rightmost bit is Offs from the word Wrd and places it in ax, right justified. The macro should be optimized so that if Wrd = ax, no mov Wrd, ax takes place, and if Offs = 0, no shift takes place. Note that the mask to extract nBits bits is (1 SHL nBits) – 1. Write a similar macro SetFld Wrd, nBits, Offs which takes the rightmost nBits bits of ax and uses it to replace the nBits of Wrd, offset from the right by Offs bits. Write a test program which uses various combinations of these macros to test each other. Note that other optimizations are also possible, for instance, when nBits = 8.

SUMMARY

We will actually summarize *everything* we have covered on macros and conditional assembly here.

Conditional Assembly

Named values can be declared and assigned values at assembly time using the = and EQU pseudo-operations. = can be used only with numeric expressions, and variables can be redefined. EQU can be used with numeric expressions, which can*not* then be redefined, or string expressions. Thus

```
x = 1 ;                          legal
x = x + 1 ;                      legal
y           EQU    1 ;           legal
y           EQU    y + 1 ;       ILLEGAL
z           EQU    BYTE PTR [si] ;    legal
```

Looping is possible in the generation of assembly code using the REPT (REPeaT), IRP (Indefinite RePeat) and IRPC (Indefinite RePeat Character)

```
REPT    n
... code ...
ENDM
```

is equivalent to placing *n* copies of … *code* … in the program, one after the other.

```
IRP     vbl, <par1, ... parn>
... prototype ...
ENDM
```

is roughly equivalent to

```
vbl = par1
        ... prototype ...
vbl = par2
        ... prototype ...
        ...
vbl = parn
        ... prototype ...
```

while

```
IRPC    vbl, string
... protype ...
ENDM
```

is roughly equivalent to

```
vbl = first character of string
        ... protype ...
vbl = second character of string
        ... protype ...
        ...
vbl = last character of string
```

```
... protype ...
```

Various tests can be performed and lines of code to be assembled included or excluded accordingly. The general form is

```
IF test
... code to include if test is true ...
ELSE ;           optional
... code to include if test is false ...
ENDIF
```

Nested IFs of the form

```
IF test1
... code to include if test1 is true ...
ELSE
    IF test2
    ... code to include if test2 is true ...
    ELSE
        IF test3
        ... code to include if test3 is true ...
        ELSE
        ... code to include if all tests are false ...
        ENDIF
    ENDIF
ENDIF
```

can be simplified using ELSEIF in place of ELSE...IF and removing all but one ENDIF:

```
IF test1
... code to include if test1 is true ...
ELSEIF test2
... code to include if test2 is true ...
ELSEIF test3
... code to include if test3 is true ...
ELSE
... code to include if all tests are false ...
ENDIF
```

Tests for definition or non-definition of an identifier, by =, EQU, or other means, is done with

```
IFDEF identifier ;       true if identifier has been defined
IFNDEF identifier ;      true if identifier has not been defined
```

Testing for whether an expression is 0 is done by

```
IF expression ;             true if expression is nonzero
```

```
      IFE expression ;                    true if expression is zero
```

Expression can contain the following relations, which evaluate to 0 if false, to nonzero if true:

EQ	EQual	NE	Not Equal
LT	Less Than	LE	Less than or Equal to
GT	Greater Than	GE	Greater than or Equal to

Macros

The basic form of a macro definition is

```
Name       MACRO  param1, param2, ...
           LOCAL  label1, label2, ... ; optional
           ...
label2:

           ...
           prototype of Name into which actual values of param1,
             param2, ... will be substituted.
           ...
label1:

           etc.
           ...
           ENDM
```

The LOCAL declaration is used for labels which are defined in the macro and which must be unique in each invocation of the macro. Parameters can be indicated within quoted strings and juxtaposed with other text by preceding and/or following them by an & character, which is stripped off.

When a macro is invoked (expanded), a parameter can be made to contain special characters (such as blank and comma) by enclosing it in <> brackets. If the invocation has too many parameters, the extras are ignored and if too few, the parameters not specified are set to blank. Testing for blank parameters can be done with

```
     IFB <parameter> ;          true if parameter is blank (or absent)
     IFNB <parameter> ;         true if parameter is non-blank
```

Tests for parameters having specific values are

```
     IFIDN[I] <arg1>, <arg2> ;    true if arg1 is exactly arg2
     IFDIF[I] <arg1>, <arg2> ;    true if arg1 differs from arg2
```

where the optional final "I" indicates case insensitivity.

The pseudo-operation EXITM can be used in macros and pseudo-macros of repetition to terminate macro expansion when EXITM is encountered.

The extent to which macro expansions appear in the .LST file optionally produced by the assembler is controlled by the three pseudo-operations .LALL and .SALL:

`.SALL` Suppress all listing of macro expansion lines

`.LALL` List all lines of macro expansion

Chapter **17**

File Processing

In this chapter, we will discuss the DOS standard file operations as used in assembly language. We will give two substantial applications, give some applications (which are isolated and can be skipped) of the macro techniques introduced in chapter 16, and introduce three useful library utilities. In addition, we will discuss some of the advanced techniques involved in memory management, redirecting I/O, and executing one program from another.

This chapter is optional. There is no strong reason for doing the operations discussed here in assembly language. On the other hand, the chapter gives a number of excellent examples of assembly language technique.

An archaeologist examining the DOS file system would discover several layers. The earliest layer was modeled, like much of the original version of DOS, on the CP/M operating system for 8-bit microcomputers. It had a method of file access using a data structure called **File Control Block** (**FCB**), and is now obsolete since FCBs can't reference files whose names include directory names. We will use the final layer, which was introduced with DOS 2.0 in about 1982. It is modeled after the UNIX file system, with files arranged in a hierarchical (tree-structured) system of directories. Files are referred to internally by an integer called the **file handle**.

Because of its heredity, the DOS file-handle calls bear a strong resemblance to corresponding standard UNIX/C file functions. File names are given by C-style character strings, which are variable-length character strings terminated by the null (binary 0) byte. We will name our DOS file call macros so that they resemble as closely as possible the corresponding UNIX/C functions.

The DOS **open** and **create** operations take as input the file name and return the file handle, a small integer. All other I/O operations use the file handle to specify the file on which they operate. The main operations are sequential reading and writing of the file from the current position (maintained by DOS), and altering the current position to effect random access to the file.

At the start of execution of each program, five standard file handles are open:

stdin	0	The keyboard (can be redirected via <*filename*; see below)
stdout	1	The display (can be redirected via >*filename*; see below)
stderr	2	The display (for error messages; can't be redirected easily)
stdaux	3	The standard AUX device; usually the serial port COM1
stdprn	4	The standard printer device PRN ; usually LPT1

The names in the leftmost column have no fixed significance to DOS; the first three are the corresponding names from the UNIX operating system[*] and the last two are names often used by analogy. Don't worry about AUX, COM1, etc. if you haven't seen them before.

One powerful property of the handle file system is **device independence**. In addition to being able to manipulate disk files, programs can also access devices such as printers, the keyboard, serial ports, etc., with exactly the same set of operations. Of course, only the appropriate operations can be applied to devices—input from the printer is not allowed, for instance, and random access is allowed only on disk files.

UNIX and DOS use device independence to implement **I/O redirection** and **piping**. If one executes a program PROG with the command line

```
PROG ... < infile > outfile
```

then standard input and output are redirected. That is, whenever PROG reads from handle 0, it actually reads from *infile* and whenever it writes to handle 1, it actually writes *outfile*. (Either input or output or both can be redirected.) For instance, the command

```
DIR > PRN
```

will print a directory listing on the standard printer.

In addition, the standard output of one program can be **piped** to the standard input of another. In the command

```
PROG1 | PROG2
```

the standard output (handle 1) of PROG1 is written to a temporary file, which is then read as the standard input (handle 0) of PROG2. (For those familiar with UNIX, since DOS doesn't have multitasking, the two programs are actually run as separate sequential jobs, one after the other.

These two concepts are very powerful when coupled with the notion of a **filter** program. A filter gets its input by reading handle 0 (stdin) and writes all its output to handle 1 (stdout). It can then be given arbitrary input and output files by redirection or piping. For example, DOS includes a standard filter program SORT which sorts ASCII text files. To get a sorted directory listing on the printer, we can execute

```
DIR | SORT > PRN
```

---

[*] Note, though, that there is a subtle difference between DOS and UNIX usage. Under UNIX, stdin, stdout, and stderr are *pointers* to file buffer areas.

For more information on the DOS file system, see any book on DOS fundamentals.

17.1 • Handles and Opening, Creating, and Closing Files

DOS file names are given by 0-terminated variable length character strings. Such a string could be declared for the file name A:\source\myprog.asm by the code

```
theName    DB      'A:\source\myprog.asm', 0
```

Such strings are sometimes called ASCIZ or ASCIIZ strings, being a string of characters terminated by a zero byte.

In order to manipulate such a file, the file name must be associated with a file handle by one of two DOS functions, the **open** function for files that already exist and the create function, called **creat** (yes, no 'e') in UNIX, which creates and opens a new file of that name. (In the latter case, if the file already exists, it's emptied and opened.)

Because only a limited number of files can be open at once, there is also a **close** file DOS call. All files are closed automatically when a program terminates, but it is good practice for the program to do so explicitly.

To keep files from being altered accidently, they can be specified as **read-only** using the DOS attrib +r filename command. Similarly, a file can be *opened* in such a way as to allow reading only, writing only, or reading and writing. It is an error to open a read-only file for writing or to create an already-existing read-only file. As many such errors can occur, some DOS functions can return an error indication.

All DOS calls introduced in this chapter indicate error by returning with the C flag set and an error number in ax.

The PCMAC.INC macros for the **open** and **creat** functions are as follows:

```
        _Open filename, accessmethod[, segment]
;;          accessmethod is one of the three integers 0, 1, or 2,
;;              or one of the corresponding symbolic values Read,
;;              Write, or ReadWrite
;;          If successful, returns carry flag clear and handle
;;              in ax

        _Creat filename[, segment]
;;          If successful, returns carry flag clear and handle
;;              in ax
```

The filename must not have any leading or trailing (or internal) white space (blanks or tabs). Accessmethod can be given numerically or symbolically as specified. The segment parameter is the segment part of the address of filename and is necessary only if the file name isn't in the ds segment. (The brackets […] indicate segment is optional, and never actually appear in either call.)

Closing a file is even simpler:

```
_Close handle
```

To encourage *always* checking for errors, and displaying a meaningful error message if one occurs, a procedure called **CCheck** is included in UTIL.LIB. (The code is discussed in Section 17.5.) CCheck (no parameters) assumes it has been called right after a DOS call which sets the C-flag, in case of error. CCheck checks the C-Flag and if set, prints an appropriate error message and _Exits. The version included here doesn't cover *all* DOS call errors, but should cover all the ones we will see in applications in this book.

Example 17.1—1. Open or create a file whose name is the first parameter on the command line.

The program is not a complete example. It just shows you how to go through very common operations that are preliminary to processing a file.

The operation of extracting a null-terminated file name (and other parameters) from the command line is repeated so frequently that we have abstracted it as another library routine called **ParseCmd**. The code required for parsing in this example isn't very difficult, but it gets trickier when the file name isn't the first parameter and when there may not be enough parameters.

The first time ParseCmd is called, it returns with a pointer to the start of the first parameter in es:si, and the blank or RETURN following the parameter has been changed to a null. With each succeeding call, es:si is returned pointing to the *next* parameter. When there are no more parameters, ParseCmd returns si = 0. There are no input parameters. Once again, the code is developed in Section 17.5.

Now we will use the various procedures and macros we have introduced to write a skeleton program to be invoked by the command

```
openskel filename
```

which will start by opening (or creating) *filename*.

```
;; OPENSKEL--Skeleton program to open or create file whose name
;;        is first parameter on the command line
;;
INCLUDE   PCMAC.INC
          .MODEL SMALL
          .STACK 100h

          .DATA
Handle    DW      ?
Usage     DB      'usage: openskel filename ...', 13, 10, '$'
          . . .

          .CODE
          EXTRN   ParseCmd : NEAR, CCheck : NEAR
OpenSkel  PROC
          mov     ax, @data
          mov     ds, ax
```

```
            call    ParseCmd ;      Returns es:si --> file name
            test    si, si
            jnz     DoOpen ;        Is there a parameter?

            _PutStr Usage ;            no
            _Exit   1
DoOpen:
            push    ds
            _Open   si, accessmethod, es ;     or _Creat si, es
            pop     ds
            call    CCheck
            mov     Handle, ax ;    Save file handle for later use

    ...process the open file...

            _Close  Handle
            _Exit   0 ;             Normal exit
OpenSkel    ENDP
            END     OpenSkel
```

Note that specifying the segment in _Open or _Creat (or anywhere else where it is optional) destroys ds, so here we saved it before the call and restored it afterwards.

Exercises 17.1

1. ✓a) Write a DB statement to define the variable DFile as the file \data\sales.dat in a manner suitable for use by the DOS _Open call.
   b) Write an assembly code fragment to open DFile for read/write access, and if successful, store its handle in the word variable FH.

2. Suppose that PFN is the address of a file name in Turbo Pascal string format—that is, the first byte is the length of the string, as in

```
        PFN         DB      15, '\data\sales.dat'
```

Write an assembly fragment to convert such a name into a zero-terminated file name suitable for use by the _Open call. Do the conversion by 'shifting the name left' one byte and inserting a zero in the vacated end position.

3. Write a separately assembled function ACCESS which takes as input a pointer to a null-terminated file name in ds:si and an _Open access method in ax. The program should return with ax = 1 if the file exists and can be accessed by the given method, 0 otherwise. Proceed by trying to open the file with the specified method, then closing the file if the _Open was successful.

4. ✓Write an assembly code procedure GetNum which takes as input the output of ParseCmd—es:si pointing to a zero-terminated parameter—and determines whether or not the parameter is a number, returning the number if it is. Use Dec2Bin from UTIL.LIB (as described in Section 11.1),

which takes as input a pointer to a byte string in **ds**:si and leaves the number found in ax, carry clear if the number is legal, and si pointing to the first character after the end of the number. GetNum should return the output of Dec2Bin if si is pointing to the zero-byte that terminates the parameter, and return with the carry flag set if not or if Dec2Bin found an error. Recall that stc sets the carry flag and clc clears it. GetNum should not alter any register except ax.

17.2 • Basic File Operations

The beauty of the file handle approach is that DOS defines two basic operations on file handles—**read** and **write**, and these operations are programmed in exactly the same way no matter what type of file is being read or written—disk file, serial port, printer, etc.—and whether input and/or output is redirected.

For disk files, DOS keeps track of the **current position** in each open file. When the file is first opened, the current position is at the beginning of the file. Each time a block of bytes is read or written, the current position is moved to the end of that block. For example, if the file's current position is at byte 123 and 10 bytes are read, then bytes 123, 124, …, 132 will be extracted from the file and the new 'current position' will be at byte 133.

The PCMAC.INC macros for reading and writing are

```
        _Read  Handle, BufferOffset, ByteCount[, BufferSegment]
        _Write Handle, BufferOffset, ByteCount[, BufferSegment]
;;            If successful, each call returns carry clear and ax
;;                equal to the number of bytes read or written
;;        End of file on _Read is indicated by successful read of
;;                0 bytes
```

BufferOffset is the address of an array containing the ByteCount bytes to be written, or at least ByteCount bytes into which bytes will be read. Handle is the value returned in ax by a successful _Open or _Creat, and BufferSegment is the (optional) segment part of the address of the buffer if it isn't already in ds.

It is possible for a valid read to read fewer than the number of bytes requested. A short read will happen if there are fewer bytes left in the file than requested, and as mentioned above, end of file is indicated by 0 bytes read.

On the other hand, it is an error if _Write writes fewer bytes than expected, even though the carry bit isn't set. A short write is usually due to disk being full. It is one of those errors that 'never occurs' but should be checked for anyway. UTIL.LIB contains a routine **WCheck** which is to be called after the _Write command. WCheck first performs a CCheck and if that is successful, compares ax, the actual number of bytes written, with cx, which _Write loaded with the number we attempted to write. (It will still be there on return from DOS.)

Let's give some simple examples of how we might use these operations. We will assume that the file to be operated on is named on the command line and that we have gone through our open procedure from the last section.

Example 17.2—1. Assume an open file with handle in memory location Handle is a text file and display its contents on the CRT. The program here combined with OPENSKEL in the previous section is equivalent to the DOS TYPE command.

The most efficient buffer size is 512 bytes, as the physical organization of disks is in 512-byte blocks and DOS always reads and writes disk files in units of 512 bytes. If a program asks for more or less, or reads or writes in such a way as to span block boundaries, DOS reads the necessary physical block(s), takes the parts needed, and rearranges them into the block asked for.

The one slightly tricky business is that *some* DOS text files are ended with a Ctrl-Z character—ASCII 26. If we _PutCh Ctrl-Z, we will get a spurious backward-pointing arrow. Therefore, we will put in a special case to check for it. Our program will use CCheck, introduced in the last section, to handle _Read errors.

```
;;   Example 17.2--1: Displaying a file--method 1
;;
            .DATA
CTRLZ       EQU     26 ;            Text file terminator
BUFFLEN     EQU     512
Buffer      DB      BUFLEN DUP (?)
            ...
ReadLoop:
            _Read   Handle, Buffer, BUFFLEN
            call    CCheck
ReadOK:
            mov     cx, ax ;        Count of bytes read
            jcxz    Done ;          End of file if # of bytes = 0
            mov     bx, OFFSET Buffer
PutLoop:
            mov     al, [bx]
            cmp     al, CTRLZ
            je      Done
            _PutCh al
            inc     bx
            loop    PutLoop
            jmp     ReadLoop
Done:
```

Notice that we can't use _PutStr to display the block, even if we put a '$' at the end, because if the block contained a '$' character, the display would be stopped prematurely.

We *could* do the display by using _Write to stdout:

```
;;   Example 17.2--1: Method 2
;;
            ...
STDOUT      EQU     1
            ...
ReadOK:
            test    ax, ax
            jz      Done
            _Write STDOUT, Buffer, ax
            call    CCheck
```

```
            jmp     ReadLoop
      Done:
```

Note: We have used `CCheck` instead of `WCheck` here, once again, because of the Ctrl-Z terminator. `_Write` to the screen will not write that Ctrl-Z and as a result, the count will appear wrong. Since that is the only reason that a `_Write` to the screen should give an incorrect count, we simply avoid the check of the count.

The `_Write` macro uses several registers. If we wish to use a register as a parameter as in `_Write STDOUT, Buffer,` **ax** above, we must be sure that the register containing the parameter doesn't get clobbered before it is used. You can check the code in the `_Write` macro and see that `ax` is safe for the byte count, and it's one of the few registers that is. In general, if the byte count is clobbered, even `WCheck` won't catch it, because `WCheck` checks to see if the number of bytes *requested* (in `cx`) was written, *not* if the *correct* number of bytes was requested. One could find such a bug by viewing the actual code generated by the macro (**Alt-V**(iew **C**(PU in TD, **Alt-O**(ptions **S**(ource1 Window… **M**(ixed Source and Assembly in CodeView). We will always make use of `ax` when a register is necessary for `_Write` length.

Example 17.2—2. Write a program

```
      create filename
```

which creates the file `filename` and fills it with text typed in at the keyboard. Stop when a line consisting of two periods (..) is entered.

The `create` program is essentially equivalent to the DOS command

```
      copy con filename
```

except that `copy` uses Ctrl-Z as its terminator.

We are going to use `_GetStr` for input (see Section 10.3.1). The basic pattern of the code is simple:

```
      Get file name from command line and _Creat it;
      while true do { that is, loop forever }
        Use _GetStr to get a line of input
        if line of input = '..' then exit loop end if
        _Write line to file
      end while
      _Close;
```

The complete program is

```
      ;;   Example 17.2--2--CREATE--text from kbd into file, stopping on
      ;;    a line consisting entirely of '..'
      ;;
      ;;     usage:  CREATE filename
      ;;
```

```
        INCLUDE   PCMAC.INC
                  .MODEL SMALL
                  .STACK 100h


                  .DATA
MAXLINE   EQU     128
InBuffer  DB      MAXLINE ;     Buffer for _GetStr
InCount   DB      ?
InLine    DB      MAXLINE DUP (?)


CrLf      DB      13, 10 ;      line-ending carriage return-line
feed
Handle    DW      ? ;               handle of open file
Usage     DB      'usage: create name-of-file', 13, 10, '$'


                  .CODE
                  EXTRN   ParseCmd : NEAR, CCheck : NEAR, WCheck : NEAR
Create    PROC
          mov     ax, @data
          mov     ds, ax
          call    ParseCmd
          test    si, si ;       Is there a parameter
          jnz     DoCreate
          _PutStr Usage ;        No; display usage and exit
          _Exit   1
DoCreate: ;       At this point, es:si --> file name
          push    ds
          _Creat  si,es ;        Destroys ds
          pop     ds
          call    CCheck
          mov     Handle, ax
MainLoop:
          _PutCh '?', ' ' ;              Prompt
          _GetStr InBuffer
          _PutCh 10 ;                Add line feed
          mov     al, InCount
          sub     ah, ah ;           Convert InCount to word
          cmp     al, 2 ;            Look for terminator line
          jne     NotDone
          cmp     WORD PTR InLine, '..'
          je      Done
NotDone:
          _Write Handle, InLine, ax ; Write InCount bytes
          call    WCheck
          _Write Handle, CrLf, 2 ;   Write end of line CR and LF
          call    WCheck
          jmp     MainLoop
```

```
Done:
            _Close Handle
            _Exit  0
Create      ENDP
            END    Create
```

As we have seen before, it is possible to define a *word* constant consisting of *two* characters, say x and y, using the notation 'xy'. We used it above for the constant '. .'.

InCount must be converted to a word because ultimately it will be loaded into cx.

Exercises 17.2.

1. ✓The first two bytes of an EXE file are 4Dh, 5Ah. Supposing that FH contains the file handle of an open file, write assembly code to determine if that file is an EXE file and goes to the label NotEXE if it is not.

2 ✓ Suppose that FH contains the file handle of a file open for write and that Date is the address of a byte string of the form MM/DD/YY containing today's date. Write assembly code to write Date into the current file at the file's current position.

3.   Rewrite Example 17.2—2 using _Read instead of _GetStr. We can also get characters from the keyboard using the _Read STDIN, ... call. When reading from the keyboard, normal keyboard editing takes place, no input comes in until a complete line has been entered, the line is echoed to the screen, and a line feed is added to both the input line and the echoed line. When *n* bytes are requested, *n* bytes or the number of bytes in the input line, whichever is smaller, are placed in the buffer. Carriage return and line feed are treated just like other characters and are included in the count and in the buffer (if there is room). If the whole line can't be read at once, the rest of it will be read on future _Reads.

4.   Write an assembly language program

```
head filename [n]
```

which displays the first *n* lines of the file filename. Use the GetNum procedure developed in Exercise 17.1—4 to get the value of *n*, and use a value of 10 if *n* is not present. (Head is present in some form in many UNIX systems.)

17.3 • Random File Accessing

So far, we have been able to access files only in sequential order, from beginning to end. With devices such as the serial and printer ports, sequential access is naturally the only type of access possible. Disk files on the other hand are **random access** devices, and allow us to jump around in the file and access any part of it at will. [*] A single new DOS call, **lseek**, and continued use of the same

---

[*] Actually a disk drive is often referred to as a **direct access** device, meaning that any part of a file can be accessed in a time which depends only slightly on the part previously accessed (the time to move the disk arm and wait for the required material to come under the read/write head). The name **random access** device is usually reserved for devices (such as RAM) in which access time is totally independent of the last item accessed. This distinction is traditionally blurred.

_Read and _Write calls is all that is required for random access.

Recall that the _Read and _Write DOS calls do their job starting at the "current file pointer" maintained by DOS. All the lseek call does is change the current file pointer! (The name "lseek" comes from the "seek" hardware command which is used to move the disk arm to the proper position. The "l" was added in UNIX because files larger than 64K bytes require a long integer (double word) to specify the position in the file.)

17.3.1 • The _LSeek Macro

The macro which performs the DOS call to relocate the current file pointer is

```
            _LSeek Handle, SeekType, LoDistance[, HiDistance]
;;              SeekType is the actual numerical value of the seek
;;              type, 0, 1, 2, or one of the corresponding symbolic
;;              values FromStart, FromCur, or FromEnd
;;          Seek distance is a double-word integer
;;              HiDistanceLoDistance.
;;              If distance is single precision, positive
;;              or negative, HiDistance can be omitted
;;          If successful, returns carry flag clear and new
;;              current position in dx|ax
```

Note the following cases for seek type:

SeekType	distance	locates to
FromStart	0	the beginning of the file (a 'rewind')
FromStart	n	absolute byte n in the file
FromCur	$n > 0$	n bytes *forward* from the current location
FromCur	$-n, n > 0$	n bytes *back* from the current location
FromEnd	0	the end of the file (and dx|ax becomes file length)
FromEnd	$-n, n < 0$	n bytes back from the end of the file
FromCur	0	File position (unchanged) to dx|ax

The construction of the _LSeek macro is a useful application of the techniques developed in Chapter 16, and will be discussed in Section 17.3.4.

17.3.2 • Applications of _LSeek I: LOG, a Message Logger

The LOG program to be developed here allows the user to record a message along with a date and time stamp in a standard file we will call LOGFILE. For instance, the following three invocations of LOG:

```
log Starting to work on Edwards contract
log Call from Smith
log Back to work on Edwards
```

might append the following lines to LOGFILE

```
10/14/90 11:24:40
      Starting to work on Edwards contract
10/14/90 13:33:24
      Call from Smith
10/14/90 13:47:15
      Back to work on Edwards
```

With only a slight stretch of the imagination, it appears that such a program might even be useful (for billing purposes, etc.).

The program that we develop makes use of _LSeek in only a fairly minor way—to move the file pointer to the end of LOGFILE so we can append to it—but the program develops some other useful techniques.

We need to determine if LOGFILE already exists (in the current directory) and if not, create it. We will use both _Open and _Creat. (If we just used _Creat and the file already existed, its previous contents would be wiped out.) To check for existence, we first try to open the file for Write Only. This open can fail for two possible reasons: either the file doesn't exist or it exists and has been marked Read Only. In the latter case, there is nothing we can do but _Exit with an error message. In the former case, we create the file with _Creat.

For our second new technique, recall the DOS call macro _GetDate which gets current date information and macro _GetTime which returns current time information. They were introduced in Programming Problems 3.1 and 7.1, respectively. They return information as follows:

_GetDate: dh = month, dl = day, cx = year, al = weekday (0 = Sunday)

_GetTime: ch = hour (24 hour clock), cl = minute, dh = second,
          dl = hundredths of a second

The only thing needed then to print the date stamp is the ability to turn small numbers into two digit decimal numbers. We could use one of our previous decimal number printing programs, but prefer to introduce a standard (dirty?) trick for doing two-digit numbers on the 80X86. Its only flaw is that it doesn't delete leading zeroes, though that would be easy enough to add.

The crucial part of the trick is a new instruction, aam.

```
        aam    ;       ASCII Adjust result of Multiplication
;                      sets ah := al / 10, al := al mod 10
```

That is to say, if we execute

```
        mov    al, 38
        aam
        add    ax, '00'
```

then ah contains '3' and al contains '8'! If we store ax directly in memory, byte swapping will put the bytes in the wrong order, but all we have to do to fix that is xchg al, ah and we have a nifty three instruction conversion routine.

The rest of the code of the LOG program is straightforward:

```
;; LOG.ASM--Program looks for a file LOGFILE in current directory
;;   and if it doesn't exist, creates one.  It then appends to
;;   this file current date and time (form mm/dd/yy hh:mm:ss), then
;;   on the following line, indented four spaces, writes the
;;   rest of the command that invoked it.
;;
;;   LOG makes use of a procedure TwoDigs defined here which takes
;;     number from 0 to 99 in al and converts it to two consecutive
;;     ASCII digits at si.  Si is then updated to point to the
;;     character after the second digit, + 1.

INCLUDE PCMAC.INC

        .MODEL SMALL
        ASSUME SS:NOTHING

        .STACK 100h

PSP       SEGMENT AT 0-256
          ORG    128
CmdLen    DB     ?
Command   DB     127 DUP (?)
PSP       ENDS

          .DATA
FileName DB       'LOGFILE', 0
AccessMsg DB      'Cannot access LOGFILE$'
NoCreate  DB      'Cannot create LOGFILE$'
WErrMsg   DB      'LOGFILE write error$'
Stamp     DB      'mm/dd/yy hh:mm:ss'
CRLF      DB      13, 10 ;     Used both for Stamp and by itself
STAMPLEN  EQU     $ - Stamp ;  Number of bytes to write for Stamp
INDENT    EQU     4
LogIndent DB      INDENT DUP (' ')

Do2       MACRO  whence
          mov    al, &whence&
          call   TwoDigs
          ENDM

          .CODE
          EXTRN  CCheck : NEAR, WCheck : NEAR
Logger    PROC
          mov    ax, @Data
          mov    ds, ax
          ASSUME es:PSP
```

```
        _Open  FileName, Write ;   Get Log File
        jnc    GotLogFile
        _Creat FileName ;     File doesn't exist (or is read-only)
        call   CCheck ;                 Try to make it
GotLogFile:
        mov    di, ax ;           Save handle in di
        _LSeek di, FromEnd, 0 ;   Seek to end of file
        call   CCheck

;   Write date and time stamp

        _GetDate
        mov    si, OFFSET Stamp
        Do2    dh ;                 Month
        Do2    dl ;                 Day
        sub    cx, 1900 ;           Reduce year to 2 digits
        Do2    cl ;                 Year
        _GetTime
        Do2    ch ;                 Hour
        Do2    cl ;                 Minute
        Do2    dh ;                 Second
        _Write di, Stamp, STAMPLEN
        call   WCheck

;   Write log message

        _Write di, LogIndent, INDENT
        call   WCheck
        push   ds ;             must have ds --> PSP for next _Write
        mov    al, CmdLen
        sub    ah, ah ;             Convert CmdLen to word
        _Write di, Command, ax, es
        pop    ds
        call   WCheck
        _Write di, CRLF, 2
        call   WCheck

        _Close di
        _Exit  0
Logger  ENDP

TwoDigs PROC
        aam    ; Standard trick to convert # <= 99 to
        add    ax, '00' ;   two ASCII digits; store at [si]
        xchg   ah, al
        mov    [si], ax
        add    si, 3 ;       skip si over digits and punctuation
```

```
                  ret
         TwoDigs  ENDP

                  END      Logger
```

17.3.3 • Applications of `_LSeek` II: `Tail`, an End of File Displayer

In this section, we are going to develop a program TAIL such that the command TAIL *filename* displays the last ten lines of *filename* on the CRT. (*Filename* is assumed to be a text file.) TAIL is a standard utility program in the UNIX operating system.

A simple-minded way to display the tail (and the *only* way to do it without random access!) is to read the whole file a line at a time, at each stage keeping track of the last ten lines read. Each time a new line is read, it replaces the oldest remaining line in our storage. The problem with this sequential method is that if the file is large, it takes a long time (and if the file is small, you can get pretty much the same result by just TYPEing it).

Since we can move around in a file at random, a more efficient method is to move to the end of the file and read backwards ten lines. Each line ends with a carriage return-line feed pair, so if we read backward and count line feeds, when we get to the eleventh line feed, it will be just in front of the tenth line from the end. The code is quite simple:

```
         mov      LFcnt, 11 ;              Line Feed Count
         _LSeek Handle, FromEnd, -1 ;      Seek to read last byte
ReadLoop:
         _Read    Handle, Buffer, 1
         cmp      Buffer, LF
         jne      NextByte
         dec      LFcnt
         jz       Found
NextByte:
         _LSeek Handle, FromCur, -2 ;      Back over byte just read
         jmp      ReadLoop ;               ...and previous byte
Found:   ;               At this point, file pointer points to
         ;                  first byte of first line to display
```

The well-educated computer scientist (such as your author) objects to the method above because he or she *knows* that it is very inefficient to read a disk file one byte at a time. Therefore, the first version of the tail program I wrote was very elegant, with 512 byte buffers and multiple precision arithmetic for the _LSeeks (and special string processing operations from Chapter 18 to find the line feeds fast). I figured though that before making wild statements about how much better my elegant method was, I'd better try the 'slow' method: one byte at a time. On my machine of the time (a moderately fast 386 with a moderately fast disk), I couldn't tell the difference! (I think the reason is that DOS does a lot of buffering of its own.) We will give the elegant solution later, in Chapter 18, but for this particular program, the 'inefficient' solution is just fine, and is shorter and easier to debug.

The only problem is how we deal with a file that contains fewer than 10 lines. There seems to be no official word as to what is supposed to happen when you lseek to a position before the start of a file. A little experimental computer science—trying it and watching the results with a debugger—

shows that _LSeek is perfectly happy to locate before the beginning of the file. It simply returns dx|ax negative. One should use **extreme caution** with such undocumented features. There is no guarantee that such features will work for other versions of DOS or that it will continue to work with future versions! (The solution in Chapter 18 does not depend on this undocumented property of _LSeek).

The program is as follows (code other than the usual boilerplate is in boldface):

```
;;   TAIL.ASM -- display the last ten lines of a text file ;
            .MODEL SMALL
INCLUDE PCMAC.INC
            .STACK 100h

CR          EQU    13
LF          EQU    10
WANTED      EQU    10 ;          Number of lines of tail desired
BUFLEN      EQU    512 ;         Still use buffer for output
STDOUT      EQU    1

            .DATA
Buffer      DB     BUFLEN DUP (?)
LFcnt       DB     ? ;           saver than using a register
Handle      DW     ?
UsageMsg    DB     'usage: tail filename',CR,LF,'$'

            .CODE
            EXTRN  ParseCmd : NEAR, CCheck : NEAR, WCheck : NEAR
Tail        PROC
            mov    ax, @data
            mov    ds, ax
            call   ParseCmd
            test   si, si
            jnz    DoOpen
            _PutStr UsageMsg
            _Exit  2
DoOpen:
            push   ds
            _Open  si, Read, es
            pop    ds
            call   CCheck
            mov    Handle, ax

            mov    LFcnt, WANTED + 1
            _LSeek Handle, FromEnd, -1 ; Prepare to read last byte
            call   CCheck
ReadLoop:
            test   dx, dx ;               Test for Beginning of File
            jge    ReadByte
```

```
              _LSeek Handle, FromStart, 0 ; Done; go to start of file
              call   CCheck
              jmp    DispLoop ;          and display the whole file
ReadByte:
              _Read  Handle, Buffer, 1
              call   CCheck
              cmp    Buffer, LF
              jne    NextByte
              dec    LFcnt ;             Number of lines still wanted
              jz     DispLoop ;          Done, display from current pos
NextByte:
              _LSeek Handle, FromCur, -2 ; Back over byte just read
              call CCheck ;                      and previous byte
              jmp    ReadLoop
DispLoop:
;  At this point, it's the 2nd version of the DISPLAY program,
;    Example 18.2--1
              _Read  Handle, Buffer, BUFLEN
              call   CCheck
              test   ax, ax
              jz     Done
              _Write STDOUT, Buffer, ax
              call   CCheck ;       Instead of WCheck since a Ctrl-Z
;                     terminating a text filc won't write
;                     and would look like an incorrect count
              jmp    DispLoop
Done:
              _Exit  0;                          Normal termination
Tail          ENDP
              END    Tail
```

17.3.4 • Writing the _Lseek Macro

In this section we will develop the _LSeek macro. It requires techniques developed in Chapter 16 and can be skipped.

First, let's look at the lseek DOS command and try to get an idea of what sort of macro we might want to write. The parameters are

Input Parameters:

ah	42h (= LSEEK function code)
al	0 = seek relative to start of file
	1 = seek relative to current file pointer
	2 = seek relative to end of file
bx	File Handle of open disk file
cx|dx	Distance to move file pointer (in bytes)

Output Parameters:

> If successful, carry is clear and dx|ax contains the new current file position (in bytes from the beginning of the file).
> If unsuccessful, carry is set and ax contains the error number.

The notations cx|dx and dx|ax here are used for double-word (32-bit) numbers (See the beginning of Chapter 15). X|Y refers to an integer whose first (high-order) 16 bits are X and whose last (low order) 16 bits are Y

A simple-minded version _LSeek macro might be as follows:

```
_LSeek    MACRO   Handle, SeekType, LoDistance, HiDistance
          mov     cx, &HiDistance&
          mov     dx, &LoDistance&
          mov     bx, &Handle&
          mov     al, &SeekType&
          mov     ah, 42h
          int     21h
          ENDM
```

The order of loading the registers was carefully chosen to try to avoid register conflicts. If the distance is already in registers, the most likely place is dx|ax—that is where it would be as a result of multiplication, the cwd instruction, or another _LSeek. The command '_LSeek *Handle, SeekType*, ax, dx' then expands into the code

```
mov    cx, dx
mov    dx, ax
. . .
```

If we had reversed the order of these two instructions, or tried to load ax first, we would have wiped something out.

To change _LSeek into the macro we specified at the start of Section 17.3.1, we need 1) to make HiDistance optional and 2) to allow symbolic values for SeekType.

The solution of the first problem is not as simple as changing the code to

```
IFNB <&HiDistance&>
          mov     cx, &HiDistance&
ELSE
          sub     cx, cx ;      BAD SOLUTION!!
ENDIF
          mov     dx, &LoDistance&
```

The solution above only works with *positive* distances. To make it work properly with negative distances, we need to use cwd, which means that LoDistance must start out in ax, and then we must shuffle the registers around properly. It is necessary to use two entirely different schemes to load the registers:

```
        IFNB <&HiDistance&>
                mov     cx, &HiDistance&
                mov     dx, &LoDistance&
        ELSE
            IFDIFI <&LoDistance&>, <ax>
                mov     ax, &LoDistance&
            ENDIF
                cwd
                mov     cx, dx
                mov     dx, ax
        ENDIF
```

We use IFIDNI to check for the symbolic versions of SeekType and get the final macro:

```
_LSeek    MACRO  Handle, SeekType, LoDistance, HiDistance
IFNB <&HiDistance&>
                mov     cx, &HiDistance&
                mov     dx, &LoDistance&
ELSE
    IFDIFI <&LoDistance&>, <ax>
                mov     ax, &LoDistance&
    ENDIF
                cwd
                mov     cx, dx
                mov     dx, ax
ENDIF
                mov     bx, &Handle&
IFIDNI <&SeekType&>, <FromStart>
                mov     al, 0
ELSEIFIDNI <&SeekType&>, <FromCur>
                mov     al, 1
ELSEIFIDNI <&SeekType&>, <FromEnd>
                mov     al, 2
ELSE
                mov     al, &SeekType&
ENDIF
                mov     ah, 42h
                int     21h
                ENDM
```

Exercises 17.3

1. ✓Write assembly code to find and display the length of the open file whose handle is in FH. Use the MPPutDec procedure developed in Section 15.1 to display the double-precision number returned in dx∣ax by an _LSeek call.

2. Let FH contain the handle of an open file.

a) Write assembly code to save the current position of the file in a double word variable IWasHere.

b) Write assembly code to reset the current position in the file to that given in IWasHere.

3. Write a variant TwoDigit of the procedure TwoDigs in LOG which takes as input a number in al, $0 \le al < 100$, and a pointer in si. TwoDigit converts al into one or two ASCII decimal digits without leading zeroes (except for al = 0) and stores them at si, updating si so that it points to the byte after the last digit stored.

4. Show how the GetNum procedure of Exercise 17.1—4 could be used to alter tail so that the command

```
tail filename [n]
```

with optional number of lines n would display the last n lines of *filename* rather than the default 10.

17.4 • A Little Something Extra: Redirecting `stderr`

As we have seen, it is possible to redirect the standard keyboard input and CRT output of a program from the command line. There is no built-in way to redirect standard error output, though. (The whole rationale behind stderr is that you probably want to *see* the error messages immediately.) The inability to redirect stderr can be a problem when you are getting too many error messages too quickly from a compiler or when you are writing an editor like ed, which wants to examine and display error messages. In this section, we are going to develop a semi-useful utility program called REDIRERR. The invocation

```
redirerr filename command
```

causes *command* to be executed in such a way that its output to stderr is redirected to *filename*. (It is possible, using the methods here, to redirect any of the other standard handles, but stderr seems the most useful.)

This section will constitute a case study of how the author wrote REDIRERR and debugged it. In the process, we will introduce some new DOS calls. NOTE: Although the program we will develop appears to make essential use of the fact that we are using assembly language, it can in fact be written more simply in any competent C/C++ or Pascal for the PC.

Before we can write the program, we have two problems to solve:

- Open a file (the replacement for stderr) in such a way that it gets a particular handle (2 = stderr).
- Execute one program from within another.

The first problem is easily solved using a standard UNIX trick: whenever a file is opened, it is given the smallest unused handle. Therefore, to open a file in such a way that its handle is n, all we have to do is make sure that all the handles 0 to $n − 1$ are in use by open files and that handle n is not in use. In the case of stderr = 2, it is normally the case that files with handles 0 and 1 are open (stdin and stdout) so all we have to do is *close* stderr and then *open* the file we are interested in.

To solve the second problem, we introduce the DOS EXEC function. When one program executes another, the program doing the executing is called the *parent* program (or process) and the program being executed is called the *child* program (or process). Under DOS, the child program is loaded above the parent in memory and executed until its conclusion, at which time control is returned to the parent program. The DOS EXEC call parameters are

> ah = 4bh
>
> al = 0 (if al = 3, the program is loaded but not executed)
>
> ds:dx is the address of the null-terminated file name of the child program. The full path name and extension (for example, .EXE) of the file name must be given. The PATH variable is not used to find the file. (The DOS program COMMAND.COM which processes typed commands searches the PATH variable and performs an EXEC to execute your program. The file COMMAND.COM must be EXECed if you wish to execute .BAT files or certain internal DOS commands like DIR. See Example 17.4—2 below.)
>
> es:bx is the address of a 7-word **parameter block**, which is in the following form:

> > word 0: The segment of the string of environment variables to be passed to the EXECed program. As we saw in Programming Problem 12.2, the segment with the environment variables for the current program is given in location 2ch of the PSP, and we will simply pass that on to the EXECed program
> >
> > words 1, 2: The segment:offset address of the tail of the command to be executed, as it would appear starting at byte 80h of the PSP. That is, a byte containing the command length, followed by all characters of the command except the command name, followed by a return (13) character.
> >
> > words 2, 3 and words 4, 5: These contain segment:offset pointers to FCBs (see the start of this chapter). The first two parameters on the command line are parsed as file names by COMMAND.COM and the data stored in two FCBs in the PSP. The pointers in these words allow that information to be set up for the program being EXECed. Since FCBs are obsolete, we will use the value –1 for each, which indicates that no FCBs are present.

The EXEC call returns with the carry flag set and an error number in ax if it was not successful, and we can use CCheck as usual. Otherwise, the parent program waits until the child program is done executing, at which time the EXEC call returns to the parent with carry clear.

The EXEC call itself saves and restores **only** the cs segment register! Therefore the parent—the program making the EXEC call—must save ss and sp itself, *and must do so in its code segment*, as that's the only segment it will be able to find when the EXEC call returns!

To get our feet wet with the EXEC call, we will construct a program whose only purpose is to execute another program.

Example 17.4—1. Write a program which executes the program CmdTail from Example 12.5—1 with the command tail ' the command tail.' The output should be

```
My command tail is | the command tail|
```

When I first tried the EXEC DOS call as described above, CmdTail was not executed and running CCheck after the call showed me that I had an out of memory error. As we saw in Debug

Workshop V, the word at 02h in the PSP is the segment address of the next memory location available, and normally that will be A000h—that is, all of available memory is allocated to the expectant parent and no memory is available for the child program. What we have to do is release the memory above the parent program which it isn't using.

We use the **realloc** DOS call (named after a similar UNIX function) to *change* the size of a memory allocation. It uses the following parameters:

> ah = 4ah
> bx = number of paragraphs (1 paragraph = 16 bytes) required in the new allocation (can be greater than or less than the original allocation)
> es = segment address of start of allocation (PSP here)

In case of error, the carry flag is set as usual and bx contains the maximum number of paragraphs actually available for the allocation. CCheck can be used to check for errors.

In order to release unnecessary memory, we must know how much memory we are actually using. The number of paragraphs is (last segment + number of paragraphs in last segment – first segment). The first segment is, of course, the PSP, whose segment address will be in es when the program starts, and the stack segment always comes last. Therefore, the number of paragraphs used by the program is (ss + (*stacksize* +15)/ 16 – es). The 15 is added to *stacksize* to round it up to a whole number of paragraphs.

The program, with parts directly involved in the EXEC call in boldface, is

```
;;   EXECER.ASM--EXEC the program CmdTail with command tail
;;    ' the command tail'  Should produce the output
;;
;;        My command tail is | the command tail|
;;
INCLUDE   PCMAC.INC
          .MODEL SMALL
          ASSUME SS:NOTHING


STACKSIZE EQU    100h ;         For later use by REALLOC
          .STACK STACKSIZE


PSP       SEGMENT AT 0-256
          ORG    2Ch
EnvirSeg  DW     ?
PSP       ENDS


          .DATA
CmdFile   DB     'cmdtail.exe', 0
CmdTail   DB     17, ' the command tail ', 13
ParmBlock DW     ? ;              For the Environment Vbls segment
          DD     CmdTail
          DD     -1, -1 ;    Null FCBs
```

```
                .CODE
                EXTRN   CCheck : NEAR
SaveSS          DW      ?
SaveSP          DW      ?
execer          PROC
                mov     ax, @data
                mov     ds, ax
                ASSUME es:PSP
                mov     ax, EnvirSeg
                mov     ParmBlock, ax

;   Code to release excess memory

                mov     bx, ss ;     Compute number of paragraphs required
;                                           (stack is last segment)
                add     bx, (STACKSIZE+15)/16 ;   stack size in paragraphs
                mov     ax, es
                sub     bx, ax ;      bx = # of paragraphs in program
                mov     ah, 4ah ;     REALLOC
                int     21h
                call    CCheck

                mov     SaveSP, sp
                mov     SaveSS, ss
                push    ds
                pop     es
                ASSUME es:@data
                mov     dx, OFFSET CmdFile ;       ds:dx --> file to EXEC
                mov     bx, OFFSET ParmBlock ;     es:bx --> param block
                mov     ax, 4b00h
                int     21h
                ASSUME ds:NOTHING, es:NOTHING
                cli
                mov     ss, SaveSS
                mov     sp, SaveSP
                sti
                call    CCheck
                _Exit   0
execer          ENDP
                END     execer
```

Making sure that both ds and es contain the proper segments is important to the working of the program above. (The author managed to foul it up in an early version, resulting in a great deal of mystery.)

If one needed to save and restore es, ds, or any other registers over the EXEC call, they can be pushed before ss/sp are saved and popped after they are restored.

Exercise 15.3—2, explained the necessity of not allowing an interrupt between mov ss, . . .

and `mov sp, ...` hence the `cli`/`sti` pair around these instructions. We must restore `ss:sp` *before* we call `CCheck` since the call itself uses the stack.

If you were to try to EXECute a DOS internal command in the manner above, you would find that it would fail. The following example shows the correct technique.

Example 17.4—2. Have the parent program execute the internal DOS command DIR *.*.

The only changes required to Example 17.4—1 are to `CmdFile` and `CmdTail`:

```
CmdFile    DB      '\command.com', 0 ; Assuming command.com is in \
CmdTail    DB      11, ' /c dir *.*', 13
```

Returning to `REDIRERR`, we need a program to execute which writes to `stderr`, so I chose to use a small modification of the `CmdTail` program cited in Example 17.4—1 which copies its command tail to `stderr`.

Example 17.4—3. A program `ErrLine` which copies its command tail to `stderr`.

The important changes to `CmdTail` (see Example 12.5—1) are shown in boldface:

```
;; ERRLINE.ASM--program to write its command tail on stderr
;;   The command line
;;
;;          errline stuff and more stuff
;;   writes the following on stderr:
;;          The command tail is | stuff and more stuff|
;;
INCLUDE    PCMAC.INC
           .MODEL SMALL
           ASSUME SS:NOTHING

           .STACK 100h

PSP        SEGMENT AT 0-256
           ORG     80h
CmdLen     DB      ?
Command    DB      127 DUP (?)
PSP        ENDS

STDERR     EQU     2
CR         EQU     13
LF         EQU     10


           .DATA
Msg        DB      'The command tail is |'
CRLF       DB      '|',CR, LF ;  To terminate line to stderr
```

```
                .CODE
                EXTRN   WCheck : NEAR
ErrLine         PROC
                mov     ax, @data
                mov     ds, ax
                ASSUME  es:PSP

                _Write STDERR, Msg, CRLF-Msg
                call    WCheck

                mov     al, CmdLen
                sub     ah, ah ;            ax := command length
                push    ds
                _Write STDERR, Command, ax, es
                pop     ds
                call    WCheck
                _Write STDERR, CRLF, 3 ;    Output CR/LF
                call    WCheck
                _Exit   0
ErrLine         ENDP
                END     ErrLine
```

It was easy enough to debug ErrLine program. Run by itself, it will display its command tail on the CRT.

The general outline of REDIRERR should now be clear. We must parse the command line to REDIRERR, extracting ErrFile, the name of the file to which stderr is redirected (null-terminated so we can use _Creat) and CmdFile and CmdTail. We need a null-terminated string for ErrFile and CmdFile, so ParseCmd sounds like the tool we need. The only problem arises in getting CmdTail, which may consist of several parameters. We recognize that after ErrFile and CmdFile have been parsed off, ParseCmd knows where CmdTail starts, so all we have to do is make the pointer to that place a PUBLIC variable, which we will call CmdTail. The general outline of the parsing code is

```
                .DATA
                EXTRN   CmdTail : DWORD
                ...
                .CODE
                ...
                call    ParseCmd
;       save es:si in ErrFile variable
                call    ParseCmd
;       save es:si in CmdFile variable
;       add an extra blank and the character count two bytes before
;             CmdTail and store CmdTail - 2 in ParmBlock
```

Error checking must be done to make sure that ErrFile and CmdFile actually point to something. Part way into the debugging, it was also realized that adding two bytes to the beginning of CmdTail (for the count and initial blank) would clobber the end of CmdFile, so CmdFile had to be moved out of the way. Therefore, rather than saving a *pointer* to the command file, the characters were moved to a byte array called CmdFile in .DATA.

Once we have found *ErrFile*, all we have to do to redirect stderr is execute

```
_Close 2 ;            stderr
_Creat ErrFile
```

After a certain amount of agony, I managed to get the following command to work successfully.

```
redirerr errfile errline.exe A Message
```

(By the way, if you need to set a breakpoint in the child program, the only way is to insert an int 3 instruction in it or call the Int3 procedure as described in Section 15.3.2.)

The next order of business was to see if the program would work with a device. My assumption was that a common application would be to redirect error output to the printer, PRN:. When I tried that, I got the error message 'File not found' when trying to create ErrFile. This error has error number 2 which, according to the DOS technical reference, isn't a valid error for the creat function. Well, I figured, that's not too surprising. Maybe _Creat doesn't work if you feed it a device name.

Next, I tried doing an _Open call on PRN:. Same results, even to the same (undocumented) error message. Taking the random approach, I tried PRN (without the colon) and the program worked fine. Apparently, whereas DOS *commands* accept device names such as 'PRN:' with the following colon, DOS *function calls* don't. To make my program accept both styles of names, too, I added code to see if ErrFile was at least three characters long (to eliminate disk names such as A:), the last character being a colon; and in that case I deleted the last character.

Here, finally, is the completed program:

```
;; REDIRERR.ASM--redirect stderr of command being executed to file
;;
;;   Form of Call:
;;
;;          redirerr <error output file> <command to be executed>
;;
;; The <command> must give the complete file name, including
;;   extension (.EXE or .COM) and the command file must either be
;;   in the current directory or its full path name must be given.
;;   The PATH variable isn't used.

INCLUDE    PCMAC.INC
           .MODEL SMALL
           ASSUME SS:NOTHING

StackSize EQU    100h ;        To avoid a magic constant
           .STACK StackSize
```

```
PSP         SEGMENT AT 0-256
            ORG     2ch
EnvirSeg DW     ? ;                 Segment containing environment vars
            ORG     128
CmdLen      DB      ?
CmdLine     DB      127 DUP (?)
PSP         ENDS


            .DATA
UsageMsg DB     'usage: redirerr errfile command [params]'
            DB      13, 10, '$'

CmdFile     DB      128 DUP (?)
ErrFile     DW      ? ;             OFFSET to err file name in PSP
            EXTRN   CmdTail : DWORD

ParmBlock DW    ? ;                     EnvirSeg transferred from PSP
TailPtr     DD      ? ;                 CmdTail moved here
            DD      -1, -1 ;        FCBs from command line; obsolete

PSPSeg      DW      ? ;             to make loading seg regs easier
STDERR      EQU     2


            .CODE
StackSave PROC
SaveSS      DW      ? ;             Storage to save and restore ss, sp
SaveSP      DW      ? ;                 over EXEC.  Must be in Code Seg!!
StackSave ENDP


RedirErr    PROC
            EXTRN   ParseCmd : NEAR, CCheck : NEAR
            mov     ax, @data
            mov     ds, ax
            ASSUME es:PSP, ds:@data
            mov     PSPSeg, es
            mov     ax, EnvirSeg ; Seg of Envir Vbls to Param Block
            mov     ParmBlock, ax
;   Parse Command Line:
            call    ParseCmd
            test    si, si ;        es will still contain PSP if si <> 0
            jnz     GotErrfile
Usage:
            _PutStr UsageMsg
            _Exit 1
GotErrFile:
            mov     ErrFile, si
            mov     di, si ;        Check ErrFile for removable ':'
```

```
FindEnd: ;                    Find end of ErrFile
         inc    di ;          ErrFile will have at least one byte
         cmp    BYTE PTR es:[di], 0
         jne    FindEnd
         add    si, 3 ;       Is ErrFile name long enough?
         cmp    si, di
         jae    GetCmd ;           no
         cmp    BYTE PTR es:[di-1], ':' ; Name ends with a colon?
         jne    GetCmd
         mov    BYTE PTR es:[di-1], 0 ;      yes, lop off the ':'
GetCmd:
         call   ParseCmd
         test   si, si
         jz     Usage
         mov    bx, OFFSET CmdFile ; Must move executable file
         sub    bx, si ;       name away from Command Tail as it
MovLoop:        ;                    will be expanded to the left
         mov    al, es:[si]
         mov    [bx + si], al
         test   al, al
         jz     MovDone
         inc    si
         jmp    MovLoop
MovDone:
         les    bx, CmdTail ; Now set up command tail
         test   bx, bx
         jz     TailEmpty ;         Must create a tail
         ASSUME es : PSP, ds : @data ;    (For doc purposes)
         mov    al, CmdLen
         add    ax, OFFSET CmdLine
         sub    al, bl ;          al = # of chars left
         inc    al ;              add a blank
         mov    ah, ' '
         sub    bx, 2
         mov    es:[bx], ax
         jmp    StoreTail
TailEmpty:
         mov    es, PSPSeg
         mov    bx, OFFSET CmdLen
         mov    WORD PTR es:[bx], (13 SHL 8) + 0 ; Empty Cmd Tail
StoreTail:
         mov    WORD PTR TailPtr, bx
         mov    WORD PTR TailPtr + 2, es

         _Close STDERR ;      Now replace stderr with ErrFile
         push   ds
         _Creat ErrFile, es ; Should give a handle of stderr
```

```
            pop     ds
            call    CCheck

            ASSUME  ds : @data, es : PSP
            mov     bx, ss ;        Stack Segment is last
            add     bx, (StackSize+15)/10h ; Number of pars in stack
            sub     bx, PSPSeg ; Release extra memory; es = start
            mov     ah, 4ah ;         address (PSP); bx = # of pars
            int     21h ;           still needed
            call    CCheck

            mov     ax, ds
            mov     es, ax
            ASSUME  es : @data
            push    ds ;    For form's sake;  Exec destroys these
            push    es
            mov     SaveSS, ss ; Explicit seg override necessary if
            mov     SaveSP, sp ;    these are declared AFTER use
            mov     bx, OFFSET ParmBlock ;    ES:BX --> Param Block
            mov     dx, OFFSET CmdFile ;      DS:DX --> Command
            mov     ax, 4b00h ;  AL = 0 indicates EXEC subfunction
            int     21h

            cli
            mov     ss, SaveSS
            mov     sp, SaveSP
            sti
            pop     es
            pop     ds
            call    CCheck

            _Close  STDERR
            _Exit   0
RedirErr    ENDP
            END     RedirErr
```

At FindEnd, when we wished to see if we needed to delete a colon from the end of ErrFile, we could have used the fact that the pointer CmdTail is pointing to the character just after the null-byte terminating ErrFile. This assumption would be dangerous for two reasons. First, if the user didn't supply enough parameters, CmdTail might be the null pointer already. Even worse, this property of CmdTail isn't a part of the specification of ParseCmd. (We might later change ParseCmd to move CmdTail to the actual beginning of the next parameter, perhaps skipping over blanks, and then the program above would cease to work.)

Note that if there is no command tail, we create one at the beginning of the command area of the PSP. Nothing else will be wiped out, though, as the earliest the ErrFile name can start is at offset 82h, and our created command tail will be in bytes 80h and 81h.

The notion of executing a command line in special circumstances shows up over and over again in DOS utilities. For instance, the `ed` editor that comes with this book EXECs masm or tasm, redirecting its `stderr` output to a file so it can read the file and display the error messages to the user. In order to do a temporary exit to DOS, it EXECs `command.com`. The program `tee.com` that comes with the `WinEdit` editor (see appendix C) works somewhat similarly to REDIRERR, executing its command line and displaying `stdout` in *addition* to allowing it to be redirected.

17.5 • The Utility Routines `ParseCmd`, `CCheck`, and `WCheck`

These routines are all rather simple but they do contain a few useful tricks.

In `ParseCmd`, introduced in Section 17.1, we have to be able to recognize three simple situations: 1) `ParseCmd` has never been called, so a pointer to the command line in the PSP must be initialized; 2) scanning is in progress and new command-line arguments are a possibility; and 3) all command-line arguments have been scanned off. We distinguish these three by keeping a segment:offset pointer `CmdTail`. Initially its segment part is 0, causing State 1 to be entered. The segment:offset pointer is set to PSP:81h, the beginning of the command line, and we proceed to State 2. Whether we enter State 2 after initializing for the first parameter, or directly, when looking for later parameters, we search for the first non-blank character, updating the segment:offset pointer as we go. If the first non-blank encountered is a Return, then we go to State 3, which is indicated by the segment part of the pointer being non-zero but the offset part being 0. If instead we found a parameter, we save its starting location for later return to the caller and continue searching for a blank, tab, or Return, which is replaced by a null byte. If a Return was the terminating character found, we also change state to 3 by setting the offset part of `CmdTail` (the first word) to 0. (In order to make sure that a Return is present, we will have to do the check mentioned in Section 12.5.)

As we saw in the last section, it is useful to have a pointer to the remaining command tail at any time (in states 2 and 3), so we will make `CmdTail` a PUBLIC double word variable in `.DATA`.

The code for scanning off the parameter in state 2 is a little tricky. In pseudo-code form, it is

```
es:si := CmdTail;
while es:[si] is a blank or tab do
        inc si
if es:[si] = RETURN then
        set state := 3 and return si = 0; { no parameter }
{ at this point, es:si is set to the final return value }
bx := si;
while es:[bx] > ' ' do  { look for end }
        inc bx
if es:[bx] = RETURN then set state := 3;
else CmdTail := es:bx+1
es:[bx] := 0;
```

The only remaining problem we have is finding the location of the PSP. We could assume that it is still lying around in `es` on first entry (as it probably is), but to make the routine more general, we make use of the Get PSP DOS command, function 62h, which is available in DOS 3.0 and after. It returns the PSP segment in `bx`. To give us a second chance at success, we check the DOS version using DOS command 30h (see Programming Problem 16.1) and if the version is less than 3.0, assume the PSP segment is in `es` and display a warning to that effect. If you expect to use the program below with DOS versions less than 3.0, you will probably want to remove the warning. The program is

```
;;   PARSECMD.ASM--A function which returns successively with es:si
;;    pointing to null-terminated command-line arguments.  When the
;;    end of the arguments is reached, returns si = 0
            .MODEL SMALL
            ASSUME SS:NOTHING

PSP         SEGMENT AT 0-256
            ORG     80h
CmdLen      DB      ?
Command     DB      127 DUP (?)
PSP         ENDS


            .DATA
            PUBLIC CmdTail ;     RedirErr uses CmdTail
CmdTail     DD      0 ;     Segment of 0 indicates CmdTail not yet
;                           initialized (state 1).  Seg <> 0 and
;                           offset = 0 indicates we've reached the
;                           end of the command line
CMDSEG      EQU     WORD PTR CmdTail + 2 ;   Low order first
CMDOFF      EQU     WORD PTR CmdTail
Warning     DB      'Warning:  ParseCmd assuming es = SEG PSP'
            DB      13, 10, '$'

            .CODE
            Public ParseCmd
ParseCmd    PROC
            push    ds
            push    bx
            mov     si, @data ;  Using si as we needn't save and
            mov     ds, si ;        restore it
            ASSUME ds : @data, es : NOTHING
            cmp     CMDSEG, 0
            jne     NotFirst ;   Not first call to ParseCmd
            push    ax ;         State 1:  Use DOS call to get PSP loc
            mov     ah, 30h
            int     21h ;              Get version
            cmp     al, 3
            jge     Version3
            _PutStr Warning
            mov     CMDSEG, es ;   Assume SEG PSP in es
            jmp     GetOff
Version3:
            mov     ah, 62h
            int     21h ;              Get PSP segment from DOS
```

```
                mov     CMDSEG, bx
GetOff:
                mov     CMDOFF, OFFSET Command

                mov     es, bx ;        Check for correct length
                ASSUME  es : PSP
                mov     bl, CmdLen
                sub     bh, bh
                cmp     bx, 126
                jbe     LenOK
                mov     CmdLen, 126
LenOK:          mov     [Command + bx], 13 ; make sure terminated with CR

                pop     ax
NotFirst: ;             State 2 or 3?
                les     si, CmdTail
                test    si, si
                jz      Done ; State 3; Offset 0 indicates no more params
ParseLoop:              ;                       State 2:  May be more params
                cmp     BYTE PTR es:[si], ' '
                je      SkipIt
                cmp     BYTE PTR es:[si], 9 ;     9 = TAB
                jne     FindEnd
SkipIt:
                inc     si
                jmp     ParseLoop
FindEnd:                ; found start of token;  now find end
                cmp     BYTE PTR es:[si], 13
                je      NoMore ;        Reached end of command line
                mov     bx, si
EndLoop:
                inc     bx
                cmp     BYTE PTR es:[bx], ' '
                jg      EndLoop
                cmp     BYTE PTR es:[bx], 13 ;    If =, last token
                mov     BYTE PTR es:[bx], 0 ;     Null-terminate parameter
                je      NoMore1 ;    Note separation of cmp and je!!!
                inc     bx
                mov     CMDOFF, bx ; Prepare for next ParseCmd
                jmp     Done
NoMore:
                mov     si, 0
NoMore1:                ;                   Go to State 3
                mov     CMDOFF, 0
Done:
                pop     bx
                pop     ds
```

```
                ret
ParseCmd        ENDP
                END
```

CCheck is straightforward. Its only difficulty is that it requires an array of error messages, which vary in length. In order to get an array of variably sized items with efficiency, the actual array will be an array of offsets into the data area containing the messages. After a fair amount of use, I decided that it would be useful if CCheck (and WCheck) wrote out some approximation to the place where the error occurred. The return address is presumably fairly close, is sitting on top of the stack when we're in either of these routines, and isn't needed any more once we know that an error has occurred, so we can just pop it and display it with PutHex. Of course, we must be careful to preserve the contents of ax, which contain the error number. The code is

```
;;    CCheck  checks for CFlag set and if so, prints error whose
;;            number is is in ax. Not all messages available
;;            (Should contain those for I/O, EXEC, and Mem Alloc)
;;            _Exits with code 1 if error
;;
                .MODEL SMALL
INCLUDE         PCMAC.INC

                .DATA
;*** first, a list of (variable-length) messages:
Inval           DB      'Invalid function number$'
NotFnd          DB      'File not found$'
;               etc.
Files           DB      'No more files$'
Unk             DB      'Unknown error number$'
;*** Then, an array Msg of pointers such that Msg[n] = offset of
;***   message for error n
Msg             DW      ?, Inval, NotFnd, ...
                ...
                DW      Device, Files
MSGLIM          EQU     ($ - Msg - 2) /2
Err1            DB      '*** DOS call ERROR at $'
Err2            DB      'h *** $'
CRLF            DB      13, 10, '$'

                .CODE
                PUBLIC CCheck
                EXTRN  PutHex : NEAR
CCheck          PROC
                jc     DoMessage
                ret
DoMessage:
                mov    bx, @data
                mov    ds, bx ;    Just in case
```

```
                mov     bx, ax ;        Save error number
                _PutStr Err1
                pop     ax ;            Return address is location of error
                call    PutHex ;        (Don't need it any more)
                _PutStr Err2
                cmp     bx, 1           bx = error number
                jl      DispUnk ;       Check range
                cmp     bx, MSGLIM
                jg      DispUnk
                shl     bx, 1
                add     bx, OFFSET Msg ;    bx --> offset of error message
                mov     dx, [bx] ;    _PutStr macro can't be used
                mov     ah, 09h ;        for this particular call
                int     21h
Finish:
                _PutStr CRLF
                _Exit  1
DispUnk:
                _PutStr Unk
                jmp     Finish
CCheck          ENDP
```

We put the code for WCheck in the same file as CCheck so we can use some of the same character strings.

```
;;              WCheck Used for _Write command. First does CCheck and if
;;                     that returns, compares ax = number of bytes
;;                     written to cx = number of bytes requested to
;;                     write and prints message and _Exits with code 2
;;
                .DATA
WrtCnt          DB      'Different number of bytes written '
                DB      'than requested$'

                .CODE
                PUBLIC WCheck

WCheck          PROC
                jnc     NoDOSErr
                jmp     CCheck ; Don't destroy original return address!
NoDOSErr:
                cmp     ax, cx
                jne     WErr
                ret
WErr:
                _PutStr Err1, @data
                pop     ax ;            Return address
```

```
                call    PutHex
                _PutStr Err2
                _PutStr WrtCnt
                _PutStr CRLF
                _Exit   2
        WCheck  ENDP
                END
```

Note that WCheck *jumps* to CCheck instead of calling it to keep the proper return address on top of the stack for displaying by CCheck. Returning to WCheck isn't necessary as we already know that a CCheck error has occurred.

Programming Problem 17.1

Write a program CheckSum *filename* which computes and displays in hex (using PutHex) the sum of all the *words* in the file *filename*—that is, the words at locations 0, 2, 4, 6, … . If the file has an odd number of bytes, then the last byte is turned into a word by giving it a zero high-order byte and adding it in. You can test your program by applying it to EXE files. The word at location 12h of an EXE file is given a value so that the file's checksum is 0FFFFh. (The checksum is wrong in EXE files with debugging information, since the word at location 12 is computed without using the debugging information.) (CheckSum is a useful utility program to have around. It provides a quick-and-dirty way of determining if two versions of the same file are different.)

Programming Problem 17.2

Write a program StakSize which can be used to alter the stack size of an EXE file to *n* bytes by giving the command

```
        stacksize filename.EXE n
```

Use GetNum from Exercise 17.1—4 to extract *n* from the command line. You must change three words in the header of the EXE file: 10h, which contains the initial value of sp (it will be changed to *n*), 0Ah, which contains the minimum number of paragraphs needed for the program, and 12h, the checksum as described in Programming Problem 17.1. To get 0Ah, you will subtract the number of paragraphs previously needed by the file (from 10h) and add the number of paragraphs required for *n*. You can recompute the checksum by looking at its old value and the old and new values at 0Ah and 10h.

Programming Problem 17.3

Write a program LineCt which is executed with the command line

```
        linect filename
```

where *filename* is a DOS text file. LineCt counts the number of lines in *filename* by counting the number of line feed characters and printing out the result in the form

```
        nnn lines
```

More challenging version: Write a DOS version of the UNIX wc utility program. The command

```
wc filename
```

prints the number of characters, words, and lines in `filename`. To count words, keep a state variable STATE which has two possible values, InWord and InSpace. Initially it is InSpace. As each character is encountered, if it is a blank, tab, or linefeed, set STATE to InSpace. If it is not and STATE = InSpace, set STATE to InWord and increment the word counter. An even more challenging version allows an optional parameter between wc and `filename` of the form *-switches*, where *switches* is any subset of the letters l, w, and c, in any order, indicating which of the counts lines, words, or characters will be printed. The default is -lwc.

Programming Problem 17.4

Write a separately translated function subprogram GetS which takes as input a file handle in ax, a maximum character count in cx, and the address of a character array of at least cx characters in ds:si. GetS reads a line of characters from file ax, up to cx characters or the next occurrence of carriage return-line feed, whichever comes first, and places them in the character array ds:si. If the carriage return-line feed pair occurs, it is replaced by a null byte; otherwise the string is terminated by a null byte. Test your function by rewriting the Display program (Example 17.2—1) using GetS. Method: Read cx characters and scan for carriage return-line feed. If found, use _LSeek to move the file pointer back to the beginning of the next line. What should you do if you read the carriage return but run out of room before the line feed?

Programming Problem 17.5

Write a utility program DUMP *filename* which displays a hex version of *filename*. Each line is of the form

```
xxxx: nn nn nn nn nn nn nn nn  nn nn nn nn nn nn nn nn | aaaaaaaa aaaaaaaa
```

where xxxx: is the hex address of the first byte on this line (taking the successive values 0000:, 0010:, 0020, etc.). The nn's are the successive bytes, in hex, and the a's are their ASCII representation. Any character out of the range 32–127 can be represented by a '.'. The last line of your dump will probably be partial. (**Note:** The DUMP program is a *very* useful utility to have around. It was helpful in debugging RedirErr, for instance.)

Programming Problem 17.6

(Harder. Rather than being a practical problem, this problem is more a demonstration of the usefulness of _LSeek and the solution to Programming Problem 17.5) The disk that accompanies this book contains a data file called STATES.DAT, which contains data about the fifty United States and the District of Columbia. Each state is represented by a line of text of at most 80 characters. You are to write a program which turns the states file into an indexed sequential file. The program should create a file STATES.IDX of 51 records of 16 characters each. The first 14 characters of each record are a state name, trailing blank filled, and the last two characters are the offset in the STATES.DAT file of the record containing that state. The records in STATES.IDX are alphabetized by state name. If you are really ambitious, then write a program STATINFO *statename* which looks up *statename* in the IDX file using a binary search (jump around in the file using _LSeek) and prints out the line of information on that state (also using _LSeek).

SUMMARY

The following DOS calls are available for file manipulation. All return with the carry flag clear, if successful, or with the carry flag set and the error number in ax if unsuccessful. The returned results given below are based on the assumption that the call is successful.

Opening a file:

```
         _Open filename, accessmethod[, segment]
; ;           returns handle in ax.  Accessmethod = Read (0)
; ;           Write (1), or ReadWrite (2)
```

Creating and opening a file:

```
         _Creat filename[, segment]
; ;           returns handle in ax
```

Closing a file:

```
         _Close handle
```

Reading or Writing a file (sequentially):

```
         _Read  Handle, BufferOffset, ByteCount[, BufferSegment]
         _Write Handle, BufferOffset, ByteCount[, BufferSegment]
; ;           returns ax equal to number of bytes read or written
; ;           (end of file on read indicated by ax = 0)
```

Relocate the file pointer for the location of the next sequential Read or Write:

```
         _LSeek Handle, SeekType, LoDistance[, HiDistance]
; ;           returns dx:ax set to new file pointer (in bytes from
; ;           the beginning of the file). SeekType = FromStart (0)
; ;           for relative to start, FromCur (1) for relative to
; ;           current pointer and FromEnd (2) for relative to end
```

Every DOS program normally starts with five open file handles: standard input (keyboard or redirected), standard output (CRT or redirected), standard error (CRT), auxiliary (generally the first serial port), and the line printer.

Three useful procedures have been added to UTIL.LIB;

ParseCmd   No input parameters.
                 Output is a pointer in es:si to the next command line argument, which
                 will be null-terminated. When there are no more arguments, si will be re-

turned as 0.

In addition, there is a public double-word variable CmdTail in the .DATA region which points to the next place ParseCmd will start its scan, that is, to the character following the last null it inserted. If there are no more arguments, the first word of CmdTail will be 0.

CCheck   Called immediately after a DOS function (other than _Write) which signifies an error by returning with the carry flag set and the error number in ax. No other input.

An error has occurred, prints an approximate error location and an appropriate error message. Has messages for all handle I/O, memory allocation, and EXEC functions.

WCheck   Serves a similar function as CCheck for _Write calls. Also checks to see if the requested number of bytes was written.

We have also introduced three non-I/O DOS Function calls: EXECute another program and resize memory allocation (see Section 17.4 for a complete description) and get PSP location (see Section 17.5).

Chapter *18*

String Processing Instructions

ah	AX	al
bh	BX	bl
ch	CX	cl
dh	DX	dl
	SI	
	DI	
	BP	
	SP	
	DS	
	ES	
	SS	
	CS	
	IP	

o **d** i t s z c

This chapter introduces 80X86 operations specifically designed for processing strings of words or bytes. Anything done using the new methods can also be done by standard array methods, but the code introduced here is often shorter and faster.

Operations on a whole array, such as moving the array or searching for a particular element in the array, are so common that most modern computers have special operations to speed up the process. A typical array processing operation might be

```
ALoop:
        ...
        mov    al, [si] ;   Get byte...
        inc    si ;       ...and update si
        ...
        jmp    ALoop
```

The 80X86 has a single instruction which accomplishes the mov and inc instructions: lodsb (load string byte), as well as various other instructions for storing, comparing, and moving. In addition, there are various rep (repeat) instructions which can be added as a prefix to a string instruction and which cause the string instruction to be repeated until some specified condition is satisfied (usually cx being reduced to 0). For instance, the following string move fragment

```
MoveLoop:
        mov    al, [si]
        mov    es:[di], al
        inc    si
```

Optional:

18.1 String Operations
The D flag
*op*s movsb/w,
lodsb/w,
stosb/w,
cmpsb/w,
scasb/w,
std, cld

18.2 REP Prefixes
*op*s rep,
repe/ne

18.3 Tail Revisited
an application

```
inc    di
loop   MoveLoop
```

can be accomplished in a single prefixed instruction:

```
rep    movsb ;        move string (byte)
```

With all this power, you may wonder why we haven't introduced these operations earlier. The answer is that you *must* learn the methods we have already studied, as there are many applications in which only they will do. In the author's experience, if you present two methods at once to do something, often neither is learned. If you still don't feel comfortable with array processing, I suggest you skip this chapter until you do.

18.1 • The String Operations

There are five string operations:

```
movsb/movsw    move string (memory to memory)
lodsb/lodsw    load string (memory to register)
stosb/stosw    store string (register to memory)
cmpsb/cmpsw    compare string (memory to memory)
scasb/scasw    compare string to byte (memory to register)
```

There are certain common principles governing all of these instructions:

- Each instruction has a word and a byte version, indicated by the terminal letter w or b, respectively.
- If an operation makes use of a register, the register is either ax (word operation) or al (byte operation).
- Any operand whose source is in memory is at address ds:[si].
- Any operand whose destination is in memory is at address es:[di].
- If si or di is involved in the instruction, it is automatically increased or decreased by 1 (byte operations) or 2 (word operations) *after* the operation is performed. Whether to increment or decrement is controlled by the **D flag** (direction flag) in the flags register. The D flag is set and cleared by the following instructions:

```
cld ; Clear D flag; that is, auto increment on string ops
std ; Set D flag; that is, auto decrement on string ops
```

WARNING: The D flag is normally 0 (auto increment) and **many library routines assume the D flag is 0**, including the printf routine in some versions of C. The interruption process, of course, automatically saves and restores the D flag (among others), but that is no proof against an operating system routine that assumes that the D flag is clear while processing the interrupt. The upshot is that by setting the D flag, you may turn up a bug in someone else's program. The fact that it is someone else's bug is cold comfort if you have no control over the program and must use it. At the very least, the following rules should be followed religiously:

1. If you are going to use string instructions with automatic **incrementing,** *always* precede the code with

Before Auto Increment
cld   ;   Set direction flag to auto increment

You need not save and restore the old value of the flag since the normally assumed value is 0.

2. If you are going to use string instructions with automatic **decrementing,** *always* precede the code with

Before Auto Decrement
pushf ;   push (save) old flag values
std   ;   Set direction flag to auto decrement

and *always* follow the string processing code with

After Auto Decrement
popf ;   restore old flag values.

That is, *always* set the value of the direction flag explicitly to 1 or 0, and if you are setting it to 1, save and restore the old value.

A detailed description of the five string operations follows. We will use a slash to separate byte and word variants, with the byte variant coming first. All instructions will assume the D flag is cleared.

```
movsb/w ;           mov   es:[di], BYTE/WORD PTR ds:[si]
;                   inc   si / add     si, 2
;                   inc   di / add     di, 2
; (of course an actual mov memory to memory is illegal)

lodsb/w ;           mov   al/ax, ds:[si]
;                   inc   si / add     si, 2

stosb/w ;           mov   es:[di], al / ax
;                   inc   di / add     di, 2

cmpsb/w ;           cmp   es:[di], BYTE/WORD PTR ds:[si]
;                   inc   si / add     si, 2
;                   inc   di / add     di, 2
; (see remarks under movsb/w)

scasb/w ;           cmp   al/ax, es:[di]
;                   inc   di / add     di, 2
```

The pseudo add/inc operations which are a part of these descriptions don't alter the flags.

Example 18.1—1. Let A, B, and C be 100 word arrays and set A[i] := B[i] + C[i] for i = 0, 1, ..., 99. Assume that all arrays are in the segment given by ds.

We can only use si and di to index two of the arrays using string instructions, but that's OK since for the third array we are going to have to add, and there is no string instruction for adding. We'll use based indexing for the addition. The code is

```
        mov   si, OFFSET B
        mov   bx, OFFSET C - 2 ; to compensate later for
        sub   bx, si ;            already having incremented si
        mov   di, OFFSET A
        push  ds
        pop   es ;               es := ds
        mov   cx, 100
        cld
AddLp:  lodsw ;                  ax := B[i]; i := i + 1
        add   ax, [bx + si] ;    ax := ax + C[i - 1]
        stosw ;                  A[old i] := ax; increment di
        loop  AddLp
```

The rest of the examples in this secion refer to optional Sections 11.2 and 14.1, so you may skip directly to the exercises if you wish.

We have done many string processing examples in the course of the book, and most of them can be quickly turned into examples of the use of the new string operations. We will show how several of the examples in Section 11.2 can be improved by using string operations. In that section, we discussed C-type variable length character strings. Such a string is an array of characters whose end is indicated by the null character 0 (not to be confused with ASCII '0')

Example 18.1—2. Code the function LenStr which returns the length of the C-string pointed to by ds:si. The length is the number of characters in the string exclusive of the terminating 0. The original code in Example 11.2—1 was

```
        mov   ax, si ;     save si to subtract at end
LenLoop:
        cmp   BYTE PTR [si], 0
        je    Done
        inc   si
        jmp   LenLoop
Done:
        neg   ax
        add   ax, si
```

Scasb uses es:di instead of ds:si, so the code can be modified to

```
        push  ds
        pop   es ;         if necessary
        mov   di, si ;     scasb uses es:di
```

```
            mov     al, 0
            cld
LenLoop:

            scasb
            jne     LenLoop

            mov     ax, di
            sub     ax, si
            dec     ax ;         scasb advances di even when =
```

Example 18.1—3. The procedure CpyStr which copies a C-type string whose starting address is in ds:si into a sequence of bytes whose starting address is in es:di. The terminating 0 byte must be copied as well. The code in Example 11.2—2 was

```
CpyLoop:
            mov     al, [si]
            mov     es:[di], al
            cmp     al, 0
            je      Done
            inc     si
            inc     di
            jmp     CpyLoop
Done:
```

We can't just use movsb because we have to know when to terminate. One way is

```
            cld
CpyLoop:
            cmp     BYTE PTR [si], 0
            movsb
            jnz     CpyLoop
```

The move is done on the terminator byte too. Here we are using the fact that movsb doesn't change the flags. If instead we had put the cmp instruction *after* the movsb, we would have had to use cmp BYTE PTR [si - 1], which is a longer and hence more time-consuming instruction.

Example 18.1—4. The function CmpStr which takes as input pointers to C strings in ds:si and es:di and returns with ax > 0, < 0, or = 0 depending on whether the di string is lexicographically greater than, less than, or equal to the si string. Comparison takes place byte by byte until an unequal pair is found or we reach the ends of the strings. If unequal bytes are found, the result comes from comparing them. The code in example 11.2—3 was

```
CharLoop:
            mov     al, [si]
            mov     bl, [di]
            cmp     al, bl ;      Are current bytes equal?
            jne     Done ;        no
```

```
            cmp     al, 0 ;         yes; are the strings terminated?
            je      Done ;          yes
            inc     si
            inc     di
            jmp     CharLoop
Done:
            sub     ah, ah ;    Must do unsigned convert BEFORE
            sub     bh, bh ;        subtracting the two characters
            sub     ax, bx ;    ax := [si] - [di]
```

We have a problem similar to CpyStr. If the two strings are of unequal length, then the shorter will have a zero byte where the longer doesn't and that will terminate the loop. If they are the same length, then checking either one of them for a zero byte, *a la* CpyStr, will work. However, now the termination check *must* be done after cmpsb or its setting of the flags will be destroyed by *cmpsb*. The new code is

```
            cld
CmpLoop:
            cmpsb
            jne     Done
            cmp     BYTE PTR [si-1], 0 ;        Either string ended?
            jne     CmpLoop
            sub     ax, ax
            jmp     Return
Done:
            mov     al, [si-1]
            mov     bl, [di-1]
            sub     ah, ah ;    Must do unsigned convert BEFORE
            sub     bh, bh ;        subtracting the two characters
            sub     ax, bx ;    ax := [si] - [di]
```

Example 18.1—5. The multiple precision addition (see Section 14.1)

```
            clc
AddLoop:
            mov     ax, es:[di]
            adc     ax, [si]
            mov     es:[di], ax
            inc     di
            inc     di
            inc     si
            inc     si
            loop    AddLoop
```

becomes

```
            clc
            cld
```

```
AddLoop:
            lodsw
            adc     ax, es:[di]
            stosw
            loop    AddLoop
```

(Note that we rearranged the order of fetching the source and destination word so that we could autoincrement both registers.)

Exercises 18.1

1. Let A, B, and C be arrays of 100 words each, with subscripts starting at 0, and assume that `ds` and `es` are set to the segment containing the three of them. Write assembly code using string-processing instructions to accomplish each of the following:

    a) ✓ Set all entries in the A array to 0.

    b)   Set `di` equal to the index (between 0 and 99) of the first entry in the B array which is equal to 123. (Set `di` = –1 if no such entry exists.)

    c) ✓ Move the A array 'down one.' That is, arrange it so that new A[0] = old A[1], …, new A[98] = old A[99].

    d)   Move the A array 'up one.' That is, arrange it so that new A[1] = old A[0], …, new A[99] = old A[98]. (Hint: the move must be done by starting from the top and working down.)

    e)   Compare A and B entry for entry and go to location `Equal` if all entries are the same.

2.   Let S and T be the addresses of the first character in two Pascal-style variable length character strings. That is, the first character of the string is the number of characters in the string (not counting the count byte). As examples, to fix ideas but not to be used for the exercises,

```
    S       DB      14, 'A short string'
    T       DB      3, 'ort'
    U       DB      0 ;             An empty string
```

Write program pieces using string-processing instructions to accomplish the following:

    a) ✓ Set `di` to the index (starting at 1) at which the character C occurs in S. Set `di` to 0 if C does not occur in S.

    b)   Set T equal to a copy of S with all lower case letters converted to upper case.

    c)   Set `bx` equal to the index (starting at 1) of the first occurrence of the entire string T in the string S. Thus in the example above, `bx` would be set equal to 5. If T isn't found within S, set `bx` to 0. (Note: In the example above, we might have to do as many as 14 – 3 = 11 string comparisons of T with various substrings of S.)

3. ✓ Write code to start a main program by moving the command line from the PSP:128 to a storage area (at least) 128 bytes long in the .DATA segment using string processing commands.

4.   Convert the following multiple precision subtraction loop (see Section 14.1) to use of string operations:

```
            clc
SubLoop:
```

```
mov     ax, es:[di]
sbb     ax, ds:[si]
mov     es:[di], ax
inc     di
inc     di
inc     si
inc     si
loop    AddLoop
```

18.2 • The REP Instruction Prefixes

The string operations introduced in the last section can be prefixed by a rep instruction which causes the string operation to be repeated, counting down cx each time until cx reaches 0. In addition, there are repe/repz (repeat while the equal or zero comparison is true and count is nonzero) and repne/repnz (repeat while the equal or zero comparison is *not* true and count is nonzero). To be more precise, we can give the following definitions, where *strop* is any of the string operations introduced in Section 18.1.

rep *strop* is equivalent to
| ```
          jcxz     stropDone
stropLoop:
          strop
          loop     stropLoop
stropDone:
``` |

repE/repZ *strop* is equivalent to
| ```
          jcxz     stropDone
stropLoop:
          strop
          jNz      stropDone  ; jnz = jne
          loop     stropLoop
stropDone:
``` |

repNE/repNZ *strop* is equivalent to
| ```
          jcxz     stropDone
stropLoop:
          strop
          jz       stropDone  ; jz = je
          loop     stropLoop
stropDone:
``` |

Notice that, unlike the loop instruction, the rep prefixes act 'correctly' when cx is initially zero. That is, the loop is not performed at all.

Let us return to the examples of the last section to see how they can be improved by use of one of the rep prefixes.
```

Example 18.2—1. Let es:di point to an array of 100 bytes. Write code to set all of the bytes to blank.

```
mov     al, ' '
cld
mov     cx, 100
rep     stosb
```

Examples 18.2—2 through 6 follow examples 18.1—2 through 6, respectively, so if you skipped those examples in Section 18.1, you can skip immediately to Example 18.2—7.

Example 18.2—2. LenStr can be altered as follows:

```
mov     di, si ;       scasb uses di
mov     al, 0
cld
mov     cx, 0ffffh;    So cx doesn't stop too soon
repne   scasb

mov     ax, di
sub     ax, si
dec     ax ;           scasb advances si even when =
```

Example 18.2—3. CpyStr can't use the rep prefix as the loop must contain another instruction, cmp, to look for a terminating zero byte. It is perfect though for copying Pascal-type strings, whose length is in the first byte:

```
CpyPascal:
        cld
        mov     cl, [si]
        sub     ch, ch ;       Convert to word
        inc     cx ;           Copy length byte too
        rep     movsb
```

Example 18.2—4. Once again rep can't be used for CmpStr as the loop must contain more than one instruction. Again though, we can use it for comparing Pascal-type strings, though the surrounding code is more complicated:

```
CmpPascal:
        lodsb   ;              al = length of left string
        mov     bl, es:[di] ;  bl = length of right string
        inc     di ;    point to actual string (si already inc ed)
        cmp     al, bl
        jbe     LeftShort ;    set cl = min(al, bl)
        mov     cl, bl
        jmp     DoCompare
LeftShort:
        mov     cl, al
```

```
DoCompare:
        sub     ch, ch ;        (convert to unsigned word)
        jcxz    Prefix
        cld
        repe    cmpsb
        je      Prefix ;        If one is a prefix of other,
;                                 simply compare lengths
        mov     al, [si-1] ;    Else compare first unequal chars
        mov     bl, es:[di-1]
Prefix:
        sub     ah, ah ;        convert char or length to word
        sub     bh, bh ;        ditto
        sub     ax, bx
```

You may not be too impressed by the code above because it is quite a bit longer than the original CmpStr, but remember that the code here has a loop consisting of a single one-byte instruction, while the loop in the original contained roughly eighteen bytes.

Example 18.2—5. Example 18.1—5 cannot use the rep prefix. You can't use a rep prefix to make a loop that must contain more than one statement. Also, a moment's thought should convince you that any time lods is used in any essential way, rep can't be.

Example 18.2—6. In MPPutDec in Example 14.1—5, we had the following code to move a multiple precision number into local storage on the stack:

```
        mov     di, sp ;        Offset to first word of dest on
stack
        lds     si, APtr ;      Pointer to source
        mov     cx, Len
MovIn:
        mov     ax, [si]
        mov     ss:[di], ax
        add     si, 2
        add     di, 2
        loop    MovIn
```

The code above is easily rewritten using rep and string operations as

```
        mov     di, sp ;        Offset to first word of dest on stack
        lds     si, APtr ;      Pointer to source
        mov     cx, Len
        mov     ax, ss
        mov     es, ax
        rep     movsw
```

Now let's consider a more elaborate example.

Example 18.2—7. Implement the insertion sort algorithm using string instructions.

The usual way to write a routine in pseudocode to sort A[1...n] is

```
for i := 2 to n do
  x := A[i]
  j := i - 1
  while (j > 0) and (x < A[j]) do
    A[j+1] := A[j]
    j := j - 1
  end while
  A[j+1] := x
end for
```

With the string instructions, sliding part of the array up one entry is easier if we do it all at once at the end. The rewritten pseudocode is

```
for i := 2 to n do
  ax := A[i]
  j := i - 1
  while (j > 0) and (ax < A[j]) do
    j := j - 1
  end while
  slide A[j+1..n-1] up 1;
  A[j+1] := ax
end for
```

Assuming A is a word array whose segment address is in *both* es and di and *n* is a constant, the code is

```
                ASSUME ds:SEG A, es:SEG A ;        documentation
                mov    bx, OFFSET A + 2 ; i := 2
                mov    dx, n - 1 ;         Number of entries to insert
                mov    si, 1 ;        Number of entries already processed
                pushf
                std    ;                   Autodecrement
InsertionSort:
                mov    ax, [bx] ;          ax := A[i]
                mov    di, bx ;            di --> A[j]…
                sub    di, 2
                mov    cx, si ;     j = number of entries to examine
FindLoop:                            The WHILE loop
                scasw
                jge    Found ;             NO repL!
                loop   FindLoop
Found:
                neg    cx ;        cx ended at number not examined
```

```
            add    cx, si ;       cx := number of entries to slide up
            jcxz   NoSlide
            mov    di, bx
            push   si ;                   Temporarily save si
            mov    si, di
            sub    si, 2
            rep    movsw ;                Slide up one
            mov    [di], ax
            pop    si
     NoSlide:
            add    bx, 2 ;                Get ready for next iteration
            inc    si
            dec    dx
            jnz    InsertionSort
            popf
```

Note that the jcxz instruction isn't really necessary here, but can save a lot of setup and cleanup if no move is needed.

Debuggers and the rep prefix: The Trace command causes one to single-step through each repetition and the Step command treats the prefixed instruction as a single instruction and does it all at once.

Exercises 18.2

1. ✓ Examine the solutions to Exercises 18.1, 1–4, and rewrite to use rep prefixes wherever possible.

2. Let S and T be two Pascal-style character strings as in Exercise 18.1—2 and write program pieces to accomplish the following, assuming that ds and es are set to the (common) segment of S and T:
   a) ✓ Set bx to the index of the *last* character in S such that all characters from 1 to bx are in T. (If no characters of S are in T, bx = 0; if all characters are, bx = length of S.)
   b) Set bx to the index of the first character of S which is *not* in T. (If all characters of S are in T, bx = length of S + 1.)

3. Pascal strings as described here usually come with a number of 'standard' operations. Write separate procedures to accomplish the following two. Assume that all parameters are pushed onto the stack in the order encountered, that strings are passed as parameters as two word segment:offset pointers, that ds must be preserved, and that subprocedures pop parameters from the stack with a ret *n* instruction when they are through. The procedures are
   a) ✓ Delete(S, m, n) deletes n characters from the string S starting at character m. If S = 'Worcestershire' then Delete(S,3,3) = 'Wostershire'. Take care of anomalous conditions by setting m = max(m, 1), m = min(m, 1 + length of S), n = min(n, 1 + length of S – m), and then exiting immediately if n = 0.
   b) Insert(S, D, m) inserts the string S into the string D starting at character position m. For instance, if D = 'I do choose to run', then Insert('not ', D, 6) = 'I do not choose to run'. If the result is greater than 255 characters long, truncate to 255. What are reasonable ways of handling m < 1 and m > 1 + length of D?

4. Requires Section 14.1. Suppose that `APtr` and `BPtr` are `DWORD` PTRs to two multiple-precision numbers of length `Len`. Write a subprogram `MPCmp` using string instructions which sets `ax` to < 0, = 0, or > 0 according as the `APtr` number is <, =, or > `BPtr`. (Hints: Numbers must be compared from high-order parts first. The low-order parts come first in memory, so the comparison must be done 'backwards', that is, with the D flag set to 1. Compare until you get non-equal (`repe`), then set `ax` := [di+2] − [si+2]. (You are already one word *past* the unequal words.) Test the sign in the initial words and negate `ax` if necessary.)

18.3 • The `TAIL` program revisited

In Section 17.3.4 we presented an 'unsophisticated' version of the UNIX `Tail` program which displays the last ten lines of a text file. In this section we will give a 'sophisticated' version which uses double-precision arithmetic to keep track of our position in the file and backwards searching with `scasb` for line-feeds. You be the judge.

```
;   TAIL -- display the last ten lines of a text file
;
            .MODEL SMALL
INCLUDE     PCMAC.INC
            ASSUME SS:NOTHING

            .STACK 100h

;                           Constants
BUFLEN      EQU     512 ;       Must be a power of 2
CR          EQU     13
LF          EQU     10
WANTED      EQU     10 ;        Number of lines of tail desired
CtrlZ       EQU     26 ;        Sometimes used to end text files

            .DATA
Buffer      DB      BUFLEN DUP (?)
Handle      DW      ? ;         The file handle
LCount      DW      ? ;         Number of Line Feeds encountered
Start       DD      ? ;         loc of buf start in file: least sig
first

UsageMsg    DB      'usage: tail filename',CR,LF,'$'

            .CODE
            EXTRN   ParseCmd : NEAR, CCheck : NEAR
Tail        PROC
            mov     ax, @data
            mov     ds, ax
            call    ParseCmd ;  Get file name from command line...
            test    si, si
            jnz     DoOpen
```

```
                 _PutStr UsageMsg
                 _Exit   2
DoOpen:

                 push    ds
                 _Open   si, Read, es ;      ...and open it
                 pop     ds
                 call    CCheck
                 mov     Handle, ax
                 mov     LCount, WANTED+1 ; Initialize line count

                 _LSeek Handle, FromEnd, 0 ;      Find length of file
                 call    CCheck

                 add     ax, BUFLEN-1 ;      Round end of file to next even
                 adc     dx, 0;                    multiple of BUFLEN (note
                 and     ax, NOT (BUFLEN - 1) ;  multiple precision
                 mov     WORD PTR [Start], ax ; BUFLEN must be a pwr of 2
                 mov     WORD PTR [Start+2], dx ;   for the 'and' to work
                 mov     ax, ds
                 mov     es, ax
                 pushf
                 std;                             set direction register to down
ReadNextRecord :
                 sub     WORD PTR [Start], BUFLEN ;       double precision
                 sbb     WORD PTR [Start+2], 0 ;   subtract with borrow
                 jge     DoRead
                 mov     WORD PTR [Start], 0 ;     if <0, we're at start
                 mov     WORD PTR [Start+2], 0 ;
                 jmp     Done
DoRead:
        _LSeek    Handle,FromStart,<WORD PTR Start>,<WORD PTR Start+2>
                 call    CCheck
                 _Read   Handle, buffer, BUFLEN
                 call    CCheck
                 mov     cx, ax;                  save number of characters read
                 jcxz    ReadNextRecord ;      (shouldn't happen)
                 mov     di, OFFSET Buffer-1 ; Set up ptr to end of buffer
                 add     di, cx

                 mov     al, LF ;                    Character to search for
LineLoop:
                 repne   scasb ;                  Stop on LF or start of buffer
                 jne     ReadNextRecord ;          LF not found
                 dec     LCount
                 jnz     LineLoop ;

                 sub     di, OFFSET Buffer-2 ;     di already one past LF
```

```
          add    WORD PTR [start], di ;    update to start of tail
          adc    WORD PTR [start+2], 0
Done:                                 ; READ and output data from Start
     _LSeek   Handle,FromStart,<WORD PTR Start>,<WORD PTR Start+2>
          call   CCheck
          cld ;                          Reset direction to up
OutputLoop:
          _Read  Handle, buffer, BUFLEN
          call   CCheck
          mov    cx, ax;              number of bytes read => cx
          jcxz   EOF
          mov    si, OFFSET Buffer
DisplayLoop:
          lodsb
          cmp    al, CtrlZ ;   Sometime text file terminator
          je     EOF
          _PutCh al
          loop   DisplayLoop
          jmp    OutputLoop
EOF:
          popf
          _Exit  0;              Normal termination
Tail      ENDP
          END    Tail
```

Exercises 18.3

1. Examine the code for the following examples given in the text and show how it can be improved by using string operations: Bin2Dec (Section 11.1), Examples 11.3—3, 12.5—2 (both methods), 14.1—3, 14.1—4, 14.3—1, 17.2—1 (first method), Log (Section 17.3.2), RedirErr (Section 17.4), ParseCmd (Section 17.5).

Programming Problem 18.1

Redo any (or all) of the following programming problems using string-processing instructions where appropriate: 10.2, 10.3, 11.2, 12.1, 12.2, 14.2, 14.3, 17.1, 17.3, 17.4

SUMMARY

New Instructions:

> **Alter Direction Flag**: (Controls whether string instructions autoincrement (DF clear) or decrement (DF set) si and/or di. The D flag should be kept cleared except when absolutely necessary.)

```
          cld   ;      clear the D flag (increment)
          std   ;      set the D flag (decrement)
```

String Processing Instructions: Byte or word version indicated by x = b or w.

```
movsx ;      move string
cmpsx ;      compare strings
lodsx ;      load string element
stosx ;      store string element
scasx ;      scan string for element in register
```

Any instruction involving an element in a register uses al or ax. ds:si is used as the source of all instructions and es:di as the destination and for scasx.

Prefixes to string instructions: Each decrements cx on each repeat and exits when cx = 0. Some can exit on other conditions.

```
rep   ;      repeat
repne ;      repeat while not equal
repnz ;      repeat while not zero
repe  ;      repeat while equal
repz  ;      repeat while zero
```

Chapter *19*

Video Basics

This chapter gives a relatively complete treatment of text mode video operations and a very brief introduction to graphics video in the form of some examples using one VGA graphics mode.

Video displays on the IBM PC can run in one of two modes, *text* or *graphics*. Normally under DOS they run in text mode, displaying 25 lines of 80 characters per line. Most PCs can also display graphic images by selectively illuminating a grid of dots on the screen called **pixels**, short for picture elements. The **resolution** of the display is typically written in the form $m \times n$ where m the number of pixels across the screen and n is the number up and down. Another facet of graphic capabilities is the number of colors that can be displayed. Typically, some relatively small number (16 or 256) can be displayed at one time from a **palette** chosen from some large number of available colors.

The display capability of a PC is determined by what type of monitor is attached to it and by the type of **display adaptor** installed. The display adaptor is usually contained on a separate board within the computer. The following are commonly used display adaptors (everything before VGA is of mostly historical interest):

- The **monochrome display adaptor** (**MDA**) which was delivered on the original PCs. This adaptor had no graphics capabilities.
- The **color graphics adaptor** (**CGA**) which delivers text mode in 16 colors and very primitive, low-resolution graphics (320×200 pixels in either of two palettes of four colors, or 640×200 pixels in monochrome).
- The **enhanced graphics adaptor** (**EGA**) which will emulate a CGA, particularly in text mode, and also has 640×350 graphics which will display 16 colors at a time chosen from 262,144 ($=2^{18}$).
- The **video graphics array** (**VGA**) introduced on PS/2s with 80286 or higher CPUs. VGA emulates CGA and, to a great extent EGA, but also

has a 640×480 graphics mode similar to the EGAs 640×350 and a 320×200 graphics mode which displays 256 colors chosen from a possible 262,144.

- **Super VGA** (**SVGA**), which is an extension of VGA allowing higher resolution (perhaps 1024×768) and more colors. SVGA Adaptors must usually be supplied with their own (generally nonstandard) drivers.

At the time of this writing, most computers sold in the last year or so have come with SVGA graphics.

In this book we are concerned almost entirely with the CGA in text mode. There are several reasons:

- All display adaptors except MDA emulate CGA in their normal (text) mode, and MDA text is very similar to CGA. There are still computers out there which can do no better, though the number is shrinking.
- Programming in graphics mode is very complex and differs from display adaptor to display adaptor. Moreover, programs like Windows, of necessity, can't allow you direct control of the computer screen. They also take over the low-level graphics programming for you.
- The IBM extended character set includes many graphic characters in text mode, making possible a quite elaborate and pleasing text-mode display, as we will see in examples below.

We will, however, also give a few simple examples of VGA graphics, just to give you the flavor.

19.1 • Display Hardware

CRTs, like television sets, work by having an electron gun aimed at a screen covered with a phosphorescent material which glows when electrons hit it. Electromagnets above and below the beam can deflect it up or down. A similar pair on either side can deflect it side to side.

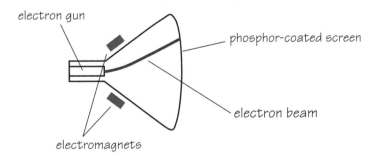

 The intensity of the beam can be altered to control the intensity of the glow on the screen. Monochrome screens are coated with a single phosphor, while color screens are coated with red, green, and blue phosphors in discrete dots, and the various colors are made up by lighting up nearby dots in varying degrees. Each pixel is made up of one dot each of red, green, and blue. An entire screen of information is obtained by causing the beam to trace rows across the screen, left to right, one after another, and when it reaches the bottom, to start all over again from the top. The electron beam is turned off during the **retrace** periods.

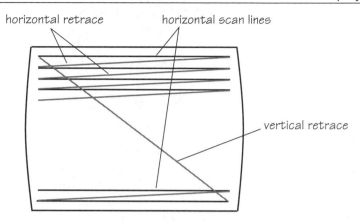

The typical CGA screen consists of 640 × 200 pixels. When used to represent text information of 25 lines of 80 characters each, each character is made up from an 8 × 8 grid of pixels (which are higher than they are wide, since characters usually are, too). Because EGA and VGA have more rows of pixels, they can either display 25 rows of characters in greater resolution, or display more rows of characters (43 and 50, respectively). VGA was the first mode to have square pixels. When in text mode, the display adaptor has a **character generator** which turns an 8-bit ASCII character into the required 8 × 8 pixel pattern and distributes the pattern out among the appropriate rows.

Computer CRTs are always equipped with **display memory**, which acts as a sort of snapshot of what appears on the screen. Although the screen appears to be a constant unflickering display, it is actually flickering too rapidly for the eye to see, as the screen is being redrawn from display memory approximately 30 times per second.

Computer *terminals* attached to large (non-personal) computers usually contain their own display memory, and characters are transmitted to the terminal one bit at a time. Even with high rates of transmission, it can take over half a second to change the entire screen in such a terminal. With more typical rates of transmission or with color information, it takes much longer. The problem is even greater in graphics modes and large screens. In text mode, an 8-bit character controls 64 pixels, whereas in graphics mode they must be controlled individually, requiring at least eight times as much information.

The clever solution used by most personal computers is to make the display memory also a part of the computer's memory, so that it can be changed at internal computer speeds. Even in the slowest PC, a text screen can be completely changed in just a little more than one screen tracing cycle, a little over 1/30th of a second. The display memory is usually physically on the display adaptor board, but appears to the PC as just another part of regular memory. Some display adaptors have several screens worth of display memory, called **pages**. The CGA, and those that emulate it, have four pages of memory in text mode. Multiple pages allow very rapid changes of the screen by simply changing which display page is being used.

In display programming of any sophistication, DOS calls are virtually worthless, even in text mode. There are three alternatives:

- The ROM BIOS `int 10h` call has a wide variety of display functions, and in this day of almost universal PC compatibility, is relatively safe to use. DOS uses these calls for its display functions, so by using them yourself, you may also speed up the display.
- Moving information directly into, and out of, display memory. This method is *very* fast but

requires the programmer to assume a lot of the functions normally assumed by DOS. Also, with certain adaptors the following technique may have to be used in conjunction with it or instead of it.

- Actual hardware I/O instructions (the `in` and `out` instructions which will be introduced in Section 19.2.3).

19.2 • Text Mode

Not only can each display adaptor show text on the screen, it can show it in a variety of forms— bright, dim, reverse video, blinking, underlined. On color displays, it can show text with a variety of foreground and background colors. In order to show characters in different modes, each of the 2,000 character positions on the screen corresponds to *two* bytes in display memory, a byte representing the character followed by an **attribute** byte. Thus the display screen is represented by 4,000, not 2,000 bytes. The format of the attribute byte for CGA (= EGA = VGA) text mode is:

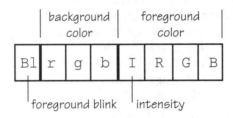

R, G, and B stand for red, green and blue. I is the high-intensity bit, and setting Bl causes the foreground to blink. The various colors produced by these bits are

000	Black (Intense mode may be dark gray)
001	Blue
010	Green
011	Cyan (a light blue-green)
100	Red
101	Magenta (a red-violet)
110	Brown (Intense mode is yellow)
111	Light Gray (Intense mode is white)

CGA color attributes

For instance, the standard attribute is 07h, light gray characters on a black background. Reverse video would be attribute 70h and high intensity (boldface) characters on a black background would be 0Fh. Normally, CGA text mode doesn't have the capability for underlining or intense background colors.

Most of these attributes are, of course, meaningless for the (monochrome) MDA. The Bl and I bits serve the same function as before and the two sets of RGB bits still relate to foreground and background "colors," but only the following combinations are meaningful:

000	Black
111	Gray (dim white)
001	Underline (foreground only)

19.2.1 • `Int 10h` **BIOS Calls for Text Mode**

Now we introduce the basic BIOS `int 10h` (video) commands for text mode. As with `int 21h` DOS calls, `int 10h` calls use a function code in `ah`. Most commands come in pairs: one command to *read* the current value of a property and another to *set* it. We can also divide the commands into four major categories:

1. **Commands concerning global display properties**.

The most important display property is its **mode**. We distinguish between text and graphics modes, and within graphics mode, various resolutions. The most commonly used text modes are 3 (CGA color, 80×25 characters) and 7 (MDA monochrome). Of the various graphics modes, we will use only 12h (VGA 640×480 pixels, 16 colors). The set command is

Set Video Mode

> input: `ah` = 00h
> `al` = desired video mode

As we mentioned earlier, CGA and the adaptors that emulate it have four **page**s of display memory in text mode; that is, four full screens of information. Very rapid screen changes can be effected by simply changing the active page number. (Debuggers can change rapidly between the debugger screen and the user's screen by simply changing page number.) Unless you change it though, you can probably assume that the page number is always 0. The BIOS calls are

Set Display Page

> input: `ah` = 05h
> `al` = display page number (0–3)

One command is used to retrieve both of these properties:

Get Video Mode and Display Page

> input: `ah` = 0fh   output: `al` = current video mode
> `ah` = chars per line
> `bh` = display page

Also useful in setting the mode is the BIOS `int 11h` call (no function number) which returns an **equipment list** in `ax`, which is coded as a pattern of bits. We are interested here only in bits 4 and 5 of `al`, which indicate the initial video mode: 10B for color and 11B for monochrome. This information can be used to determine whether a monochrome or color video adaptor is installed.

Example 19.2—1. Determine whether a monochrome or color video adaptor is installed and print an appropriate message. The code is:

```
.DATA
```

```
Mono      DB      'Monochrome adaptor', 13, 10, '$'
Color     DB      'Color adaptor', 13, 10, '$'
          ...
          .CODE
          ...
          int     11h ;         BIOS get equipment list call
          test    al, 10000B ;  Bit 4
          jnz     MDA
          _PutStr Color
          jmp     Done
MDA:
          _PutStr Mono
Done:
```

In IBM PCs and very compatible clones, the information obtained with these two calls is stored in standard locations in BIOS RAM memory: The byte at location 40h:49h contains the current video mode, the word at location 40h:4Ah contains the screen width in characters, and the byte at location 40h:62h contains the current page number. The word at location 40h:10h contains the equipment list.

2. **Display of Characters**.

There are several BIOS methods of displaying characters, none of which is totally adequate for normal needs. One of them displays characters and attributes, but does *not* move the cursor, while the other (like _PutCh) displays a character *without* changing the attribute at that character position, but *does* advance the cursor.

Display Character and Attribute, NO cursor change

input: ah = 09h
         al = ASCII character
         bl = attribute
         bh = display page (0–3; 0 usually)
         cx = number of copies to display (1, probably)

Display Character using Present Attribute and Advance Cursor

input: ah = 0eh
         al = ASCII character
         bh = display page (0–3; 0 usually)

Example 19.2—2. One can combine these two calls to get the BIOS call-that-should-have-been: display character and attribute and advance cursor. We first display the character with the attribute we want (09h) and then display it again (0eh) to advance the cursor. We skip the first call on characters less than blanks so they can be used for their usual control purposes. The following is a macro that does the job (IFNB, if non-blank, is described in Section 16.2):

```
PutCA      MACRO   char, attr, page ;  put char with attr on page
           LOCAL   SecondCall
           mov     al, &char&
IFNB <&page&>
           mov     bh, &page&
ELSE
           sub     bh, bh
ENDIF
           cmp     al, ' '
           jb      SecondCall
           mov     ah, 09h
           mov     bl, &attr&
           mov     cx, 1
           int     10h
SecondCall:
           mov     al, 0eh
           int     10h
           ENDM
```

Get Character and Attribute at Cursor Position

input: ah = 08h   output :   al = ASCII character
        bh = display page   ah = attribute

3. Cursor Manipulations.

There are two things you can do with the cursor—affect its position and affect its size. We will only discuss the former.

Set Cursor Position

input: ah = 02h
        dh = row (0–24)
        dl = column (0–79)
        bh = display page (0–3; 0 probably works)

The meaning of the cursor location is as follows:

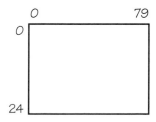

Text Screen Coordinates

One can hide the cursor simply by setting its position outside the screen.

Get Cursor Position

input:	ah = 03h	output:	dh = row
	bh = display page		dl = column

(The call above also returns the cursor size in ch and cl; the cursor size can be *set* using function 01h.)

Example 19.2—3. Display the message 'Error' in flashing red letters on a black background in the center of the screen without altering the current cursor position.

The code is

```
        .DATA
ErrMsg  DB      'Error$'
ERRLEN  EQU     $ - ErrMsg - 1
        ...
        .CODE
        ...
        sub     bh, bh ;        Assume page 0
        mov     ah, 03h
        int     10h ;           Cursor position in dx...
        push    dx ;              ...saved on stack
        mov     dh, 12 ;        Row = 12
        mov     dl, 40 - ERRLEN/2 ; Col
        sub     bh, bh
        mov     ah, 02h
        int     10h ;           Set cursor in middle of page
        mov     cx, ERRLEN
        mov     bx, 0084h ;     Page 0, red foreground, blink
        mov     ax, 0920h ;     Display blanks (char doesn't matter)
        int     10h ;           Doesn't advance cursor
        _PutStr ErrMsg ;        Insert Message
        pop     dx ;            Old cursor position from stack...
        sub     bh, bh
        mov     ah, 02h
        int     10h ;              ...and restore cursor to it
```

4. Scrolling

One can specify arbitrary windows on the screen and scroll them up or down with the appropriate BIOS functions:

Scroll Window

input:
al = number of lines to scroll (0 to clear window)
ch = row number of upper left-hand corner (0-24)
cl = column number of upper left-hand corner (0-79)
dh = row number of lower right-hand corner (0-24)
dl = column number of lower right-hand corner (0-79)
bh = attribute for cleared lines

ah = 06h (scroll up)
ah = 07h (scroll down)

Example 19.2—4. A macro to clear the whole screen, setting all attribute bytes to a specified value, by scrolling.

```
ClearScr  MACRO  attr ;          attr is optional
IFNB <&attr&>
          mov    bh, &attr&
ELSE
          mov    bh, 07h ;       Black background, gray foreground
ENDIF
          mov    ax, 0600h ;     Scroll up, whole window
          mov    cx, 0000h ;     Upper left corner = 0, 0
          mov    dx, 184Fh ;     Lower right corner = 24, 79
          int    10h
          ENDM
```

19.2.2 • Direct Access to Display Memory

The video memory for the monochrome display adaptor is at location 0B000h:0 and that for CGA and adaptors emulating CGA is at location 0B800h:0.

Example 19.2—5. Set es to the segment of the correct display memory.

The program below is a simple modification of Example 19.2—1:

```
VideoSeg  EQU     0B000h
Video     SEGMENT AT VideoSeg
Page      DB      25 DUP (80 DUP (?, ?))
;                 25 rows of 80 cols of char, attr
Video     ENDS
          . . .
          .CODE
          . . .
          int     11h ;          Get equipment list
          mov     bx, VideoSeg
          test    ax, 10000B ;   Bit 4
```

```
            jnz     Monochrome
            add     bx, 800h
Monochrome:
            mov     es, bx
            ASSUME es : Video
```

The reason for the definition of `Page`, which is really for documentation purposes only, is that a page of display memory is organized as a string of character-attribute pairs (character first), with the first 80 pairs making up the first screen row, the next 80 pairs, the next screen row, and so on. MDA display memory consists of a single page of 4,000 bytes and CGA memory consists of 16,000 bytes divided into four pages of 4,000 bytes each.

Example 19.2—6. Choosing from a pop-up menu.

We will create a pop-up menu in the middle of the screen—with graphic characters to give it a double-line border and one of four choices highlighted. The user can change the highlighted option by using up and down cursor keys, and make a choice with the Enter key, after which the program restores the area occupied by the menu, informs the user of his or her choice, and exits. The rather fanciful menu choices are as follows:

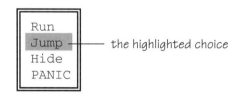

We start with a copy of the menu, complete with border, attributes, and highlighted first line, in our own storage. To simplify matters, we will assume CGA (or EGA or VGA) color text mode, and that page 0 is the current page. Our first actions will be to save the current contents of video memory at the place where our popup will go, and then move the menu into that location. For speed, we use the `rep movsw` instruction from Chapter 18. Each row of the menu must be done separately, as the rows are separated by almost 160 bytes in display memory. (You may wonder why we didn't use another display page. That method would have involved copying everything in page 0 to the new page or initializing it in some other way, which is much more time-consuming than just saving the area covered by our menu.)

Once the menu is displayed, we use the `_BIOSCh` macro (see Section 5.5) to 'listen' for up and down cursor arrows and the Enter key. The scan codes for these keys are 72 (up), 80 (down), and 28 (Enter). In addition, on extended keyboards, which most keyboards now are, there is an extra set of cursor keys which produce *two* scan codes, a first scan code of 0E0h followed by the scan code of the corresponding key in the numeric keypad. Thus the up arrow on the cursor keypad produces 0E0h, then 72. If any key other than up, down, or Enter is pressed, or if the user tries to move off the top or bottom of the menu, a beep (Ctrl-G, ASCII 7) is echoed.

The mechanism for handling the highlighting of the menu choice is simple: just change the attribute bytes of the previously highlighted line back to normal. Then change the attribute bytes of the new highlight line to the highlight attribute.

The program is

```
;; MENU.ASM—A program to demonstrate a pop-up menu with
;;    highlighted menu choice via direct access to display memory.
;;    Assumes CGA, EGA, or VGA

INCLUDE    PCMAC.INC
           .MODEL SMALL
           ASSUME SS:NOTHING ; Safety first; see Section 12.4


           .STACK 100h


           .DATA
NO         EQU    1Eh ;          Normal attribute (yellow on blue)
HI         EQU    5Fh ;      Highlight attribute (white on magenta)
; Double outlining characters:
UL         EQU    0C9h ;        Corners
UR         EQU    0BBh
LL         EQU    0C8h
LR         EQU    0BCH
V          EQU    0BAH ;        Vertical
H          EQU    0CDh ;        Horizontal
;   The menu, with attributes:
MLines     DB     UL, NO, 7 DUP (H, NO), UR, NO ; top border
LINELEN    EQU    $ - MLines
           DB     V, NO, ' ', HI, 'R', HI, 'u', HI, 'n', HI
           DB        3 DUP (' ', HI), V, NO ; First line highlighted
           DB     V, NO, ' ', NO, 'J', NO, 'u', NO, 'm', NO
           DB        'p', NO, ' ', NO, ' ', NO, V, NO ; 2nd line
           DB     V, NO, ' ', NO, 'H', NO, 'i', NO, 'd', NO
           DB        'e', NO, ' ', NO, ' ', NO, V, NO ; 3rd line
           DB     V, NO, ' ', NO, 'P', NO, 'A', NO, 'N', NO
           DB        'I', NO, 'C', NO, ' ', NO, V, NO ; 4th line
           DB     LL, NO, 7 DUP (H, NO), LR, NO ; bottom border
NUMLINES EQU      ($ - MLines) / LINELEN
;    Where the menu starts in a video page:
MENULOC    EQU    ((25 - NUMLINES)/2)*160 + 80 - 2 * (LINELEN / 2)
;    Storage for previous contents of menu area
SaveArea DB       LINELEN * NUMLINES DUP (?)
YouChose DB       'You chose line '
ChoiceNo DB       ?, 13, 10, '$'

EnterSC    EQU    28 ;          Scan code of enter key
UpSC       EQU    72 ;          Scan code of up cursor key
DownSC     EQU    80 ;          Scan code of down cursor key
Extend     EQU    0E0h ;        Prefix for extended keyboard keys

Video      SEGMENT AT 0B800h
Page0      DB     25 DUP ( 80 DUP (?, ?))
```

```
Video       ENDS

            .CODE

;   MoveBlock procedure; Used to move FROM menu display area TO
;     SaveArea (bx <> 0) or vice-versa (bx = 0). On entry, ds:si
;     and es:di are assumed properly set up for the movsw
;     instruction (see chapter 18). The only reason we need to know
;     which way the move is going is that the SaveArea is contiguous
;     and the parts of the display area we're using aren't, so we
;     have to move by rows and si or di is incremented differently
;     if it corresponds to the display area. cx, dx, si, and di are
;     destroyed.

MoveBlock PROC    ;         Move memory block to or from display mem
          mov     dx, NUMLINES
MoveLoop:
          mov     cx, LINELEN/2 ;     Because I'm moving WORDS
          rep     movsw
          test    bx, bx ;      If bx = 0, moving from display mem
          jnz     IncDI ;          if <> 0, moving to it
          add     si, 160 - LINELEN ; Move to next line of video
          jmp     IncDone
IncDI:
          add     di, 160 - LINELEN
IncDone:
          dec     dx
          jnz     MoveLoop
          ret
MoveBlock ENDP

; NewAttr; Set all the attributes on the menu line pointed to by
;   es:di to the attribute given in al; cx is destroyed

NewAttr   PROC
          push    di
          mov     cx, LINELEN/2 - 2 ; Don't highlight border
NewLoop:
          mov     es:[1+di], al
          add     di, 2 ;        Only changing alternate bytes
          loop    NewLoop
          pop     di
          ret
NewAttr   ENDP

;***************************
;*  Main Program
```

```
        ;***************************

Menu            PROC
                mov     si, MENULOC
                mov     ax, Video ; TASM users see footnote on p. 312
                mov     ds, ax
                mov     di, OFFSET SaveArea
                mov     ax, @data
                mov     es, ax
                ASSUME ds:Video, es:SEG SaveArea ;     for documentation
                sub     bx, bx ;       Indicates si is screen
                call    MoveBlock ;   Save menu area of display page

                mov     si, OFFSET MLines
                mov     di, MENULOC
                mov     ax, es ;       es <-> ds
                mov     bx, ds
                mov     ds, ax
                mov     es, bx
                ASSUME ds : SEG SaveArea, es:Video
                call    MoveBlock ;   Display menu (bx will be nonzero)

                mov     bx, 1 ;        Currently highlighted line
                mov     di, MENULOC + 160 + 2
;           (pointer to current highlight in di)
Choose:
                _BIOSCh
                cmp     ah, Extend ; Is it a new extended kbd key?
                jne     notExtendedKey
                _BIOSCh ;             Eat the prefix
notExtendedKey:
                cmp     ah, UpSC ;    Up Cursor?
                jne     C1
                cmp     bx, 1 ;       If =, can't go up
                je      BadKey
                mov     al, NO ;      Un-highlight current line
                call    NewAttr
                dec     bx
                sub     di, 160 ;     Move to previous line
                mov     al, HI ;      Highlight new line
                call    NewAttr
                jmp     Choose
C1:
                cmp     ah, DownSC ; Down Cursor?
                jne     C2
                cmp     bx, NUMLINES - 2
                jge     BadKey ;      IF =, can't go down
```

```
              mov    al, NO
              call   NewAttr
              inc    bx
              add    di, 160 ;     Move to next line...
              mov    al, HI
              call   NewAttr ;        ...and highlight it
              jmp    Choose
C2:
              cmp    ah, EnterSC ; Enter Key?
              je     Done
BadKey:
              _PutCh 7 ;                      Beep
              jmp    Choose


Done:
              mov    si, OFFSET SaveArea ;      Restore menu area
              mov    di, MENULOC
              add    bl, '0' ;     Easy conversion to decimal
              mov    ChoiceNo, bl
              call   MoveBlock ;   Display menu
              _PutStr YouChose
              _Exit  0
Menu          ENDP
              END    Menu
```

19.2.3 • Hardware I/O: CGA Snow

For various reasons, one occasionally has to use actual hardware I/O instructions to do video programming properly. Examples of such situations are extreme speed requirements, when one wishes to do something nonstandard, or when one wishes to get around a limitation in the hardware. The subject is far beyond the scope of this text, but it is worth pursuing at least to a minor degree as we will otherwise have no excuse to introduce the hardware I/O instructions at all.

Hardware I/O is, in principle, very simple. The 80X86 recognizes up to $2^{16} = 65,536$ I/O **ports**. A port can be used to input or output a byte or a word of information using two basic instructions:

```
    in      ax or al, port;     Read a word or a byte from port
    out     port, ax or al;     Write a word or a byte to port
```

The order of the operands is determined, as usual, on the 80X86: $op\ dest,\ source$. For port numbers less than 256, *port* can be the literal port number. For larger port numbers and variable port numbers, the port number must be in dx, which is the *port* operand. **Note: There is no relationship whatever between ports and interrupt numbers!**

On such a seemingly simple base, a very complicated I/O structure can be built. In the first place, each I/O device may have *several* associated ports, which can be categorized as **data ports**, **status ports**, and **control ports**. The use of a data port is obvious—that's how the actual data gets in and out. Writing to control ports is used to control the action of the device. For instance, the serial ports (COM1:, etc.) each have a control port for setting Baud rate (rate of transmission), parity bit, etc. Programs can read from the status port to find out the state of the I/O device. As we will see below, the display adaptor has a status port which makes it possible to determine what the electron beam is doing in 'painting' the CRT screen.

Example 19.2—7. Avoiding CGA snow.

IBM's original CGA had a problem: If the CPU and the chip that was redrawing the screen tried to access display memory at the same time (in text mode), 'snow' appeared on the screen. The BIOS routines avoid this problem, and it is not a problem on EGA, VGA, or any CGA clone the author has seen. Hence there's not a lot of practical value to the code to avoid it. (Many programs still include such code. When you are installing such a program, it may ask you at some point if you see snow on the screen. If you say yes, the program then uses the following slower but non-snowy method of moving bytes to display memory.)

The trick to avoiding snow is writing to display memory only during horizontal or vertical retrace, when the electron beam is off. To determine when that is, we must read a byte from the video adapter status port, 03DAh. Bit 0 of that byte is 1 during horizontal retrace.

It isn't enough, though, simply to wait for bit 0 to go to 1. We might have come in at the very end of horizontal retrace, and by the time we move our character, we may already be out of it. Therefore we need *two* waits, one for horizontal retrace to *end*, then one for it to begin again. The first wait guarantees us that we have a full retrace period at our disposal. That is, of course, if interrupts are disabled. If interrupts are enabled, all bets are off, because we could get an interrupt in the middle of either of our waits which could use up part of our retrace time. The correct code is

```
VideoStat EQU    03DAh ;        Video Status Port
HRetrace  EQU    1 ;            Horizontal Retrace Bit
          ...
          mov    bx, char and attribute to store
          mov    dx, VideoStat
          cli    ;              Can't be any later
WaitForNoRetrace:
          in     al, dx ;       al := video status byte
          test   al, HRetrace
          jnz    WaitForNoRetrace
WaitForRetrace:
          in     al, dx
          test   al, HRetrace
          jz     WaitForRetrace

          xchg   bx, ax
          stosw  ;    or movsw without the xchg and mov bx,...
          sti    ;              Can't be any earlier
```

According to Wilton's book on PC video systems (p. 73, see the bibliography) the horizontal retrace interval is just long enough to copy one word to or from display memory, and on the very slowest PCs, even an ordinary mov is too slow. A movsw or stosw must be used (see Chapter 18). One can also write many more characters during the less frequent) vertical retrace interval (bit 3 of the status byte.) See Wilton's book for more information.

Note that a CGA does roughly $30 \times 200 = 6,000$ horizontal retraces per second, each horizontal cycle therefore taking about 160 microseconds (μsec, or millionths of a second). We would expect, on the average, to wait about half that long, or 80 μsec. On even the slowest PCs, many instructions take less than 1 μsec, so the code above can really waste a lot of time that could otherwise be spent on computing!

Exercises 19.2

1. ✓Using the IRPC pseudo-operation (Section 8.4), give shorter definitions of the menu display lines (MLines) in Example 19.2—6.

2. ✓Write assembly language code to do cursor movement up, down, left and right as would be done by a full-screen editor. Use the get cursor position call, followed by the set cursor position call. Do not move beyond the top, bottom, left, or right edges of the screen.

3. a) ✓ Write a subprocedure InsertLine which takes as input a line number (0-24) in ah and an attribute inFYl and shifts everything on the screen from the specified line number down one, inserting a new line at the specified line number with the specified attribute.
   b) Write a subprocedure DeleteLine which takes as input a line number (0-24) in ah and an attribute in al and shifts everything on the screen, from the specified line number down, up one line, deleting the specified line inserting a new line at the bottom of the screen with the specified attribute.

4. Suppose that we have CGA Video with the following declarations:

```
VideoSeg   EQU     0B800h
Video      SEGMENT AT VideoSeg
Screen     DB      25 DUP (80 DUP (? ?))
Video      ENDS


           .DATA
Row        DW      ? ;            0..24
Col        DW      ? ;            0..79
           . . .
           ASSUME ds : @data, es : Video
```

In what follows, assume that snow is not a problem.
   a) ✓ Write assembly code to change the attributes of every byte on the screen to green background, bright red blinking foreground.
   b) Write assembly code to change all the displayed characters in row Row to blanks without changing the attributes of any of these bytes.
   c) Write assembly code to change the attributes of all characters in column Col to black background, light gray foreground.

19.3 • Simple VGA Graphics

Video graphics is an extremely complicated area, particularly on the IBM PC, and far beyond the scope of this book. However, it is worthwhile to give an example just to give a little of the flavor of the subject. It is an area which can be treated in high-level languages, but because speed is essential, assembly language is often used, at least for graphics functions. Use of hardware I/O instructions is also frequent for the same reason, but we will limit ourselves to the BIOS `int 10h` calls.

To fix our ideas, we will program only in VGA 640 × 480, sixteen color mode (mode 12h). This mode is something that only a hardware designer could love, but it is the highest-resolution standard VGA mode. The determination of pixel color has the following overall structure:

VGA Mode 12h Overview

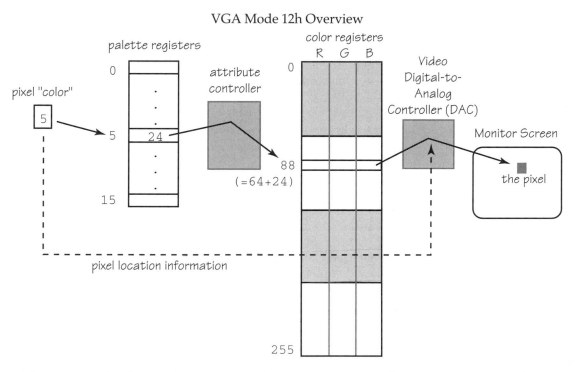

There are two levels of indirection. Specifying a pixel color (in the diagram, 5) causes the corresponding one of sixteen **palette registers** to be chosen, which in turn specifies one of 256 **color registers**, which in turn specifies the actual Red, Green, and Blue values for the pixel in question. As you might expect, there are BIOS `int 10h` calls for setting and reading the palette and color registers. In addition, the 256 color registers are either divided up into four banks of 64 registers each (as above) or 16 banks of 16 registers each. The particular bank chosen (in the picture above, the second one) and whether there are four or sixteen banks is controlled by the **attribute controller**. The attribute controller can be programmed with its own set and read commands, but we will ignore this technicality. The **default** is four sets of 64 banks, with bank 0 chosen. *In any case, at most the low-order 6 bits of a palette register value are meaningful.*

Each color register is 18 bits long, allowing 6-bit red, green, and blue fields for a total of 262,144 colors. When you switch modes, the palette and color registers are assigned default values, which result in the palette registers 0–15 mapping into the standard 16 CGA foreground text colors coded in four bits as IRGB. Thus, palette register 5 maps to a color register whose value is a medium magenta, RGB values (42, 0, 42), and palette register 0bh maps to a color register whose value is a bright cyan, RGB values (21, 63, 63). The default values for the palette registers are

palette register	color register	palette register	color register
0	0	8	56
1	1	9	57
2	2	10	58
3	3	11	59
4	4	12	60
5	5	13	61
6	20	14	62
7	7	15	63

We have already seen how to get into and out of VGA mode 12h with the function 00h call. In addition, we will need three other int 10h functions. The three levels of set instructions, in order, are

Set Pixel to Specified Palette Entry

input: ah = 0ch
al = palette register number (0–15 in this mode)
bh = display page (should be 0)
cx = x coordinate of pixel (0–639 in this mode)
dx = y coordinate of pixel (0–479 in this mode)

Set Palette Register to Specified Color Register

input: a**x** = 1000h
bl = palette register number (0–15)
bh = color register number (0–63)

Set Color Register Values

input: a**x** = 1010h
bx = color register number (0–255 in this mode)
dh = red value (0–63)
ch = green value (0–63)
cl = blue value (0–63)

The three corresponding calls to get the current values are

Get Palette Entry for Pixel

input: ah = 0dh
bh = display page (should be 0)
cx = x coordinate of pixel (0–639 in this mode)
dx = y coordinate of pixel (0–479 in this mode)
output: al = palette register number (0–15 in this mode)

Get Palette Register Color Register Value

input: ax = 1007h
            bl = palette register number (0–15)
output: bh = color register number (0–63)

Get Color Register Values

input: ax = 1015h
            bx = color register number (0–255 in this mode)
output: dh = red value (0–63)
            ch = green value (0–63)
            cl = blue value (0–63)

The screen coordinates used in call ah = 0ch are as follows in this mode:

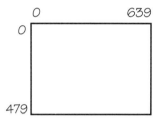

VGA 640 × 480 mode Screen Coordinates

Note that by using the second or third Set call above (ax = 1000h or ax = 1010h), we can instantaneously change the colors of *all* pixels on the screen with a given palette entry number, *even in text mode*. Thus, we can reprogram the 'standard' CGA colors to be any group of 16 colors that we want. See Example 19.3—5.

Example 19.3—1. Draw the following figure full-screen in VGA graphics.

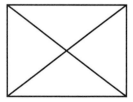

Getting into and out of VGA mode and selecting the color palette register for the points of our figure are straightforward. The interesting part is that the pixels for the diagonal lines must occur at discrete positions, and since the ratio of horizontal to vertical dimensions on the screen is 4 to 3, something special must be done to get the diagonal lines. (That is, we can't put a pixel at x = 1, y = 1.3.) We choose to increase the y (up-and-down) coordinate every time we increase the x coordinate (side to side) *except* when the x coordinate is divisible by 4, which is easy to check on a binary machine. Thus, a magnified view of one of the lines would be

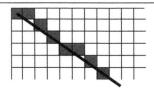

We can plot all of the points we need with one loop if we're careful. Consider the following pseudocode version:

```
y := 0
for x := 0 to 639 { x = column }
  Plot(x, y)
  Plot(x, 479 - y)      { display points on diagonals }
  Plot(x, 0)
  Plot(x, 479)          { plot top and bottom of column }
  if (x mod 4 <> 0) then
    Plot(0, y)
    Plot(639, y)    { plot left and right end of row...}
    y := y + 1          { ...and increment row }
  end if
end for
```

We can make use of the fact that the 'draw pixel' BIOS call preserves registers and use cx for x and dx for y. Once the diagram has been drawn, the program waits for a keystroke and then returns to normal text mode and exits. The code is

```
;; PATTERN.ASM--rectangle with cross in VGA 640x480 16 color mode.
;;
INCLUDE    PCMAC.INC
           .MODEL SMALL
           ASSUME SS:NOTHING

           .STACK 100h

ROWS       EQU     480
COLS       EQU     640 ;       Rows and cols on VGA screen
PixColor   EQU     1011B ;     Bright Cyan

           .CODE
Pattern    PROC
           mov     ax, 0012h ; Video mode 640x480 16 colors
           int     10h ;                 Set Video Mode

           mov     ah, 0ch ;   Plot point in PixColor
           mov     al, PixColor
           mov     cx, 0 ;     Start at x = 0,
           mov     dx, 0 ;        y = 0
```

```
                sub     bh, bh ;        Necessary to avoid weirdness
                mov     si, COLS ;      Number of times through loop
        PlotLoop:
                int     10h ;           Plot(x, y)
                push    dx
                neg     dx
                add     dx, ROWS - 1
                int     10h ;           Plot(x, 479 - y)
                sub     dx, dx
                int     10h ;           Plot(x, 0)
                mov     dx, ROWS - 1
                int     10h ;           Plot(x, 479)
                pop     dx
                test    cx, 3 ;         y goes up only 3/4 ths of the time
                jz      NoUpY ;            ...when x isn't divisible by 4
                push    cx
                sub     cx, cx
                int     10h ;           Plot(0, y)
                mov     cx, COLS - 1
                int     10h ;           Plot(639, y)
                pop     cx
                inc     dx
        NoUpY:  inc     cx
                dec     si
                jg      PlotLoop

                _BIOSCh ;               Wait for keystroke

                mov     ax, 0003h ;     Normal 80X86 text mode
                int     10h
                _Exit   0
        Pattern ENDP
                END     Pattern
```

Programs using VGA graphics modes can be debugged using CodeView or the Turbo Debugger. Not too surprisingly, it isn't an entirely satisfactory experience. CodeView should be invoked with the /S switch and TD with the /ds switch, as in

```
    cv /S Pattern      or      td /ds Pattern
```

Example 19.3—2. Construct a general line-drawing procedure.

We want our procedure to take as input the coordinates of two points (x1, y1) and (x2, y2) and draw the line between those points. Formulas from analytic geometry tell us that the equation of the line is

$$y - y1 = m*(x - x1)$$

where m, the *slope* of the line, is given by the formula

$$m = (y2 - y1) / (x2 - x1)$$

($x1 = x2$ is a simple special case.) Using the line equation directly is very inefficient. In order to compute m, we would have to use real arithmetic, then perform a real multiplication, and finally convert the resulting value of y to the nearest integer. Luckily, most of this effort can be avoided by using a method known as **Bresenham's algorithm**, which is presented in most books on computer graphics. The algorithm involves no multiplication or division whatever! We'll give just a brief introduction to the method before presenting the code, which is a somewhat altered version of the program given in the article 'Smooth Views', by Michael A. Covington (see the bibliography.)

First of all, the algorithm works only when the slope m satisfies $|m| \leq 1$. ($|m|$ is the absolute value of m, that is, m with its sign removed.) This condition is easy enough to arrange—if it is greater than 1, we interchange x's and y's, keeping track of the fact we have done so in a variable called Steep, and then plot (y, x) instead of (x, y).

As with Example 19.3—1, x will be altered by xincr = ±1 each time through the plotting loop, but y will be altered by yincr = ±1 only on certain times through the loop. Whether y is changed will be determined by whether a variable, which I have called ErrDiff, is ≥ 0. ErrDiff is computed for the starting point and then updated incrementally at each successive x in a rather simple manner. To give you some idea where ErrDiff comes from, consider the following:

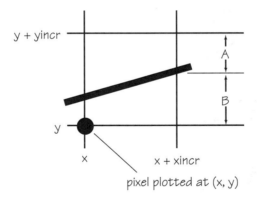

pixel plotted at (x, y)

The next point will be plotted at (x+xincr, y) or (x+xincr, y+yincr) depending on whether B is greater than A. ErrDiff is just (B – A) times an appropriate positive number which makes it integral. The general form of the code is:

```
x := x1; y := y1              { the running coordinates }
delx := |x2 - x1|
xincr := sign(x2 - x1)        { x2 - x1 = delx * xincr }
dely := |y2 - y1|
yincr := sign(y2 - y1)

if (dely > delx) then
   set Steep to true and swap all x and y values
end if
ErrDiff := 2*dely - delx        /* initial value */
```

```
  for counter := 0 to delx        /* plot delx+1 points */
    if Steep then Plot(y, x) else Plot(x, y) end if
    if (ErrDiff >= 0) then
      y := y + yincr
      ErrDiff := ErrDiff - 2*delx
    end if
    x := x + xincr
    ErrDiff := ErrDiff + 2*dely
  end for
```

It turns out to be easier simply to plot (x, y), swapping x and y before and after the operation if Steep is true. Also, we will use delx as the counter, counting it down to 0. The procedure, called BLine, which takes as input the two points and a color number on the stack and pops its parameters at the end, is:

```
;; BLINE.ASM—display line from (x1, y1) to (x2, y2) in color Color
;;   using Bresenham's algorithm. This program a modified form of
;;   the algorithm in Covington's May 1990 Byte article.
;;
;;   Calling Sequence
;;         push    x1
;;         push    y1
;;         push    x2
;;         push    y2
;;         push    color
;;         call    BLine
;;
;;   Preserves seg registers and si and di
;;
            .MODEL SMALL

            .CODE
x1          EQU    WORD PTR [bp+12] ; Passed parameters
y1          EQU    WORD PTR [bp+10]
x2          EQU    WORD PTR [bp+8]
y2          EQU    WORD PTR [bp+6]
Color       EQU    BYTE PTR [bp+4]

delx        EQU    WORD PTR [bp-2] ;  Local variables on stack
twodelx     EQU    WORD PTR [bp-4]
twodely     EQU    WORD PTR [bp-6]
Steep       EQU    BYTE PTR [bp-8]
xincr       EQU    WORD PTR [bp-10]

x           EQU    cx ;                Variables in registers
y           EQU    dx
ErrDiff     EQU    si
```

```
yincr       EQU     di

            PUBLIC  BLine
BLine       PROC
            push    bp
            mov     bp, sp
            sub     sp, 10
            push    si
            push    di

            mov     x, x1 ;         Initial point —> registers
            mov     y, y1

            mov     ax, x2
            sub     ax, x
            mov     bx, 1
            jge     xOK
            neg     ax ;            delx := ax := abs(x2 - x1)
            neg     bx ;            xincr := bx := sign(x2 - x1)
xOK:
            mov     si, y2
            sub     si, y
            mov     yincr, 1 ;      yincr = di
            jge     yOK
            neg     si ;            dely := si := abs(y2 - y1)
            neg     yincr ;         yincr := sign(y2 - y1)
yOK:
            mov     Steep, 0 ;      Steep := 0;
            cmp     si, ax ;        if (dy > dx) then
            jng     notSteep
            mov     Steep, 1 ;          Steep := 1
            xchg    x, y ;              Swap(x, y)
            xchg    ax, si ;            Swap(delx, dely)
            xchg    bx, yincr ;         Swap(xincr, yincr)
notSteep:
            mov     delx, ax ;      (store stuff from registers)
            shl     si, 1 ;         si := 2*dely
            mov     twodely, si
            sub     si, ax ;        ErrDiff := si := 2*dely - delx
            shl     ax, 1
            mov     twodelx, ax
            mov     xincr, bx

            mov     ah, 0ch ;       Prepare for BIOS light pixel call
            mov     al, Color
            sub     bh, bh
PlotLoop: ;                         while delx >= 0 do
```

```
              cmp    Steep, 0 ;                if Steep then
              jz     noSwap
              xchg   x, y ;                          Swap(x, y)
              int    10h ;                           Plot(x, y)
              xchg   x, y ;                          Swap(x, y)
              jmp    SHORT update
noSwap:
              int    10h ;                else  Plot(x, y)


update:
              test   ErrDiff, ErrDiff ; if (ErrDiff >= 0) then
              jnge   SHORT NoYIncr
              add    y, yincr ;                 y := y + yincr
              sub    ErrDiff, twodelx ; ErrDiff := ErrDiff - 2*delx
NoYIncr:
              add    x, xincr ;          x := x + xincr
              add    ErrDiff, twodely ; ErrDiff := ErrDiff + 2*dely
              dec    delx ;               delx := delx - 1
              jge    PlotLoop ;       end while (delx >= 0)

              pop    di
              pop    si
              mov    sp, bp
              pop    bp
              ret    10
BLine         ENDP
              END
```

Example 19.3—3. Change screen colors 'continuously.'

By changing the color palette, we can change items drawn on the screen with them. This process is called **animating the color palette**. We will demonstrate it with a single color, starting with red = 63, green = blue = 0. Each time the Animate routine is called, it decrements red and increments green. When red gets to 0, it then continues the process with green and blue, then blue and red, then starts all over again. We make Animate a separate procedure so that it can be called among other actions. We also write another procedure InitCol to start out the process.

```
;; ANIMATE.ASM—Cycle through two-color combinations,
;;   one change per call
;;
          .MODEL SMALL

SetColor  MACRO  Reg, red, green, blue
          mov    bx, &Reg&
          mov    dh, &red&
          mov    ch, &green&
          mov    cl, &blue&
```

```
                mov     ax, 1010h
                int     10h
                ENDM


                .DATA
Red             DB      63
Green           DB      0
Blue            DB      0
UpColor         DW      Green ;      Pointer to color to increment
DownColor DW          Red ;        Pointer to color to decrement

                .CODE
                PUBLIC InitCol, Animate
InitCol         PROC    ;                    Initialize color
                mov     ax, 1000h ;  Set palette regs 0, 1 to color
                mov     bx, 0000h ;   regs 0, 1 (These are the
                int     10h ;         defaults but could have been
                mov     ax, 1000h ;   changed)
                mov     bx, 0101h
                int     10h
                SetColor 0, 0, 0, 0 ;    Register 0 is black
                SetColor 1, red, green, blue
                ret
InitCol         ENDP

Animate         PROC
                mov     si, DownColor
                mov     di, UpColor
                cmp     BYTE PTR [si], 0 ;  Is DownColor all the way down?
                jne     DoIt
                mov     si, di ;          DownColor := UpColor
                cmp     di, OFFSET Blue;  if old UpColor = Blue then
                jne     Add1
                mov     di, OFFSET Red ;       UpColor = Red
                jmp     Store
Add1:
                inc     di ;             else UpColor := next color
Store:
                mov     DownColor, si
                mov     UpColor, di
DoIt:
                inc     BYTE PTR [di]
                dec     BYTE PTR [si]
                SetColor 1, Red, Green, Blue
                ret
Animate         ENDP
                END
```

We will collect the last two examples in one grand and glorious example which does nothing particularly useful. (You might use it as a screen saver). It does show how to erase lines, so it isn't totally frivolous.

Example 19.3—4. Write a program which generates a certain number of random lines (say 10), and then continues generating lines, each time erasing the oldest line on the screen. As each line is generated, call `Animate` to change the color of the lines. Stop when a key is struck.

The main program is quite simple, if we assume a procedure `Randline` to erase the oldest line (if ten lines have been generated) and generate a new one:

```
initialize display;
repeat
  RandLine
  change to next color
until key pressed
restore display
```

The assembly code is:

```
;; CRAZY.ASM—Displays random lines in modulating color
;;
INCLUDE    PCMAC.INC
           .MODEL SMALL
           .STACK 100h

           .CODE
           EXTRN   RandLine : NEAR, Animate : NEAR, InitCol : NEAR
Crazy      PROC
           mov     ax, @data
           mov     ds, ax
           mov     ax, 0012h ;   Video mode 640x480 16 colors
           int     10h ;                   Set Video Mode

           call    InitCol ;     Initialize screen colors

PlotLoop:
           call    RandLine ;    Draw random line and erase old one
           call    Animate ;     Change to next color

           mov     ah, 1 ;       Key Struck?
           int     16h
           jz      PlotLoop

           _BIOSCh ;             Eat up the character

           mov     ax, 0003h ;   Normal 80x25 text mode
```

```
              int     10h
              _Exit   0
Crazy         ENDP
              END     Crazy
```

For `RandLine` we will make a table `LineTab` of 10 (or however many we choose) line coordinates and use an index `NewLine` to circulate through the `LineTab` entries: `LineTab[1]`, … `LineTab[10]`, `LineTab[1]`, … . Each time we reuse an entry in the table, we will erase the previous entry by generating the line again (with `BLine`) using color 0, black. This method of erasure is not quite a perfect solution to the problem because if the line we're erasing intersects another line still on the screen, it will erase a dot out of the second line too. The general form of the program is:

```
if LineTab[NewLine] has been used then
   BLine(coordinates from LineTab[NewLine], color = Black);
Generate new random coordinates and store in LineTab[NewLine];
BLine(coordinates from LineTab[NewLine], color = 1, which changes);
if NewLine = 10 then NewLine := 1
else NewLine := NewLine + 1;
```

In order to be able to tell when we're reusing a table entry, the first word of each entry is initialized to –1, which would not be a legal line coordinate.

We will generate the random coordinates of the lines using the function `Random` developed in Section 14.2. This function generates numbers between 1 and $2^{31} - 1$ and what we need are numbers between 0 and 639 or 0 and 479. It would seem that we could get numbers in the correct range by dividing the random number by 640 or 480—it even comes back from `Random` in the right registers—and taking the remainder. The problem is that *the random number is usually too big for the quotient to fit into* `ax`, so we get a divide error. We use a quick-and-dirty way to get around this problem. We simply zero `dh`, the high-order byte of the output from `Random`, which makes the random number small enough that the divisions works.

The code for `RandLine` is

```
;;    RANDLINE.ASM—Generate a new random line in color 1 and save
;;       its coordinates in LineTab.  When a LineTab entry is reused,
;;       first erase the previous line.
              .MODEL SMALL
              .DATA
NLINES        EQU     10
LineTab       DW      NLINES DUP(-1, 0, 0, 0)
EndTab        LABEL   WORD
NextLine DW           LineTab

              .CODE
              PUBLIC RandLine
              EXTRN  Random : NEAR, BLine : NEAR
RandLine      PROC
              mov     si, NextLine
              cmp     WORD PTR [si], 0
```

```
                jl      NewLine
                push    [si] ;          Erase old line
                push    [si+2]
                push    [si+4]
                push    [si+6]
                sub     ax, ax
                push    ax ;            Color black
                call    BLine
NewLine:
                call    Random
                sub     dh, dh ;        make smaller so no divide overflow
                mov     bx, 640
                div     bx
                push    dx ;            Random number mod 640, x1
                mov     si, NextLine
                mov     [si], dx
                call    Random
                sub     dh, dh ;        make smaller so no divide overflow
                mov     bx, 480
                div     bx
                push    dx ;            Random number mod 480, y1
                mov     si, NextLine
                mov     [si+2], dx
                call    Random
                sub     dh, dh ;        make smaller so no divide overflow
                mov     bx, 640
                div     bx
                push    dx ;            Random number mod 640, x2
                mov     si, NextLine
                mov     [si+4], dx
                call    Random
                sub     dh, dh ;        make smaller so no divide overflow
                mov     bx, 480
                div     bx
                push    dx ;            Random number mod 480, y2
                mov     si, NextLine
                mov     [si+6], dx

                mov     ax, 1
                push    ax
                call    BLine
                add     NextLine, 8
                cmp     NextLine, OFFSET EndTab
                jb      Done
                mov     NextLine, OFFSET LineTab
Done:
                ret
```

```
RandLine  ENDP
          END
```

All the lines between `NewLine` and `mov ax, 1` can be replaced by four calls to the `GetCoord` macro, defined below (the `IF/ELSE/ENDIF` calls are described in Section 16.1).

```
coordno = 0
GetCoord  MACRO
          call    Random
IFE (coordno AND 1)
          mov     bx, 640
ELSE
          mov     bx, 480
ENDIF
          sub     dh, dh ;     make smaller so no divide overflow
          div     bx
          push    dx
          mov     si, NextLine
          mov     [2 * coordno + si], dx
coordno = coordno + 1
          ENDM
```

The code `IFE … ENDIF` could be replaced by the line

```
          mov     bx, 640 - 160 * (coordno AND 1)
```

Perhaps a less mysterious version would be to use *two* assembly-time variables and rewrite the macro as

```
coordloc = 0
coordsize = 640
GetCoord  MACRO
          call    Random
          mov     bx, coordsize
          sub     dh, dh ;     make smaller so no divide overflow
          div     bx
          push    dx
          mov     si, NextLine
          mov     [coordloc + si], dx
coordloc = coordloc + 2
coordsize = (640 + 480) - coordsize ;     toggle coordsize
          ENDM
```

It is also possible to change the text and background colors in *text* mode by changing the palette or color register settings. For instance, CodeView uses an olive green background color and the Norton Utilities uses a baby blue one.

Example 19.3—5. Write a macro `ChgColor PalReg, R, G, B` which changes the color referred to by palette register `PalReg` to the color specified by R, G, B. Only the palette color register referred to by the contents of `PalReg` are to be changed.

```
ChgColor  MACRO   PalReg, R, G, B
          mov     ax, 1007h ;  Get palette register color register
          mov     bl, PalReg
          int     10h ;        Returns color register in bh
          mov     bl, bh ;     Put it in bx
          sub     bh, bh
          mov     dh, R
          mov     ch, G
          mov     cl, B
          mov     ax, 1010h ;  Set color register value
          int     10h
          ENDM
```

In order to cause color (that is palette register) 5 (normally magenta) to produce baby blue, we could use the macro call

```
ChgColor 5, 27, 41, 63
```

To get a baby blue background for a character, we would then set its attribute to x101xxxxB (the x's represent other character attributes). The color characters on the screen with foreground or background attribute 5 would have their corresponding color changed to baby blue.

Programming Problem 19.1

The French national flag consists of three vertical stripes colored blue, white, and red, from left (the flagpole) to right. Write a program to use CGA text mode to draw the flag. (Hint: The easiest way is to clear windows to the appropriate background attribute.) Harder: Also draw the flagpole in yellow.

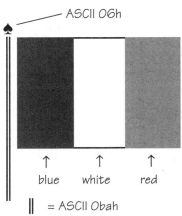

Even Harder: Do an American flag instead. (Don't try to draw the stars!)

Programming Problem 19.2

Redo programming problem 15.2 except that instead of displaying a pair of notes at the cursor to indicate a beep, display the letters 'BEEP' in flashing white letters on a red background in the center of the screen. When the time has elapsed or a key is struck, restore these four characters to their original condition.

Programming Problem 19.3

(Requires VGA or better.) Write an assembly program MIX, which can be optionally called with three command line numbers between 0 and 63 representing the original red, green, and blue component of a color mixture. If no parameters are supplied, assume 32, 32, and 32 (a medium gray). Your program should display a 50 × 50 square of the specified color (register 1), as well as three 10 × 10 squares of pure red, green, and blue (registers 2, 3, and 4). One of these squares, initially the red one, is the 'chosen' color, indicated by surrounding it with a larger white square in outline two pixels wide.

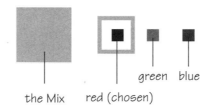

the Mix   red (chosen)   green   blue

The text and lines do not appear on the screen. Which color is chosen can be altered by the user using the left and right arrow keys. The amount of the chosen color in the mixture can be increased or decreased with up and down arrow keys. The Enter key causes the program to exit, displaying the final red, green, and blue values. Extra: Have *shifted* up or down arrow keys increase or decrease the chosen color by 8.

SUMMARY

Rather than simply repeating information from the chapter, we will refer you back to where it was originally given.

General terminology is considered in the chapter introduction and hardware concepts in Section 19.1. Section 19.2 discussed the use and format of attribute bytes in determining how text is displayed on the CRT. Section 19.2.1 gave a detailed description of the BIOS int 10h calls for text-mode video, as well as calls to switch between text and graphics modes. Section 19.2.2 showed how display memory can be accessed directly. Section 19.2.3 showed how hardware I/O could be used to solve a particular display problem. We introduced the unique hardware I/O instructions

```
in    al or ax, port;    read from port into al or ax
out   port, al or ax;    write to port from al or ax
```

where *port* is either a constant in the range 0…255 or the register dx, containing the port number. An I/O device typically has three types of ports: data, status, and control. Several BIOS int 10h calls necessary for VGA graphics were introduced in Section 19.3.

Chapter 20

Floating Point

This chapter gives a brief introduction to the IBM PC facilities for manipulating **floating point** numbers. These numbers are the ones with decimal points, perhaps times a power of ten, which are termed `float` or `double` in C/C++ and **real** in Pascal. Manipulation of these numbers takes place in a logically separate unit called the **Floating Point Unit** (**FPU**). In addition to performing arithmetic on floating point numbers, the FPU also computes square root, log, exponential, and trig functions, as well as converting back and forth between various other numeric formats.

The FPU is actually physically separate for the 8086, 8088, 80286, 80386, and 80486 SX chips, and requires that an additional chip, called a **numeric coprocessor**, be purchased and installed. The numeric coprocessors for the above CPUs had the numbers 8087 (8086 and 8088), 80287, 80387, and 80487 SX. The 80486 (DX) and Pentium chips actually contain the FPU themselves. The operation of all of these FPUs is very similar, but not identical.

The reader should be warned that the FPU is quite a bit more complicated than presented here. The *i486 Processor Programmer's Reference Manual* (see the bibliography) spends 214 pages discussing the 486 FPU and spends virtually no time on the underlying numerical analysis necessary to understand and perform floating point computations properly. You are probably better off, in most situations, using a high-level language to do floating point.

20.1 • FPU Data

The FPU manipulates five forms of data, which will be discussed in more detail below:

- **short floating point** (the `float` type of C/C++), which is 32 bits long.
- **long floating point** (the `double` type of C/C++), which is 64 bits long.
- **integer** (ordinary 80X86 word), which is 16 bits long.
- **long integer** (80X86 double word), which is 32 bits long
- **BCD (Binary Coded Decimal)**, a form which is 'nearly' an integer in ASCII format and is used for translating floating point numbers to and from ASCII. It is 80 bits long.

Inside the FPU, all numbers are converted to a sixth form:

- **extended floating point**, which is 80 bits long

20.1.1 • Floating Point Numbers

All three floating point formats are set up analogously to ordinary scientific notation. A number in scientific notation is of the form $\pm n.nnnnnnn \times 10^{\pm eee}$, which in computer notation would normally be written $\pm n.nnnnnnE\pm eee$. That is, -123456.78 is $-1.2345678 \times 10^5 = -1.2345678E5$. Internally, floating point numbers on the PC are done similarly, except that the n.nnnnnnn and $\pm eee$ parts are in binary and a power of 2 is used instead of a power of 10. The floating point number is divided up into three groups of bits:

- The sign bit $(1 = -, 0 = +)$
- The exponent bits—the positive or negative power of two to multiply times the third group,
- The **significand** (sometimes called the mantissa or fraction).

It isn't really necessary to understand how the representation works in detail. To fix ideas, we'll look at the specific format of long floating point numbers. You can skip down to the heading 'Range of Floating Point Numbers' without significant loss.

The general form of a long floating point number is:

The sign bit is s and exp is the exponent. Sign-magnitude representation is used; that is, the representation of $+x$ and $-x$ differ only in the s bit. The sign of the exponent part is handled a little differently. A **bias** is added to the exponent and the resulting positive number stored in the exp field. The bias for long floating point numbers is 1023, and the exponents represented must lie in the range

$$-1023 \le \text{exponent} \le 1024$$

so that when the bias is added, $0 \le exp \le 2047$, which is precisely the unsigned quantities that will fit into the 11-bit exp field. (Biasing is used instead of some other sign representation because it allows the last 63 bits of the number to be compared as a whole in determining the magnitude of the floating point number.)

As to the significand, first note that for any nonzero number in scientific notation, we can arrange it so that there is exactly one nonzero digit to the left of the decimal or binary point. Such a number is said to be **normalized**. For binary numbers, there is only one nonzero digit, of course, 1.

Since the first digit of a normalized number is always 1, it can be omitted from the representation. Thus if the significand is

$$b_{51}b_{50}b_{49}...b_2b_1b_0$$

(b_i a binary digit) then the number represented is

$$(-1)^s \times 1.b_{51}b_{50}b_{49}...b_2b_1b_0 \times 2^{(exp-1023)}$$

($(-1)^s$ is just a tricky way of turning 0 or 1 into a + or – sign.)

▶ **Range of Floating Point Numbers**

Binary digits and exponents do not correspond exactly to decimal digits and exponents, but the following are the approximate ranges of the three types of floating point numbers, in decimal:

	decimal digits of precision	range of exponent
short	7	10^{-38} to 10^{38}
long	15	10^{-308} to 10^{308}
extended	19	10^{-4932} to 10^{4932}

The reason for the larger size of extended floating point numbers is that it allows partial results to be computed with relatively little loss of accuracy.

It is important to understand the difference between **precision** and **accuracy**. Precision is the number of digits represented starting with the first nonzero digit. Thus 104, 10400000000=1.04E+10, and 0.0000104=1.04E–5 may all have three digits of precision. Accuracy on the other hand is the number of digits which are correct *for the number you are trying to represent*. For the (finite number of) numbers that can be represented exactly by floating point numbers, accuracy is complete, but for the infinite number that can't, precision is the upper limit on accuracy. Accuracy may also be less than precision, and usually is in the results of computations. 3.140000 could be a short floating point representation of π with seven digits of precision, but only three digits of accuracy. Also, when a short floating point number is loaded into the FPU, and thus becomes an extended floating point number, its precision is increased from seven to nineteen digits, but its accuracy is not increased.

As an example of what computation can do to accuracy, consider what can happen when you subtract nearly equal numbers. 1.000049 represents 1 to 5 digits accuracy and 1.000051 represents 1.0001 to 5 digits of accuracy, but 1.000051 – 1.000049 = 0.000002 = 2.000000E–6, which represents 0.0001 = 1.000000E–4, to *no* digits of accuracy! Computational accuracy is a very important field in the subject of Numerical Analysis, and is far beyond the scope of this book.

▶ **Declaring Floating Point Variables**

Short floating point variables—being double words—are declared using the DD pseudo-op. There is a corresponding pseudo-op DQ to define **quad words**, consisting of four words or eight bytes, which is used to define long floating point variables. For example:

```
A         DD      -1.23 ;        A negative short fp number
B         DD      54E23 ;        A positive short fp number
```

```
C        DD       -5432 ;      A negative long integer
D        DD       ? ;          A variable which can hold either
;                                   a short fp or long integer
E        DQ       -1.23 ;      A negative long fp number
```

20.1.2 • Integers

The FPU uses the usual 2's complement binary integers defined by DW or DD. The way to distinguish between integers and floating point numbers for DD is that floating point numbers must contain a decimal point or an E-part.

20.1.3 • BCD Numbers

BCD numbers are integers and consist of 18 decimal digits and a sign. Decimal digits are coded, two per byte and the sign is the left bit of the final byte, giving a total of ten bytes. Decimal digits occupy four bits, sometimes called a **nibble**, and are equal to their hex representation. The pseudo-operation used to declare BCD variables is DT, for define **ten-byte**. For instance, the declaration

```
A        DT       -12345
```

will produce the following memory layout:

```
A+9 A+8 A+7 A+6 A+5 A+4 A+3 A+2 A+1   A
 1 █ 0 0 0 0 0 0 0 0 0 0 0 0 0 0 1 2 3 4 5
```

The minus sign is the leftmost bit of byte A+9. As usual with the 80X86, the ordering of bytes is least-significant first.

The main use of BCD numbers is in doing I/O on floating point numberss.

20.2 • Form of Floating Point Instructions

All floating point operations, and *only* floating point operations, start with an initial 'f'.

Floating Point Instructions
f*operation*   *zero or more operands*

If the operation has a BCD or integer operand, that is indicated by the second letter of the operation code:

Types of Operands	
f**b***operation* *operand* ;	**BCD** operand
f**i***operation* *operand* ;	**Integer** operand

Other second letters indicate floating point arguments.

If the last letter of the operation code is 'p', the FPU stack is popped on completion of the operation. (See the next section for a description of the FPU stack.)

Pop FPU Stack after Operation	
`foperationp`	`zero or more operands`

20.3 • The FPU Stack

The most important registers in the FPU are a stack of eight extended floating point numbers and a 2-bit tag field for each of the eight.

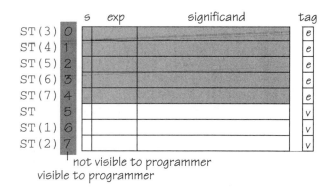

The most important tags indicate that the entry is empty or that it contains a value.

The stack entry numbers to the left in the diagram above are unavailable to the programmer. Instead, one entry is designated the stack top, specified by ST, and all the other entries are specified relative to it: ST(1), ST(2), ..., ST(7). A typical situation might be as shown in the diagram below:

This stack has three actual entries. The top, ST, is at actual entry 5 and the next-to-top entry is ST(1). The entries ST(3)–ST(7) are empty. If we push a new entry onto the stack above (called a **load** in FPU parlance) then the picture is as at the left below, and if we pop the stack above, it is as at the right below. Note that popping the stack causes the old top of stack entry to be marked as empty.

s	exp	significand	tag		s	exp	significand	tag
ST(4)			e	ST(2)			e
ST(5)			e	ST(3)			e
ST(6)			e	ST(4)			e
ST(7)			e	ST(5)			e
ST			v	ST(6)			e
ST(1)			v	ST(7)			e
ST(2)			v	ST			v
ST(3)			v	ST(1)			v

after push   after pop

Initially ST is 0 and all entries in the FPU stack are marked empty. The first load (push) is into entry 7 (though the actual locations in the stack are unimportant to the programmer).

There are a number of important differences between the FPU stack and the 80X86 stack.

- The FPU stack is in the FPU. The 80X86 stack is in main memory.
- The FPU stack is always exactly 8 registers long, though it may appear to be less when registers are marked as empty.
- In every FPU computation, one of the operands is ST.
- Trying to load (push) into a non-empty entry in the FPU stack is an error and trying to compute using an empty entry of the FPU stack is an error. (We will not discuss how to deal with such errors.)

The rest of this section will be spent introducing the various load (push), store, pop, and FPU other FPU stack manipulation instructions.

FPU Load (Push)
fld   *mem32 or mem64* ;   short or long fp load
fld   ST(*n*) ;   load from another stack entry
fild   *mem16 or mem32* ;   int or long int load
fbld   *mem80* ;   BCD load

Memnn represents the address of a memory location of length *nn*. In all cases, the argument is converted to the internal extended format of the FPU and pushed onto to the stack. Assuming the former ST(7) is empty, it is loaded with the operand and the new ST points to the old ST(7).

Any of the standard 80X86 memory addressing modes can be used for *memnn*, as well as those to be introduced in Section 21.2.2 for the 80386 and above. However, a simple register cannot be used as the operand. That is

fild ax ;   ILLEGAL!

Various commonly used constants can also be loaded:

FPU load (push) constants

```
fld1   ;          load 1
fldz   ;          load zero
fldpi  ;          load π
fldl2t ;          load log₂10
fldl2e ;          load log₂e
fldlg2 ;          load log₁₀2
fldln2 ;          load logₑ2
```

The following instructions store ST, performing whatever type conversions are necessary. Most of the instructions optionally allow you to pop the FPU stack after storing, and are shown with an op code followed by [p], meaning that the 'p' is optional. The [] brackets aren't written.

FPU Store [and pop] ST

```
fst[p]  mem32 or mem64  ;   store [and pop] ST
fst[p]  ST(n) ;           copy [then pop] ST to ST(n)
fist[p] mem16 or mem32 ; store [and pop] ST as int
fbstp   mem80 ;           store and pop ST as BCD
```

Note that there is no non-popping version of fbstp. The destination register in the second form of fst can be empty or contain a value.

There is no instruction which simply pops the FPU stack, but a reasonable substitute is a version of the comparison instruction which we will discuss in Section 20.6. Other occasionally useful instructions are also given below:

FPU Miscellaneous Stack Instructions

```
fcomp  ST ;           pop FPU stack
fld    ST, ST ;       load duplicate of stack top
fxch   ST(n) ;     exchange contents of ST and ST(n)
fxch   ;           exchange contents of ST and ST(1)
```

20.4 • Floating Point Arithmetic

The FPU implements what is called a **stack machine**, that is, arithmetic is performed by pushing the two operands onto the stack, then executing an arithmetic op code, which in effect pops the two top items off the stack, performs the operation on them, and pushes the result.

The arithmetic operations available are of the form f*op*, where *op* = add, sub, subr (subtract reverse), mul, div, and divr (divide reverse). The result executing f*op* (no operands) is

1. Pop the top of the stack into a temporary extended floating point number I will call arg2.
2. Set ST = ST + arg2   if *op* = add;
   ST − arg2   if *op* = sub;
   arg2 − ST   if *op* = subr;
   ST × arg2   if *op* = mul;
   ST / arg2   if *op* = div;
   arg2 / ST   if *op* = divr;

Note: The Intel documentation in the *i486 Microprocessor Programmer's Reference Manual* incorrectly reverses the operands.

When we show stack contents in program comments, we will do it in the order ST(2) ST(1) ST because it makes it easy to see the order of the arithmetic operands. For example,

```
;                                 ST(2) ST(1) ST
        fld     A ;                             A
        fld     B ;                       A     B
        fop       ;                       A op B
```

in particular,

```
        fld     A ;                             A
        fld     B ;                       A     B
        fsub      ;                       A  -  B
```

As an example, in Section 14.2, we developed a procedure for computing a 'random' 32-bit integer r satisfying $0 \le r \le 2^{31}-1$. The usual standard random number generator produces a floating point number x satisfying $0 \le x < 1$. Such a number can be obtained by dividing r by 2^{31}, which motivates

Example 20.4—1. Let Seed be a 32-bit integer between 0 and $2^{31}-1$. Set Rand := Seed/2^{31}. (See Section 14.2)

```
Power       DQ      2147483648.0 ;      = 2**31; exact since it is an
;                                       integer with fewer than 15 digits.
            . . .
            fild    Seed ;      Load integer and convert to float
            fdiv    Power
            fstp    Rand
```

Using the arithmetic instructions, it is very easy to program the evaluation of complex formulas by converting the formula into **Reverse Polish Notation**. In Reverse Polish Notation, the operator is written *after* the operands instead of between them. Thus a + b becomes ab+ and (a + b) × (c – d) becomes ab+cd–×. To evaluate a Reverse Polish expression using the FPU, just read it left to right, pushing any operands as encountered and executing any arithmetic operations as encountered.

Example 20.4—2. For floating point numbers A, B, C, D, and E, use the FPU to set E: = (A + B) × (C – D). Using the Reverse Polish form of the formula shown above, we write

```
;   Example 20.4-2: Solution 1
;                               ST(2)         ST(1)         ST
        fld     A ;                                         A
        fld     B ;                           A             B
        fadd      ;                                         A+B
        fld     C ;                           A+B           C
        fld     D ;             A+B           C             D
```

```
                    fsub    ;                           A+B         C-D
                    fmul    ;                                   (A+B)*(C-D)
                    fstp    E ;             Pop to clear the stack
```

The pairs of instructions

```
                    f[i]ld memaddr ;        optionally an integer operand
                    fop
```
and
```
                    fld     ST(n)
                    fop
```

occur frequently, so the FPU allows them to be abbreviated by the single instruction

```
                    f[i]op memaddr ;        equivalent to f[i]ld memaddr/fop
                    fop     ST, ST(n) ;     equivalent to fld ST(n)/fop
```

In the second case, both operands must be written. Thus, the code above could be rewritten

```
    ;   Example 20.4-2: Solution 2
    ;                               ST(2)       ST(1)           ST
                    fld     A ;                                 A
                    fadd    B ;                                 A+B
                    fld     C ;                     A+B         C
                    fsub    D ;                     A+B         C-D
                    fmul    ;                               (A+B)*(C-D)
                    fstp    E ;             Pop to clear the stack
```

Note that the second method has the advantage that it uses one less stack entry, which can be important when evaluating complicated expressions.

Example 20.4—3. Use the FPU to compute $X := (A + 1) / (A - 1)$.

We could proceed in a straightforward manner as above, producing the code

```
    ;   Example 20.4-3: Solution 1
    ;                               ST(2)       ST(1)           ST
                    fld     A ;                                 A
                    fld1    ;                         A         1.0
                    fadd    ;                                   A+1
                    fld     A ;                     A+1         A
                    fld1    ;         A+1           A           1.0
                    fsub    ;                       A+1         A-1
                    fdiv    ;                               (A+1)/(A-1)
                    fstp    X
```

Using the technique of the second version in the last example and reversing the addition and subtraction, we get:

```
;   Example 20.4-3: Solution 2
;                                    ST(2)        ST(1)         ST
        fld1    ;                                               1.0
        fadd    A ;                                             1+A = A+1
        fld1    ;                                 A+1           1.0
        fsubr   A ;                               A+1           A-1
        fdiv    ;                                             (A+1)/(A-1)
        fstp    X
```

For a third version, we might try to speed things up by loading A only once:

```
;   Example 20.4-3: Solution 3
;                                    ST(2)        ST(1)         ST
        fld     A ;                                             A
        fld1    ;                                 A             1.0
        fadd    ST, ST(1) ;                       A             A+1
        fxch    ST, ST(1) ;                       A+1           A
        fld1    ;                     A+1          A             1.0
        fsub    ;                                 A+1           A-1
        fdiv    ;                                             (A+1)/(A-1)
        fstp    X
```

Finally, we might try a fourth approach, using yet another option for operands of the f*op* instructions:

```
        fop[p] ST(n), ST ;   does ST(n) := ST(n) op ST
;                                 and [optionally] pops ST
```

Using the popping version, we could write

```
;   Example 20.4-3: Solution 4
;                                    ST(2)        ST(1)         ST
        fld     A ;                                             A
        fld     ST ;                              A             A
        fld1    ;                     A            A             1.0
        fadd    ST(2), ST ;           A+1          A             1.0
        fsubp   ST(1), ST;                         A+1           A-1
        fdiv    ;                                             (A+1)/(A-1)
        fstp    X
```

We can summarize the arithmetic instructions as follows:

FPU Arithmetic Instructions
op = add, sub, subr, mul, div, divr
fop ;   pop ST into extended fp arg2...
fop memop ;   convert fp memop to extended fp arg2...
fiop memop ;   convert integer memop to extended fp arg2...
fop ST,ST(n) ; copy ST(n) to extended fp arg2...
;   ...then in all four cases, set ST := ST op arg2
fop[p] ST(n),ST ; set ST(n) := ST(n) op ST [and then pop ST]

In addition, there are some other useful instructions:

FPU Miscellaneous Arithmetic	
fabs ;	Absolute value. Set ST := |ST|
fchs ;	Change sign of ST. ST := $-$ST
fsqrt ;	Square root. ST := $\sqrt{ST}$

Exercises 20.4

1.   Assume that all variables are long or short floating point unless otherwise specified. Write FPU code to do the following:

   a) $A := B + C - 4.4$
   b)   ✓ $Area := \pi R^2$
   c) $Vol := (4/3)\pi R^3$
   d) $Arith := (A + B)/2$
   e) $Geom := \sqrt{A \times B}$
   f) $Harmonic := 1/(1/A + 1/B)$
   g)   ✓$AbsDif := |A - B|$

2.   A three-dimensional vector is specified by a triple (x, y, z) of floating point numbers. The distance between two such vectors (x1, y1, z1) and (x2, y2, z2) is given by the formula

$$dis\tan ce := \sqrt{(x2 - x1)^2 + (y2 - y1)^2 + (z2 - z1)^2}$$

Write FPU code to compute distance assuming everything in sight is a floating point variable.

20.5 • Floating Point I/O

As you might expect, it is much more difficult to convert floating point numbers to and from human-readable form than it is for integers. I have supplied four routines in UTIL.LIB that should simplify the task of writing programs using floating point.

   The first two are analogous to GetDec and PutDec from Chapter 3:

   GetFP input: none
          output: a decimal real number in ASCII form is read from the keyboard, converted
             to floating point and left loaded on top of the FPU stack.

PutFP input: ST on the FPU stack
       output: the number is displayed and popped from the FPU stack.

With both of these functions, all 80X86 registers are preserved, as are all FPU stack registers except as indicated. GetFP requires three empty entries on the FPU stack, including one to contain the result, and PutFP requires no empty entries on the FPU stack.

Example 20.5—1. Read floating point numbers A, B, and C from the keyboard and compute and display the solution to the equation $Ax + B = C$.

```
;; LINEAR.ASM--Read fp numbers A, B, and C from the keyboard
;;  and compute and display the solution to Ax + B = C.
;;  We actually don't need any variables as everything can
;;  take place on the FPU stack.
INCLUDE   PCMAC.INC
          .MODEL SMALL
          .STACK 100h
          .DATA
PromptA   DB      'Type A: $'
PromptB   DB      'Type B: $'
PromptC   DB      'Type C: $'
OutMsg    DB      'The solution of Ax + B = C is x = $'
          .CODE
Linear    PROC
          EXTRN  GetFP : NEAR, PutFP : NEAR
          mov    ax, @data
          mov    ds, ax
          _PutStr PromptA ;          ST(2) ST(1) ST
          call   GetFP ;                         A
          _PutStr PromptB
          call   GetFP ;                   A     B
          _PutStr PromptC
          call   GetFP ;             A     B     C
          fsubrp ST(1), ST ;               A     C-B
          fdivr  ;                               (C-B)/A
          _PutStr OutMsg
          call   PutFP
          _PutCh 13, 10
          _Exit  0
Linear    ENDP
          END    Linear
```

A typical run might be

```
C:\>linear
Type A: 2
Type B: 2
```

```
Type C: 5.5
The solution of Ax + B = C is x = 1.75
```

The following example shows how arrays of floating point numbers can be used.

Example 20.5—2. Read in a number $n \leq 100$ and n data points $x_1, x_2, \ldots, x_n$. Then compute and display the mean m and the standard deviation s of the data points using the following formulas:

$$m = \frac{x_1 + x_2 + \cdots + x_n}{n}$$

$$s = \sqrt{\frac{(x_1 - m)^2 + (x_2 - m)^2 + \cdots + (x_n - m)^2}{n - 1}}$$

The outline of the code is straightforward:

> read and check integer n ($2 \leq n \leq 100$)
> loop to read the x_is, summing as we go
> compute m from running sum
> loop to compute sum of squares of differences
> compute and display s.

The actual code is as follows:

```
;; STDDEV.ASM—This program reads a sequence of N(>1) real numbers
;;  and computes and displays its mean and standard deviation.
INCLUDE    PCMAC.INC
           .MODEL SMALL
           .STACK 100h
           .DATA
Prompt1    DB      'Number of Data Points = $'
Prompt2A   DB      'X[$'
Prompt2B   DB      '] = $'
OutMsg1    DB      'The Mean is $'
OutMsg2    DB      13, 10, 'The Standard Deviation is $'

NMAX       EQU     100
X          DQ      NMAX DUP (?) ;        Storage for data points
N          DW      ? ;                   Storage for N

Err1       DB      'N must be greater than 1', 13, 10, '$'
Err2       DB      'N must be less than $'

           .CODE
StdDev     PROC
           EXTRN   GetDec:NEAR, PutDec:NEAR, GetFP:NEAR, PutFP:NEAR
```

```
            mov     ax, @data
            mov     ds, ax

            _PutStr Prompt1 ;       Get N
            call    GetDec
            cmp     ax, 1 ;             and check it
            jle     tooSmall
            cmp     ax, NMAX
            jle     NOK
tooBig:
            _PutStr Err2
            mov     ax, NMAX
            call    PutDec
            _PutCh 13, 10
            _Exit   2
tooSmall:
            _PutStr Err1
            _Exit   1
NOK:        ;                       Now read in the data points
            mov     N, ax
            mov     di, OFFSET X
            mov     cx, ax
            mov     bx, 1 ;         input index
            fldz    ;               initialize sum of X[i]s
inLoop:
            _PutStr Prompt2A ;      Prompt for X[i]
            mov     ax, bx
            call    PutDec
            _putStr Prompt2B
            call    GetFP ;         Read X[i]
            fadd    ST(1), ST ;     ST(1) := ST(1) + X[i]
            fstp    QWORD PTR [di] ; and store X[i]
            add     di, 8
            inc     bx
            loop    inLoop

            fidiv   N ;             ST = mean
            _PutStr OutMsg1 ;       Output Mean
            fld     ST ;            Duplicate mean so we don't lose it
            call    PutFP

;                                   Now, compute sum of difs squared
            mov     si, OFFSET X
            mov     cx, N
            fldz    ;               initialize sum of squares
sqLoop:
            fld     QWORD PTR [si]
```

```
            fsub    ST, ST(2) ;    at this point, ST(2) = mean
            fmul    ST, ST ;       square ST = X[i] - mean
            fadd    ;               and add to sum of squares
            add     si, 8
            loop    sqLoop

            fld1    ;              now compute N-1
            fchs    ;              ST = -1
            fiadd   N ;            ST = N - 1
            fdiv    ;              ST = sum of squares / (N - 1)
            fsqrt   ;              ST = standard deviation

            _PutStr OutMsg2 ;      output standard deviation
            call    PutFP
            _PutCh 13, 10

            fcomp   ST ;           pop mean off stack

            _Exit   0
StdDev      ENDP
            END     StdDev
```

A typical run might be:

```
C:\>stddev
Number of Data Points = 10
X[1] = 1
X[2] = 2
X[3] = 3
X[4] = 4
X[5] = 5
X[6] = 6
X[7] = 7
X[8] = 8
X[9] = 9
X[10] = 10
The Mean is 5.5
The Standard Deviation is 3.0276503541
```

In addition to GetFP and PutFP, there are more general functions which convert to and from strings of characters, corresponding to the functions Bin2Dec and Dec2Bin introduced in Section 11.1:

FP2Bin   input: ds:si points to a string of ASCII characters
         output: a decimal real number from the input string is converted to floating point
             and left loaded on top of the FPU stack. ds:si is left pointing to the first char-
             acter after the end of the converted number.

Bin2FP   input: ST on the FPU stack; es:di points to the first character of a string of characters in which the converted number will be stored

output: the converted number is stored starting at the specified location and the original number is popped from the FPU stack. es:di is left pointing to the first character after the last character stored.

As before, FP2Bin requires three empty stack locations, including the one in which the number is finally left pushed.

Exercises 20.5

1. ✓ Write code to read a positive integer from the keyboard and compute and display the square roots of all numbers from 2 to the number read. A typical line, with the actual value replacing the dots, would read

```
The square root of 2 is 1.414...
```

2. What do you think would be displayed by the following code? Try it out and see.

```
OutMsg    DB       '1/0 = $'
          . . .
          _PutStr OutMsg ;      ST(1)         ST
          fld1    ;                            1
          fldz    ;             1              0
          fdiv    ;                            1/0
          call    PutFP
          _PutCh 13, 10
```

3. Do Programming Problem 20.1.

20.6 • FPU Comparing and Branching

There is a serious problem with comparing and branching on floating point numbers. The comparing part takes place in the FPU and the branching takes place using the flags in the 80X86, which until the 80486 was a completely separate chip! Because of the separation, we have to go through an awkward sequence of instructions to transfer the results of the compare from the FPU to the 80X86 flags.

The FPU comparison instructions are reminiscent of the arithmetic instructions, except that they all have a pop option, and there is even one that pops both ST and ST(1):

FPU Compare Instructions
fcom[p] *mem32* or *mem64* ;   compare ST to operand [and pop]
fcom[p] ST(*n*) ;   compare ST to ST(*n*) [and pop]
fcom[p]   ;   compare ST(1) to ST [and pop]
fcompp   ;   compare ST(1) to ST and pop twice
ficom[p] *mem16* or *mem32* ;   compare ST to converted
;   integer operand [and pop]
ftst   ;   compare ST to 0.0

Note that once again, the Intel documentation incorrectly reverses the order of operands on `fcom[p[p]]` without operands. Note also that I have recommended using `fcomp ST` to pop the FPU stack without storing anything. `fcomp` with no operand works, but could generate an error indication if `ST(1)` were empty, for instance.

The FPU compare and test instructions set bits in an FPU register called the **status word**. The next step is transferring these bits to the 80X86 flags.

Transferring the FPU Status Word to Flags		
StatWd	DW	? ; defined in the .DATA segment
	. . .	
	fstsw	StatWd ; Store status word in StatWd
	mov	ax, StatWd
	sahf	; Transfer ah to the flags register

After execution of the code above, the flag bits will be properly set from the FPU comparison for use of the *unsigned* jump instructions.

Example 20.6—1. Set A to the larger of the floating point numbers B and C.

```
;                              ST(1)      ST
        fld    B ;                        B
        fld    C ;             B          C
        fcom   ;              B          C
        fstsw  StatWd
        mov    ax, StatWd
        sahf
        jbe    OrderOK ;       Note unsigned jump
        fxch   ;              C          B
OrderOK:                       smaller    larger
        fstp   A ;                        smaller
        fcomp  ST ;            pop remaining item
```

Example 20.6—2. Write a complete program `quadroot` which inputs the three coefficients A, B, and C of the quadratic equation $Ax^2 + Bx + C = 0$ and computes and displays its roots. Handle the usual special cases intelligently: if the **discriminant** $B^2 - 4AC$ of the equation is less than 0, there are no real roots, and if it is equal to 0 there is one double real root. Moreover, if A = 0, the equation reduces to the linear equation Bx + C = 0, and if B is 0 too, the equation degenerates, having either no roots or infinitely many.

By keeping careful track of the stack, we are able to keep all of our computations there. Note too that we can make things more efficient by replacing A by 2A and B by –B early on, and can throw away C as soon as we have used it to compute 4AC. The program is:

```
;; QUADROOT.ASM--Read A, B, and C and solve the quadratic equation
;;  Ax**2 + Bx + C = 0. Consider all special cases
```

```
INCLUDE    PCMAC.INC
           .MODEL SMALL
           .STACK 100h
           .DATA
Two        DD     2.0
PromptA    DB     'Enter coefficients of the quadratic equation'
           DB     13, 10, 'Type A: $'
PromptB    DB     'Type B: $'
PromptC    DB     'Type C: $'
Err1       DB     'Error--both A and B are 0', 13, 10, '$'
Err2       DB     'Error--there are no real roots', 13, 10, '$'
Out2A      DB     'The two roots are $'
Out2B      DB     ' and $'
OutDub     DB     'There is one double root $'
OutLin     DB     'The equation is linear with root $'

StatWd     DW     ?


           .CODE
QuadRoot PROC
           EXTRN  GetFP : NEAR, PutFP : NEAR
           mov    ax, @data
           mov    ds, ax
           _PutStr PromptA ;    ST(2)          ST(1)          ST
           call   GetFP ;                                     A
           ftst
           fstsw  StatWd
           mov    ax, StatWd ; If A = 0, go to Linear
           sahf
           jnz    nonZero
           jmp    Linear
nonZero:
           fmul   Two ;                                       2*A
           _PutStr PromptB
           call   GetFP ;                     2*A            B
           fchs   ;                           2*A            -B
           _PutStr PromptC
           call   GetFP ;      2*A            -B             C
           fmul   ST, ST(2) ; 2*A            -B             2*A*C
           fmul   Two ;        2*A            -B             4*A*C

           fld    ST(1) ;      -B             4*A*C          -B
           fmul   ST, ST ;     -B             4*A*C     (-B)*(-B)=B*B
           fsubr  ;                           2*A            -B             B*B - 4*A*C
;                                                                          = disc
           ftst   ;
           fstsw  StatWd
```

```
                mov    ax, StatWd ;  if disc < 0, Err2
                sahf
                jb     NoRoots
                jz     OneRoot
TwoRoots:
                fsqrt  ;               2*A          -B            sqrt(disc)
                _PutStr Out2A
                fld    ST(1) ;       -B      sqrt(disc)        -B
                fadd   ST, ST(1) ;   -B      sqrt(disc)    -B+sqrt(disc)
                fdiv   ST, ST(3) ;   -B      sqrt(disc)(-B+sqrt(disc))/2*A
                call   PutFP ;        2*A          -B          sqrt(disc)
                fsubp  ST(1), ST ;                2*A        -B-sqrt(disc)
                fdivr  ;                               (-B-sqrt(disc))/2*A
                _PutStr Out2B
OutST:          ;              Common final output and return
                call   PutFP
                _PutCh 13, 10
                _Exit  0
NoRoots:
                _PutStr Err2
                _Exit  2
OneRoot:  ;                         2*A          -B            disc
                fcomp  ST ;                      2*A          -B
                fdivr  ;                                    -B/(2*A)
                _PutStr OutDub
                jmp    OutST
Linear:        ;                                                    A
                fcomp  ST ;        pop off A (= 0)
                _PutStr PromptB
                call   GetFP ;                              B
                ftst   ;           if B = 0 too, Err1
                fstsw  StatWd
                mov    ax, StatWd
                sahf
                jnz    LinOK
                _PutStr Err1
                _Exit  1
LinOK:
                _PutStr PromptC ;                          B
                call   GetFP ;              B              C
                fchs   ;                    B             -C
                fdivr  ;                                 -C/B
                _PutStr OutLin
                jmp    OutST

QuadRoot  ENDP
          END    QuadRoot
```

A typical run might be

```
C:\>quadroot
Enter coefficients of the quadratic equation
Type A: 2
Type B: 3
Type C: -2
The two roots are 0.5 and -2
```

Exercises 20.6

1. Write code fragments to do the following, assuming A, B, C, and X are floating point variables:
   a) ✓ Set X equal to the largest of A, B, and C.
   b) If A >= 0, set X equal to the square root of A.

2. ✓ Let N be a word integer and let A[1], ..., A[N] be an array of N short floating point numbers. Write a program fragment which sorts the array using your favorite method. (Insertion sort is recommended.)

20.7 • Transcendental Functions and the FPU

The FPU has op-codes to compute the sin, cos, and arctan of numbers on the stack. It is therefore possible to compute all of the trigonometric functions. It also has op-codes to compute 2^x and $\log_2 x$ for any number x. These instructions, together with the instructions to `fld` log constants allow easy computation of e^x, $\log_e x$, 10^x, and $\log_{10} x$. To get a very simplified idea of how these computations work, see Programming Problem 20.1. With a little more work, it is possible to compute exponentials of any number or logs to any base.

20.8 • The FPU and the Debugger

Each debugger has a window which can be opened to display the contents of the FPU stack (and other information which we haven't discussed). Open the TD FPU window by executing **Alt-V**(iew N(umeric coprocessor, and the CV FPU window by executing **Alt-W**(indows 8(. 8087. The CV window doesn't display any useful information until an FPU instruction is actually executed by the program.

Programming Problem 20.1

Write a program `DecDig` which takes as input an integer n and produces as output the approximate number of decimal digits x represented by n binary digits. You must solve the equation

$$2^n = 10^x$$

As

$$10^x = \left(2^{\log_2 10}\right)^x = 2^{x \log_2 10}$$

we have $n = x\log_2 10$, and so $x = n/\log_2 10$. Notice that $\log_2 10$ is one of the constants which can be loaded with a special `fld` instruction. Have your program print the approximate number of decimal digits of precision of short (24 bits of significand), long (53 bits of significand) and extended (64 bits of significand) floating point numbers.

Programming Problem 20.2

Write a program `Heron` which takes as input the three (floating point) sides a, b, and c, checks to see if they can be the lengths of the three sides of a triangle, and if so, displays the area of the triangle. If the sides do not form a triangle, display an appropriate error message. Compute the area using **Heron's formula**:

$$area = \sqrt{s(s-a)(s-b)(s-c)}$$

where s, the **semiperimeter** of the triangle, is given by s = (a + b + c)/2. To test that the three numbers form the sides of a triangle, you must check that the sum of each pair of sides is strictly greater than the third side, which requires three compare and branches. (In the process, it also guarantees that each side is greater than 0. If a ≤ 0, then either b ≤ c or c ≤ b. If the former, a+b ≤ 0+c = c, etc.) The following is a typical test case:

```
C:\>Heron
A = 3
B = 4
C = 5
The area is 6
```

Also test with sets of sides (5, 10, 15), (10, 15, 5), and (10, 5, 15), all of which do not form triangles.

Programming Problem 20.3

An array of n floating point numbers is sometimes called a **vector**. The length of the vector $(x_1, x_2, \ldots, x_n)$ is given by the formula

$$length = \sqrt{x_1^2 + x_2^2 + \cdots + x_n^2}$$

A vector is said to be **normalized** if its length is 1. Any vector which is not all 0s can be normalized by dividing each of its entries by the length of the vector. That is, if L≠0 is the length of $(x_1, x_2, \ldots, x_n)$, then the normalized version of that vector is $(x_1/L, x_2/L, \ldots, x_n/L)$. Write a program `Normal` which reads n, an integer, and then the n floating point numbers $(x_1, x_2, \ldots, x_n)$ to form a vector. If all of the entries are 0, display a suitable error message. Otherwise compute and display the normalized version of the vector elements. A sample test run might be:

```
C:\>Normal
Program to normalize a vector of length n
n = 2
x[1] = 3
x[2] = 4
The normalized version of the vector is
x[1] = 0.6
x[2] = 0.8
```

(The length of the given vector is 5.) Your program should handle vectors with up to 20 elements.

Summary

The 80X86 uses the FPU to perform arithmetic operations and compute transcendental function values on floating point numbers. It handles five types of data: short and long floating point numbers, BCD numbers (used for converting to and from ASCII representations) and short and long signed integers. Internally the FPU holds all such numbers converted into extended floating point form in a stack of eight floating point registers. The register which is currently the stack top is specified by `ST`, the register just below it as `ST(1)`, and so on down to the last register, `ST(7)`.

Pushing onto the FPU Stack: Accomplished by various forms of the `fld` instruction (`fild` to load integers, `fbld` to load BCD integers). Memory items of any of the five handled types can be pushed, as well as items from the stack itself and various constants such as 0, 1, π, and various useful logarithms. The old `ST(7)`, which becomes the new `ST` as a result of `fld`, must have been previously empty.

Storing the FPU Stack Top: Use `fst` or `fist` (no `fbst`) to store and convert into any of the four floating point or binary integer types in memory, or to another location in the stack itself.

Popping the FPU Stack: Use `fstp` (or `fistp` or `fbstp`) to store and pop or `fcomp ST` to pop without storing.

Exchanging the Top of the FPU Stack and Another Item: Use `fxch`.

Arithmetic: Four ordinary operations `fadd`, `fsub`, `fmul`, and `fdiv`, and two operations `fsubr` and `fdivr` that reverse the operands where reversal makes a difference. If we represent the operation code as `fop`, there are the following forms of addressing:

```
fop              ;    pop stack; new ST := old ST(1) op old ST
fop mem          ;    ST := ST op fp operand in mem
fop ST, ST(n)    ;    ST := ST op ST(n)
fiop mem         ;    ST := ST op signed integer operand in mem
fop[p] ST(n), ST ;    ST(n) := ST(n) op ST [and pop]
```

There is also

```
fsqrt            ;    ST := √ST
fabs             ;    ST := |ST|
fchs             ;    ST := − ST
```

Comparison: Various comparison instructions set flags in the FPU status word:

```
fcom[p[p]]       ;    compare ST(1) to ST [and pop [twice]]
fcom[p] mem      ;    compare ST to fp operand in mem [and pop]
fcom[p] ST(n)    ;    compare ST to ST(n) [and pop]
ficom[p] mem     ;    compare ST to int operand in mem [and pop]
ftst             ;    compare ST to 0.0
```

The status word flags must then be transferred to the 80X86 flag register via the instruction sequence

```
fstsw   memloc ;      memloc is a word in memory
mov     ax, memloc
sahf
```

after which *unsigned* jump instructions can be used for the decision making.

Four UTIL.LIB routines are available for converting floating point numbers to and from human-readable format:

GetFP   corresponds to GetDec, but loads the number onto the FPU stack.

PutFP   corresponds to PutDec, but takes the number to display from the FPU stack, popping the stack.

FP2Bin   corresponds to Dec2Bin, and takes as input a pointer to a character string containing the ASCII representation of a floating point number in ds:si. It returns with ds:si pointing to the first character after the floating point number and the converted number loaded onto the FPU stack.

Bin2FP   corresponds to Bin2Dec, and takes as input a number on top of the FPU stack and a pointer in es:di to the character string in which the ASCII representation is to be stored. On exit, the number is popped from the FPU stack and es:di points to the first location in memory after the converted ASCII representation.

Chapter **21**

Other CPUs: 286, 386, 486, and Pentium

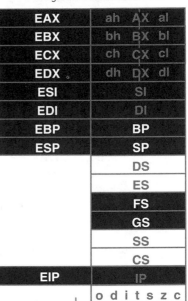

In this chapter, we will treat the various features in the higher-numbered 80X86 CPUs (counting the Pentium as 80586). These chips are almost entirely upward compatible, so features introduced for one level of CPU will also be available in higher-numbered CPUs.

21.1 • The 80286

The most substantial difference between the 80286 and the 8086-88 is the addition of a **protected mode**. In protected mode, segment registers become pointers into a table of **memory descriptors** rather than being a direct part of the address. Among other things, the protected mode allows up to 16 MBytes of memory to be addressed and allows safe execution of multiple programs at once by *protecting* each program in memory so that it cannot be interfered with by other programs. DOS normally operates in **real mode**, in which segment registers act just as they do in the 8086-88. The use of protected mode is extremely complex and far beyond the scope of this book. In operating systems such as Microsoft Windows, OS/2 and UNIX which use protected mode, the applications programmer is not allowed to manipulate the protection features anyway!

The 80286 also adds a few instructions useful to the general programmer, notably:

```
        push    constant ;  for example, push 3 or push OFFSET
A
        shl     reg-or-mem, constant ; for example, shl ax,
14,
                ; or any of the other shift ops
                ; shr, sal, sar, ror, rol, rcr, rcl
```

The assemblers will not recognize these or any of the other new 80286 instructions unless they are preceded by the `.286` pseudo-operation somewhere in the program. A program assembled with these new instructions can be assembled on any 80X86, but of course, won't run on an 8086 or 8088.

Example 21.1—1. Rewrite `PutHexB` From Exercise 9.3—1 using 80286 instructions. Recall that `PutHexB` displays the contents of `al` as two hex digits.

```
;; PUTHEXB.ASM--program to display the contents of al as two hex
;;    digits.  Uses 80286 instructions.
;;
;;    Calling Sequence:
;;          mov    al, theNumber
;;          PUBLIC PutHexB
;;          call   PutHexB
;;
;;    all registers but ax are preserved
                .286
INCLUDE    PCMAC.INC
                .MODEL SMALL

                .DATA
HexDig     DB     '0123456789ABCDEF'

                .CODE
                PUBLIC PutHexB
PutHexB    PROC   ;             al = xy = digits to display
                shl    ax, 4 ;      ax = ?xy0
                shr    al, 4 ;      ax = ?x0y
                and    ax, 0f0fh ;  ax = 0x0y
                push   bx ;         Don't destroy bx
                push   dx ;           or dx
                mov    bx, OFFSET HexDig
                xlat   ;             0y --> ASCII hex digit in al
                push   ax
                xchg   ah, al
                xlat   ;             0x --> ASCII hex digit in al
                _PutCh al
                pop    ax
                _PutCh al
                pop    dx
                pop    bx
                ret
PutHexB    ENDP
                END
```

There is also a new multiply instruction

```
imul  reg, reg-or-mem, constant ; reg := reg-or-mem * constant
```

and a shorthand form

```
imul  reg, constant ;   short for imul reg, reg, constant
```

This new form of the `imul` instruction is not really an extension of the original `imul` instruction. It does do signed multiplication, but the multipliers are always 16 bits long and the result must fit in a single word register *reg*.

Example 21.1—2. Bx is assumed to contain the month number (1–12). Display the month name. We will assume we have declared an array

```
MoName    DB       'January$  '
          . . .
          DB       'September$'
          . . .
          DB       'December$ '
```

where each entry is ten characters long. The code is

```
imul   bx, 10
_PutStr [MoName - 10 + bx]
```

Other new instructions of interest are related to procedure entry and exit. Registers can be saved on entry and restored on exit with the new instructions

```
pusha ;      push all regs
popa ;       pop all regs in reverse order of pusha
```

Pusha pushes all ordinary and segment registers onto the stack in a specified order and popa pops them off in reverse order. However, since one seldom needs to save more than a few registers, it is usually better just to use the individual push instructions, as before.

A more important new pair of instructions for procedure entry and exit are enter and leave, which assist in maintaining **stack frames** in block-structured languages such as Pascal, C/C++, Ada, etc. These instructions require a fair amount of explanation, which will occupy us for the rest of this section.

The instruction

```
enter  n, 0 ;      Enter subprocedure
```

is equivalent to our standard procedure entry code

```
push   bp
mov    bp, sp
```

```
        sub     sp, n ;          Allocate n bytes of local storage
```

The instruction

```
        leave   ;                Leave subprocedure
```

is equivalent to the code

```
        mov     sp, bp
        pop     bp
```

Note that the `ret` instruction is still required.

Enter becomes even more interesting when its second parameter is nonzero. It then is very useful for implementing languages like Pascal and Ada that have nested procedure and function declarations. (C and C++ do not.) The discussion of this nesting is fairly complex though, and if you have no particular interest in it, you might prefer to skip the rest of this section.

In languages with nested procedure and function declarations, every such subprocedure has a **lexical level**, or **lex level**. Procedures and functions declared at the outermost level have lex level 1. Those declared directly inside such procedures have lex level 2, and so on. In general, a procedure or function declared at the top level of a procedure or function with lex level n has lex level $n + 1$. Consider the following example, which we will use throughout:

```
procedure A         { lex level 1}
   procedure B      { lex level 2}
     procedure C    { lex level 3}
       begin { C }

         . . .

       end  { C }
     begin { B }

       . . .

     end   { B }
   procedure D       { lex level 2 again }
     procedure E     { lex level 3}
       procedure F { lex level 4}
         begin { F }

           . . .

         end { F }
       begin { E }

         . . .

         F; { execute F }

         . . .

         B; { execute B }

         . . .

       end   { E }
     begin { D }

       . . .
```

Note: In procedure D at lex level 2, we can call procedure E at lex level 3, but no procedures at higher lex levels, as their names would be hidden. It can also call procedures D, B, and A at lex levels 2, 2, and 1, irrespectively. It is easy to see that if a procedure or function at lex level m can call a procedure or function at lex level n, then $m \leq n + 1$. (But not conversely; E can't call C for instance, even though they are at the same lex level.)

The reason for considering lex levels is that the procedure E above can access not only its own local variables, but also the local variables of the containing procedures D and A as well. Since these procedures could be recursive, there might be several stack frames corresponding to different active calls of A, D, and E, and procedure E needs some way of determining which version of these local variables to use. The choice is generally made using some form of a **display**, which is an array of pointers in the stack of the following form:

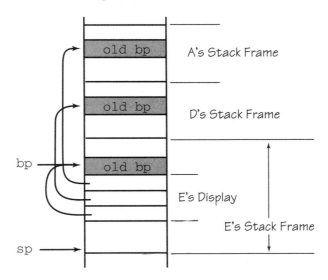

The diagram above assumes a situation in which the main program called A, which called D, which called E.

If now E calls F, F can simply use a copy of E's display with a pointer to F's stack frame appended to the end, as is seen in the top diagram on the next page. When E calls B, only the first entry of its display is copied to B, and once again a pointer to B's stack frame is attached to the end of the new display, as is seen in the bottom diagram on the next page.

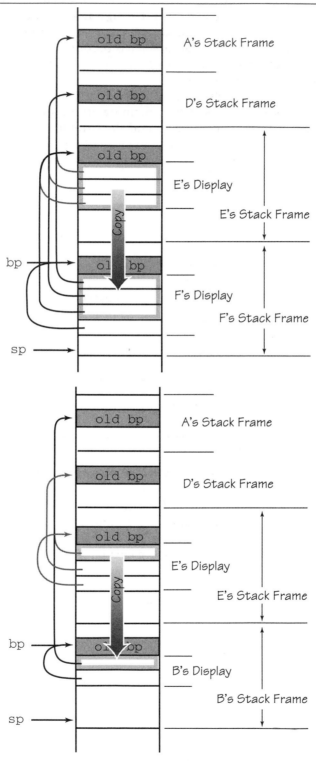

Setup of the display can be automated by the `enter` command. Upon entry, a procedure executes

```
enter  n, lexlevel ; n = number of bytes of local storage
```

which is roughly equivalent to the following pseudocode:

```
push bp
mov  bp, sp
if (lexlevel > 0) then
  for i := 1 to lexlevel - 1 do
    push [oldbp - 2 * i]; { copy lexlevel-1 entries from previous }
  end for
  push bp                 {  display and add new entry }
end if
sub sp, n
```

Note that since the called procedure can have a lex level at most one higher than its caller, there will in fact be enough entries from the old display to copy.

Exercises 21.1.

1. ✓ Suppose that we have declared the following procedures in Pascal or a similar language:

```
procedure Outer;     { Lex Level 1 }
  var
    x, y : integer; { display at bp - 2, x at bp - 4, y at bp - 6 }
  procedure Inner(a : integer); { a at bp + 4, display at bp - 2 }
    begin { Inner }
      x := a + y
    end;   { Inner }
  . . .
```

Write code for the procedure `Inner` using `enter` and `leave` and referencing the non-local variables `x` and `y` through the display in the stack.

2. ✓ Suppose that a language with nested procedure and function declarations wished to pass procedures and functions as parameters. To work properly, the display in force when the procedure or function is passed should somehow be passed along with it. The passing should be done in a fixed length of storage, since procedures receiving such a parameter need have no idea of the lex level of the caller or of the procedure or function passed. Suggest a mechanism for passing the display. **Note:** The passed procedure is going to do an `enter` and that `bp` will therefore have to be faked in some way before the passed procedure or function is actually called.

21.2 • The 80386 and 80386 SX

The 80386 represents a substantial break with previous 80X86 architecture. It will emulate its predecessors, but it is also possible to go far beyond their capabilities. It is a true 32-bit CPU, for instance, which means that it can fetch, store, and do all arithmetic on 32-bit quantities in a single instruction. By comparison the 8086-80286 does virtually all operations on 16-bit or smaller operands. The 80386 comes in two varieties, the original 80386, sometimes called the 80386 DX, and the 80386 SX, which is slower and cheaper but which appears identical to the programmer.

The difference between the two 80386s is that whereas the 80386 DX can fetch 32 bits from memory in a single operation, the 80386 SX economizes by being able to fetch or store only 16 bits at a time; if it needs to fetch a double word, it does so in two consecutive fetches, which is transparent to the programmer but takes twice as long. Thus not only is the 80386 SX slower because of its generally slower clock cycle time, it would be somewhat slower than an 80386 at the *same* clock cycle time. We say that the 80386 DX has a 32-bit **band width**, while the 80386 SX has a 16-bit band width. (The 8088 is to the 8086 as the 80386 SX is to the 80386 DX, in that the 8088 appears identical to the 8086 to the programmer but has only an 8-bit band width, as opposed to the 8086's 16-bit band width.)

As we said earlier, the 80386 *et. al.* will emulate earlier processors nearly exactly, but also has powerful extensions. It has a **protected mode** similar to the 80286, but in which 32-bit offsets can be used, thus allowing segments of up to four *Giga*Bytes (four *billion* bytes). It also has a **real mode**, in which DOS normally executes, and a **virtual mode**, which allows it to execute a DOS program as an individual task as though it were on an 8086-88, even though it is in effect running in protected mode. As before, we will restrict our attention to the real mode.

As with the 80286, there is a special pseudo-operation, `.386`, which must be used before any 80386 operations or registers can be used. `.386` also enables the 80286 instructions. Note that a program with the `.386` directive can be *assembled* on a machine with *any* 80X86 processor, but can be *executed* only on one with an 80386 or above processor.

21.2.1 • The 80386 Register Set

The 80386 has the same set of registers as its predecessors, but its register set is embedded in a much larger register set. Each of the registers ax, bx, cx, dx, si, di, sp, bp, and ip is embedded as the least significant part of an **extended register**, whose name is given by prefixing the original register by 'e', as in eax, ebx, ecx, edx, esi, edi, esp, ebp, and eip. For instance,

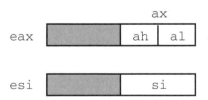

The shading in the left-hand (high-order) portion of the registers is to indicate that there is no way of accessing this part of the register directly, by itself, as one can access the upper half of ax by ah. In addition, there are two more **segment registers**, fs and gs.

CV and TD normally display only the 16-bit 8086-88-286 registers in its register window. To display the full extended register set in CV, choosing **Alt-O**(ptions 3(2 bit Registers. You will have to widen the Registers window to show the full 32 bits of registers. To display the extended registers in TD, choose **R**(egisters 32 bit from the Register Window SpeedMenu (**Alt-F10** or click right), or hit **Ctrl-R** when the Registers window is active. For both debuggers, these commands toggle.

21.2.2 • Addressing

80386 instructions can have addresses which are either 16 or 32 bits long (that is, can address 64 KBytes or 4 GBytes). The CPU expects a default address length—16 bits in real or virtual mode (and in particular, in DOS) and 32 bits in protected mode. If you use the wrong default address size in your code for the particular mode you are running in, the code generated will quickly degenerate into what appears to the CPU to be unrecognizable gibberish!

Just as the default *segment* used with instructions can be overridden, so also there is a byte which when placed in front of an instruction means 'use the non-default address length.' The assembler adds the address length byte automatically, if necessary, and it is entirely transparent to the programmer.

What good are 32-bit addresses? It is illegal to use a 32-bit memory address which is greater than 65,535 (= 2^{16} – 1) in real or virtual mode (that is, while running DOS)! * Even with this limitation, though, it is worthwhile using (small) 32-bit addresses, as there is a whole powerful new set of 32-bit addressing modes. With the use of the (automatic) overrides, you can use both the old 16-bit modes and the new 32-bit ones. The assembler determines which mode is the default for simplified segments (.DATA and .CODE) from the location of the .MODEL statement:

Default to 16-bit Addresses	
.MODEL SMALL ;	BEFORE .386, .486, or .586
.386	

Default to 32-Bit Addresses	
.386 ;	or .486 or .586
.MODEL SMALL ;	AFTER .386, .486, or .586

Choosing one of the sequences above makes for really mysterious coding, and TASM allows the much clearer option of specifying USE16 or USE32 in the .MODEL statement, as in .MODEL USE16 SMALL.

Masm and Tasm differ on the defaults for non-simplified segments, so to be safe, you should always specify the address size with a USE16 or USE32 modifier in all non-simplified segments.

DOS requires that all code segments use 16-bit addresses, and since, as we saw above, you gain nothing by using 32-bit data segments with DOS, I suggest that

---

All segments for .386 programs to be run under DOS should default to 16-bit addresses.

This class of programs includes those to be run from the DOS prompt in Windows.

Even though any conceivable protected-mode program (using 32-bit addressing) would run in a single segment, protected mode operating systems still use multi-segment programs. Having separate code and data segments allows the code segment to be marked as read-only, for instance.

As mentioned above, 32-bit addressing in the 80386 allows much more powerful indexing than

---

* It causes an interrupt 13 = 0Dh, which is a General Protection Violation. This is another of those interrupts which IBM shouldn't have used but did. It is an undocumented interrupt which, as my machine is configured, is used to handle the mouse. Trying to use a large 32 bit address causes my machine to lock up.

older processors. All eight 32-bit extended registers can be used as base registers, and all except esp can be used as the index register in based (double) indexing What's more, the index (second register) in based indexing can be automatically multiplied by 1 (of course), 2, 4, or 8 for ease of indexing into arrays of bytes, words, double words, or quad words. (Double words and quad words (8 bytes) can be used to contain short and long real, or floating point, numbers. See Section 20.1.) The most general form of memory reference on the 80386 is

32-bit Addressing	
[address + reg1 + n*reg2]	(n = 1, 2, 4, or 8)

where any combination of address, reg1, n, or n*reg2 can be omitted. Reg1 can be any of the eight 32-bit general registers and reg2 can be any of these except esp. (If you just want to add esp, you can make it reg1. Adding n * esp for $n \neq 1$ isn't meaningful because esp is *always* a memory address.) Thus, the following are legal 80386 memory references:

```
[A - 2 + ebx + 4 * eax]
        [esp]
     [eax + ebx]
     [esi + 3]
```

Example 21.2—1. Write code to implement setting a[i] := b[i] + c[i] for i = 1, ... 100, where each of the arrays is an array of double words indexed starting at 1. Assume all arrays are in the segment in ds.

One version of the code is

```
          mov     ecx, 100
AddLoop:
          mov     eax, [b - 4 + 4*ecx] ;    Start at the top...
          add     eax, [c - 4 + 4*ecx] ;    ...and work down
          mov     [a - 4 + 4*ecx], eax
          loop    AddLoop
```

(On the 80386, the loop instruction uses the entire ecx register.)

Example 21.2—2. In the code at the end of Section 15.3, we wished to turn on the T Flag, bit 9 of the flags register. The original code was

```
;; Turn the T flag on
          pushf   ;              Push flags register
          pop     ax ;           and move it --> ax
          or      ax, 0100h ;     T Flag := 1
          push    ax ;           Reload flags register--
          popf ;                 all other flags unchanged
```

On the 80386, the code above could be rewritten as

```
;;  Turn the T flag on
            pushf
            or      WORD PTR [esp], 0100h
            popf
```

21.2.3 • New Instructions

First of all, all previous instructions that had both byte and word versions now have a third, double word version. For fastest memory access, it is desirable that words and double words in memory be **aligned**—that is, words start on addresses divisible by 2 and double words start on addresses divisible by 4. The ALIGN pseudo-op can be used for this purpose. ALIGN 2 or ALIGN 4 rounds the location counter up to the next multiple of 2 or 4, respectively.

The string processing instructions of Chapter 18 have the double-word forms lodsd, stosd, movsd, cmpsd, and scasd.

Example 21.2—3. Redo Example 21.2—1 using string processing instructions.

The new code is

```
            mov     ecx, 100
            mov     esi, OFFSET b ;    Assuming ds is seg of b and c
            mov     edi, OFFSET a ;     and es is seg of a
AddLoop:
            lodsd
            add     eax, [c - b - 4 + esi] ; Already advanced by
lodsd
            stosd
            loop    AddLoop
```

Similarly, push and pop come in single and double word varieties, so when pushing a constant (but not when pushing an OFFSET, whose size is known from its segment's USE type), size must be specified:

```
            push  WORD PTR 3  or  push  DWORD PTR 3
```

The instructions pusha and popa for pushing and popping *all* registers also come in double word versions pushad and popad.

The cbw and cwd have been augmented with various other sign-extending instructions:

```
cwde ; word to double word; eax := ax by sign extension
cdq ; double to quad word; edx,eax := eax by sign extension
```

Even more useful is the addition of the instructions

```
movzx reg, reg-or-mem ; move to reg and extend with zeros
movsx reg, reg-or-mem ; move to reg with sign extension
```

Cwde is equivalent to `movsx eax, ax`.

Example 21.2—4. Instead of using the `xlat` instruction, part of Example 21.1—1 can be rewritten for the 386 without using bx as

```
    . . .
    push    edx ;           Don't destroy edx
    movzx   edx, ah ;       Convert left digit
    _PutCh [HexDig + edx]
    movzx   edx, al
    _PutCh [HexDig + edx]
    pop     edx
    . . .
```

Note that we must use **e**dx in order to be able to index with it, but the resulting addresses are still limited to the range 0-65,535 in DOS.

Another useful group of instructions is

```
    setcc byte reg-or-mem ; set reg-or-mem to 1
;                       if condition cc is true, to 0 otherwise
;                       cc = l, ge, ne, nbe, etc.
```

Example 21.2—5. Set eax := Sign of x, that is, eax = –1 if x < 0, eax = 1 if x > 0, and eax = 0 if x = 0.

```
    movsx   eax, x ;        So we don't have to worry about
    test    eax, eax ;       the size of x
    setg    al ;            al = 1 if x > 0, otherwise 0
    setl    ah ;            ah = 1 if x < 0, otherwise 0
    sub     al, ah ;        al is the Sign of x
    movsx   eax, al ;       extend it to all of eax
```

Finally, the 80386 has a variety of instructions for testing and setting individual bits in memory:

```
    bt     mem-or-reg, reg-or-constant ; Bit Test
    bts    mem-or-reg, reg-or-constant ; Bit Test and Set (to 1)
    btr    mem-or-reg, reg-or-constant ; Bit Test and Reset (to 0)
    btc    mem-or-reg, reg-or-constant ; Bit Test and Complement
```

The second operand specifies a bit number in the first. The specified bit is placed in the C flag, after which all instructions but the first alter the specified bit as stated. (Complement sets 1 to 0 and 0 to 1.). If the second operand is a register, it must be the same size as the first operand—word or double-word. When the bit specifier is a constant, it should be in the range 0–31. When the bit specifier (second operand) is a register and the first operand is memory, the full range of the register can be used the test takes place by counting that many bits forward in memory! For instance

```
    mov     eax, 32015
    bt      MemDWd, eax
```

will test bit 15 of the double word at location MemDWd + 4000.

Two useful instructions for finding one bits are

```
bsf    reg, mem-or-reg ;              Bit Scan Forward
bsr    reg, mem-or-reg ;              Bit Scan Reverse
```

The word or double-word specified by *mem-or-reg* is scanned—from low order end (bit 0) up in the forward case, from the high order end (bit 31 or 15) down in the reverse case, and the number of the first nonzero bit encountered is placed in *reg*. If the entire word or double-word is 0, the Z flag is set. The operands must be the same size and that if *mem-or-reg* has only one1 bit, the results of bsf and bsr will be the same. Note that only a single word or double-word is scanned, even if the second operand is in memory. This is because scasw or scasd can be used to find a word or double-word with a non-zero bit in it.

Example 21.2—6. Example 9.1—1 has various examples of manipulating the bits that indicate the status of the various shift keys. We can redo that example with the bt instructions.

The byte KbdStatus is assumed to contain the status of the shift keys.

- Process the Ctrl key down action by *setting* bit 2 of KbdStatus:

```
bts    KbdStatus, 2 ;       Set Ctrl bit
```

- Process the Alt key up action by *clearing* bit 3:

```
btr    KbdStatus, 3 ;       Clear Alt bit
```

- Process the Num Lock key down action by *complementing* bit 5:

```
btc    KbdStatus, 5 ;       Toggle Num Lock bit
```

In the first three examples, we have ignored the test result of the instruction.

- Convert the lower case letter in al to upper case if 1) the caps lock key (corresponding to bit 6) is up and either shift key (bits 0 and 1) is down or 2) the caps lock key is down and both shift keys are up.

```
            test   KbdStatus, 00000011B ;    If a shift key down...
            jz     TestCaps
            btr    eax, 5 ;                       change to upper case
TestCaps:
            bt     KbdStatus, 6 ;            Is Caps Lock down?
            jc     Done
            btc    eax, 5 ;                  Toggle case
Done:
```

Example 21.2—7. Finally, let's do a complete example showing off the power of some of the 80386 instructions. We will write a program much favored by computer science instructors (and textbook writers) to find all the primes less than some number N, using a method known as the **Sieve of Eratosthenes**.

First, recall that a prime number is a whole number which is divisible only by itself and 1, and 1 usually isn't counted as a prime. The first few primes are 2, 3, 5, 7, 11, 13, 17, 19, 23, ... Our method for finding all the primes less than N is to write out the numbers from 1 to N. Cross out 1 as not being a prime and then search for the first uncrossed-out number (2). It will be a prime. Cross out all multiples of 2 and search for the next uncrossed-out number after 2, which will be the next prime, 3. Continuing in this manner, we repeatedly search out the next uncrossed number after the last prime, which will be the next prime, and then cross out all of its multiples.

We will implement the Sieve of Eratosthenes using an array of bits, with the nth bit representing the nth whole number. Thus, all numbers from 0 to N–1 will be represented. The largest such array we could put in a single segment under DOS would be 64K bytes, or 2^{19} bits, which is approximately 500,000. We will use `scasd` and `bsf` to find the next prime, the next 1 bit, and use `btr` repeatedly to 'cross out' all multiples of the prime by setting the corresponding bit to 0. When searching for the next 1 bit, we might have to deal with an earlier prime in the double word we are searching, so it's easier if we cross out each prime as it is found, as well.

When setting up our array, we may as well start with 0, 1, and all multiples of 2 crossed out. The initialization is done with

```
PSeg        SEGMENT USE16
Bits        DD      0AAAAAAA8h, 16383 DUP (0AAAAAAAAh)
;                   0, 1 and multiples of 2 already crossed out
PSeg        ENDS
```

(TASM gives a spurious warning about location counter overflow here.)

According to the **Prime Number Theorem**, the number of primes less than N is approximately $N/\log N > N/\log_2 N =$ (in our case) $2^{19}/19$, which is roughly $500,000/20 = 25,000$. Clearly, writing all these numbers out isn't very practical. At eight numbers per line and 25 lines per screen, this display would be 125 screens full. It's also a pretty good sized file, too. If we wrote out the primes in binary, at four bytes each, it will be a 100K file. Therefore we will satisfy ourselves with merely reporting the *number* of primes less than N. We will want to print out N, which can be larger than a single word, and so will use `MPPutDec` (see Chapter 14).

Crossing off multiples is simple using `btr`. Assuming we have the current prime in an extended register *CurPrime* and compute the multiples in an extended register *Multiples*, we can use the code

```
        mov     Multiples, CurPrime
CrossOffMultiples:
        btr     Bits, Multiples
        add     Multiples, CurPrime
        cmp     Multiples, UpperBound
        jl      CrossOffMultiples
          Find Next Prime
```

Since all the even numbers have already been crossed out, there is no reason to cross out *even* multiples of the current prime, so the code could be altered as follows to cross out only odd multiples:

```
        mov     Multiples, CurPrime
        shl     CurPrime, 1 ; Need only cross out odd multiples
CrossOffMultiples:
        btr     Bits, Multiples
        add     Multiples, CurPrime
        cmp     Multiples, UpperBound
        jl      CrossOffMultiples
        shr     CurPrime, 1 ; Get CurPrime back to last prime
            Find Next Prime
```

The code to find the next prime is quite a bit more difficult and caused the author a substantial amount of grief in finding it. The general idea is as follows:

```
FindNextPrime:
        mov     edi, address of DWORD containing CurPrime
        mov     ecx, Number of DWORDs left in the table
        sub     eax, eax ;   scan for nonzero
        repz    scasd ;       Repeat until nonzero DWord found
        jz      Done ;        If none found, done
        bsf     eReg, the double word found
        mov     CurPrime, (number of the bit corresponding to
;                   bit 0 of found DWord) + contents of eReg
        cmp     CurPrime, UpperBound
        jge     Done
            Cross Out Multiples
```

We have to do the comparison on *UpperLimit* because if we take an *UpperLimit* $< 2^{19}$, we may have some extra 1 bits left over in the last double word if *UpperLimit* isn't divisible by 32.

There are two reasons for scanning from DWord boundaries (that is, from addresses divisible by 4). In the first place, accessing things at DWord boundaries is supposed to be faster on the 80386, but more importantly, when we get to the end of the Bits array, if we aren't on a DWord boundary, we will either miss some bytes or scan off the end of the segment, causing the General Protection Violation mentioned earlier (about which more later).

Now let's begin to fill in the code in FindNextPrime. We may as well use edi for *CurPrime*, so the first two instructions can be replaced by

```
        shr     edi, 3 ;       shifts by consts <> 1 legal in 386
        and     di, 0fffch ; zero last 2 bits to get DWord addr
        mov     ecx, total number of bytes, rounded UP to a DWord
        sub     ecx, edi ;    total number of bytes to scan
        add     ecx, 3 ;      Round up to DWords
        shr     ecx, 2
```

The total number of *bytes* in the table is (*UpperBound* + 7) SHR 3. We can get rid of the final add ecx, 3 by initially adding 3*8 + 7 = 31 instead of 7 to *UpperBound*. Therefore, the code is

```
shr     edi, 3 ;        shifts by consts <> 1 legal in 386
and     di, 0fffch ; zero last 2 bits to get DWord bdry
mov     ecx, (UpperBound + 31) SHR 3
sub     ecx, edi ;      total number of bytes to scan
shr     ecx, 2
```

The final SHR acts to complete the rounding.

The two lines starting bsf … are quite a bit trickier. When the scan is completed, edi is left pointing to the DWord *after* the desired one, that is, to (*DWord address*) + 4. Getting really fancy with 80386 addressing modes, we could try the following code:

```
bsf     eReg, [-4 + edi] ;         BAD CODE!!!
lea     edi, [-32 + eReg + 8 * edi] ;   edi := Next Prime
```

The reasoning is that –32 + eReg + 8 * edi = eReg + 8 * (–4 + edi) = *bit #* in eReg + ((*DWord address* –4 + edi) converted to a bit #). We were just lucky that 8 was the number we needed to multiply by.

The trouble is that the code above has two *very* serious problems. If you try to execute a program using this code, it hangs and you have to reboot your machine. There are, in fact, two bugs here, both tricky to find (see the end of this section for debugging tips).

The first problem is that when you get to the last double-word of Bits, at address 0fffch, and the scasd instruction causes you to go a DWord beyond, it adds 4 to *di*, giving 0, so –4 + edi = –4 = 0fffffffch, which is an illegal address causing a protection violation. This problem is easy to fix: simply replace the bsf instruction with bsf eReg, [-4 + **di**].

The second problem is not so easily solved. When edi hits 0, –32 + eReg + 8 * edi = –32 = 0ffffffc0h and we are crossing out negative prime numbers; we will 'never' get bigger than *UpperLimit*. We can't change to …8 * di] because that isn't a legal addressing mode. We could simply mask off the high-order 12 bits in edi, but as long as we're going to add an extra instruction, it seems more straightforward simply to subtract 4 from di to begin with, to get it to point to the *correct* DWord. The code is

```
sub     di, 4 ;                  GOOD CODE!!!
bsf     eReg, [di]
lea     edi, [eReg + 8 * edi]
```

Finally, all we have to do is choose names for the registers we have referred to symbolically up to now. We choose *eReg* = edx, *UpperLimit* = esi, *Multiples* = ecx, and use ebx to count primes. Also, when I was debugging this program, I frequently got into trouble with the various shift amounts. At last, I did what I should have done in the first place: give symbolic names to the amount to shift a bit number to get a byte address (3) and the amount to shift a byte address to get a double-word number. The code is

```
;;; SIEVE.ASM--Program to compute number of primes <= 524288 =
;;; 2**19 using the sieve of Eratosthenes and 80386 bit
;;; instructions
INCLUDE   PCMAC.INC

        .MODEL SMALL ;         This order defaults to 16-bit
```

```
            .386    ;                       addresses

            .STACK 100h

UPBOUND    EQU     80000h
BitNo2ByteNo EQU 3 ;        Amount to shift bit # to get byte #
ByteNo2DWordNo EQU 2 ;      Amount to shift byte # to get dword #

            .DATA
Msg1       DB      'The number of primes less than $'
Msg2       DB      ' is $'
Msg3       DB      13, 10, '$'
PrimeCt    DD      ?
UBound     DD      UPBOUND

PSeg       SEGMENT USE16 ;       Default may not work here
Bits       DD      0AAAAAAA8h, 16383 DUP (0AAAAAAAAh)
;                  0, 1 and multiples of 2 already crossed out
PSeg       ENDS

            .CODE
Sieve      PROC
            mov     ax, PSeg
            mov     ds, ax
            mov     es, ax
            ASSUME ds : PSeg, es : PSeg
            mov     edi, 2 ;                Initial 'last' prime
            mov     ebx, 1 ;        Initial count of primes (not incl 1)
            mov     esi, UPBOUND ;        Highest prime to look for
            sub     eax, eax ;        Compare to 0 in scasd
FindNextPrime:
            shr     edi, BitNo2ByteNo ; Byte to start search from
            and     di, 0fffch ;        Round down to nearest Dword
            mov     ecx, (UPBOUND+7) SHR BitNo2ByteNo ; Bytes in Bits
            sub     ecx, edi ;                Number of bytes to scan
            shr     ecx, ByteNo2DWordNo ;     Number of Dwords to scan
            repz    scasd ;           Scan for nonzero dword
            jz      SHORT Done ;      No more primes
            sub     di, 4 ;           EDI already one dword beyond
;   (must sub from di instead of edi as when edi trips over to
;   (0, subtracting 4 gives fffffffch which kills the machine on
;   (the next instruction)
            bsf     edx, DWORD PTR [di] ;     Find bit... (scasd
;                   leaves us a double-word beyond what we found)
            lea     edi, [edx + 8 * edi] ;    ...and get the prime
            cmp     edi, esi
            jge     Done
```

```
            inc     ebx ;                   ...and count it
            mov     ecx, edi ;     ecx is index for cross-out loop

            shl     edi, 1 ;       Need only cross out odd multiples
CrossOffMultiples:
            btr     Bits, ecx
            add     ecx, edi
            cmp     ecx, esi
            jb      CrossOffMultiples
            shr     edi, 1 ;                Get edi back to last prime
            jmp     FindNextPrime
Done:
            mov     ax, DSeg ;              Write out output message
            mov     ds, ax
            ASSUME ds : DSeg
            mov     PrimeCt, ebx ;          Save prime count
            _PutStr Msg1
            push    ds
            push    OFFSET UBound
            push    2
            call    FMPPutDec
            _PutStr Msg2
            push    ds
            push    OFFSET PrimeCt
            push    2
            call    FMPPutDec
            _PutStr Msg3
            _Exit   0
Sieve       ENDP
            END     Sieve
```

When run, the `Sieve` program displays

```
The number of primes less than 524288 is 43390
```

As mentioned earlier, it was difficult to find some of the bugs in `Sieve` because they occurred so late in the program, that is, after going through the main loop many thousands of times. The `btr eReg, [-4+edi]` was a real tough one. After flailing around, I finally convinced myself that it was something that happened after a lot of iterations. One could, of course, set a breakpoint in `FindNextPrime` and then sit there and hit the run key over and over again. 43,385 times, to be exact! The way around that is to place a **pass count** on the breakpoint. Setting a pass count of n on a breakpoint at a statement means that the break will be taken only the nth time that the statement is executed.

In CodeView, set the pass count at the same time you set the breakpoint by putting the cursor on the breakpoint line and executing **Alt-D**(ata **S**(et breakpoint... **P**(ass count n **Enter** or by entering

```
bp location /Ppasscount
```

in the dialog window. You can alter the pass count of an existing breakpoint using **Alt-D**(ata **E**(dit breakpoint..., scroll to the breakpoint you want, and type **M**(odify **P**(ass count *n* Enter. After breaking at the breakpoint, the pass count is, in effect, reset to 1, even though it will still show as *n* in the Modify window. To restore it in fact to *n*, use **Alt-D**(ata **E**(dit breakpoint... **M**(odify and hit Enter. (You needn't reenter the pass count.) Reset the pass count to another value, as above. The largest pass count for CV is 65,535.

In the Turbo Debugger, move the cursor in the program to the line on which the breakpoint is desired and choose **Alt-B**(reakpoint **A**(t... . Then type c**H**(ange **P**(asscount *n* Enter. When the break is taken, the passcount is automatically reset to 1. The largest pass count for TD is 32,767.

Experimentation with the buggy `Sieve` program showed that the problem occurred after 43,385 = 0A979h passes through the `FindNextPrime` loop. Finding this number is quite tedious as the program runs very slowly when running through a breakpoint with a pass count. To get to the bad place in TD, first set a pass count of, say 30,000, then a pass count of 13,385.

After unmasking the `btr eReg, [-4+edi]` problem, I ran into a further rather frightening bug. At that time, the `jge Done` instruction was `jae Done`. The following `lea` instruction caused a negative number to be loaded into `edi`, which compared *above* `esi`, causing the program to terminate, seemingly normally, showing 43,385 primes. This bug is one of those boundary problems which can't be detected by trying smaller cases, either. It just so happened that I knew from an earlier, different version of the program that the number of primes should be 43,390, so I once again had to go through 43,000 odd iterations and trace to find the problem.

Exercises 21.2

1. ✓ Given the array

```
ShortMo    DB      'Jan$'
           DB      'Feb$'
           etc.
```

and a month number (1–12) in `al`, write 80386 code to display the three-character abbreviation for the month name.

2. ✓ Redo example 21.2—3 using a `bt` instruction.

3. Rewrite using 80386 instructions the code to compare two C strings as in Example 19.1—3.

4. A set can be represented as an array of bytes, with each bit in the array representing whether a particular element is in (bit = 1) or not in (bit = 0) the set (see Section 12.3). Write 80386 code to solve Example 12.3—2 (determining whether an element is in a set) using `bt` and Exercise 12.3—4 (determining the cardinality, the number of 1 bits in a set) using `btr` and `bsf`.

21.3 • The 80486, 80486 SX and Pentium

The 80486 is essentially a fast 80386 with the floating-point processor built in (it must be added to the 80386 with the 80387 numeric coprocessor; see Section 20.1). Because of built-in cache (fast) memory and faster internal processing speeds, the 80486 can be on the order of twice as fast as an 80386 *running at the same clock speed*. The 80486 SX is a slow 80486 with the floating-point processor disabled. There is a corresponding 80487 SX, which is the same slow 80486 with the regular processor disabled. The Pentium is essentially a fast 80486 with some ability to process instructions in two parallel streams.

Most of the new instructions in these CPUs are for protected mode. There are only three new 486 instructions and one more for the Pentium for the applications programmer, which appear to be of very limited benefit. As with the 80386, the pseudo-operation .486 must be used before any 80486-only instructions are used. .486 also enables the 80386 instructions discussed in the last section. The .586 pseudo-operation enables Pentium, as well as 80386 and 80486 instructions.

The new 80486 instructions are bswap *extended-reg*, which reverses the order of bytes in *extended-reg* and which appears to have been intended to simplify data transfers with machines that don't byte swap, and two rather mysterious instructions cmpxchg and xadd which appear to have been intended for implementation of semaphores (see Section 15.7).

The most important application of the xadd instruction, defined by

```
xadd mem/reg, reg ;      xchg mem/reg, reg then add mem/reg, reg
```

seems to be that it gives 80486 the world's most powerful capability to compute perhaps the least useful commonly computed numbers, the Fibonacci numbers. Recall that the **Fibonacci numbers** (0, 1, 1, 2, 3, 5, 8, 13, 21, …) (see Programming Problem 14.1) are defined by $F_0 = 0$, $F_1 = 1$, and $F_n = F_{n-1} + F_{n-2}$. To put the Nth Fibonacci number into eax, we use

```
;   Put the Nth Fibonacci number into eax (N >= 3)
            .486
            mov    ecx, N-2
            mov    edx, 0
            mov    eax, 1
FibLoop:
            xadd   eax, edx
            loop   FibLoop
```

The new instruction for the Pentium is cmpxchg8b, which is an eight-byte version of cmpxchg.

21.4 • The FPU with 80286 and above.

This section discusses a few of the differences that the FPU has with the higher numbered CPU chips. It assumes a fairly detailed knowledge of Chapter 20.

Perhaps the most useful improvement is in the transfer of comparison flags from the FPU to the 80X86. Instead of having to store the status word in memory and then load it into ax, it is possible to do the fstsw into ax directly.

FPU Flags to 80X86 flags for 286 and above		
.MODEL SMALL		
.286 ;		or .386 or .486 or .586
...		
fstsw **ax** ;		Store FPU status word in **ax**
sahf ;		Put ah into flags register

Also, there is another reason for specifying 286 or higher. The early FPUs were on separate chips, called coprocessors, and their operation had to be synchronized with that of the main CPU. The main CPU would send out coprocessor instructions (`fld`, `fadd`, etc.) and then issued an `fwait` instruction which caused the 80X86 CPU to stop until the FPU had finished executing all of its instructions. These `fwait` instructions are generated automatically by the assembler. (You can see them in the debugger by choosing mixed assembly and machine language (**F3**) in CV or viewing the CPU window in TD.) The point of interest is that more `fwait` instructions are required for the 8087 coprocessor, and lacking any other information, the assembler generates enough `fwait`s for it. If you specify a higher numbered main CPU, as in the code above, the assembler may generate fewer `fwait`s.

Of course when you specify a higher numbered CPU, you limit yourself to running on that CPU and above.

SUMMARY

The 80286 chip used on PC-ATs and clones introduced protected mode addressing, allowing access to more than 1MByte of memory. It also introduced a few new instructions

```
    push   constant
    shr    reg-or-mem, constant; also shl, sar, rol, etc.
    imul   reg [, reg-or-mem] , constant
    enter  n, lexlevel ;     Set up stack for procedure at lex
;                  level lexlevel with n bytes of local storage
    leave ;       un-set up stack
```

The 80386 added 32-bit addressing, enormously increasing the size of a segment, and *orthogonalized* the addressing scheme; that is, made virtually all conceivable indexing combinations legitimate. It also added automatic multiplication of an index register by 2, 4, or 8. The eight general registers were extended to 32-bit registers with original names prefixed by 'E'. The original 16-bit registers form the low-order 16-bits of these registers.

Double word forms of appropriate instructions were added, along with many new instructions, the most useful perhaps being

```
    movzx reg, reg-or-mem ; move to reg and extend with zeroes
    movsx reg, reg-or-mem ; move to reg and with sign-extension

    setcc byte-reg ;  set byte-reg to 1 if condition cc is true

    bt    mem-or-reg, reg-or-constant ; bit test
    bts   mem-or-reg, reg-or-constant ; bit test and set
    btr   mem-or-reg, reg-or-constant ; bit test and reset
    btc   mem-or-reg, reg-or-constant ; bit test and complement
```

Mem-or-reg contains the bit to be tested and `reg-or-constant` is the bit number. The original value of the bit goes to the C-flag.

```
    bsf   reg, mem-or-reg ;            bit scan forward
    bsr   reg, mem-or-reg ;            bit scan reverse
```

Mem-or-reg is the item to be scanned and the resulting bit position is put into *reg*.

The 80486 and Pentium are virtually identical to the 80386 from the application programmer's standpoint.

Along with a general increase in function, CPU chips also tend to get faster as their numbers get larger. Representative clock rates for the various processors are

8086-88	4.77–8 MHz
80286	6–12 MHz
80386SX	16–20 MHz
80386	16–40 MHz
80486 SX	25 MHz
80486	33–100 MHz
Pentium	60–200 MHz

Answers
to Selected Exercises

Chapter 1

1.2—5, first example. F + D = 15 + 13 = 28 = 16 + 12 = 1Ch, so the final digit of the result is C and there is a carry of 1 into the next position. The sum in that digit position is 0, carry 1, etc.

1.3—1 Since the sign (=leftmost) bit of 00101101B is 0 = +, it is the same whether considered to be signed or unsigned, and = 32 + 8 + 4 + 1 = 45.

As an unsigned number, 11111111B = 128 + 64 + … + 4 + 2 + 1 = 255, and as a signed number, it is –(2's complement of 11111111B) = –(00000001) = –1.

1.3—2 As an unsigned number, 88h = 8 × 16 + 8 = 128 + 8 = 136. As a signed number, it is negative since its first hex digit is ≥ 8, so its value is –(2's complement of 88h) = –(78h) = –(7 × 16 + 8) = –120.

3Fh has a positive sign bit, so its value is 3×16 + 15 = 63 whether considered as a signed or unsigned number.

1.3—3

```
  -47 = -(00101111B) = 11010001B
   38 =                00100110B
                       11110111B
```

which is a negative number since its first bit is 1. Therefore the answer is –(2's complement of 11110111B) = –(00001001) = –9, as was expected. Note that this arithmetic must involve *exactly* eight bits (or however many bits you are assuming) to work properly. There is no overflow here since the addends have different signs.

```
  -47 = -(00101111B) = 11010001B
  -88 = -(01011000B)  10101000B
                     1 01111001B
```

The carry bit out the left end is discarded and here we have overflow because the signs of the addends are both the same (1's) while the sign of the result is different (0).

1.3—4 A signed byte represents values from –128 to 127. An unsigned byte can represent values from 0 to 255. The two interpretations represent the same value in the range 0…127.

1.3—5 a) 33h is positive as its first hex digit is < 8, hence its first bit is 0. Therefore the 16-bit value is 0033h. On the other hand, AEh is negative so its extended version is FFAEh. If we add an initial 0 in assembly language to indicate that the number is hex, giving 0FFAEh, it is *still* negative, because the sign bit is the *actual* left-hand bit as the number is stored, and when the number is stored, the leading 0 would be omitted.

1.3—5 b) 00A9h is a positive number but if shortened to 8 bits, the resulting number A9h would be negative. Therefore 00A9h ≠ A9h. On the other hand, 003Bh is positive and equals 3Bh. FCF3h and F3h are both negative, but in shortening FCF3h we have discarded significant bits, so FCF3h ≠ F3h. (In fact, FCF3h = – (2's complement of FCF3h) = –030Dh = –((3× 16 + 0)×16 + 13) = –781 and F3h = – (2-s complement of F3h) = –(0Dh) = –13.

1.4—1 '3' + 2 = '5'

1.4—2 'b' – 'A' = 'b' - 'a' + 'a' – 'A' = 1 + 32 = 33

Chapter 2

2.2—2 b)

```
            DB     5 DUP (5, 10)
```

2.2—3 a)

```
    All on one line
    _
```

2.2—3

```
    mov W, 'J' ; OK; 'J' = 74 is either word or byte
    mov 74, W ;  ILLEGAL; moving to a constant doesn't make sense
    mov W, ah ;  ILLEGAL; can't move byte to word
    mov al, B ;  OK; B contains SOMETHING, even if unknown
    mov A, B  ;  ILLEGAL; can't move memory to memory
```

2.2—4

```
            mov    ah, AByte
            mov    al, Another ;      ax = 9abch
            mov    ax, 1234h
            mov    ax, 'A' ;          ax = 0041h
            mov    ah, 1
            mov    al, 2 ;            ax = 0102h
```

2.2—5 a)

```
    All on one line
    _
```

2.2—5 d)

```
    One _
```

2.2—5f)

```
    * * * * *
    * * * * *
    * * * * *
    * * * * *
    _
```

2.2—6 g)

```
    * * * * * * * * *
    *               *
    *               *
```

```
        *          *
     * * * * * * * * *
```
2.2—6 c)
```
     One if by land,
     Two if by sea.
     Two if by sea.
```

2.2—7
```
     Msg      DB      'down',13,10,' down',13,10,'   down',13,10,'$'
```

Chapter 3

3.1—1 Ex4Msg:
```
     strange_lso
     Ex5Msg:
     Ex5 is not

     ‾
     Ex7Msg:
     The 64 _
```
3.1—3
```
     DestBSP  DB      8, ' ', 8, '$'
```
3.2—1
```
     Msg1     DB      'The 64 $'
     Msg2     DB      ' question', 13, 10, '$'
              ...
              _PutStr Msg1
              _PutCh '$'
              _PutStr Msg2
```

Chapter 4

4.1—1
```
              mov    ax, 0FFFFh ; = -1; ax = FFFFh

              inc    ax ;          ax = 0000h
              mov    ax, 0FFFFh
              inc    al ;          ax = FF00h
              mov    ax, 0FFFFh
              inc    ah ;          ax = 00FFh
              mov    ax, 1234h
              sub    ax, 35h ;     ax = 1234+FFCB = 11FFh
              mov    ax, 1234h
              sub    al, 35h ;     ax = 12FFh (no borrow from ah)
              mov    ax, 1234h
              neg    ax ;          ax = EDCCh
              mov    ax, 1234h
              neg    al ;          ax = 12CCh
              mov    ax, 1234h
              mov    al, -1 ;      ax = 12FFh
```

```
              inc     AX ;            ax = 1300h
              mov     ax, 12FFh;
              inc     AL ;            ax = 1200h (no carry into ah)
              mov     ax, 1200h
              dec     AX ;            ax = 11FFh
              mov     ax, 1200h;
              dec     AL ;            ax = 12FFh
              mov     ax, 1234h
              sub     ax, ax ;        ax = 0000h
              mov     ax, 1234h
              sub     al, al ;        ax = 1200h
```

4.1—2

```
    a
    d
    —
```

4.2—1

```
              mov     al, -1
              mov     bl, -1
              mul     bl ;            ax = FE01h (=255*255=256*255-255=
    ;                                 100h * FFh - FFh = FF00h - 00FFh)
              mov     al, -1
              mov     bl, -1
              imul    bl ;            ax = 0001h (-1 * -1 = 1)
              mov     ax, -1
              mov     bx, -1
              imul    bx ;            ax = 0001h
    ;                                 dx = 0000h  ( 32-bit 1)
              mov     ax, -1
              mov     bx, 2
              imul    bx ;            ax = FFFEh
    ;                                 dx = FFFFh  (32-bit -2)
              mov     ax, 0FF80h ;  = -128
              mov     bl, 2
              idiv    bl ;            al = C0h = -64, ah = 00h
              mov     ax, 0FF80h
              mov     bl, 2
              div     bl ;            Gives divide overflow because as an
    ;                                 unsigned number, 0FF80h = 65,408,
    ;                                 and 65,408/2 is too large to be
    ;                                 represented in a single byte.
```

4.2—2 b)

```
              mov     ax, B
              neg     ax ;            ax := -B
              mov     bx, D
              dec     bx ;            bx := D - 1
              imul    bx ;            ax := -B * (D - 1)
              mov     A, ax
```

5.2—3 f)

```
              mov     ax, Minutes
              cwd
              mov     bx, 60 ;      Can't idiv 60
              idiv    bx
              mov     Hours, ax
              mov     Minutes, dx
```

4.2—2 h)

```
              mov     ax, 22
              imul    R ;           ax := -B
              imul    R ;           dx, ax = 22*R*R
              mov     bx, 7
              idiv    bx
              mov     Area, ax
```

Chapter 5

5.1—1 a) The necessary **if** statement, with decorations, is

$$\textbf{if } A \geq 0 \textbf{ then } X := A \textbf{ else } X := -A \textbf{ end if}$$

which gives us the following skeleton

```
              cmp     A, 0
      ;                             hole for jump
              mov     ax, A
              mov     X, ax ;       since mov X, A is illegal
      ;                             hole for jump
      Lab1:
              mov     ax, A
              neg     ax
              mov     X, ax
      Lab2:
```

Inserting the necessary jumps, we get

```
              cmp     A, 0
              jnge    Lab1 ;        if (A >= 0) then
              mov     ax, A
              mov     X, ax ;           X := A
              jmp     Lab2
      Lab1:   ;                     else
              mov     ax, A
              neg     ax
              mov     X, ax ;           X := -A
      Lab2:
```

We could quit here, but there are several interesting optimizations. First of all, note that `mov ax, A` occurs at the *beginning* of both the **then** part and the **else** part, so it could be factored out ahead of the **if**, and `mov X, ax` occurs at the *end* of both parts, so it could be factored out after the **if**. This would give us the code

```
        mov     ax, A
        cmp     A, 0
        jnge    Lab1 ;          if (A >= 0) then
        mov     ax, A
        mov     X, ax
        jmp     Lab2
Lab1:   ;                       else
        mov     ax, A
        neg     ax
        mov     X, ax
Lab2:
        mov     X, ax
```

Since A is already in `ax`, `cmp A, 0` should be replaced by `cmp ax, 0`, and the `jnge` around the jump should be removed, also allowing us to remove `Lab1`. When all these things are done and the blank lines are removed (and the code recommented), we have the code a 'fluent' speaker of assembly language would write

```
        mov     ax, A
        cmp     ax, 0
        jge     Lab2
        neg     ax
Lab2:   mov     X, ax ;         X := |A|
```

5.1—1 f) The flags are preserved until an instruction comes along which changes them (see Section 5.4). Therefore we can write

```
        cmp     X, 0 ;          if (X > 0) then
        jng     Lab1
        mov     SgnX, 1 ;           SgnX := 1
        jmp     Done
Lab1:
        jnl     Lab2 ;          else if (X < 0) then
        mov     SgnX, -1 ;          SgnX := -1
        jmp     Done
Lab2:
        mov     SgnX, 0 ;           else SgnX := 0
Done:
```

5.1—2 b) The decorated version of the **if** statement is

```
if ((X > 5) and (Y < 0)) or (Z <= 13) then A := 10 else A := 2 end if
```

The final answer is given after that of 5.1—6b). Try to work it out for yourself before looking there.

5.1—3 c)

if (A <= 100) **and** (A >= 10) **then** A := A / B **end if**

5.1—4 c)

```
              cmp    ax, 0
              jng    over
              inc    ax
              jmp    through
     over:    dec    ax
     through:
```

5.1—5.

```
              mov    ax, D
              cmp    ax, 9
              jg     Letter
              add    al, '0'
              jmp    Store
     Letter:
              add    al, 'A' - 10 ;       so 10 --> A
     Store:
              mov    HEXD, al
```

5.1—6 b)

```
              jnz    GoOn
              js     SFSet
              jno    Lab ;       since SF = 0 if we get here
              jmp    GoOn ;      NOT a jump around a jump
     SFSet:
              jo     Lab ;       since SF = 1 if we get here
     GoOn:
```

5.1—2 b), concluded. The code is

```
              cmp    X, 5
              jng    Lab1 ;      if ((X > 5)
              cmp    Y, 0
              jl     Lab2 ;          and (Y < 0))
     Lab1:
              cmp    Z, 13
              jnle   Lab3 ;              or (Z <= 13) then
     Lab2:
              mov    A, 10 ;        A := 10
              jmp    Lab4
     Lab3:    ;                   else
              mov    A, 2 ;         A := 2
     Lab4:
```

5.2—1

```
              mov    ax, Time1
              cmp    ax, Time2
```

```
                    jA       Time1Later ;  UNSIGNED comparison must be used
                    mov      ax, Time2
          Time1Later:
                    mov      Late, ax
5.2—3
                    cmp      al, 'A'
                    jb       notLetter
                    cmp      al, 'Z'
                    jbe      Letter
                    cmp      al, 'a'
                    jb       notLetter
                    cmp      al, 'z'
                    jbe      Letter
                    cmp      al, 128 ;      Note: 128 appears negative
                    jb       notLetter
                    cmp      al, 154 ;        as does 154, etc.
                    jbe      Letter
                    cmp      al, 160
                    jb       notLetter
                    cmp      al, 167
                    jbe      Letter
          notLetter:
```

5.2—4 Suppose we are comparing two n-bit unsigned numbers X and Y. The computer does this by computing $X - Y = X + (2\text{'s complement of } Y) = X + 2^n - Y = 2^n + (X - Y)$ where the computation is done considering X and Y to be positive numbers. Then $X \geq Y$, i.e., X is ae Y, precisely when the comparison sets the carry bit. In fact `jae` and `jc` are the same instruction. Thus the "above" condition is CF = 1 *and* ZF = 0.

5.3—1 a) We can use `cx` for a counter as well as the numbers to be squared. We must use a register other than `ax` and `dx` to accumulate the sum since multiplication uses both of them.

```
                    mov      cx, N
                    mov      bx, 0 ;        use bx to accumulate sum
          SqSum:
                    mov      ax, cx
                    mul      cx
                    add      bx, ax
                    loop     SqSum
                    mov      ax, bx ;       put the sum where required
```

5.3—1 b) The following is a rather clever method, if I do say so myself:

```
          EvenRow   DB       '* '
          OddRow    DB       '  *   *   *   *    *', 13, 10, '$'
                    . . .
                    mov      cx, 4
          StarLoop:
```

```
            _PutStr EvenRow
            _PutStr OddRow ;     omit first star
            loop    StarLoop
            _PutStr EvenRow
```

5.4—1 b)

```
            dec     ax
            jge     NonNeg
```

5.4—2

```
            sub     al, '0'
            jl      NotDigit
            cmp     al, 9 ;         NOT '9'!
            jge     NotDigit
        ;                   When we get here, conversion already done!
```

5.6—3 There are several foreign lowercase letters whose values are above 128, and therefore appear negative, but which must be converted to their uppercase equivalents. For example, character 135, "ç", must be converted to character 128, "Ç".

5.7—1

```
            jge     FarAway
```

becomes

```
            jnge    Lab
            jmp     FarAway
        Lab:
```

Chapter 6

6.2—1

```
        A       DW      1111h
        B       DW      2222h
                  . . .
                push    A
                mov     ax, 3333h
                push    ax
                push    B
                pop     ax ;        ax = 2222h
                pop     B ;         B  = 3333h
```

6.2—3 Because in order to pop the saved value back into sp, sp has already have the correct value. Hence there is no point to saving and restoring sp by this method.

6.3—1

```
                call    procA
            ;                   order of execution of this line: 3
                  . . .
        procA   PROC
                call    procB
            ;                   order of execution of this line: 2
                ret
```

```
procA       ENDP
procB       PROC
;                           order of execution of this line: 1
            ret
procB       ENDP
```

6.3—2 a) The pop ax instruction actually pops the return address of the call to procB, so the following ret instruction does the return from procA instead, and we never return to procA.

6.3—2 b) At the ret instruction, the stack is wrong and the program will try to return to whatever garbage was in ax.

6.3—2 c) No return address for procX was pushed onto the stack, so the program will try to return to whatever happens to be next on the stack, whether or not it is a return address.

6.4—1

```
;; SPACE.ASM--A procedure which takes as input an integer in ax
;;    and displays that number of space characters on the CRT
;;    screen. If ax <= 0, no spaces are displayed. All registers
;;    are preserved.
;;
INCLUDE     PCMAC.INC
            .MODEL SMALL


            .CODE   ; No .DATA required
            PUBLIC Space
Space       PROC
            push    ax
            push    cx
            push    dx ;            _PutCh destroys ax and dx
            cmp     ax, 0
            jle     Done
            mov     cx, ax
SpaceLoop:
            _PutCh ' '
            loop    SpaceLoop
Done:
            pop     dx
            pop     cx
            pop     ax
            ret
Space       ENDP
            END
```

Chapter 7

7.3—1

```
            mov     ax, 1234h
            mov     bx, 5678h
            xchg    ah, bl ;     ax = 7834h
;                                bx = 5612h
```

7.3—8 Changed parts of the code are in boldface. A complete version of the code is in the file
GETDECC.ASM in CHAP07 on the disk that comes with this book.

```
;; GETDECC.ASM -- a function to read a decimal number (with
;;    optionalminus sign) from the keyboard and return the binary
;;    value in ax
;; Program returns carry flag clear if no error
            . . .
Counter   DB    ? ;              In the .DATA segment
            . . .
          mov   Counter, 0 ;
            . . .
          sub   al, '0' ;  Yes, cvt to DigitValue and extend to a
          inc   Counter ;    A digit has occurred; count it.
            . . .
          mul   cx ;          NumberValue * 10 ...
          jo    Error
          add   ax, bx ;        + DigitValue ...
          jc    Error
          mov   bx, ax ;        ==> NumberValue
            . . .
NoLF:
          cmp   Counter, 0
          je    Error ;        No digits occurred
          cmp   bx, 8000h ;  tricky way to do only one compare
          ja    Error ;     gets all negative numbers except 8000h
          jne   OK
          cmp   Sign, '-' ;  MUST be - for number to be OK
          je    Positive ;  Needn't negate this number
Error:
          stc   ;              Set carry bit to indicate error
          jmp   Return ;        and return to caller
OK:
          cmp   Sign, '-'
            . . .
          mov   ax, bx ;      Returned value --> ax
          clc   ;             Clear carry bit to indicate no error
Return:
          pop   dx ;          restore registers
            . . .
```

Chapter 8

8.1—1 MoreBytes DEF, 10 DUP (?), Y, Z produces the code

```
DEF       DB    10, DUP, (?)
```

```
MoreBytes DEF, <10 DUP (?)>, Y, Z produces the code
```

```
DEF       DB       10 DUP (?), Y, Z
```

```
MoreBytes , 'A', 'B', 'C' produces the code
```

```
DB       'A', 'B', 'C'
```

(The first comma indicates that the first parameter is the empty string.)

8.1—2 `Display2 13, 10` expands to

```
mov     ah, 02h
Display <13>
Display <10>
```

which finally expands to

```
mov     ah, 02h
mov     dl, 13
int     21h
mov     dl, 10
int     21h
```

8.1—3 a) If `Abs` is used more than once, `valPos` will be multiply defined. Fix the macro with the insertion

```
Abs       MACRO  aValue
          LOCAL  valPos
          cmp    aValue, 0
          . . .
```

8.1—3 b)

```
          cmp    ax, 0
          jge    ??0000
          neg    ax
??0000:
          cmp    dl, 0
          jge    ??0001
          neg    dl
??0001:
          cmp    MemLoc, 0
          jge    ??0002
          neg    MemLoc
??0002:
```

8.2—2

```
ErrMsg    MACRO  errNo, returnVal
          LOCAL  theMessage
```

```
            .DATA
theMessage DB      '*** ERROR &errNo& ***', 13, 10, '$'
            .CODE
            _PutStr theMessage
            _Exit   <&returnVal&>
            ENDM
```

8.3—1

```
            DB      2
            DB      3
            . . .
            DB      17

Number1     DB      1
Number2     DB      2
            . . .
Number9     DB      9

            DB      0ah
            DB      1ah
            . . .
            DB      9ah

            DB      11h
            DB      12h
            DB      13h
            DB      21h
            . . .
            DB      53h
```

Chapter 9

9.1—1

```
            mov     al, 11010110B
            and     al, 01111000B ;          al = 01010000B
            mov     al, 11010110B
            or      al, 01111000B ;          al = 11111110B
            mov     al, 11010110B
            xor     al, 01111000B ;          al = 10101110B
            mov     al, 11010110B
            not     al ;                     al = 00101001B
            mov     al, 0C9h ;               al = 11001001B
   ;                                         1Eh = 00011110B
            and     al, 1Eh ;                al = 08h = 00001000B
            mov     al, 0C9h
   ;                                         15 = 00001111B
            and     al, 15 ;                 al = 09h = 00001001B
```

```
        mov     al, 0C9h
        or      al, 1Eh ;              al = 0DFh = 11011111B
        mov     al, 0C9h
        xor     al, 1Eh ;              al = 0D7h = 11010111B
        mov     al, 0C9h
        not     al ;                   al = 36h = 00110110B
```

9.1—2 The field in question is shown as follows:

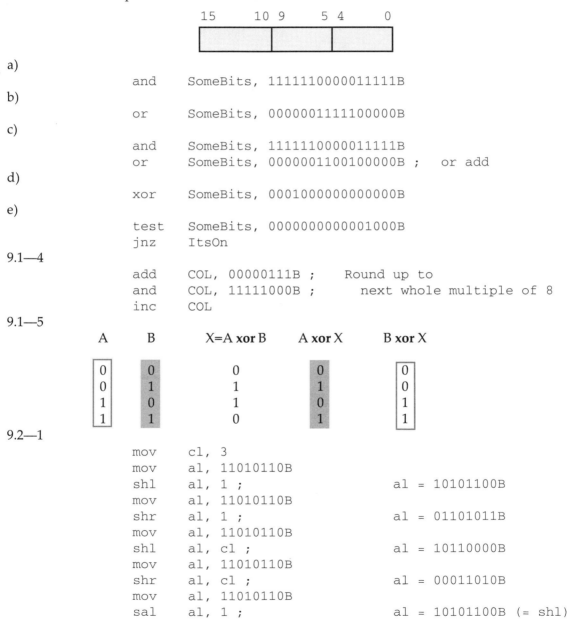

```
             15        10 9    5 4      0
```

a)
```
        and     SomeBits, 1111110000011111B
```
b)
```
        or      SomeBits, 0000001111100000B
```
c)
```
        and     SomeBits, 1111110000011111B
        or      SomeBits, 0000001100100000B ;   or add
```
d)
```
        xor     SomeBits, 0001000000000000B
```
e)
```
        test    SomeBits, 0000000000001000B
        jnz     ItsOn
```

9.1—4
```
        add     COL, 00000111B ;   Round up to
        and     COL, 11111000B ;       next whole multiple of 8
        inc     COL
```

9.1—5

A	B	X=A xor B	A xor X	B xor X
0	0	0	0	0
0	1	1	1	0
1	0	1	0	1
1	1	0	1	1

9.2—1
```
        mov     cl, 3
        mov     al, 11010110B
        shl     al, 1 ;                al = 10101100B
        mov     al, 11010110B
        shr     al, 1 ;                al = 01101011B
        mov     al, 11010110B
        shl     al, cl ;               al = 10110000B
        mov     al, 11010110B
        shr     al, cl ;               al = 00011010B
        mov     al, 11010110B
        sal     al, 1 ;                al = 10101100B (= shl)
```

```
            mov     al, 11010110B
            sar     al, 1 ;                 al = 11101011B
            mov     al, 11010110B
            sal     al, cl ;                al = 10110000B (= shl)
            mov     al, 11010110B
            sar     al, cl ;                al = 11111010B
            mov     al, 11010110B
            rol     al, 1 ;                 al = 10101101B
            mov     al, 11010110B
            ror     al, 1 ;                 al = 01101011B
            mov     al, 11010110B
            rol     al, cl ;                al = 10110110B
            mov     al, 11010110B
            ror     al, cl ;                al = 11011010B
            mov     al, 3Ch ;                  3Ch = 00111100B
            shl     al, 1 ;                 al = 78h = 01111000B
            mov     al, 3Ch
            shr     al, 1 ;                 al = 1Eh = 00011110B
            mov     al, 24 ;                   24 = 00011000B
            shl     al, 1 ;                 al = 48 = 00110000B
            mov     al, 24
            shr     al, 1 ;                 al = 12 = 00001100B
            mov     al, 99h ;                  al = 10011001B
            rol     al, 1 ;                 al = 33h = 00110011B
```

9.2—2

```
            sal     ax, 1 ;         ax := ax * 2

            sar     ax, 1 ;         ax := ax / 2

            mov     cl, 3
            sal     ax, cl ;        ax := ax * 8

            sar     ax, cl ;        ax := ax / 8

            mov     bx, ax
            sal     bx, 1
            add     ax, bx ;        ax := ax + ax * 2 = ax * 3

            mov     bx, ax
            sal     bx, 1
            sal     bx, 1 ;         bx := ax * 4
            add     ax, bx ;        ax := ax + ax * 4 = ax * 5
            sal     ax, 1 ;         ax := ax * 10

            mov     bx, ax
            sal     bx, 1 ;         bx := ax * 2
            add     ax, bx ;        ax := ax + ax * 2 = ax * 3
```

```
                    saR    ax, 1 ;        ax := ax * 1.5  (truncated)
9.2—3 a)
                    mov    ax, X
                    mov    cx, N ;        loads shift quantity in cl
     ;                                       mov cl, BYTE PTR N also works
                    shr    ax, cl ;       Nth bit is now rightmost
                    test   al, 1
                    jnz    NBitOn
       ; or
                    mov    ax, 1
                    mov    cx, N
                    shl    ax, cl ;       ax contains a 1 only in the Nth bit
                    test   X, ax
                    jnz    NBitOn
9.2—3 b)
                    test   X, 1 SHL N ;  works only if N EQUated
                    jnz    NBitOn
9.2—5 a)
                    mov    ax, Time
                    and    ax, 0000011111100000B ;   Extract minutes
                    mov    cl, 5
                    shr    ax, cl ;       and shift to right end of the word
                    mov    Minute, ax
9.2—5 b)
                    mov    ax, Time
                    and    ax, 1111100000011111B ;   Zero out minutes field
                    mov    bx, Minute
                    and    bx, 0000000000111111B ;   Get rid of stray bits
                    mov    cl, 5
                    shl    bx, cl ;  and shift mins to the correct position
                    add    ax, bx ;       or OR ax, bx
                    mov    Time, ax
9.3—1
     ;;   PUTHEXB.ASM--Display al as two hex digits
     ;;
     INCLUDE    PCMAC.INC
                .MODEL SMALL
                .CODE
                PUBLIC PutHexB
     PutHexB    PROC
                push   ax ;            ax = wxyz as four hex digits
                push   cx
                push   dx
                mov    cl, 4
                sub    ah, ah ;        ax = 00yz
                ror    ax, cl ;        ax = z00y
                shr    ah, cl ;        ax = 0z0y
```

```
                 mov      cx, ax ;        Preserve digits for later display
                 add      cx, '00' ;      Yes, this works
                 cmp      cl, '9' ;       Convert digits > 9 to ABC...
                 jle      Doch
                 add      cl, 'A'-'0'-10
        Doch:
                 cmp      ch, '9'
                 jle      DispIt
                 add      ch, 'A'-'0'-10
        DispIt:
                 _PutCh cl, ch ;          y, z converted to ASCII hex digits
                 pop      dx
                 pop      cx
                 pop      ax
                 ret
        PutHexB  ENDP
                 END
```

9.4—2 a)

```
                 cmp      A, 10
                 jng      NoInc
                 cmp      B, 14
                 jnle     NoInc
                 inc      A
        NoInc:
```

9.4—2 b)

```
                 sub      ax, ax ;        Initial guess for (A > 10)
                 cmp      A, 10
                 jng      TryB
                 inc      ax ;            ax := (A > 10)
        TryB:
                 sub      bx, bx
                 cmp      B, 14
                 jnle     AndIt
                 inc      bx ;            bx := (B <= 14)
        AndIt:
                 and      ax, bx
                 jz       DontInc
                 inc      A
        DontInc:
```

An optimizing compiler would probably produce similar code for both statements.

9.5—1

```
        TimeRec  RECORD Hour:5, Min:6, Sec2:5
        Time     RECORD <>

                 mov      ax, Time ;       9.2—5 a)
                 and      ax, MASK Min ;   Extract minutes
```

```
            mov    cl, Min
            shr    ax, cl ;       and shift to the rt end of the word
            mov    Minute, ax

            mov    ax, Time ;            9.2—5 b)
            and    ax, NOT MASK Min ; Zero out minutes field
            mov    bx, Minute
            mov    cl, Min
            shl    bx, cl ;   Shift minutes to the correct position
            and    bx, MASK Min ;       and get rid of any stray bits
            add    ax, bx ;      or OR ax, bx
            mov    Time, ax

AttrRec     RECORD Blink:1, BackCol:3, Inten:1, ForeCol:3
Attr        AttrRec <>

            and    Attr, NOT MASK BackCol ; 9.2-6 a)
            or     Attr, 100B SHL BackCol

            xor    Attr, MASK Blink ;        9.2-6 b)

            mov    al, Attr ;               9.2-6 c)
            and    al, MASK ForeCol
            not    al
            mov    cl, BackCol
            shl    al, cl
            and    Attr, NOT MASK BackCol
            or     Attr, al

            mov    al, Attr ;               9.2-6 d)
            and    al, MASK BackCol
            mov    cl, BackCol
            shr    al, cl
            mov    Back, al

            mov    al, Back ;               9.2-6 e)
            mov    cl, BackCol
            shl    al, cl ;     Shift background color into position
            and    al, MASK BackCol ;   and mask it to size
            and    Attr, NOT MASK BackCol ; Zero background color
            or     Attr, al ;                    and insert Back
```

Try to understand why some operations could be performed as address arithmetic while others had to be performed with machine instructions.

Chapter 10

10.1—1 a)

```
            mov     ax, A ;                 ax = 0A00h
            mov     ax, [A] ;               ax = 0A00h
            mov     ax, [A + 4] ;           ax = 2A02h
            mov     ax, [B + 4] ;           ax = 2B02h
            mov     ax, [A + 10] ;          ax = 2B02h
            mov     ax, [B - 4] ;           ax = 1A01h
            mov     al, [C + 2] ;           al = 2Ch
            mov     al, [C + 7] ;           al = 1Dh
            mov     al, [D] ;               al = 0Dh
            mov     al, [D - 3] ;           al = 3Ch
```

10.1—1 b) $B - A = 6, C - A = 14, D - C = 6, A - B = -6$.

10.1—2

```
            mov     al, [E + 3] ;           al = 'o'
            mov     al, [E + 5] ;           al = 13
            mov     al, [F + 2] ;           al = '$'
            mov     al, [E + 9] ;           al = 'K'
            mov     al, [F - 2] ;           al = 10
```

10.1—3

```
    Ground round
    ‾
```

10.1—4

```
    abcdefghijkl
    dbcdefghijkl
    dbcdkfghijkl
```

10.1—5 a) In case 1, al = 29; in case 2, al = 18

10.1—5 b) The second add adds the contents of memory location A − 444 to al. If that location, happened to contain 42, the second add would also add 42 to al.

10.1—6

```
    Mellow friends!
    ‾
```

10.1—7

```
    3135        (Number + 2 is the address of the character '1'; Dumber + 2 = '3' + 2 = '5')
```

10.1—8 c)

```
            mov     ax, WORD PTR Alpha ;        ax = 4241h
            mov     ax, WORD PTR Alpha+1 ;      ax = 4342h
```

10.1—10

```
            mov     ax, [A + (C - B)] ;         ax = 1B01h
            mov     al, [D + (A - B)] ;         al =   0Ch
            mov     ax, [A + 3] ;               ax = 021Ah
            mov     ax, [B - 3] ;               ax = 021Ah
            mov     al, [C - 2] ;               al =   03h
```

```
            mov     al, [C - 11] ;              al =    1Ah
            mov     al, BYTE PTR [A + 3] ;      al =    1Ah
            mov     ax, WORD PTR [C - 11] ;     ax = 021Ah
```
10.2—1
```
            mov     bx, 3
            mov     al, [CArray + bx] ;         al = 'e'
            mov     bx, N
            mov     al, [CArray + bx] ;         al = ' '
            mov     al, [CArray + 2 + bx] ;     al = '0'
            mov     bx, N
            shl     bx, 1
            mov     ax, [WArray + bx] ;         ax = -11
            mov     ax, [WArray - 2 + bx] ;     ax = 2
            mov     bx, OFFSET Carray
            mov     al, [bx] ;                  al = 'I'
            mov     al, [3 + bx] ;              al = 'e'
            mov     bx, OFFSET WArray
            mov     ax, [bx] ;                  ax = 4
            mov     ax, [8 + bx] ;              ax = 2
            mov     bx, OFFSET Carray
            mov     si, 3
            mov     al, [bx + si] ;             al = 'e'
            mov     al, [3 + bx + si] ;         al = '8'
            mov     bx, OFFSET WArray
            mov     si, 6
            mov     ax, [bx + si] ;             ax = 87
            mov     ax, [4 + bx + si] ;         ax = -11
```

10.2—2 b) Sets ax to the largest element in WArray.

10.2—3 b) Changes in boldface:

```
            mov     ax, [WArray]
            mov     bx, OFFSET WArray + 2
            mov     cx, 5
    Mystery2:
            cmp     ax, [bx]
            jge     M2
            mov     ax, [bx]
    M2:     add     bx, 2
            loop    Mystery2
```

10.2—4 c) This is one method, using based indexing:

```
            mov     bx, 0 ;         The subscript
            mov     di, OFFSET A
            mov     si, OFFSET B
            mov     cx, 100
```

```
SumLoop:
                mov     ax, [bx + si] ;       B[i]
                add     ax, [C - B + bx + si] ;   + C[i]
                mov     [bx + di], ax ;              --> A[i]
                add     bx, 2
                loop    SumLoop
```

10.2—7

```
                _GetDate
                mov     bl, al ;        Day number to bl
                sub     bh, bh ;          and convert it to a word
                shl     bx, 1 ;              and multiply by 2
                mov     ax, [Days + bx]
                _PutStr ax
```

10.2—8 M can be considered to be an array of 3 five-byte elements. Therefore the address of M[i] is [M + 5 * i]. That is in turn an array of 5 bytes, so its jth element, M[i][j] = M[i, j] has address [M + 5 * i + j].

10.3—1

```
Prompt      DB      'Enter your name: $'
Hello       DB      'Hello, $'
NAMELEN     EQU     50
NameBfr     DB      NAMELEN
NameLen     DB      ?
Name        DB      NAMELEN DUP (?)
            . . .
            _PutStr Prompt
            _GetStr NameBfr
            mov     bl, NameLen
            sub     bh, bh ;      Convert length to word
            mov     [Name + bx], '$'
            _PutStr Hello
            _PutStr Name
            _PutCh 13, 10
```

10.3—2 Search method:

```
Vowel       DB      'aeiouAEIOU'
NumVowels   EQU     $ - Vowel
            . . .
            mov     bx, OFFSET Vowel
            mov     cx, NumVowels
FindVowel1:
            cmp     al, [bx]
            je      aVowel
            inc     bx
            loop    FindVowel1
```

Conversion array method:

```
IsVowel  DB      'A' DUP (0)
         DB      1
         DB      ('E' - 'A' - 1) DUP (0)
         DB      1
         etc.
         . . .
         mov     bl, al
         sub     bh, bh ;      convert character to word
         test    [IsVowel + bx], 1
         jnz     aVowel
or
         mov     bx, OFFSET IsVowel
         xlat
         test    al, al
         jnz     aVowel
```

The first method has slightly longer code, but much shorter data, so the second method takes more space. On the other hand, the first method contains a loop which may be executed up to 10 times, so it is the costlier method in terms of time.

10.4—1 a) The address of A[N + 3] is [A0 + 2 * (3 - 1) + bx] = [A0 + 4 + bx].

10.4—1 b) [A0 + 32 + bx] is the address of A[N + c], whose address is [A0 + 2*(c - 1) + bx]. Therefore 2*(c – 1) = 32 and c = 17.

10.4—1 d)

```
         mov     bx, OFFSET A0
         mov     ax, 1 ;       ax = N
         mov     cx, 100
SetLoop:
         mov     [bx], ax ;    A[N] := N
         inc     ax
         add     bx, 2
         loop    SetLoop
```

10.4—2

```
MoName   DB      'Jan$Feb$Mar$Apr$May$Jun$'
         DB      'Jul$Aug$Sep$Oct$Nov$Dec$'
         . . .
;  The part the displays the month (from dh) is
         mov     bl, dh
         sub     bh, bh
         shl     bx, 1
         shl     bx, 1 ;       bx := 4 * bx
         _PutStr [MoName - 4 + bx]
```

10.4—4 c)

```
         mov     bx, OFFSET Count+2*('A'-' ')
;                             bx := address of Count['A']
         mov     cx, 26
```

```
CombineLoop:
        mov     ax, [2*('a' - 'A') + bx]
        add     [bx], ax
        mov     [2*('a' - 'A') + bx], 0
        add     bx, 2
        loop    CombineLoop
```

Chapter 11

11.1—1

```
;;   PRINTLEN.ASM--Function which takes as input a binary number in
;;    ax and as output produces the number of character positions
;;    PutDec would use to print it.
;;
;;   Calling Sequence:
;;        EXTRN   PrintLen:NEAR
;;        mov     ax, theNumber
;;        call    PrintLen
;;
;;   On exit, ax contains the result. All other regs preserved
;;
            .MODEL SMALL

            .DATA
PowersOf10 DW     10000,1000,100,10

            .CODE
            PUBLIC PrintLen
PrintLen   PROC
            push    si
            push    cx
            push    bx
            mov     bx, ax ;        bx holds input, ax the result
            mov     ax, 1 ;         At least one posit always required
            mov     cx, 4 ;         Number of entries in PowersOf10
            mov     si, OFFSET PowersOf10
            test    bx, bx
            jge     NoSign ;        If > 0, no space needed for sign
            neg     bx ;            Procedure will work even for -32768
            inc     ax
NoSign:
            cmp     bx, [si]
            jae     Done
            add     si, 2
            loop    NoSign
Done:
            add     ax, cx
```

```
                pop     bx
                pop     cx
                pop     si
                ret
       PrintLen ENDP
                END
```

11.2—4 Changed lines from `CmpStr` are in boldface:

```
;; CMPSTRI.ASM--return ax < 0, = 0, > 0 according as string at si
;;   is <, =, or > string at di. Case of letters ignored
;;
;;   Calling Sequence:
;;       EXTRN   CmpStrI:NEAR
;;       mov     di, OFFSET rightString
;;       mov     si, OFFSET leftString
;;       call    CmpStrI
;;
;;   On exit, ax contains the result and all other registers are
;;     preserved
;;
            .MODEL SMALL

            .DATA
            EXTRN   UpIt:BYTE

            .CODE
            PUBLIC CmpStrI
CmpStrI     PROC
            push    bx
            push    si
            push    di
            push    cx
            mov     bx, OFFSET UpIt
CharLoop:
            mov     al, [di]
            xlat
            mov     cl, al
            mov     al, [si]
            xlat
            mov     bl, [di]
            cmp     al, cl ;    Are current bytes equal?
            jne     Done ;          no
            ...
Done:
            sub     ah, ah ;    Must do unsigned convert BEFORE
            sub     ch, ch ;        subtracting the two characters
```

```
                sub     ax, cx ;       ax := [si] - [di]
                pop     cx
                pop     di
                pop     si
                pop     bx
                ret
CmpStrI         ENDP
                END
```

11.4—1 The suggested approach could be implemented as follows:

```
                .DATA
State           DW      ?
EEState         EQU     0
EOState         EQU     2
                etc.

                .CODE
                ...
                mov     State, EEState ;   Initialize State
                jmp     FSMLoop
StateSw         DW      EE, EO, OE, OO
FSMLoop:
                _GetCh ;               al := _GetCh
                cmp     al, 13 ;       if char = 13, done
                je      Done
                mov     bx, State ;  switch State
                jmp     [bx + StateSw]
EE:                     ;                   case EE:
                cmp     al, 'a'
                jne     EEb
                mov     State, OEState
                jmp     FSMLoop
EEb:
                mov     State, EOState
                jmp     FSMLoop
EO:                     ;                   case EO
                ...
Done:
                cmp     State, OEState
                jne     BadString
                ...
```

In this particular example we can simplify things a bit by making the value of State a pointer to the place where the case statement jumps:

```
                .DATA
```

```
State       DW      ?
EEState     EQU     0
EOState     EQU     2
            etc.

            .CODE
            . . .
            mov     State, OFFSET EE ;  Initialize State
            jmp     FSMLoop
StateSw     DW      EE, EO, OE, OO
FSMLoop:
            _GetCh ;            al := _GetCh
            cmp     al, 13 ;    if char = 13, done
            je      Done
            jmp     State ;     switch State
            jmp     [bx + StateSw]
EE:                 ;                   case EE:
            cmp     al, 'a'
            jne     EEb
            mov     State, OFFSET OE
            jmp     FSMLoop
EEb:
            mov     State, OFFSET EO
            jmp     FSMLoop
EO:                 ;                   case EO:
            . . .
Done:
            cmp     State, OFFSET OE
            jne     BadString
            . . .
```

Chapter 12

12.1—1 1035h:3a22h corresponds to 10350h + 3a22h = 13d72h. 0a355h:9211h corresponds to 0a3550h + 9211h = 0ac761h. 3133h:0c3a4h = 31330h + 0c3a4h = 3d6d4h.

12.1—2 7b3ch:0fh, 7000h:0b3cfh, 7b00h:3cfh, and many others.

12.1—3 023ah:2130h corresponds to 44d0h; 044bh:0002h corresponds to 44b2h; 033ah:1137h corresponds to 44d7h. Therefore the locations in increasing order are 044bh:0002h, 023ah:2130h, 033ah:1137h.

12.1—4 $1K = 1024 = 2^{10} = 10000000000B = 400h$. $640 = 64 * 10 = 40h * 0ah$. $640K = 400h * 40h * 0ah = 0a0000h = 0a000:0h$. Other answers include 9fffh:10h, etc.

12.4—2
```
;   Subscript Method
;           mov     ax, CSeg
            mov     es, ax
            ASSUME  es:CSeg
            mov     bx, 0
```

```
            mov     cx, 20
SetLoop:
            mov     [C + bx], 0 ; No explicit Seg Override needed
            add     bx, 2
            loop    SetLoop

;   Pointer Method
;           mov     ax, CSeg
            mov     es, ax
            ASSUME  es:CSeg
            mov     bx, OFFSET C
            mov     cx, 20
SetLoop:
            mov     es:[bx], 0 ;  Seg Override needed!!!
            add     bx, 2
            loop    SetLoop
```

12.4—3

```
            mov     ax, X ;              override: es
            mov     ax, U ;              override: none
            mov     ax, P ;              override: cs
            mov     ax, [X + bx] ;       override: es
            mov     ax, [U + bx] ;       override: none
            mov     bx, OFFSET X
            mov     ax, [bx] ;           override: none
;                            (ds would be used erroneously)
;                   (programmer should have written es:[bx]])
            mov     bx, OFFSET U
            mov     ax, [bx] ;           override: none
```

12.5—2 Because ds and es would not be set pointing to the beginning of PSP2. One could reset ds properly by executing mov ax, ds/add ax, 128/mov ds, ax at the beginning of the program but to what purpose? This adds instructions to the program and doesn't save any space, because a SEGMENT AT declaration reserves no space anyway. (It is simply describing space that already exists.)

12.5—3

```
;;  FILES.ASM--Program to display the maximum number of open files
;;
;;    Gets this number from word 32h of the PSP
;;
INCLUDE    PCMAC.INC
           .MODEL SMALL
           ASSUME SS:NOTHING
           .STACK 100h
PSP        SEGMENT AT 0-256
           ORG     32h
NFiles     DW      ?
```

```
PSP       ENDS

          .DATA
Msg       DB     'The maximum number of open files is $'

          .CODE
          EXTRN  PutDec:NEAR
Files     PROC
          ASSUME ds:PSP
          mov    bx, NFiles ;  Put NFiles in a 'safe' register
          _PutStr Msg, @data ; Set ds while we're at it
          ASSUME ds:@data
          mov    ax, bx
          call   PutDec
          _PutCh 13, 10
          _Exit  0
Files     ENDP
          END    FILES
```

12.7—1 The opening instructions specified in the exercise have the effect of pushing the far return address ds:0 = PSP:0 onto the stack. Since the PROC is declared FAR, the ret instruction will perform a far return, so the next instruction executed after the ret will be int 20h, a return to DOS.
12.7—2 The stack segment uses 256/16 = 16 paragraphs, as does the PSP. The .CODE and .DATA segments together use (436 + 26)/16 rounded up to the nearest whole paragraph, = 29, for a total of 16 + 16 + 29 = 61 paragraphs.

Chapter 13

13.1—1

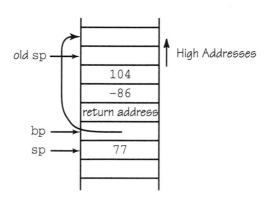

13.1—2

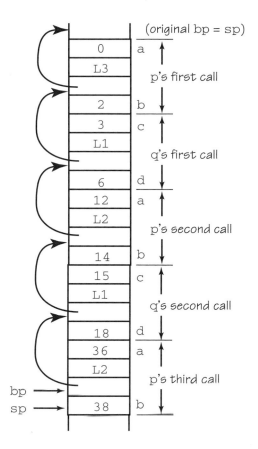

13.1—4 a)

```
;;   ABSDIF.ASM--Pascal function to return the absolute value of
;;   the differrence between its two arguments

             .MODEL SMALL

             .CODE
             PUBLIC absdif
x            EQU     [bp + 6]
y            EQU     [bp + 4]
absdif       PROC
             push    bp
             mov     bp, sp ;       No local storage
             mov     ax, x ;        Can't do cmp x, y (= cmp mem, mem)
             cmp     ax, y
             jng     elsepart
             sub     ax, y
             jmp     Done
elsepart:
             neg     ax
```

```
                    add     ax, y
          Done:
                    pop     bp
                    ret     4
          absdif    ENDP
                    END
```

13.1—4 b)

```
                    mov     ax, x
                    add     ax, 3
                    push    ax
                    mov     ax, 14
                    push    ax ;          push const is illegal
                    EXTRN   absdif : NEAR
                    call    absdif
```

13.1—4 c) The changes in the code for absdif are

```
          ;;    ABSDIF.ASM--C function to return the absolute value of
          ;;       the differrence between its two arguments
                    . . .
          x         EQU     [bp + 4]
          y         EQU     [bp + 6]
                    . . .
                    ret
                    . . .
```

The changes in the call are

```
                    mov     ax, 14
                    push    ax ;          push const is illegal
                    mov     ax, x
                    add     ax, 3
                    push    ax
                    EXTRN   absdif : NEAR
                    call    absdif
                    add     sp, 4 ;       Pop parameters from stack
```

13.2—2 a) Turbo Pascal version:

```
          ;;  CARDP.ASM--Turbo Pascal version; Card(s) returns the number of
          ;;    1 bits in s
                    .MODEL SMALL

                    .CODE
                    PUBLIC Card
          s         EQU     WORD PTR [bp+4]
          Card      PROC
```

```
            ASSUME cs : CODE
            push    bp
            mov     bp, sp
            mov     dx, s ;        dx needn't be preserved
            sub     ax, ax
            mov     cx, 16 ;       cx needn't be preserved
CountLoop:
            shr     dx, 1
            jnc     TestForDone
            inc     ax
TestForDone:
            loop    CountLoop
            pop     bp
            ret     2
Card        ENDP
            END
```

A Visual C/C++ or Borland C/C++ version:

```
;; CARDC.ASM--C/C++ version; Card(s) returns the number of
;;  1 bits in s
            .MODEL SMALL

            .CODE
            PUBLIC _Card
s           EQU     WORD PTR [bp+4]
_Card       PROC
            push    bp
            mov     bp, sp
            mov     dx, s ;        dx needn't be preserved
            sub     ax, ax
            mov     cx, 16 ;       cx needn't be preserved
CountLoop:
            shr     dx, 1
            jnc     TestForDone
            inc     ax
TestForDone:
            loop    CountLoop
            pop     bp
            ret
_Card       ENDP
            END
```

Using the extra syntactic sugar in Section 13.2.3, we could write

```
;; CARDCP.ASM--either version; Card(s) returns the number of
;;  1 bits in s
```

```
                    .MODEL SMALL, C or Pascal

                    .CODE
                    PUBLIC Card
        Card        PROC    s : WORD
                    push    bp
                    mov     bp, sp
                    mov     dx, s
                    sub     ax, ax
                    mov     cx, 16
        CountLoop:
                    shr     dx, 1
                    jnc     TestForDone
                    inc     ax
        TestForDone:
                    loop    CountLoop
                    pop     bp
                    RET
        Card        ENDP
                    END
13.4—1
                    .MODEL SMALL
                    .CODE
        x           EQU     DWORD PTR [bp + 6]
        y           EQU     WORD PTR [bp + 4]
        SetIt       PROC
                    push    bp
                    mov     bp, sp
                    push    ds
                    push    si
                    lds     si, x
                    mov     ax, y
                    mov     [si], ax ;    ds (correctly) assumed
                    pop     si
                    pop     ds
                    ret     6
        SetIt       ENDP
                    END
13.4—2 a)
                    .MODEL SMALL
        x           EQU     WORD PTR [bp + 4]
        y           EQU     WORD PTR [bp + 6]
        sum         EQU     DWORD PTR [bp + 8]
        diff        EQU     DWORD PTR [bp + 12]
                    .CODE
                    PUBLIC _SumDiff
        _SumDiff    PROC
```

```
                push   ds
                push   di
                lds    di, sum
                mov    ax, x
                add    ax, y
                mov    [di], ax
                lds    di, diff
                mov    ax, x
                sub    ax, y
                mov    [di], ax
                pop    di
                pop    ds
                ret
      _SumDiff  ENDP
                END
```

or

```
                .MODEL SMALL, C
                .CODE
                PUBLIC SumDiff
      SumDiff   PROC   USES ds di x:WORD y:WORD sum:DWORD diff DWORD
                lds    di, sum
                mov    ax, x
                sub    ax, y
                mov    [di], ax
                lds    di, diff
                mov    ax, x
                add    ax, y
                mov    [di], ax
                RET
      SumDiff   ENDP
                END
```

13.4—3 Pascal order:

```
                mov    ax, @data
                push   ax
                mov    bx, OFFSET A + 4
                push   bx ;          seg:offset of a[3]
                push   ax
                mov    bx, OFFSET A + 34
                push   bx ;          seg:offset of a[18]
                call   Swap

                mov    ax, @data
                push   ax
                mov    bx, i
                shl    bx, 1
                lea    dx, [a - 2 + bx]
                push   dx ;          seg:offset of a[i]
```

```
            push    ax
            lea     dx, [a + bx]
            push    dx ;            seg:offset of a[i+1]
            call    Swap
```

Chapter 14

14.1—1

```
       ;                               ds = wxyzh; dx = mnoph; ax = qrsth
            mov     si, 0Fh
            and     dx, si ;        dx = 000ph (all that's meaningful)
            and     si, ax ;        si = 000th = final offset
            mov     cl, 4
            sub     ax, si ;        ax = qrs0h
            add     ax, dx ;        ax = qrsph
            rol     ax, cl ;        ax = pqrsh
            mov     bx, ds ;        bx = wxyzh
            add     bx, ax ;        bx = wsyzh + pqrsh
            mov     es, bx
```

14.1—2 The code for MPSAR is

```
       ;; MPSAR.ASM--Multiple precision arithmetic shift A right 1
       ;;
       ;;  Calling Sequence:
       ;;          push pointer to A
       ;;          push number of words in A
       ;;          EXTRN  MPSAR: NEAR
       ;;          call   MPSAR
       ;; Return shift out right end as value in ax. Only ds preserved
       ;;
                .MODEL SMALL

                .CODE
                PUBLIC MPSAR
APtr            EQU     DWORD PTR [bp+6]
Len            EQU     WORD PTR [bp+4]
MPSAR          PROC
                push    bp
                mov     bp, sp
                push    ds
                lds     si, APtr ;     ds:si --> A
                mov     cx, Len
                dec     cx
                mov     ax, cx
                shl     ax, 1
                add     si, ax ;       ds:si --> left end of A
```

```
                sar    WORD PTR [si], 1 ;  Get the ball rolling
                jcxz   Done ;       Just in case Len = 1
        SARLoop:
                dec    si
                dec    si
                rcr    WORD PTR [si], 1
                loop   SARLoop
        Done:
                mov    ax, 0 ;       sub ax, ax would destroy carry
                adc    ax, 0 ;       return final carry flag
                pop    ds
                pop    bp
                ret    6
        MPSAR   ENDP
                END
```

14.1—3

```
                mov    ax, x
                neg    ax
                mov    ax, 0 ;       sub ax, ax would foul up the carry
                adc    ax, 0
```

14.2—1 a) $a + b = q(n - 1) + r$ where $0 \le r < n - 1$ and $r = (a + b) \bmod (n - 1)$. Then $an + b = q(n - 1) + r + a(n - 1) = (a + q)(n - 1) + r$, so r also $= (an + b) \bmod (n - 1)$

14.2—1 b) $((((an + b)n + c)n + d)n + e) \bmod (n-1) = (((an + b)n + c)n + d + e) \bmod (n-1) = ((an + b)n + c + d + e) \bmod (n-1) = \dots$ (One really should do an inductive proof, but this is the idea.)

14.3—1

```
                ...
        APtr    EQU    DWORD PTR [bp+6]
        Len     EQU    WORD PTR [bp+4]
        NZD     EQU    ch
        DecPut  PROC
                push   bp
                mov    bp, sp
                sub    NZD, NZD ;   Indicate no non-zero digits yet
                push   ds
                ...
        PutLoop:
                mov    bh, [si] ;   bx = xy??
                test   NZD, NZD ;   if there has been a non-zero digit
                jnz    NoTest ;        don't test for one any more
                test   bh, bh
                jz     Next
                inc    NZD
                cmp    bh, 09h
                jg     NoTest
                add    bh, '0' ;    Right digit is first non-zero digit
                _PutCh bh
```

```
                    jmp     Next
        NoTest:     ;                       Display both digits
                    shr     bx, cl ;        bx = 0xy?
                    . . .
                    _PutCh bl
        Next:
                    dec     si
```

Chapter 15

15.2—2 Use the debugger to examine the segment:offset address at location 84h (= 4 * 21h) and set a breakpoint at *that* segment:offset. (The segment is the second word.)

15.3—1 We will end up with dx|ax = 0:0, rather than its true value of 0h|0FFFFh or 1h|0h.

15.3—2 a) If an interrupt occurs after ss has been loaded but before sp has been loaded, the interrupt process will push information onto a 'stack' whose segment corresponds to one stack and whose offset corresponds to another. When the stack is changed, the two instructions to set up ss and sp should be preceded by cli and followed by sti.

15.3—2 b) Sp is often changed without changing ss (for instance, every time something is pushed onto or popped off the stack). Disabling interrupts frequently slows the processing of these interrupts and in extreme cases can even lead to the loss of an interrupt. Therefore to move the stack, the programmer must either change ss first or disable interrupts explicitly.

15.3—2 c)

```
        Name        PROC
                    mov     ax, @data
                    mov     ds, ax ;        As usual
                    mov     bx, ss
                    sub     bx, ax
                    mov     cl, 4
                    shl     bx, cl ;        bx = amount to add to sp
                    cli
                    mov     ss, ax
                    add     sp, bx
                    sti
```

15.3—4 If the instruction being Stepped isn't a call, trace as usual. If the op-code is one of several for the call instruction, determine how long the instruction is and set an int 3 break at the first byte beyond it, then start running at the call instruction. The next time a breakpoint occurs, remove the int 3 break previously set (which may or may not have caused the break.)

15.7—1

```
        W:          sub     al, al
        W1:         **lock** xchg **s**, al ; set al := **s**, **s** := 0 indivisibly
                    test    al, al
                    jz      W1

        S:          mov     **s**, 1
```

15.7—2 An integer semaphore could consist of a binary semaphore **s** and a global counter n. In addition, each program using the semaphore would need its own private variable, say `tester`, to record the value of n. The code for the integer semaphore operations could be

```
intW:  repeat                          intS: W(s)
           W(s)                              n := n + 1
           tester := n                       S(s)
           if n > 0 then n := n - 1 end if
           S(s)
       until tester > 0
```

Chapter 16

16.1—1

```
           mov     cl, 3
           shl     ax, cl
           mov     cl, 5
           shr     ABC, cl
```

16.1—4

```
     ctr = 1
     ctr = ctr + 1
     ctr = ctr + 1
```

16.2—1

```
     A         DW      5 DUP(18)
     B         DW      24
               DW      -18
     C         DW      ?
               DW      100 DUP (?)
     D         DW      50 DUP (20 DUP (1, 0))
```

Chapter 17

17.1—1 a)
```
     DFile     DB      '\data\sales.dat', 0
```
17.1—1 b)
```
           _Open DFile, ReadWrite
           call  CCheck
           mov   FH, ax
```
17.1—4
```
     ;;  GETNUM.ASM--input is a pointer in es:si to a zero-terminated
     ;;   byte string. Returns with ax = value of string as a decimal
     ;;   number and carry clear, or carry set if entire parameter
     ;;   isn't a number. Uses Dec2Bin to translate number
     ;;
               .MODEL SMALL
               ASSUME SS:NOTHING

               .CODE
               PUBLIC GetNum
```

```
            EXTRN  Dec2Bin : NEAR
GetNum      PROC
            push   ds
            push   si
            test   si, si ;      Is a string actually present?
            jz     Error
            mov    ax, es
            mov    ds, ax ;      Dec2Bin requires seg in ds
            call   Dec2Bin
            jc     Exit ;        if carry set, Dec2Bin got an error
            cmp    BYTE PTR [si], 0 ; Did Dec2Bin use up string?
            je     OK
Error:
            stc    ;                          no; set carry flag
Exit:
            pop    si
            pop    ds
            ret
OK:
            clc    ;             take no chances
            jmp    Exit
GetNum      ENDP
            END
```

17.2—1

```
            _Read  FH, Buffer, 2
            call   CCheck
            cmp    ax, 2
            jl     NotEXE
            cmp    WORD PTR Buffer, 5A4Dh ; Swap bytes to get word
            jne    NotExe
```

17.2—2

```
            _Write FH, Date, 8
            call   WCheck
```

17.3—1

```
FileLen     DD     ?
            ...
            _LSeek FH, FromEnd, 0
            call   CCheck
            mov    WORD PTR FileLen, ax ;    WORD PTR necessary or
            mov    WORD PTR FileLen+2, dx ;  assembler will
            mov    ax, SEG FileLen ;         complain of size error
            push   ax
            mov    ax, OFFSET FileLen
            push   ax
            mov    ax, 2 ;       Length of number in words
            push   ax
            call   MPPutDec
```

Chapter 18

18.1—1 a)

```
                cld
                mov     ax, 0
                mov     cx, 100
                mov     di, OFFSET A
      ZeroLoop:
                stosw
                loop    ZeroLoop
```

18.1—1 c)

```
                cld
                mov     si, OFFSET A + 2
                mov     di, OFFSET A
                mov     cx, 99
      MovLoop:
                movsw
                loop    MovLoop
```

18.1—2 a)

```
                cld
                mov     di, OFFSET S+1
                mov     cl, S ;         Length byte
                sub     ch, ch ;        Convert to word
                jcxz    Done ;          Empty string
                mov     al, C ;         Character to find
      FindLoop:
                scasb
                je      Done
                loop    FindLoop
                mov     di, OFFSET S+1 ;    Not Found
      Done:
                sub     di, OFFSET S+1 ;    When found, si --> one beyond
```

18.1—3

```
      PSP       SEGMENT AT 0-256
                ORG     80h
      CmdPSP    DB      128 DUP (?)
      PSP       ENDS

                .DATA
                ...
      CmdLen    DB      ?
      Command   DB      127 DUP (?)
                ...
      Name      PROC
                mov     ax, @data
                mov     ES, ax ;    MUST use es here because of movsw
      ;                             No point in ASSUMEing since the
```

```
        ;                                assembler would get it wrong anyway
                mov     si, OFFSET CmdPSP
                mov     di, OFFSET CmdLen
                mov     cx, 64 ;        Moving words rather than bytes
        MovLoop:
                movsw   ;               Word move faster than byte
                loop    MovLoop
                mov     ax, es
                mov     ds, ax
```

18.2—1

   18.1—1 a)

```
                . . .
                mov     di, OFFSET A
                rep stosw
```

   18.1—1 d)

```
                . . .
                mov     cx, 99
                rep movsw
```

   18.1—2 a)

```
                . . .
                jcxz    Done
                mov     al, C ;         Character to find
                repne scasb
                je      Done
                mov     di, OFFSET S+1 ;   Not Found
                . . .
```

   18.1—3

```
                mov     cx, 64 ;        Moving words rather than bytes
                rep movsw               ;       Word move faster than byte
                mov     ax, es
                . . .
```

18.2—2 a)

```
                sub     bx, bx ;        bx = number of contiguous chars in T
                mov     dl, S
                sub     dh, dh ;        dx = length of S string
                mov     cl, T
                sub     ch, ch ;        cx = length of T string
                jcxz    Done ;          If T is empty, NO chars are in it
                mov     si, cx ;        si := length of T string
        ScanLoop:
                mov     al, [S + 1 + bx] ; Next character from S
                mov     cx, si ;                cx = length of T string
                mov     di, OFFSET T+1 ;    di --> first char of T
                repne scasb ;                   Search for al in T
                jne     Done ;                  Not there
                inc     bx
                dec     dx
```

```
                jge     ScanLoop
        Done:
18.2—3 a)
        ;;    DELETE.ASM--Pascal-type deletion of characters from a string
        ;;
        ;;    Calling Sequence:
        ;;          push    SEG Strng
        ;;          push    OFFSET Strng
        ;;          push    StartDeletion
        ;;          push    DeletionLen
        ;;          EXTRN   Delete : NEAR
        ;;          call    Delete
        ;;
        ;;    Only ds is preserved
                .MODEL SMALL

                .CODE
                PUBLIC Delete
        Strng          EQU    DWORD PTR [bp + 8]
        StartDeletion EQU WORD PTR [bp + 6]
        DeletionLen EQU  WORD PTR [bp + 4]
        Delete    PROC
                push    bp
                mov     bp, sp
                cmp     StartDeletion, 1 ; make parameters right
                jge     StartOK1
                mov     StartDeletion, 1 ; StartDeletion >= 1
        StartOK1:
                push    ds
                lds     di, Strng ;   ds:di --> Strng
                mov     cl, [di]
                sub     ch, ch ;       cx := length of Strng
                mov     ax, cx
                inc     ax ;            ax := 1 + length of Strng
                cmp     StartDeletion, ax
                jle     StartOK2
                mov     StartDeletion, ax ; StartDeletion <= Strng len+1
        StartOK2:
                sub     ax, StartDeletion ; ax := 1 + Strng len - Start
                cmp     DeletionLen, ax
                jle     LenOK
                mov     DeletionLen, ax ; DeletionLen <= # of chars left
        LenOK:
                cmp     DeletionLen, 0
                jle     Done ;          No characters to remove
                mov     ax, DeletionLen
                sub     [di], al ;    Cut down length of Strng
```

```
                sub     cx, DeletionLen
                sub     cx, StartDeletion
                inc     cx ;            Number of characters to shift left
                jcxz    Done
                add     di, StartDeletion ; Indexing from 1 compensates
                mov     si, di ;                    for size byte
                add     si, DeletionLen
                mov     ax, ds ;       es must contain seg of Strng too
                mov     es, ax
                rep movsb ;            Finally!
        Done:
                pop     ds
                pop     bp
                ret     8
        Delete  ENDP
                END
```

Chapter 19

19.2—1

```
                DB      V, NO, ' ', NO, 'J', NO, 'u', NO, 'm', NO
                DB      'p', NO, ' ', NO, ' ', NO, V, NO
```

becomes

```
                DB      V, NO
                IRPC    c, < Jump  >
                DB      '&c&', NO
                ENDM
                DB      V, NO
```

19.2—2 Code to do cursor up:

```
                mov     ah, 03h
                mov     bh, 0 ;        Assume current display page 0
                int     10h ;          Get Cursor Position
                test    dh, dh ;       Is row 0?
                jz      UpDone
                dec     dh ;           Row isn't 0; move cursor up one row
                mov     ah, 02h
                int     10h;           Set cursor to new position
        UpDone:
```

19.2—3 a) We want to shift the window (ah, 0)—(24, 79) down one line. The code is

```
                mov     bh, al ;       attribute of cleared line
                mov     ch, ah ;       upper row of scrolled window
                sub     cl, cl ;       left col of scrolled window
                mov     dx, 184Fh ;    lower right corner = (24, 79)
```

```
                    mov     ax, 0701h ;   scroll down 1 line
                    int     10h
19.2—4 a)
                    mov     al, 10101100B ;    green backgr, bright red
            ;                                      blinking foregr attribute
                    mov     di, 1 ;            Offset to first attr position
                    mov     cx, 25*80 ;        Number of attributes to store
            XmasLoop:
                    stosb   ;         or    mov     [di], al
                    inc     di ;            add     di, 2
                    loop    XmasLoop
```

Chapter 20

20.4—1 b)
```
            ;                                   ST(1)        ST
                    fldpi   ;                                π
                    fld     R ;                π             R
                    fmul    ST ;               π             R*R
                    fmul    ;                                π*R*R
                    fstp    Area
```
20.4—1 g)
```
            ;                                   ST(1)        ST
                    fld     A ;                              A
                    fsub    B ;                              A - B
                    fabs    ;                                |A - B|
                    fstp    AbsDif
```
20.5—1
```
    Prompt      DB      'Enter upper limit for square root (> 2): $
    OutMsg1     DB      'The square root of $'
    OutMsg2     DB      ' is '
                ...
                EXTRN   GetDec : NEAR, PutFP : NEAR
    GetLim:
                _PutStr Prompt
                call    GetDec
                dec     ax ;            Get number of square roots
                jl      GetLim
                mov     cx, ax
                fld1    ;               initial 'last argument'
    RootLoop:
                fld1    ;               find next argument...
                fadd
                fld     ST ;            ...and save it
            ;                           ST(2)        ST(1)        ST
                fld     ST ;            ST           ST           ST
                _PutStr OutMsg1
```

```
          call    PutFP ;                           ST            ST
          fsqrt   ;                                 ST            √ST
          _PutStr OutMsg2
          call    PutFP ;                                         ST
          _PutCh 13, 10
          loop    RootLoop
20.6—1 a)
      StatWd  DW      ?
              ...
      ;                                   ST(1)             ST
          fld     A ;                                       A
          fld     B ;               A                       B
          fcom
          fstsw   StatWd
          mov     ax, StatWd
          sahf
          jae     NoXch1 ;       jump if A >= B
          fxch    ;              B=max(A, B)               A
      NoXch1:        ;           max(A, B)           A or B
          fcomp   ST ;                               max(A, B)
          fld     C ;            max(A, B)                 C
          fcom
          fstsw   StatWd
          mov     ax, StatWd
          sahf
          jae     NoXch2 ;       jump if max(A, B) >= C
          fxch    ;              C=max(A, B, C)            C
      NoXch2:        ;           max(A, B, C)              ?
          fcomp   ST ;                               max(A, B, C)
          fstp    X
20.6—2
      StatWd  DW      ?
              ...
          mov     bx, 1 ;        for i := 1 to N - 1
          mov     dx, N
          mov     si, OFFSET A
      loopi:      ;                                ST(1)             ST
          cmp     bx, dx
          jge     Done
          fld     DWORD PTR [si + 4]                       A[i+1]
          mov     cx, bx ;       j := i
          mov     di, si
      loopj:      ;                     while 'j >= i and...
          fld     DWORD PTR [di] ;           A[i+1]        A[j]
          fcom    ;                          A[i+1]        A[j]
          fstsw   StatWd
          mov     ax, StatWd
```

```
                sahf
                jae     jDone ;             ...and A[i+1] < A[j]
                fstp    DWORD PTR [di + 4] ; A[j+1] := A[j]
                sub     di, 4 ;             j := j - 1
                loop    loopj ;         end while
        jDone:
                fstp    DWORD PTR [di + 4] ; A[j+1] = old A[i+1]
                inc     bx
                add     si, 4 ;             i := i + 1
                jmp     loopi ;        end for
        Done:
```

Chapter 21

21.1—1

```
        Inner   PROC
                enter   0, 2 ;                  no locals, lex level 2
                mov     bx, [bp - 2] ;          display entry for lex level 1
                mov     ax, ss:[bx - 6] ;   y
                add     ax, [bp + 4] ;       + a
                mov     ss:[bx - 4], ax ;        --> x
                leave
                ret     2
        Inner   ENDP
```

21.1—2 The necessary procedure information is found by passing the procedure's address and the address of the current display. The procedure being passed must be visible so its lex level is ≤ current lex level + 1, and the items necessary for constructing its display are in the current display. Assuming small model, we could push the procedure information onto the stack as follows:

```
        push    OFFSET theProcedure
        push    bp
```

If this procedure parameter were to be passed on to other procedures, that would be done by simply copying the two parameter words. To specify the code that the receiving procedure uses to call *theProcedure*, assume that the items pushed above are at bp + n and bp + n + 2. We have to fake the value of bp so that when *theProcedure* uses the enter instruction to set up its display, and the fake value we need is at bp + n. The code to call *theProcedure* is

```
        push    bp ;            save current value of bp
        push the parameters to theProcedure
        mov     bp, [bp + n]
        call    WORD PTR [bp + n + 2]
        pop     bp ;            callee has already popped parameters
```

21.2—1

```
        movzx   eax, al
        _PutStr [ShortMo - 4 + 4 * ax]
```

21.2—2

```
;;  Turn the T flag on
        pushf
        bts     WORD PTR [esp], 9
        popf
```

Appendix A

The IBM Extended ASCII Character Set

Dec	Hex	Char	Dec	Hex	Char	Dec	Hex	Char	Dec	Hex	Char
0	00		32	20		64	40	@	96	60	`
1	01	☺	33	21	!	65	41	A	97	61	a
2	02	☻	34	22	"	66	42	B	98	62	b
3	03	♥	35	23	#	67	43	C	99	63	c
4	04	♦	36	24	$	68	44	D	100	64	d
5	05	♣	37	25	%	69	45	E	101	65	e
6	06	♠	38	26	&	70	46	F	102	66	f
7	07	●	39	27	'	71	47	G	103	67	g
8	08	◘	40	28	(	72	48	H	104	68	h
9	09	○	41	29	)	73	49	I	105	69	i
10	0A	◙	42	2A	*	74	4A	J	106	6A	j
11	0B	♂	43	2B	+	75	4B	K	107	6B	k
12	0C	♀	44	2C	,	76	4C	L	108	6C	l
13	0D	♪	45	2D	–	77	4D	M	109	6D	m
14	0E	♫	46	2E	.	78	4E	N	110	6E	n
15	0F	☼	47	2F	/	79	4F	O	111	6F	o
16	10	►	48	30	0	80	50	P	112	70	p
17	11	◄	49	31	1	81	51	Q	113	71	q
18	12	↕	50	32	2	82	52	R	114	72	r
19	13	‼	51	33	3	83	53	S	115	73	s
20	14	¶	52	34	4	84	54	T	116	74	t
21	15	§	53	35	5	85	55	U	117	75	u
22	16	■	54	36	6	86	56	V	118	76	v
23	17	↨	55	37	7	87	57	W	119	77	w
24	18	↑	56	38	8	88	58	X	120	78	x
25	19	↓	57	39	9	89	59	Y	121	79	y
26	1A	→	58	3A	:	90	5A	Z	122	7A	z
27	1B	←	59	3B	;	91	5B	[	123	7B	{
28	1C	∟	60	3C	<	92	5C	\	124	7C		
29	1D	↔	61	3D	=	93	5D	]	125	7D	}
30	1E	▲	62	3E	>	94	5E	^	126	7E	~
31	1F	▼	63	3F	?	95	5F	_	127	7F	⌂

Dec	Hex	Char	Dec	Hex	Char	Dec	Hex	Char	Dec	Hex	Char
128	80	Ç	160	A0	á	192	C0	└	224	E0	α
129	81	ü	161	A1	í	193	C1	┴	225	E1	β
130	82	é	162	A2	ó	194	C2	┬	226	E2	Γ
131	83	â	163	A3	ú	195	C3	├	227	E3	π
132	84	ä	164	A4	ñ	196	C4	─	228	E4	Σ
133	85	à	165	A5	Ñ	197	C5	┼	229	E5	σ
134	86	å	166	A6	a	198	C6	╟	230	E6	μ
135	87	ç	167	A7	o	199	C7	╟	231	E7	γ
136	88	ê	168	A8	¿	200	C8	╚	232	E8	Φ
137	89	ë	169	A9	⌐	201	C9	╔	233	E9	Θ
138	8A	è	170	AA	¬	202	CA	╩	234	EA	Ω
139	8B	ï	171	AB	½	203	CB	╦	235	EB	δ
140	8C	î	172	AC	¼	204	CC	╠	236	EC	∞
141	8D	ì	173	AD	¡	205	CD	═	237	ED	Ø
142	8E	Ä	174	AE	«	206	CE	╬	238	EE	∈
143	8F	Å	175	AF	»	207	CF	╧	239	EF	∩
144	90	É	176	B0	░	208	D0	╨	240	F0	≡
145	91	æ	177	B1	▒	209	D1	╤	241	F1	±
146	92	Æ	178	B2	▓	210	D2	╥	242	F2	≥
147	93	ô	179	B3	│	211	D3	╙	243	F3	≤
148	94	ö	180	B4	┤	212	D4	╘	244	F4	⌠
149	95	ò	181	B5	╡	213	D5	╒	245	F5	⌡
150	96	û	182	B6	╢	214	D6	╓	246	F6	÷
151	97	ù	183	B7	╖	215	D7	╫	247	F7	≈
152	98	ÿ	184	B8	╕	216	D8	╪	248	F8	°
153	99	Ö	185	B9	╣	217	D9	┘	249	F9	•
154	9A	Ü	186	BA	║	218	DA	┌	250	FA	·
155	9B	¢	187	BB	╗	219	DB	█	251	FB	√
156	9C	£	188	BC	╝	220	DC	▄	252	FC	ⁿ
157	9D	¥	189	BD	╜	221	DD	▌	253	FD	²
158	9E	₧	190	BE	╛	222	DE	▐	254	FE	■
159	9F	ƒ	191	BF	┐	223	DF	▀	255	FF	

Appendix

80X86 Instructions

The format of each instruction description is

INS
full name of instruction `INS`

<u>O S Z A C</u>
<u>flags set</u>

Brief description of `INS`.

All non-privileged mode, non-FPU instructions. Precise flag settings.

Op codes which are available only in the 80286 and after are followed by a ② symbol, those available only in the 80386 and after are followed by a ③ symbol, those available in the 80486 are followed by a ④ symbol, and those available in the Pentium by a ⑤. (The 80286 instructions listed here were also available on the 80186, but few computers were constructed with that chip.) No op codes related to protected mode or FPU are listed. Some of the op codes related to decimal arithmetic (`aaa`, `aas`, `daa`, `das`) are complicated to describe in detail so sample usages are given instead.

Use of 80286, 80386, 80486, or Pentium instructions must have been previously enabled with a `.286`, `.386`, `.486`, or `.586` pseudo-operation

If an operation has operands, they will be listed in their general form at the beginning of the 'brief description.' If no such form is given, the instruction has no operands.

The format of the flags register is

Bit number:

11	10	9	8	7	6		4		2		0
O	D	I	T	S	Z		A		P		C

where

  C   Carry flag.
  P   Parity flag, 1 if the low byte of the last result had an even
       number of 1 bits.

A   Auxiliary carry flag. A sort of decimal carry between four bit nibbles for decimal operations.
Z   Zero flag.
S   Sign flag. The sign of the last operation that set it.
T   Trap flag. If 1, an `int 1` occurs after execution of each instruction (see Chapter 15).
I   Interrupt flag. Interrupts are enabled if this flag = 1 (see Chapter 15).
D   Direction flag. Direction (decreasing addresses = 1) of string operations (see Chapter 18).
O   Overflow flag.

Effect of operation codes on the flags Overflow, Sign, Zero, Auxiliary carry, and Carry, in that order, are given to the right of the instruction description. The following symbols are used to indicate flag settings:

symbol	flag setting
	flag unaltered
√	flag set according to results of instruction
1	flag set to 1 by instruction
0	flag cleared to 0 by instruction
?	flag left with unpredictable value by instruction

In operands, *reg* stands for any of the eight word registers (ax, bx, cx, dx, sp, bp, si, di), or any of the eight byte registers (al, ah, bl, bh, cl, ch, dl, dh) or, on the 386/486/Pentium, any of the eight extended registers (eax, ebx, ecx, edx, esp, ebp, esi, edi). *Reg/mem* stands for a *reg* or one of the memory references

16-Bit Addressing				
simple	**indexed**		**based indexed**	
	[bx]	[bx+*Addr*]	[bx+si]	[bx+si+*Addr*]
Addr	[bp]	[bp+*Addr*]	[bx+di]	[bx+di+*Addr*]
(or [*Addr*])	[si]	[si+*Addr*]	[bp+si]	[bp+si+*Addr*]
	[di]	[si+*Addr*]	[bp+di]	[bp+di+*Addr*]

where *Addr* stands for an address, constant, or expression involving these. For the 386/486/Pentium, *Reg/mem* can also have the form

32-Bit Addressing
[*Addr* + *ebase* + *n* * *eindex*]

where *Addr* is as above, *ebase* is any of the extended registers, *n* is 1, 2, 4, or 8, and *eindex* is any of the extended registers except esp. In this form, *Addr*, *ebase*, *n*, and *eindex* can be omitted in any reasonable combination.

Use of extended registers or 32-bit addressing must be enabled with a `.386`, `.486`, or `.586` pseudo-operation.

Certain instructions (such as loop and the string instructions) use registers implicitly, and on the 386/486/Pentium, the register used depends on whether the computer is in 16-bit mode (always used by DOS) or 32-bit protected mode. Syntax of the form [e]cx or [e]si will always be used to specify such a register, indicating that cx or si is used in 16-bit mode and ecx or esi in 32-bit mode.

Always ignore the [e] in [e]rr in instruction descriptions when running in DOS.

The instructions are

		O S Z A C
AAA		
ACII Adjust al after Addition		? ? ? √ √

Normal Usage: A and B are bytes containing single BCD digits (0..9):

```
mov     al, A
add     al, B ;        or adc
aaa
```

Leaves al containing the decimal digit sum. Decimal carry (if any) added to ah and placed in C.

		O S Z A C
AAD		
ASCII Adjust ax before Divide		? √ √ ? ?

al := al + 10 * ah; ah := 0. (ah:al would normally be two BCD digits (0..9).

		O S Z A C
AAM		
ASCII Adjust ax after Multiply		? √ √ ? ?

ah := al **div** 10; al := al **mod** 10. (quotient and remainder, respectively).

		O S Z A C
AAS		
ASCII Adjust al after Subtract		? ? ? √ √

Normal Usage: A and B are bytes containing single BCD digits (0..9)

```
mov     al, A
sub     al, B ;        or sbb
aas
```

Leaves al containing the decimal digit difference. Decimal borrow (if any) subtracted from ah and placed in C.

ADC
ADd with Carry

O	S	Z	A	C
√	√	√	√	√

adc *dest, source* sets *dest* := *dest* + *source* + C flag. The following combinations of source and destination are allowed:

        adc   *reg, reg/mem*
        adc   *reg/mem, reg/const*

ADD
ADD

O	S	Z	A	C
√	√	√	√	√

add *dest, source* sets *dest* := *dest* + *source*. The following combinations of source and destination are allowed:

        add   *reg, reg/mem*
        add   *reg/mem, reg/const*

AND
AND

O	S	Z	A	C
0	√	√	?	0

and *dest, source* sets *dest* := *dest* **and** *source* bit by bit. The following combinations of source and destination are allowed:

        and   *reg, reg/mem*
        and   *reg/mem, reg/const*

BOUND ②
Check subscript for BOUNDary violations

O	S	Z	A	C

bound *reg, mem* checks to see if *reg* [*mem*] and *reg* [*mem* + 2] or [*mem* + 4], depending on size of operands. If either test fails, an interrupt 5 is signaled.

BSF ③
Bit Scan Forward

O	S	Z	A	C
		√		

bsf *reg, reg/mem* scans *reg/mem* for a 1 bit from right to left (i.e., from bit 0). If there are no 1 bits, Z is set. If there is a 1 bit, Z is cleared and *reg* is set to its number. Must be 16- or 32-bit operands.

BSR ③
Bit Scan Reverse

O	S	Z	A	C
		√		

bsr   *reg*, *reg/mem* scans *reg/mem* for a 1 bit from left to right (i.e., from bit 15 or 31). If there are no 1 bits, Z is set. If there is a 1 bit, Z is cleared and *reg* is set to its number. Must be 16- or 32-bit operands.

BSWAP ④
Byte SWAP

O S Z A C

bswap   *reg* reverses the order of the bytes in *reg*, which must be a 32-bit register.

BT ③
Bit Test

O S Z A C
√

bt   *reg/mem*, *reg/const* stores the bit specified by address *reg/mem* and bit number *reg/const* in the C flag. Regs and mem must be 16 or 32 bits and *const* must be 8 bits.

BTC ③
Bit Test and Complement

O S Z A C
√

btc   *reg/mem*, *reg/const* stores the bit specified by address *reg/mem* and bit number *reg/const* in the C flag. Then specified bit is complemented. Regs and mem must be 16 or 32 bits and *const* must be 8 bits.

BTR ③
Bit Test and Reset

O S Z A C
√

btr   *reg/mem*, *reg/const* stores the bit specified by address *reg/mem* and bit number *reg/const* in the C flag. Then specified bit is set to 0. Regs and mem must be 16 or 32 bits and *const* must be 8 bits.

BTS ③
Bit Test and Set

O S Z A C
√

bts   *reg/mem*, *reg/const* stores the bit specified by address *reg/mem* and bit number *reg/const* in the C flag. Then specified bit is set to 1. Regs and mem must be 16 or 32 bits and *const* must be 8 bits.

CALL
CALL subprocedure

O S Z A C

call   *reg/mem* , if a far call, pushes the current cs register, then in any case pushes the current [e]ip. It then resets [e]ip, and perhaps cs, from *reg/mem*, depending on its type.

CBW

O S Z A C

Convert Byte to Word

$ax := al$, sign extended.

CDQ ③

O S Z A C

Convert Double word to Quad word

$edx:eax := eax$, sign extended.

CLC

O S Z A C

CLear Carry

0

C flag := 0.

CLD

O S Z A C

CLear Direction flag

D flag := 0.

CLI

O S Z A C

CLear Interrupt flag

Disable interrupts; i.e., set the I flag to 0.

CMC

O S Z A C

CoMplement Carry flag

√

C flag := **not** C flag.

CMP

O S Z A C

CoMPare

√ √ √ √ √

cmp *dest, source* subtracts *source* from *dest*, sets the flags accordingly, and discards the result. The following combinations of source and destination are allowed:

```
cmp     reg, reg/mem
cmp     reg/mem, reg/const
```

CMPSB
CMPSW
CMPSD ③
CoMPare Strings

O S Z A C
√ √ √ √ √

Compare string items at ds:[e]si (left operand) and es:[e]di (right operand), set flags, and advance [e]si and [e]di to next (D flag = 0) or previous (D flag = 1) string item.

CMPXCHG ④
CoMPare and eXCHanGe

O S Z A C
√ √ √ √ √

cmpxchg *mem/reg1*, *reg2* compares *mem/reg1* to al/ax/eax according to the size of *mem/reg1* and sets the flags. If equal, performs mov *mem/reg1*, *reg2* ; otherwise, performs mov al/ax/eax, *mem/reg1*.

CMPXCHG8B ⑤
CoMPare and eXCHanGe 8 Bytes

O S Z A C
√ √ √ √ √

cmpxchg8b *mem* compares *mem* to edx:eax and sets the flags. If equal, moves ecx:ebx to *mem* and otherwise moves *mem* into edx:eax.

CWD
Convert Word to Double word

O S Z A C

dx:ax := ax, sign extended.

CWDE ③
Convert Word to Double word Extended

O S Z A C

eax := ax, sign extended.

DAA
Decimally Adjust al after Addition

O S Z A C
? √ √ √ √

Normal Usage: A and B are bytes containing two BCD digits (0–9) each:

```
mov    al, A
add    al, B ;      or adc
daa
```

Leaves al containing the two decimal digit sum. Decimal carry out the left end is placed in C.

DAS
Decimally Adjust `al` after Subtraction

$$\underline{O\ S\ Z\ A\ C}$$
$$?\ \surd\ \surd\ \surd\ \surd$$

Normal Usage: A and B are bytes containing two BCD digits (0–9) each:

```
mov     al, A
sub     al, B ;        or sbb
daa
```

Leaves `al` containing the two decimal digit difference. Decimal borrow out the left end is placed in C.

DEC
DECrement

$$\underline{O\ S\ Z\ A\ C}$$
$$\surd\ \surd\ \surd\ \surd$$

`dec` *reg/mem* performs *reg/mem* := *reg/mem* − 1. Note that the C flag is not altered.

DIV
DIVide unsigned

$$\underline{O\ S\ Z\ A\ C}$$
$$?\ ?\ ?\ ?\ ?$$

`div` *reg/mem* divides by *reg/mem*, treating both numbers as unsigned. The dividend and locations of quotient and remainder are determined by the size of *reg/mem*:

size	dividend	quotient	remainder	
byte	ax	al	ah	
word	dx:ax	ax	dx	
double word	edx:eax	eax	edx	(386/486/Pentium)

ENTER ②
create stack frame upon ENTERing a subprocedure

$$\underline{O\ S\ Z\ A\ C}$$

`enter` *n*, *m* sets up a stack frame at lex level *m* with *n* bytes of local storage. See Section 21.1 for a more detailed description.

HLT
HaLT processing

$$\underline{O\ S\ Z\ A\ C}$$

Stops instruction execution. An interrupt causes its interrupt handler to be executed and a subsequent `iret` instruction causes execution to be resumed at the instruction following the `hlt`.

IDIV
sIgned DIVide

<u>O S Z A C</u>
? ? ? ? ?

idiv *reg/mem* divides by *reg/mem*, treating both numbers as signed. The dividend and locations of quotient and remainder are determined by the size of *reg/mem*:

size	dividend	quotient	remainder	
byte	ax	al	ah	
word	dx:ax	ax	dx	
double word	edx:eax	eax	edx	(386/486/Pentium)

IMUL
sIgned MULtiply

<u>O S Z A C</u>
√ ? ? ? √

Does signed multiply in various forms depending on operands:

instruction	size	multiplicands	result	comments
imul *reg/mem*	byte	al, *reg/mem*	ax	
	word	ax, *reg/mem*	dx:ax	
	dword	eax, *reg/mem*	edx:eax	386–Pentium
imul *reg*, *reg/mem*	word	*reg*, *reg/mem*	*reg*	386–Pentium
	dword	*reg*, *reg/mem*	*reg*	386–Pentium
imul *reg*, *const*	word	*reg*, *const*	*reg*	286–Pentium
	dword	*reg*, *const*	*reg*	386–Pentium
imul *reg*, *reg/mem*,	word	*reg/mem*, *const*	*reg*	286–Pentium
const	dword	*reg/mem*, *const*	*reg*	386–Pentium

IN
INput

<u>O S Z A C</u>

in al/ax/eax, dx/*const* performs byte, word, or double word (80386/486) input into al, ax, or eax from a port specified by dx or the *const* (255).

INC
INCrement

<u>O S Z A C</u>
√ √ √ √

inc *reg/mem* performs *reg/mem* := *reg/mem* + 1. Note that the C flag is not altered.

INSB ②   <u>O S Z A C</u>
INSW ②
INSD ③
INput into String

Inputs from the port specified by dx to the memory location specified by es:[e]di and advances [e]di to next (D flag = 0) or previous (D flag = 1) string item.

INT   <u>O S Z A C</u>
software INTerrupt

int *const* (*const* 255) causes interr upt *const*; that is, the flags, cs, and [e]ip are pushed onto the stack, interrupts are disabled, and control is passed to the interrupt handler whose location is determined by a segment:offset pointer at location 4 * *const* in unprotected mode and at the appropriate entry in the Interrupt Descriptor Table in protected mode. Int 3, the breakpoint interrupt is a single byte and all other int instructions are two bytes. Normally, return from interrupt is effected by an iret instruction.

INTO   <u>O S Z A C</u>
INTerrupt if Overflow

If the overflow flag is set, execute an int 4 instruction.

IRET   <u>O S Z A C</u>
Interrupt RETurn   <u>? ? ? ? ?</u>

Pop [e]ip, cs, and flags from stack. Some actions depend on whether or not in protected mode (80286/386/486/Pentium).

J*cc*   <u>O S Z A C</u>
Jump if condition *cc* is true

j*cc* *address* jumps to *address* if condition *cc* is true. *Address* is stored as an 8-bit offset relative to the ip (**short** jumps) or on the 80386/486/Pentium, as a 16- or 32-bit offset (**near** jumps). The following conditions and meanings are recognized:

instruction	meaning
ja	jump if above (unsigned greater than)
jna	jump if not above (= jbe)
jae	jump if above or equal (unsigned greater than or equal to)
jnae	jump if not above or equal(= jb)
jb	jump if below (unsigned less than)
jnb	jump if not below (= jae)

jbe	jump if below or equal (unsigned less than or equal to)
jnbe	jump if not below or equal (= ja)
je	jump if equal
jne	jump if not equal
jz	jump if zero (= je)
jnz	jump if not zero (= jne)
jg	jump if greater (signed comparison)
jng	jump if not greater (= jle)
jge	jump if greater than or equal to (signed comparison)
jnge	jump if not greater than or equal to (= jl)
jl	jump if less (signed comparison)
jnl	jump if not less (= jge)
jle	jump if less than or equal to (signed comparison)
jnle	jump if not less than or equal to (= jg)
jc	jump if carry flag set (= 1)
jnc	jump if carry flag clear (= 0)
jo	jump if overflow flag set (= 1)
jno	jump if overflag clear (= 0)
jp	jump if parity flag set (= 1)
jnp	jump if parity flag clear (=0)
jpe	jump if parity even (= jp)
jpo	jump if parity odd (= jnp)
js	jump if sign flag set (= 1)
jns	jump if sign flag clear (= 0)
jcxz	jump if cx register is zero (short form only)
jecxz	jump if ecx register is zero (short form, 80386/486/Pentium)

JMP   O S Z A C
JuMP
                                                                   ‾‾‾‾‾‾‾‾‾

jmp *address* jumps to the code at location *address*. *Address* is stored as an 8-bit offset relative to the ip (**short** jumps), a 16-bit offset (**near** jumps), the segment:offset address of the destination (**far** jumps), the address of a word containing the offset of the destination, or the address of the segment:offset address of the destination. The 80386/486/Pentium have other combinations as well, for instance, a 32 bit near jump.

LAHF   O S Z A C
Load the AH register from the Flags register
                                                                   ‾‾‾‾‾‾‾‾‾

ah := low byte of the flags register.

LDS   O S Z A C
LES
LFS ③
LGS ③
LSS ③
Load segment register and another register from far pointer

lxs *reg*, *mem* loads register *reg* with the first word of double word at *mem* and loads segment
register *xs* with the second word.

LEA   O S Z A C
Load Effective Address

lea *reg*, *mem* computes the offset specified by *mem* and loads it into *reg*. On the 80386/486/
Pentium, *reg* can be either 16 or 32 bits.

LEAVE ②   O S Z A C
prepare to LEAVE subprocedure by resetting stack

Does the equivalent of

```
            mov     [e]sp, [e]bp
            pop     [e]bp
```

LOCK   O S Z A C
LOCK memory access for next instruction

Keeps any other processor from accessing memory during execution of the following instruction.
For a more complete description of the use of this instruction, see Section 16.7.

LODSB   O S Z A C
LODSW
LODSD ③
LOaD al/ax/eax from String

Load al/ax/eax from byte/word/dword at ds:[e]si and advance [e]si to next (D flag = 0) or
previous (D flag = 1) string item.

LOOP   O S Z A C
LOOPE
LOOPZ
LOOPNE
LOOPNZ
LOOP while [condition is true and] [e]cx not 0

`loop` *address* is roughly equivalent to

```
        dec    [e]cx
        jnz    address ;      short jump only
```

`loopcc` *address* is roughly equivalent to

```
        dec    [e]cx
        jz     Done
        jcc    address ;      short jump only
Done:
```

That is, the loop continues as long the condition *cc* is true *and* [e]cx is non-zero *after* it is counted down. Cx is used in 16-bit address mode and `ecx` in 32-bit address mode. Note that the `loop` instructions do not alter the flags.

MOV   O S Z A C
MOVe

`mov` *dest, source* sets *dest* := *source*. The operation is actually a *copy* rather than a move. The following combinations of source and destination are allowed:

```
        mov    reg, reg/mem
        mov    reg/mem, reg/const
        mov    segreg, reg/mem
        mov    reg/mem, segreg
```

MOVSB   O S Z A C
MOVSW
MOVSD ③
MOVe a String of data

Moves a string item at `ds:[e]si` to `es:[e]di` and advances [e]si and [e]di to next (D flag = 0) or previous (D flag = 1) string item.

MOVSX ③   <u>O S Z A C</u>
MOVe with Sign eXtension

`movsx reg, reg/mem` sets *reg* := *reg/mem* with sign extension, where *reg/mem* specifies a byte or word and *reg* specifies a longer register.

MOVZX ③   <u>O S Z A C</u>
MOVe with Zero eXtension

`movzx reg, reg/mem` sets *reg* := *reg/mem* extending to the left with zeroes, where *reg/mem* specifies a byte or word and *reg* specifies a longer register.

MUL   <u>O S Z A C</u>
unsigned MULtiply   √ ? ? ? √

Does unsigned multiply in various forms depending on operands:

instruction	size	multiplicands	result	comments
mul *reg/mem*	byte	al, *reg/mem*	ax	
	word	ax, *reg/mem*	dx:ax	
	dword	eax, *reg/mem*	edx:eax	386/486/Pentium

NEG   <u>O S Z A C</u>
NEGate   √ √ √ √ √

`neg reg/mem` negates (replaces with the 2's complement) the operand. Sets C flag := (operand 0). If the operand is its own 2's complement, sets O flag = 1; otherwise clears it.

NOP   <u>O S Z A C</u>
No OPeration

The instruction does nothing except fill one byte of space. Its chief use is in filling in a forward near or far jump which is subsequently discovered to require less space.

NOT   <u>O S Z A C</u>
NOT

`not reg/mem` replaces *reg/mem* with its bit-by-bit logical complement.

OR	O S Z A C
OR	0 √ √ ? 0

or *dest, source* sets *dest* := *dest* inclusive **or** *source* bit by bit. The following combinations of source and destination are allowed:

    or   reg, reg/mem
    or   reg/mem, reg/const

OUT	O S Z A C
OUTput	————

out dx/*const* , al/ax/eax performs byte, word, or double word (386/486/Pentium only) output from al, ax, or eax to a port specified by dx or the *const* (255).

OUTSB ③	O S Z A C
OUTSW ③	————
OUTSD ③	
OUTput from String	

Outputs to the port specified by dx the memory location specified by es:[e]di and advances [e]di to next (D flag = 0) or previous (D flag = 1) string item.

POP	O S Z A C
POP from stack	————

pop *segreg/reg/mem* must have a word or double word (386/486/Pentium) argument. The word or double word on pointed to by the stack pointer is placed in *segreg/reg/mem* and the stack pointer incremented by 2 or 4.

POPA ②	O S Z A C
POPAD ③	————
POP All general registers	

Popa pops all general registers in the order di, si, bp, sp (discarded), bx, dx, cx, and ax. Popad pops the corresponding extended registers edi, ... eax. The order is the reverse of the order they are pushed by pusha[d].

POPF	O S Z A C
POPFD ③	————
POP stack into Flags register	

Popf[d] pops the single- or double-word flag register off of the stack.

PUSH O S Z A C
PUSH onto stack

push *segreg/reg/mem/const* must have a word or double word (386/486/Pentium) argument. A *const* argument can only be used on the 286/386/486/Pentium. The stack pointer is decremented by 2 or 4 word or double word *segreg/reg/mem/const* is stored at the memory location pointed to by the new value of the stack pointer.

PUSHA ② O S Z A C
PUSHAD ③
PUSH All general registers

Pusha pushes all general registers in the order ax, cx, dx, bx, sp, bp, si, and di. Pushad pushes the corresponding extended registers eax, ..., edi.

PUSHF O S Z A C
PUSHFD ③
PUSH Flags register onto stack

Pushf[d] pushes the single or double word flag register onto the stack.

RCL O S Z A C
RCR √ √
Rotate with C flag Left/Right

rcl/r *reg/mem*, *amount* rotates the $n + 1$ bits made up of the n bits of *reg/mem* and the C flag left or right by the specified *amount*. *Amount* is 1, cl, specifying an amount in the cl register, or (286/386/486/Pentium) *const*.

REP O S Z A C
REPE
REPZ
REPNE
REPNZ
REPeat string instruction while [condition is true and] [e]cx not 0

Rep*cc* can be applied as a prefix to any of the string instructions lods, stos, movs, cmps, scas, ins, and outs. Rep*cc* *strop* is roughly equivalent to

```
aLabel:
        strop
        loopcc ALabel
```

As such, the combinations rep*cc* cmps and rep*cc* scas can alter the flags.

RET   O S Z A C
RET

Ret returns from a subprocedure by popping the top of the stack into [e]ip and, if in a far procedure, the next word from the stack into cs. The form ret *const* performs the ret as above and then pops *const* bytes from the stack (presumably the parameters used to call the procedure).

ROL   O S Z A C
ROR   √   √
Rotate Left/Right

rol/r *reg/mem, amount* rotates *reg/mem* left or right by the specified *amount*. Amount is 1, cl, specifying an amount in the cl register, or (286/386/486/Pentium) *const*.

SAHF   O S Z A C
Store the AH register in the Flags register   ? ? ? ?

Sets the low-order byte of the flags register to the contents of ah.

SAL   O S Z A C
SAR   √ √ √ ? √
Shift Arithmetic Left/Right

sal/r *reg/mem, amount* shifts *reg/mem* left or right by the specified *amount*. Amount is 1, cl, specifying an amount in the cl register, or (286/386/486/Pentium) *const*. On sal, 0 bits are shifted in at the right of the item and the last bit shifted out of the left end is placed in the C flag. On sar, sign bits are shifted in at the left of the item and the last bit shifted out the right end is placed in the C flag. Sal is the same as shl.

SBB   O S Z A C
SuBtract with Borrow   √ √ √ √ √

sbb *dest, source* sets *dest* := *dest* − *source* − C flag. The following combinations of source and destination are allowed:

           sbb   *reg, reg/mem*
           sbb   *reg/mem, reg/const*

SCASB   O S Z A C
SCASW   √ √ √ √ √
SCASD ③
SCAn String for al/ax/eax

Compare `al`/`ax`/`eax` to the byte/word/dword at `ds:[e]di` (right operand), set flags, and advance `[e]di` to next (D flag = 0) or previous (D flag = 1) string item.

SET*cc* ③   O S Z A C

SET byte according to whether condition *cc* is true
                                                                    _____

`Setcc` `reg/mem` sets the byte *reg/mem* to 1 if condition *cc* is true, to 0 otherwise. The following conditions and meanings are recognized:

instruction	meaning
seta	set if above (unsigned greater than)
setna	set if not above (= `setbe`)
setae	set if above or equal (unsigned greater than or equal to)
setnae	set if not above or equal(= `setb`)
setb	set if below (unsigned less than)
setnb	set if not below (= `setae`)
setbe	set if below or equal (unsigned less than or equal to)
setnbe	set if not below or equal (= `seta`)
sete	set if equal
setne	set if not equal
setz	set if zero (= `sete`)
setnz	set if not zero (= `setne`)
setg	set if greater (signed comparison)
setng	set if not greater (= `setle`)
setge	set if greater than or equal to (signed comparison)
setnge	set if not greater than or equal to (= `setl`)
setl	set if less (signed comparison)
setnl	set if not less (= `setge`)
setle	set if less than or equal to (signed comparison)
setnle	set if not less than or equal to (= `setg`)
setc	set if carry flag set (= 1)
setnc	set if carry flag clear (= 0)
seto	set if overflow flag set (= 1)
setno	set if overflag clear (= 0)
setp	set if parity flag set (= 1)
setnp	set if parity flag clear (= 0)
setpe	set if parity even (= `setp`)
setpo	set if parity odd (= `setnp`)
sets	set if sign flag set (= 1)
setns	set if sign flag clear (= 0)

	O	S	Z	A	C
SHL
SHR
SHift Left/Right
$$\begin{array}{ccccc} O & S & Z & A & C \\ \sqrt{} & \sqrt{} & \sqrt{} & ? & \sqrt{} \end{array}$$

`shl/r` `reg/mem`, `amount` shifts `reg/mem` left or right by the specified `amount`. `Amount` is 1, `cl`, specifying an amount in the `cl` register, or (286/386/486/Pentium) `const`. Zero bits are shifted in at the right or left end of the item and the last bit shifted out is placed in the C flag.

SHLD ③
SHRD ③
SHift Left/Right Double
$$\begin{array}{ccccc} O & S & Z & A & C \\ ? & \sqrt{} & \sqrt{} & ? & \sqrt{} \end{array}$$

`shl/rd` `reg/mem`, `reg`, `cl/const` shifts `reg/mem` left or right a number of bits given by `const` or the contents of `cl`. Vacated bit positions are filled from the right or left of `reg`. The result is used to set S and Z and the last bit shifted out is used to set C. `Reg/mem` and `reg` must either both be words or both double words.

STC
SeT Carry flag
$$\begin{array}{ccccc} O & S & Z & A & C \\ & & & & 1 \end{array}$$

C flag := 1.

STD
SeT Direction flag
$$\begin{array}{ccccc} O & S & Z & A & C \end{array}$$

D flag := 1.

STI
SeT Interrupt flag
$$\begin{array}{ccccc} O & S & Z & A & C \end{array}$$

Enable interrupts; i.e., set the I flag to 1.

STOSB
STOSW
STOSD ③
STOre `al`/`ax`/`eax` in String
$$\begin{array}{ccccc} O & S & Z & A & C \end{array}$$

Store `al`/`ax`/`eax` in byte/word/dword at `es:[e]di` and advance `[e]di` to next (D flag = 0) or previous (D flag = 1) string item.

SUB
SUBtract
$$\begin{array}{ccccc} O & S & Z & A & C \\ \sqrt{} & \sqrt{} & \sqrt{} & \sqrt{} & \sqrt{} \end{array}$$

sub *dest, source* sets *dest := dest – source* . The following combinations of source and destination are allowed:

```
sub     reg, reg/mem
sub     reg/mem, reg/const
```

TEST

TEST value against register or constant

O	S	Z	A	C
0	√	√	?	√

test *reg/mem, reg/const* does a bit-by-bit **and** of *reg/mem* and *reg/const*, sets the flags according to the result, and discards it.

WAIT

WAIT for 80X87 to complete execution

O	S	Z	A	C

Suspends execution until the 80x87 signals that it has completed execution.

XADD ④

eXchange and ADD

O	S	Z	A	C
√	√	√	√	√

xadd *mem/reg, reg* performs xchg *mem/reg, reg*, followed by add *mem/reg, reg*, setting the flags.

XCHG

eXCHanGe operands

O	S	Z	A	C

In either of the two forms xchg *reg, reg/mem* or xchg *reg/mem, reg*, the two operands are interchanged.

XLAT

transLATe byte

O	S	Z	A	C

Uses al as an index into a table at ds:[e]bx, setting al := [[al] + [e]bx].

XOR

eXclusive OR

O	S	Z	A	C
0	√	√	?	0

xor *dest, source* sets *dest := dest* **xor** *source* bit by bit. The following combinations of source and destination are allowed:

```
xor     reg, reg/mem
xor     reg/mem, reg/const
```

Appendix

Two Programming Editors

C.1 • the Ed Editor

Ed is a simple DOS-based editor written by the author which is particularly useful for writing assembly language programs. It can be distributed freely as long as the author's copyright notice is maintained.

This section contains a brief description of how to install and use ed in writing assembly programs. Complete documentation for ed is available in the file ed.doc on the disk accompanying this book.

▶ **Installing ed**

Simply copy ed.exe from the diskette that accompanies this book to a directory in your PATH or to your working directory.

▶ **Creating a source file**

To edit a new or previously existing file, enter

        ed *name-of-file*↵ (↵ represents the **Enter** key)

at the prompt. For instance, to create the first assembly program, type

        ed first.asm↵

The text is entered in much the same manner as with a typewriter, but the arrow (cursor) keys can be used to move the cursor (the flashing block or underline). Text is inserted by typing the new text and deleted by hitting the **Del** or gray left arrow = **Backspace** key. You can get a help screen similar to the one

651

```
↑ cursor up          ↓ cursor down       → cursor right      ← cursor left
Ctrl → right to next tab                   Ctrl ← left to last tab
Home to line start     Home-Home to screen start    PgUp scroll screen up
End  to line end          End-End  to screen end        PgDn scroll down
Home-Home-Home file start    End-End-End file end    Ctrl-Enter open line


Alt-S search fwd  Alt-B search backwards  Alt-N repeat last search
Alt-F search and replace fwd         Alt-B search and replace backwards


Gray ← erase char before cursor     Del erase character under cursor


Alt-A toggle autoindent Alt-D delete line Alt-G go to line  Alt-H help
Alt-K kill rest of line Alt-M toggle block      Alt-F change file name
Alt-W write file  Alt-Q quit ED      Alt-L leave to DOS (with return)


Alt-T compile/assemble  Ctrl-N go to next error line


Alt-X cut to clipboard  Alt-C copy to clipboard Ins insert clipboard
```

ed commands

above by typing **Alt-H**, that is, hold down the key labeled **Alt** and type **H** . You can exit the help screen and abort most editing commands with the **Esc** key.

▶ **Translating a source file**

When the file has been created to your satisfaction, you can assemble the file by typing **Alt-T**. This command causes ed to save your source file, find and invoke your assembler (its directory should be in your PATH), and return to ed, informing you either that the assembly was successful or putting the cursor on the line with the first error and the error message at the bottom of the screen. Further error messages, if any, can be viewed by typing **Ctrl-N**, that is, holding down the key labeled **Ctrl** and typing **N**. Edit and reassemble your file if necessary until there are no more errors.

▶ **Creating the .EXE file**

You can exit *temporarily* to DOS by typing **Alt-L** and link and execute your program as above. Return to ed by typing exit↵ at the C> prompt. If you are done, you can exit ed; otherwise, make corrections and repeat the process of translating and executing your program.

> **If you get a message saying you have run out of memory,** it probably means that you have done ed *file*, **Alt-L**, ed *file*, **Alt-L**, etc. without ever typing exit. This process will fill up memory with several copies of ed. Typing exit↵ to get back to ed and **Alt-Q** to get out of ed a few times and things should return things to normal.

Be sure your source file is saved before typing **Alt-L**, either as a result of the **Alt-T** command, which saves and assembles, or of the **Alt-W** command, which only saves the file

▶ **Exiting** `ed`

Exit from `ed` by typing `Alt-Q`.

C.2 • The `WinEdit` Editor

`WinEdit` is a very capable shareware editor for use with Windows 3.1, '95, or NT. Being "shareware" means that you can download a copy free from the Internet, but if you like it and make substantial use of it, you are morally obligated to purchase a license for it. `WinEdit` is "smart" in that it can color code keywords for several languages (including hypertext for the WEB) and decode error messages from various translators, including MASM and TASM. **Getting it to work properly can be a fairly tricky process**. I have only been fully successful with MASM 6.11 and Windows '95, which immediately worked like a charm, but I haven't tested other combinations exhaustively. For some guidance in solving problems, see the end of this section.

I am assuming some prior experience with Windows here.

▶ **Installing** `WinEdit`

Download `WinEdit` from the internet from `http://www.windowware.com`. You can purchase it direct from the manufacturer but I suggest you make sure you can get it up and running to your satisfaction before you do so. In the `Program Manager`, choose **Run** from the file menu and execute the usual `setup` program. Then use the `File Manager` to copy the files from the `\winedit` directory on the disk accompanying this book to the `\winedit` directory on your hard disk.

▶ **Starting** `WinEdit`

Start `WinEdit.exe` (Windows '95 or NT) or double-click `WinEdit16.exe` (Windows 3.1) from the `WinEdit` group.

▶ **Configuring** `WinEdit`

- First, you must arrange it so that the File Open command will look for assembler source files. Choose **Preferences...** from the File menu and click on the **File Filters** button. Then enter "Assembly Programs" as the type of files and "`*.asm, *.inc`" as the filter, no quotes in either case. Click on the **Add** button. This will make Assembly programs the last choice. To make them the default choice, first select and delete the supplied filters, then add "Assembly Programs", then add any other file groups you would like to have.
- Second, you must set up the proper assembly, link, and execute commands. Such a set of commands is called a **Project** by `WinEdit`. Projects are saved in files with the extension `.wpj`, and the project `default.wpj` is automatically loaded when `WinEdit` starts. To manipulate the project, choose **Configure...** from the Project menu. As a starting point, you may want to open one of the two simple projects `masm.wpj` or `tasm.wpj`

that you copied over earlier. I suggest that you make whatever changes are necessary for your environment. (In particular, choose your own working directory, say `c:\assembly`.) Then save the project as `default.wpj`. For more advanced work, using `util.lib` and a debugger, you can use the included projects `masmadv.wpj` or `tasmadv.wpj` for suggestions.

Several of the project commands make use of an interesting program `tee.com` that comes with `WinEdit`. `Tee.com` is reminiscent of the program `redirerr` developed in Chapter 17 in that both merely execute the rest of their command line, but its output is mucked about. In the case of `tee`, the output that normally goes to the screen also can be sent to a file, so that `WinEdit` and read and interpret error messages. (See below.)

▶ **Creating a source file**

Start `WinEdit` as above. Choose **New** from the File menu. Type in your program. The usual Windows editing functions, and Help, are available. Save your program by choosing **Save** or **Save As...** from the File menu). If you want to edit an already existing file, `WinEdit` keeps a list of recently edited files at the bottom of the File menu, or choose **Open...** from the File menu.

▶ **Translating a source file**

First make sure that you have done the Project configuration properly, as above. Then choose **Compile** from the Project menu. WinEdit opens up a DOS window and assembles the file you just created. When it is done, close the DOS window. You should then be presented with a dialog box allowing you to view error messages, if any. Go through the standard cycle of correcting errors (choosing **Next error** from the Search menu) and reassembling until there are no more errors.

▶ **Creating the `.EXE` file**

Choose **Make** from the Project menu. As in translating, you will get a DOS window in which the linker will be run. Close it when it is done and view error messages. As before, edit, reassemble, and relink until there are no more errors.

▶ **Executing the `.EXE` file**

Choose **Execute** from the Project menu and view the output in the resulting DOS window. When you have properly configured the **Debug** entry in the Project menu (see above), you can also run an interactive debugger to aid fixing your program. See Debug Workshop I after Chapter 4 for more information.

▶ **If Things Go Badly**

• Under Windows 3.1, when you try to assemble or link, you may get a cryptic message from `WinEdit` saying that you need to "reduce your PIF KB value." To do so, start the `Pif Editor` in the Main program group. Open the file `EDTEMP.PIF` that `WinEdit` Setup has installed in your `\windows\system` directory and reduce the value in the

"KB required" window. You can either experiment until you find a value that works, or in `WinEdit` you can temporarily change the "Execute" entry in your project configuration to "`mem`" and click the "Capture Results" box if it isn't already chosen. Then choose execute and view the output to see approximately how much regular memory you have available.

- Again, under Windows 3.1, if your DOS windows don't stay open, use the PIF Editor on EDTEMP.PIF and check the "keep windows open" entry.
- I have had a lot of trouble getting either linker to work with Windows 3.1. You may be able to do so by scavenging more memory. Get rid of all the TSRs (from `autoexec.bat`) and device drivers (from `config.sys`) that you can. Run `memmaker` (in DOS) to try to free up more memory. Then reboot, increase the KB value above, and try again.
- In Windows '95 or NT you may chance to use a long file name as part of the name of your working directory. This can produce strange error messages. Stick to the tried and true 8+3 character directory names.

Appendix

Selected DOS and BIOS Functions, Formats, and Memory Locations

This appendix covers the firmware- and DOS-related items introduced in this book. Many books are available which give a complete and detailed description of them, for instance, Norton and Wilton's *Programmer's Guide to the IBM PC & PS/2* (see the bibliography).

D.1 • BIOS Calls

D.1.1 • Int 10h (Video) Calls

00h   Set video mode

input: ah = 00h
            al = desired video mode (03 = CGA text, 07 = MDA text,
                  12h = VGA 640 × 480 16 color graphics

02h   Set cursor position

input: ah = 02h
            bh = display page (0–3; 0 probably works)
            dh = row (0–24)
            dl = column (0–79)

03h   Get cursor position

input: ah = 03h   output: dh = row
            bh = display page   dl = column

05h   Set display page

input: ah = 05h
            al = display page number (0–3)

06h and 07h   Scroll window up or down

input: ah = 06h (up) or 07h (down)
            al = number of lines to scroll (0 to clear window)
            bh = attribute for cleared lines (see Section D.5)
            ch = row number of upper left-hand corner (0–24)
            cl = column number of upper left-hand corner (0–79)
            dh = row number of lower right-hand corner (0–24)
            dl = column number of lower right-hand corner (0–79)

08h   Get character and attribute at cursor position

input: ah = 08h   output :   al = ASCII character
            bh = display page   ah = attribute (see Section D.5)

09h   Display character and attribute; no cursor change

input: ah = 09h
            al = ASCII character
            bl = attribute (see Section D.5)
            bh = display page (0–3; 0 probably works)
            cx = number of copies to display (1, probably)

0ch   Set pixel to specified palette entry

input: ah = 0ch
            al = palette register number (0-(number of colors – 1))
            bh = display page (should be 0)
            cx = x coordinate of pixel
            dx = y coordinate of pixel

0dh   Get palette entry for pixel

input: ah = 0dh   output: al = color value
            bh = display page (should be 0)
            cx = x coordinate of pixel
            dx = y coordinate of pixel

0eh   Display character using present attribute and advance cursor

input: ah = 0eh
              al = ASCII character
              bh = display page (0–3; 0 probably works)

0fh   Get video mode and display page

input: ah = 0fh   output: al = current video mode
                                                ah = chars per line
                                                bh = display page

10h   Set palette register to specified color register

input: ax = 1000h
              bl = palette register number
              bh = color register number

Get palette register color register

input: ax = 1007h   output: bh = color register number
              bl = palette register number

Set color register values

input: ax = 1010h
              bx = color register number (0-(number of colors – 1))
              dh = red value (0–63)
              ch = green value (0–63)
              cl = blue value (0–63)

Get color register values

input: ax = 1015h   output: dh = red value (0–63)
              bl = color register number   ch = green value (0–63)
                                                 dl = blue value (0–63)

D.1.2 • Int 11h (Get Equipment List) Call

                                  output: ax = coded equipment list.
                                                bits 4-5 are the initial video mode:
                                                    10 = 80 × 25 color
                                                    11 = 80 × 25 monochrome

D.1.3 • Int 16h (Keyboard) Calls

00h   Get key from keyboard

input: ah = 00h   output: al = ASCII code of key, or 0
                                                 ah = scan code of key

macro: _BIOSCh

01h   Check if key pressed

input: ah = 01h   output: ZF set if no character waiting
                                                 if ZF is clear, al and ah as in function 0

02h   Get shift status

input: ah = 02h   output: al = shift status bits:
                                                      bit 0 = Right shift key
                                                      bit 1 = Left shift key
                                                      bit 2 = Ctrl key
                                                      bit 3 = Alt key
                                                      bit 4 = Scroll Lock
                                                      bit 5 = Num Lock
                                                      bit 6 = Caps Lock
                                                      bit 7 = Insert mode on

D.2 • Int 21h (DOS) Calls

The number of available DOS calls, and the functionality of already existing calls, increase with each new version of DOS. These are all available at least from DOS 3.3 (the latest version as of this writing, not including Windows '95, is DOS 6.22) and should work on any PC even vaguely capable of running modern software.

01h   Get character from keyboard with echo

input: ah = 01h   output: al = the ASCII character
                                                           if 0, char is not ASCII and
                                                           next call returns scan code

macro: _GetCh

02h   Display character

input: ah = 02h
              dl = the character

macro: _PutCh   char1, char2, ...

08h Get character from keyboard without echo

input: ah = 08h   output: al = the ASCII character
                                                 if 0, char is not ASCII and
                                                 next call returns scan code

macro: _GetCh   noEcho

09h Display string of characters

input: ah = 09h
          ds:dx = segment:offset address of string of characters to be displayed,
                      terminated by a '$' character.

macro: _PutStr   StrOffset [, StrSeg]

0ah Get string of characters from keyboard

input: ah = 0ah   output: filled buffer
          ds:dx = address of buffer of the form:
                      byte 0 = n = maximum number of bytes to fill
                      byte 1 = number of bytes actually filled by call
                      bytes 2–n+1 = bytes to fill from keyboard

macro: _GetStr   BufOffset [, BufSeg]

25h Set interrupt vector

input: ah = 25h
          al = interrupt number
          ds:dx = address of interrupt handling routine

macro: _SetIntVec Intno, Handler

2ah Get date

input: ah = 2ah   output: al = day of week (0..6)
                                                 cx = year (e.g., 1980)
                                                 dh = month (1..12)
                                                 dl = day (1..31)

macro: _GetDate

2ch   Get time

input: ah = 2ch   output: ch = hour (0–23)
                                                       cl = minute (0–59)
                                                       dh = second (0–59)
                                                       dl = hundredth of second

macro: _GetTime

30h   Get DOS version number

input: ah = 30h   output: al = major version number
                                                       (0 for DOS 1.x, 3 for DOS 3.2)
                                                       ah = minor version number
                                                       (20 for DOS 3.2)

31h   Terminate and stay resident

input: ah = 31h
             al = return code
             dx = number of paragraphs needed for this program, including PSP

34h   Can DOS be called? (undocumented)

input: ah = 34h   output: es:bx points to a byte which is 1
                                                       if DOS cannot be called

35h   Get interrupt vector

input: ah = 35h   output: es:bx = interrupt vector
             al = vector number

macro: _GetIntVec IntNo, DoubleWord

3ch   Create file

input: ah = 3ch   output: ax = handle if C Flag clear
             cl = file attribute byte   ax = error number if C Flag set
             ds:dx = address of null-terminated file name

macro: _Creat   FileNameOffset [, FileNameSegment]

3dh   Open file

input: ah = 3dh   output: ax = handle if C Flag clear
                 al = 0 for read only   ax = error number if C Flag set
                       1 for write only
                       2 for read/write
                 ds:dx = address of null-terminated file name

macro: _Open   FileNameOffset, AccessMethod [, FileNameSegment]
                       (AccessMethod = Read, Write, or ReadWrite)

3eh   Close file

input: ah = 3eh   output: ax = error number if C Flag set
                 bx = file handle

macro: _Close   Handle

3fh   Read from file

input: ah = 3fh   output: ax = bytes read if C Flag clear
                 bx = handle   ax = error number if C Flag set
                 cx = number of bytes to read
                 ds:dx = address of buffer to read into

macro: _Read   Handle, BufferOffset, ByteCount [, BufferSegment]

40h   Write to file

input: ah = 40h   output: ax = bytes written if C Flag clear
                 bx = handle   ax = error number if C Flag set
                 cx = number of bytes to read
                 ds:dx = address of buffer to write from

macro: _Write   Handle, BufferOffset, ByteCount [, BufferSegment]

42h   Move disk file position pointer

input: ah = 42h   output: dx|ax = new ptr if C Flag clear
                 al = 0 seek from start   ax = error number if C Flag set
                       1 seek from current position
                       2 seek from end
                 bx = handle
                 cx|dx = amount to move pointer

macro: _LSeek   Handle, SeekType, LoDistance [, HiDistance]
                       (SeekType = FromStart, FromCur, or FromEnd)

4ah   Reallocate memory block

input: ah = 4ah   output: if C Flag is set, ax contains error
                   es = segment of block to be changed   number and bx contains
                   bx = desired size of new block   maximum size available

4bh   Load and execute a program

input: ah = 4bh   output: ax = error number if C Flag set
                   ds:dx = pointer to null-terminated path-and-file name of program
                   es:bx = pointer to parameter block:

                                word at 0:   segment of environment variables
                                double word at 2:   pointer to command tail with length
                                double word at 6:   pointer to first FCB or –1
                                double word at 10:   pointer to second FCB or –1

4ch   Return to DOS

input: ah = 4ch
                   al = return code (0 = normal return)

macro: _Exit   [ReturnCode]

62h   Get PSP address

input: ah = 62h   output: bx = segment of PSP

D.3 • PSP Format

word at 0:	int 20h (old-style return to DOS instruction)
word at 2:	segment of first paragraph above this program's allocation
word at 2ch:	segment containing environment variables for this program
word at 32h:	maximum number or open files for this program
byte at 80h:	number of bytes in command line, excluding command and terminating carriage return
bytes 81h-0ffh:	the command line

D.4 • BIOS Data in Low Memory

word at 410h:	equipment list; bits 4-5 are 10 for color, 11 for mono
byte at 417h:	shift status keys (see int 16h, function 2 for format)
word at 41ah:	offset of head of keyboard input queue
word at 41ch:	offset of tail of keyboard input queue
words at 41eh-43ch:	keyboard input queue in ASCII-scan code pairs
byte at 449h:	current video mode (returned by int 10h function 0fh call)
word at 44ah:	screen width in characters

byte at 462h:	current display page number (returned by `int 10h` function `0fh` call)
double-word at 46ch:	time in ticks since midnight (approx. 18.2 ticks/sec.)
byte at 470h:	set to 1 when clock (above) passes midnight.

D.5 • Video Memory

Text video memory is located at 0B000h:0 in monochrome systems, 0B000h:8000h in all other systems. Which one is used can be determined by looking at the equipment list (see above).

A text screen is represented as 2000 text-attribute pairs (text in the first byte, attribute in the second) listed by rows. Each attribute byte has foreground attribute in bits 0-2, background attribute in bits 4-6, intensity in bit 3 and blink in bit 7. Color attributes are

000	Black (Intense mode may be dark gray)
001	Blue
010	Green
011	Cyan (a light blue-green)
100	Red
101	Magenta (a red-violet)
110	Brown (Intense mode is yellow)
111	Light Gray (Intense mode is white)

and monochrome attributes are

000	Black
111	Gray (dim white)
001	Underline (foreground only)

Appendix  E

Debugger Summary

Menus and windows are manipulated in the debuggers using a mouse or the keyboard in what has become the standard fashion for windowing applications, exemplified by Microsoft Windows. A general description is contained in Debug Workshop I, Section I.1.

E.1 • CV (CodeView)

To assemble, link, and debug using CV, use the statements

```
        masm /zi myfile;
        link /cv myfile+myfile1+...
or
        ml /Zi myfile.asm myfile1.asm ...
and
        cv myfile rest of command line
```

To use a 50-line screen with VGA execute the following (once):

```
        cv /50 myfile rest of command line
```

If you wish to switch back and forth between the CV screen and a graphics output screen, execute CV with the /s switch:

```
        cv /s myfile rest of command line
```

Type **F1** for **help**. The bottom line of the screen is a **help line** showing the purpose of some functions keys. You can also perform the function by clicking left on the appropriate entry on the help line.

Each window has a window number in the upper right-hand corner, and the window with number *n* can be brought to the front and made the **active window** by typing **Alt-n**. This command can also be used to **open** a window and make it the active one. Cycle from among the windows making each window in turn the active window using **F6**.

Executing the program

Run	**F5**
Step (over call)	**F10**
Trace (into call)	**F8**
Restart Program	**Alt-R**(un **R**(estart
View object code	**Alt-O**(ption **S**(ource1 window... **M**(ixed *or* **F3**
View Register Window	**Alt-W**(indows 7(. registers *or* **Alt-7**
View User (output) screen (any key then returns to CV)	**F4** *or* **Alt-W**(indows **V**(iew output
View a second source window	**Alt-W**(indows 4(. Source 2 *or* **Alt-4**
View another source code module	**Alt-F**(ile open **M**(odule... then choose from list. You may have to activate the particular module window before being able to open into it.

Viewing Data Values

Watch	**Alt-W**(atch **A**(dd watch *variable-name* [,*x*]*or* **Ctrl-W**. Default for *variable-name* is the one under the cursor. *x* can be d(decimal), c(character) x(hex), or s(C-type string)
Open Watch window	**Alt-W**(indows 2(. watch *or* **Alt-2**
Open Memory window	**Alt-W**(indows 5(. memory 1 *or* 6(. memory 2 *or* **Ctrl-5** or **Ctrl-6**.
Change location or format of display in memory *n* window	**Alt-O**(ptions **M**(emory *n* window... and choose **A**(ddress or **D**(isplay format. You may have to activate the memory window first to get the Options menu to refer to it.
Inspect current variable value	**?** *variable-name*[,*x*] (in command window), *x* as above
Dump [*n*] bytes starting at *address*	**db** *address* [**L** *n*] (in command window). If *n* not specified, 16 will be dumped. *Address* can be symbolic or hex, with or without segment part.
Dump [*n*] words starting at *address*	**dw** *address* [**L** *n*] (in command window). If *n* not specified, 8 will be dumped.
Dump [*n*] words of stack	**dw** ss:sp [**L** *n*] (in command window). If *n* not specified, 8 will be dumped.

Manipulating Breakpoints

Breakpoint toggle at cursor line	**F9** *or* double click left in line *or* **Alt D**(ata **S**(et Breakpoint...
Here (temporary breakpoint at cursor line)	**F7** *or* click right on line
Set Breakpoint...	**Alt-D**(ata **S**(et Breakpoint... **L**(ocation *address,* where *address* can be label or hex numeric, with or without segment, *or .linenumber* (note period). Location defaults to cursor line
...with pass count	... **P**(asscount *n*
Edit Breakpoint	**Alt-D**(ata **E**(dit Breakpoint... Scroll to desired breakpoint. **R**(emove to delete, **M**(odify to change. In Modify, you can reset the **P**(asscount
Breakpoint command	**bp** *address* [/**P***passcount*] (in command window) address as above

Manipulating Windows

Change active window	Click left on new window or **F6**
Open a window	**Alt-W**(indows and choose window *or* **Alt-***n*
Close window	Click left on close box in top left-hand corner *or* **Ctrl-F4**
Iconize (minimize) window	Click left on down arrow in upper right-hand corner *or* **Alt-W**(indows miN(imize *or* **Ctrl-F5**
Zoom (maximize) window	Click left on up arrow in upper right-hand corner *or* **Alt-W**(indows maX(imize *or* **Ctrl-F10**
Restore iconized window	Double-click on icon *or* **Alt-W**(indows **R**(estore *or* **Ctrl-F5**
Restore Zoomed window	Click left on double arrow in upper right-hand corner *or* **Alt-W**(indows **R**(estore *or* **Ctrl-F10**
Move Window	Drag upper bar of window to new position *or* **Alt-W**(indow **M**(ove *or* **Ctrl-F7** and use cursor keys to move, **Enter** to terminate.
Resize Window	Drag lower right-hand corner of window *or* **Alt-W**(indow **S**(ize *or* **Ctrl-F8** and use cursor keys to resize, **Enter** to terminate.

Miscellaneous

Toggle between 16- and 32-bit registers	**Alt-O**(ptions 3(86
Make normal number base hex	**n16** in command window
Make normal number base decimal	**n10** in command window

Exit CV

   Alt-F(ile eX(it *or* **Alt-F10** *or* **q** in the command window

E.2 • TD (Turbo Debugger)

To assemble, link, and debug using TD, use the statements

```
tasm /zi myfile
tlink /v myfile+myfile2+...
td myfile rest of command line
```

If you wipfLíØ@switch back and forth between the TD screen and a graphics output screen, execute TD with the /ds switch:

```
td /ds myfile rest of command line
```

   Type **F1** for **help**. The bottom line of the screen is a **help line** showing the purpose of some functions keys. Holding down the **Alt** key causes the corresponding Alt-function key operations to be listed. You can also perform the function by clicking left on the appropriate entry on the help line.

   Each window has a window number in the upper right-hand corner, and the window with number *n* can be brought to the front and made the **active window** by typing **Alt-***n*. Cycle from among the windows making each window in turn the active window using **F6**.

   Some windows are divided into panes. You can cycle through the panes, making each in turn active, using the TAB key, or click left on the desired pane. Each window, or pane within a window, has a **SpeedMenu**, brought up by clicking right on the window or pane or hitting **Alt-F10**. A shortcut to opening the SpeedMenu is to hold down the **Ctrl** key and hit the shortcut letter. Holding down the **Ctrl** key causes a selection of letter functions to appear on the help line without opening the SpeedMenu.

Executing the program

Run	**F9**
Step (over call)	**F8**
Trace (into call)	**F7**
Restart Program	**Alt-R**(un **P**(rogram reset
View Object Code	**Alt-V**(iew **C**(pu
View Register Window	**Alt-V**(iew **R**(egisters
View User (Output) Screen (any key then returns to TD)	**Alt-F5** *or* **Alt-W**(indow useR(screen
View Another Code Module	**Alt-V**(iew **M**(odule... *or* **F3**, then choose from list

Viewing Data Values

Watch [C-type string]	**Alt-D**(ata **W**(atch *variable-name* [**,s**]*or* **Ctrl-F7**. Default for *variable-name* is the one under the cursor.
CPU multi-pane window with code, registers, stack, and memory.	**Alt-V**(iew **C**(pu **Tab** between subpanes. **Ctrl G**(o to change address in memory or code subpanes.
Dump Window	**Alt-V**(iew **D**(ump. Like the memory pane of the CPU window. **Ctrl-G**(o to change address.
Variable Window	**Alt-V**(iew **V**(ariables Switch between panes with **Tab** and use scroll keys to go up and down.

Manipulating Breakpoints

Breakpoint Toggle at Cursor Line	**F2** *or* click left in first two columns *or* **Alt B**(reakpoint **T**(oggle
Here (temporary breakpoint at cursor line)	**F4**
Set Breakpoint...	**Alt-B**(reakpoint **A**(t... *label* **Alt-B**(reakpoint **A**(t... *SourceFile.Label* **Alt-B**(reakpoint **A**(t... *address,* where *address* is hex offset or segreg:offset
...with Pass Count	... **cH**(ange **P**(asscount *n*

Manipulating Windows

Change Active Window	Click left on new window or **F6**

Open a Window	**Alt-V**(iew and choose window
Close Window	Click left on close box in top left-hand corner *or* **Alt-W**(indow **C**(lose
Iconize (Minimize) Window	Click left on down arrow in upper right-hand corner *or* **Alt-W**(indow **I**(conize/restore
Zoom (Maximize) Window	Click left on up arrow in upper right-hand corner *or* **Alt-W**(indow **Z**(oom *or* **F5**
Restore Iconized Window	Double-click on icon *or* **Alt-W**(indow **I**(conize/restore
Restore Zoomed Window	Click left on double arrow in upper right-hand corner *or* **Alt-W**(indow **Z**(oom *or* **F5**
Move Window	Drag upper bar of window to new position *or* **Alt-W**(indow **M**(ove/resize and use cursor keys to move, **Enter** to terminate.
Resize Window	Drag lower right-hand corner of window *or* **Alt-W**(indow **M**(ove/resize and use **Shift**-cursor keys to resize, **Enter** to terminate.

Miscellaneous

Save Window Layout	**Alt-O**(ptions **S**(ave **L**(ayout *filename* (best choice for *filename* is TDCONFIG.TD in the same directory as the TD.EXE file)
Toggle between 16- and 32-bit Registers	With register window active, **Ctrl-R**
Make TD Resident (for debugging TSRs)	**Alt-F**(ile **R**(esident

Exit TD

Alt-X *or* **Alt-F**(ile **Q**(uit

Appendix

How Assemblers Work

In this appendix we will explain how assemblers work. The assembler is the computer program (in our case MASM or TASM) which translates symbolic assembly language source code (the `.ASM` file) into a machine language object file (the `.OBJ` file) suitable for use as input to a linker program. We will start with an oversimplified description and then refine it. Some sketches of data structures will be given in C/C++.

F.1 • Introduction

In their simplest form, assemblers are really nothing more than table lookup programs. They have a fixed table of symbolic opcodes (such as `mov`, `add`, `jmp`, etc.) and a **symbol table** which is used to store information about the labels in the particular program being translated.

For each symbolic opcode, the opcode table will contain such information as the corresponding machine numeric operation code, internal format of the instruction, etc. This information can get quite complex on a CPU like the 80X86 where a single symbolic opcode such as `mov` may correspond to many different numeric codes depending on the operands used with it.

The symbol table will contain a numeric value for each symbol, usually the location of the symbol in memory.

The chief difficulty with the simple table lookup view is that symbols may be used before they are defined, as in

```
        jmp     aLabel
        . . .
aLabel:
```

Here we don't know how to fill in aLabel in the `jmp` instruction until the assembler has processed some further indeterminate number of lines of source code. The most common solution to this problem is a **two-pass algorithm**, that is, the assembler makes two complete passes through the source program it is translating. The first pass fills in the symbol table with the locations of all the labels and the second uses that symbol table to translate the program.

In the next section we will give a fairly detailed description of a very simple two-pass assembler. In later sections we will describe the details which must be added to make the assembler work on a CPU such as the 80X86, and then will discuss how to construct a one-pass assembler and optimize forward jumps.

F.2 • A Simple Two-Pass Assembler

Our assembler will assume a very simple CPU structure, though we will sometimes give examples from the 80X86 because it is so familiar.

▶   **The First Pass**

The assembler keeps track of the location in memory following the code or data we have just assembled in a variable called the **location counter**, or LC. (MASM and TASM allow the programmer to refer to it as $.) LC is initialized to zero at the beginning of the first pass.

For each line of source code, the assembler first pass performs the following operations:

1.   Delete any comments from the line. If the resulting line is blank, ignore it.
2.   Is there a label on the line? If so, enter the label into the symbol table and give it the value LC. Delete the label from the line. If the resulting line is blank, do not consider it further.
3.   Find the first non-blank field on the line—the opcode—and look it up in the opcode table. Examine the remaining operands if necessary to determine the number n of bytes that the line will occupy. Note that on the 80X86, this analysis can get quite complex:

cmp	ax, 100	occupies three bytes
cmp	[A + bx], 100 ; (A a word)	occupies five bytes
cmp	[A + bx], 400	occupies six bytes

and

DB	'Bill Jones', 13, 10, '$'	occupies thirteen bytes

The actual numeric operation code could also be determined at this time, though it isn't needed until the second pass. For instance, the three cmp instructions above have the numeric operation codes 3Dh, 83h, and 81h, respectively.

4.   Add the n computed above to LC.
5.   Although it isn't strictly necessary, it will probably save a lot of time if we write the results of analyzing each line onto an intermediate file so that our analysis doesn't have to be repeated on the second pass. In order to make it easy to generate a listing file, we might also keep a complete copy of the source line here too.

▶   **The Second Pass**

For each record in the intermediate file (which corresponds to one line of the source file) do the following:

1. From the information in the opcode and symbol tables, translate the various operands of the instruction into the string of bytes which is their internal representation.
2. Write the generated code or data bytes out into the object file.

F.3 • Making the Assembler More Realistic

Our simple assembler has a number of problems, some of which may already have occurred to you.

1. Not all labels are set to the value of LC—for instance in

```
aLabel      EQU      1000
```

and

```
aProc       ENDP
```

Also consider the case of

```
aLabel      ORG      80h
```

On the first pass, the location counter LC is changed *first* as a result of some instructions and then aLabel is given the new value of LC. Therefore we have to look up the opcode before we process the label and sometimes alter our standard label processing accordingly.

2. In the 80X86 architecture, the machine opcode for an instruction manipulating a symbol A depends on the size of A—BYTE, WORD, DWORD or QWORD, etc. (DWORD and QWORD are used for short and long precision floating point numbers, respectively; see Section 20.1.) In addition, PROCs and EXTRNs are specified as NEAR or FAR, which affects the length of the call instructions used to reference them. This information as to type must be collected in the symbol table during the first pass when the symbol is defined, for use in actually generating the code during the second pass.

3. For each symbol, an 80X86 assembler must be able to determine what segment it is in, so that it can determine (from ASSUME statements) whether there is a segment register containing the appropriate value and whether or not it is necessary to generate a segment override byte (see Chapter 12).

Whether or not to use a segment override must be determined on the *first* pass because the override takes up a byte and therefore affects the locations of any symbols that occur after it in the program. Therefore if a program uses a symbol not yet defined, the assembler must make an assumption about it. Ours assume the most likely case: that no segment override is necessary. (Similarly, a jmp to a label which isn't yet defined is assumed to be NEAR.)

The above assumptions place some responsibility on the programmer, namely, that a symbol which isn't in the default segment must be declared before it is used. Declarations of EXTRN symbols must be placed in the correct segment, as that is the way the assembler determines which segment they are in. Thus to declare A to be an external WORD variable in segment DSeg, you must use something like

```
DSeg        SEGMENT PUBLIC
            EXTRN  A : WORD
DSeg        ENDS
```

An assembler usually makes it easy to define labels before use by allowing the programmer to intersperse code and data segments and enter and leave any segment over and over again, at will. For example

```
DSeg        SEGMENT PUBLIC
A           DW      ?
            . . .
DSeg        ENDS

            .CODE
            . . .
            mov     A, 100
B:

            . . .


DSeg        SEGMENT PUBLIC
Ptr         DD      B
DSeg        ENDS
            . . .
```

4.   Problem 3 shows that it may be necessary to enter and leave segments over and over again, which means that we can't make do with a *single* location counter LC. Rather each segment must have one, and at any time there will be a current segment, whose location counter is represented by LC.

We have come far enough that we can suggest a more substantial table structure to be set up on the first pass. If you do not wish to go into this level of detail or are uncomfortable with the amount of C used, skip to Problem 5, perhaps skimming as you go.

First of all, we need a **segment table**, each entry of which might be defined in part by the following C/C++ code:

```
struct SegTabEntry {
    char name[N];
    enum {PUBLIC, PRIVATE, AT, ...} SegType;
    int AtLoc; // if of type AT
    int LocCtr, Size;
        . . .
};
```

The Size field is the number of bytes currently in the segment. Most of the time Size will be the same as LocCtr, but a separate field is necessary since it is possible to move the location counter *back* from its current location using the ORG pseudo-operation.

We declare a segment table as an array of SegTableEntrys, and also make associated declarations:

```
struct SegTabEntry SegTable[MaxSeg];
int NSeg = 3;    // Number of segments currently defined
int CurSeg;      // Current segment
int LC;          // = SegTable[CurSeg].LocCtr
```

NSeg starts at 3 since we always have the standard segments .STACK, .CODE, and .DATA. We can assume they are the first three entries of SegTable and their indices are defined by constants

```
enum {
  StdStackSeg,  // = 0;  Entry for standard stack seg
  StdCodeSeg,   // = 1;        Entry for standard code seg
  StdDataSeg};  // = 2;        Entry for standard data seg
```

In addition we can keep a table of the currently ASSUMEd contents of the segment registers in an array declared by

```
#define NOTHING -1  // Seg register has unknown contents

enum {CS, DS, ES, SS}; // Give symbolic names to Seg Regs

int Assumes[4]; // one for each Seg Reg above
```

The code above is a lot to digest for all but the most fluent C programmers, so perhaps some examples will help. Assumes[DS] tells us the segment that DS currently points to by giving its entry number in SegTable. If Assumes[DS] = -1 = NOTHING then the contents of DS are unknown. Initially we set

```
Assumes[DS] = StdDataSeg;
Assumes[SS] = StdStackSeg;
Assumes[CS] = StdCodeSeg;
Assumes[ES] = NOTHING;
```

We can now declare the symbol table entries:

```
enum Boolean {FALSE, TRUE};
struct SymTabEnt {
  char Name[M];
  int Seg;    // index into SegTable; -1 if no seg
              // if symbol EQU const, it will have no seg
  int Value;
  enum {BYTE, WORD, DWORD, QWORD, ... } Size;
  enum Boolean EXTRN;
```

```
enum Boolean PUBLIC;
enum {NEAR, FAR} Distance;
    . . .
};
```

(Of course Distance and Size will never both be used so we could save space putting some of the data in a union.)

5. Suppose an 80X86 program is to be constructed from three source files: P1.ASM, P2.ASM and P3.ASM, and that each use the following amounts of space:

	.STACK	.CODE	.DATA
P1	200	100	50
P2		150	500
P3		100	50
Totals	200	350	600

The linker must combine the .OBJ files into the three final segments of size 200, 350, and 600 bytes. Thus the various segments in the original .OBJ files must be shuffled together, which has several implications on the information the assembler must include in the .OBJ file. Clearly the .OBJ file must contain

- A description of all the segments in the file, including their names (so they can be matched up with those in other .OBJ files) and their sizes.
- A way of indicating which segments the various code and data bytes in the .OBJ file belong to.

These problems are generally dealt with by defining different types of records in the .OBJ file. Each record will consist of a byte telling its record type followed by a length byte or word followed by the record data. So far we need records which are (lists of) segment descriptions and records saying 'I am code or data to be put in segment n.'

Assembly programs are arranged so that *all* of the .CODE segment must go before *all* of the .DATA segment. Therefore segment size information in all of the files to be linked must be collected before any actual linking begins. In order to make it unnecessary for the linker to search the entire .OBJ file for size information, it would be best to place it near the beginning of the file. That is in fact easily done. At the end of the first pass (and not earlier), before any code or data has been generated, all segment information is known and can be written into the .OBJ file as a single record.

6. Similarly, we need to have a list of all the EXTRNs used by the code in the .OBJ file, as well as the PUBLIC symbols defined in it. The linker, in order to determine what files are to be included in the linking process, may have to search one or more libraries for EXTRN symbols not defined in files it already has. Once again though, EXTRN and PUBLIC symbols are known at the end of the first pass, and so can be written near the beginning of the .OBJ file where they can be found efficiently by the linker. It merely means that we need two new types of .OBJ file records, for EXTRN and PUBLIC symbols.

7. Problems 5 and 6 also have implications on the actual code and data records in the file, too. Suppose that P1 and P2 in the example in Problem 5 have the following general form:

```
;    P1

                .DATA
A               DB      . . .
                . . .

                .CODE
                EXTRN   Y. . .
B               PROC
                . . .
                mov     al, A
                . . .
                call    Y
                . . .
B               ENDP
                END     B
```

and

```
;    P2

                .DATA
X               DW      . . .
                . . .

                .CODE
                PUBLIC Y
Y               PROC
                . . .
                mov     ax, X
                mov     bx, 0
                . . .
                call    Y
                . . .
Y               ENDP
                END
```

In P1 the assembler will assign A to the location 0 in .DATA and B to location 0 in .CODE. In P2, X will be assigned location 0 in .DATA and Y to location 0 in .CODE. When these programs are linked together, we can't have both A and X in location 0 of .DATA and B and Y in location 0 of .CODE! Suppose P2 is placed after P1. Then there three 0's in the three mov instructions, one and only one of which (the one involving X) must be altered by the linker. The linker must also change the 0 in the call instruction in P2 to the correct value for Y.

The problem now becomes apparent. The code contains several different kinds of zeroes: those which are actually numeric 0 and should never be changed and those which refer to the 0 offset in any of several different segments. There is nothing magic about 0 either. The same could be true of any other number that might occur in the .OBJ file.

Therefore in addition to records containing code and data bytes, we must also have **relocation records** telling how some of those bytes must be altered if the code or data is relocated. Typically a code or data record is followed immediately by a record giving its relocation information. **Note:** Data records may need relocation because they may contain pointers to other code or data locations.)

Each entry in a relocation record must have the following information:

- the offset of the word being relocated.
- the type of relocation. Either 'I am the nth EXTRN' or 'I am in the mth segment'. In the latter case, the actual code or data word can contain the original offset.

Relocation information is all readily available during pass 2 from the symbol and segment tables collected during pass 1. However it needs to be **buffered**. That is, we will keep two arrays in memory, one for the current code or data segment and one for relocation information. When one or the other of these areas fills up (or we end the current segment), both of these arrays will be written to the .OBJ file and we will start all over with empty arrays. If we simply wrote out code or data and relocation information unbuffered, they would be interleaved and we would have to waste a lot of space in the .OBJ file identifying which is which.

Putting all the information together on Problems 5, 6, and 7, we see that the .OBJ file will have the following general form:

        Record containing segment list
        Record containing EXTRNs referenced
        Record containing PUBLICs defined
        Code/data record 1
        Relocation record for code/data record 1
        Code/data record 2
        Relocation record for code/data record 2
        ...
        Last code/data record
        Relocation record for last code/data record

In fact, the .OBJ files generated by MASM and TASM are quite a bit more complicated than the structure above.

F.4 • One-Pass Assemblers

TASM normally assembles in one pass. In this section we will discuss the modifications necessary to do that.

The most obvious problem with doing assembly in one pass is handling forward references. After all, that was the original reason for two passes.

Perhaps the simplest solution requires making a minor restriction on forward references: a forward reference must use only the symbol by itself, rather than an expression involving the symbol.

That is, if the symbol `FwdRef` is not yet defined,

```
jmp     FwdRef ;      is legal
```

but

```
jmp     FwdRef + 3 ;  is illegal (under this restriction)
```

Forward references almost always refer to code labels and use of a code label like `FwdRef + 3` is dangerous anyway since it involves detailed knowledge of how many bytes instructions take (which can change with even minor changes in the code). Therefore forward references involving expressions will almost never occur anyway.

With the restriction to forward referencing of symbols alone, we go through the first (and only) pass as before, except that now we generate code and data and write it into the `.OBJ` file as we go. For code involving purely backward references, we need merely to move the code-generation part of the second pass into the first pass. When a reference to an undefined symbol occurs, code is generated with the symbol's position taken up by some sort of placeholder (0, perhaps). The symbol is entered into the symbol table if it isn't already there, with an indication that it is not yet defined. The `value` field in its symbol table entry can be used for a pointer to a list of places where the undefined symbol is used. These places will be absolute locations in the `.OBJ` file containing the filler that must be replaced by the actual reference to the symbol when it is finally defined. Schematically, the view partway through the pass might be

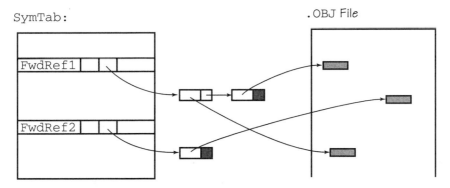

Each time a new label is encountered, it is looked up in the symbol table to see if forward references to it already exist. If so, we follow the list of forward references, `_LSeeking` to each location in the `.OBJ` file and filling in the value (see Section 17.3). Then the symbol table entry can be marked defined and the actual value entered. At the end of the (only) pass, we can run through the symbol table and make sure that all undefined symbols were eventually defined.

The assembler can use a linked representation for the forward references, and once a forward reference is resolved, reuse the list elements for other forward references. Since there aren't very many forward references and they tend to be resolved fairly quickly, there is very little storage overhead, though the overhead of jumping around in the `.OBJ` file could be fairly high. (To write two bytes, one has to read 512 bytes—or 1024 bytes if the two bytes happen to span two 512-byte disk segments—change the bytes in question, and then rewrite all 512 or 1024 bytes.)

The Turbo Assembler is a one-pass assembler in its default mode, and allows arbitrary expressions to contain forward references. Thus if `FwdRef1`, `FwdRef2`, and `FwdRef3` are all forward references,

```
jmp    FwdRef1 + (FwdRef2 - FwdRef3)
```

is legal in TASM. As with some other features of TASM, I'm not sure the ability to handle forward references like the above in one pass is worth the effort, but it is worth asking how TASM does it.

One method of solving the forward-reference-to-expressions problem is an extension of our method of handling simple forward references. We keep a list of forward references with the locations to be filled in the .OBJ file, and generate code/data with place holders. Since forward references can be included in arbitrary expressions, our list entries must now contain the actual expression containing the forward reference. Therefore we must use variable length character strings in the list entries. (Expressions could be quite long, but are typically short and we don't want to waste space.) Since a forward reference expression might include several undefined labels as in the example above, we can't tie it to a single entry in the symbol table. Therefore we will keep a single list of all the forward references. As before, a view partway through the pass might be

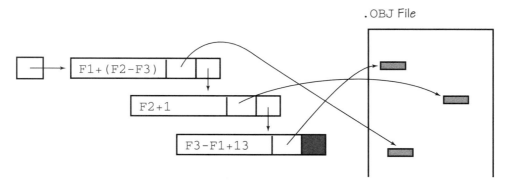

As the undefined symbols are gradually defined, there is no way to tell which of the expressions in the list of forward references has become completely defined, and searching and translating each expression on the list each time a new symbol is defined would be very time-consuming. It would therefore seem reasonable to keep adding to the list until the entire program text has been scanned and then make a single pass through the list trying to compute all forward reference expressions. Thus we can solve the general forward reference problem, at the expense of requiring more memory than we did for the solution of the simplified problem we gave first.

There is one other difficulty with a single-pass assembler which must be mentioned. As was discussed in the solutions to problems 5 and 6 in the last section, we need to put a list of all the segments, EXTRNs, and PUBLICs at the beginning of the .OBJ file, but this information isn't known until we have passed completely through the source file. In a single-pass assembler we will already have generated all the object code and data by that time. Even the length of these three lists isn't known until the end of the pass, so we can't leave space for them at the beginning of the .OBJ file.

In order to put the above information at the beginning of the .OBJ file, our one-pass assembler becomes a sort of one-and-a-little-pass assembler. The code and data generated on the first pass is written to a temporary or **scratch file**. At the end of the first pass, the header information with segment table, EXTRNs, and PUBLICs is written into the actual .OBJ file and then the scratch file is copied to the .OBJ file and deleted.

The use of a scratch file isn't a total loss, though, since it can be used to make the forward reference expression fixups more efficient. In the last diagram above, we have shown the forward references occurring in the list in the reverse order that they occur in the .OBJ (actually scratch) file. This ordering is the easiest way to add items to a linked list, but with only a slight amount of additional effort (keeping a pointer to the last item on the list as well as the first), items could be added to the *end* instead of the beginning of the list, with the result that they occur in the list in the same order that they occur in the scratch file. Then instead of _LSeeking into the scratch file to fix up the forward references, we could fix them up as we copied the scratch file to the .OBJ file. The result would be *no* file overhead for the fixup operation.

Exercise F.4

1. Some forward references contain the actual value of the symbolic expression (e.g., mov ax, OFF-SET F). Some contain the *difference* between that value and the location of the instruction following the reference (e.g., jmp F). The instruction location referred to is in the code segment, *not* in the .OBJ file. In fact, there is no relationship between the location of code in the code segment and its location in the .OBJ file. Also, when the address is a difference, it can be either a byte or a word. Suggest additions necessary to the linked list items so that this translation can be done correctly.

F.5 • Optimizing Forward Jumps

As we saw in Section 5.7, conditional jump instructions, such as jne A are represented internally as two bytes, one for the opcode and one for the *displacement* to the jump destination (in this case, A). The displacement is treated as an 8-bit signed number. If the jump is taken, the CPU sign-extends the displacement to 16 bits and adds it to the IP to give the actual location of the next instruction to be executed. Thus if jne A is a forward jump, it can be pictured in memory as follows:

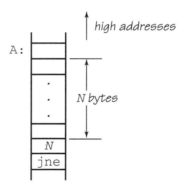

As a result of this design, one can do a conditional jump forward by at most 127 bytes (and backward by at most 128 bytes).

This limitation on the range of conditional jumps is a common feature in the architecture of many mini- and microcomputers. It shortens the code while putting only minor limitations on the programmer. Most jumps *are* in fact to near code locations, and as we have seen (Section 5.7), a conditional jump over a longer distance is easily crafted with a five-byte jump, a jump around an unconditional jump. That is, if A is too far away, jne A can be replaced by

```
        je      Around
        jmp     A ;             A is too far away for a jne A
Around:
```

One could of course always code jumps this way, but the longer jump takes more space and takes longer to execute.

There are also two forms of the unconditional jmp instruction, a two-byte instruction with a one-byte offset to the destination and a three-byte instruction with a word offset. Again, it is worthwhile to use the shorter instruction if possible.

Many assemblers, including TASM and MASM (6.0 and above), have been designed to choose the optimal jump instruction automatically. (With TASM, you tell it to optimize jumps with the JUMPS pseudo-operation and /m on the command line.) As stated in Section 5.7, I consider this capability a solution in search of a problem, but once again doing the optimization does present an interesting programming problem for the assembler writer. We will spend the rest of this section discussing it.

Optimizing backward jumps is easy (except when encountered in the process of optimizing forward jumps). We know our current location and the location of the jump destination, so it is easy to see whether a large or small jump is required. As usual, it is the forward jumps that present the problems.

Let's suppose that on the first (or only) pass, the assembler encounters a conditional jump to an as yet undefined label. The assembler can then start a look-ahead process, adding up the lengths of subsequent instructions. It only has to do look forward until it finds the undefined label or until it finds 128 bytes of code, whichever comes first. During the look-ahead, the assembler can't define the values of any other labels it encounters because it doesn't know how long the jump instruction is going to be. Perhaps the most straightforward way to delay definition of labels would be to save the location in the source file of the line after the conditional jump (using _LSeek 0 bytes from current location), doing the look-ahead without adding symbols to the symbol table, _LSeeking back to the location previously saved, and then processing the code normally.

Optimizing jumps as above would be fairly easy, and could even be done in a one-pass assembler, if it weren't for the fact that the area between the jump and its destination can contain other jumps (both forward and backward) which need to be optimized!

We can attack the problem of jumps within the range of jumps by keeping *two* values for number of bytes encountered in the look-ahead, a maximum number and a minimum number. Non-jump instructions simply cause their length to be added to both numbers. A jump whose size cannot yet be determined adds 2 to the minimum and 3 or 5 to the maximum. The look-ahead stops when the *minimum* value reaches 128 (telling us that a short jump is impossible) or when the jump destination is encountered (telling us if a short jump *might* be possible). If the *maximum* distance to the jump destination is 127 or less, then the original jump can be made a two-byte jump and we can proceed as before. If the minimum distance hit 128, then the five-byte (or three-byte) jump must be used. We have a problem though when we get

$$\text{minimum displacement to destination} < 128 \leq \text{maximum displacement}$$

There are two reasonable solutions to the above problem. The first is simply to make all jumps in this situation big ones. We could justify this decision on the theory that this ambiguous situation won't happen very often and that when it does it may be the right choice anyway. On the other hand, MASM automatically makes multiple passes over the source file to optimize such jumps, and

TASM allows us to specify multiple passes if necessary with the /m switch on the command line. (TASM has an upper limit n to the number of passes, which is specified with /mn. /m by itself is equivalent to /m5.)

A method for optimizing jumps using multiple passes is as follows. Once one jump which can't be optimized is encountered, defining of symbols is suspended for the rest of the pass. Any further jumps which can be optimized are optimized and marked as being optimized so we won't have to worry about them again. Each pass through the source file is going to optimize at least one jump—the *last* unoptimized one—so this process will eventually terminate. If the number of passes is restricted, on the last pass, we will simply assume a big jump in the cases that are still ambiguous.

There are of course substantial bookkeeping problems to be solved, particularly if we try to be efficient and do as little repeat translation as possible. As I have indicated before, I'm not at all sure it is worth the effort on the part of the assembler writer.

Bibliography

Carta, David G., "Two Fast Implementations of the 'Minimal Standard' Random Number Generator," *Commun. ACM* **33**, 1 (Jan. 1990), pp. 87-88.

Chappell, Geoff, *DOS Internals*. Reading, MA: Addison-Wesley, 1994.

Covington, Michael A., "Smooth Views," *BYTE*, **15**, no. 5 (May 1990), pp. 279-83.

Crawford, John H. and Patrick P. Gelsinger, *Programming the 80386*. Alameda, CA: SYBEX, 1987.

Duncan, Ray, *Advanced MS-DOS Programming*, 2nd ed. Redmond, WA: Microsoft Press, 1988.

Duncan, Ray, ed., *Extending DOS*. Reading, MA: Addison-Wesley, 1990.

Holzner, Steven, *Creating Utilities with Assembly Language*. New York, NY: Brady, 1986.

Hummell, Robert L., *PC Magazine Assembly Language Lab Notes*. Emeryville, CA, Ziff-Davis Press, 1992

Intel Corporation, *I486 Microprocessor Programmer's Reference Manual*. Berkeley, CA: OSBORNE/McGraw-Hill, 1990.

Knuth, Donald E., "An Empirical Study of FORTRAN Programs," *Software — Practice and Experience*, **1**, 2 (1971), pp. 105–133.

Lafore, Robert, *Assembly Language Primer for the IBM PC & XT*. New York, NY: Plume/Waite, 1984.

Marsaglia, George, and Sullivan, Stephen J., "Technical Communications Concerning the Papers of Carta and Park and Miller" (with responses from Park, Miller, and Paul K. Stockmeyer), *Commun. ACM* **36**, 1 (July 1993), pp. 105–110.

McKeeman, W. M., "Symbol Table Access," in Bauer, F. L, and J. Eickel, *Compiler Construction: An Advanced Course*. Berlin: Springer-Verlag, 1974, pp. 253–301.

Norton, Peter and Richard Wilton, *Programmer's Guide to the IBM PC & PS/2*. Redmond, WA: Microsoft Press, 1988.

Park, Stephen K. and Keith W. Miller, "Random Number Generators: Good Ones are Hard to Find," *Commun. ACM* **31**, 10 (October 1988), pp. 1192-1201.

Rector, Russell, and George Alexy, *The 8086 Book*. Berkeley, CA: OSBORNE / McGraw-Hill, 1980.

Schmit, Michael L., *Pentium Processor Optimization Tools*. Cambridge, MA: AP Professional, 1995.

Schulman, Andrew, ed., *Undocumented DOS*. Reading, MA: Addison-Wesley, 1990. 2nd ed., 1993. (Unfortunately, the first edition seems to be a prerequisite to the second.)

Tannenbaum, Andrew S., *Modern Operating Systems*. Englewood Cliffs, NJ: Prentice-Hall, 1992.

van Gilluwe, Frank, *The Undocumented PC*. Reading, MA: Addison Wesley, 1994.

Williams, Al, *DOS 6, A Developer's Guide: Advanced Programming Guide to DOS*. New York, NY: M & T Books, 1993.

Wilton, Richard, *Programmer's Guide to PC and PS/2 Video Systems*. Redmond, WA: Microsoft Press, 1987.

Index